BIZET and His World

BIZET
and His World

by Mina Curtiss

VIENNA HOUSE
New York

This Vienna House edition,
first published in 1974,
is reprinted by arrangement
with Alfred A. Knopf, Inc.

International Standard Book Number: 0-8443-0085-3
Library of Congress Catalog Card Number: 58-10973

Printed in the United States of America

To Marc

Acknowledgments

First and foremost I must thank M. and Mme Daniel Halévy, without whose generosity, kindness, and friendship this book could not have been written. Not only did M. Halévy open to me the archives of his father, Ludovic Halévy, one of Bizet's collaborators on *Carmen,* but Mme Halévy, over her hospitable tea table, evoked for me, by recalling conversations with her father-in-law, a family picture indispensable to an understanding of Bizet's character.

Mme Bouts Réal Del Sarte, Mlle Géraldy, Mme de Roux-Glandy, M. Gustave Del Sarte, M. André Réal Del Sarte, great-nieces and nephews of Bizet's mother, were most helpful in permitting me the use of their family papers, thereby enabling me to give a picture of the background of Bizet's childhood hitherto neglected.

Mme Suzanne Reiter kindly gave me permission to reproduce family photographs, and M. Jean-Jacques Simart graciously put at my disposal the commentary of his grandfather, Jean Reiter, on Pigot's life of Bizet.

I am also indebted to Mme Emile Henriot for her gracious permission to quote unpublished material from the letters of her grandfather, Charles Gounod; to M. Bessand-Massenet for permitting publication of letters of his grandfather, Jules Massenet; to Mme Lafont-Ferrare, the niece of Ambroise Thomas, for similar permission; also to Mme Vouillon, daughter of Camille du Locle, Mme de Juge, granddaughter of Carvalho; and to the Messrs. Heugel and Beck, who permitted me to copy the Bizet correspondence in the files of Heugel et Cie.

M. Jean Paladilhe's permission to quote from the unpublished journal and letters of his great-grandfather and his grandfather, the composer Emile Paladilhe, has made possible a clearer understanding of the problems that beset all the young composers of Bizet's generation.

To Mmes Brugère, Madier, and Charles Richet, descendants of Madame Trélat, and to her former pupils, Mlle Letellier and Mme Gaudibert, I am grateful for the information they so graciously gave. I am specially indebted to Mlle Letellier for the letter from Léo Delibes to Mme Trélat.

Others who were kind enough to let me copy, or to supply copies or photostats of documents or information related to Bizet include Messrs. Jacques Barzun; Jean-Paul Changeur; Alfred Cortot; Winton Dean; Roger Hauert; Jean Lapeyre, Director of the Musée de Dieppe; Marc Pincherle; Francis Steegmuller; and Albert Willemetz; and Mmes Mary Benjamin and O'Donnell Hoover. Mme de Chambure, the distinguished musicologist who owns Bizet's music library, graciously allowed me to check it with his own catalogue. Kapten Rudolf Nydahl of Stockholm afforded me the privilege of viewing his rare collection of Bizet memorabilia and autographs.

The late M. François Galabert, former archivist of the city of Toulouse and son of Bizet's friend, Edmond Galabert, placed at my disposal all of Bizet's letters to his father and gave me much valuable information. The late M. Henry Malherbe kindly put me in touch with the late Dr. Eugéne Gelma of Strasbourg, who supplied me with several useful documents and the photograph of Bizet in National Guard uniform.

For their interest and help I am also indebted to Mmes Beaufreton and André Marix-Spire, to Messrs. Gerard Bauër, Stéphane Wolff, and the late M. J.-G. Prod'homme. I must thank, too, the Director of the Théâtre Nationale de l'Opéra-Comique for permission to use the log-books of the rehearsals of *Carmen*.

I owe a special debt to Winton Dean. I have drawn freely, and not always with acknowledgment, on his research and opinions as expressed in his publications on Bizet. And he has been personally most generous in helping to solve problems that arose during the writing of this book.

I wish also to express my gratitude to M. Julien Cain, Director of the Libraries of France, to M. Jacques Suffel and the staff of the Bibliothèque nationale, as well as to the librarians and staff-members of the following libraries in Paris: the Conservatoire Nationale de Musique, the Institut de France, the Arsenal, the Opéra, the

Beaux-Arts, the Ville de Paris, the Institut d'Art et d'Archéologie, and the Bibliothèque municipale of Versailles. I am also indebted to the Director of the Services des Recherches of the Archives nationales, the Director of the Archives de la Seine, and the archivists of the Archives du Ministère des Affaires Etrangères. The staff of the Dartmouth College Library kindly supplied me with photostats of the François Delsarte-Steele Mackaye correspondence.

I have been most fortunate in having the co-operation of a research assistant, Mlle Liliane Yacoël, whose gifts include not only thoroughness, imagination, and tact, but also a well-dowser's instinct for hidden sources. My former secretary, Mrs. Nellie M. Sickman, displayed great patience and accuracy in the initial stages of the writing of this book. Her successor, Mrs. Elenor Fardig, has been endlessly patient and careful in copying and recopying the many drafts of the manuscript. For his suggestions and help over and above the call of duty I am grateful to Herbert Weinstock, Executive Editor of Alfred A. Knopf, Inc.

M. C.

Preface

The focal center in the foreground of this work is Georges Bizet, depicted whenever possible in his own words or those of his friends and contemporaries. The method I have used seems to me comparable to the weaving of a tapestry designed by a pointillist, or perhaps more accurately to a historical painting carried out in *montage*. To a large extent I have abjured the author's right to interpretation except as it expresses itself in the juxtaposition of documents, although I know that the average reader prefers to accept an author's opinion rather than to formulate his own. My unwillingness to bow to this preference is based not on a sense of irresponsibility toward the reader, but rather on a desire to project as truthfully as possible the life of a great composer. The sources for this biography are largely unpublished, and the very fact of their having been ignored for more than eighty years after Bizet's death is in itself a relevant commentary on his life. I have felt, therefore, that only by including as many original documents as possible could I fill in the dearth of information about him which has hitherto existed. These documents came into my possession in a rather extraordinary manner.

While translating a selection of the letters of Marcel Proust, I found that the published version of his correspondence was frequently garbled; omissions were not indicated and many meanings were falsified. (This is also true of Bizet's published correspondence.) Because the letters of Proust which most interested me were written to Bizet's widow, Mme Emile Straus, I asked the aid of her closest living relative, M. Daniel Halévy. He was kindness itself and showed me the proof-sheets of the published letters Proust had written to Mme Straus, his cousin. He did not inherit the original letters. Because Bizet's son and widow both predeceased her second husband, Emile Straus, he became the heir to the family papers. He, dying childless in 1928, left the documents to his sister's son, René Sibilat, who, at his death in 1945, left them to his widow, Mme Magda Sibilat. She then became the owner also of the libraries of Mme Straus and of Mme Straus's father, Fromental Halévy, composer of *La Juive*, as well as of a large part of his correspondence and Bizet's.

Unfortunately Mme Sibilat was subject to recurrent attacks of mental illness, as a result of which her whereabouts were unknown when, soon after the War, I tried to find her. After weeks of searching, I found myself one day at a party talking to a gentleman who had only recently ceased to be in charge of her business affairs. Learning from him that the only person she trusted was her American doctor, who happened also to be my doctor, I was able to arrange a meeting. Subsequently I spent much time with her copying out the deleted portions of Proust's letters to Mme Straus. On one such occasion Mme Sibilat opened a cupboard in the hotel apartment where she was living temporarily and literally tossed into my lap volume after morocco-bound volume of holographs. These documents turned out to be letters from Bizet to his parents, his wife, and his mother-in-law; from Gounod, Saint-Saëns, Massenet, and other composers and artists to Bizet; letters to Fromental Halévy from Rossini, Verdi, Meyerbeer, Berlioz, and many other important contemporary figures—letters which had never before been seen by anyone but the correspondents themselves or their heirs. The experience was breathtaking and disturbing to someone who, having in childhood been severely punished for delving into a trunkful of her parents' love letters, has retained the notion that the clue to the creative process, the secret of life, lies in letters. When Mme Sibilat saw my excitement, she revealed to me that she had a whole unused apartment full of other such treasures. At this point I had to leave France. But she accepted my evaluation of her possessions and promised to keep the collection together until I could return to catalogue it.

When I returned the following winter, Mme Sibilat, who has since died, was in a state of acute depression, obsessed with the mistaken idea that she had lost her fortune. She wished to sell everything piecemeal as rapidly as possible. In order to keep the Bizet-Halévy collection together, I persuaded her to let me catalogue all her books and documents with the understanding that she would give to the Bibliothèque nationale everything not salable in dollars. After four months of cataloguing, I returned to the United States with the Bizet-Halévy collection which, in due course, will also go to the Bibliothèque nationale.

While attempting to sell the collection for Mme Sibilat, I started to read the letters. Knowing nothing of Bizet's life, not even having heard *Carmen* sung in years, I became fascinated, and overwhelmed with curiosity about the character of the writer of these extraordinarily revealing letters. I read Winton Dean's excellent short biography of Bizet and realized suddenly that I had in my hands the answers to countless questions that occurred to me while reading it. I then decided to acquire the collection myself.

For eight years the pursuit of the truth about Bizet led me back into the world of the Second Empire: its lyric theatres, its eccentric managers, its composers and artists, its family life, and the terrible year of the Siege of Paris and the Commune, but most of all to a revelation of the integrity as a man of this great composer who died at the age of thirty-six, only three months after the *première* of his masterpiece.

In this book I have tried to set Bizet against the background of his age, while communicating to the reader some of the excitement I have experienced in digging for the material necessary to a projection of Bizet's life and times as seen through his eyes and those of his contemporaries rather than through my own.

MINA CURTISS

Chapelbrook
Ashfield, Mass.
January 8, 1958

Contents

	Preface	x
I	The Bizets and the Delsartes	3
II	The Conservatoire	15
III	Bizet and Gounod	26
IV	Symphony in C: *Le Docteur Miracle:* Prix de Rome	38
V	Villa Medici: Victor Schnetz: Edmond About	51
VI	Rome: *Don Procopio:* Italy	68
VII	*Vasco de Gama:* Return from Rome	92
VIII	Death of Aimée Bizet	105
IX	Gounod's *La Reine de Saba: Erostrate* by Ernest Reyer	113
X	Scherzo: *Les Pêcheurs de Perles:* Choudens	124
XI	Meyerbeer: Galabert: *Ivan IV*	146
XII	Hard Times: The Princesse Mathilde: Céleste Mogador	158
XIII	*La Jolie Fille de Perth:* I	172
XIV	Paul Lacombe: Competition: Bizet, Music Critic	185
XV	*Malbrough s'en va-t-en guerre: La Jolie Fille de Perth*: II	203
XVI	Mme Trélat: *La Coupe du Roi de Thulé*: The *Roma* Symphony	216
XVII	Geneviève Halévy	235
XVIII	Marriage	251
XIX	The Year of Terror I: The Siege of Paris	259
XX	The Year of Terror II: The Commune	279
XXI	Family Problems	296
XXII	*Djamileh*	318
XXIII	*L'Arlésienne*	331
XXIV	Toward *Carmen*	342
XXV	Galli-Marié: Delaborde	357

XXVI   *Carmen* I: Rehearsals   371
XXVII *Carmen* II: *Première*   388
XXVIII Death of Georges Bizet   410
XXIX   *Carmen* III: Success   426
XXX   Postscript   438
       BIBLIOGRAPHICAL NOTES   443
       APPENDIX I: Unpublished Letters   457
       APPENDIX II: Works of Georges Bizet   465
            Chronologically Listed with Dates of
            Composition and Publication
       APPENDIX III: Posthumous Presentations of Bizet's
            Dramatic Works   470
       APPENDIX IV: Bizet's Music Library   472
       APPENDIX V: Selected List of Reading on the Life
            and Works of Georges Bizet   475
       INDEX   *follows page* 477

Illustrations

FOLLOWING PAGE 112

1. a. Georges Bizet, 1859. *Portrait by F. Giacomotti.*
   b. Georges Bizet, 1860. *Sketch made on return journey from Rome by G. Planté.*
2. Fromental Halévy. (*Bibliothèque de l'Opéra*)
3. François Delsarte. (*Bibliothèque de l'Opéra*)
4. Charles Gounod, 1857. (*Collection of author*)
5. a. Ernest Guiraud. (*Bibliothèque de l'Opéra*)
   b. Antoine-Louis Clapisson. (*Bibliothèque de l'Opéra*)
6. Page from Bizet's outline for music lessons. (*Collection of author*)
7. Caricature from cover of *Diogène,* September 28, 1863. (*Bettmann Archive*)
8. a. Georges Bizet. (*By courtesy of the late M. F. Galabert*)
   b. Edmond Galabert. (*By courtesy of the late M. F. Galabert*)

FOLLOWING PAGE 176

9. Page showing Bizet's corrections in libretto of *La Jolie Fille de Perth,* Act III. (*Collection of author*)
10. a. Céleste Vénard, La Mogador.
    b. Céleste Mogador, Comtesse Lionel de Moreton de Chabrillan, *c.* 1866. (*Bibliothèque Nationale*)
11. a. Marie Reiter, *c.* 1900. (*By courtesy of Mme Suzanne Reiter*)
    b. Jean Reiter, 1886. (*By courtesy of Mme Suzanne Reiter*)
    c. Esther Halévy. (*By courtesy of M. Daniel Halévy*)

[xv]

d. Jacques Bizet, 1882. (*By courtesy of M. Daniel Halévy*)

12. a. Bizet in National Guard uniform. (*By courtesy of the late Dr. Eugène Gelma*)
   b. Sketch of Geneviève Halévy by her mother. (*Collection of author*)

13. a. Letter from Bizet to his wife. (*Collection of author*)
   b. Letter from Bizet to his mother-in-law. (*Collection of author*)

14. Page from Bizet's music catalogue. (*Collection of author*)

15. a. Alphonse Daudet, c. 1870. (*Bibliothèque Nationale*)
   b. Léon Carvalho. (*By courtesy of Mme de Juge*)

16. a. Geneviève Bizet, 1876. *Portrait by Elie Delaunay.* (*Louvre*)
   b. Geneviève Bizet, c. 1880.

FOLLOWING PAGE 368

17. Manuscript of the *"Habanera"* from *Carmen* in Bizet's handwriting. (*Collection of author*)

18. Henri Meilhac and Ludovic Halévy, 1866.

19. a. Camille du Locle. (*Bibliothèque de l'Opéra*)
   b. Galli-Marié in unidentified role. (*Bibliothèque de l'Opéra*)

20. a. Galli-Marié as Carmen.
   b. Lhérie as Don José.

21. Page from manuscript of *Grisélidis* showing original version of *"La fleur que tu m'avais jetée"* from *Carmen*. (*Collection of author*)

22. Proofsheet of piano score of *Carmen*. (*Collection of author*)

23. Georges Bizet, 1875. (*Bettmann Archive*)

24. a. Telegram from Ludovic Halévy to Hippolyte Rodrigues announcing Bizet's death. (*Collection of author*)
   b. Geneviève Bizet-Straus, 1886. *Portrait by Auguste Toulmouche.* (*Collection of author*)

BIZET and His World

CHAPTER I

The Bizets and the Delsartes

On October 25, 1838, in Paris, at 26 rue de la Tour d'Auvergne, a male child was born whose name on his birth certificate was to read Alexandre-César-Léopold Bizet. But because this certificate was among the records destroyed by fire during the Commune, the grandiose nomenclature with which Georges Bizet started his short life might never have been known to posterity had it not appeared in the records of the Conservatoire and of the French Académie in Rome, on his marriage license, and on the birth and baptismal certificates of his son. He was baptized Georges on March 16, 1840, in the church of Notre Dame de Lorette, and Georges he called and signed himself throughout his life. It is perhaps symbolic of the many puzzling problems confronting a biographer of Bizet that the very first of them should be the mystery of his name. Why this child, born into an unpretentious and humble household, should have been named after three emperors remains unexplained.

Aimée-Marie-Louise-Léopoldine-Josephine Delsarte, Bizet's mother, born December 22, 1815, at 69 Place d'Armes, Cambrai, came from a family of doctors and lawyers on her father's side, and on her mother's of landed gentry reduced to poverty by the Revolution. The spelling of her family name varied.[1] Contemporaries—for example, Delacroix in his *Journal*—wrote the name as a single word. But Aimée's brother, François Delsarte, the best-known member of the family, in signing his name capitalized the second syllable, perhaps because natives of his birthplace, Solesmes, in the

---

[1] On her birth certificate Aimée Bizet's name stands as Delsarte; on her marriage license it appears as Delzart.

north of France, cherished a legend of the residence there, at some time long past, of a famous Italian painter. And because Andrea del Sarto spent part of 1518 and 1519 in France, he became identified as the legendary artist forebear. Although the Delsarte family has clung to this legend as well as to another claiming a Spanish ancestor, we need trace it no farther back than Bizet's maternal grandfather, Jean-Nicolas-Toussaint Delsarte, who was born in 1778, the son of Dr. Nicolas Delsarte. A man of eccentric temperament, the second Nicolas appears to have been unsuccessful as a lawyer in the town of Solesmes, his birthplace. Shortly before the birth of his only daughter, Aimée, the family had moved to the nearby city of Cambrai, where the father's occupation was listed as *"marchand caffetier."* Little suited to a career as either wine-merchant or proprietor of a café, Nicolas Delsarte was unable to support his family. According to one of his descendants, "he was so driven by his genius for invention that he spent all his time and money in studies and experiments." But because he lacked a practical financial sense, any profit from his inventions went to the investors with enough capital to launch them.[2]

Bizet's grandmother, Aimée-Albertine-Roland Delsarte, came from a family of some wealth, and is described by her descendants as "an ambitious little *bourgeoise* who, caring only for a life of ease, made the mistake of marrying a creative genius, far more interested in his inventions than in his clients, and who spent all of his wife's dowry on patent fees." He reduced his family to such penury that his wife, in desperation, left him, accompanied by her four small children, the two youngest of whom, Aimée and Camille,[3] she eventually took to the home of her mother, Mme

---

[2] During the first decade of Bizet's life, his grandfather was working on a device which, he wrote, could "bring about an economically advantageous revolution in the steam engine, a saving in fuel . . . as well as a drastic lowering of the cost, volume and weight of the machines; many fewer and certainly much less deadly explosions." In another letter Nicolas Delsarte told of developing a miner's lamp "to prevent the explosion of hydrogen gas caused by the carelessness of workers in the coal mines." (Unpublished, undated letters from Nicolas to François Delsarte, in the collection of Mme Bouts Réal Del Sarte.) François Delsarte inherited his father's gift for invention and originated a device for tuning stringed instruments which he called the *Phonoptique*. (See Hector Berlioz, *A Travers Chant*, Paris, 1880, 255–57.)

[3] Camille Delsarte, Bizet's youngest uncle, whom he may never have known, was also a musician. After having taught singing profitably at Mézières in the Ardennes he had great success as first tenor in the Opera at Rheims. He eventually migrated to Australia and lost touch with his family in France. (See Appendix I, p. 457.)

Roland, at nearby Raillencourt. Mme Roland refused to receive her son-in-law, Nicolas Delsarte, so it is unlikely that Bizet's mother ever saw her father after she was old enough to remember him. When Mme Delsarte died in 1837, the younger Aimée fled to the Paris home of her brother, François, who had been married four years earlier. There, soon after her arrival, Aimée Delsarte encountered her future husband, Adolphe-Amand Bizet.[4]

Born at 3 rue des Trois Pucelles in Rouen on August 16, 1810, Adolphe-Amand was descended on his father's side from Louis-Guillaume Bizet, a master rope-maker, and Guillaume-Michel-Jérôme Bizet, a linen-weaver. On his mother's side, Adolphe Bizet's great-grandfather was Charles Gaumont, a master-carpenter. Adolphe's mother, Catherine-Geneviève Cornu, had been a cotton-spinner before her marriage to Georges Bizet's grandfather, the linen-weaver. At the time of Adolphe's birth, his father was listed as "absent" and was later "presumed" killed while fighting in Napoleon's army. As the only son of his widowed mother, who continued to live in Rouen, Adolphe Bizet, "hairdresser and wig-maker, residing in Paris," was granted exemption from military service on October 2, 1837.

Two months later, on December 26, when he married Aimée Delsarte at the Church of Saint-Laurent, he had become a singing teacher. Family legend and gossip offer no explanation of this rapid change of vocation, or indeed of his meeting with Aimée Delsarte. There is a certain irony in the thought that the composer whose masterpiece has been the backbone of the Opéra-Comique for more than seventy years sprang from a union that suggests the plot of an opera, either *comique* or *bouffe*. Picture a young girl with musical talent, a stranger in Paris, who, while searching for a hair-dressing establishment, overhears a *coiffeur* singing in a melodious but uncultivated voice. She falls in love with him and marries him against strong family objections, with the understanding that he will study with her brother in order to become a singing teacher.

The family objections were not hypothetical. Some five months before the wedding, in a letter to François Delsarte and his wife, their uncle protested against Aimée's remaining with her

---

[4] Biographers have always added an "r" to the middle name of Bizet's father, thereby changing it to Armand. But on all official documents it is spelled without the "r."

brother and sister-in-law in Paris while their grandmother needed her care. "Good God," he wrote, "what a moment to choose for a marriage! You, my good friends, who know your grandmother's antipathy to this marriage,[5] why must you choose this time, when she is in need of consolation and care, to *make plans so opposed to her views? . . .* Your sister, you say, cannot stay alone in Paris. I quite agree with you that the thing is impossible. But as against this impossibility, I balance the fate that your sister can expect if she marries a man who as yet has no profession, no money, and who, in spite of all his good qualities, may not succeed. . . . The time that you choose, my good friend, is in every way inopportune. At least let the remains of my poor sister cool off before plans are made for a union which, later on, I should be far from opposing if the man you wish to present to me as a nephew can, through his work, make your sister happy; her unhappiness would be the sorrow of my life. I know, my good friend, from what I have been told that the young man you mention can succeed. . . . I know that he is very steady, but isn't he mortal? And then what would happen to your sister? Wait . . . that is my deliberated ultimatum. Even if I do not agree with you, follow your inclinations and may God lavish his blessings upon you! That is how I feel!!!" "

Aimée's marriage against her family's wishes is indicative of her strength of will and capacity for devotion. Yet there was much to be said for the family point of view. The grandnieces of Adolphe Bizet describe him as *"un brave homme, ni plus, ni moins."* One of the grandnieces was told by her mother, who knew the elder Bizet well, that he was "neither very remarkable, nor very much respected, nor very intelligent; slightly ridiculous and not talented musically, but a very upstanding and handsome man. In the Delsarte family he was valued as a decent human being, but not as an artist."

Judging by the three or four letters from Bizet to his father preserved among dozens to his mother and to his wife's relatives, his opinion of Adolphe Bizet coincided fairly closely with that of his mother's family. In spite, or perhaps partly because, of Adolphe Bizet's devoted admiration for his son, Georges implied from time

---

[5] Aimée Bizet apparently bore no ill-will toward her grandmother: at the time of Mme Roland's death, she traveled alone all the way north to her bedside. A letter she wrote at that time is the only one of hers extant. (See Appendix I, p. 458.)

to time, after he was grown up, that his father was rather a bore, kindly and well-meaning, but something of a nuisance, not extremely intelligent, and more interested in his vegetable garden than in ideas.

Although Adolphe Bizet was sufficiently gifted musically to compose a few pieces,[6] it was his mother's criticism of his work that Georges Bizet valued. As a child, he learned the rudiments of harmony from his father, but his mother, a talented pianist, taught him his notes and his letters simultaneously, and probably gave him his first piano lessons. Although both parents were musical, there can be little doubt that Georges's intelligence and much of his early musical training came predominantly from his mother's side of the family.

This influence has been largely ignored by Bizet's biographers because his early intimacy with the Delsartes did not survive his mother's death in 1861; later, as a result of the Delsartes' objections to his marrying a Jewess, the relationship dwindled into a formality. When Bizet's letters to his parents were published some thirty years after his death, most of the references and messages to the Delsartes included in nearly every letter were deleted by the editor, a close friend of Bizet's widow. Among his private papers only one document indicative of the family connection remains, a torn and yellowed sheet of music bearing the inscription: "Page torn from the manuscript of *Pré-aux-clercs,* Autograph of Hérold, to my dear nephew Bizet, Delsarte." But in Delsarte's daily record for January 1, 1856, he notes a payment of 100 francs by Georges Bizet for lessons given.

The Delsarte household was dominated by a passionate preoccupation with music and a highly personal Catholicism that on occasion brought the family into open conflict with the Church. Materially the family existed in a state of cultivated poverty which the grandchildren still mention with pride as *"la misère Delsarte."* Bizet's early determination to earn money by his works, and his intense aversion to clericalism were no doubt in part a reaction against the self-imposed hardship and the exaggerated mysticism that formed the background of his uncle's family.

At the beginning of the reign of Napoleon III, a pupil of

---

[6] A cantata, *Imogine,* a string quartet (dated February 1, 1853), some fugues, piano works, and songs, at least one of which was published, as well as two fantasies for military band on themes from Fromental Halévy's *La Reine de Chypre.*

Delsarte's approached a cabinet minister, urging him to secure an
official post for his teacher. "Where or how could we help him?"
the minister replied. "Delsarte is an innovator and we have no
place for him. We have round holes for round men, and square
and oval holes for square and oval people, but where in all conscience do you want me to put a man who is all three?" [7] The pattern of Delsarte's childhood and youth was certainly not calculated
to shape him for any of the normal disciplines of life. In his own
account, it often sounds like an excerpt from *Jane Eyre*. Indeed
there is a quality reminiscent of Rochester in both the temperament and bearing of this proud and passionate man.

François, born in 1811, was the oldest of the children who
had accompanied their mother when she left her husband. For a
reason undisclosed in family legend he was left, at the age of
seven, with his younger brother at a *pension* in Paris. Because
funds for the support of the children were not forthcoming, they
were transferred to an unheated garret, where the younger boy
contracted pneumonia and died. François followed his brother's
coffin on foot across a cold and wintry Paris. On his way back
from the cemetery, he fainted from hunger and exhaustion. As he
regained consciousness, snow was falling all around him; he heard
what seemed to him angelic voices and imagined himself in heaven
with his brother. But the voices were those of streetsingers who
befriended the child. In rapture at the sounds he had heard, he
determined there and then—so the legend goes—to become a
musician.

His musical education began quite as fortuitously. While sup-
porting himself as apprentice to a brick-maker, he ate his meals
with the other workers in a little *bistro* frequented by an old
Italian called Bambini, a music teacher whom François "boldly
accosted" for information as to how he, too, could become a
musician. The old man took over the boy's care and education;
Delsarte lived with him throughout his years at the Conservatoire
and until his marriage. Delsarte's descendants describe Bambini as
"un Italien exalté," a kind but eccentric man. He would pace the
floor of an evening, balancing a heavy load of books on his head.
"These are the works of Gluck, my child," he explained to his

---

[7] This and all subsequent unidentified quotations in this chapter are from
the unpublished journal of Delsarte's youngest daughter, Madeleine Réal Delsarte. Collection of Mlle Géraldy.

pupil. "They are monumental, the creation of a genius. By carrying them on my head, some of their greatness will penetrate my brain." Thus, perhaps, began Delsarte's passion for Gluck, which was in part responsible for the revival of interest in that master's work in Paris in the 1850's.

Delsarte entered the Conservatoire in 1825 at the age of fourteen. He minimized the value of his studies there and blamed the loss of his voice on the official method of teaching singing. He won only a second prize in the vocalization examination in 1828 and failed in the final competition for opera singers in 1829. Two of the judges, however, perceived the extraordinary quality of his art. The celebrated singer Adolphe Nourrit is reported to have said to Delsarte: "I gave you my vote for the first prize and my children shall have no singing-master but you." And La Malibran herself assured him that one day he would be a great artist. By the time he had become, if not a great, at least a distinguished artist, it pleased him to hear the comment that "he sang without a voice the way Ingres painted without color." " But according to his pupil and biographer, Angélique Arnaud, the comparison was inexact. "Delsarte was not without a voice; on the contrary, his voice had great range and power, with an impressive and eminently sympathetic timbre. Only it was not a healthy organ." "

After Delsarte's failure at the Conservatoire, he made several attempts to sing light roles at the Comique and the Ambigu. But it soon became clear that his voice was too undependable for a career on the operatic stage. So in 1831 he took up teaching as a profession. His success was immediate, and his prestige grew with the years. Jenny Lind came from Sweden to hear him sing. Rachel asked his advice on the interpretation of her roles. He coached Coquelin and Jean-Baptiste Faure. His lectures on expression and interpretation were crowded not only with his own pupils, but also with composers, clergymen, lawyers, and members of society. Although the Princesse de Chimay, Mme de Lamartine, the Comtesse d'Haussonville, and many other titled ladies adored the master and spread his fame, "his favorite students," his daughter said, "were generally those who paid nothing. There were so many that in the end he gave a special course for them. He even went so far as to collect needy students. . . . He could say 'no' only in anger, and my mother was forced to intervene daily to get rid of people who tried to exploit him. We always kept open house in the kitchen, and each poor person had a day assigned to him. 'Our guests,' Mama would call them with a wry smile. They were mostly unsuccessful musicians who . . . lived off my father's generosity." Obviously the *"misère Delsarte"* stemmed from the temperament of the artist himself.

In 1847, the year Bizet started his studies at the Conservatoire, his uncle was invited to sing for a large fee at the court of Louis-Philippe. He refused, not out of pride, he maintained, but because he valued his art too highly to treat it as merchandise. "I do not sell my loves." On the occasion of this invitation from the King, Delsarte capitulated when he learned that the concert was to be a birthday celebration given by the Duc d'Orléans in honor of his father. But he imposed three conditions: that there should be no other singer; no accompaniment other than the chorus of the Opéra; and no compensation. At court, we are told, he was "respectful, but not humble . . . so noble and so simple that before he had spoken a word, he had won the hearts of all. The family of Louis-Philippe showered him with such delicate attentions and the King was so charming and cordial . . . that M. Ingres could not refrain from remarking: 'It could indeed be said that it is Delsarte who is King of France today.' " [n]

The painter's comment may well have been made after Delsarte sang, "sobbing, Gluck's *Laissez-vous toucher par mes larmes,* while the King, weeping, arose and in a voice drowned in tears cried, 'That is sublime.' Delsarte, when he came home, remarked to his children, 'I wished to sing without remuneration, but the King paid me well.' " [n]

Louis-Philippe's successor, Napoleon III, although his musical predilections hardly included Gluck, did nevertheless, soon after his accession, invite Delsarte to sing at court. He accepted, under the same conditions as in 1847. But after the concert the monarch despatched a courier to the artist's house with the following message: " 'The Emperor has ordered me to tell you that every time you give a paying concert he wishes a ticket reserved for him.' . . . And on the eve of every concert he received a letter from the Emperor's secretariat asking for a ticket for the concert in exchange for an enclosed thousand-franc note." [n]

These commands from the Court were, of course, the high points in Delsarte's career—recognition of the position he occupied among a small, very distinguished group of admirers. The leaders of this circle were the Bertins, publishers and editors of the *Journal des Débats*. The music critic of their paper, Hector Berlioz, carried on a running controversy over Delsarte's interpretations of Gluck, and disapproved of his predilection for "antiquated and childish" music. But Berlioz was not a powerful influence in the Bertin circle, which, having first been dedicated to romanticism, subsequently devoted itself to reviving the classics. Napoléon-Henri Reber was musical arbiter, Ingres intellectual leader of this group.

Although Reber seemed to be "not of our time . . . but a contemporary of Haydn, the Boccherini of our day," he became an admirer of Bizet who, many years later, wrote: "If I occupied the musical position assigned to me by Reber, I should no longer have anything to wish for." Professor of composition at the Conservatoire, Reber also wrote operas, songs, ballets, and chamber music. His greatest work was his *Traité d'harmonie*. His consciously archaic wit and the exquisite urbanity of his manners evoked a sense of the past. His white hair, like a powdered wig, and his anachronistic style of dress, gave him the air of a man dropped out of the eighteenth century into the nineteenth, surprised and slightly shocked by the music and customs of the day.

"In this quite special world," writes Saint-Saëns, "there were no *soirées* without Delsarte. He would arrive, pretending to have a hideous sore throat in order to justify his chronic loss of voice; and without any voice, by some sort of magic, he would make everyone thrill to the accents of *Orphée* and *Iphigénie*. I often accompanied him, and he would always ask for *pianissimo*.

" 'But,' I would say to him, 'the author has indicated *forte*.' 'That's true,' he would answer, 'but at that time the keyboard had very little sonority.' It would have been too easy to reply that the accompaniment had been written not for keyboard, but for an orchestra. . . .

"To spread the cult of the ancient masters, Delsarte had the idea of publishing a collection of pieces chosen here and there from their works, and he created the *Archives du chant*. He had special plates cast for this publication, which was a triumph of typographical beauty, accuracy, and good taste. But to be successful a work of this kind needed the backing of an influential publisher. Delsarte published his own work with no success at all.

"Voiceless singer, unequaled musician, questionable scholar, guided by an intuition that sprang from genius, Delsarte played, in spite of his numerous deficiencies, an important role in the evolution of French music of the nineteenth century. He was not an ordinary man. He left the impression on all who knew him of an illuminator, an apostle." "

Less sympathetic than Saint-Saëns, Delacroix, who dined frequently at Bertin's, thought Delsarte "basically mad." For Delsarte regarded Mozart "as a great corrupting influence. . . . That nice Delsarte said that Mozart had pillaged Galuppi outrageously . . ." Delacroix wrote in his *Journal*. "I told him that *what was Mozart* had not been taken from Galuppi or anyone else. . . . Delsarte behaves like a kind of madman; his plans for the welfare of mankind, his tremendous perseverance in attempting to become a homeopathic doctor . . . his ridiculous and exclusive preference for old music, as well as the eccentricity of his behavior, put him in a class with Ingres, whose preferences and antipathies are just as silly. . . ." " Bizet's opinion of his uncle did not differ greatly from Delacroix's. After having studied with his uncle, he concluded that his own father was "the only professor who understands *the art of the voice.*"

But whatever Bizet's feelings for his uncle may have been, his affection for his aunt and cousins was positive and warm. Mme Delsarte, a woman of extraordinary musical gifts, a truly noble character, patient, kind, and endowed with a much needed sense of humor, had married her husband in 1833, when she was sixteen. Rosine-Charlotte Delsarte was the daughter of Martin-Joseph Andrien, first basso at the Opéra and a great friend of Cherubini, then director of the Conservatoire. At Andrien's death, Cherubini took charge of the musical education of Rosine and her older sister.[8] Although family legend claims that Rosine entered the Conservatoire at the age of five, the records show that she had reached the required age of ten. During her five years at the Conservatoire she won first prizes in solfeggio and piano, a second prize in solfeggio when she was only eleven, and honorable mention in harmony and as accompanist at fourteen. Her harmony professor was Bizet's future teacher and father-in-law, Fromental

---

[8] Atala-Thérèse-Annette Andrien (1806–82) was an even more brilliant musician than her sister. Having won all possible prizes while a student at the Conservatoire, she was the first woman instrumentalist to play the piano at the Conservatoire concerts. She taught piano at the Conservatoire and married a singer, Pierre Wartel.

Halévy. From the time Rosine was thirteen until four years after her marriage to Delsarte, she held the post of assistant professor of solfeggio at the Conservatoire at a salary of 1000 francs per year. Her force of character asserted itself early for she is said, after a stubborn battle, to have brought about the enactment of a regulation forbidding the presence of the pupils' mothers during classes. These women, according to Rosine's granddaughter, were on "the social level of *concierges,* and fought like shrews over the success or failure of their daughters in classroom competition."

Rosine was less successful in combating her own mother. The widow Andrien wished to marry off her daughters as young as possible. When Delsarte fell in love with the thirteen-year-old Rosine, his fellow-student at the Conservatoire, she was as beautiful as she was gifted. But she was not in love with her future husband, and managed to postpone the marriage until, after three years, she reluctantly submitted to her mother's wishes, weeping profusely on her wedding day. Although neither she nor her husband had had a religious upbringing, Mme Delsarte experienced a miraculous conversion soon after her marriage. Tired, one day, after the private lessons she gave in addition to her teaching at the Conservatoire, she stopped to rest in the church of Saint-Etienne du Mont. She was moved to pray at the tomb of Saint Geneviève, the patron saint of Paris, who then appeared to her in a vision. Henceforth, according to her granddaughter, she became a "saintlike person," and later converted her husband, who, although less saintly than his wife, was even more of a mystic.

Three sons were born to Mme Delsarte before she was twenty, and another son and two daughters followed in the next few years. She taught her children the principles of music and the piano. Bizet, too, shared in these lessons with his cousins Henri, Adrien, and Gustave. His early exercises in solfeggio were copied on discarded proof-sheets of the *Archives du chant,* the collection that occupied Delsarte and his wife during Bizet's early childhood.

In the intervals between Bizet's frequent visits to the Delsartes, his mother supervised his practicing at home so assiduously that on one occasion, it is said, she changed his shirt for him while he was at the piano to prevent his losing any time from his work. Mme Bizet was undoubtedly aware that without continual practice on a standard piano, her son's technique could hardly develop normally. For the instruments in use in the Delsarte house-

hold were peculiar unto themselves. Delsarte admitted readily that
he was no connoisseur of the piano, that he could listen only to
Chopin. "When a piano was brought to the house," his daughter
tells us, "he immediately removed the pedals, to the horror of the
pianists who came to see him. They would invariably gasp with
surprise and lean over to make sure that there was really nothing
there. 'Don't look for pedals,' Papa would say, 'it's useless. I never
keep pedals on my pianos. The way they are misused exasperates
me.' "

Delsarte's treatment of his pianos varied from time to time.
In 1865 an American pupil reports that "the piano is of pre-
Raphaelite construction, and stands in the middle of the room
like an island in a lake, with a footstool placed over the pedals.
. . . The lid of the piano was absent, and to judge from the
inside, I should say that the piano was the receptacle for everything that belonged to the Delsarte homestead. There were ink-
stands, pens, pencils, knives, matches, toothpicks, half-smoked
cigars, even remnants of his luncheon, which seemed to have been
black bread and cheese, and dust galore." " (This statement belies
his daughter's claim that Delsarte lunched each day off new-laid
eggs, a luxury that forced the family to keep chickens.)

The master's favorite keyboard instrument, a harpsichord
that had belonged to Queen Hortense, mother of Napoleon III,
was used for the instruction of Bizet and his cousins. Although
Delsarte, occupied with morning and evening classes as well as
with private lessons, spent little time with his nephew, he did
bring to bear sufficient influence to enable the nine-year-old boy
to become an auditor in classes at the Conservatoire a year before
he was old enough to be officially enrolled as a student.

CHAPTER II

The Conservatoire

In the records of the Conservatoire for the term 1847–48, Bizet's name is written in pencil in a list without heading at the end of the volume, but it does not appear on any official class list. The only account of his early entrance to the Conservatoire was published nearly thirty years later in a hastily written obituary article for which no sources were given. It has been quoted in every biography of Bizet, and is repeated here.

From the time Bizet had been a small child, he had listened outside the door of the room in which his father gave singing lessons. When he was only eight, his father called him in and gave him a song to sing at sight. The boy astonished him by singing it correctly without looking at the music. By the time he was nine, the family had decided that he was ready for the Conservatoire. So, according to the accepted account, his father went to consult Louis Alizard, a singer at the Opéra,[1] as to how best to persuade the authorities to waive the rule that no pupil could enter the Conservatoire before the age of ten.

"After a short conference," wrote Charles Pigot, Bizet's earliest biographer, "the two friends, with our candidate for the Conservatoire in tow, went straight to [Joseph-Jean] Meifred, who was then a member of the Committee on Studies. 'Your child is very young,' said Meifred, eying the little fellow with a condescending sneer. 'That is true,' replied the father, refusing to be disconcerted. 'He may be small in stature, but his knowledge is

---

[1] Adolphe Bizet was at this time a member of the *Comité de lecture* of the Opéra.

great.'—'Oh, really! And what can he do?'—'Sit down at the piano, strike some chords, and he will name them for you without a mistake.'—The test was carried out on the spot. His back turned toward the instrument, the child, without hesitating, named all the chords struck for him, chords deliberately chosen in the most recondite tonalities. At the same time, he rapidly enumerated, with surprising facility, the various functions of these chords in the order in which they were struck. Meifred was unable to restrain his admiration. 'You, my boy,' he cried, 'you will go straight to the Institut.' " [n]

The account of Bizet's precocious virtuosity and his ability to convince Meifred of his gifts is unquestionably true. But the curious part of this oft-told tale is the professor's "condescending sneer" before he had heard the child play. For Meifred was a great admirer of Delsarte, who was using his influence to help his nephew into the Conservatoire. Indeed, only a few months before this incident, Meifred had written to Bizet's uncle asking his opinion of one of his pupils, remarking on Delsarte's "gift for finding the vein of gold in any metal." In thanking him, Meifred wrote: ". . . if you do me this favor I should be happy if an occasion arose that would enable me to show my gratitude." [n] Surely sneering condescension toward the nephew would hardly have been a way to repay the uncle's favor.

In any case, Meifred's prediction of possible future election to the Institut did not simplify Bizet's immediate problem, for all the classes at the Conservatoire were full. His uncle, however, was able to arrange for his admission as an auditor in the piano class of Antoine-François Marmontel, who regarded his childhood friend Delsarte as "a musician of taste, but lacking in judgment as a scholar."

While Bizet was an auditor in Marmontel's class, he experienced at first hand the violence of the Revolution of 1848. In a street near his house a barricade was erected and reinforced by a grille stolen from the church of his baptism, Notre-Dame de Lorette.[2] In front of the Conservatoire, during the June rioting, a company of the National Guard, raw recruits barely able to fire

---

[2] César Franck and his bride were forced to climb this barricade in order to be married in the church on February 22, and were "willingly helped in this delicate operation by the insurgents who were massed behind the improvised fortification." (Vincent d'Indy, *César Franck,* London, 1910, 39.)

a gun who had been summoned hastily to quell the workers' riots, halted to dress their ranks. Among the rawest of the recruits drafted at this time was François Delsarte, whose resentment at the attacks on the Archbishop's Palace by members of the National Guard as well as by civilian anti-clericals caused him to welcome rather than, as earlier, to evade military duty. "It was in June of '48 . . ." his daughter writes, "when my father, along with all the men of his age, was obliged to do military service. . . . His post was near the Seine. One day the troops arrested a foreigner whom they regarded as a suspicious character. The man was forced to the sentry box with blows and insults. Pale and terrified he made no resistance. By his appearance, my father judged him to be a Pole. He was searched, but the only seditious object found in his pockets was a cheap little rosary. 'A Jesuit!' the crowd shouted. 'Down with the Jesuit! Toss the Jesuit into the river!' And the mob started pushing him toward the Seine. . . . My father . . . summoning all his talents, advanced resolutely toward the noisiest section of the crowd. With that attitude, those gestures with which he was so well able to move and influence an audience, he pulled from his pocket the large rosary a Trappist had given him, and waving it in their faces, cried, 'Citizens, I claim my share of your wrath. You see I am even more of a fool than Monsieur.' Nothing more was necessary. His great presence of mind and the authority of his personality were enough to disarm the crowd." "

The impact of all this violence on the nine-year-old Bizet was strong enough so that twenty years later a pupil's work reminded him of "a horrible patriotic song sung all over Paris in 1848. Perhaps the memory of that futile, ridiculous, stupid revolution makes me unfair to your song." "

On October 9, 1848, Bizet, a fair little boy with a pink, plump, very alert face, was taken to the Conservatoire to compete in the examinations for the piano class. Entering the old building facing the rue du Faubourg Poissonnière which then housed the Conservatoire, he found a large hall, the walls of which, like those of most other similar institutions at the time, were painted a blue-gray dotted roughly with black. The only furniture in this waiting-room consisted of some old benches. The usher, M. Ferrière, a stern, rude man always decked out in a funereal top hat, would call the candidates in his policeman's voice, shouting their names into the midst of the crowd of emotional friends and relatives who accompanied them. It was a little like the summons to the condemned. To each candidate he gave a number denoting his place among those waiting to appear before the jury already in session in the concert hall.

"This hall, intended for examinations, was built like a sort of little theatre, with a row of boxes and a circular gallery," Massenet wrote. "It was decorated in the style of the Consulate. . . . In this same little hall—not to be confused with the well-known hall of the Société des Concerts du Conservatoire—all examinations of all the classes, including those in comedy and tragedy, were given. Several times a week, organ classes were conducted there too, for at the back a large, two-manual organ was hidden behind a huge tapestry. Next to this shrill, worn, old instrument stood the fatal door through which the pupils came onto the platform that formed the little stage. In this room, too, for many years, the competitions for the Prix de Rome were held." [n]

Competing with Bizet that October morning in 1848 were twenty-one other boys. Four were accepted as pupils and five as auditors; thirteen were rejected. Bizet was one of the two students accepted for Marmontel's class, probably the only one who, according to his teacher, could play all of Mozart's piano sonatas "with taste and without affectation."

The curriculum and teaching at the Conservatoire have sustained sharp criticism for a hundred and twenty years or more, ever since Berlioz expressed himself forcibly on the subject. The dissatisfaction continues today,[n] for no basic changes appear to have materialized. Committees of reform and reorganization have been appointed from time to time, the first by Cherubini in 1835. The report of this committee, signed by Auber, Halévy, and Marmontel among others, was submitted in 1848. The curriculum therein outlined was adopted and remained in force during Bizet's student years.

There were seven divisions of teaching:
1. elementary studies: solfeggio, oral harmony, keyboard studies, study of dramatic roles
2. singing
3. lyric declamation
4. piano, harp

5. string instruments
6. wind instruments
7. composition, harmony, organ

In addition, there were complementary courses in music, declamation, literature, and history related to the lyric and dramatic arts; the history of music; and the Italian language. Astonishing as it may seem to anyone unfamiliar with the idiosyncrasies of official French records, the Conservatoire kept no lists of the members of these classes. Nor is there any report of how they were taught.

The Director at this time was Daniel-François-Esprit Auber, who, although friendly with Bizet's father, was never admired by the son (see Appendix I, p. 459). From the time he was old enough to have any critical sense, Bizet felt bitterly about the results of Auber's long regime as director of the Conservatoire, which lasted from the time he became Cherubini's successor in 1842 until his death in 1871 at the age of 89. The laxity of Auber's standards resulted not so much from a weakness in moral values or a lack of taste as from the fact that, according to a contemporary, "he is never very deeply affected by anything . . . never has any passions, but simply preferences, and those never very strong. He is a ladies' man, but never in love; he has women, but no mistresses; acquaintances, but no friends. . . . When he dies, he will kiss himself most tenderly, clasp himself in his own arms, and say to himself, '*Adieu*, my friend. I have never loved anyone but you; I am miserable at leaving you.' " "

When Bizet entered the Conservatoire, Auber was sixty-five. The son of a wealthy banker, Auber had shown musical gifts from childhood. His first work, a comic opera, was produced in 1813 without success, and, indeed, he had no success until his father's death, when the loss of his fortune forced him to earn his living. Of the nearly fifty operas Auber composed, *Fra Diavolo,* first produced in 1830, is the only one performed at all frequently today.

The only muse Auber knew was the muse of boredom, he admitted to a friend, and even his happiest ideas, he said, were created between yawns. His lifelong collaboration with Eugène Scribe spared him the libretto trouble common to most composers, a difficulty that might well have silenced him altogether had it not been for Scribe, whom he regarded as "the greatest librettist who ever lived. I only had to place the words on the piano, put on my hat, and go out. When I came back, the music was all written—the words had done it alone." [n] As Bizet remarked, "Auber, who had so much talent with so few ideas, was almost always understood, while Berlioz, who had genius without talent, almost never was."

The director of the Conservatoire taught no classes. Bizet was trained by the best professors, two of whom, at least, he both loved and admired. He remained as an auditor in Marmontel's class until the beginning of 1849, when he was listed as a member of a "Special class for 'Men,' taught by Marmontel, successor to Zimmerman."

Pierre-Joseph-Guillaume Zimmerman, the father-in-law of Charles Gounod, became outside examiner of piano classes after his retirement as professor. He was so struck by Bizet's gifts that when the boy won a first prize in solfeggio only six months after he had entered the Conservatoire, Zimmerman offered to give him private lessons. The pupil, always devoted to his master, wrote after his death: ["I have not forgotten that my dear and regretted master,] Zimmerman, had plenty of trouble at home on my account. They were always reproaching him for wasting his time on a little idiot who would never amount to anything. [Then, when I made the slightest showing, all these people would go into ecstasies while at the same time retaining the privilege of changing their minds again at the first failure."] [n]

Zimmerman, Marmontel wrote, "had a kind, sweet face that beamed with good will; his eyes, clear and lively, were shaded by shaggy eyebrows; a straight nose, a smiling mouth, combined to bring out his strength of will and his rare gift of observation. . . .

"As a professor Zimmerman left a reputation for popularity with everyone. . . . His word and his advice were authoritative. An erudite musician, capable, a man of wit and taste . . . he was one of the great piano teachers. His broad and remarkable influence was due to the skill of his teaching and the eclecticism in the choice of works that he adapted." [n]

Unfortunately Mme Zimmerman and her daughters in no way resembled the father of the family. ["They are capable of unparalleled pettiness . . ."] Bizet said. ["Gounod's loyal nature does not easily adapt itself to these small people whose inept advice, which he accepts wholeheartedly, sometimes makes him pull a boner, as they say. . . ."] "

When Zimmerman retired from his professorship, a strong rivalry naturally arose among his possible successors, and it was through his influence that Marmontel won the post. Marmontel, too, was one of those rare, born teachers whose joy and fulfillment it is to give everything to their pupils. They are the lifeblood of generations of students. Their memory remains green as long as a single member of one of their classes is alive. But it is as difficult to re-create their personalities as to revive the spell of long-dead actors who have swayed great audiences in their day.

Antoine-François Marmontel, born in 1816, was the nephew of Jean-François Marmontel, the author of *Contes moraux* and *Mémoires d'un père pour servir à l'instruction de ses enfants*. A brilliant pupil at the Conservatoire, professor at an early age, Antoine Marmontel interrupted his sixty years of teaching only once, when he fought in the same infantry regiment as his son during the War of 1870.

His teaching had a very special significance for Bizet, which the latter expressed in a letter written to his master a year after he had left the Conservatoire for the Académie in Rome: "In your class one learns something besides the piano; one becomes a musician. The farther I go, the more I understand how large a part of the little I know I owe to you. Your method of teaching has suggested many ideas to me which I will develop for you when I return. Just as you make the weakest pupils play Haydn's first symphonies, couldn't you use for solfeggio the easy works of the great masters instead of the ABC of Monsieur X [3] . . . whom I like a great deal—and whom I should be most unhappy to see as a member of the Institut." "

Marmontel was only thirty-two in 1848 when Bizet, six or seven years younger than any of the other pupils, entered the class that he attended during the next five years. It met on Mondays, Wednesdays, and Fridays at 11.30. At 9 o'clock on the same days, Bizet had a class in solfeggio with Croharé, for which

---

[3] Probably François-Emmanuel-Joseph Bazin (1816–78), professor of solfeggio at the Conservatoire and author of a treatise on harmony used in all French schools at that time. He composed a number of works for the Opéra-Comique of which only *Maître Pathelin* and *Voyage en Chine* are still occasionally given.

Charles-Henri-Valentin Alkan, the pianist, was accompanist. Six months after his entrance, when he was only ten and one half years old, Bizet won a first prize in solfeggio. In 1851 he won a second prize in piano, and the following year the first prize in the piano-playing competition. Marmontel was indefatigable in coaching his pupils to win these competitions. Shortly before the contest one year, he held a secret audition in the afternoon at Erard's, the piano manufacturer's, so that his pupils could play the piano they would use in the competition. And that same evening he invited a number of guests to his house, among them two members of the jury, to hear Bizet and two other competitors play from their own manuscript compositions.

For one competition the pupils were given for study the E flat Concerto by Ignaz Moscheles. "But, alas, in what a broken, fragmentary fashion!" the celebrated pianist complained. "Auber, the director, does not allow more than four or five minutes to each pupil . . . eight bars, therefore, are taken from the *tutti*, and half of the first solo [is] jumbled together with the second half of the third. . . . I was invited to sit on the jury with Auber, Ambroise Thomas, and others, but declined. Now I am beset with troops of fair pianists about to contend for the prize, who wish me to hear their rendering of my dislocated concerto. Like jockeys before the race, they all hope to get the first prize, and ask for my protection, as one asks for a vote when canvassing for a seat in Parliament." [n]

In October 1852, Bizet entered the class of François Benoist, which met Tuesdays, Thursdays, and Saturdays at 2. Benoist was then in the thirty-third of his fifty-three years of teaching organ at the Conservatoire. Bizet won an honorable mention in his first year in Benoist's class and a first prize in the following year. He was also appointed assistant organ accompanist in 1854. Benoist, although "the most mediocre of organists, was," according to Saint-Saëns, "an admirable teacher. . . . He spoke little, but his taste was discerning and his judgment sure. He collaborated in several ballets given at the Opéra. And though it is hard to believe, he brought 'his work' to class and scribbled orchestrations while his pupils played the organ, which did not prevent his hearing and supervising their work, laying aside his own to give them the necessary criticism." [n]

The professor whose composition course Bizet entered in

October 1853 also divided his time between the theatre and teaching, but his pupils, unlike Benoist's, suffered from this duality of interests. Jacques-François-Fromental-Elie Halévy "during the final years of his career continually wrote operas and comic operas that added nothing to his glory, and which disappeared, never to reappear, after a respectable number of performances. . . ." Saint-Saëns wrote. "He greatly neglected his classes, coming to them only when he could find the time. The pupils came anyway, and taught each other, and were much less lenient than the master, whose great defect was exaggerated kindness. And even when he did come to class, he was incapable of defending himself against intruders. Singers came for auditions . . . ridiculous tenors who made him lose his precious time," [n] and the precious time of his students, also.

Halévy had started teaching at the Conservatoire while himself still a pupil. His classes were always popular, for he was by nature cordial and friendly. But after the success of *La Juive* in 1835, when he was thirty-six years old, he became the most sought-after teacher at the Conservatoire. Even after he had produced many failures and was preoccupied with his career in the theatre, his prestige and the eclecticism of his teaching continued to attract many aspiring young composers. He himself has left an illuminating description of his pedagogical method or lack of method. When a friend told him that one of his pupils had said that his work was going well except for counterpoint, which was troubling him, Halévy replied, " 'What does he know about it? He has never done any.'

" 'What do you mean?' I replied. 'If he is in your class, he must be required to do it.'

" 'Not at all,' Halévy answered. 'I require nothing. I deal with grownup young people who have reached the age of reason and who should know what they need. I am always ready to listen to them. I examine and correct what they bring me—overture, symphony, waltz, romance. When the famous [Louis-Antoine] Julien was in my class, he brought me nothing but quadrilles. I corrected his quadrilles. I have always made it a matter of duty not to thwart their inclinations.' " [4n]

Much has been written of Halévy's influence on Bizet, a sub-

---

[4] For further information on Halévy as teacher see Mina Curtiss, "Fromental Halévy," *The Musical Quarterly*, XXXIX, No. 2, April 1953.

ject on which Bizet never expressed himself. Indeed, not until seven years after Halévy's death, when Bizet married his master's daughter, did he begin to understand and sympathize with the complexities and problems that had beset his father-in-law. At the Conservatoire he had found his professor of composition ["a devilish man with whom you never know where you stand . . . such a slippery gentleman that you don't know how to handle him."] There was, as Halévy himself admitted, no question of his "handling" his students. Perhaps if Bizet had been submitted to a more positive discipline against which he could have rebelled, he might have avoided the pattern of starting and abandoning one work after another which he followed for so much of his life. Halévy's music, "free," as Heine said, "of the faults or errors which sometimes occur in the works of original genius . . . pleasant, beautiful, respectable, academic, and classic," appears to have left Bizet more or less untouched. In any case, he never commented on it until after he had become a member of the Halévy family.

Halévy's complex character puzzled the boy, as indeed it puzzled Sainte-Beuve, who found in this "judicious" man "something of La Bruyère's *honnête homme,* which made it possible for him to chat interestedly with you throughout a dinner or a whole evening without saying a single word about music, or even introducing his own special subject. . . . He was like a bee who, having found himself not wholly at home in the hive, was in search of some place outside where he could make his honey. . . . He had an instinct for languages . . . a passion for dictionaries. . . . His curiosity was insatiable. Everything interested, attracted, inspired him with the desire, or rather the regret that he had not made the subject in question his life's work. If he read history, he would wish he had been a historian; if military tactics, the general of an army; if geology, a geologist; if politics, a man involved in world affairs. . . ."

Halévy's election as Permanent Secretary of the Académie des Beaux-Arts in 1854 provided him with a wide range of expression for his scholarly interests. His intellectual curiosity and questing mind undoubtedly influenced Bizet far more than his musical ideas or compositions. Quite possibly the passion for literature which Bizet developed at this time, which caused his parents to fear that he might even abandon his musical career, was inspired or at least encouraged by his many-sided professor. Yet even on this level Bizet maintained a sense of values lacking in his teacher. For when Halévy, profoundly impressed by his pupil's gifts during the first year he taught him, wanted Bizet to try for the Prix de Rome at the age of fifteen, the boy refused on the grounds of his immaturity and his need for additional background.

Halévy's outstanding qualities were kindness, friendliness, and generosity to young composers. To Offenbach, when he was still merely a member of the orchestra at the Opéra-Comique, the master gave free lessons. When Wagner was penniless in Paris in 1841, Halévy hired him to make the piano reduction of his very successful opera, *La Reine de Chypre.* Halévy's kindness to Bizet expressed itself not only in the natural interest he took in the work of a pupil whose talent he immediately recognized, but also in using his influence to secure for him free tickets for the Opéra-Comique, which Bizet could not afford to buy. For Halévy's connection with the lyric theatres was not restricted to the comparatively minor one of composer. Over a period of many years he held the posts of *chef du chant* and, subsequently, of vice-regent at the Opéra. When one of his friends expressed surprise that he continued his administrative work after the triumph of *La Juive,* he replied: "You can't compose operas all day long." This was not the man to mold or influence the artistic development of a boy who in his own life would ask nothing better than the opportunity to "compose operas all day long." Charles Gounod, whom Bizet then regarded as "the only man among our modern musicians who really adores his art," [n] was to become the strongest musical influence in Bizet's life.

CHAPTER  III

Bizet and Gounod

As with many important events in Bizet's life, his first meeting with Charles Gounod is blurred behind a haze of false information. Biographers have always claimed that the friendship between the older man and the boy started when Gounod acted as substitute teacher in the classes Zimmerman was said to have been too ill to teach during his final years at the Conservatoire. In fact, however, when Bizet entered the Conservatoire, Marmontel had already taken over Zimmerman's classes. He was at pains in his biographical essay on his master to point out that "Zimmerman at the time of his retirement was still in the fullness of his strength and energies, but he had the feeling that there was a secret hostility to his teaching which came from artists he himself had trained. . . . He was dissatisfied, too, because on several occasions, the jury was inclined to slight his class in favor of the rival class. . . . Distressed by all these minor worries, he resigned at the height of his powers and was appointed inspector of piano classes." [n] So it was at Zimmerman's house that Bizet took his lessons in solfeggio in 1850 and 1851. And it was probably during Gounod's courtship of Anna Zimmerman, whom he married in June 1852, that Bizet met him, soon after the *première* of Gounod's first opera, *Sapho*. This work, although a financial failure, served to launch the composer on a career in the theatre in which Bizet, even at the age of thirteen, participated.

Bizet's enthusiasm and talent, Gounod's warmth and charm, and their similar family backgrounds drew the older man and the boy into a close friendship. Like Bizet's mother, Mme Gounod was an excellent pianist. She had supported her two sons by giving lessons from the time their father died in 1823, when Charles was only five years old. The attachment between Gounod and his mother seems to have been even more intense than the relationship between the Bizets. For Mme Gounod was a far more active and dominating woman than Aimée Bizet. "Your mother," a friend of Gounod wrote to him, "is not only a Christian . . . she is also edifying and strong; as generous as a saint. We speak of her often as a miracle of divine grace and one of the most remarkable examples of the omnipotent mercy of God." [1]

Gounod tells us in his *Mémoires* that he learned music at his mother's breast, that even before he could speak, he could distinguish between and recognize perfectly the different tunes of the lullabies she sang as she nursed him. Gounod held strong convictions on the subject of breast-feeding, believing that it is "the means of transmitting a host of instincts, aptitudes, bents that add just that much more to the resemblance between mother and child." Although Mme Gounod was proud of her son's musical gifts, she was absolutely opposed to his becoming an artist. She had suffered considerably from the vagaries of her husband, twenty-two years her senior, who, even at the age of sixty, when Charles was born, remained an unsuccessful and unambitious portrait painter. Mme Gounod never actually tried to thwart her son's passion for music, but during the early part of his education she placed as many obstacles as possible in the way of his becoming a professional musician. Eventually she capitulated and Gounod entered the Conservatoire in 1836, at the age of eighteen.

He won no prizes except the Prix de Rome, the only one he wanted. We first hear of the impact of his personality from Rome. Fanny Mendelssohn Hensel, who was on her honeymoon in Italy in 1840, found him "hyper-romantic and passionate." If his high spirits one evening impelled him to climb an acacia tree and throw down whole branches of flowers so that his companion "looked like Birnam Wood coming to Dunsinane," within a few days he could transform his enthusiasm into excessive religious exaltation. Indeed, his friend Georges Bousquet confided to Fanny Hensel "how far

[1] J. G. Prod'homme et A. Dandelot, *Gounod*, Paris, 1911, I, 95. This biography and *Mémoires d'un artiste* by Charles Gounod, Paris, 1896, are the chief sources of the information on Gounod. Subsequent quotations in this chapter from these works will not be separately noted.

Gounod had allowed himself to be drawn into religious ties, the result of which he much feared for one of his weak character. . . . Exalted, and subject to every influence as [Gounod] was," Bousquet was afraid that he would "exchange music for the cowl." "

Bousquet's fears for his friend were well grounded, but he underestimated the more practical side of Gounod's pliable nature, a capacity for compromise suggested in the French aphorism, "Marriage is such a heavy burden that it takes three to bear it." For if Gounod was wedded to the Church while his grand passion was music, wife and mistress were never mutually exclusive and both were always essential to him. The shift in Gounod's attitude toward Rome is typical of the emotional extremes to which he was subject throughout his life.

On his arrival in Rome in 1839, Gounod had been disappointed. "Instead of the city I had pictured," he wrote, "a city of majestic character, striking appearance, an air of grandeur, full of temples, ancient monuments, picturesque ruins, I found myself in a really provincial city—vulgar, colorless, and dirty practically everywhere. I was completely disillusioned, and it would have taken very little to make me give up my grant, repack my trunk, and escape as quickly as possible back to Paris and everything I loved." But he was so overwhelmed with emotion two years later, when he was about to leave Rome, that long afterwards he wrote: "I shall not try to describe my sorrow when the time came to say good-bye . . . to that Rome where I felt I had taken root. . . . I fell into a profound depression and cried like a child," an experience duplicated some twenty years later by the far more restrained Bizet.

After an absence abroad of more than three years, Gounod returned, in May 1843, to Paris, where his mother's welcome to her son reminded the Abbé Gay of "the Holy Virgin receiving one of her children into Heaven after his earthly journey." Gounod's time for entering the Kingdom of Heaven had not yet arrived, but he nevertheless spent the next few years almost wholly removed from the temptations of this world.

Through the influence of the Abbé Dumarsais, curate of the Chapel for Foreign Missions, Mme Gounod had arranged, even before her son's return, his appointment as musical director of the Chapel. In this position Gounod, for almost the only time in his life, acted on principle, motivated more strongly by his musical convictions than by his eagerness to please. He accepted the position on condition that he need not "take advice, much less orders, from the curate or the vestry, nor from anyone. I had my ideas, my feelings, my convictions. In a word, I intended becoming the curate of music. . . . Palestrina and Bach were my gods, and I came to burn up what until now had been adored." In this task Gounod was encouraged and assisted by François Delsarte, whose friendship with the Archbishop of Paris and membership in the Third Order of Saint Dominic gave him the position of unofficial consultant on church music. The parishioners vociferously opposed the changing of their taste, but at the end of one year Gounod had not only won over the parish, but, according to his brother, himself wished "to do nothing for the theatre, and to devote himself exclusively to religious music."

The dramatic in Gounod triumphed, however, even if he was to postpone for a few years work in the theatre itself. In February 1846, a number of newspapers announced that "M. Gounod, composer, former Prix de Rome, has entered orders." From that time until the Revolution of 1848, Gounod prefixed the date of his letters with a cross and signed himself "Abbé Charles Gounod."

In 1847 Gounod entered a Carmelite monastery, where he devoted himself to reading, translating, annotating, and commenting on the works of the Church fathers. Although he emerged from his retreat only once a week, this period of marking time, as he remembered it in the days of his fame, was endurable, at least in part, because his seclusion enabled him to clarify his conflicting ideas about the function of the artist.

"The society of artists is dying on its feet," he wrote to a friend. "Each member pivots around his neighbor. There is no progress toward an avowed purpose, toward a clearly perceived end. . . . This anarchy is a sad spectacle; time will put an end to it, but when will that time come?—I think it will be when the *masses* develop a tendency of some kind to opinions of their own. . . . The public accepts an infinite number of productions, varied and even opposed to their points of view; and they enjoy the very contradictions. They split their affection and their sympathies, and necessarily divide the effectiveness of their stimulus to such a degree that they no longer even give an impetus to artists. . . . It seems to me that the principle of evil lies in this absence of a universal need. I believe, in a word, that the artist's growth stems from all the power and all the moral, intellectual, and religious energy of the epoch to which he belongs, and that society expresses itself through him in proportion to the vitality and activity it transmits to him."

Holding these views, Gounod could hardly have remained permanently removed from the main stream of the life of his time, particularly as his monastic propensities were apparently not strong enough to cause him to risk continuing to wear priests' robes during the Revolution of 1848. Thirty or more years later he was to write of this period: "For four and a half years I carried out duties which, while being very useful and profitable for musical studies, nevertheless had the disadvantage of leaving me to vegetate from the point of view of my career and my future. For a composer there is only one road to follow: the theatre." Gounod found little difficulty in overcoming the obstacles existing along this road. In addition to talent and ambition, he possessed great personal magnetism and good looks.

His striking head was framed in a black beard. "His fiery eyes shone with liveliness and spirit, his broad, high forehead revealed the depth of thought of a man of genius; but besides these attractive qualities, his marvelously expressive and intensely vital face was above all suffused with a feeling of such charm, such good will, that one was captivated, pervaded by a sense of understanding as strong as it was immediate."

Even as a novice in the world of the theatre, where charm is the stock in trade, he triumphed. "I met a M. Gounod," writes Edmond Got the great comic actor, "former Prix de Rome, a philandering monk, so they say, and as talented musically as he is exuberant and shamelessly pushy as a man. He actually kissed me on both cheeks the first time I ever met him! His opera,[2] which was given a few days ago, was received creditably; less so, however, than one would have expected from hearing the score sung and played by him at the piano, with no voice—but what charm!"[n] Voice or no voice, the charm was to endure into old age—along with the weakness for kissing—as we know from a description of him at seventy.

"Gounod spent all day Wednesday, and Thursday morning,

---

[2] *Sapho.*

with us," wrote Henri Meilhac, one of Bizet's librettists for *Car-men.* "Never in my life have I been kissed so often in so short a time. He brought M. Dalicot and Mme Dalicot with him. M. Dalicot kisses even more than Gounod, but he kisses only Gounod, flinging himself at the master from time to time and kissing him three or four times in succession. The master does not appear surprised by this; he returns the kisses and says, 'My son.' Mme Dalicot he calls 'my daughter,' so that the relationship isn't really very clear. Gounod sat down at the piano and played all Wednesday evening; because of that I forgave him his kissing bouts." "

This combination of amiability, talent, and charm soon made Gounod, still unknown as a composer, a most welcome guest in society. At the house of the homeopathic doctor Hoffman, at whose fashionable parties Gounod was surrounded by a bevy of admiring women patients of the doctor, he collaborated on a comic opera with a brother-in-law of the mistress of the house. Fragments of this work Gounod sang at intimate gatherings. At one of these parties he met the great singer Pauline Viardot who, after arranging for Emile Augier to write the libretto of *Sapho,* opened the doors of the Opéra to Gounod.

Were God to have made an exception for Gounod, permitting St. Cecilia to substitute for St. Peter as usher into the kingdom of heaven, he could have had no more golden guide into that formidable stronghold, the Paris Opéra, than Pauline Viardot-Garcia.

"With Mme Viardot we enter another world," wrote Saint-Saëns," from his youth a favored denizen of that sphere. Studded with great names and a legend, restricted neither by space nor time, the Garcia family was a vital force in the musical life of Europe for over a century. Its greatest star, Maria, the fabulous Malibran, dead tragically young, was immortalized by Musset in a poem, although it was the younger sister, Pauline, with whom he fell in love. Turgenev was for many years Pauline's lover and friend. Berlioz, also a close friend and almost daily visitor in Paris, fell in love with her late in life. He deemed Mme Viardot "one of the greatest artists in the past or present history of music." " Moscheles heard her sing in Berlin and found her "one of the greatest phenomena of our time. I seem to realize and understand a character after seeing Viardot in it—not before. She creates her role." "

But "her voice, with its enormous power and its prodigious range, that voice inured to all the difficulties of the art of singing, did not," according to Saint-Saëns, "please everyone. It was not a velvet or a crystal voice, but rather harsh, pungent, like the taste of a bitter orange, made for tragedy or epic verse, superhuman rather than human. Light things, Spanish songs, Chopin's mazurkas transcribed by her into songs, became the chit-chat of a giant. To tragic measures, to the severe strains of the oratorio, she gave incomparable grandeur." [n]

Even in middle age, after she had lost her voice, she seemed to a highly critical young American writer "a most fascinating and interesting woman, ugly, yet also very handsome, or, in the French sense, *très belle*." [n] Henry James was struck, too, in Mme Viardot's salon, by "that spontaneity which Europeans have," a quality of which Gounod was surely the embodiment. He soon endeared himself to the Viardots, who introduced him to that influential and unscrupulous character, the current director of the Opéra, the fantastic dandy, Nestor Roqueplan, who more than a decade later took an interest in Bizet's career.

The most spectacular of the group of *boulevardier*-journalist-theatre-managers who were the life and death of the theatre under Louis-Philippe and Napoleon III, Roqueplan was noted for his fads and eccentricities. Everyone knew of the collection of bed-warmers which lined the walls of his room and that his nervous facial tic was supposed to have been acquired in a duel with a German colonel to whom he said while fencing, "My God, you are ugly! Hairy as an ape!" His passion for display, his dedication to the life of pleasure, gave rise to bizarre stories, such as his supposed invention of an ingenious mechanism that raised from the floor below his office at the Opéra either a sumptuously laden table or a voluptuously decorated Oriental-style bed.

"My dream is to die insolvent and in style," Roqueplan was in the habit of remarking. It was a dream that came true shortly before the end of the Empire in 1870. At that time Bizet's future collaborator, Ludovic Halévy, described Roqueplan as "very, very witty. . . . What he said was much better than what he wrote. He was an execrable theatre director; people no longer kept track of the theatres that succumbed to his management. This passion of his for theatre management cost his friends a lot of money. He never went bankrupt. Someone always paid up for him. His great preoccupation was to be well dressed, to be stylish, to invent hats, etc. He liked me a lot. I think I know why. . . . When others said to him: 'What a witty remark you just made! . . . What a splendid article that was this morning!' . . . I would merely say: 'Oh, Nestor, what trousers!' Immediately he would turn his back on the others, take me in a corner, and say: 'Quite a green, isn't it? I had a lot of trouble getting it from my tailor. He had to have three different shades dyed in England. It isn't everybody's green, is it? A very special green! It really struck you!' " "

Because of his aversion to any musical innovations, Roqueplan's sense of color determined the only drastic changes he made at the Opéra. The claque had always come to work wearing red, green, or yellow ties. Now they could appear only in black, as opposed to the members of the orchestra, who were required to wear white ties. Their salaries, however, remained unchanged. Roqueplan did not squander on lesser fry the 900,000-franc deficit that finally lost him the directorship of the Opéra. His meat was Meyerbeer. "With him," the director enjoyed saying, "I never argued. Everything he asked for I gave him, and sometimes I even annoyed him by my insistence on signing his contracts without reading them." "

Just after Mme Viardot's great success in Meyerbeer's *Le Prophète,* she persuaded Roqueplan to receive Gounod. "He agreed to desert the performance for part, but not all, of one evening," Gounod remembered. "He wanted a subject that combined three essential conditions: 1, it must be short; 2, it must be serious; 3, a woman must have the principal part. We decided on *Sapho.*"

The opera was not a success, but this debut gave Gounod a certain standing in the lyric theatre. "The work, while showing inexperience in what is known as theatre sense, a lack of knowledge of scenic effects, of the resources and practices of instrumentation," the composer admitted, "did have a real feeling for expression, a generally sound instinct for the lyric side of the subject, and a tendency to nobility of style. . . . Berlioz . . . . coming up to my mother at the *première,* said: 'Madame, I can't remember having experienced a similar emotion in twenty years.' "

Yet *Sapho* closed after nine performances; Mme Viardot sang in only the first six. But the replacement of the great singer was not the only problem that confronted the management. For the tragic opera *Sapho* was, curiously enough, a forerunner of Offenbach's highly popular pseudo-classic operettas, *Orphée aux enfers* and *La Belle Hélène,* which hid political implications behind an accepted classic plot. Gounod's heroine was a combination of the poetess Sappho and the legendary Sappho who committed suicide for love of Phaon. Yet at a time when the Prince-President was so soon to become the Emperor Napoleon III, the voluntary exile of Phaon rang a danger signal in the office of censorship. The political commissioner, therefore, licensed *Sapho* for a single performance, the license to be renewed only after changes had been made in the text.

"It seemed," said Théophile Gautier, "that *Sapho* was a dangerous and subversive subject, politically speaking. . . . We would never have suspected it, and in reading M. Emile Augier's libretto, the sale of which was forbidden at the Opéra the opening night, we understood less than ever the motive of this interdict, even from the censor's point of view. Our firm conviction is that society would not have been violently overthrown in the night had one been able to read, on April 16, 1851, the words on which M. Gounod had embroidered his music. . . . It is easy to recognize, hearing M. Gounod's music, his habit of writing for the Church and his constant preoccupation with the classic masters. . . . In music as in painting we like unity of coloring, and M. Gounod's score seems to us comparable to a beautiful woman whose torso and face were painted by Ingres, her legs and arms by Delacroix."

Less than a year after the failure of *Sapho,* Gounod was commissioned by the Comédie-Française to write the choruses for François Ponsard's five-act tragedy, *Ulysse.* While the rehearsals of this play were in progress, Bizet worked on a transcription of the choruses for voice and piano, the first of countless pieces of hack-work by which he would suppport himself for many years to come. He retained a lifelong enthusiasm for both *Ulysse* and *Sapho.* Even after the established success of *Faust* and *Roméo et Juliette,* he wrote: "When I used to say that *Sapho* and the choruses from *Ulysse* were masterpieces, people laughed in my face. *I was right* and I am right today. Only I was destined to be right several years too soon."

The *première* of *Ulysse* in June of 1852, shortly after Gounod's marriage, could hardly have been more painful. For the fourteen-year-old Bizet it was a shocking, but perhaps salutary preparation for the suffering he would endure on the opening nights of *L'Arlésienne* and *Carmen*. The attitude toward music of the large and distinguished literary audience is best characterized by Théophile Gautier's reply to the Brothers Goncourt when they admitted to him their "musical deafness," their ability to listen only to martial music. " 'Good! . . .' he said. 'I am like you. I prefer silence to music. Only after having lived part of my life with a singer was I able to distinguish between good and bad music, but it doesn't matter to me. Nevertheless, it is curious that all writers of this period are like that. Balzac execrated it. Hugo can't bear it. Lamartine . . . has a horror of it. Only a few painters have a taste for music.' " [n]

Saint-Saëns, who attended the opening of *Ulysse,* wrote: "The play seemed boring, and certain brutally realistic lines shocked the audience; they whispered and laughed. . . . This bizarre tragedy . . . deserved more patient spectators. . . . After the failure of *Sapho* and *Ulysse,* Gounod's future could have seemed dubious to the uninitiated, but not to the elite, which places artists where they rightly belong. He was marked with the sign of the chosen," [n] marked, in fact, by Berlioz, the one critic who was also to appreciate Bizet's earliest work.

"Quel homme élégant que Berlioz!" Gounod remarked during Berlioz's lifetime to Saint-Saëns, who regarded the statement as a profound comment on the fiber of the younger man's music. Gounod's own "impeccable elegance sometimes covers a certain stock in trade of vulgarity," Saint-Saëns found. "He is occasionally plebeian, appealing for that very reason to the common people, and thereby winning popularity long before Berlioz did." [n]

Leaving aside the nature of musical elegance, the question of moral elegance, or elegance of feeling and behavior, is inevitably raised by Gounod's acceptance of the libretto of his next work. The book of *La Nonne sanglante* had been in Berlioz's hands from 1841 to 1847. The music had been commissioned by Roqueplan's predecessor at the Opéra. The new director, however, was less concerned with fulfilling inherited obligations than with ridding himself of a difficult composer. After a variety of delays and evasions on Roqueplan's part, Scribe, the librettist of *La Nonne,* demanded the return of his work, which he then offered in turn to Halévy, Verdi, and Albert Grisar. All of them, according to Berlioz, "were scrupulous enough to decline his offer; knowing how matters stood and considering Scribe's treatment of me not far from dishonest. M. Gounod finally accepted it. . . ."ⁿ

The libretto of *La Nonne* had been familiar to Gounod for some time. A scene he composed for baritone, chorus, and orchestra, entitled *Pierre l'Hermite,* later incorporated into the opera, was played in 1853 at the same concert of the Société Sainte-Cécile as the second part of Berlioz's *L'Enfance du Christ.* The latter piece was applauded, but "M. Gounod's work," wrote the critic of *La France musicale,* "was coldly received by the audience, which expected something entirely different. He owes himself a prompt revenge; that he will take it we have no doubt."

Not, however, in *La Nonne sanglante,* which had its *première* at the Opéra on October 18, 1854. A week earlier Gounod, apparently in the throes of an attack of conscience over his treatment of Berlioz, appealed to him for reassurance and received the following reply:

"Paris, October 11, 1854
"My dear Gounot [*sic*],
"Four or five years ago I made my radical decision about *La Nonne,* and I am astonished that you should have felt a moment's embarrassment because of it or me. You should have spoken to me about it sooner; this cloud would then immediately have vanished from your mind.

"I assure you, and you will believe me, that I feel neither regret nor the slightest latent bitterness, and for a long time you have had my most sincere good wishes for the success of your new work. Don't forget that I owe you very real gratitude for the profound and noble emotions your *Sapho* made me feel, and I am bent on paying that debt! Hang it all! We're artists, aren't we?

"I am not sure of being free this Saturday evening; however, if you send me seats for the dress rehearsal and don't give me disagreeable neighbors, I shall make every effort to come in spite of my aversion to the stupid way this important ordeal is always conducted at the Opéra.

> *"Adieu, bon courage,*
> and have no doubts
> about your wholly devoted
> Hector Berlioz" [n]

This letter, found among Bizet's private papers nearly a century after it was written, was perhaps the most valuable reward he received for his labors on the piano and voice reduction of the score of *La Nonne.* Choudens published Bizet's version a few months after the opera closed. And for many years Bizet played to his friends the Overture, *"La Symphonie des ruines,"* and *"La Marche des morts"* from the work that initiated him into the mysterious functioning of the Opéra and the hazards inherent in writing for the lyric theatre. It is unlikely, however, that as a mere student at the Conservatoire he was aware of the true significance of Berlioz's letter. And many years were to go by before Bizet became disillusioned in Gounod.

CHAPTER IV

Symphony in C: *Le Docteur Miracle*: Prix de Rome

From the time Bizet first heard *Sapho* when he was fourteen years old, he fell under the spell of Gounod, and became steeped in Gounod's music. His piano reduction for four hands of *La Nonne sanglante* was published a few months before his seventeenth birthday and was followed shortly by a similar arrangement of Gounod's First Symphony in D, which the composer wrote to "console" himself, he said, for his disappointment over the failure of *La Nonne*. Four days after his seventeenth birthday, on October 29, 1855, Bizet started composing his own first symphony, which he finished by the end of November. Because he himself never mentioned this delightful piece and persisted in calling *Roma,* written many years later, his *first* symphony; because this symphony in C remained undiscovered until 1933 and unperformed until 1935, the composer's attitude toward this early work has remained problematic. Yet anyone familiar with Gounod's First Symphony, which met with great success when it was performed in the spring of 1855, is bound to recognize at once the impact it had on Bizet's imagination.

"Gounod is an entirely original composer, and as long as one imitates him one remains on the level of a pupil," Bizet wrote a few years later while, as a student in Rome, he was rejoicing at having "completely extricated" himself from the master's influence. That this exultation was premature Bizet himself realized very soon. Even after he had written *L'Arlésienne* in 1872 he confessed to Gounod: "You were the beginning of my life as an artist. . . . I can now admit that I was afraid of being absorbed." At the beginning, then, there was every reason why Bizet's First Symphony should so closely resemble Gounod's. And the resemblance is striking. Not only are there passages in the first movement that are almost identical note for note with Gounod's Symphony, but there are structural features copied from Gounod throughout Bizet's work.[1] One need only hear the two symphonies played in chronological order to understand why Bizet chose to dismiss his as an exercise too derivative for public performance. Yet, whereas the eclecticism in both compositions is striking, Bizet's already bears the individual mark of the future composer of *Carmen*.

Whether or not Bizet ever showed the symphony to Gounod is an open question, for Gounod was hard driven during 1855 and 1856. Since 1852, when he had accepted the directorship of the Orphéon de la Ville de Paris, he had been making a tremendous effort to reorganize it and to improve "the wretched condition" of this organization, originally founded to teach singing in the schools and to supervise classes in choral singing for working people. In 1855 he conducted three large choral concerts, one of which was honored by the presence of the Emperor and Empress, who heard two works Gounod had composed for the occasion: *Hymne à la France* and *Vive l'empereur*. This patriotic effort brought him the Cross of the Legion of Honor early in 1856. Later in the year he decided to try for the chair at the Académie des Beaux-Arts left vacant by the death of Adolphe Adam, an honor that could be achieved only by endless letter-writing and the paying of formal calls on the other thirty-five members of the Académie. During the spring of 1856, he also composed the incidental music for a revival of Molière's *Le Bourgeois-gentilhomme* at the Comédie-Française. All this activity may well have decided Bizet not to burden his master further by showing him the Symphony in C. If Gounod did find time to look at it, he surely saw at a glance the echoes of his own work and perhaps dismissed the tribute politely. But when an event took place which at the time seemed far more important in Bizet's life, Gounod did not fail his friend.

In May 1856, when Bizet entered the competition for the

---

[1] For further information on this subject, see Howard Shanet, "Georges Bizet: Symphony in C," *More Background,* Book of the Month Club, New York, 1955.

Prix de Rome, he immediately wrote Gounod about the text for the cantata to be set to music by the competitors: *David* by "Gaston d'Albano," the pseudonym of Mlle de Montréal. "Thank you for having let me know so quickly and so promptly the subject that will be keeping you busy for the next 20 or 25 days," Gounod replied. "No, you are mistaken—I am quite sure that you will finish on time, perhaps even before the time set. On the first day, a cantata seems like an opera in five acts, as though there would never be enough days and nights to get to the end of it. I know something about this; I have gone through it, and nevertheless I finished, so did my comrades, and the time allowed was enough for the job. *Don't hurry too much.* Everything will come in its own good time. Don't rush into using an idea on the pretext that you might not be able to find another. Ten will occur to you for every one. Be severe with yourself. I am enchanted by your subject for the sole reason that the characters are set and clear. . . . *Bon courage;* above all, be calm. Hurrying only stifles everything. And if I were to give you just one piece of advice, it would be not to work at night. It shrivels and contracts the mind, and that feverish kind of work leads, most of the time, to only one thing: dissatisfaction the next day, and a consequent need to start the previous day's work over again." [n]

The competition ended in a stalemate, and after long deliberation, the judges decided to give no first prize. Bizet was awarded a second prize that did not entitle him to the grant for study in Rome, but did provide him with free tickets to all the lyric theatres of Paris—an appurtenance particularly useful at this time, as his next effort at composition was to be a theatre piece.

During the summer of 1856, Offenbach, whose works had several times been rejected by the Opéra-Comique, launched a prize competition in an effort to build up his own theatre, the Bouffes-Parisiens. In a page-long article in *Le Figaro,* he announced the rules of the competition and defined his concept of *opéra-comique,* which he regarded as a pre-eminently French invention although, he said, "it grew out of the Italian *opera buffa.* . . . The differences between the two spring from the temperament of the nation that adopted the form. Where the Italians indulged in verve and imagination, the French have prided themselves on their cleverness, their common sense and their good taste. Where originally everything was sacrificed to liveliness, the French have sacrificed everything to wit. . . . What is *opéra-comique* but a comedy with song? The very name implies it: a gay, amusing, light work." Offenbach proposed, therefore, through this competition, to revive the original form "in an opera that runs a barc three-quarters of an hour, can use only four characters, an orchestra of at most thirty musicians, and a plot and tunes that must 'click.' " *

The jury to choose the winning opera consisted of Fromental Halévy, Scribe, Auber, Ambroise Thomas, and Gounod. The prize of 1200 francs was divided between Bizet and Charles Lecocq, of whose many works, successful in his lifetime, only *La Fille de Madame Angot* and *Le Petit Duc* are remembered today. Lecocq,[2] who claimed never to have found in any other composer "such sure judgment, perfect taste and common sense" as Bizet's, wrote many years later a description of the competition and its outcome. If neither accurate nor detached, it is, nevertheless, illuminating. *"Le Docteur Miracle,"* he writes, "was a little *opéra-bouffe* in the Italian style, with no orginality of plot: a guardian; a lover who disguises himself to be near his beloved; rage of tutor on discovering them together; false contract and final forgiveness. All the usual situations, worn to the bone, but the lines very cleverly adapted to the requirements of the musician." *

The plot of the libretto by Léon Battu and Ludovic Halévy actually concerns a young officer in love with the daughter of a magistrate who loathes soldiers. To carry out his suit the officer disguises himself as a cook and serves the magistrate such a bad omelette that he thinks himself poisoned. A doctor (again the officer disguised) is summoned and promises to cure the magistrate in return for the hand of his daughter.

"Altogether feeble," Lecocq continues, "this piece was a godsend to the contestants. . . . The prize was awarded *ex-aequo* to Bizet and me. This division of the prize . . . could only be embarrassing, as it required the performance of two scores written for the same text. . . . Halévy, whose pupils Bizet and I both were, strongly influenced this jury in favor of my opponent, and without his insistence (I have since learned) I would have had the prize all to myself. . . . This bizarre decision only half satisfied

---

[2] Lecocq dedicated two piano mazurkas to Bizet, and also sent him affectionately inscribed copies of songs published under the pseudonym Georges Stern.

me, and visibly annoyed Bizet. In order to give us an equal chance with the public, the piece had to be performed by the same actors . . . one day with Bizet's music, the next with mine.

"Bizet's was to be played first. I protested, and at a meeting in Offenbach's office, we drew lots out of a hat; it was I who drew number 1.[3] This caused considerable difficulty between me and Offenbach. . . . He tried to make me change part of my music, which I refused to do. . . . The hard feelings between us . . . lasted many years. . . . *Le Docteur Miracle* had a very minor, though double, success—a run of twenty-two performances, eleven of mine and eleven of Bizet's. . . . Bizet's score was not bad, but rather heavy, and he failed with almost all of the little couplets I was able to bring off. He rewrote them before the first performance, and as this sort of thing was not at all his style, he had the devil of a time finding out how to do it. One day, when he told me this, I suggested jokingly that he let me take over the job. . . . Finally the first performance of *Le Docteur Miracle,* music by Charles Lecocq, was given on April 8, 1857. The following day the same *Le Docteur Miracle,* music by Georges Bizet, had its *première.* Halévy did not do me the honor of attending my performance, but he did come to Bizet's. I must say that during the two or three years that I attended Halévy's class he taught me absolutely nothing; and his lessons, if they can be called that, tended to turn me against composing, for invariably, when I submitted a composition to him, he would say to me in his sullen way, 'That isn't bad, but I don't like it.' Never would he tell me why he 'didn't like it.' "

The adjective "sullen" applied to the friendly and amiable Halévy is surprising. But he probably took little interest in a pupil who entered the Conservatoire at the late age of seventeen, and whose talent certainly lacked the quality of "elevation" so essential an element in the work of Halévy's favorites. Also, there rankled in Lecocq's memory the post-Conservatoire years during which he struggled for the success in the theatre which eluded him until he was thirty-four. When he was sixty he often, in his dreams, reverted to his school-days at the Conservatoire. "I see Halévy's class," he wrote to Saint-Saëns, "and the sullen way he used to wipe his spectacles. . . . But the last time I dreamed of the Conservatoire my nightmare was strangely complicated. It was

---

[3] This incident is verified in a letter written by Bizet many years later, now in the possession of Kapten Rudolf Nydahl, Stockholm.

Halévy's class with his old square piano, but the composer of *Charles VI* was seated among the pupils with Auber, Ambroise Thomas, Gounod, etc. I think even *Il Povero Mascagni* was there." [n]

Bizet's half of the prize brought him advantages over and above the small monetary award and the experience, valuable to a student, of seeing a score and a libretto transformed into a three-dimensional production. His prestige at the Conservatoire was immediately enhanced. Soon after he won the prize, we find his name quoted in the diary of Alcide Paladilhe, a man interested primarily in successful or potentially successful celebrities. This very Leopold Mozartian father kept a detailed history of the career of his son, Emile, who, when he entered the Conservatoire at the age of nine in 1853, was regarded as an infant prodigy. On January 7, 1857, the father noted that Emile played his third Nocturne in Halévy's class. "Bizet and a lame young man with whom he had jointly won the Offenbach prize, were carried away while Emile played, as were all the other pupils. M. Halévy said: 'That's very good . . . a very pretty piece.' . . . Bizet advised him strongly to have the work engraved, saying that it was bound to be successful." [4]

The publicity Bizet gained through the eleven performances of *Le Docteur Miracle,* in addition to his natural gaiety and high spirits and his extraordinary gifts as pianist and sight-reader, widened his social life. He became a welcome guest at Offenbach's famous Friday evenings, which were among the most crowded and popular parties in Paris. At one fancy dress ball, Bizet played the accompaniment for a parody of *Il Trovatore* by Edmond About. The author, who later became a close friend of Bizet's, joined Offenbach, Ludovic Halévy, and Léo Delibes in singing the leading roles. For this performance the artists' names were translated to Edmundo Abutti, Jacomo Offenbacchio, Luigi Halévy, Léo Delibestino, and *il maestro Bizetto.* At a party to celebrate "the imminent end of the world" the star performance was a solo polka danced by Delibes.

This composer, "restless, fidgety, slightly befuddled, correcting and excusing himself, lavishing praise, careful not to hurt any-

---

[4] Alcide Paladilhe, unpublished journal. Subsequent quotations from this work, which is in the Paladilhe collection, will not be individually noted in this chapter.

one's feelings, shrewd, adroit, very lively, a sharp critic," ⁿ was a classmate of Bizet's at the Conservatoire. While trying to gain a foothold in the theatre, he supported himself by serving as accompanist at the Théâtre-Lyrique where, on at least one occasion, Bizet substituted for him at a rehearsal of *Così fan tutte*. But they were never close friends. Indeed, before *Coppélia* brought Delibes recognition as a serious composer in 1870, he had reason on several occasions to regard Bizet as a more fortunate rival.

As winner of the Offenbach prize, Bizet also entered the category of promising young composers who were, more or less as a matter of course, presented to Rossini at one of his Saturday evening parties. To be seen at these *soirées* gave a cachet of distinction to the professional career of any young artist. Rossini greeted them all with superficial cordiality, but was impressed by few. He received Saint-Saëns with routine politeness when the young man was first presented to him. But when Rossini discovered that his guest was an artist of undoubted promise, he invited him to pay him a morning call to discuss his work. The maestro's study, in which he received his visitors, was an extraordinary room. A panoply of musical instruments grouped around a stomach pump that Rossini declared was "the best of all instruments" adorned the walls. Tall stands held Rossini's famous wigs, one for each day of the week, it was said, and two or even three for Sundays— one on top of the other for warmth in church.

Bizet was introduced to Rossini during the winter of 1857 by Mme Simart, wife of the well-known academic painter. By the end of March he was sufficiently at home at Rossini's Saturday parties to assure M. Paladilhe, boastful of his son's invitation to one of these gatherings, that he would keep an eye out for young Emile and mention him to Rossini.

When Emile at thirteen was presented to Rossini, the old composer exclaimed, "What a pretty child!" Paladilhe *père*, who was, of course, present, speaks of the host's "little court of fanatical devotees, of whom he makes fun and rightly so. . . . Before hearing Emile play," the father continues, "the maestro examined him, felt his forehead and his temples carefully, remarking, 'What a fine head! He has everything inside it that he needs for success!' And when someone mentioned Mendelssohn, he added, 'In there are the makings of another Mendelssohn.' . . . Emile played his *Fughette* and his third Nocturne. Rossini stood by the piano and listened attentively. He interrupted often, exclaiming at the charm, the grace, and the distinction of the compositions. 'There is a youngster who will certainly go far,' he said.

"And turning toward the circle of his admirers, he said: 'The admirable thing about him is that he is so firmly built, with a fine, strong, well-developed chest. I have rarely seen so talented a young creature who also looks so healthy. That will help him to live and make his way.' From time to time he took Emile's hand and kissed him affectionately on the brow. . . . Mme Rossini went to get a bag of pralines which she presented to Emile, saying: 'Take these pralines. There is, after all, nothing more Christian, nothing that I prefer to these pralines.' One of the admirers said: 'Those are Rossinian pralines. You must frame them.' To which Rossini replied, 'There's where you'll frame them,' pointing to his stomach. . . . Then he showed him a picture of Mozart and, pointing out his head-dress, said, 'That is how you will wear your hair one day, do you hear?' "

At Rossini's Saturday evenings, Mozart was performed most frequently. But Liszt and Rubinstein played their own works; when Verdi came, he was honored by a special performance of the Quartet from *Rigoletto;* Saint-Saëns's Tarantella for flute and clarinet had its *première* at Rossini's. The most successful evenings, however, were those when Rossini, in spite of the fact that he regarded himself as a "fourth-class" pianist, played the charming little works he was continually composing, many of which have never been published.

The room in which these gatherings were held was elaborately furnished, in keeping, no doubt, with the taste of Mme Rossini, the maestro's second wife. Although Rossini adored his Olympe, she was generally regarded as vulgar, ordinary, and pretentious. On one wall of the salon hung a large photograph of Rossini in a porcelain frame, along the sides of which were inscribed the names of his works. In the center of the room stood the Pleyel piano. "Rossini's house," wrote Eduard Hanslick, "is far from possessing the amenities necessary to such an innumerable quantity of guests. The heat is sometimes intolerable and the crowd so thick that when a fair singer . . . has to approach the piano to sing, she is literally forced to fight her way to it.

"Rows of ladies glittering with jewels occupy the whole of the music room; the men stand, so jammed against one another that they cannot move. The doors remain open, and from time to time a servant with refreshments pushes his way through the dense mass, though it is well known that very few people (and those for the most part strangers) take advantage of them: the lady of the house is said not to approve! I have nothing to say about the present Mme Rossini except that she is well off and once was beautiful. A haughty Roman nose, like some tower that has escaped the ravages of time, rises from the ruins of her former beauty. The rest is covered with diamonds." "

Early in May 1857, Rossini presented Bizet with an inscribed photograph of himself, perhaps as a good-luck token for the ordeal he was about go go through. For on May 16, Bizet, for the second time, entered the competition for the Prix de Rome. The libretto of the cantata to be set to music was *Clovis et Clotilde* by one Amédée Burion. "The candidates, supplied with this luminous libretto, were then isolated with a piano in a room called a *loge* until their scores were finished," wrote Berlioz, who that year was serving on the jury for the first time. "At eleven o'clock in the morning and at six in the evening the *concierge,* to whom the keys were entrusted, came to unlock the captives, who then met to take their meals together; but they were forbidden to go outside the building of the Institut.

"Everything sent in from outside—newspapers, letters, books, laundry—was carefully inspected so that neither advice nor help from anyone could be given the candidates. They were not, however, prevented from receiving visitors in the courtyard of the Institut every evening between six and eight, nor from inviting their friends to lively dinners at which God knows what might not have been communicated in conversation, between the claret and the champagne. The time allowed for composition was twenty-two days; composers who finished early were permitted to leave after having deposited their *signed* and *numbered* manuscripts." "

The choice of *Clovis et Clotilde* as libretto aroused Gounod's enthusiasm. "I am enchanted by the subject assigned for this year's competition," he wrote to Bizet. "It is simply wonderful. The three characters are equally charming, and I find no padding in the sequence of the scenes, *all* of which seem to be remarkable. What a subject for characterization! Splendid! I am very eager to know how you will come out of this. I am sorry not to be one of the candidates myself. I would willingly go back *en loge* to work on that libretto. Its color is superb and the style worthy of a great historical painting." [n]

The cantata, which is divided into five scenes, deals with the early Frankish king's conversion to Christianity. In addition to Clovis and his queen, Clotilde, there is, as the third character, her father, Rémy. The work opens with a recitative by Clotilde. "Noble Clovis," she sings, "my husband and my glory, he who causes the ancient world of Rome to tremble, behold, thou returnest to me consecrated by victory, thy brow with laurel crowned, palms in thy hand. I see thy proper courser with ebony mane, bearing thee toward me like a hurricane."

In the second scene Clotilde, in the company of her father, "honored member of the Christian faith," prays that following the King's baptism of glory, Rémy may "make him a Christian." In the next scene Clotilde's solitary prayer for her husband's salvation is interrupted by his return. A duet of love and faith between the royal pair reveals Clovis's conversion to Christianity. Rémy joins his daughter and Clovis in a final scene and proclaims his vision of a glorious future for the now Christian Clovis. The cantata ends with a hymn to God. [n]

Bizet's score for this exhilarating text won him the Prix de Rome for 1857, but not without a battle behind the scenes. On July 3, at the first meeting of the jury, which consisted entirely of members of the Music Division of the Académie, Bizet received one vote on the first ballot, two on the second and third, and none on the fourth. On the following day, however, when the cantatas were played before thirty of the thirty-six members of all sections of the Académie, Bizet's won sixteen votes on the first ballot. As soon as he received the good news, he rushed to Gounod's country place at Saint-Cloud, to report his victory, ignorant probably of the narrow margin by which he had won it.

Gounod, away from home for the day, wrote Bizet a letter of congratulations the same evening, July 5: "No one except your parents is happier than I am at the news you came to bring us at Montretout, and for which I should have liked to congratulate you with a kiss on both cheeks. . . . Now your school life is over. Your real life as an artist is about to begin—a severe and serious life, because you will now be able to come to grips with yourself comfortably without any worries. . . ." [n]

The ceremony that initiated Bizet into the "serious and severe" life of an artist was very impressive. "In honor of the great event," Berlioz wrote, "the academicians don their green-embroidered uniforms; they are dazzlingly radiant. They are about to crown a painter, a sculptor, an architect, an engraver and a musician. There is great joy in the abode of the Muses. . . ." [n]

At the annual public session of the Académie des Beaux-Arts on October 3, 1857, the program consisted of:

1. Performance of the piece by the Second Grand Prize in Musical Composition—composed by M. [Charles] Colin. . . .
2. Report on the work of the students at the Académie Impériale Française at Rome.
3. Awarding of the Grand Prizes.
4. Historical account of the life and work of M. David d'Angers.
5. Performance of the piece by the First Grand Prize in Musical Composition, composed by M. Bizet. . . .
6. Presentation of the Grand Prize for Musical Composition.

Gounod was prevented from hearing this ceremonial performance of Bizet's cantata because he was undergoing one of his more or less chronic attacks of nervous prostration. During the master's rest cure at Dr. Blanche's sanatorium, Bizet, a week after his official recognition as Prix de Rome, substituted for him as organist at the church in Bougival, where he played Gounod's Sanctus. By December, when Bizet left for Rome, Gounod had fully recovered. He presented his young friend with letters to friends in Rome, an autographed photograph, and a copy of his Serenade for piano and organ harmonium inscribed, "To my dear and good friend, Georges Bizet, *souvenir* and *adieu.*"

Rossini, too, gave Bizet letters of introduction: one to Felice Romani, the author of over one hundred librettos for Rossini, Bellini, and Donizetti; the other to Francesco Florimo, librarian of the Conservatory at Naples. In the latter he described the young composer as "an excellent student of composition [who] made his successful debut here in Paris with an operetta, is also a good pianist and a very charming young man." [n] In the letter to Romani, he adds that *"il Signor* Bizzet [*sic*] has an outstanding talent that deserves your nurturing and mine." [n]

In addition to letters, Rossini also gave advice to many of the

Prix de Rome. "Both in your music and in the conduct of your life," he told Emile Paladilhe, "take Mozart and the Italians as your models. Value melody and inspiration most. Don't compromise a fine future by dubious connections. Choose your acquaintances among those most eminent in the arts and among the wealthiest people. In that way you can only profit by the former and have nothing to lose through the latter. . . .

"Go to Rome and absorb that genius for melody which one breathes with the air of the sky of Italy. But go without preconceptions. Make no comparisons. Profit without bias from both the good and the bad that you hear. Listen carefully to everything without taking sides. Above all, don't criticize, and always be very prudent, very circumspect when it comes to expressing an opinion. Also act as though you were very tolerant. Even be it, if you can, for there is no one who doesn't need understanding.

"When I heard Palestrina's masterpieces played in Rome, they seemed to me deadly boring. I found in them neither melodic ideas nor skill. A second hearing didn't change my opinion, which I took care not to reveal to a living soul. I didn't understand any more than I had the first time, and I went humbly to confess this to the singer who directed the performance. He showed me the written work. I saw great skill there and fine food for the eyes. All this is obscured by the execution and does not produce the effect one would tend to expect. As for the idea, it must be pursued. It cannot be grasped in melodic scraps. Seek for a fine simplicity, but naturally without vulgarity. Skill will bring you appreciation from very few. The true successes are those that the public reveres. And the public likes to be moved, to be touched, and to understand without trouble or effort."

If Rossini was generous and gracious in the letters of introduction he gave to Bizet, the same cannot be said of his boon companion, Michele Enrico Francesco Vincente Paolo Carafa di Colobrano. This shadow of Rossini had attained, entirely through the glory reflected upon him by his devoted and loyal friend, a musical position in France quite disproportionate to his gifts. Their conflicting opinions of Bizet stand out as a rare example of disagreement between them. The letter of introduction to Giuseppe Mercadante which Carafa wrote for Bizet caused him great amusement.

"I am against ever presenting sealed letters of introduction," he wrote to his mother from Italy. "The one *père* Carafa gave me has taught me a lesson. I had sense enough to open it first. Sometimes indiscretion pays. There was an expression in *père* Carafa's letter which cannot be translated into our chaste language. My dear papa can amuse himself by translating it in his spare moments: 'The young man who will bring you this letter has had great success with his studies. He has won the important prizes at our Conservatoire. But, in my humble opinion, he will never be a dramatic composer, as he hasn't a f . . . . . . bit of enthusiasm.'

"I promise you, *père* Carafa," Bizet continued," that one day I shall write your biography, and put this letter at the end instead of a facsimile score. That would be edifying." [n]

Enlivening, if not edifying, a biography of Carafa might well be. Born in Naples in 1787, he fought on both sides in the Napoleonic wars, and was decorated for his part in the Russian campaign. The wars over, he supported himself by composing innumerable piano pieces and operas. After becoming a naturalized Frenchman, he was appointed professor of composition at the Conservatoire in spite of the protests of Cherubini, then the director. This friend and compatriot admonished Carafa: "Since the minister has given you the preference over the three candidates I sponsored, I hope that you will set yourself to studying counterpoint and fugue before teaching them to others." [n] Carafa preceded Berlioz by some twenty years as a member of the Institut. When the great composer was finally elected he remarked: "Like Banquo's ghost at Macbeth's banquet—Carafa is invisible to me. We rub shoulders, but we don't speak." [n]

Rossini and Carafa could be seen any day proceeding along the boulevards, Rossini on foot and Carafa astride a horse which, people claimed, had been bought from the proceeds of his opera *Thérèse,* produced nearly twenty years earlier. It was perhaps during one of these expeditions that Bizet, after his return from Rome, encountered Carafa, who inquired whether he had used his letter of introduction. "When one has the good luck to own the autograph of a man like you, M. Carafa, one keeps it," Bizet replied.

Bizet left for Rome on December 21, 1857.

CHAPTER  V

Villa Medici: Victor Schnetz: Edmond About

Seventy-six letters that Bizet wrote to his mother and father during his sojourn in Italy between 1858 and 1860, have been published under the title *Lettres de Rome*. Like most schoolboy letters, they are a mixture of impulsive confidences, superficial impressions, and reassuring reports to parents on health and work. The few letters to friends dating from this time reveal much more about Bizet the artist than does the mass of detail written to his mother and conditioned by her nature. For Aimée Bizet, partly no doubt because of ill health and continual financial insecurity, was above all else a worrier. She worried about the physical, social, and material details that preoccupy the average mother, but, judging by her son's replies, showed no more than average understanding of problems arising from his development as a composer. She brooded over his well-being as he did over hers, spared him no details of her illnesses or financial difficulties. The development of Bizet's genius is therefore not easily discernible in the record of his life in Italy as presented to his family. There does emerge, however, the picture of an ebullient, enthusiastic, genial boy; a *bon bourgeois* and family man; an artist, neither analytical, introspective, nor unduly narcissistic; a sharp, quick, perceptive human being with a gift for reportage.

Bizet started the first stage of his journey to Rome on the evening of Monday, December 21, 1857, when, with his three fellow prize-winners—Heim, an architect; Sellier, a painter, and

[51]

Charles Colin, an oboist—he left Paris by express train for Lyons, arriving the next morning at seven-thirty. These entries he conscientiously made in his diary, which, although formally entitled *Voyage de Paris à Rome,* was obviously intended only as a calendar or reminder. In it he notes that before leaving Lyons for Vienne, on the afternoon of the twenty-first, he visited the museum and saw "2 Peruginos, a fine Flandrin, a Heim," the last painter being the father of his traveling companion. Continuing their journey by train, the young men arrived four days later, on Christmas Day, at Avignon. From there Bizet, in his first letter home, declared: "I am the happiest of all the young people I know, and it would be madness to feel sorry for me." [1]

Another four days' traveling by stagecoach took the travelers to Toulon by way of the Provençal cities of Nîmes, Tarascon, Arles, and Marseilles. Provence, as exotic to a Parisian as a foreign country even in its language, made an impression on Bizet which echoed years later in the authentic local color of his score for *L'Arlésienne.* "These ancient and medieval ruins," he wrote to his mother, "these mountains, these valleys, these imposing sites, and, over and above everything, the sea, which is for me a wholly new experience. I have seen more, I have thought more in a week than in all the rest of my life. The spectacle of nature is so unfamiliar that I find myself unable to analyze its effect on me. . . . Tonight we took a little boatride in the roads of Toulon, which greatly impressed me. I had no idea of the grand and strange effect of the sea."

From Nice, the party traveled by *voiturin*—the driver's name, Bizet noted in his diary, was M. Reybaud—a sort of horse-drawn wagonette or "dusty carriage, part coach, part *fiacre,* packed with human beings, overloaded with trunks and boxes. . . . All artists strapped for money gratefully remember the convenience of this unpretentious vehicle." [n] Arriving at Savona after a two-day journey, Bizet, disillusioned by the "horrible" *trompe-l'oeil* architecture of Piedmont, finds "the churches look like painted cardboard monuments. . . . Unfortunately the priests' party is very powerful. The owner of the hotel where we are spending the night told

---

[1] Georges Bizet, *Lettres, Impressions de Rome (1857–1860), La Commune (1871),* Paris, 1907, 3. Subsequent unidentified quotations in this chapter are from this work. Unpublished portions of the letters, in the collection of the author, are enclosed in square brackets and individually noted, except for short quotations, which are noted by square brackets only.

us, only an hour ago, the most incredible things about these damned Jesuits. In all the small cities the women are bigots and ferociously virtuous except in relation to their confessors. . . . The Piedmontese beg in a variety of ways, humbly by day, with a bludgeon at night. . . ."

Through Genoa and Pisa the travelers continued to Florence, where Bizet was less articulate about the obvious beauties of the city than about the dishonesty of the Tuscans. On January 27, the group finally arrived at the Villa Medici, that beautiful palace built in 1540 which in 1803 had become the official domicile of the French Académie in Rome. Bizet spent no time describing this landmark, but labeled it "paradise" and sent a photograph of it to his parents. A friend of his, however, who came to the Villa soon after Bizet's arrival, has described the building. "The first view . . ." wrote Edmond About, "is grand and majestic, but without much ornamentation. From afar, you recognize above the door the arms and the flag of France. The only thing luxurious about the entrance consists of an avenue of holm oak trees and a jet of water playing in a large fountain. You pass between very rare, very beautiful, but very modest antique marble pillars. They wouldn't fetch more than six thousand francs.

"The first floor is given over to vast, magnificent reception rooms lined with the most beautiful Gobelins tapestries, worthy in every way of the grandeur of France. . . . But the most elegant part of the building is the façade at the back. It ranks among the masterpieces of the Renaissance. The architect seems to have exhausted a mine of Greek and Roman bas-reliefs to cover his palace. The garden is of the same period. . . . You see nothing but masses of greenery, plotted out with the most scrupulous care. Six lawns, surrounded by hedges, breast-high, spread out in front of the villa. . . . To the left four-times-four squares of turf are framed by high walls of laurel, by gigantic woods and holm oaks. The walls meet beyond the tree-lined walks and envelop them in cool, mysterious shade. . . . Both large and small gardens are dotted with statues of Hermes and marbles of all sorts." [n]

High up in the right-hand tower of the Villa, at the top of a spiral staircase, remains the fabulous "Turkish" room decorated by Horace Vernet in Oriental style with Arabic inscriptions painted on plaster over the bed, the doors, and the windows. Even today multi-colored birds flit above the chandeliers, although a leaking roof has dampened their plumage. Bizet was fortunate enough to occupy this room, said to be the highest in Rome, during the first month of his stay at the villa. The view from its windows, which give on four-fifths of the city and on the surrounding country, is breathtaking. But the occupant of *la chambre turque* during February 1858 was more interested in the human than in the aesthetic aspect of life at the Villa Medici.

"We were magnificently received by our comrades, who felt impelled to indulge in charming practical jokes," he wrote home, "apple-pie beds, bedside tables propped up so that there was a terrible racket every time you touched one, etc. It is an old custom, so the last thing you do is to take any offense at it. Soumy, the engraver, covered one eye with a bandage and deluded us into thinking he had a knife-wound, thus giving us an ominous picture of the city of Rome after seven in the evening. But now all that is over. When things calmed down, I met a dozen highly distinguished young people, five or six insignificant ones, and three who are rather vulgar.

"I was lucky enough to sit at table between the pleasantest boys at the Académie. M. Schnetz, our director, is a fine man; he is very nice to me."

Victor Schnetz, like Pierre Véron and Roqueplan at the Opéra and Auber at the Conservatoire, was one of those striking eccentric figures who, born at the time of the Revolution, grew up under the first Napoleon, flourished through the successive monarchies, and died with the fall of the Second Empire. Endowed with a certain amount of talent, but with more personality than character, these artists or dilettantes turned administrators gave off in their own day that kind of bright theatrical aura which in the light of history casts a barely perceptible shadow. Schnetz, seventy years old when Bizet arrived at the Villa Medici, had long been a fixture in the social life of the Eternal City. "When a good Frenchman arrives in Rome, the first person he asks to be shown is the Pope, the second 'M. Schnetz.' " [n]

A large, ruddy mountaineer of a man, dark-complexioned, "with a face that was gentle and benevolent in spite of the thick hedge of black eyebrows that spread all the way to his abundant hair," [n] Schnetz had a gruff manner, but he was a shrewd observer, witty and surprisingly tactful. "Under his rugged exterior and ebullient good nature was hidden the discernment of a critic whom nothing escapes and an indefinable mixture of diplomacy and indiscretion which led him to make fun of everything, including himself. . . ." [n]

A favorite pupil of David's, Schnetz in his youth had been taken seriously as a painter. Delacroix, in 1824, said that he was enchanted by the *Brigand's Wife* by Schnetz, which he saw in the gallery of the Duc d'Orléans, and more than thirty years later he advised a pupil of his to call on Schnetz in Rome because "he deserves this mark of respect for his great talent." [n] Schnetz himself did not place a very high value on his own work. Each year when the students at the Villa were invited to inspect the canvasses he was about to send to the Salon in Paris, the painter would stand erect on the threshold of his studio, clad in a vast dressing-gown and a Greek cap adorned with gold tassels. "Holding his maulstick like a scepter, he would never permit his guests to enter without first remarking, 'Gentlemen, I warn you that I do not value frankness.' " [n]

The predominating passion of Schnetz's life was his love for Italy and for Rome. In his early youth, with Géricault and Léopold Robert, he had walked through the country, climbed the mountains, and lived with shepherds, smugglers, and brigands. "Everyone knows," wrote an attaché at the French Embassy in Rome, "that . . . in Léopold Robert's *The Reapers,* the women leading the procession are two young sisters greatly cherished by our two friends. One of them, Maria Grazia, is still alive and lives in the town of Sonino. M. Schnetz, from time to time, makes an excursion into the Sabine to see this old friend, who every month receives a little pension of 15 francs.

"In exchange, full and complete protection is assured the pensioners of the Villa Medici. Thanks to the influence of the old mountain-woman, no bandit would dare touch a French artist. Every year at the same time Maria sends her benefactor long ropes of Sonino figs. Anyone who finds Maria Grazia's atrocious figs hard and dry is most unwelcome at the director's table." [n]

The dried figs were more or less typical of the food served at the Villa. For the domestic staff consisted largely of the friends of Schnetz's youth, brigands to whom he accorded one of the ancient privileges of the Villa Medici, the right of asylum. Although not a gourmet's dream, M. Schnetz's Sunday evening dinners, served on a Sèvres service presented by Louis-Philippe, were among the most favored social events in the city. Roman aristocrats, French officers, diplomats of all countries, visiting artists and celebrities flocked to them. Nowhere else did the French mingle with the Italians. For after 1850, when Napoleon III had stationed a garrison in Rome, France had been so unpopular that Schnetz remained the only Frenchman received in Roman society, welcomed everywhere by princes and beggars alike.

The first of his two terms as director of the Académie began in 1841. Gounod, a student at the Villa at the time, had harbored certain doubts about Schnetz's suitability as successor to his beloved Ingres. "My mother tells me," he wrote to a friend a week before Schnetz's arrival, "that he will arrive with his sister, who will be our hostess. This is all to the good, for at first I heard a rumor of something *altogether unlike* a sister; nothing could have discredited the Académie more than such a mess." [n]

Schnetz's first act as host to the students at the Villa was an evening party that he enlivened by transforming the large salon of the Académie into a sort of café-smoking-room with card-tables. "There, where the previous night Haydn and Mozart had been played *con amore,* the young artists were offered the pleasures of the games of *manille* and backgammon; all this in the presence of M. and Mme Ingres, 'silent and impassive, like statues in the midst of false gaiety. . . .' The incident was never repeated." [n]

Music did not appeal to the Director, possibly because of his deafness. But Bizet's attraction for *"ce papa exquis"* of all the children of the Académie was apparently responsible for the introduction of musical entertainment at the Villa. Ten days after his arrival, he played the piano at one of the regular Sunday evening parties. "I had a great success," he wrote. "It was the first time since M. Schnetz has been director that a musician has been heard and applauded at the Académie. It is fair to say that there are no pianists in Italy, and if you can play your scales with both hands you are regarded as a great artist." At the end of his stay in Rome, he advised Paladilhe, then a newcomer at the Villa, to "make as little music as possible in M. Schnetz's salon. But if you do, and want a success, say that you are going to play a piece by Verdi. Once you have taken this precaution, play Beethoven, Bach, Chopin. It doesn't matter which. It will always be taken for Verdi, that is to say for good music." [n]

During his first few months away from home, Bizet concentrated far more on the pleasures and excitements of meeting new people than on the composition of new pieces. Sightseeing, too, was secondary, for the first few months of the winter of 1858 were exceptionally rainy. And unlike the gray stone buildings of London and Paris, which reveal their structural splendor in any weather, the yellow, the orange, the brown churches and palaces of Rome need light and sunshine to illumine their beauty. So except for a *Te Deum*, on which he worked from mid-March to mid-May, Bizet spent his time discovering people and paintings, while his thoughts were preoccupied with Gounod and the preparations for *Faust* in Paris. Not even Gounod's sad letter bearing the news of his mother's death, which greeted Bizet on his arrival in Rome, quenched his high spirits for long.

"Life here is too happy," he wrote in a letter to his mother dated "*lunedi, 8 febbraio.* . . . The food is excellent. There is a splendid garden that we can't take advantage of now because the rain is coming down in torrents. In the evening we meet at table, and after dinner we usually spend our time in the students' salon. We chat, we keep warm, we play a hand at twenty-one. In short, we couldn't have a better time. The Académie has an excellent library, of which I am making use. I am taking Italian lessons. My professor, whom I pay 10 frs. 70 c. a month . . . is very pleased with me. . . . To all your good advice I shall reply with just one word; dapper is what they label me here and they are astonished at my *extraordinary neatness.* . . . Tell papa not to be too critical of my letters. I write in a great hurry and haven't the courage to reread. So I probably leave in a lot of nonsense. I wrote to Halévy. With him I was careful and didn't make a single mistake in French, a rare thing in the 19th century. . . ."

Having reassured his mother about his personal habits, Bizet, in his next letter, proceeded to allay her worries on another level. "Go in for politics, *mon Dieu!* Why we don't even know what's going on, and care less. We live entirely the life of artists, which means that any interests foreign to art and to the well-being of the individual artist are completely banished from our lives. But you were not mistaken in thinking that I greatly enjoyed myself at the Carnival. I went in a carriage with several companions, and we threw bouquets and confetti with both hands. Nothing is more charming than the Carnival in Rome. All the windows are lined with charming women, almost all of them dressed in Roman costume. There is a rain of flowers and confetti (bags of flour) which adorns and blanches you. But when you are wearing a gray domino you can exchange bouquets with the ladies and flour-bags with the men and not worry about getting dirty. M. Schnetz gave a masquerade ball. The wife of one of our servants made me a *ravishing costume,* a *baby's* dress. My wild success redounded entirely to the credit of the dressmaker. I am saving all my trappings to show you and to disguise myself again, should the occasion arise."

Félix-Henri Giacomotti, who painted the portrait of Bizet which he presented to his parents on his return to Paris, remembered, when he was old, his friend's joy of living, his certainty that he would conquer all obstacles. "The very embodiment of adolescent genius, his proud, virile brow was haloed in ash-blonde hair. He had rosy cheeks . . . a delicate nose with quivering nostrils and an eye full of mischief when it wasn't alight with inspiration." If there is a certain discrepancy between Giacomotti's brush and his pen portraits of Bizet, an unfinished painting by Sellier still hanging in the Villa Medici suggests the more romantic creative aspect of the composer which is lacking in Giacomotti's portrait. But it is very remote from the young man who, during the spring and summer of 1858, spent more time dining out than composing incipient masterpieces.

The precautions Bizet took to preserve his wardrobe and to insure a "smart" appearance in society were meticulous. ["M. Schnetz has had a very fine chest made for me,"] he told his mother. ["My belongings are laid in it in layers of pepper and camphor like pickled herrings in their salt. One of the pensioners who neglected taking these precautions found nothing but holes where his clothes had been. I had my collars all cleaned, so you see I am tidy. If you came into my room, there would be nothing for you to straighten. Marvelous to relate, not one button has come off a single shirt, but, of course, the laundry here is done to perfection and nothing is ever spoiled. I have very convenient, large drawers; in one I put my shirts in 4 piles of 6 each. I have numbered them so as not to put more in one pile than in the others. In the 2nd drawer are my socks, my handkerchiefs, my nightshirts, etc.; in the 3rd are my summer clothes. I have not yet torn or spoiled anything and I've lost only two handkerchiefs and not a single pair of gloves! In six months! You see, I have improved.

"I am a great deal thinner, which means that my two new

suits are just right for me.—My summer trousers fit me very well, and I have three complete outfits: my blue suit, my black-and-white suit, and my other blue trousers with my white jacket. Not counting my new suit (from the Palais d'Industrie) I *most certainly* have enough for three years. I have tried to let my beard grow, but M. Schnetz won't hear of such a thing; he doesn't think my face is the right shape for it. . . . I am the dandy (*sic*) of the Académie. . . ."] *

Bizet's adjustment to his particular world was, at this time, quite perfect: "I go out in society practically every evening. [M. Schnetz's friendship for me and my minor social successes are provoking a little jealousy on the part of several of my companions. But I make fun of it. I would rather provoke envy than pity.] At M. Sampayo's [2] I met Monsieur le Comte de Kisseleff, the Russian Ambassador. He is a charming man. I have already dined with him twice, and am going again tomorrow." The dinners at M. de Kisseleff's continued to delight Bizet throughout his stay in Rome. "I dine every week at Kisseleff's, which flatters pleasantly the remains of my sensuality as a gourmand," he wrote nearly two years later. "I say the remains, for in that way, too, I have changed a good deal. I no longer like cakes or candy or ices (except *marrons glacés*). I have become a model child."

This naïve concern with the pleasures of the flesh undoubtedly attracted the debonair M. de Kisseleff. For the Russian Minister Plenipotentiary in Rome, brother of the better known Ambassador to Paris, "was far more interested in his entertainment and comfort than in any political success. M. de Kisseleff had the best-appointed establishment as well as the best cook in Rome. A rather egotistical bachelor, he invited only the gayest and most amusing guests to his dinners." [3]

---

[2] Antoine-François-Oscar Sampayo (1818–62), son of an Irish father and a French mother, was first secretary of the French Embassy in Rome.

[3] "Kisseleff was living very peacefully when love descended upon his already white but still attractive head. The subtle diplomat could not resist the charms of a very seductive widow, Donna Francesca Torlonia, the most beautiful and unquestionably the best of the great ladies of Rome. Daughter of a younger son of the Ruspoli family, Donna Francesca had only her beauty as dowry. So she resolutely accepted the hand of the Russian minister. The marriage of a member of the highest aristocracy to a schismatic, against the will of the Pope, was a great event, a scandal. So the fiancés were forced to leave Rome and to go and be married in France. The minister changed his post to Florence. . . ." Henry d'Ideville, *Journal d'un diplomate en Italie: Rome 1862–1866*, Paris, 1873, 55–6.

Bizet's association with this attractive man of the world supplied his mother with fresh fuel for anxiety over its possible effect on her son's relations with his companions at the Villa. ["Mama urges me to get on well with my fellow-students,"] he wrote in one of the few letters addressed to his father. ["I have succeeded in living very peaceably with fifteen of them; the other five are utterly ridiculous, as I keep telling them, to their considerable irritation. But I have the majority on my side, and I don't care a rap for the rest. M. de Kisseleff counts me among his friends. I have dined there twice this week, and what dinners!!!! They compensate for the meals at the Académie, which are not up to much; in my opinion there is no good meat here. I am feeling very well. I take lots of baths, as they are free at the Académie."] "

Fortunately for Bizet, medical care was also free. "My health is still just as poor as it is in Paris although my appetite has developed," he had written home at the end of February; and a month later, "I lost a lot of weight while traveling, and I am not regaining it, which worries me." By the end of March he was suffering from the throat ailment that dogged him all his life and was ultimately in part responsible for his early death. He took illness gaily. "I have caught a sore throat that is progressing more rapidly than I am. Fortunately I am treated like a spoiled child here, and the many people who come to see me help me to be patient about staying in bed.[4] M. Venti, an Italian doctor, has bled me and put twelve leeches on my throat, which didn't even tire me. But M. Meyer, a French doctor, gave me an excellent gargle, and today I am better. I hope you won't worry. There is really no reason to. As for M. Schnetz, he is in my room all the time. I am sure that you will think that I have been imprudent. It isn't true. I was only careless. But starting today I shall be as careful as an old man. . . . I needn't tell you one is perfectly taken care of here except for the

---

[4] Among the visitors who came to cheer Bizet while he was ill was the painter Gustave Moreau, who was studying in Rome. Moreau, besides his talent as a painter, had "a delightful tenor voice," Bizet wrote. "This charming boy comes to see me often, and we do whole scores together." Another caller was Jean-Jacques Ampère, son of the great scientist and himself a distinguished historian. Ampère, according to his colleague Gregorovius, who was also in Rome at this time, was "one of the most brilliant Frenchmen, good-natured, kind, versatile and, what is rare among Frenchmen, devoid of vanity. While still young, he visited Goethe at Weimar, and with Thiers and Guizot took part in the editing of *The Globe*. He has visited many countries, studied many branches, and can talk on all subjects." Ferdinand Gregorovius, *Roman Journals*, London, 1907, 42.

mistakes of the doctors, who, along with the pharmacists, are paid by the government. But anyway I am M. Schnetz's favorite. . . ."

A few days later, aware that his rather light-hearted attitude toward his illness might worry his parents, he wrote again, making it clear that in the future he would revert to the usual fortnightly interval between letters. "A slight indisposition," he admits, "at a distance of a thousand miles, looks like a grave illness. I am much better, though it still hurts me a little to swallow. . . . I have lost an enormous amount of weight in a week and can now see a lot of bones I didn't know I had. My room is a procession . . . of visitors. All my fellow-students come to see me every day except two whom I don't much care for. . . . The tonsilitis I had in Paris was a midsummer night's dream compared to this one. Everybody advises me to have my tonsils out, but that step requires reflection. . . ."

Within a fortnight his desire to reassure both himself and his parents had induced in him a not wholly convincing philosophic approach. Although he had grown "frighteningly thin," although his trousers were "a thousand times too big," he was "still chubby. . . . This little illness," he wrote, "has done me lots of good. I feel more robust, stronger, and my mind is fresher and freer. The monotony of happiness and health was beginning to be tedious, and this fortnight in bed has been a good thing. . . . You seem to worry perpetually about my financial situation," he continues. "What can I say to reassure you? I don't know, so I give up.

"You talk a lot about religious ceremonies, too. Here is what they consist of: putting on your best suit in the morning, going and standing four hours in the entrance to the Sistine Chapel, all in order to listen to the most boring music. There you have it. Inspiration here lies in the great works of the masters, and even more in those of the good Lord, in the countryside, in relics of the past, but not at all in these ridiculous ceremonies, in which a magnificently dressed dummy presents a spectacle for a curiously stupid crowd. One thing alone is great and makes a fine impression; that is the benediction in the square of St. Peter's. So now you are informed about Holy Week in Rome. Poor music combined with unworthy play-acting for which the Pope and the cardinals are responsible; that is what I have seen and heard.

["You know how much I share your opinion of society. After several valuable discussions on this subject with the misanthropes here at the Académie I am regarded as an opportunist. I don't care."]

Bizet's opportunism, if indeed it existed, was soon to be challenged by the presence in Rome of the arch-opportunist of his day, whom Bizet had met at Offenbach's parties. "[Edmond] About has arrived," Bizet wrote to his mother. "He flung his arms around me as though I were an old friend. He is charming to me. I was convalescent when he arrived, and he came every day and spent three hours with me. He is here on some artistic mission. He is coming, I believe, to live at the Académie. He will be a delightful companion. [He was charged with all sorts of messages for me by M. and Mme Offenbach. About was unaware of our dispute,[5] and said that Mme Offenbach particularly seemed very well disposed toward me. You see it is always wise to assert your rights. No one thinks of holding it against you.]"[n]

Bizet's immediate plunge into intimacy with the new arrival is not surprising. About, propagandist for the advantageous cause, journalist, art-critic, novelist, playwright, and man of the world, was one of the most attractive and notorious young men in France. This careerist, who had transformed himself from an impecunious student into "the prince of *boulevardiers*," dabbled in every field and acquired money and influence rapidly. His wit was as cutting as his foil; even his fencing-master reproached him for fighting too many duels.

About's first book, *La Grèce contemporaine*, published in 1854 after a visit to Greece, when he was only twenty-six years old, won a great *succès de scandale*. No less a critic than Flaubert called it "a nice little book, very exact, full of truths, and most witty. . . ." *Tolla*, About's first novel, which Henry James found a "truly beautiful little novel, a masterpiece of the fantastic," was published in 1855, to be followed in 1857 and 1858 by three other novels, among them *The King of the Mountains*, which is still read in schools. As a result of the success of these books, the author was awarded the Cross of the Legion of Honor at a dinner party at the Princesse Mathilde's shortly before he left for Rome.

About's opinions on painting veered as frequently and were often as unsound as his political views. Manet he regarded as a failure, his painting "an enormous dunghill." Corot was no

---

[5] This dispute apparently had to do with the payment of the award for *Le Docteur Miracle*.

draughtsman. After devoting an admiring chapter to Delacroix's paintings in 1855, ten years later, when the great painter was dead and his reputation at a low ebb, About characteristically trimmed his praise to "Delacroix painted half a dozen masterpieces and horrors by the hundred." Bouguereau he then found "one of the most complete artists." But in spite of his limitations, About served Bizet as a knowledgeable guide through the museums of Rome and unquestionably opened his young admirer's eyes, and stimulated in him an appreciation of painting unusual in a composer.

"About has found all doors closed to him," Bizet wrote home in May 1858, "and the few French people who do receive him can't avoid it. His reputation as a scandalmonger has done him a lot of harm, and it will be difficult for him to write an *honest* and *serious* book on Italy. He will manage by dint of his wit." It was rather by dint of Schnetz's wit and social position that About's articles, which soon started appearing in the official *Moniteur,* were so successful. The Romans blamed Schnetz for having given the visitor too intimate information about their society. "The terrible traveler had in fact spent barely a fortnight in Rome before he had cleverly reported and made use of all the old Director's conversation and anecdotes. . . . 'Oh, what a serpent I nursed in my breast!' old Schnetz would say. And from his tone of voice it was hard to tell whether the Director was not perhaps pleased at having nursed this poisonous snake whom he had himself guided into the mountains." "

Schnetz's sponsorship of About probably tended to postpone Bizet's awareness of the flaws in the writer's character, while About's conversation was sufficiently intoxicating to foster the illusion of originality. Having cultivated a gift for bestowing what the Goncourts called critical "caresses," About lost no time in flattering the young composer. When, soon after About's arrival, Bizet, in doubt about the value of his *Te Deum,* played it for him, the newcomer's words could hardly have been more reassuring. "If you don't achieve one of the finest positions in the musical world, you will certainly fall short of all opportunities and expectations, because except for Gounod and Gevaert there no longer is anybody." When Mme Bizet questioned About's standards of judgment, Bizet replied, "I shall probably have much less talent and less dogmatic convictions than Gounod. In these days that means more chance of success. [Don't repeat this to anyone. Peo-

ple are already too disposed to treat me like a man without convictions.]"

But convictions were in no way involved in the project that
occupied Bizet's attention for the next month. About had suggested
a plot for a one-act operetta. "It is charming, but a little too comic
for the Opéra-Comique. However I don't attach any importance to
it except as an amusing exercise, although About wants to have
this little number produced by Roqueplan." This "very pretty
opéra-bouffe" continued as a topic of conversation throughout
the month of April, and then, like many another love duet to improvised piano-accompaniment, evaporated into thin air. Although no word or note of it was ever put on paper, the talk about
it must have been as sympathetic to Bizet as were About's attacks
on the Vatican.

Only one thorn in the flesh irritated Bizet during these first
months of exuberant social success—his fellow prize-winner in
music. Charles Colin appears to have been one of those maddening bores who, for some inexplicable reason, always occupy a disproportionate amount of their associates' conversation. "This cre-
tin," as Bizet usually calls him, seems to have been a born scapegoat—the embodiment of the gauche, unpopular clown, the figure
of fun who lurks beneath the surface of every insecure adolescent
and must, at all costs, be suppressed. From the outset of their stay
at the Villa, Bizet had enlarged upon and contrasted his own
savoir-faire with Colin's boorishness. The week after their arrival,
when Bizet's performance at Schnetz's Sunday *soirée* introduced
a new era of entertainment at the Académie, Colin had played his
oboe. "He played very well, only he behaved so stupidly with the
other fellows that the poor boy was most disastrously teased. Bonnet (the architect) said yesterday to several people. 'That impossible Colin terrifies me. Every time he plays that *leek* of his, he
gets red as a rooster. I'm always afraid his eyes will pop out of his
head.' This running fire of gibes resulted in the boorish Colin's
refusing to accept decently the hazing that is always practiced on
newcomers, and which consists of a yeá or nay vote to decide who
pays for the coffee. He declared that this was no way to do things,
and formally refused to pay. We all laughed like crazy and added
a coffee with *brandy* and *cigars* as penalty for his having disobeyed
the majority. Anyway, this group of young people will develop his
character. He certainly needs it. [I need hardly tell you that] I

came off well. I let them charge me for eight coffees, the result of which was that, seeing my indifference, they no longer had any fun teasing me. So they wreaked their vengeance on poor Colin." Colin's turgid stubbornness was perhaps the chief cause of his unpopularity. On one occasion, for instance, when the Director asked him to play at a Sunday evening musicale, Colin refused, saying, "I won't play because I don't want to, and that's all there is to it." Understandably enough, he was not asked to perform when the students organized a celebration in honor of Schnetz's promotion to the rank of Commander of the Legion of Honor.

For Bizet that evening was a triumphant success. The work he performed was a brilliantly humorous parody of Clapisson which he had improvised in 1854 when that violinist and tenth-rate composer had been elected to the Institut in preference to Berlioz. Antoine-Louis Clapisson, a native of Naples, where he was born in 1808, was a good violinist. Starting out as a composer of romances, songs, and salon pieces, he wrote six operas before he achieved success in 1846 with *Gibby la cornemuse* and again in 1854 with *La Fanchonette*. The public, undismayed by his bombastic and uninspired style, enjoyed his gift for melody. His contempt for the new young composers he expressed freely during a visit to the Villa Medici. "Here are Clapisson's ideas about us," wrote one of the Prix de Rome. "We . . . laugh at the most respected reputations and at the men who have managed to attract the ear of the public. . . . Our mad conceit drives us, young as we are, to write music for the theatre as though it were easy to do. He advises us to spend at least ten years writing nothing but collections of romances and comic songs, and to attract the ear of the public by composing for the audiences of the *cafés chantants*. Quotation: 'You must realize that reputation and glory consist of nothing more than hearing your name spoken often and seeing it in print. That is as powerful as 300 horses.' " [n]

Bizet's improvisation on Clapisson's works, which he frequently played at musical gatherings, stemmed from his contempt for the composer and a more or less personal feud with the man himself which had originated while Bizet was still a pupil. Clapisson had presented to the Conservatoire a collection of ancient musical instruments of which he was appointed curator. In order to guard his *rebecs* and *viole d'amore,* he slept in a room at the Conservatoire. Around two o'clock one morning, a group of young men gathered under his window and shouted "Clapisson! Clapisson!" The newly appointed curator woke with a start. Thinking that a fire threatened his precious instruments, he rushed to the window, a grotesque, Falstaffian figure in his nightshirt. At the sight of him, the voices died down, and when he cried, "What is it? What's the matter?" there was a profound silence. Then one voice was heard to proclaim, "You write rotten music!" After another silence, the boys burst into roars of laughter and fled, leaving poor Clapisson flabbergasted. Next day, the author of the insult failed to divulge his identity, and Bizet became the scapegoat. He "strongly and sincerely" denied having made the offensive remark, and a friend insisted that Bizet "was incapable of any meanness, great or small. His high spirits were never aggressive and his teasing was always good-natured." [n] But the elder composer's hostility is implicit in the rough draft of a letter Bizet penned.

"Sir and Illustrious Master," begins this document, hurriedly scrawled and filled with abbreviations, "You are one of the leading lights of the art of music—you are a member of the Institut, *ch.* of the L. of Honor. You have composed the admirable scores of *la Promise,* of *la Fanch* [*onette*], of *Gibby* [*la cornemuse*], and of a host of operas that have rightly won you great popularity.—I, Sir, am but the lowliest of your admirers. Today, Sir, I greeted you, and you did not acknowledge my greeting.—The immeasurable distance that separates us, in both age and position, does not justify your ignoring me nor what I hardly dare call your impoliteness. You occupy too high a position to permit my finding fault with your behavior. I leave it to you to decide whether you should not acknowledge in some kindly or polite way the so sincere expression of my respect and, I repeat, of my admiration. I should have liked to persuade myself that your—forgetfulness was involuntary, Sir. But nothing could have prevented your seeing me this morning, unless perhaps it was the halo of glory encircling your brow.

"I am, Sir and very illustrious Master, with the most profound respect, your v. humble and v. devoted servant.

G. B." [n]

It seems unlikely that this draft was ever copied and sent.
The version of *The Burial of Clapisson,* the parody with

which Bizet regaled his Paris friends, "began with a funeral march on Clapisson's most banal theme: first the procession of mourners with the members of the Académie in solemn state at their head, then the funeral oration delivered by Ambroise Thomas, then the cheerful departure of the company, glad to have the tiresome ceremony over. The second part was called '*Apothéose.*' Clapisson's soul, clad in the full-dress attire of the Académie, sword at its side, finding itself alone, flies from the cemetery up to heaven. God, surrounded by the most celebrated composers, receives him with honor among the immortals (here the ceremony of admission to the Académie was parodied). Beethoven . . . greets him with the opening bars of his Fifth Symphony, which Clapisson interrupts with a theme from *La Fanchonette.* Beethoven, only momentarily disconcerted, resumes his Symphony (left hand), but Clapisson is not to be outdone and pours forth a stream of his choicest melody (right hand). So for some time the contrapuntal battle continues, till Beethoven as the wiser of the two gives in and *La Fanchonette* is carried to a swelling apotheosis." [n]

When Bizet played this work at the Villa Medici in honor of Schnetz's promotion to Commander of the Legion of Honor, he changed the scene of the "*Apothéose.*" The program announced the *Reception of Clapisson by Beethoven,* not into heaven, but *into the Underworld.* A member of the audience recalled many years later "the staggering zest and brilliance of the performance . . . the screamingly funny medley of the anemic and antiquated motifs of *La Fanchonette* with broad improvisations on the Fifth Symphony. . . . On retiring Schnetz said to Bizet, 'You have created an inspired epic out of a parlor trick. You made me laugh so much I feel fifty years younger.' " [n]

After Clapisson's death in 1866, Bizet never again played this parody.

CHAPTER  VI

Rome: *Don Procopio:* Italy

During Bizet's first six months in Rome, he devoted a comparatively small amount of time to work. The *Te Deum* he composed was inspired wholly by his desire to win the fifteen-hundred-franc Rodrigues Prize for a religious work. "If I get the prize . . ." he had written a week after his arrival in Rome, "I shall ask Papa to invest it for me and I shall ask him for a *tiny bit* of it with which to see Switzerland on my way to Germany. But let's not build castles in Spain, or rather in Switzerland!" [1]

From the end of February to mid-April 1858, Bizet worked on the *Te Deum* with very little satisfaction. It is "frightfully difficult." He "digs away at it like a slave." It is "devilishly hard, and I am longing to finish it so that I can start a three-act Italian opera to a libretto that I like very much." He had worked on it during his illness, and hoped that it wouldn't sound "too feverish." Cheered by About's praise, he could write on April 17: "My *Te Deum* is finally finished. I only have to orchestrate. I don't know what to think of it. Sometimes I find it good, at others, detestable. The one sure thing is that I was not cut out for religious music." After a fortnight of orchestrating, he still had his doubts. "At certain moments it enchants me, at others I am bored with it. In any case, the Académie will judge."

The less demanding labor of orchestration left Bizet free to

---

[1] Bizet, *Lettres de Rome*, 30. Subsequent unidentified quotations in this chapter are from this work. Unpublished portions of the letters, in the collection of the author, are enclosed in square brackets and individually noted, except for short quotations, which are noted by square brackets only.

enjoy the fair spring weather, "happy as a fighting cock. . . . I am becoming more and more attached to Rome," he wrote. "The better I know it, the more I love it. Everything is beautiful here. Every street, even the dirtiest, has its individuality, its special character, or some reminder of the ancient city of the Caesars. Astonishingly enough, the things I found most offensive when I arrived in Rome now are part of my very existence: the ridiculous madonnas above every streetlight, the laundry hanging out to dry in every window, the dung piled up in the middle of the square, the beggars, etc. All this I enjoy, it amuses me, and I would yell bloody murder if a single pile of dirt were removed."

During this early summer, Bizet also explored some of the Italian countryside. When the *Te Deum* was copied, he went on a two-week holiday in the Sabine hills with his friend Heim, the architect. They left at four o'clock on the morning of May 27 for a tour of Albano, Tivoli, Gensano, Frascati, and Norma, and returned full of enthusiasm for everything Italian except climate, women, and musical instruments. "I had a superb journey!" Bizet wrote to his mother. "What a wonderful country! We saw so much. You learn more about the Italian language and character traveling a fortnight in the mountains than spending six months in Rome. Besides, we were lucky. We saw the most amusing and interesting things in the world; sometimes it was a characteristic procession, sometimes a wedding or a funeral. Everywhere we found the people frank and kindly. The native Italians do not detest the French, and besides they appreciate the slightest attention. In exchange for a cigar or two, you acquire a partisan. The women are often pretty, sometimes ugly, and always dirty. We visited several monasteries, and were always welcome. We were received, among others, by a charming man with a cultivated mind and a splendid face. Nothing could have been more beautiful than his grave and kindly head. He wore his monk's robes with unbelievable ease and elegance. Most of the cities we visited had a very unhealthy climate. Malaria is prevalent in all the swampy regions, and you see the traces of fever in every face. . . . I played organs several times in churches and convents. They were horrible!"

The high mood in which Bizet returned to Rome from his fortnight in the hills was of short duration. Troubled by his mother's perpetual anxiety about him, he too became anxious and uncertain about his work. Early in February, he had found a seemingly good libretto for his Italian opera—*Parisina,* a forgotten work of Donizetti's—but by the end of June he discovered that the libretto he had chosen did not suit him at all. "So I looked for, and found, an Italian farce in the manner of *Don Pasquale.* It is very amusing to do, and I hope to carry it off with honors. I am decidedly made for *bouffe* music, and I am giving myself over to it completely. I can't tell you the trouble I had finding this libretto. I went to every bookseller in Rome, and read over two hundred pieces."

Bizet's discovery of the right libretto did not, however, serve to launch him into concentrated work. "I have become very critical," he told his mother, "and am rarely satisfied with what I do, which means that in spite of my great facility I don't progress any faster than anybody else. Quite the contrary. . . . For the last fortnight I have had insomnia, which has tired me a little. I couldn't go to sleep until three or four in the morning. I forced myself to get up at seven so as to store up sleep for the next night, but always in vain. Now I have reverted to my former habits, and go to bed regularly at eleven so I can fall asleep by midnight. . . ."

The distress of mind Bizet tried not to communicate to his mother he revealed to Gounod. After asking his "dear Master" for detailed news about *Faust,* which was soon going into rehearsal, he wrote: "What can I tell you about myself? Very little. I am studying Rome to the best of my ability and I dare believe that my studies will be fruitful. I often go to the mountains; down there, you know, behind Rivoli, to Subiaco, to Vicovaro, to Cervaro. Oh, how I wish you could be here, if only for a few days! What good you would do me! For three months I have been in a state of profound apathy toward my art. I have much preferred to stroll about, to read, to observe, rather than expose myself to committing some miserable *pezzo di musica.* However I have had to think about my envoi and have chosen an *opéra-bouffe* (2 acts) entitled *Don Procopio.* It is gay; above all, it is very musical. I hope to do something tolerable with it. *Oh, how difficult it is to make good music!* And besides I have been left to myself for the nine months, unable to hear one note of good music, so I no longer know how to judge. . . . I am rather like a poor swimmer in deep water. I splash a lot and make little progress. I have always been very much the schoolboy; you don't become *yourself* easily. I am sure of overcoming this obstacle, but when? . . . I hope it will be soon because I am in a hurry to show some result. Perhaps you experienced something analogous to this when you were in Italy? I doubt it.—If you know a cure for musical spleen, tell it to me. . . ." [n]

The most immediate cure would, of course, have been victory in the Rodrigues competition. But the prize went to the only other competitor. "I have just this minute learned that Barthe has the Rodrigues prize," Bizet wrote to his mother. "I must say I am very much upset!!! Oh, well, I shan't die of it." He merely had "an atrocious attack of dysentery for a week." Barthe's victory, he wrote later, did not greatly affect him. His absence from Paris had been disadvantageous, he believed; he doubted whether there actually had been a competition and thought that Barthe's cumulative work had won him the award. "For all these reasons," he concluded, "I don't have to console myself for a failure that is not a real one and is given no publicity."

The failure of the *Te Deum,* which he himself knew to be a feeble work, reinforced his determination to substitute an *opéra-bouffe* for the Mass required as his next *envoi.* "How can they oblige me, a non-Christian, to do a work that would be uninspired and insincere?" Bizet fulminated to a group of his fellow-students. "Mozart's Requiem fills me with admiration. But look how inferior academic fugal music is to the high Gregorian Lamentations of the *Stabat,* the *Vexilla,* or the *Dies Irae.* During Holy Week, when I listen to the simple children in the choir of the poorest village church singing the splendid prose that shines with the aura of Christianity, of penitence and remorse, I emerge with the illusion that I am a Christian. When I hear a Mass by Cherubini, I come out feeling like a dilettante." [n]

The shock of losing the Rodrigues prize lasted about ten days. Then Bizet wrote to his mother: "I am working very hard because I am beginning to realize that my little opera could well become a first-rate thing, and the more I am convinced of this, the more effort I must put into what is left to do. I should like, as far as possible, to do a really polished work. I don't want any mistakes in it, which is difficult. Fortunately, I have improved tremendously; I can *rewrite,* and I take advantage of it. You know that in Paris when I had composed something, I couldn't start it over again, Here, on the contrary, I am delighted to. Another sign of improvement: it seems as though all my skill and my musical slickness are no longer of any use to me; now I can only do something that has an idea behind it, which means that not one of the pieces in my opera will be *worthless*. I am convinced that to do bad work is better than to do mediocre; I am trying to do good work, which would be even better. I have great trouble composing, which is natural enough; I have no basis of comparison to depend on, and I can only be satisfied with a thing when I believe it is *good*— while in class, or at the Institut, it was sufficient if my work was better than my fellow-students'. . . .

"I feel, too, that I am strengthening my artistic taste. Comparisons between painters and sculptors and musicians are useful. All the arts are related, or rather there is only one art. Whether one expresses one's thought on canvas, in marble, or on the stage matters little; the thinking is always the same. I am more than ever convinced that Mozart and Rossini are the two greatest musicians. While I admire Beethoven and Meyerbeer mightily, I feel that my nature tends to make me like pure and *spontaneous* art more than the passionately dramatic. So in painting Raphael is the same man as Mozart; Meyerbeer feels as Michelangelo felt. Don't think that I am exclusive; on the contrary. I have come to recognize that Verdi is a man of genius moving in a most deplorable direction.

"There, in general, is my line of thought; it will show you which way my taste as an artist has gone since my departure. As for my personal morale, it has not changed, and I congratulate myself. I am still gay, although more serious. My companions say that I have wit; modesty precludes my believing it. But everyone certainly believes that there are no obstacles in my way, that my road is all mapped out for me. I wish it were true, but I dread my return; I dread the first contact with the directors and the manufacturers of pieces, whom I no longer honor with the name of *poet*. I fear [those cretins] the singers. I fear, in a word, that tacit ill-will which, without disagreeable expression, obstinately hinders one from going ahead. Well, that concerns Providence, not me.

["I hope that today you will not complain of my verbosity. You may find me a little naïve in paying myself so many compliments, but I tell you the truth so that you can know where I stand and not worry about me."]

Georges's mother, in turn, told him the truth. "The news about your health distresses me profoundly," he wrote to her in October. "You needn't try to persuade me that you look after yourself. . . . It is not a habit of yours! . . . Take care of yourself, I beg of you; see a doctor; in a word, act like everybody else. You are the only person I know who refuses to believe that being careful can have a salutary effect on health."

Bad news, undue emotional or nervous strain, always reduced the youthful Bizet's self-confidence to a low ebb. As a kind of shock-absorber or anodyne to his distress over Mme Bizet's recurrent attacks of illness, knowledge of which she never spared him, he would almost automatically engage in a quarrel or brawl with fellow-pensioners he disliked. Subsequently a despatch would go off to Paris, fully reporting his triumph, as if to show that his strength counterbalanced Mme Bizet's weakness.

Immediately after receiving the October bulletin, Bizet picked a quarrel with Colin and ["Doublemard, a sculptor, a boy with plenty of common sense, but both despicable and despised."] These two, after seeing Bizet in the Russian ambassador's box at the Argentina Theatre, had the "impudence" to address some "unsuitable remarks" to him. "Several of these jokes," he wrote, "were very clear allusions to my association [with aristocrats] and my customary social life."

Bizet's subsequent attempt to avenge with fisticuffs this affront to his vanity was interrupted by other residents of the Villa Medici, but he himself tended to regard his outbursts of temper as a chronic ailment. "My natural quarrelsomeness persists," he wrote in a moment of detachment. "A jab from an elbow in the street, someone staring at me longer than I like, and brrrrrrrrrr . . . off I go. I do my best to control it, but it is hard for me, in fact very hard. All my comrades lecture me, including those, naturally, who are more easily offended than I am. Well, time is a great teacher and will perhaps reform me, if that is possible."

Calmed by his purge of violence, housebound by the rains and snows of November, Bizet settled down to work. At New Year's he wrote to his parents: "I have only two more years in which to be peacefully happy. I haven't spent my year so badly. . . . I have composed as much music as can be done in four months' constant work. . . . My *envoi* continues to jog along nicely; it will be completely finished, orchestrated, and copied by the first of April (perhaps a month earlier). Sum total, all goes well.—Provided that, on my return I find three, or even two nice acts for the Théâtre Lyrique, which I have every reason to hope for." This hope was naturally related to the subject of money. "I have a little plan about that lovely metal to which we are all subject," he wrote. "When I have a hundred thousand francs put by, Papa will not give any more lessons, nor shall I. We will start life on an income that will not be bad. A hundred thousand francs— that's nothing; just two successful little *opéras-comiques*. A success like *Le Prophète* brings in nearly a million. So what I am saying is no castle in Spain."

While making plans for the future, Bizet had also been delving into the past. "I have read some fifty [good] books," he wrote in this summary of his first year in Rome, "as much history as literature." His choice of books was catholic, conditioned, no doubt, by the contents of the library at the Villa Medici and the influence of his friend About. He made copious notes on the works of Greek and Latin authors which he read in French translation: a volume of selections from *Odes, Satires,* and *Letters* of Horace, sixteen *Satires* of Juvenal, the *Prologues* of Persius, the poems of Catullus, the *Elegies* of Propertius, etc. He read *Notes sur le Théâtre grec et sur le Théâtre latin* in sixteen volumes, which included analyses of the plays of Aeschylus, Sophocles, Euripides, Aristophanes, Menander, Plautus, Terence, Seneca, and many lesser writers. He filled two notebooks with a detailed synopsis of the *Aeneid*. Bizet's digests of the classics savor of school exercises or lecture notes. Only when he writes of authors related to his own immediate interests does he express personal opinions. Beaumarchais, as the author of *Le Mariage de Figaro* and *Le Barbier de Séville*, naturally appealed to him. His notes on Beaumarchais's complete works published in 1837 by Ledentu cover both sides of a long piece of foolscap in small, compressed handwriting.

"*Le Barbier de Séville* comedy 4 acts. Prem. Comédie Française (Tuileries) 23 February 1775— . . . to be read and reread over and over, both the play and the preface—the plot is extremely simple—how light and at the same time how firm! MASTERPIECE—the preface includes a quite new conception of music for the period—Beaumarchais felt and understood the flaws in this art—he should have had *Wagner* for a collaborator.

"*Le Mariage de Figaro* comedy 5 acts. Prem. Comédie Française Tuesday 27 April 1784—Superb preface—but inferior to the one for *Le Barbier*—nothing frivolous about it—to be studied endlessly! It should be learned by heart! . . .

"*Report*—I support this petition about the rights of authors—interesting from every point of view—Directors haven't changed—the theatre then was neither worse nor better than today—

"*Letters.* . . . No. *33*—to the authors of the *Journal de Paris*—touching!—fine analysis of charity! use of figures of speech like About's— . . . *39* reply to the *curé* of St. Paul who reproaches him for having permitted work to be done at his house on Sunday! This is an admirable piece! to be reread often! What a pity this century doesn't study these masters!—*44* long letter to his daughter about the riot in which Beaumarchais escaped being the 1st victim—simple—earthy—but full of wit! *he is frightened!* Decidedly the forerunners of the revolution had no idea of the violence of the passions they would have to curb. . . ." [2]

The successors to the Revolution of 1789 appealed to Bizet less. His comments on the prose works of the great romantic poets are largely exclamatory, his emotions about them mixed. In his notes on the first volume of Lamartine's *Voyage en Orient* Bizet carries on a sort of dialogue with the author:

" '*A world in an insect's tear!*' What exquisite form! Why does M. de Lamartine spoil his splendid descriptions by his crushing personality?—Your landscapes are admirable—but you take up too much space in them!

"P. 64. Gently!—you are pretty hard on Virgil! make room for Alfred de Musset!—*ridiculous yet pious Aeneas!* Ah! If only he had been a Catholic! . . .

"—118 *Museums—Graveyards of the arts* (nice!)

"These pages are exquisite—and dangerous!— . . ."

No memorable sentences attracted Bizet in Chateaubriand's *Itinéraire de Paris à Jérusalem.* "Immense erudition," he recognized, but "dry as a catalogue. . . . Not the book of a poet! Cold gaiety—Catholic gaiety. *Me*, again *me*, always me.—Apology for slavery—*A man cannot be a superior being unless he has the rights of life and death over his servants. How I deplore this!* Maybe it is true, but one doesn't write such things. . . ." The preface to the *Mémoires* the young critic found, in spite of the

---

[2] Bizet, unpublished notes in collection of the author. The three quotations immediately following are from the same source.

"slightly pretentious style, superb, great, really liberal! Fine and wholesome philosophy!"

The work Bizet read with the most interest and care, judging by the bulk and detail of his notes, was the *Correspondence* of Baron von Grimm in seventeen volumes. The bi-monthly news letters that this German-born, Francophile friend of Rousseau and the Encyclopedists wrote to various German sovereigns, to Catherine II of Russia and the King of Poland, give a vivid picture of the social, political, and artistic life of Paris during the third quarter of the eighteenth century. Ignoring the political events reported in the letters, Bizet copied carefully the opening dates of important plays, operas, the activities, witticisms, and demises of the great, as well as spicy anecdotes. For example, a letter in which the Comte de Lamaquais described his mistress: "She cooked my soup and ate it with me. She made my bed and enjoyed it with me. As she had beauty but no style, kindness but not sweetness, humor without caprice, and the charm, in my eyes, of being ridiculous without being awkward, foolish without being stupid, she was a far healthier ferment for my spirit than is tea for my stomach." The remark of an elderly duchess on the subject of actors also attracted Bizet: "You mean a lady receives them as guests in her salon? Fie, how shocking! In my day we received them in the antechamber or in bed, never in the salon!"

Few of Bizet's notes on his reading, his private diaries, his letters to his parents, show the struggles inherent in the artistic development of a musician. But at the end of his first year in Rome he wrote a most revealing letter to a young painter, Emile Diaz: "We were made, I think, to understand each other. I, too, am frightened. I, too, start lots of things with enthusiasm and get discouraged at the end when I see that *I have not done what I set out to do.*

"Nevertheless, I have improved tremendously since I left Paris. At the Conservatoire I was a good pupil; here I begin to think of myself as an artist. I stand alone, but how I stumble! What falls I take! Anyone who doesn't break his neck in the dark forests of art is lucky. Well, I have a bright light to guide me. I have a purpose; I know what is good, what is beautiful. There are moments when you think you attain them and then—where are you?—a big cloud looms, and you have to start feeling your way all over again. It is aggravating. You see, *mon cher,* we both have somewhat the same problem. We are searching. Will we find something? Why not? We are young and intelligent. Let's have courage and hope in spite of anything, always hope. . . .

"It would be wonderful indeed to succeed in having one's name inscribed even in the margin of the golden book of the mind. But, hush! If we were overheard, we would be misunderstood; our ambition would be mistaken for arrogant foolishness. Let us await the future in silence while saying to ourselves: whatever happens, we shall always be among the privileged because we know and understand the beautiful. Indeed, I thank God every day for having made me as I am. I feel very proud when I see that I can be happy without all the usual pleasures of my age. My wonderful mountains, my beautiful Italian sky keep me from being bored even for a moment. But I see many who don't feel as I do. They may not have my worries and doubts as an artist, but they don't have my joys either, and I feel sorry for them." [n]

As the year drew to a close, Bizet became more and more preoccupied with the progress of Gounod's *Faust,* which had been in rehearsal since the early autumn. In spite of what Bizet wished to believe, a year's separation had in no way diminished the older man's influence on him. Soon after Bizet's arrival in Rome, Gounod had sent him the score of his *Le Médecin malgré lui,* which the young composer found "decidedly the most charming thing in the vein of comedy that has been done since Grétry. . . ." At the same time, Gounod wrote: "Although the distance between us is great, you are nevertheless very often here with me; more than often—*habitually,* I should say. . . . I think of you with memories of the past, with loving concern for the present, and with lively hope for your future. And from this triple point of view, I love you doubly, since your dear first master [3] left no one closer than me (at least on the practical career side) to inherit his very warm, paternal interest in you. On that side, I can say without vanity that no one can take his place as well as I can, and I hope you are convinced of this." A few months later, Gounod assured Bizet that "your letter shows a perceptible growth in all the faculties that you as a man must use to sustain your gifts as an artist. In every field, character is the backbone of intelligence and gives it scope. By all means admire, admire as much as you can.

[3] Zimmerman.

Admiration is a noble faculty, and at the same time one of man's most vital capacities . . . to admire is to grow, and if Italy is so powerful in our development, it is because she stimulates us to live fully, which is an essential part of admiration." [n]

Early in 1858, when the title role in *Faust* was given to Hector Gruyer, Bizet was elated. Gruyer, or Guardi as he later called himself, a Provençal with an attractive personality and a promising voice, was outstanding among Adolphe Bizet's pupils, most of whom were singers rejected by better-known or more established professors. "I think the whole business is superb," Bizet wrote to his mother. "Gounod is perhaps the only composer who can give *useful* advice to a singer; he is the only one capable of understanding the insecurity and discouragement of a young artist. . . . Oh, if only I could transmit a little of my self-confidence to [Hector]! . . . Encourage him for me. Let him try, to surmount all the little obstacles that undermine his self-confidence. . . . In spite of everything, he must have courage. . . . I have high hopes for the Théâtre-Lyrique; Gounod's music should suit Hector. So let him develop self-confidence—in a word, character—and his success will be assured."

Although Bizet continued to indulge in high hopes for Gruyer, he worried about the chances for success of the opera itself. [*"Faust* at the Théâtre-Lyrique is one of those terrific mistakes that Gounod unfortunately can't avoid. (Complete silence about this, even to Hector.)] Well, I hope that luck will prove me wrong! And besides, the music must be so beautiful."

In his New Year's letter to Hector, Bizet wrote: "I am waiting with feverish impatience an event of such importance to my two best friends. . . . Your next letter will undoubtedly tell me of a success for both of you. I shall certainly feel strong emotions in my life, but never shall I wish for anything more than I do for the success of *Faust*. I see no announcement in the papers, yet the moment should be at hand. You mustn't be lazy about this sort of thing! Write to me the very day after the opening. I don't want to learn of your success from the papers before I hear about it from you. . . .

"Here, I am building up a solid stock of patience for the beginning of the battle I shall have to sustain in Paris. I expect plenty of rebuffs, but I hope to have the courage to face them, and then woe betide those who put obstacles in my path. I promise you they will have to deal with a wild man. [Your little tiffs with the Zimmerman family surprise me not at all: I expected them. . . . Gounod is not a man of action; he has that in common with the majority of great artists. He needs someone close to him with the right point of view and sure, sane judgment.]

"I am happy to see that you already like Gounod as much as I do. What a sympathetic nature! How delightful it is to come under the influence of that warm imagination! For him 'art is like a priesthood': those are his own words. And I would add that he is the only man among our modern musicians who really adores his art.

"You ask for all sorts of details about me. I am afraid I can't satisfy you. . . . I shall only say that my *opéra-bouffe* will not be among the poorest. It is Italian music, but the good kind of Italian. I am very hard on myself, which makes me hope to get somewhere. Next year I shall do Victor Hugo's *Esmeralda,* a French opera, and my third year will be spent on a symphony. My taste draws me definitively to the theatre, and I feel the vibrations of certain dramatic elements that I had been unaware of until this day. So I am hopeful.

"Another good thing: up to this moment, I floated between Mozart and Beethoven, Rossini and Meyerbeer. Now I know what to adore. There are two kinds of genius: natural genius and rational genius. While I admire the second tremendously, I shall not disguise the fact that I am wholly drawn to the first. Yes, *mon cher,* I have the courage to prefer Raphael to Michelangelo, Mozart to Beethoven, and Rossini to Meyerbeer. . . . It is a matter of taste; one order of ideas influences and attracts my nature more strongly than the other. When I look at *The Last Judgment,* when I hear the *Eroica* or the fourth act of *Les Huguenots,* I am moved, surprised, and haven't eyes, ears, brains enough to admire them. But when I look at *The School of Athens, The Dispute of the Holy Sacrament,* the *Virgin of Foligno,* when I hear *Le Nozze di Figaro* or the second act of *Guillaume Tell,* I am completely happy, I experience a well-being, a complete satisfaction that make me forget everything else. Ah, but a man is fortunate to be thus endowed! Well, let's try not to be too idiotic; that would at least be quite an accomplishment. . . . Midnight tolls!!! We are in 1859. Another year to go. In twenty years we shall be saying, 'Another year gone by!'—This one, I hope, dear Hector, will be the best of your life."

Besides his anxiety over the success of *Faust,* Bizet was having trouble with his own work. "I see that you are already worried about my *envoi,*" he wrote to his mother. "If you knew with what difficulty I work, you would easily understand why I am not as far along as I had hoped. Yes, I mistrust my facility. I am surrounded by ten intelligent boys who will never be anything but mediocre artists because of the fatal confidence with which they abandon themselves to their great skill. Skill in art is almost indispensable, but it ceases to be dangerous only at the moment when the man and the artist are formed. I do not want to do anything *chic:* I want to have *ideas* before starting a piece, which is not how I worked in Paris. This results in a certain paralysis that it will take me a year or two to overcome. . . . I repeat, I am satisfied with my opera; only right now I am taking infinite pains with a very difficult air. . . . I played several fragments to Colin, who seemed pleased with them. The opinion of David, whose arrival I am impatiently awaiting, will be most illuminating for me."

Bizet's wish for criticism from a peer was granted a few days later when Samuel David, winner of the Prix de Rome for 1858, came to the Villa bearing letters to Bizet from Gounod and Halévy. No sooner had David arrived than Bizet played him his *envoi,* with which David was "well satisfied." Bizet, on the other hand, found David's cantata "bad," but his chorus, *Génies de la terre,* "splendid in style, pure and elevated in feeling." The letter David brought from Halévy, the first acknowledgment of the many letters Bizet had written to his professor during the previous year, was disappointing. ["My dear Bizet,"] he wrote, ["Your comrade, David, who leaves tomorrow for Rome, will give you this short note, which I had intended making longer, but there is no time. I want to thank you for you letters and messages, and to tell you, my dear Bizet, that I am always interested in you and in your work. Send us some good things this year. Your affectionate, F. H."] [n] In the margin of the copy of Halévy's letter which Bizet sent to his parents, he scribbled: "Oh, what a rascal! I'll show him!!!!"

Gounod's letter, on the other hand, brought him the greatest satisfaction and reassurance, but if he had had less faith in Gruyer he might have sensed in it a forewarning of impending disaster. "My poor *Faust* that you want me to tell you about has taken so much time," Gounod wrote, "that it has been impossible to snatch fifteen minutes even to devote to the friendship I bear you. Your charming comrade, Samuel David . . . is destined to a fine future. . . . You will have the opportunity of going with him on those splendid expeditions which you will remember later as the most beautiful time of your life, my dear boy; profit well by them . . . as though you were really a child. Soak up everything like a sponge. Lay yourself open to all the varied influences that surround and protect you. Without sacrificing time for reflection, without forgetting the unalterable rights of your personal work, be like a plant; believe in what you feel: don't ask yourself questions while you are working; wait until *after work.* . . .

"My *Faust* is in full rehearsal. Guardi is, as you know, a fine and worthy lad, full of the elements and high qualities that form an artist. He is, above all, absolutely without vanity; his lack of self-esteem is the best frame of mind to help him amount to a good deal. He is excellent in his part at certain times; at others he is weak; but it will turn out well, I hope. . . .

"As for me, I can't very well tell you whether my score is good. I am so tied up with it that I am a very bad judge. Nothing any longer has any effect on me. I am saturated with my music. The execution is for the time being very much hampered by the production. People think about their arms, their legs, and no longer sing or phrase. The orchestra saws . . . but all that will work itself out in the final rehearsals and in the performance. They seem to be very happy. I hope, God willing, that they are not mistaken. The sets will be splendid." "

This heartening letter and Bizet's inclination to ally himself with a fellow-admirer of Gounod's launched him into a new "friendship." "David is a charming boy in every sense of the word," he told his mother. "He is sensitive, witty and demonstratively affectionate. . . . We don't always agree on questions of music. . . . His *musical education* (*not instruction*) has been a little neglected. As a result he is . . . a passionate Mozartian one day, and the next proclaims Verdi as the only genius the art of music has ever had. . . . Since he has been here, he has already tried out twenty styles, none of which is good, for none of them is his own. . . . We have already had dozens of discussions about

Verdi. . . . My opinion of him is very different from what I thought in Paris, but here I judge dispassionately and am therefore more likely to be right.—Verdi is a man of great talent who lacks the essential quality that makes *great masters:* style. But he has marvelous bursts of passion. His passion is brutal, it is true, but it is better to be passionate that way than not at all. His music is sometimes exasperating, but never boring. All in all, I understand neither the idolizers nor the detractors he has aroused. To my mind, he merits neither the one nor the other."

Bizet's opinion of Verdi continued to fluctuate. *Un Ballo in Maschera,* which had its *première* in Rome in 1859, he found "foul." He was, of course, too young to grasp the trend of Verdi's development. Yet, in several of Bizet's operas there are traces of Verdi's influence; unlike Gounod's, it was not an influence he feared. Now he was "delighted" because David "was very much surprised to see me completely freed of the influence of *Gounod.* . . . Gounod is an essentially original composer; imitating him, you remain a pupil."

The deliberately Italian style of *Don Procopio* had indeed temporarily freed Bizet of Gounod's musical influence. But the material fortunes of the Bizet family continued to be tied up with the success of *Faust.* This opera suffered more than the usual number of postponements. Apart from the normal amount of cutting and rewriting during rehearsals and of anxiety about the singers, political complications arose. The entry of France into the war for the unification of Italy made the Paris government particularly eager to refrain from any unnecessary friction with the Vatican. At a moment as significant in the foreign relations of France as in the fortunes of *Faust,* the Ministry of Beaux-Arts decided that the scene of Marguerite in the cathedral must be cut lest it cause a "diplomatic incident." The situation was saved by Monseigneur de Ségur, the Papal nuncio, a close friend of Gounod's, who was present at the rehearsal interrupted by the censorship order. When Léon Carvalho, the director, requested the Monseigneur to express to the government emissary his opinion of the church scene, the cleric remarked, "I wish the theatre were filled with scenes like this one." The order to censor was promptly rescinded.

But there was no mentor with sufficient prestige to plead the cause of Gruyer when he developed a hoarseness in rehearsal which resulted in the omission of one of his arias. This bad news shocked Bizet violently. "I am not fooling myself about the misfortune that has struck all of us," he said. "Tell Hector . . . he must get well and do everything possible to get back the aria they have cut. I am on pins and needles, feverishly impatient. How will this come out? . . . It isn't possible that such a splendid opportunity should change into a catastrophe. . . .

["I think my dear Papa was wonderfully right to *snub* Mme Gounod a little. She is a good woman, but she loves her husband in a *stupid* way. She does him great harm and is a disastrous influence. . . .

"Gounod said the best possible things in his letter about Hector both as man and artist; he had no reservations.] But he is the weakest man in the world where friendship is concerned. . . . A man has only a certain number of virtues, and all of Gounod's are concentrated on his art. He is a very passionate man, and when he was here his love for the wife of one of his friends drove him to commit the shameful act of deceiving the friend who nursed him night and day through a serious illness. [Naturally all of this is wholly between ourselves. One can really only judge people from a distance.]

"This in no way changes my friendship for Gounod, only he has a nature that can't *resist*. [A wise wife would have been a great help to him. This man, who is absorbed by his imagination, needed an intelligent curb. His poor mother knew it well! I wanted to tell you this so that you would know that any weakness of Gounod's is carefully cultivated by his wife's family; she is the one who is responsible for the *frailties* he indulges in. So I shan't be at all surprised if he abandons Hector. . . . Anyway, let's continue to hope that the result of twenty years of effort won't be lost, and that my dear father will not see his hopes blasted. . . ."] "

At the dress rehearsal of *Faust*, Gruyer, whose stage presence and brilliant singing in the first act were striking, lost his voice in the middle of the evening and was forced to withdraw. The *première* was postponed, and Barbot, a pupil of François Delsarte, sang the role on March 19, when *Faust* finally opened.

Bizet believed that *Faust* was lost. "It is a terrible blow. . . ." he wrote to his mother. "You attribute to the librettos the succession of failures of which our best composers have been the victims for several years. You are right, but there is also another reason: not one of these composers has a complete talent. . . . Not even the strongest [Gounod among others] has the only means through which a composer can make himself understood by the public today: the *motif*, which is very mistakenly called the 'idea.' A man can be a great artist without having the *motif;* then he must renounce money and popular success. But he can also be better than other men and possess this precious gift; witness Rossini. Rossini is the greatest of all because, like Mozart, he has all the virtues—elevation, style, and finally . . . the *motif*. I am absolutely convinced of what I am saying, that is why I have hope. I know my own capacities. I orchestrate well. I shall never be common, and I have finally discovered this much-sought-after *sesame*. In my opera I have a dozen motifs, but real, rhythmic ones, easy to remember, and at the same time I have made no concession to taste. . . . Next year I shall look for the *motif* in grand opera. That is much more difficult. But it is already an advantage to have found it in *opéra-comique*.

"If other people could hear me, they would think I was mad, but you who know that I am not a fool will understand what I am trying to tell you. Remember that when I was *en loge* I was never mistaken about the relative merit of my cantatas. I am conscious of what I do, of what I am worth, and when the time comes that I can say, 'I have succeeded,' there will be many people to agree with me.

"I have been waiting for a letter from Gounod since *Faust;* in my reply I shall be ironical with him. I shall deplore the accident that forced him to take that dreadful Barbot, as though I didn't for an instant suppose that he could be satisfied with him."

The favorable reviews of *Faust* surprised Bizet; he was disconcerted by Berlioz's praise of Barbot, and longed to see the score. But Gounod remained silent. ["I shall not be the first to write,"] Bizet assured his father. ["After what has happened, I must stay completely on guard, and I shall. If I wish to know *Faust*, it is more as a musician than as a *friend* of Gounod's. I ask you to believe this.] I am convinced that the tenor's role is badly written for the voice. [This is a defect of Gounod's.] But I am also convinced that *Faust* is a masterpiece."

By the end of April, Bizet was "swimming in joy." With only twenty-two more pages of *Don Procopio* to copy, he was looking forward to a journey into Tuscany and Umbria. After a week's postponement because of "a very painful ulcerated sore throat," he set out on this adventure with the painter Didier and "his adorable dog, which doesn't know which of us he likes best." The dog was in the nature of a substitute for Samuel David, who, after following Colin into Bizet's bad graces, had been discarded as a traveling companion.

Bizet's two-month holiday, which started May 17, was a continual joy to him. Although he was still convalescent from his throat infection when he left Rome, his energies were restored by a week of daily swimming and long walks in the woods at the Port of Anzio. He studied Italian while Didier sketched. And he took an enthusiastic interest in the natives. "Here, at the Port of Anzio, we are in constant contact with Italian convicts, who are splendid people. One prisoner, a shoemaker to whom we gave work, told us how a priest had had him sentenced for fifteen years because of a mere peccadillo. However, the convicts are very happy. Those who are able to work earn a lot of money. They are free and respected by everyone. The Port of Anzio has a population of fifteen hundred, divided as follows:

Convicts	250
Priests	60
Military	60
Fishermen	800
Merchants, laborers, farmers, *bourgeois*, *rentiers,* etc.	330
Total	1500

The convicts are the happiest and the best behaved. There isn't a single thief among them. I sing my *envoi* to myself from time to time, and it sounds well, but we won't know what to think of it until October."

From Anzio the travelers proceeded to Terracina via San Felice, where they spent a week climbing the rocky hills, walking in the forests, and enjoying the magnificent views. At Terracina, Bizet found a letter from his mother reproaching him for his lack of interest in the war that the Italians, with their French allies, were waging against Austria for the unification of Italy.

On June 4, the day of the Battle of Magenta, he replied: "Although you accuse me of indifference about the war, I assure you that if I knew mathematics and a little strategy, I would already be in Piedmont, where I would doubtless lose no time in winning my epaulettes. Meanwhile, I am taking the most wonderful journey in the world and swimming well enough to save myself from drowning should the necessity arise."

The sights and sounds Bizet chose to jot down each day in his travel diary frequently evoke the theatre or the opera. On a May Sunday in Anzio, while lunching and walking in the woods, he sees a "comic parody of a preacher by a peasant; very amusing scene." At Sonino on St. Anthony's Day he is struck by the costumes in the "barbaric procession." From the carriage window he catches a glimpse of "a delightful ravine where women were doing their washing, their blue and white aprons giving a charming color to the scene." At Terracina he notes the "surprising, very original, striking effect of litanies sung in the square by the convicts to the accompaniment of their clanking chains." [n] After visiting the Magician's Grotto at Cape Circe, he conceived the idea for an ode-symphony entitled *Ulysse et Circe*.

"As soon as I am back in Rome," he wrote, "I shall reread the passage in Homer. . . . There are charming things to be done with this subject; the chorus of Ulysses' companions, the scene of Circe's spells, the drunken scenes. There will be four purely symphonic orchestral pieces and five or six with voices and chorus." But like *Parisina,* like *Esmeralda,* like About's operetta, *Ulysse et Circe* failed to materialize. His next idea was a sounder one. "I am convinced," he wrote to his mother, "that an intelligent musician should find the ideas for his librettos himself, and I am working at it. Get Hoffmann's tales from the library and read *Le Tonnelier de Nuremberg*. I want to do three acts on this delightful story. The singing contest will be a very original and undoubtedly effective scene.—There are also certain things in Voltaire's tales which I like very much.—You see I am not too big a fool, and I do think about my work. Don't tell anybody about my idea for *Le Tonnelier* for a very good reason."

The idea of using Hoffmann's tale had occurred to Wagner as early as 1845. But as he postponed work on the libretto until 1861 and did not finish the score until 1867, Bizet naturally knew nothing of the German composer's prior claim to the work. In any case, by midsummer he had decided that *Le Tonnelier* was impossible. "There is no one to do the three acts for me," he told his mother. "I am annoyed that the success of this story does not seem as sure to you as it does to me. The scenes of the *portrait*, the *singing contest*, the *games*, and the *workshop* are certainly effective. And besides, it's so attractive, so German! Read it again, and you will discover that touch of sentiment which only the Germans know how to find, and that is so popular with us."

Early in July, Bizet became war-conscious: "I am in a city of 12,000 inhabitants, and have been able to read the details of our victories. I agree with you; all this is marvelous. The only regrettable thing is that our men are sacrificing themselves for the Italians. In France you may think that there is enthusiasm in Italy. Disabuse your mind. . . . Italy is, as you know, composed of seven different states. The Kingdom of Naples, the most important, has not sent one man to the war. The Neapolitans are not at all inclined to make common cause with the Italians of the North. In the *first* place, in the Papal states there have been few enlistments. In Rietri . . . there have been six volunteers. In the *second* place, in Tuscany the soldiers find it better to stay at home than to go split a gut. And *thirdly* the two duchies of Parma and Modena have advanced enough, but their population is only several hundred thousand. As for Lombardy, it was sufficient to applaud and throw flowers. You can't set your country free that way. In short: in Italy, where there are 25 million inhabitants, Garibaldi has not been able to raise 10,000 volunteers. [It's a disgrace.] . . . Piedmont alone has behaved with great courage, but Piedmont isn't a fifth part of Italy.

"In any case, this war will serve to show that France is the first nation of the world, that Napoleon III is a great man and Victor Emmanuel a very courageous prince. . . . Mac Mahon made a wonderful showing at Magenta." This victory Bizet and his companions celebrated by "giving the name Magenta to a very pretty dog we found. When we call him in the street the priests thumb their noses at us in fine fashion."

By the time Bizet returned to Rome on July 14, the war was over. "This magnificent campaign . . . is another splendid page in our history," was his patriotic comment. He had intended merely to pass through Rome on his long-planned visit to Naples. But an icy bath gave him "a slight rheumatic ailment," and he delayed starting for Naples until he was cured. With him on this expedition went his former traveling companion Didier, two other pensioners, and the sculptor Paul Dubois, who, only sixteen years

later, would make the portrait bust for Bizet's tomb. Except for a
stay in Pompeii, the visit to the south was disappointing. "When
you have seen Rome, you are hard to please! The Gulf of Naples
is marvelous, but the city is hideous. . . . The best thing about
Naples is the sea. So we have rented a boat and will go swimming
and sailing twice a day.

"The inhabitants of this part of the country are not good-
looking. They are active and intelligent. Unfortunately they are
one and all thieves! . . . We have already taken several walks. I
was looking forward to the historic and poetic reminders of our
ancient authors, but I was completely disillusioned. The inferno
that Virgil describes in his *Aeneid* is today an insignificant, boring
place."

Pompeii, where they boarded with farmers and spent the
evenings picking cotton, was "amazing! Here you live with the
ancients; you see their temples, their theatres, their houses in
which you find their furniture, their kitchen utensils, their surgical
instruments, etc. . . . All the Latin authors take on an immense
interest here."

The delights of Pompeii were, alas, soon interrupted by bad
news from Paris. At the revival of *Faust* on September 10, Hector
Gruyer had suffered an even worse failure than at the dress rehearsal. After three performances his voice had failed him. *Faust*
was removed from the repertory for two months until a successor
to Gruyer could be found. In one of the few letters addressed
directly to his father, Bizet wrote: "I needn't tell you that even
from far away I feel as deeply as you do your sorrow over Hector's
failure. I am horribly depressed today. The disappointment is all
the more cruel because we hoped for so much. I wish I were there
to share your distress and to do my best to console you. . . . The
hope I continue to feel in no way lessens my disappointment. I
detest in advance all this breed of directors and artists I shall have
the pleasure of associating with. People can't forgive failure, and
I can see from here all of Hector's difficulties. . . ." [n]

In this mood Bizet wrote to Hector: "If you had succeeded,
mon cher ami, I would perhaps have delayed writing to you, but
as fate is against you, I hasten to tell you how much I sympathize
with you. . . . My mother tells me that you bear your reverses
with courage. . . . As for me, I am furious; sorrow takes that
form with me. I am furious at the directors; they are nothing but

money-making machines. I am furious and at the same time heartbroken over the behavior of a man in whom I had faith— you know whom I mean. He must be aware of this, for he has not written to me. . . ." [n]

As in the past, the cycle of failure or anxiety, followed by rage and violence, terminated in illness. As Bizet was about to return to Rome, he developed "a magnificent cold accompanied by grippe, sore throat, pain, and God knows what else. In the beginning I refused to see a doctor and, thanks to this brilliant idea, I was let in for twelve days of starvation diet. I lost some weight, but I dare say this little accident has done me lots of good. . . ."

His enforced rest gave him time to read the French newspapers, in which he discovered that Gounod was working on a *Don Quixote,* "a tragi-comic-heroic" version of which Bizet had been "caressing for some time." "It has always been impossible for me to judge Gounod," he wrote. "Dominated by my empathy with this man who is so much older than I am both in years and in extent of intellectual development, I have been completely subject to his influence. But when I come back we shall find out just what his opinions are. In any case, he is the most remarkable musician we now have (except Rossini and Meyerbeer) and that proves again that to be a great artist it is not necessary to be an honorable man." [n]

Bizet's return to Rome early in November was triumphant. The Académie report on his *Don Procopio* was "not only the best report of the year but even one of the best there has ever been." He copied it out verbatim for his parents.

"M. Bizet (first year)
"M. Bizet has sent to the Académie, as his first *envoi,* an *opéra-bouffe* entitled *Don Procopio.*

"We are glad to record here notable improvement over the first attempts of this young artist.

"We have noted in the first act: an *introduction,* a *trio,* an elegant *cavatina,* and a *finale,* in which the *adagio,* ensemble, very well handled, is followed by a warm allegro *motif* sung in unison by all the characters, the effect of which is very lively.

"The second act, better than the first, starts with a *serenade,* a very charming melody, very delicately accompanied by *guitar* and *tenor oboe.*

"We note also: a *duo* for soprano and bass, in which the

pace and the motifs are very elegant; a little chorus for men's voices, sung *mezza voce,* and finally a very good trio (for three basses), lively, witty, and well written for the voice.

"To sum up: this work is distinguished by an easy and brilliant touch, a youthful and bold style, precious qualities for the genre of comedy toward which the composer has shown a marked propensity. These qualities open the way to novel effects, and M. Bizet will not forget the obligation he has undertaken as much to himself as to us."

Elated by this flattering report, Bizet began to write the symphony he had in mind. By the end of the first fortnight's work, however, his confidence again had dwindled. "I am becoming very critical," he wrote to his mother. "I looked at my Italian opera again yesterday and found it very weak. Between ourselves I can admit that it is better than Clapisson's music and certain things by Auber, but that doesn't mean it's good." Recurring uncertainty about his work sent him back to the social life he had enjoyed the year before. Again he dines weekly with the Russian ambassador and is entertained by the Sampayos at the French Embassy. But he has, he says, become very severe with himself on the subject of dissipation. "My comrades think that I am incapable of judging this subject because I have never felt any sort of passion. [True, the things that ordinarily dominate the lives of young people my age leave me quite unmoved. Gambling alone has some attraction for me, but it is nothing more than an amusement.] . . . As for the *fair sex,* I am less and less the French cavalier. I see nothing in them but the satisfaction of one's self-esteem. I would gladly risk my life for a friend, but would consider myself a fool to lose a hair of my head for a woman. I confide these things only to you, for if they were generally known, they would harm my chances of future success."

Success had not preoccupied Bizet during his journey. But on his return to Rome his insecurity again gave rise to his sense of competition. "[David is a sad creature,]" he writes to his mother early in December. "The imbecile has fallen madly in love with Donna [Francesca Torlonia],[4] a rather pretty little coquette; and as this creature is Italian, he is doing music *alla Verdi,* undoubtedly to please his love. Like me, he wished to write an *opéra-bouffe.* . . . It lacks only three things: gaiety, taste, and wit. [I think he

---

[4] The future Countess Kisseleff.

will have a complete failure.] . . . He has acquired a loathsome habit of making fun of people he talks to. To be sure, I like to tease people myself, but I can't stand being teased. I told him so outright, and since that time he no longer dares disagree with me. [He has tried to establish himself here as a wit, but he has taken a beating. We are really perfectly friendly, but we avoid the subject of music.]" Shortly after Bizet wrote this letter, David presented him with the manuscript score of his *Les Génies de la terre* inscribed "to my dear friend Georges Bizet, as a mark of staunch affection."

As 1859 neared its end, Bizet needed more than anything the advice and support of another musician—so much so, in fact, that he overcame his anger at Gounod and wrote to him asking for help. Gounod ignored the letter, "which is all the more ridiculous," Bizet said, "because when he sees me again he will be overcome by tears of affection. And so, indeed, shall I. For there is nothing as contagious as friendship, whether feigned or real. For me it is a great joy to see even the externals of friendship. It is so seductive and so rare."

CHAPTER  VII

Vasco de Gama: Return from Rome

Bizet spent his last six months in Rome in a gradually accelerating state of nervous tension and instability. His mother's health continued to deteriorate. He dreaded the loss of freedom his return to Paris would mean. He could not bear the thought of leaving Rome. He was involved in a love affair with a girl identified only as "Zeph." He started two symphonies and burned them both. His "hellish career" seemed to him "more and more prickly. If it weren't for my intelligence," he wrote, "there are times when I would regret not being in the oil or the cinnamon business."[1] Above all, his second *envoi* became increasingly difficult to finish. Therefore, in order to spend additional time in Rome, he petitioned the Minister of Beaux-Arts for permission to waive the rule which required Prix de Rome to spend their third year in Germany. In the margin of the petition, Schnetz added a note which, no doubt, influenced the Minister into granting Bizet's somewhat irregular request. "M. Bizet . . ." wrote the Director, "is very studious and highly intelligent. He believes, as I do, that the blue skies of Italy would have a fortunate influence on the work he has undertaken. . . . I take the liberty of recommending this young composer's petition to your Excellency's favor. . . . November 26, 1859."

The work Bizet had started was an ode-symphony. The words had been supplied by one Louis Delâtre, a French poet resident

---

[1] Bizet, *Lettres de Rome,* 219–20. Subsequent unidentified quotations in this chapter are from this work. Unpublished portions of the letters, in the collection of the author, are enclosed in square brackets.

in Rome, "a very learned man who knows and speaks twenty-five languages, but writes his own not very intelligently." In spite of this handicap, Bizet had Delâtre rhyme Luiz Vaz de Camões's *The Lusiad;* he himself wrote the scenario based on this poem, envisaging a work in the manner of Félicien David's *Le Désert,* an ode-symphony much admired by Berlioz.

"Until now," Bizet admitted to his mother early in January 1860, "I have given you only half-hearted news of my *envoi.* I was hesitating, I was searching, and I was not at all satisfied with my efforts. Today . . . I am finally on the way. . . . I have done half of the first part of my ode-symphony, and I am pleased with it. The rest will go the same way, I hope. . . ." A fortnight later he reports, "My *Vasco de Gama* (that is the definite title of my symphony) would be going perfectly well if my collaborator's verses weren't so absurd. Sometimes I have to rewrite them, which serves to show me that if necessary I could get along without a collaborator. . . .

"I am, I think, making great progress. I rewrite very easily and I know the value of what I am doing: two good signs. . . . I feel that the more I keep going, the more I advance. Let's hope I shan't stop again. I mustn't, because the very good is so difficult that a lifetime isn't long enough to approach it."

In spite of his high resolutions, Bizet grew bored. So early in February he started to write both music and libretto for an *opéra-comique* based on Molière's *L'Amour-peintre,* hoping that this opera might serve as the second part of his *envoi* instead of the completed *Vasco de Gama.*

"You tax me with having little stability in my ideas," he wrote to his mother early in March, "and judging by appearances you are right. When you read the lines I have had to work with, you will understand why I have postponed the piece. . . . To make a stew, you must at least have a cat. And to make music, you must have words that are not too much worse than bad; the utterly ridiculous is embarrasing. Don't worry, my *envoi* will be all the fuller because it will be much more important than last year's. Let's hope that the report will be equally good."

Before the end of the month, however, Bizet again changed his plans. In a further report on his first *envoi,* Ambroise Thomas, representing the Music Division of the Académie des Beaux-Arts, now pointed out that "M. Bizet should have submitted for his first *envoi* to the Académie a religious composition. But we have received an *opéra-bouffe* from him, an Italian opera, *Don Procopio,* which the regulations required for his second *envoi.* We must censure this pensioner for having inverted the order of his works, although we accord praise to his score. We should tell him, nevertheless, that he would do well, no matter in what direction his inclination may lure him, to practice composing something of a different character. The study of severe and poetic subjects ennobles the mind, purifies the taste, and develops, even in lively natures, an elevated feeling for art." [n]

Although the opinion expressed in this routine auxiliary report in no way vitiated the praise of *Don Procopio* in the previous report, Bizet immediately abandoned the proposed Molière opera and went scurrying off in a direction he knew to be false and had sworn never to try again. "The simplest course," he wrote, "would be to complete my *envoi* by a *Credo.* . . . But this would be repugnant to my beliefs. I don't want to do a Mass before I am in a state of mind to do it well, that is to say, as a Christian. So I have taken an odd way of reconciling my ideas to the requirements of the Académie. They ask me for religious music. All right! I will do something religious, but Pagan religious. [The marvelous] *Carmen Saeculare* (Secular song) by Horace has been tempting me for a long time; there is nothing more beautiful in classic Latin, and not even Virgil or Lucretius or Horace himself has ever written anything so great, so pure, so elevated. It is a song to Apollo and to Diana for two choruses. From the literary and poetic point of view it is finer than the Mass. . . . Besides, to tell the truth, I am more Pagan than Christian. I have always read the classic writers with infinite pleasure, while in the Christians I have found only dogmatism, egotism, intolerance, and a complete absence of any taste for the arts. Naturally I except the works of St. Paul and St. John. . . .

"Here I am, then, saddled with an enormous and extremely difficult task. It may be impossible, but at least I shall have attempted it. I don't know of any musician up to the present time who has risked doing a comparable piece."

During an attack of grippe which followed Thomas's rebuke, Bizet gave considerable thought to the procedure employed in judging *envois* by the "five *bourgeois* who are annoyed at having to spend their Sundays reading music instead of going to the country.

. . . As for *Vasco de Gama,* I am taking the criticism of these
gentlemen with a grain of salt in advance. My score is complicated
and, consequently, difficult to read. To judge a work of such
length it would be necessary to study it at home, coolly and, above
all, without a piano. But the gentlemen of the section entrust the
reading of the *envois* to a reader—good or bad doesn't matter.
. . . The work is played hurriedly and only once; then the
Areopagus brings its judgment to bear on a young man who is
equal, if not superior, to his judges (this applies not just to me, but
to everybody). . . . Either these gentlemen don't understand, in
which case their negligence, even their injured vanity, prompts
them to a savage attack; or, seduced by a certain form, a certain
taste, they approve without knowing why. . . . You may find me
slightly disposed to look on the dark side of things but . . . what
can one expect from those creatures? Reber is silent, Berlioz away,
Auber asleep; Carafa and Clapisson listen, alas! There is only
Thomas, but he is so lazy!

"Otherwise I am very pleased with what I am doing with the
Carmen Saeculare, but it is for me—and for you. . . ."

This very personal *Carmen Saeculare* evaporated into thin
air and was never again mentioned. But in late June, after re-
reading *Vasco de Gama,* Bizet decided that he had never produced anything as good. "Whatever the gentlemen of the
Académie des Beaux-Arts may say, my opinion is formed; and it is
good, even very good. . . . I need hardly say that *Vasco de Gama*
is way below the level of the great works of art; but if I want to
compete with our good contemporaries [I mean Thomas, Verdi,
Halévy], I think I have, if not the advantage, at least the right to
try.

"I wouldn't risk confiding a thing like this to anybody but
you," he assured his mother. "But I am happy at present. . . .
I can declare, at last, that I am a musician, which I doubted for
a good long time. Whether I succeed in two, four, or ten years
is unimportant. I am young enough not to lose the hope that I
shall live to enjoy my success. . . . Besides, the time is ripe.
Gounod alone is a man; on the lower level—nothing. Verdi will
not write any more, they say, and if he does write I doubt if he
will again show the kind of flashes of genius he showed in *Il
Trovatore, La Traviata,* and the fourth act of *Rigoletto.* He has
a fine artist's nature lost through negligence and cheap success.

[In short his gifts are quite different from those of the members of our Institut. I like *La Juive* better than *Il Trovatore* musically; but I reverse my opinion in the matter of emotional content. When it comes to feeling, neither one of them has any.]

"It takes a lot of strength to be an artist. It is hard, very hard indeed, particularly in Rome. The wind of the sirocco has an unheard-of effect on the nerves. You know me, and you know that I haven't at all a nervous temperament. Well, on the days when the sirocco blows, I can't touch *Don Giovanni* or *Le Nozze* or *Così fan tutte*. Mozart's music affects me so directly that it actually makes me very sick. Certain of Rossini's works produce the same effect."

Fortunately for his equilibrium, Bizet found during his last six months in Rome the friend he had longed for, a man who would remain devoted to him throughout his life and even after his death. Ernest Guiraud, Bizet's classmate in Marmontel's and Halévy's classes at the Conservatoire, was a mediocre composer who is remembered today only in relation to other musicians. He orchestrated *Contes d'Hoffmann* after Offenbach's death, and after Bizet died he composed the recitatives for the grand opera version of *Carmen*. As professor of harmony at the Conservatoire he taught Debussy, Erik Satie, and Paul Dukas. Born in New Orleans in 1837, while his father, Jean-Baptiste Guiraud, was serving as director of music in that city, Ernest returned to France at the age of fifteen to enter the Conservatoire. In 1859 he was awarded the Prix de Rome for a cantata that Bizet considered "very good . . . infinitely superior to Colin's and to mine . . . better constructed, better felt, more the work of a man."

Although pleased when he learned that Guiraud had won the award, Bizet abjured any high hopes of friendship after his disillusionment with Colin and David. But when the new Prix de Rome arrived, Bizet immediately found him "pleasant, modest, frank and loyal. We have the same ideas about music, which places him in formal opposition to David. I am delighted with him. . . . We are already playing duets. I am convinced that from now on he will compensate me for Colin and David." Bizet soon gave proof of his friendship by taking Guiraud to one of M. de Kisseleff's dinner parties. There the newcomer appeared "somewhat shy. They thought his playing was cold, and it is rather true," Bizet confided to his mother. "But he is so nice, so friendly, such a good fellow that I excuse these defects. Unfortunately the public judges less fairly, and Guiraud, in his approach to life, his playing, his music, is a little soft, a little apathetic. I am trying to liven him up a bit."

Bizet had small success in energizing Guiraud, who remained all his life the vaguest of men. His phlegmatic, good-humored indolence complemented Bizet's quick temper and abundant nervous energy; his naturally generous, warm nature and his real intelligence made him a delightful companion. With Guiraud, Bizet started at the end of July on his long-anticipated journey through northern Italy. He had looked forward tremendously to this holiday "with a friend, a colleague who shares my tastes and who likes me, I think, with a sincere and frank friendship—a very rare thing, by the way, among musicians." But when the moment of departure came, he was in no holiday spirit. His grief was uncontrollable. "It was time for me to leave Rome," he wrote. "I loved it too much. I have never wept so much. . . . Many reasons forced me to decide never to return. . . . Money was the least important. I was getting too used to that independent life. I acquired habits that I had to break. Decidedly it is not a good thing to be too happy. . . . My leavetaking from the Académie was very warm. I have seen no other like it. Even boys I thought indifferent to me shook my hand with tears in their eyes. As for me, I had an appalling attack of nerves. I cried for six hours without stopping. I realized that I was well liked at the Académie, and it moved me very much."

On the journey back to Paris, Bizet jotted down musical ideas in a little notebook. "It might be useful," he wrote. "In any case it will serve as a souvenir of Italy." Apparently for this same reason, he kept a very detailed journal or diary which he labeled simply *Notes de voyage*. They are written in his smallest handwriting on both sides of fifteen sheets of finely lined flimsy paper, $8\frac{1}{2}''$ x $10\frac{1}{2}''$. The ink, turned dark brown with age, has frequently seeped through the paper, painfully reducing the legibility. Unlike most private diaries, nine tenths of Bizet's reads like an annotated guidebook, a kind of outline for a recitative on the splendors of the architecture and painting of the Italian Renaissance. The remainder is given over to succinct accounts of Bizet's nocturnal adventures, which form a curiously divergent coda to each day's aesthetic experience. The language is frequently unprintable. For on an aesthetic or spiritual level women had no place in Bizet's life at this time. He divided them simply into good or bad. "The women here have about one franc's worth of virtue," he had written to his mother soon after his arrival in Italy. "The same applies to the upper classes, only it's more expensive. . . . A virtuous Italian woman has all my admiration. I esteem and admire her more than Jeanne d'Arc or Lucretia. . . . You rare really virtuous women who live by [duty], devotion, and love of family are a thousand times more valuable than the holy martyrs. . . ."

The category in which Bizet placed his Roman mistress is not revealed in the stenographic style of his journal.

"Friday—July 27, 1860

"Tender, agonizing night. Finally I leave her. I wait at the station. I depart with Guiraud. From Rome to *Palo*— At *Palo* a swim at the beach. The sky clouds over—sad— We try to lunch with some fishermen; impossible. It was too awful. We lunched off a few eggs at the *locanda*. I keep feeling horribly sad. We leave on foot for *Cerveteri*. I arrive there with a fever. I go to bed and sleep. Horrible awakening. I am miserably unhappy. The calm of evening brings me a little relief. We are present at a quarrel between [illegible] and the inn-keeper. Despair of the child. I try a hand at piquet, which makes me sick. I sleep.

"Saturday 28

". . . I feel better. The weather is quite cool. From *Palo* to *Civita Vecchia*. In the train we met two sweeties. I would almost have **** one, but was still thinking of her. Arrival at *Civita Vecchia*. Excellent swim. A coachman asked fifty francs to take us to *Viterbo*. He took us for ten. . . .

"We arrive at *Viterbo*

"Sunday 29 at 5 in the morning. . . . I sleep. I breakfast and sleep some more. *Viterbo* looks picturesque. We go to *S. Francesco* to see the del Piombo Christ. It is splendid, marvelous drawing. This painting is extraordinarily impressive. The Virgin is very inferior. Beautiful fountains in the city. Theatre in the evening. (Goldoni) . . . The performance diverted me. . . . I think 20 times a day of Zeph. . . .

"Friday, August 3, Orvieto

". . . The Cathedral was started in 1290. The façade is decorated with sculpture and mosaics. The rose window is marvelous. There are twelve statues above it and as many surrounding it. . . . The sculpture, executed by Orlando, Guido, etc. (see the Guidebook) under the direction of Ramo of Siena, is divided into . . . subjects from the old and new Testaments. . . . These astonishing works are very primitive, and yet one feels that imagination, even genius prevails in these curious carvings. . . ." After drawing a sketch of Luca Signorelli's frescoes in the chapel of the Madonna di San Brizio, Bizet concludes his entry for August 4 with "Ouf! ah! I nearly forgot. We played the organ, an instrument with 42 registers and 32 pedals. It must have been excellent, but now it is refurbished. We returned to the hotel, drank a good deal, and now we long to go to bed with the fat *padrona* but the family has just come in. Zut! Tomorrow will do." [2]

By tomorrow the travelers had arrived at Citta della Pieve: "Very tired. We drink two carafes; we eat. Then, after having cast a covetous glance at the daughter of our hostess we sleep until noon, Monday, the 6th. Decidedly the young girl is charming." At Chiusi the equally charming sister of the hostess not only resisted their blandishments, but added injury to insult by stealing from them. After an "appalling" night journey by *diligence,* in the company of "a polite gentleman who would tolerate neither tobacco nor fresh air," the travelers arrived on August 8 at the "enchantingly picturesque, delightful" city of Perugia, where they remained three days. Bizet, in the five pages of orderly lists and notes he devoted to the wonders of Perugia, permitted himself to speculate on the relations between Perugino and his pupil Raphael, the painter he most admired. In the Collegio del Cambio, "the Erythrean and Libyan Sybils, as well as the head of Christ in the *Transfiguration* are attributed to Raphael," Bizet writes. "He may undoubtedly have worked on them. But is it possible that the master would have left his pupil absolute master of such an important part of his work? . . . The ceiling representing the Sun and the planets is also attributed to Raphael, and is indeed worthy

---

[2] Bizet, *Notes de voyage,* unpublished journal in collection of author. Further quotations from this source will not be individually noted in this chapter.

of him. . . . This whole room, one of the glories of Italy, is the finest expression of a talent which, if not of the first order, has its own special charm and a strong feeling of religious ecstasy."

In the evenings there is the usual "search for women, in vain, alas!" However, on their final night in Perugia, they encounter "a rather bizarre woman. We toast Garibaldi, we eat melon, I steal two kisses, and on we go."

At Assisi, Bizet found the upper church somewhat disappointing: "a thing interesting from the archaic or even decorative point of view is not always artistically so." By the lower church he was "truly moved, astonished. All of the Middle Ages with their poetic and metaphysical aspirations are enclosed in this sanctuary. . . . Once you have recovered from your astonishment, you look for Giotto and find him above the choir. The work of the old master is composed of five frescoes telling the story of St. Francis. . . . These compositions are remarkable. Dante passed by here. The elongated heads, so long that they are almost misshapen, have an extraordinary feeling. . . . This is not *painting*, neither is it *color* nor *design*, yet it is *art* and great art. . . . The memory of this church is ineffaceable in spite of the horrible music!!!!"

At Rimini, "a city without antiquarian interest," Bizet found time to write a long letter to his mother. He enjoys bathing in the Adriatic, makes unsuccessful efforts to teach Guiraud to swim. "Guiraud takes to Italian life very well, but perhaps a little too much on the dawdling, unproductive side. He sleeps too much. I am very stimulating to him, perhaps too much so, but I have become excessively nervous, quite the opposite from what I was in Paris. I can't stay still; after seven hours of sleep, bed becomes unbearable and . . . for some time I have been indifferent to the pleasure of eating. I am in a continual state of irritation; I feel some need, some desire that I can't define.

"I have fussed a good deal the last few days because the servitors of the Pope are intolerable. . . . I would have been delighted . . . to beat up one of these wretches, but the poor devils are terribly frightened of the French. . . . Guiraud laughs when I scream at them, which only makes me scream the louder.

"On the whole, we are having a delightful journey. We sing Mozart all day long. I am very happy to have such a charming traveling companion; his excellent disposition is more and more sympathetic to me."

In Ravenna, Guiraud was stricken with a bad sore throat, and Bizet, reduced to solitary sightseeing, found the city "sad and colorless." He was, of course, impressed by the mosaics in the churches of San Apollinare Nuovo and San Vitale, though he found that "the ridiculous perspective of the exterior of San Vitale serves to diminish the beautiful effect of the interior, where the Byzantine capitals and the enormous proportions transport you to the Orient." From Ravenna the travelers made their way to Bologna, where Bizet admired the paintings in the museum but failed to appreciate Giovanni da Bologna's splendid fountain: "an upstanding figure of Neptune and 4 sirens pressing streams of water from their breasts, *c'est cochon.*" Ferrara he found "a rather sparsely inhabited large city, sad and with no particular character," its cathedral "an ugly Gothic *bibelot.*" A day spent in the museum and the library ended with a night in a bordello. The servant of the establishment, probably selected by Bizet for reasons of economy, he found "a little on the skinny side!!! Oh, Berlioz, why wert thou not here?" An unanswerable riddle.

At Padua, Bizet was again enchanted by the Giottos. He felt a sense of Dante in the beautiful *grisaille* allegories of the virtues and vices, was horrified at catching sight of a prison in which criminals and political prisoners were held, "some of the latter in chains. It is infamous!!!"

During his travels, Bizet began to conceive the symphony he would go on composing for some eight years. He planned to call it *Rome, Venice, Florence, and Naples.* "It works out wonderfully. Venice would be my andante, Rome my first movement, Florence my scherzo, and Naples my finale. It is a new idea, I think." The novelty of the idea is less striking than his need to create a symbol or permanent souvenir of Italy. "When I think that this is my last summer here, my heart still aches a little. . . ." he wrote. "I sympathize sincerely with those who have not won the prize or who have received it before they are mature enough [like Paladilhe. The poor kid is, I think, too ignorant, musically speaking, to profit now by a stay in Rome.]" Bizet's own immaturity did not lie in the field of music.

At Venice he suffered a shock that gave violent release to his latent nervous tension. A letter from his mother drove him briefly quite out of his mind. "It was terribly rash of you to date your letter from a hospital," he wrote to her two hours after his arrival. "That letter was the first one the post office employee gave me. I opened it and saw those two lines. The blood rushed to my head and to my heart. I could no longer read the rest of the letter or throw off this terrible state of mind. Then, after a quarter of an hour of rage, I managed to find sufficient provocation to quarrel with the gondolier; I hurled myself at him with the firm intention of strangling him. My kind Guiraud snatched him out of my hands. Two minutes later I arrived at St. Mark's. The sight of this enchanted splendor brought me to my senses, and I decided to leave at once for Paris. Again Guiraud was helpful. 'Read the letter preceding that one,' he said. And in the earlier letter I found some small comfort. I read the others, compared the handwriting, and could see no change.

"In spite of the effort you made to seem gay in your letters, I could see the sadness. Do stop trying to deceive me this way. For some time your letters have made me fear this crisis. I count on the Providence that you talk about to bring you through this illness soon, triumphantly and completely. For I would consider myself freed of any gratitude toward that Providence if, after the success and high hopes it has given me, it did not grant me my mother's health, the one benefit I desire, the only one I ask of God. As for me, I can take care of myself and need nobody. . . .

"If you have the slightest desire for me to return immediately, say so frankly. . . . In spite of my longing to see you again, I am staying here because I think that my presence in Paris would be useless and I am even afraid of bothering you. But if I do stay, I require, in exchange, complete frankness. *Adieu,* dear, beloved Mama; I am overcome with sleep, with fatigue. For two nights I haven't slept, thanks to the insects that ornament the hotels of Padua. All this, combined with the blow of your letter and the sharp regret that a certain letter from Rome caused me, has exhausted me physically."

In the same envelope Bizet included an almost identical letter to his father, demanding additional information. "Force the doctor to give a sincere opinion of what there is to fear. Tell me whether your financial condition is sound enough to permit of the necessary care. Why is she in a six-bed room? Your reply will determine my decision. But write to me by every post. . . ." [n]

While waiting in Venice, Bizet wrote very little in his journal. For the third time he described the shock of his mother's letter and the attack on the gondolier, as though the act of recounting this incident somehow purged him. On Thursday, September 6, he made the final entry: ". . . We climb the Campanile. Superb view. You can really understand the plan of Venice. We visit the bordellos. I find a ravishing woman. She wants 10 francs. What nerve! . . . Decidedly this St. Mark's Square is the most marvelous of all marvels. Tomorrow the real details. . . ."

But by "tomorrow" Bizet had started the journey north, spurred on, no doubt, by the letter for which he had been hoping for a year and a half. Gounod, who was in Baden-Baden for the performance of his opera *La Colombe,* informed him that he would be back in Paris before the end of August. "I understand only too well the tears that you shed the day you left . . ." he assured Bizet. "I remember as exactly as though it were yesterday the tears I wept under the same circumstances. . . . Rome is a being; it is more than a friend. It is a truth, a profound and multiple revelation. It is the key to a host of questions which can be summed up in the good, the true, and the beautiful. Rome isolates you, through self-communion, from all the pettiness of daily life, allows you to soar in the great domain of things eternal. This aspect, absolutely devoid of any narrow preoccupation, forms the most exquisite, the most divine charm of the memory you will keep and that we will revive for each other when we resume those lovely, long talks we used to have.—If I have seemed to neglect you, dear child, it was because when you wrote to me you spoke of an immediate departure for Naples, but gave me no address. . . . You know that I love you too much to be capable of any apathy toward you.

"You inform me that you intend merely crossing Germany. I would rejoice in this news if I considered no one but myself and my happiness at the thought of seeing you and embracing you again. But I do not want you to make this decision lightly or irrevocably. Here is what I would say about it: after Italy, Germany; which means that after contemplation, after that kind of beatitude of thinking, above all, of dreaming, you must withdraw into yourself even if it is hard work and plough the ground that your stay in Italy will have seeded. You will not in any immediate or practical way sense this relationship, which will unite the two sides of your mind. Because only after it has happened are we aware of what has gone on inside us. Yet this relationship will exist, and only the hard work I speak of can fertilize the germs you will have brought from Rome; without that work, they will remain absolutely sterile. I heard some one say to M. Ingres, 'There is no art without skill.' It is a profoundly true remark. Question Germany before you leave there. If you find an answer, listen; and you may be sure that you will find it supremely useful to have acquired habits of *work* which have become an essential part of you, and also the *strength* to withstand all the onslaughts that await you here in this horrible Paris, all paved with distractions and interruptions of every kind. Otherwise *Rome* would merely have been a *Capua.* If there is nothing in Germany to hold you, come back and we will work hard here right away.

["You talked to me last year about your friend Gruyer (Guardi). I was formerly fond of this young man and expressed my affection for him, as you know I do when I feel it. But it didn't last. It was one of my disappointments (I have had several of this kind), and if my conscience is not deceiving me, I think I have every reason to be greatly surprised by his attitude toward me. It would be a long, boring story to write, and fifteen minutes of talk will tell you more than twenty letters. . . . Your ever devoted friend, Ch. Gounod."] "

CHAPTER  VIII

Death of Aimée Bizet

Bizet did not hurry back to Paris. Although no further news of his mother's condition arrived before he left Guiraud in Venice, he tarried several days at Nice. He explained to his father that his traveling companion, Heim, was "slightly indisposed and has asked me to stay with him two days longer. . . . I am doing him a great favor, considering how necessary it is for me to be in Paris now." The state of Heim's health seems to have been subject to precariously sudden changes, judging by the conclusion of Bizet's letter: "I think he is lost, which does not make me feel very cheerful." As a postscript he added: ["Things will have changed a lot at home."] [1]

Bizet's reluctance to face the changed situation in Paris is understandable, all the more as the changes did not suit his own plans. During his final months in Rome he had repeatedly tried to persuade his mother to find adjoining but separate living quarters for him to occupy when he returned to Paris. "I like my freedom," he explains. "I am irregular in my habits. Sometimes I go out walking by moonlight until all hours. My freedom of action would be hampered by my fear of inconveniencing you, and that must be avoided." He does not wish to burden her with having to receive callers such as "directors, singers, etc.," who will be shown the door five minutes later. He needs only two rooms and a little vestibule. The furnishing he wishes to do himself gradually

---

[1] Bizet, *Lettres de Rome,* 276. Unpublished portion letter LXXV. Subsequent unidentified quotations in this chapter are from this work. Unpublished portions of the letters, in the collection of the author, are enclosed in square brackets.

because "I have developed a horror of mahogany, and little by little I shall buy artistic furniture that I will enjoy looking at. . . . [I dislike coal, and shall heat with a wood-burning fireplace. Please, above all, be careful about choosing the wallpaper. It should be deep red in the salon-study and brown in the bedroom.]"

Mme Bizet was not in sympathy with her son's carefully worked-out plans. The rent for a separate apartment would be too high. She suspects that George's motives for wishing a separate dwelling are based less on consideration for her than on a desire to entertain unsuitable guests freely. "There is no problem there," he assures his mother. "I don't like women of questionable morals; if from time to time I am willing to amuse myself by going to see them, they aren't so important to me that I would enjoy having them come to my house. It is merely a question of my *individual* liberty. . . . [Although I have never given you any reason to lack the utmost confidence in me . . . I think you have always taken me for a humbug. But I assure you that the influence of this fine Italian climate acts as a deterrent to this trait, which, forgivable in a child, is unbearable in a man. . . . We agree, then, that nothing will be decided until I return. But I shall keep hoping that my plan can be worked out."]

His mother's condition when Bizet reached Paris toward the end of September precluded any thought of his living alone. "My mother is very ill," he wrote to his friend Ernest L'Epine.[2] "We have given up all hope of being able to save her. I have no time for anything but tears. What a sad homecoming, and how hateful Paris is!" ⁿ

Yet friends tried to help him. Gounod immediately arranged with the publisher Choudens for Bizet to make a piano reduction of the score of his opera *Philémon et Baucis,* unsuccessfully performed while Bizet was in Rome. At the same time, Bizet asked Ludovic Halévy to write the libretto for the one-act opera that he

[2] Ernest L'Epine (1826–93), a member of the Duc de Morny's secretariat, collaborated with Alphonse Daudet on a number of plays. He also wrote humorous sketches under the name of "Quatrelles" and composed a number of songs and piano pieces, several of which were included in Bizet's music library. On November 26, 1851, Bizet presented a manuscript composition to L'Epine inscribed: "To M. Ernest L'Epine, souvenir from his young friend Georges Bizet." On January 7, 1859, Bizet wrote to his mother from Rome: "L'Epine is a man whom I like infinitely in every way. His turn of mind, his taste as an artist, and that marvelous musical aptitude will always make me seek him out." Bizet, *Lettres,* 121.

intended to submit as his final *envoi* for the Prix de Rome. But Halévy's willingness to cooperate was fruitless because, as Bizet wrote him a month or so after his return from Italy, "I can't think about work. . . . My mother's health is causing me the greatest anxiety. . . . But I am not abandoning the hope of collaborating with you." [n] Twelve years went by before that hope materialized in *Carmen.*

In the winter of 1861, Bizet received an excellent report on *Vasco de Gama.* Fromental Halévy, speaking for the Académie, found "elevation of style, spaciousness of form, fine harmonic effects, rich and colorful orchestration," in the ode-symphony. He predicted a brilliant future for the composer, but warned him "to beware of certain harmonic audacities that might at times be described as harshness." During that same winter, the Opéra-Comique, which, by the terms of its subsidy, was required to produce annually a one-act opera by a Prix de Rome, commissioned Bizet to write a score for *La Guzla de l'Emir.* This libretto, probably far less satisfactory than Ludovic Halévy's would have been, was the product of Michel Carré and Jules Barbier, the successful pair who supplied most of Gounod's librettos. Bizet had no choice but to accept it. For several months he worked sporadically on *La Guzla,* but his mother's increasing weakness prevented his accomplishing any serious work.

In the spring, Bizet participated in an event as significant in the history of the Opéra as in his own musical development. The impact of hearing for the first time an opera by Wagner, and witnessing the brutal reception of *Tannhäuser* by the Paris audience, initiated a change in his opinion of the German composer. After reading two of Wagner's scores, probably *The Flying Dutchman* and *Lohengrin,* he had written to his mother from Rome: [*"There is absolutely nothing there.* They . . . are the work of a man who, lacking melodic inspiration and harmonic inventiveness, has created eccentricity; extraordinary that this innovator should have no originality, no personality. I like Verdi or Adam a hundred times better."] Ten years later, Wagner had become "that great immense musician . . . above and beyond all living composers."

The *première* of *Tannhäuser* at the Opéra is a saga unto itself: the diplomatic stroke by which Wagner's friend, the Princess Metternich, Austrian ambassadress, intimate of the Empress, and self-described *"singe à la mode,"* persuaded Napoleon III to command the production; the hundred and sixty-nine turbulent rehearsals;[3] the preliminary hissing and booing at the opening; the stampede by the members of the Jockey Club, outraged at finding no ballet in progress when they arrived for the second act; the Emperor sitting back in his box and enjoying the bedlam. Prosper Mérimée, who did not live long enough to attend the equally unsuccessful, if chillier, reception of the opera based on his *Carmen,* found *Tannhäuser* "a colossal bore. Some say that . . . Wagner has been sent to force us to admire Berlioz. Actually it was monstrous. It seems to me I could write something like it tomorrow, inspired by my cat walking over the keyboard of the piano. . . . The Princess Metternich made a terrific effort to have people think she understood it and to start applause that wouldn't come. Everybody was yawning. . . . The fiasco is enormous. Auber calls it Berlioz without melody."[n] Gounod on the other hand commented: "May God give me a failure like that!"

Liszt's arrival in Paris after his friend's disaster provided Bizet with the opportunity of fulfilling a wish he had expressed when the great virtuoso was in Rome: "I would rather like to meet this strolling player." The meeting took place on May 24, 1861, at the house of Fromental Halévy. After dinner, Liszt's brilliant performance of a new and spectacularly difficult composition of his own evoked overwhelming praise from his fellow-guests. " 'Yes,' Liszt admitted, 'this piece is difficult, horribly difficult and I know only two pianists in Europe capable of playing it as it is written and at the proper tempo—Hans von Bülow and myself.' Halévy, who sat near the piano and . . . knowing well Bizet's remarkable memory . . . said to him, 'Did you notice this passage?' which he indicated by playing a few notes. Bizet

[3] During the rehearsals of *Tannhäuser,* Wagner wrote the following letter to Alphonse Royer, director of the Opéra: "Sir: It appears that you are to see His Excellency the Minister today. Would you take advantage of this occasion to tell him that it is not true that I threw my snuffbox at M. Monelli's head, and that on the contrary I took every suitable means to direct this singer for a very good performance of my role of Wolfram. Also will you be good enough to confirm to the Minister that instead of no one's being able to get along with me, I have a full and cordial understanding with all the competent heads of the Opéra. And even with the only incompetent conductor I have until now been very long-suffering and indulgent. So that if I now ask for a change in the conducting of the opera, it is only in order to avoid delays and fatigue that would be fatal to the presentation of my work. . . ." Unpublished letter, collection of author.

then sat down at the piano, and without the slightest hesitation played the passage from memory. . . . Liszt then produced the manuscript, and Bizet played the work through with great brilliance, no hesitation, and no mistakes. The company was astonished. 'My young friend,' said Liszt, 'I had thought that there were only two men capable of surmounting the difficulties with which it pleased me to ornament this piece. I was wrong. There are three of us, and to be fair I should add that the youngest of the three is perhaps the boldest and the most brilliant.' " [n]

One of the guests, Eugène d'Eichthal, future economist and banker, found Bizet's playing far less brilliant than Liszt's, but much "pleasanter." There was no doubt in Bizet's own mind, or in the minds of any of his musical friends, that he could have made a career for himself as a virtuoso pianist had he so chosen. But showmanship was repellent to his nature, and he believed, bearing in mind Liszt's own career, that the public never takes seriously the compositions of a concert pianist. Bizet's whole range of temperament and talent found expression at the piano. "As others imitate the mannerisms and the diction of celebrated actors, he would parody, with a malicious wit and incomparable mastery, the style of famous composers of every school. He was the first person to do an entire newspaper in music, including even the advertisements, a marvelous act that many have copied but no one has equaled. Nothing could be more amusing than to hear him . . . loosing the orchestral tempests of Wagner. . . . He amplified his improvisations with impeccable skill, inexhaustible harmonic richness; his marvelous talent as a pianist alone would have been enough to assure him a brilliant future, but he hid it as though it were a vice. . . . He took as much pains to conceal his prowess at the piano as others take to show off theirs." [n]

Bizet the musician did not minimize the usefulness of his gifts as a pianist. A composer, he felt, should never relax his piano practice; it served as training for precision in the structure of his work. As examples of great composers who were also excellent pianists, Bizet cited Bach, Mozart, Beethoven, and Meyerbeer. He gave specific direction for serious study of the piano to his pupil Edmond Galabert: "watch yourself, criticize yourself, listen to yourself attentively, and play passages again and again until your touch produces the sound you wish; never be satisfied with the nearly right; learn the discreet use of the pedal so that the sound is sustained even during the brief periods when the hand is forced to let go of one or more keys and chords must continue vibrating." Bizet himself, Galabert tells us, "achieved marvelous effects of softness by the simultaneous use of two pedals and in the *fortissimo* always combined the mellow, the velvety tone with force and brilliance." The pupil was struck, too, by the effectiveness of his teacher's interpretations of the various roles in his operas while he accompanied himself at the piano. He would sing the female roles in a tenor voice, the male parts in a baritone or a bass. "It was a great artistic experience, too," Galabert recalled, "to hear him perform certain splendid passages chosen from the masterworks that formed part of his rich music library: certain superb stresses of the role of Cassandra in Berlioz's *Prise de Troie,* *'Tu ne m'écoutes pas, tu ne veux rien comprendre';* and, farther on, the vision of the prophetess, her interrupted words, and the sketches of the orchestra filling in Cassandra's silence. Or Heller's *Etude de la Chasse,* or his number 14 in F minor of the *Nuits Blanches,* Beethoven's 32 *Variations* on a theme in C minor, Chopin's *Funeral March,* fugues and preludes from *The Well-Tempered Clavier* of Bach. He made a great point of the double benefit to technique and expression to be derived from this last collection if one worked hard at it. . . . He thought that in order to feel deeply the aesthetic emotion and to express the proper nuances, a pianist should hum, so that the voice carries, animates, colors his playing. He himself used the voice, particularly when he was playing an orchestral piece, to imitate by singing or humming the timbre of the different instruments, filling out or underlining the details and the counter-melodies. But he was so accomplished in the art of making the whole range of the piano vibrate simultaneously, and in varying its tones, that he could render admirably orchestral transcriptions like the Wedding March from Mendelssohn's *Midsummer Night's Dream;* and he could evoke the idea of an orchestra even in works written for the piano, like the *Funeral March,* No. 3, in the fifth book (op. 62) of the same composer's *Songs without Words.* He also thought that to deepen and perfect a piece, it must be learned by heart. His memory, however, was extraordinary, and he could compose long works without writing a note." "

During the summer of 1861, Bizet worked on both *La Guzla de l'Emir* and the scherzo for his symphony. He also helped Gounod with the preparations for *La Reine de Saba,* the five-act opera begun a year earlier. From his country house, where he spent the month of August, Gounod thanked Bizet for consenting to coach the basso Belval for his role: "You see, my dear child, your affection and your talent have spoiled me, and I am no longer able to get along without you. You are so perfectly the expression of all my intentions that I can't translate or interpret myself as well as you do. . . . And what about you, you rascal, [you happy rascal!] Two loves! How the devil do you do it? As for me, I have never been able to. I find that two add up to less than one! [Well, it would seem to depend on how you handle them.] In any case, attend to your symphony and your overture. I am impatient to hear it all." [n] Before Bizet could complete these works, the blow he had been dreading fell.

At half past eight on the morning of September 8, 1861, Aimée Bizet died at the age of forty-five. Georges and a young fellow-tenant at 18 rue de Laval signed the death certificate. "The undersigned witnesses," one paragraph reads, "declare that they do not know the names of the father and mother of the deceased." This curious "lapse" of memory indicates the extent to which Bizet's early intimacy with the Delsarte family had dwindled away.

A week after his mother's death, he received a note of condolence from Fromental Halévy: "My dear Georges, I have been away from Paris, and heard only yesterday of the misfortune that has struck you. I need not tell you how much I share your sorrow. Time alone can soften it—Count, too, on the sympathy of your friends, on their devotion and affection." [n]

Cold comfort here for a boy who was literally haunted by his mother's spirit! Gounod, on the other hand, wrote from the heart: "What can I say, my dear, dear child, compared with what your heart is telling you every moment of the day? 'You no longer have your mother.' And a mother is irreplaceable. You know the part my friendship plays in anything that affects you. You know how freely and sincerely I offer you anything you could or would wish from me, if not to console you, at least to sympathize with you. The most consoling friend in this kind of grief is work. Work alone has a stern enough voice and a gentle enough hand to express and to touch the greatest sorrows as well as the greatest joys of life. For work alone is exempt from the flaws and imperfections of our poor humanity! . . ." [n] Gounod kept Bizet constantly busy with choral rehearsals and the orchestration of *La Reine de Saba.* "Help, my Bizet," he cried in one of the many short notes he wrote at this time. "I spent half the night working and I shall need your assistance."

"At night," Bizet told Galabert years later, "I would feel a terrible agony. I would be forced to fling myself down in an armchair, and then I would think that I saw my mother come into the room. She would cross and stand beside me and put her hand on my heart. Then the agony would increase. I would suffocate, and it seemed to me that her hand, weighing on me so heavily, was the true cause of my suffering." [n]

Soon after his mother's death, Bizet submitted to the Académie his long-overdue third *envoi.* He had intended to offer the Italian symphony conceived on his journey from Rome, but his mother's illness had prevented its completion. So instead of the complete symphony he presented only the Scherzo, along with the funeral march he had just composed and an overture called *La Chasse d'Ossian.* The Scherzo was first played at the Cercle de l'Union Artistique, more popularly known as the Cercle des Mirlitons or the Jockey Club of musicians. Its members, amateur composers and players, among them Prince Poniatowski and Prince Edmond de Polignac, applauded the work enthusiastically. That same autumn, the Académie, too, put its stamp of approval on the third *envoi,* finding nothing too "audacious" in the harmony. Indeed the Scherzo was one of the few works by Bizet performed during his lifetime which escaped the stigma of "Wagnerism."

Georges Bizet, 1859.
Portrait by F. Giacomotti

Georges Bizet, 1860.
Sketch made on return
journey from Rome
by G. Planté.

Fromental Halévy.

François Delsarte.

Charles Gounod, 1857.

Ernest Guiraud.

Antoine-Louis Clapisson.

Page from Bizet's outline for music lessons.

Caricature from cover of *Diogène,* September 28, 1863.

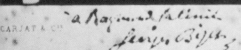

Georges Bizet.

Edmond Galabert.

CHAPTER  IX

Gounod's *La Reine de Saba:*
Erostrate by Ernest Reyer

For an artist in any medium the Paris of 1862 offered a harsh, forbidding terrain. *"The moral sense,"* wrote Flaubert in April of that year, "is more and more on the decline. People wallow in mediocrity. Small works, small passions, and small people: one is surrounded by nothing else." [n] And Baudelaire echoes his friend: "You can't imagine to what extent the race of Parisians is degraded. Paris is no longer that charming, pleasant world I used to know. The artists know nothing, the writers know nothing, not even how to spell. This whole world has become contemptible, inferior even to the world of high society. . . . They bear me a grudge because I am less ignorant than other men. What decadence!" [1][n] From the time five years earlier when these authors had been brought to trial for the so-called immorality of *Madame Bovary* and *Les Fleurs du Mal*, resentment against the government had spread from the minority of intellectuals and artists to many of the younger generation of students. They attacked where they

---

[1] In October 1862, two months after Baudelaire wrote these remarks to his mother, Ludovic Halévy met him at the office of the publisher Michel Lévy. "The conversation turned to Edward Ourliac," Halévy reported in his journal. "I had just been reading his novel *Susanne,* and had been charmed by it. I said so, and added that I found in this book a clarity and frankness of style that existed in very few works of that period. 'But, Monsieur,' Baudelaire interrupted, 'I was writing at that time.'" L. Halévy, *Carnets,* Paris, 1935, I, 5. Years later, when Halévy was revising his journal, he wrote on the margin of this entry: "I was wrong to find this remark ridiculous. It is true that I had not read any of the works of Baudelaire."

could, made their antagonism felt *en masse* as an audience, cared little for justice in their critical standards.

On January 3, 1862, *Gaëtana,* a play by Edmond About, Bizet's friend of Roman days, offered such an opportunity for mob action. As About's relations with the court grew increasingly cordial, he became more and more a symbol of betrayal to the students and younger men who had admired him in the past. To give him a lesson in liberalism, they organized a protest meeting for the opening night of *Gaëtana.* The insignificance of the play— "by turns turgid and witty, imitative, improbable, but lively"— did not concern them. Their resentment was focussed against the author as a symbol of the government. A crowd of over one thousand people made such a scene under the windows of About's house that he withdrew the play and never attempted another.

During the first two months of the year, Bizet's time was entirely given over to the hack-work involved in the preparation of Gounod's *La Reine de Saba,* a work as mediocre as *Gaëtana.* "My Bizet," Gounod wrote on January 14, "All my *airs de ballet* are sufficiently orchestrated so that you can arrange them, more or less. But before this piano arrangement I want to ask you to make another one for me, a provisional one, but none the less urgent. I mean the monstrous arrangement for two violins which they are using for the dance rehearsal at the theatre. . . ." [n]

The first performance of *La Reine de Saba* on February 28 was honored by the presence of the Emperor and Empress. It lasted from quarter to eight until twenty minutes past midnight. When it was over, the audience heaved a sigh of relief. "I am trying to hold up our unhappy Gounod who has had a fiasco worse than any yet seen," Berlioz wrote. "There is nothing in his score, nothing at all. How can I hold up what has neither bone nor sinew? Still, I have got to find something to praise." [n]

Gounod's distress over his failure was intensified by the death of his master and friend, Fromental Halévy, only three weeks after the opening of *La Reine de Saba.* For Halévy's funeral, he collaborated with three now-forgotten composers in setting to music the 23rd Psalm. Immediately after Halévy's funeral, Gounod departed for Italy, leaving Bizet at work on the piano arrangement, or what the composer called "the amputation" of *La Reine de Saba.*

Before Bizet had finished this task, his services as coach,

director of rehearsals, and general factotum were again commandeered, this time by a new friend, a composer very different from Gounod. Ernest Reyer, whose *La Statue* Bizet had greatly admired at its *première* the year before at the Théâtre-Lyrique, had been commissioned to write an opera, *Erostrate,* to be performed in the summer of 1862 at Baden-Baden. Reyer was then thirty-eight years old. Described as a miniature Flaubert, whose *Salammbô* he later made into an opera, he wore the same style of heavy mustache, had a piercing eye, carried himself stiffly, and spoke brusquely. More like a cavalry officer than a musician, he complained that the friends who called him "Colonel" might at least give him the rank of general. A native of Marseilles, a kind and affectionate man, gay and amusing, Reyer became embittered later in life by years of neglect in his own country. At the time of Bizet's early friendship with him he was enjoying the only success in the theatre he was to know for nearly thirty years. A passionate admirer and devoted friend of Berlioz, whom he succeeded as critic on the *Journal des Débats* in 1864, Reyer owed to the great composer's influence the commission to write *Erostrate* for the theatre at Baden-Baden where Berlioz had for many years been conducting concerts.

Apart from Bizet's admiration for *La Statue,* which he regarded as the most remarkable opera presented in France in the previous twenty years, he had a more personal reason for welcoming the chance to serve as Reyer's alter ego at the rehearsals of *Erostrate* while the composer himself escaped to Baden to complete his opera "in a state of tranquillity" never to be found in Paris. As early as January 1859, Bizet had had it in mind to go to Baden "to arrange a little business with Bénazet for an *opéra de salon.* Even though it would pay only three or four thousand francs, it would always be good to have," he had written to his mother from Rome. Now Reyer promised to arrange with Bénazet, the director of the Baden theatre, to produce a work of Bizet's the following summer.

From Baden, early in May, Reyer sent Bizet the orchestral manuscript of the first act of his new work with detailed instructions to be communicated to the copyist, Lemorne. Joseph Méry, the poet and librettist of *Erostrate,* "adores you," Reyer wrote, "and you needn't worry. We will look after you with Bénazet. Thank you always, my dear Bizet, for your zeal in my behalf and your affection for me. And count always on the very sincere friendship of your *bon vivant* E. Reyer." [2]

By June, Reyer had moved to "a pretty little house in the village of Lichtenthal, half an hour from Baden. I am surrounded by trees," he wrote, "and near at hand are a convent, a forest and a mill. I am told that the nuns in the convent are real artists. On Sundays a crowd comes to mass to hear them sing. . . . I am alone. I have no neighbors, men or women (alas!), and no one will disturb me. . . .

"I shall take a room for you next to mine if you don't want to spend a lot of money at a hotel and don't mind not being in Baden proper. The Theatre is charming. The seating will be more comfortable than at the Opéra. I hope that next year you will be able on your own account to try out the acoustics. We will arrange this with Bénazet. . . ."

A more careful examination of the new theatre, which was to open with the *première* of Berlioz's *Béatrice et Bénédict,* disclosed certain basic imperfections. "Would you believe that the orchestra pit is too small?" Reyer fumed. "Berlioz is furious. This negligence on the part of the architect is outrageous. When his mistake was pointed out to him, he replied that the important thing was for the public to be comfortable. This mason doesn't bother about musicians. You will see how I shall make him tear down his barrier and shove his tier of seats back into the foyer. . . ."

By the end of June, Bizet was complaining of the infrequency of Reyer's letters. "My dear, good Bizet," Reyer replied, "you must not keep too much track of my letters because I prefer talking to writing. We will talk a lot when you are in Baden, and you may be certain that at the opportune moment I shall do everything I can to make sure that you come here under the most favorable conditions. Bénazet is a man who must be dealt with in his own good time, but a good man at that, and not at all stingy. I don't know whether some excerpts from my score which I sang before Her Majesty, appealed to her, but I do know that she will refuse me nothing that has to do with *Erostrate*—and it seems to me that you have a great deal to do with it. . . . My trio is still as

---

[2] Ernest Reyer to Bizet, n.d. All of Reyer's letters quoted in this chapter, unpublished and undated, are in the collection of the author, and will not be individually noted.

unborn as though it weren't needed. Reassure Lemorne. Tell him that it will not take long to copy. It will take much more time to compose. . . . It is unbelievable that Mlle Saxe should flinch at a B natural, her finest note! The population would be stupefied if they read this in the *Badenblatt*. Tell her that her fear that the words will not be understood is justified not only for that passage, but for many others. There will be many Russians, Germans, and English in the audience. If she finds it easier to pronounce '*Et l'éclat de sa pierre illumine mon cou,*' and Méry does not object, neither do I. I guarantee that the public will not be scandalized and the curtain will not be lowered before the end of the first act. The end of the act naturally brings to mind the end of the next act. Before the week is out, you will receive another package. If the trio is in it, all the better. If not, it will come later. . . . Thank you a thousand times for what you say about my score. Your friendship for me makes you see the thing through a telescope, but I am, nevertheless, flattered and pleased."

Finally, in mid-July, Reyer managed to finish and despatch half of the awaited trio. Along with it came a note saying, "Choudens has written to me and I have replied. . . . You will travel to Baden in the company of our dear publisher, and we will make him climb to the summit of Mount Mercury—without his realizing it, I need hardly say, for I know he doesn't like walking."

Late in July, Bizet received the conclusion of the trio, about one hundred pages. "There is no accompaniment at the end," Reyer wrote, "just a few chords to guide you. I didn't think there was any use in sending you more than that. . . . Write to me quickly what I should do about the introduction, which will certainly not be an overture. . . . The situation in Paris doesn't sound madly gay. If Cazaux is in tears, if Mlle Saxe is in a rage, what the devil shall we do? . . . Two rehearsals will never be enough, and a postponement is impossible. . . . Here, only one stage-set was forgotten; the burning of the temple at the end. . . . The scene designer was notified by telegraph, and the set will be made. 'Around the ruined temple. Dost thou hear, etc.,' and there were neither ruins nor temple, barely a little stump of a column supposed to be the goddess's altar. . . . I have not yet seen Berlioz. You and he, fellow mountaineers, will no doubt leave here in the same compartment. Don't forget Choudens. We will abandon him on Mount Mercury. A publisher, a businessman, can't get out of taking this climb. The god is no longer there, but the polite gesture will have been made.

"Berlioz will conduct his opera, and I shall probably conduct mine. Only, as I am extremely bald, I am worried because a bald head reflects the chandeliers brightly, and the audience behind me in the upper galleries will fire at me with pea-shooters.

"The weather is fine, and the breastworks of Baden are reinforced by a young Russian girl with an enormous bosom. I am holding a gigantic Gretchen in reserve for Choudens. . . . Give Gounod a handshake for me. . . ."

Gounod, however, was not within handshaking distance of Paris. Still recuperating in Italy from the failure of *La Reine de Saba,* he wrote Bizet from Florence on his forty-fourth birthday: "My dear Bizet, my child . . . I promised to write you from Rome, but . . . I looked at Rome in despair, like a lover about to depart. I should never have left there. I might have amounted to more—at least a little more. . . . You already know, perhaps, through Choudens, that I have done nothing at all. I think this sterility will continue for some time. I feel that I am in the process of demusicalization. My spirit is like a body disintegrating. I am no longer capable of any thought. And you? What is happening to you? What are you doing? You are young and free. You must live and be happy and stay happy. I expect and want something new from you on my return." [n]

Gounod's gloom soon lightened at the prospect of a performance of *La Reine de Saba* in Brussels. On his way home from Italy, he stopped at Baden-Baden to go to the *première* of *Béatrice et Bénédict.* " 'What are you doing here?' Jouvin asked him. 'I am traveling because of a death in the family,' Gounod replied. 'You have lost a relative?' Jouvin asked. 'Yes, a woman I loved very much: *La Reine de Saba.'* " [n]

Owing to Reyer's procrastination, the first performance of *Erostrate* was postponed until August 23. Bizet, forced to wait in Paris so that he could bring the parts, which were still being copied, was, therefore, unable to get to Baden in time to hear Berlioz's opera. Immediately after the opening of *Béatrice et Bénédict* on August 9, Reyer wrote to him: "Gounod is here. I saw him for a moment at Berlioz's performance. *Succès d'estime* for the music, *succès d'ennui* for the libretto. What an audience!

I had to charge like a raging bull on the Princess Battera's box, from which loud-mouthed jokes resounded continually throughout the two acts. To my mind Berlioz's work is a marvel of art and craftsmanship. Mlle Charton's duet and andante are beyond all admiration. However Papa Haydn, of whom Berlioz has made so much fun, has played him the nasty trick of whispering into his ear the most ravishing phrases from *The Creation.* And Berlioz has used them, sumptuously and literally. This has not harmed the duet. . . . But what difference does it make? No one has ever written anything sweeter, purer, more adorable than that duet. . . ."

Gounod, too, admired the duet. "It is absolutely beautiful and perfect," he wrote to his wife. "It is as immortal as the sweetest and most profound music of the great masters. . . . Berlioz is a genius with both the innocence of a child and an extraordinary intellectual complexity. . . . I love Berlioz for the art he expresses, and he would have to do me considerable harm before I could forget the good he has done me. We are leaving here together on Wednesday." [n]

Before the two masters departed, Bizet at last arrived in Baden-Baden. This small city in the valley of the Black Forest, on the banks of the river Oos, was, during the fifties and the sixties, the most fashionable and popular watering-place in Europe. Partly because the Grand Duchess, born a Beauharnais, was a cousin of Napoleon III, the French regarded Baden-Baden as the summer capital of the Continent. In the Meilhac-Halévy play *Frou-Frou,* when the heroine's husband tells her that he has been named minister to Baden, she replies, "Oh, but you told me you had been appointed to a foreign country." If the Parisians regarded Baden as a second home, it also attracted from all over Europe visitors on every social level, among whom only the middle classes came primarily to take the cure. The Parisians, those inveterate city-dwellers, found in Baden just enough scenery to satisfy their illusions of being in the country; the Russians were attracted by the gambling casino, the British by the horse-racing. One Irish visitor found in "the fairy city of Baden . . . all the fascination of a grand scale *opéra-comique.* . . . King Bénazet has the showiest, most glittering, most costly, and perhaps wickedest *troupe* in the world! . . . It is difficult to get a glimpse of this secret and mysterious power. King Bénazet keeps himself

shrouded like a veiled prophet. . . . At home there are people
who would call this illustrious man the keeper of a gambling-den.
Here he has a lovely palace and gives delightful *soirées* and balls to
choice artistic guests. . . . It is a gay kingdom, and we must not
look this gift horse too closely in the mouth." "

The gambling casino, known as the Conversation House,
supplied the fortune of this Maecenas. It resembled, according
to Alfred de Musset, for years a devotee of the resort: "a Greek
temple covered with tiles, a kind of barn with a peristyle, formless
and nameless, a kind of hayloft, bastard of the Pantheon." If
Bénazet's palace lacked the beauty of Versailles, he was, nevertheless, *le roi soleil* of his kingdom. He distributed his wealth
with no mean hand. "If he resembled Louis XIV," said Reyer,
"it was on his good side. He honored artists, and rewarded them
generously. Every concert Berlioz gave cost Bénazet some twenty
thousand francs. And when he heard some facetious tourist remark that the harmonic sounds of the violins and the vibrations
of the little antique cymbals in the *Queen Mab* Scherzo sounded
like badly oiled hinges or the carillon of little bells in an inn, he
smiled and continued in his lively admiration of the great composer." "

Bizet unfortunately was in no state of mind to enjoy the
pleasures of Baden when he finally arrived there. Reyer speaks
of his "ill-timed bursts of temper and his irritation at the most
trifling difficulty. Once he had launched an attack, he championed
the person or cause even in the absence of any provocation or
offense." " His quarrel with Emilien Pacini, the librettist who
collaborated with Méry on *Erostrate,* has often been reported.
Pacini, Reyer said, was "a rare spirit with an open nature, one of
the most obliging of men, who writes lyrics with a facility that
Scribe must sometimes have envied." Usually one of those mild,
accommodating men who frequently serve as a butt for the jokes
of their companions, on this occasion he had apparently been
ridden to exasperation. In the presence of Gounod and several
others he remarked that the failure of *La Reine de Saba* was
deserved.

No sooner had Pacini spoken than Bizet, leaping up like a
jumping-jack, red in the face with rage and indignation, proceeded
to threaten him in the most violent language. Before anyone had
time to stop him, Bizet challenged Pacini to a duel. Seconds

were appointed, and all of Gounod's tact and diplomacy was needed to persuade his rampant disciple that if anyone had been insulted, it was not Bizet, but he himself. Pacini, equally set on defending his honor, was finally calmed down, and the crisis evaporated in apologies.

During another less belligerent conversation, Bizet made a remark to Jouvin which the critic of the *Figaro* quoted a year later in his attack on *Les Pêcheurs de Perles*. Describing a dinner in Baden at which he was present, Jouvin wrote: "In this coterie of demi-gods, or those aspiring to be, Hector Berlioz represented the venerable Nestor, Charles Gounod the prudent Ulysses, Ernest Reyer the fiery Ajax, and the author of *Les Pêcheurs de Perles*, the young and already impetuous Achilles. . . . The fiery sword had revealed to Achilles his vocation of hero. The shock of the *harmonies,* like sword-points with which the author of *Tannhäuser* had pierced the ears of his audience, had worked an analogous miracle on my young friend Bizet. Moreover, except for Berlioz —a protestant from the other side of the Rhine—all sang Wagner's praises. What's more, as they were convinced that only proselytizing faith is the true faith, they wanted, between dessert and cheese, to give me a role in this Hosanna—perhaps the one that the composer of *Béatrice et Bénédict* would under no circumstances assume. Georges Bizet, believing he could convince me by a white lie that should have burned his tongue, went so far as to say, 'You like Verdi's music. Well, Wagner is Verdi with style.' . . . I can still hear this captious remark, still see Reyer's indignation at this sacrilegious comparison. The devil would fit more comfortably into an overflowing holy water stoup than the name of Verdi on the lips of the intolerant author of *La Statue.* Reyer looked askance at Bizet. The latter, lowering his eyes, seemed to say, to justify himself, 'You have to lie a little in fighting for a good cause.' " [n]

On Bizet's return to Paris, the difficulties in his relationship with his father, which were partly responsible for his nervous tension, were intensified. The previous June, just nine months after the death of Mme Bizet, Marie Reiter, the maid who nursed her during her illness, had given birth to a son. The child, Jean, always tacitly regarded as the son of Adolphe Bizet, was brought up as a sort of cousin in the household. Marie, who was a tall, handsome girl of twenty-four at the time of Mme Bizet's death, remained as housekeeper to the elder Bizet until his death in 1886. From then until the end of her life she was in the service of Georges Bizet's widow. Just before Marie's death in the second decade of this century, she confided to her son—by this time a man in a respected position, with a wife and a family—that he was the son, not of Adolphe, but of Georges Bizet.

When Marie went back to her native village in Alsace to give birth to her child, the feelings between Georges and Adolphe were naturally strained. A letter to Choudens perhaps best shows Bizet's state of mind in the autumn of 1862: "I wish I were in a position never to have to raise these questions of money, which fill me with horror. However, if you know me well, you know what to think about this subject. A day will certainly soon come when my courage and my talent will be rewarded. And you can then count on a conscientious artist and an excellent friend for everything pertaining to your business of publishing. In the meantime I am extremely embarrassed financially, and I should be most obliged if you would help me.

"The sum you offer me is insufficient. My minimum is 1800 francs; that is to say my board and lodging at my father's.

"I ask this amount of you because I am convinced that I am able to earn it. In fact, *cher ami*, if we put our accounts in order rigorously, we shall arrive at a total slightly larger than I myself believed; for instance:

Erostrate	200
Le Cabaret	100

The symphony for four hands (two weeks of work) something none of your friends would do for you 200

Id for two hands 100

"Putting together the parts of the Italian arrangements of *Faust*, of *Philémon*, correcting the proofs at 2 frs. per hour, amounts to a lot more than 100
and I am not mentioning *The Merry Wives of Windsor*,[3] for which I wrote more than sixty pages of orchestration, which would seem to be poorly paid at the price of 100
                                                                    ⎯⎯⎯
                                                                    800

"Let me make it clear that I am not demanding this. . . . I promise that I will do everything—polkas, dance-hall pieces,

<hr />

[3] See Appendix II, p. 469.

quadrilles, proof-correcting, transcriptions, signed or unsigned, arrangements, derangements, transpositions, and scores for two flutes, two trombones, two cornets, even two pianos. I give you my word that we will make a good thing of this for both of us. . . .

"It isn't possible that I am not worth 1800 frs. a year to you. Let me know quickly, so that in case it is impossible, I can turn to you know whom: it is urgent. But, I repeat, aside from the fact that you want to help me, which I know you do, this will not be bad business for you, I am sure.

"In any case and whatever happens, always your devoted friend

"Georges Bizet

"Don't write. The letter might by chance get into my father's hands." [n]

Later in the year, Bizet received the final payment of his Prix de Rome grant as well as praise for his fourth *envoi*, *La Guzla de l'Emir*. The Académie report notes: "a 'prelude,' happy in form and very neatly orchestrated, some 'couplets,' a 'duet,' interrupted by an elegant 'serenade,' a tenor 'aria' and finally a very pretty 'song' followed by a scenically effective 'trio.'

"Although there is still a little affectation in this score and a certain tendency to sacrifice vocal interest to wealth of accompaniment, we are glad to praise its elevated feeling, its vivacious style, its sound execution—in a word, the solid virtues which M. Bizet has already shown, and which today give sure proof of a brilliant future." [n]

Bizet's gifts were further recognized at the year's end by Ambroise Thomas, who had accepted a commission from Fromental Halévy's widow to complete her husband's unfinished opera, *Noë*. Thomas, however, soon abandoned the project and invited Bizet to meet him and the librettist, Saint-Georges, at Madame Halévy's house at "two o'clock sharp" on December 23 and "exactly at noon" on Christmas day to discuss the plans for *Noë*. This was Bizet's first encounter with the librettist who was to serve him badly and with the opera he would complete only after his marriage to the daughter of its composer. Now, fortunately, the opportunity came to him to create an opera of his own.

CHAPTER  X

Scherzo: *Les Pêcheurs de Perles:* Choudens

The year 1863 could hardly have started more promisingly for Bizet. Two of his compositions were played at concerts, and his first opera was recognized as the work of an artist by the only great music critic of the day. His achievement was a symbol of hope to all serious young French composers. Yet achievement and success were, in this instance, far from synonymous. And before we can grasp the full significance of that paradox it is necessary to understand the decadence of French music at the time and the extraordinarily complex situation in the lyric theatres of Paris.

The official title of the Opéra has varied under the different forms of government which have granted its subsidy. Today it is the Académie *Nationale* de Musique et de Danse. Under Napoleon I and Napoleon III, it was the Académie *Impériale.* Académie *Royale* in the beginning, it was founded by Louis XIV in 1669. No sooner had the first performance taken place in 1671 than the precedent for managerial intrigue and dictatorship was established. Jean-Baptiste Lully, through his influence with Mme de Montespan, succeeded at the start in ousting the original directors and in dominating the French lyric drama from 1672 to his death in 1687. Even after his death, only works by composers of his school were played. This first of the cycles of stagnation which were recurrently to restrict or bar the natural development of French opera ended only when Jean-Philippe Rameau succeeded in overcoming Lully's successors as well as the unjust, prejudiced criticism that is inevitably the lot of every French innovator. Until Rameau's death in 1764, his and Lully's works predominated in the repertory. But in the 1770's, Niccola Piccinni and Gluck came to Paris. The latter, who tried to revolutionize serious French opera, roused the usual violent antagonists. A gradually increasing band of followers split the public in a feud between Gluckists and Piccinnists in which neither composer participated. The events of the Revolution and the Consulate were not conducive to new creative works, and only under the stimulus of the second foreign invasion, consisting of Cherubini, Spontini, and later Rossini, did French composers begin to create works of any stature. During the first two decades of the nineteenth century, French adaptations of German and Italian operas by Mozart, Weber, and Rossini were popular. And after the Revolution of 1830, the foreigners, no longer invaders, but welcome guests, became the dominating force in French opera. Meyerbeer set the pattern that Halévy adopted, and under the bourgeois king Louis-Philippe the Opéra knew its greatest days. But the quality of the works given owed far more to the talent of the composers and the singers than to the standards of the directors of the theatre.

As unscrupulous and domineering as Lully, they were, however, with one or two exceptions, neither musicians themselves nor even lovers of the arts—only of the *artistes*. *Boulevardiers*, gamblers like Véron and Roqueplan, they regarded the government subsidy as a stake for self-enrichment. Bankruptcies were recurrent. By the time the Second Empire reached its height, the Opéra was a kind of club of the upper classes, desiring no new members and requiring no fresh forms of entertainment. For a young composer it took courage indeed to batter through the walls of this tight, reactionary organization.

On a slightly different social level, the Opéra-Comique, also state-subsidized, was almost as formidable. Growing out of the *spectacles de la foire*, which were parodies of the lyric tragedies, the Comique was founded in 1715. The French word *comique* is closer to the English words *comedy* or *comic spirit* than to *comic*. The difference between "grand" and "comic" opera was primarily the substitution of spoken dialogue for recitative and an inevitably happy resolution of the plot. In the twenties and thirties of the nineteenth century, a large repertory was built up by Auber, Adam, Boïeldieu, Hérold, and Halévy. The same works, or replicas of them, were performed hundreds of times before the same bourgeois family audiences, who were more interested in each other and their match-making than in the operas they ostensibly came to see and hear.

Among the non-subsidized theatres were the Théâtre-Italien, which from time to time gave second-rate Italian works with Italian singers, and the operetta theatres, where Offenbach flourished. The only house open to the works of serious young composers was the Théâtre-Lyrique, which led an adventurous and frequently disastrous existence between 1847 and 1870. Located first in one building, then in another, it was directed by imaginative men who avoided the conventions that bound the other theatres and who tried wholeheartedly to encourage original works and to build up an enterprising audience.

The condition of the concert stage at the time was perhaps best described by Berlioz, writing in 1858: "There are two Societies, one already ancient, the other very young, each of them playing once every two weeks during only three and a half months. Their public performances amount to about six or seven every year. The first, the Société des Concerts du Conservatoire, was founded under the best possible conditions. It has, gratis, an excellent hall, in which it can rehearse at any time. The personnel of the executants of this society is composed of the ablest musicians in Paris. The works they perform are almost always studied with the greatest care. But the Société du Conservatoire restricts its function to *conserving* a certain number of the masterpieces of a few illustrious dead; for them the living do not exist. Nevertheless . . . composers who pass by the hall of the Concerts du Conservatoire should salute the threshold with respect, as did the French officers when they saw the great Pyramid in which the Egyptians, during so many centuries, have preserved the mummies of their Pharaohs.

"The other organization, the Société des Jeunes Artistes, which M. Pasdeloup directs with zeal and devotion, has no hall of its own. . . . The associated musicians, drawing only a very small salary from the six or seven annual concerts, and obliged to live by employing their talents in all sorts of ways elsewhere, are rarely present at all rehearsals. They almost never come to the preparatory rehearsals, at which the orchestra should be complete. . . . These gentlemen played at a ball the night before and went to bed at five o'clock in the morning. A little sleep is necessary. Some have lessons to give, others are detained by a theatre-rehearsal, etc. . . . And frankly, one can't blame them. But what torture for the conductor of the Société! And for the composer whose work is being played, if he is present. Indeed he may be present. For the Société des Jeunes Artistes, while proving their respect for the illustrious dead, have not declared war against the living. Far from it. Considering their limited resources they have already rendered important service to modern art." [n]

One important service that Jules Pasdeloup rendered was the playing of Bizet's Scherzo on January 11, 1863. The work itself was minor, but as a symbol, both to Bizet and to all his young colleagues, it was a triumph. The Concerts Populaires, which Pasdeloup conducted every Sunday in the Cirque d'hiver, then called the Cirque Napoléon, had been founded by him in 1861, succeeding the Société des Jeunes Artistes. Pasdeloup, to whom Bizet fourteen years later dedicated the score of *Carmen*, had the courageous aim of introducing to his very conservative audience previously unplayed works of foreign composers such as Schumann, as well as new works by young French composers. At each performance of an unfamiliar composition, his audience protested either by hissing or by threatening to cancel subscriptions. Although the rest of the program that included Bizet's Scherzo could hardly have been more orthodox—Mozart's E flat Symphony, Beethoven's *Egmont* Overture and the adagio from Haydn's Quartet No. 6—Pasdeloup was deluged the following day by irate letters protesting his playing of the new work.

The critics on this occasion gave the Scherzo brief but friendly notices. "It sounded charming," said the critic of the *Revue et Gazette Musicale,* "and was applauded by the audience. We can only encourage this happy attempt, which will no doubt be advantageous to young composers." J. Lovy, in *Le Ménestrel* found the piece "pleasant, written with a certain verve, but with an inadequate peroration," in spite of which "the composer received wholehearted applause." The following week, when the Scherzo was repeated by an even more adventurous and shorter-lived organization entitled the Société Nationale des Beaux-Arts, another critic on *Le Ménestrel,* Paul Bernard, wrote, "M. Bizet's Scherzo is the work of a consummate musician. But in it we looked in vain for the melodic inspiration necessary for this kind of piece, and of which there are so many examples in Haydn, Mozart, Beethoven, and Mendelssohn. The first measures, though imitative, were promising. Unfortunately the rest of the work becomes a little heavy and seemed to us prolix above all."

At the second playing of the Scherzo, Bizet conducted his own work; at the same concert Saint-Saëns also conducted one of his own compositions. "A man may be very talented, write correctly, knowledgeably, in a very closely knit, conscientious style, and lack the tact, the experience, and the special art necessary to a good orchestra conductor," wrote the critic of the *Gazette.* "M. C. Saint-Saëns proved this point very well that afternoon when he conducted two excerpts from one of his symphonies. . . . The execution could hardly have been more hesitant, duller, or more uneven. M. Bizet, when his turn came, tried to conduct a Scherzo he had composed, but he succeeded no better. His music is not at all distorted, far-fetched as in general is M. Saint-Saëns's. On the contrary, it is remarkable for a wholly French clarity and grace, far preferable to all the combinations usually employed to hide the absence of melody." [n]

The Scherzo was never again played in Bizet's lifetime, but this joint participation in what must have been a rather disastrous performance launched an enduring friendship between the two young composers. When Saint-Saëns heard the Scherzo played years after Bizet's death, he recalled the earlier occasion: "While listening to Georges Bizet's delightful Scherzo . . . seeing the audience excited and admiring, applauding the work and the composer, encoring until they were out of breath, I looked back twenty years to the first performance of this same Scherzo, badly played, badly listened to by an inattentive and indifferent audience. . . . Failure then, for us young Frenchmen, was synonymous with death! Even success did not insure a second hearing at these concerts. 'Write masterpieces like Beethoven and I will play them,' the conductor told me. . . . A few years later conditions changed, and we were no longer denied performance at the concerts. . . . 'Since they don't want us in the theatre,' I used often to say to Georges Bizet, 'let us take refuge in the concert-hall.'

" 'That is all right for you,' he would reply, 'but I am not made for the symphony. I need the theatre. Without it I don't exist.'

"One wonders now . . . why this charming musician, this lovable and jolly lad, found so many obstacles in his way. The public naturally enough finds difficulty in approaching a brusque genius like Berlioz, who dwelt on inaccessible heights. But Bizet, the embodiment of youth, of vigor, of gaiety and good nature! . . . Loyal and sincere, he never disguised his friendships or his antipathies. This mutual characteristic drew us together. Otherwise we differed completely and pursued different ideals. He sought above all things, passion and life, whereas I ran after the chimera of purity of style and perfection of form. So our conversations never ended. Our friendly discussions had a liveliness and charm that I have never again found with anyone else.

"Bizet was not a rival; he was a brother in arms. I used to acquire new strength from contact with that high intelligence which expressed itself with endless humor, that character so strongly wrought that no disappointment could weaken it. Before he was a musician, Georges Bizet was a man, and that, more than anything else, perhaps, is what did him harm." [n]

Saint-Saëns as a young man was far from prepossessing. "He was short and always strangely resembled a parrot; the same sharply curved profile, a beak-like hooked nose, lively, restless, piercing eyes. . . . He strutted like a bird and talked rapidly, precipitately, with a curiously affected lisp. But his external lack of charm was soon dispelled by the quickness of his wit and the extraordinary breadth of his interests and culture. . . ." [n]

In addition to these qualities, which would inevitably have attracted Bizet in spite of the difference in musical principles of the two men, Saint-Saëns had a capacity for loyalty and devotion which Bizet alone in their own generation evoked in him. Although loyal in his friendships with the accepted masters—Rossini, Berlioz, Gounod—Saint-Saëns was hostile to most of his contemporaries. His enmity to Massenet increased with the years. Between him and Reyer there was a state of armed truce. To César Franck he was indifferent. But even in his old age, when his own reactionary attitude toward the revolutionary works of young composers resembled so closely the prejudice of the old guard of his youth against *Carmen,* he continued to go to listen to his friend's work. It was fortunate for both Saint-Saëns and Bizet that they could together laugh off the criticism heaped upon them in the winter of 1863.

For Bizet was soon again a butt for the critics. Only three weeks after the second performance of the Scherzo, he conducted another of his works at a concert of the Société des Beaux-Arts. This time it was his second *envoi* from Rome, *Vasco de Gama*. The high praise lavished on this work by the members of the Music Section of the Académie did not influence the critics.

The writer for the *Revue et Gazette Musicale,* after praising "the grace, freshness and originality" of Félicien David's Symphony in E flat (he found this composer's conducting satisfactory) remarks that the same thing could not be said of the performance of *Vasco de Gama*. "It is true," he writes, "that in this work voices were introduced and brought disorder, confusion, even chaos. It is also true that the composer is far from being as much at ease in his vocal as in his instrumental style.

"We do not believe that because certain subjects have already been used, they are necessarily outlawed. We find it quite natural that M. Bizet wanted to have a *Vasco de Gama,* just as Spontini had a *Fernando Cortez* and Félicien David a *Christophe Colomb*. Only we regret that he has failed so lamentably. . . . Comparisons are useless when one is confronted with a work of such limited scope and, even worse, imperfection. Except for a rather pretty horn solo, skillfully accompanied by the orchestra, an elegant bolero sung by Mlle Girard, and a prayer, too involved in dissonances and not supplely enough harmonized, everything . . . from the chorus of soldiers and sailors, which, pretending to be honest and frank, is full of banal phrases and common rhythms, to the storm, with the shrill sound of the piccolo, the additional chromatic rather than dramatic whistling and rumbling of the ascending and descending scale, everything lacks breath, color and originality." [n]

If we remember Bizet's difficulties in composing *Vasco de Gama,* it seems unlikely that this particular criticism greatly disturbed him. But the general lack of enthusiasm did not engender a state of mind conducive to the creation of new works. Indeed, it is not yet clear just what he was composing during the winter of 1863. But it seems probable that soon after Bizet returned from Baden, he started work on the score of the opera *Ivan IV*.

The libretto of this work, by Arthur Leroy and Henri Trianon, had been in Gounod's hands since 1855 or 1856. He apparently finished the score in 1857, but became discouraged when the management of the Opéra continued to ignore his work. He took from *Ivan* the Soldiers' Chorus for *Faust,* a march for *La Reine de Saba,* and later an aria for *Mireille.* Yet in May 1862, a little over a fortnight before writing to Bizet that he was sterile and *"démusicalisé,"* he gave a reading of it to his traveling companion in Italy. Very likely, then, Gounod, seeing Bizet at loose ends in Baden, offered him the libretto, in which he himself had lost interest. But in April, before Bizet had time to finish *Ivan IV,* Léon Carvalho commissioned him to write *Les Pêcheurs de Perles* for September production.[1]

He wrote the good news to Gounod, who replied: "Although I received your splendid, friendly letter on Sunday, it just happened that I couldn't find a free moment to tell you immediately all the pleasure, all the joy I feel at the news of your commission for three acts for the Théâtre-Lyrique. My satisfaction in whatever you do stems both from the friendship I bear you and from the confidence your debut inspires in me. You have, my dear child, in your bag of tricks a great deal more than is needed for a mere attempt. You have, moreover, *your* name to establish, and that is the point to which I wish particularly, even exclusively, to draw your attention.

"1. You will, you tell me, be brief. That is an important first point to decide; it is excellent. But the very short time you tell me you have before your work is scheduled for performance prompts me to recommend this to you: *'Don't drive yourself* with the excuse that you are in a hurry.'

"In the first place, the faster you want to go, the slower you will actually be because your partial and successive criticisms of your work will force you to *rewrite,* which is tantamount to double the work. Let your work mature as though you had twice the time, only work *without stopping.* That was the method of the Tortoise and he won over the Hare.

---

[1] Until recently it has been assumed that *Les Pêcheurs de Perles* was the subject of a letter dated March 28, 1863, from Berlioz to Marmontel, Bizet's former teacher, acknowledging receipt of the score of an opera by one of Marmontel's pupils. (See *Revue de musicologie,* November 1938, 140–1.) But as Berlioz specified neither the name of the composer nor the title of the work, there is no proof that the opera referred to in his letter was not composed by another of Marmontel's protégés.

"I urge you, besides, to envisage several pieces before writing a single one; because 1, the unity of your work will profit by it; 2, you will insure variety both in the conception of your pieces and in their *execution*.

"2. Your subject, you tell me, is Mexican. I don't know the story so I can tell you nothing from that point of view. But as far as possible make your *tone light*. The Mexican does not tend to be *dark*, or so it seems to me.

"3. Now, don't pay any attention to any assured or known successes. Be *very much yourself*. That way you may be very much alone today, but it will mean your having plenty of people around you tomorrow. A first original work is always a *Duel;* a second becomes a *Battle;* a third is a *Victory*, not always apparent, but certainly in Reality and in Truth. Have faith *in your own emotion*, that it is a success and a *promise*.

"You regret that the law does not permit the assassination of certain musicians? But surely it does permit it, and the Divine Law *commands* it. Only the method must be decided upon. We all kill: butchers kill meat; the lazy kill time or flies; journalists kill the dead; and good works kill bad ones. Twenty years from now, Wagner, Berlioz, Schumann will reckon plenty of victims. Don't we already see some names, famous ones at that, half demolished by the last blows of Beethoven? There was a great assassin!

"Carré, in one of his letters, made me hope that a visit from you would coincide with his. How nice that would be! What a lot of work you would get through here in a week, and without driving *yourself*, I would almost say without knowing it! In the quiet of this security, the long hours are enormously reassuring. Time that you know in advance to be protected from interruption is immeasurably fruitful. What makes creation slow in our usual environment is perpetual interruption. It is like a train that never gets anywhere because it stops at every station. *Continuity* is real speed. Again the tortoise!—Write to me. It makes me happy. Tell me *if* and *when* you are coming. I will shut you up next to my room, and you will see how you work. And besides, you will have no expenses; good business.

"*Adieu,* I embrace and love you.
              "Your
                 "Gounod." "

Bizet settled down to composing *Les Pêcheurs de Perles* with a tenacity and concentration quite foreign to him in his Roman days, when his deadline had been academic rather than professional. "I have not forgotten," a friend wrote to him after the opera opened, "the driving work you imposed on yourself, nor the existence of a recluse I always found you leading when your score was still entitled just *Leïla*." [n] Gounod tried to extricate Bizet from his isolation early in the summer. "Won't you spare me a few moments," he asked his Bizet *"chéri,* so that I can soon hear that music which, because it is yours, somehow affects my own innards? I know that this is a lot to ask while you are working, and I don't want to annoy you. But think of my eagerness and how happy you would make me if you took pot-luck with us one day at Saint-Cloud and served us your work as dessert. . . . I am beginning the orchestration of *Mireille* and have a lot to do, too!" [n]

By the time Bizet had finished his score early in August, new problems confronted him. His publisher was reluctant to sign a contract for *Les Pêcheurs de Perles*. Antoine de Choudens (he felt as strongly about the "de" in his name as did Honoré de Balzac), the grandson of Antonio Francesco Pacini, Rossini's early publisher, had entered the family business at the age of twelve. Married at seventeen, he started his own firm when he was only eighteen, and built up a successful business that collapsed in the Revolution of 1848. The road back to solvency was slow, and not until he published the score of Gounod's *Faust* did he again make money on a large scale. His contract with Gounod became legendary. At the time of the initial unpopularity of the work, the flat 15,000 francs Choudens paid Gounod appeared generous. But the publisher retained all profits from the sale of scores and sheet music, which paid him fabulously well.

Years later, when *Faust* was established in the repertory and Choudens was still profiting by the sale of the music, Gounod came to call on him one day, wearing a very worn and shabby hat. "Why, Master, should such a famous man wear a hat like that?" Choudens asked. "I have to," Gounod answered. "It's my *Faust* hat."

Shortly afterwards, Choudens returned Gounod's visit to commiserate with him on the failure of his latest opera *Le Tribut de Zamora,* the score of which Choudens had also published.

Choudens then wore a hat even shabbier than Gounod's, and when the composer remarked on it, the publisher replied, "This is my *Zamora* hat."

The specter of *Faust* stalked the Choudens household. For, as Antony Choudens, the younger son and a devoted pupil of Bizet, told his teacher, whenever he and his older brother, Paul, were naughty as children, their father could immediately make them behave by threatening to take them to see *Faust* again.

Choudens *père* was brusque in manner, but hospitable. He gave frequent parties at which the guests, many of them musicians, played cards and billiards. Music was his business, and Choudens never pretended any interest in the purely artistic side of the works he published. When he was awarded only a bronze medal at one of the Universal Expositions, a friend expressed his astonishment. Choudens replied, "It is not surprising. After all, I gave myself the gold medal years ago!"

Choudens's delay in signing the contract for *Les Pêcheurs de Perles* intensified Bizet's nervousness during the rehearsals of his first opera. And when a notice in the gossip column of *Le Ménestrel*, a paper owned by the rival publisher, Heugel, stated that Bizet's opera was the "property" of Choudens, the composer was outraged. "I by no means asked M. Heugel to insert the notice about me in his paper," he wrote to Choudens. "If anyone was untruthful in this business, it is you who let it be thought, who even said, that you had bought my score. I have witnesses. . . . You didn't offer me 500 frs. for it. That my music should be antipathetic to you *va bene*. I shall try to console myself. Let that go.—You seem for some time to have been irritated with me. Why? Yesterday you didn't come to shake hands with me. Why? . . . Don't consider yourself in any way bound by our conversation, but I would be very sorry to have our relation broken off without understanding your behavior. . . . I am waiting for news from you and, if you please, I am always yours, Georges Bizet." "

Choudens huffed and puffed his reply at nine o'clock on the morning of August 26. "Your letter surprises and amazes me," he wrote. "Where have I publicly talked of your work, which I don't know, and which it is impossible to understand or estimate after hearing only one incomplete performance of a few excerpts?

"Why, after the evidences of friendship I have always given you, would I do harm to your score which I am committed to publishing? . . .

"I have nothing urgent on hand at the moment and I am quite willing to wait to see you as long as you find it necessary.

"I can only repeat that I did not expect to receive a letter such as the one you sent me." [n]

Meanwhile, readers of *Le Ménestrel* were informed that "the statement that M. Choudens had secured the rights to *Les Pêcheurs de Perles* was an error. M. Georges Bizet, author of the score, has the honor of informing the editors that that announcement is completely inaccurate."

Rehearsals of *Les Pêcheurs de Perles* began early in August. The locale of the opera had been changed from Mexico to Ceylon; the libretto remained unfinished until a few days before the opening. The librettists seem never to have heard the music until the final orchestral rehearsals. One of them, Eugène Cormon (pseudonym for Pierre-Etienne Piestre), author of some two hundred stage pieces, one hundred and seventy-seven of which were written in collaboration with other authors, remarked that had he and Carré realized Bizet's talent, they would never have given him "that white elephant." Their banal book, which imitated *La Vestale* and *Norma,* has as heroine Leïla, a sacred virgin who breaks her vows for love. Until a fortnight before the scheduled opening, *Leïla* was also the title of the opera. Carré, who seems to have been in charge of the plot, was unable to decide how to terminate the third act, which satisfied no one. During rehearsals he kept asking for suggestions, until finally Carvalho said to him one day, "Throw it in the fire." This remark was literally transposed into the action of the opera which ends with a fire being set to the pearl fishers' tents so that Leïla and her lover Nadir can escape. As a last-minute notion, Zurga, Nadir's rival, was killed. Numerous changes during rehearsal were predictable in any work directed by Carvalho, whom Gounod called the "Zouave" of directors.

Léon Carvalho, whose real name was Carvaille, was born on the island of Mauritius around 1825. Like many other French colonials, he was suspected of having mixed blood. During his difficulties with Reyer over the production of *La Statue,* the com-

poser remarked to a friend: "Carvalho has all the defects of the
mulatto and none of the virtues of the Negro." [n] But whatever
his faults, Carvalho was by far the most enlightened impresario of
his day, more civilized than Roqueplan or Véron, more imaginative than Perrin, and, until he became director of the Opéra-
Comique in 1877, more daring than du Locle. As a young man,
after studying at the Conservatoire, he sang at the Opéra-
Comique, where he was a failure. Offered the directorship of the
Comique at that time, he refused it in order to found the Théâtre-
Lyrique.

He himself had no passion for the new music. He preferred
the works of Auber, Hérold, and Clapisson, the last perhaps because he provided the first great success of the Théâtre-Lyrique,
La Fanchonette, in which Carvalho's wife, Caroline Miolan, sang
the leading role. But Carvalho's personal taste for traditional light
music did not lessen his enjoyment in sponsoring and encouraging the works of young composers. At the Opéra and the
Comique they were treated like beggars, made to wait for hours,
often without being granted an interview. But Carvalho made it
a practice to welcome them cordially and himself see them out
to the top of the stairs. His charm and amiability were outstanding.
But these qualities were insufficient to sustain his composers and
authors through the nervous strain he engendered by the perpetual changes he demanded during rehearsals. Wagner and
Berlioz, as well as Flaubert, whose plays he produced, all started
out enraptured by his charm, his enthusiasm, his perceptiveness,
only to end in exasperation at his insistence on leaving the mark
of his own frustrated creative urge on their creations. Saint-Saëns
speaks of his "mania" for changing any work he presented, ancient
or modern. For *Così fan tutte* he commissioned a new libretto
based on Shakespeare's *Love's Labour's Lost.* In an original work
he would insist that the authors shift the period or the background or the country in which the action took place. He wanted
a dancer's part changed to a singer's so that his wife could play
the rôle. At the rehearsals of Saint-Saëns's *Le Timbre d'argent*
(piano reduction by Bizet), Carvalho would one day wish to introduce wild animals into a dream sequence; on another he would
decide that all the music except for choruses and ballet should be
cut. He was horrified when Massenet, obviously to avoid any
tinkering with his work, gave him for use in rehearsals of *Manon*

a complete score of the work, engraved and bound. "My friend," the director said to the composer, "your work will be performed as though you were already dead."

The only fault Carvalho admitted, the one he called his besetting sin, was his love of good food and wine. His guests were royally entertained at table and served with wine bought in Pauillac, despatched to Mauritius, and returned to Paris because he believed that it was improved by a sea voyage. Unlike Roqueplan, who was also a gourmet, Carvalho adored the country and spent as much time as possible at his châlet near Dieppe, overlooking the sea, near the villa of his friend, the younger Dumas. An enthusiastic gardener, he took great pride in showing off the trees and flowers he planted with his own hands.

Carvalho's most admirable quality, rarely found in a Frenchman of his day, was also the most self-destructive: he lacked any ambition to acquire wealth. Money for him was primarily the medium necessary to the production of new works in the theatre. He was always hopelessly in debt. The state subsidy of 100,000 francs granted him in June 1863, on the strength of which he had undertaken to put on *Les Pêcheurs de Perles* and part of Berlioz's *Les Troyens,* was not due to be paid until January 1864. The winter season of 1863 was therefore crucial for him and for his composers. With the rehearsals of *Les Pêcheurs de Perles* still in full swing and the readings of Berlioz's work just begun, Carvalho opened the Théâtre-Lyrique on September 1 with *Le Nozze di Figaro.* His wife sang Cherubino. "No words can express such talent, such charm, such artistry!" wrote Ludovic Halévy. "Cherubino's song, sung, murmured, sighed by Mme Carvalho surpasses anything else."

A week later, Carvalho gave a triple bill consisting of Reyer's *La Statue,* Grétry's *L'Epreuve Villageoise,* and Méhul's *Joseph.* This triple bill scandalized the critics, who attacked Carvalho for unnecessary financial recklessness. The performance of *La Statue* was so poor that two months later Reyer sued Carvalho to force its removal from the repertory. *Les Pêcheurs de Perles* was to have had its *première* on September 14 but it was postponed to the 20th because of the illness of the Leïla, Léontine de Maësen, who had still not entirely recovered on the opening night.

Nevertheless, the applause at the end of the performance was most enthusiastic. Bizet responded to it by appearing on stage with the singers, "a little dazed. His head was lowered and revealed only a forest of thick, curly, fair hair above a round, still rather childish face, enlivened, however, by the quick bright eyes that took in the whole audience with a delighted but embarrassed look." The composer's appearance on stage elicited almost as much disapproval from the press as did the unfortunate libretto. Indeed, one critic claimed that without the private claque of Bizet's friends scattered through the audience there would have been no ovation. This is quite untrue. But had there been a personal claque, it would have been no ordinary venal group. A member of the audience at the *première* was struck by the fact that, "although he was then only a glorified schoolboy ready for the great test . . . he was already treated like a master; and the elite among those young men who . . . would also become masters pointed him out to me as their chief, who would show them the way and lead the new young school of French music to its glorious destiny. And this opinion was unanimous. I cannot remember hearing a discordant note in the chorus of universal praise that was raised around his name. . . . To know him was enough to explain this phenomenon. In the man himself there were such rare and charming qualities that one forgave the artist his disturbing superiority." ⁿ

Bizet's inner awareness of his value and his potentialities as an artist probably irritated the press. For if one were to strain through a sieve the many thousands of words written by critics of *Les Pêcheurs de Perles,* eliminating the personal prejudices of the writers and their infatuation with their own witticisms, leaving only the actual opinions of the music, the residuum would not be unduly harsh or mistaken. The shocking thing is the violence of their tone, their obvious resentment against youth and originality, the assumption that it is their duty to criticize not only a man's music, but his manners and morals as well.

"We will make a little observation," wrote the critic of *Le Ménestrel,* "which has to do not with his talent, but with his tact and modesty. There was general surprise at seeing him come on stage to greet the audience at the end of the work. With us this sort of exhibition is admissible only for a most extraordinary success, and even then we prefer to have the composer dragged on in spite of himself, or at least pretending to be."

Johannès Weber of *Le Temps* was even more carping: "In

announcing the names of the authors at the end of the piece, M. Ismaël added to M. Bizet's name 'Prix de Rome for the year 1857.' Of what interest is that to the public? When *Les Troyens* is given, will they say M. Berlioz, Prix de Rome for 1830, Knight of the Legion of Honor, Member of the Institut, Librarian of the Conservatoire, etc., etc? . . . If the claque has the impudence to demand M. Berlioz's appearance to pay his respects to them, he will be at pains to vanish. . . . But M. Bizet was forced to appear on stage.

"Oh, friends, *claqueurs,* clumsy, intriguing, nauseating climbers! This was not the first time that I was seized by the desire to write my own treatise on *De Amicitia,* which would differ tremendously from Cicero's."

In the *Figaro,* Jouvin wrote: "There were neither fishermen in the libretto nor pearls in the music. . . . M. Georges Bizet, as a beginner, was condemned to accept gratefully the libretto of *Les Pêcheurs de Perles.* . . . He has great assurance in the way he deals with the orchestra and mass vocal effects. . . . But *Les Pêcheurs de Perles* betrays on every page, along with the talent of the composer, the bias of a school to which he belongs, that of Richard Wagner. Everything M. Bizet has written spontaneously bears the hallmark of really estimable virtues. The rest is written by a disciple with his eyes on the Master. . . . M. Bizet, I hasten to add, is far from being altogether a Wagnerite. . . . I know him to be intelligent enough to season his admiration. . . ." After recounting Bizet's remarks about Wagner made the previous year at Baden, Jouvin concludes: "I have no desire to harm the newcomer for whom, on the contrary, I feel a very lively sympathy. . . . But I must say to him, like Léopold to Rachel, 'Thy God is not my God.' "

Gustave Bertrand noted in *Le Ménestrel* the influence of Gounod and Félicien David on *Les Pêcheurs de Perles.* Gounod's influence was, of course, inevitable and Bizet undoubtedly had learned something from David's work. "David," he said, "is a mirror that reflects the Orient admirably. He went there. What he saw impressed him strongly, and he renders it very well. What he does ordinarily is feeble. But give him a text about the Orient in which the words palm tree, minaret, camel, etc., appear, and he does some very nice things." [n]

Bertrand also found in Bizet's opera "a feeble imitation of

the funeral march in *La Juive*" as well as "shocking and violent effects worthy of the new Italian school," meaning, of course, Verdi. "There is too much shrieking in the score of *Les Pêcheurs de Perles*. . . . Nevertheless," he admits, "there is talent floating in the midst of all these regrettable imitations, and one feels that one is dealing with a musician capable of a striking revenge. His greatest mistake is preoccupation with too many celebrated works and the failure to make sufficient demands on his own personal inspiration."

Bizet was far less distressed by the reviews than were his friends. For the only critic whose opinion he valued, Hector Belioz, devoted his final review in the *Journal des Débats* to *Les Pêcheurs de Perles:*

"The score of this opera had a real success," Berlioz wrote. "It includes a considerable number of beautiful, expressive pieces full of fire and rich coloring. There is no overture, but an introduction sung and danced with great verve and spirit. The duet that follows, '*Au fond du temple saint*' is well carried out in a simple and sober style. The chorus for the arrival of Leïla seemed rather ordinary, but the one that follows is, on the contrary, majestic and pompous in a remarkably harmonious way. Much of Nadir's aria, with its obbligato accompaniment of violoncellos and horn, is praiseworthy; besides, Morini sang it delightfully. We must mention also a pretty chorus sung in the wings and a triple-rhythm passage in which a violin solo produces an original effect. I like less Leïla's aria on the mountain. It is accompanied by a chorus with the kind of rhythm one dares no longer write today. Another aria of Leïla's, with a horn solo, is full of grace; the intervention of a group of three wind instruments introduced and re-introduced superlatively well produced a ravishingly original effect. There are fullness and fine dramatic movement in Nadir's and Leïla's duet, '*Ton coeur n'a pas compris le mien.*'

"I would reproach the composer only for having abused in this duet the device of doubling the voices in octaves. The chief's aria in the third act has character; Leïla's prayer is touching. It would be even more so without the exercise in vocalization, which to my mind spoils the beauty of the end.

"M. Bizet, laureate of the Institut, took the journey to Rome; he has come back without having forgotten the nature of music. Since his return to Paris, he has rapidly acquired the very rare special reputation of an incomparable reader of scores. His talent as a pianist also is great enough so that, in his transcriptions of orchestra music, which he does at sight, no mechanical difficulty can stop him. . . . The score of *Les Pêcheurs de Perles* does M. Bizet the greatest honor, and he will have to be recognized as a composer in spite of his rare talent as a pianist." "

Among his contemporaries Bizet's first work was discerningly appreciated. Gounod, whose wife had presented him with a daughter early in September, came to a rehearsal, but could not attend the opening, as by that time he was recovering at Dr. Blanche's sanitorium from another of his periodic nervous breakdowns. Ludovic Halévy wrote, after hearing *Les Pêcheurs de Perles:* "The music represents the theatrical debut of Georges Bizet, grand Prix de Rome for 1857. Bizet must be 26 or 28 years old.[2] Bear this name well in mind. It is that of a musician. . . . The score is of a superior quality. There is in this first work an assurance, a calm, an easy, powerful handling of the choruses and the orchestra which certainly announce a composer. . . . The score is already greatly criticized, widely discussed. After listening to the work seriously three times, I persist in finding in it the rarest virtues." "

To Bizet's fellow Prix de Rome, Guiraud and Emile Paladilhe, who lived close by him in the rue Fontaine Saint-Georges, the performance of a three-act work by their friend and contemporary had a double significance. Bizet's opera "had a fine and very well-deserved success . . ." young Paladilhe wrote to his father. "This score is very remarkable and far superior (between ourselves) to anything Auber, Thomas, Clapisson, etc., are doing today. If this work had not succeeded, we Prix de Rome would have been completely ruined. As things now stand, Carvalho . . . is enchanted by this success, and has told Bizet and Gounod (secretly) that he had not wanted to play the works of the Prix de Rome who returned to Paris before Bizet; that he had made inquiries and found that all these young men were without talent; that he was going to try to shelve Samuel David and play Guiraud and then me, as he had heard good things about me. You see that our position as Prix de Rome is not too bad just now." "

---

[2] Actually he had not yet passed his twenty-fifth birthday.

Les Pêcheurs de Perles alternated with *Le Nozze di Figaro* for eighteen performances, the last of which was given on November 23. It was not played again until eleven years after Bizet's death. Although the opera was not a financial success, Carvalho appreciated Bizet's talent sufficiently to commission him immediately to finish or rewrite *Ivan IV* as soon as possible. And on October 11 an announcement in *Le Ménestrel* put an end to the controversy in its columns about the publication of the score. "It is definitely Choudens," the notice read, "who is still the publisher of *Les Pêcheurs de Perles,* as we announced in the first place. We congratulate the author of this score, the beauty of which the public appreciates more and more every evening. The superior performance of this work . . . would be enough to warrant its success, but in all fairness the composer can claim his own fine and splendid share."

The next opera to be given at the Théâtre-Lyrique was part of Berlioz's *Les Troyens.* The performance of this work, based on Virgil's *Aeneid,* was the climax of some five years of agonizing postponement for the great composer. The opera is divided into two parts, *The Fall of Troy* and *The Trojans in Carthage,* and requires five hours to perform. Carvalho presented only the second part, and this dismemberment of the work was only the beginning of a series of further amputations which caused Berlioz great distress. The theatre was too small for so tremendous a work; the singers, the chorus, and the orchestra were inadequate. Berlioz paid the essential extra musicians himself, and the artist who sang Dido's part accepted far less salary than she would have been paid elsewhere. The scenery, "which Carvalho insisted upon arranging, was quite unlike what I had directed," Berlioz wrote. "It was absurd . . . and ridiculous. . . . On the opening night, the scene-shifter nearly spoiled everything and upset the whole piece by his clumsiness in the hunting-scene. . . . I cannot describe the way in which Carvalho, while protesting that he wished only to conform to my wishes, positively tortured me into giving my consent to the cuts he thought necessary. . . ." [n] Aeneas could not wear a helmet because Mangin, a beggar who sold pencils in the street, wore one, and if Aeneas appeared helmeted, the gallery might shout, "Hello, here's Mangin!"

Musically, Carvalho's ideas were even more devastating. He

directed the singers with no regard for the music, and thought nothing of asking Berlioz to alter the tempos, to add or suppress measures to suit the stage business he had contrived. "At the dress rehearsal on November 2, the preparation was visibly inadequate. Though some passages were magnificently sung . . . many others required constant aid from the prompter. . . . The bulky scenery on which the producer counted so heavily made the show last from eight o'clock to half past twelve." [n] But neither the lateness of the hour nor the lack of integration in the production dampened the ardor of one member of the small, invited audience. Bizet, immediately after the dress rehearsal, wrote Reyer, in Germany, a long, enthusiastic account of the music.

On the opening night, November 4, the singers forgot their parts, lost their places, and floundered about. The intervals lasted fifty-five minutes. During one of them, the gallery expressed its impatience or disapproval of Berlioz's music by chanting the Soldiers' Chorus from *Faust*. Berlioz, fortunately, was not too much distressed by the demonstration.

"My friends and I expected a stormy evening and all sorts of hostile demonstrations," he wrote, "but nothing of the kind happened. My enemies dared not show themselves; a solitary hiss was heard at the end, when I was called for, and that was all. . . ." [n]

Although his enemies may have stayed away, many members of the audience failed to show either tolerance or sympathy for the man himself and for the illness and suffering he had endured. Nor were they moved by the amazing beauty of the music. "Yesterday they performed those Trojans, those famous Trojans, those Trojans who for the last ten years have been proclaimed as a masterpiece by the friends of M. Berlioz and by M. Berlioz himself, especially by M. Berlioz . . ." wrote Ludovic Halévy in his journal. "The theatre was full of fanatics crying 'Bravo, Bravo, Sublime!' during the first acts. This enthusiasm died down into a calm and fell away at the end." [n]

Among the most articulate of the irrepressible fanatics was Bizet. His vociferous calls for the author on the opening night, his "bravos" at succeeding performances of *Les Troyens,* his belligerent defense of Berlioz in any gathering he attended, nearly involved him in a duel. Victor Chéri the challenger, may well have been somewhat inebriated when he scrawled the following communication: "Sir, I have just heard that in a house you frequent, and where naturally I am unknown, you permitted yourself in connection with one of those musical platitudes that you call your works, to remark that it was as much like Auber as the sublime *Troyens* was like—'oh, what's its name?'—*Turlurette!* But, M. Biset [*sic*] (Georges), I am, and you know very well that I am, the ridiculed although popular author of this tune, which I recognize at its true worth. I have promised myself as well as my friends who were good enough to report your platitudes to try to find the occasion to correct you.

"The occasion is quite naturally here today when there is a performance of *Les Troyens,* which you relish—those other fishermen of who knows what. Well, if you are unfortunate enough to shout for this Berlioz, your fetish, and to repeat your scandalous and ridiculous behavior, I shall regard it as a personal affront. And if you have a behind, I shall have boots! (And they won't be soft!)

"If you are prudent enough to remain silent, and if you refrain from expressing the slightest approval, I shall see the expression of one who repents, who knows his age, and who regrets behavior that I leave to your judgment. I salute you. Victor Chéri. Orchestra Director of the Variétés." "

The author of this inflammatory and inflamed document had started his career as a child actor in the company of his older and better-known sister, Rose Chéri. Although not untalented musically, he was refused admittance to the Conservatoire, and for several years had difficulty in finding work even in a small orchestra. He became a pupil of Pasdeloup and a protégé of Gounod, who called him "a boy whom I like for every possible reason—heart, talent, intelligence, wit." "

"Sent two seconds to V. Chéri," Bizet scrawled across the challenge. "(Nephtali Mayrargues and Ernest Guiraud). V. Chéri gave his word of honor that he had nothing to do with this dastardly action."

The violent controversy evoked by *Les Troyens* stimulated sufficient interest on the part of the public to keep the theatre reasonably well filled for the twenty-one performances following the *première,* even though Carvalho charged a higher admission price. Admirers like Bizet went more than once. "Meyerbeer was present night after night, 'for my pleasure,' he said, 'and my instruction.' " Corot became a devotee, knew the score by heart, and sang it at his easel. *Les Troyens* earned enough money to save the Théâtre-Lyrique for the time being, and Berlioz's own share, amounting to fifty thousand francs, enabled him to give up his labors as critic on the *Journal des Débats.*

For the younger musicians, however, the end of the year was less encouraging. Bizet, of course, had his commission from Carvalho to finish *Ivan IV.* But the date for the production was not set. The young composers, hopeful of seeing their work staged at the Opéra-Comique or the Opéra, again had reason to be pessimistic. Emile Paladilhe, encouraged by the seeming success of *Les Pêcheurs de Perles,* went to call on de Leuven, director of the Comique, soon after the government had issued an edict granting freedom, so-called, to the theatres. " 'In the last two days,' " de Leuven told the young man, " 'the Ministry has laid open great opportunities to young composers by granting them the freedom of the theatres. This leaves us a single policy to follow, which is to produce only the works of *established composers.* The same holds true for the Opéra.' I left in a rage," Paladilhe continues, "because I thought he was pulling my leg. So then I went to find C. Doucet.[3] I told him the story as though de Leuven had invented an excuse for not playing a work of mine. But imagine my astonishment when Doucet said, 'He is right. *Moreover the Minister has forbidden him to play a single piece by a beginner.*' And he added, 'You have nothing left but the Théâtre-Lyrique, which is subsidized to present annually three acts by a Prix de Rome. Those who have not won it will never be played. What is called the freedom of the theatres means the right of any individual to build a theatre and to stage whatever he likes in it.' . . . The Théâtre-Lyrique has about ten prizewinners to play before it plays us. And as they want to liquidate those arrears, we can look forward to being produced in ten or twelve years." [n]

In any light then, Bizet was better off than his contemporaries. If *Les Pêcheurs de Perles* was a failure, at least he had had the advantage of performance. He himself said in retrospect that the opera was "very much discussed, attacked, defended—a failure in short, honorable and brilliant, if I may use that expression, but nevertheless a failure." [n]

---

[3] Camille Doucet was Director-General of State Theatres.

CHAPTER  XI

Meyerbeer: Galabert: *Ivan IV*

However honorable and brilliant the failure of *Les Pêcheurs de Perles* may have been, it hardly served as challenge or stimulus to Bizet's creative faculties. In 1864, when not occupied giving lessons, doing hack-work for publishers, and serving as accompanist at rehearsals of various kinds, he managed to do some work on *Ivan IV*. With Guiraud he alternated as pianist at the rehearsals of the soloists for the performance of Berlioz's *L'Enfance du Christ*, directed by the composer himself, early in April. He and Saint-Saëns supplied the accompaniment on the piano and harmonium for an audition of *Mireille* at Gounod's house.

The leading parts were sung by Gounod himself and the Vicomtesse de Grandval, a lady Bizet frequently encountered during the next few years. Although today Mme de Grandval's descendants are unaware of their ancestor's musical gifts, she wrote scores for a number of one-act operas produced at the Comique which were quite as accomplished as many works by her professional competitors.[1] Although not a trained singer, she seems to have had the qualities needed for a successful portrayal of the role of Mireille. Both performers and guests at the audition expected an immediate success for the work.

The opening night, March 19, when Mme Miolan-Carvalho sang the title role, was therefore a great disappointment. This star had forced Gounod to rewrite her part so many times during rehearsals that much of its original charm was lost. The audience

---

[1] Mme de Grandval presented Bizet with an inscribed copy of her *Messe*. The scores of several of her other works are included in Bizet's music library.

applauded the first act enthusiastically. But the rest of the opera seemed to Ludovic Halévy "gloomy, dismal and ineffectual," an opinion concurred in by most of the critics, apart from Gounod's personal friends. One member of the press, irrelevantly but not unpredictably, accused Gounod of "flirting with Wagnerism, of systematically manipulating dissonances, harmonic lags, and other chemical brews from the laboratory of *Tannhäuser* and *Lohengrin.*"

Gounod's failure was soon followed by the success of a work closer to Bizet's heart than *Mireille. Sylvie,* a one-act operetta composed by Guiraud while he was still in Rome, had its *première* at the Opéra-Comique on May 11 before an audience that liked the little piece, encored two of the songs, and agreed that its composer showed wit, restraint and taste.

While this miniscule work was in rehearsal, a major event shook the foundations of the musical world—the death of Giacomo Meyerbeer on May 2 at the age of seventy-one. The public of today, which rarely, if ever, sees Meyerbeer's works performed, finds it difficult to understand the exalted and influential position he occupied during his lifetime and for many years after his death. When Bizet, writing from Rome, places Meyerbeer in the same category as Beethoven and Michelangelo, he seems to be expressing the exaggerated judgment of a young musician who confuses success with popularity and genius with skill. But greater and more experienced composers than Bizet, rivals of Meyerbeer, expressed equally startling opinions of his work. If in his later years Berlioz remarked that Meyerbeer not only had the luck to be talented, but the talent to be lucky; if he wrote that "Meyerbeer's influence, and the pressure exercised by his immense fortune, no less than by his *genuine* eclectic talent, on managers, artists, critics and public alike, have rendered any serious success at the Opéra almost impossible," he had expressed himself quite differently after first hearing *Les Huguenots* in 1836: "The effervescence of emotion excited by this masterpiece makes one long to be a great man in order to place one's glory and one's genius at the feet of Meyerbeer." [n] And even a quarter of a century later, Berlioz found the score of *Le Pardon de Ploërmel* (*Dinorah*), which bored Bizet, "ingenious, subtle, piquant and often poetic." [n] Wagner, who repaid Meyerbeer's friendship with more than his usual ingratitude, wrote: "This last epoch of dramatic art has ended with Meyerbeer.

. . . Like Gluck, Mozart, and Beethoven, in turn, he, too, achieved the ideal of his period; it is no longer possible to surpass him." More succinctly than any of Meyerbeer's fellow composers, Théophile Gautier defines the essence of his power. "Apart from his outstanding musical gifts," wrote Gautier, "Meyerbeer possesses to the highest degree an instinct for the theatre. He is pervaded by the plot, he identifies himself with the meaning of the words, he adheres to the historic and local color of his subject." "

A generation unfamiliar with the works of Meyerbeer may assume that the operatic clichés common to Verdi, Bizet, Gounod, and the early Wagner were spontaneously created by them. But an audience that knew Meyerbeer's operas recognized their common origin. Bertram in *Robert le Diable,* says a modern critic, "is the father of all the operatic devils of the nineteenth century. . . . Berlioz would never have written the *Marche au supplice* without Meyerbeer's example, and the Mephistos of Gounod's opera and Liszt's *Faust* symphony come from the same stock." " In the quarrel scene between the Montagues and Capulets in the third act of Gounod's *Roméo et Juliette;* in the first act of *Carmen,* when the cigarette girls denounce Carmen to Zuniga, the debt to the chorus of the rival factions in the third act of *Les Huguenots* has been noted. Curiously enough, Meyerbeer was one of the few composers whose influence contemporary critics failed to find in *Les Pêcheurs de Perles.* Yet the overall quality of the work, its emphasis on situation rather than character, its attempted grandiosity, derived more from Meyerbeer than from Wagner. *Ivan IV,* too, falls into this category. The impact of Meyerbeer's music on the works of both his contemporaries and his immediate followers is undeniable. "One portion of our little musical world, the one I belong to, is melancholy," wrote Berlioz, "the other is glad because Meyerbeer is dead."

He died after only a week of an illness that had seemed not at all serious. "I saw him barely a month ago, at one of the dress rehearsals for the last revival of *Les Huguenots* with Mlle Saxe," Ludovic Halévy noted in his journal. "For the last month Meyerbeer spent his time in the lyric theatres. You saw him at the Opéra, at the Opéra-Comique, at the Italiens, at the Théâtre-Lyrique. He seemed determined to present his long-awaited and long-deferred *L'Africaine* this winter. [2] The copyists from the Opéra

---

[2] Meyerbeer started composing *L'Africaine* in 1838 and finished it in 1863.

went to his house every day and had already copied a large part of the opera. He supervised the work himself with the care and the passion that he brought to everything that had to do with his art. . . . He was alone in Paris when he died. Louis Brandies, his business manager, stayed with him throughout his illness. Saturday, when he saw that Meyerbeer was growing seriously worse, Brandies suggested notifying Mme Meyerbeer. 'No, no,' Meyerbeer replied, 'it would be pointless. I am not that sick. Besides,' he added, 'it is impossible to be a universal man. You must be either a family man or a worker. I have been a worker. Do not notify my family.' A man of work he certainly was. No one deserves the title more. He was preoccupied with what he had done, and after what he had done, with what he would do. He nursed his fame with indefatigable zeal. He maintained the public interest with his continually promised, continually postponed *L'Africaine*. He subsidized the critics. He went alone to see his works, sitting at the back of a little box. He would arrive on time for the first act and leave only after the last note. He had but one thought—his music, again his music, and always his music. After Meyerbeer was dead they found under his pillow a little notebook in which he had written in pencil in a trembling handwriting: 'To be opened after my death.' This notebook contained the following instructions: 'I am to be left lying on my deathbed with my face uncovered four days. My legs and arms are to be bled. After the four days have elapsed, I am to be taken to Berlin and to be buried in my family tomb. My will is not to be read until Berlin.' . . . Only his acquaintances were aware that his greatest fear was of being buried alive.

"Meyerbeer's remains were taken with great ceremony from the Rond Point des Champs-Elysées to the Gare du Nord. There, in front of the railway carriage waiting to carry the body to Berlin, six or seven eulogies were pronounced—a ridiculous one by Saint-Georges, a mediocre one by Beulé, and a very neat one by Perrin, claiming *L'Africaine* as the property of the Opéra." [n]

Emile Olivier, member of the Chamber of Deputies and future premier, friend of Wagner and Liszt, "declared in the best official style that Meyerbeer's music . . . had forged a bond that linked 'the fatherland of Beethoven, Mozart, and Meyerbeer with that of Hérold, Halévy, and Auber.' " [n] The last, as head of the delegation from the Institut, followed the family in the procession to the mourning-draped station, where a band played excerpts from *Robert le Diable* and *Le Prophète*. Second in line was the delegation of composers and dramatic writers with which Bizet, Guiraud, and Paladilhe marched.

Soon after Meyerbeer's funeral, Bizet moved to the country to live, for the first time, on the property his father had bought three days after the opening of *Les Pêcheurs de Perles*. For the sum of 3800 francs, Adolphe Bizet had acquired just under an acre of land at Le Vésinet, about twelve miles from Paris. Until a few years earlier this land had been a state forest. But with the introduction of the railroad the woodland was split up into small lots to be sold with the inducement of a three-year free railroad pass to any landholder who built on his property. Immediately after his purchase, Adolphe Bizet started the construction of two small cottages. They stood at either end of a garden shaded by ancient trees and enclosed in an iron grilled fence. The cottage on the right as one entered from the garden contained the kitchen, dining-room, and Adolphe Bizet's bedroom. Georges's cottage consisted of one room, longer than it was wide and barely large enough to hold a piano, three chairs, a table, and a small cupboard. His bed- and dressing-room was curtained off at the back. In front of the cottages a lawn was planted and clumps of bushes set out. In the back, Georges's father made a vegetable garden, which included an asparagus bed and strawberry patch. The fruit was one of Bizet's delights. To Galabert, who remembered helping him pick them before an *al fresco* dinner, he wrote: "Decidedly the garnering of lucre disrupts the head and the heart. I prefer my strawberries, my worries, and my creditors."

Edmond Galabert, who became, with Guiraud, Bizet's most trusted friend, first visited Le Vésinet in the spring of 1865, brought by Lécuyer, a singer and former pupil of Bizet's father. A young man just Bizet's age, Galabert journeyed to Paris for a month every year from his home in Montauban, where his father was a winegrower. With more passion than talent for music, he was quiet, modest, and serious. To the utmost degree he embodied the qualities Bizet required in friendship: loyalty, sincerity, and a capacity for unquestioning devotion. Galabert was more studious than Guiraud, but less light-hearted. Conscientious about his work, in contrast to Guiraud's laziness and procrastination, Galabert, too, had the passive, non-competitive, non-challenging nature essential to the continual reassurance of Bizet's self-confidence.

Before accepting his new pupil, Bizet put him through a serious oral examination. Although Galabert knew some harmony, Bizet examined him chiefly on the subject of literature. And when Galabert spoke of a number of French and foreign authors he had read, mentioning particularly Goethe and Schiller, Bizet said: "That settles it. People think you don't have to be well-read to be a musician. They are wrong. You must, on the contrary, have a very broad knowledge of things." [3] The lessons in counterpoint started immediately, and when Galabert returned to Montauban at the end of one month, he took with him twenty songs Bizet had annotated for the first lesson by correspondence. Later he sent his pupil the texts of several cantatas used in past Prix de Rome competitions. When Galabert again came north a year later, he brought with him the fully orchestrated score of a cantata called *Imogine,* which Bizet had him play for Guiraud one day when the three of them were lunching together at Le Vésinet. "I wanted Guiraud to hear your cantata," Bizet explained, "so he could give me his opinion of it. I knew what I thought, but I might have been mistaken, and I didn't want you to go on working if it was useless."

Bizet's conscientious criticism of Galabert's efforts, which continued by mail for several years, stemmed more from his affection as a friend than from any illusions about his pupil's talent. At the end of three or four years, when Galabert decided to abandon the idea of coming to Paris to pursue a musical career, Bizet wrote: "Your decision is as good for your spiritual as for your physical health. . . . Live out of doors, cultivate your vines, .work, and raise the moral standards of your community. Picture where we would be in twenty years if there were a hundred agriculturists of your caliber in every department of France.—What you have done is not lost! You have provided yourself with a kind of enjoyment that will seem all the more rewarding in contrast to your ordinary occupations. Music will keep your nervous system sensitive and farming will strengthen your muscles. You can exert your influence over a certain number of men, and you will be conscious of the

---

[3] Georges Bizet, *Lettres à un ami,* intro. by Edmond Galabert, Paris, 1909, 5. Subsequent unidentified quotations in this chapter are from this work. Unpublished portions of the letters are enclosed in square brackets.

good you are doing every day. From the point of view of human progress you will accomplish a hundred times more than you would in this wearing, enervating, and, alas, often futile struggle. . . ."

Bizet obviously appreciated Galabert's simple moral goodness, his balance and steadfastness; his correspondence with the provincial vintner, so removed from the procrastination, dishonesty, and intrigue of the theatre, served as a relief from tension. The question of fees was not mentioned until a year after the lessons started. Then Bizet cut Galabert short. "Don't ever mention that to me again," he said. "I accept money for lessons because they bore me; people don't understand that I take trouble about them. You and I just talk about things that interest us, that we love. We swim in the same waters. I have been at it longer than you. I know the bad places and I only say to you: 'Don't go there, it's dangerous.' " Actually Galabert paid for his lessons by supplying Bizet through the years with wine from his father's Montauban vineyards. The details of this arrangement, which occupy a large part of their correspondence, were omitted in publication by Galabert, who seems to have regarded this barter as a possible reflection on his master's memory.

The effort Bizet put into his more mundanely remunerated lessons is evident in the fragments of a series of outlines that he wrote out for children's classes. They were not to be read aloud, he notes, but to be spoken naturally. Lessons 1, 3, 10, and 12 remain among his private papers, a sad commentary on the inadequacy of his financial resources, for the instruction offered in these outlines was available in any elementary textbook. How many *Jeux d'enfants* were lost in the hours Bizet spent copying out these lessons for children?

"1. You will learn, my children, to read music," the series begins. "For the tunes of the music that you sing or hear sung can be written as easily as you write the words. 2. Let us open our music books. What do we see there? Some lines drawn in fives, and on these lines different kinds of marks. 3. Each of these lines is called a stave and the chief marks that you see on the stave are called: notes, rests, clefs, and accidentals. 4. The notes are used to write the sounds. 5. The rests, as the name implies, are used to replace the notes when the voice or the instrument must be interrupted or silent. . . ." And so forth and so on.

Bizet also worked during 1865 on the first two volumes of

Le Pianiste chanteur, a five-volume series of piano arrangements of operatic songs and arias; a piano solo transcription of Gounod's "*Ave Maria*," and a new edition of some of the Thalberg variations. These were all published by Heugel, "a very gentle, very shrewd, gracious man, hospitable and eager to please, emanating self-satisfaction while also taking an interest in the satisfaction of others." ⁿ Heugel paid 2100 francs for *Le Pianiste chanteur*. "I do not think such a collection of piano pieces has ever been made at a price so advantageous to the consumer," ⁿ Bizet assured the publisher.

From this drudgery Bizet found relief during what the French somewhat arbitrarily call *la belle saison*. Of the simple, idyllic routine of the long summers at Le Vésinet, Galabert gives us a charming glimpse: fruits and vegetables picked from the garden by the composer and his friends for meals cooked by Bizet's father; delightful walks along the banks of the Seine in the company of friends and two romping dogs. A large black-and-white watch dog, named Zurga after the character in *Les Pêcheurs de Perles*, lived in a kennel outside Bizet's cottage, and had as companion a smaller reddish-brown dog called Michel. Life was wholly informal, and Galabert tells of one summer evening when Bizet, working in this room, suddenly heard a tenor voice outside singing "*Je crois entendre encore*" from *Les Pêcheurs de Perles*. He went out through the garden into the lane, where he found Saint-Saëns, who, unable to find Bizet's house, had taken this sure way of attracting his friend's attention.

During the summer of 1865, although occupied with finishing the score of *Ivan IV*, Bizet sent Galabert carefully annotated and analyzed criticisms of his exercises and compositions. On one cantata Bizet commented: "I see nothing there to change . . . only the idea is a little dull. Let yourself go, aim at emotion, avoid dryness; don't turn up your nose at the sensuous, you austere philosopher. Provide yourself with *Don Giovanni*, *Le Nozze*, the *Flute*, *Così fan tutte*. Read Weber too. Long live the sun and love! Don't laugh and don't curse me out. This philosophy can be raised to a very high level. Art has its exigencies. Be yourself and your work will be good. Thank you for the pleasure you have given me by sending me these few pages. Intelligence is a rare thing in this century of Boeotians, and it is pleasant to get a big dose of it."

By the end of the summer Bizet had sent *Ivan* to the copy-

ist, and he hoped for its production in late January or early February. The score was in due course submitted to Carvalho, who
turned to Roqueplan for help in raising the money to produce the
opera. In November the old war-horse invited Carvalho and Bizet
to his house for "an important meeting." Some ten years earlier,
when Bizet had first met Roqueplan as director of the Opéra during the rehearsals of *La Nonne sanglante*, this meeting might indeed have been important. But the Opéra was now in the steadier
hands of Perrin, and the former director, for the time being, occupied no official position in the theatre. His influence lay largely
in his newspaper articles. Gone were the days when he inhabited
a palace, splendid with its yellow salon hung in gold damask as a
background for his collection of paintings; a blue salon filled with
Louis XIII furniture upholstered in red damask and a dining-room
decorated with antique Gobelin tapestries. The little apartment on
the second floor of a two-story house where Bizet came to call on
him was "furnished with mediocre eighteenth-century furniture
and some paintings and sketches by his brother, and looked like
the nest a kept woman had inherited from a painter." [n] The coarse-
featured, apoplectic-looking old man, with a tic that continually
distorted his face and terrified strangers, was not usually cordial
to young composers. After merely glancing at the score of one
young man, he made all sorts of promises, assuring him that nothing would be easier than to put his work into rehearsal in no time.
As he showed the elated composer to the door, Roqueplan hesitated for a moment. " 'One more thing,' he said. 'You are M.
Meyerbeer, aren't you?' 'Of course not. My name is Dupieu,
Monsieur.' 'Oh,' was the reply. 'I am so sorry. Because you see
there is absolutely nothing I can do for you. *The* composer, at
present, is Meyerbeer.' " [n]

Meyerbeer remained for Roqueplan *the* composer, a prejudice
that at the moment weighed in Bizet's favor. For Carvalho would
have been shrewd enough to emphasize the spectacular, grandiose
aspects of *Ivan IV* even if he himself had not valued them more
than the possible merits of the score. But Roqueplan's influence, if
he exercised it, failed to crystallize the fate of the opera.

"*Ivan* is delayed again," Bizet complained early in December.
"The Théâtre-Lyrique hasn't a sou [and I have to wait until the
powers that be gild the intelligent director a little]." But he was in
no mood to wait. "M. Bizet had the idea today that he would have

more of a chance of seeing his work produced at the Opéra and under better circumstances. M. Bizet is mistaken," Camille Doucet informed the Minister on December 11. "The Opéra has works by Verdi and others, as well as ballets, which will run through and beyond the year 1866. Besides, by its very subject matter, this *Ivan IV* has more chance of success at the Théâtre-Lyrique than at the Opéra. M. Bizet is still very young, and in order to be produced at the Opéra he would need to have a work that carried more guarantees for the theatre. With *Ivan IV* he would no doubt succeed at the Théâtre-Lyrique; at the Opéra he would run a great risk of failure. This is the opinion of M. Perrin, with whom I have discussed the matter, and who is not at all disposed to compete with the Théâtre-Lyrique in a way dangerous to the work and its young composer, who could later on be presented at this higher level with surer ammunition and under more favorable circumstances." [n]

The hypocrisy of this memorandum is puzzling because Doucet was friendly to Bizet and fully aware of the financial straits of the Théâtre-Lyrique. In any case, Bizet himself not only presented the score of *Ivan* to the director of the Opéra, but also later reminded Perrin: "You have the manuscript of *Ivan*. Let me thank you again for the time you will spend reading this opera, and also for the kind way you received me. It is clear that there are thorns without roses in the charming career I wish to pursue. A word from you is all I need to take me from *nothing to everything.* Forgive these reflections, which will serve as a preface to my bulky parcel." [n] This optimism over Perrin's omnipotence was ill-founded. Indeed, Bizet's version of *Ivan* probably suffered the same fate as Gounod's, which Perrin's predecessor had allowed to languish unread. For Perrin had troubles of his own.

Three months after Bizet importuned him, he was forced to resign. Perrin's independent way of functioning and the resultant financial difficulties had for some time dissatisfied the ministry. His insistence on maintaining in the repertory Meyerbeer's posthumous *L'Africaine* finally brought about his downfall. The work had first been produced the previous April in the hope of restoring to the Opéra the prestige and success so long synonymous with Meyerbeer's name. But without the composer's all-guiding presence, his orphaned work became a white elephant. The composer's heirs had forced Perrin to pay a fantastically high price for the score. The general public was disappointed in it, and the regular subscribers to the Opéra were outraged at being forced to see repeated performances of *L'Africaine,* which Perrin insisted on giving more than one hundred times in eight months. Meyerbeer was indeed dead. It was not the moment for a historical opera in the Meyerbeer manner by a young composer who already had one failure behind him.

"Nothing new from the Opéra," Bizet reported to Galabert at the end of the year. "One must still wait and always intrigue. What fun!" But no amount of patience or scheming, or even a long life, would have enabled Bizet to see the *première* of *Ivan.* It took place in Germany during the Second World War (see Appendix III, p. 470).

In his disappointment over the final rejection of *Ivan* by the Opéra, Bizet reverted to the pattern of behavior which defeat or distress had induced during his Roman days. This time he picked a quarrel with his publisher. "I have never done harm to anyone," he announced to Choudens at New Year's. "I have always, in all my relationships, acted with great good will; and in some, including mine with you, with true friendship and no ulterior motives. My position does not enable me to be useful to my friends. I try sometimes to be nice to them, and if I don't succeed, it isn't my fault. I started out on my career with my head high and a confident heart. Sometimes my manner is brusque. My tongue runs away with me, controlled by my nerves rather than my intelligence. But I don't know of one man who can reproach me with having deliberately caused pain to anyone. I am, at the moment, learning the hard way. More and more rebuffs and disappointments surround me, and I can't understand why. So be it. I shall bear everything. I shall fight everything. . . .

"What do you hold against me?

"You are not a child. I don't think you are capable of an unconsidered act. Choudens, I will believe whatever you tell me. I count on the truth. I bear you no grudge. The tone of this letter proves that. There is no wounded pride or affectation or strategy here. Once again, be sincere; tell me everything. If discretion is necessary, I give you my word of honor not to repeat a word you say. Don't come to my house. Not because I wouldn't be very happy to have you there, but for a reason that I shall explain. Write to me or make an appointment at your house.

"I am astonished, flabbergasted, and, above all, heartbroken.

"I shall await word from you and be glad if that word permits me to be, as I have been until now, your friend, Georges Bizet." "

Chouden's response, written on January 8, 1866, served to re-establish Bizet's equilibrium—but not for long.

CHAPTER XII

Hard Times: The Princesse Mathilde: Céleste Mogador

I am convinced from our conversation yesterday that somewhere around me there is hidden dung," Bizet wrote to Choudens on March 31, 1866. "I sense it, I feel it. It smells to high heaven. Where is it? What form does it take, what color? That's what I don't know. Am I not considered sufficiently responsible to share honorably in whatever trouble there is? That would be a mistake. I don't deserve this lack of confidence. Whatever it's about I shall lie low, completely passive, because I am convinced that the first step I take will land me on all fours in the mess I have described above. *I trust you.* I am sure if the slightest suspicion arose touching my reputation as a *scrupulous, irreproachable* man, you would enable me to clean up the situation vigorously and thoroughly, *regardless of the consequences of the mopping up.* This, *cher ami,* I have the right to exact of your friendship on which I count absolutely in this case, with the understanding that I would do as much for you. I assure you that if ever you need a similar service, come to me, and all my affection, devotion, energy, and intelligence will be dedicated to you. Now I am waiting quietly." "

Was there, in fact, a conspiracy against Bizet, describable only in foul language? Or was this suspicion of malicious intrigue merely the expression of an unwarranted sense of persecution? It would appear to have been so. For the cooperation and friendship proffered him during the first three months of 1866 prove the groundlessness of his suspicions.

Choudens, late in January, had acceded to Bizet's request for a three-hundred-franc advance on a piano reduction of Six Famous Choruses from Gounod's operas. Heugel paid a hundred-franc advance on a solo piano version of excerpts from *Don Giovanni* which was completed in mid-March, when Bizet received an additional five hundred francs for the Mozart work, as well as five hundred for the second volume of *Le Pianiste chanteur*. Subsequently Bizet also made piano arrangements for four hands of the overture and the best known arias, duets, and trios from *Don Giovanni* and a solo-piano version of the whole score of the opera. Had these reductions been paid on a royalty basis, Bizet's financial worries would have been considerably mitigated. For the Opéra, the Théâtre-Italien, and the Théâtre-Lyrique all gave productions of the Mozart opera during the first half of 1866. Paris went mad over Adelina Patti's Zerlina and Christine Nilsson's Donna Elvira.

These much-discussed performances of *Don Giovanni* undoubtedly increased the sale of Bizet's "carefully revised and fingered" piano arrangements of the score. But the profits went to Heugel, and Bizet's income continued to be sharply inadequate for his needs. However, another friend in the musical world came to his rescue during this difficult winter. Alfred Godard, a successful piano-manufacturer who also played his instruments, composed music, and wrote musical criticism, was helpful to many impecunious young composers. He and his wife established a shop where musicians could rent instruments and scores, and Godard also served as intermediary between artists and patrons. Early in February, in notifying Bizet of the gift of a thousand and twenty francs from the Comte de Bourey, he wrote: "Burn this bit of paper, which concerns only you and your obliged and affectionate Alfred Godard." *

Gounod, too, was concerned about Bizet's melancholy. "I don't want you to be *sad* and *discouraged,* my very dear child," Gounod wrote to him a few days later. "If you are free this evening, come and see me in my study, which I never leave. If not, come tomorrow morning to embrace me and to stay for lunch." *
For the past year Gounod has been either in the south of France composing *Roméo et Juliette* or in Paris suffering a nervous breakdown and undergoing the ministrations of Dr. Blanche. Even after he had finished the score of *Roméo* and was sure of its production, his disillusionment with the lyric theatre was profound. "I have

made the very clear-cut and irrevocable resolution no longer to work in the theatre," he wrote at this time to Meilhac, who had asked Gounod to collaborate with him and Halévy. *"La Colombe* at the Opéra-Comique and *Roméo* at the Th. Lyrique will be the last two works I shall put on the stage, my farewell to the dramatic art. . . ."* n* Gounod did not, of course, hold to his resolution, but subsequently produced *Cinq-Mars, Polyeucte,* and *Le Tribut de Zamora.* But for the moment he was quite as disgusted as Bizet with the hazards of writing opera. He did what he could to cheer his *"cher enfant."* By introducing him into the salon of the Princesse Mathilde Bonaparte, Gounod both broadened Bizet's social life and gave him the opportunity to profit by his talents as a pianist.

["I play the piano well,"] Bizet wrote to an unidentified Belgian composer, ["and live off it very badly. For nothing in the world would make me decide to play in public. I find the profession of performer odious! A ridiculous aversion, which costs me about fifteen thousand francs a year. I sometimes play at the Princesse Mathilde's and in a few houses where the artists are friends, not servants."]* n* At the Princesse Mathilde's, artists, far from being servants, were the very backbone of her salon.

Laetitia-Mathilde-Frederica-Aloissia-Elizabeth Bonaparte was one of the most remarkable women of her day. Had her early engagement to marry her cousin Louis, later Napoleon III, not been broken, the history of late nineteenth-century France might well have been very different. Only slightly more French by blood and early upbringing than the Empress Eugénie, she possessed essential virtues lacking in her Spanish rival. Mathilde was the daughter of Jérôme, King of Westphalia, youngest Bonaparte brother and least responsible of all Napoleon's erratic kin, and of Princess Catherine of Württemberg. Mathilde was born in Trieste in 1820. Niece of Napoleon I and of George III of England, as well as a cousin of Alexander I of Russia, she was brought up in exile in Florence and Rome. She developed early a love of the arts second only to her pride in her Bonaparte ancestry and her devotion to the memory of the Emperor uncle she had never known. Her longing to set foot on French soil influenced her into marrying Count Anatole Demidov, a Russian nobleman as fabulously rich as he was sadistic, jealous, and dissolute. After a few years of marriage,

Mathilde left her husband, and with an adequate separation allowance led a life of elegance and freedom in Paris.

The mixture of German and Corsican strains in her nature, combined with her undisciplined upbringing, resulted in an unconventionality of behavior and freedom of thought rare in a princess. She was a beautiful woman even in her late forties, when Bizet knew her. But far rarer than her beauty were her warmth, her graciousness, and an imaginative generosity not often found in rich and powerful patrons of the arts. As hostess to Sainte-Beuve, Flaubert when he was in Paris, Gautier, who was her official librarian and favorite poet, the Dumas, *père* and *fils,* and sometimes Taine and Renan, whose presence was proof enough of her anticlericalism, she enjoyed the most brilliant conversation of the day. And she was an excellent listener. For five afternoons Flaubert read aloud to her the manuscript of *L'Education sentimentale.*

In a limited way the Princess was an artist herself, for in spite of a very meager talent, she was a serious and hard-working painter. Although she had little taste for music, she was a conscientious, if not wholehearted, patroness of musicians. After having been exposed to twelve music teachers, she admitted that good music grated on her ears like sand. Her piano was usually out of tune. Indeed, the only sound she found really gratifying was the noise of a barrel-organ. Nevertheless, at her large Sunday evening gathering she always had music after dinner.

"The Princesse Mathilde's . . . salons are always crowded," wrote one of her musical guests. "It is the only salon in Paris where one can meet all nationalities. There are diplomats, royalists, imperialists, strangers of importance passing through Paris, and especially all the celebrated artists." On one occasion "Gounod played most enchantingly some selections from *Roméo et Juliette,* the opera he has just composed. I hear that he wants Christine Nilsson to sing it. The music seems to me even more beautiful than *Faust.* . . . Gounod is, I think, the gentlest, the most modest and the kindest-hearted man in the world. . . ." [n]

Whether because Gounod confided to the Princess the material and spiritual distress of his protégé, Bizet, or whether because she immediately took a liking to the young man, he was, soon after his introduction to her salon, asked by her lover, Count Niewekerke, who was Superintendent of Fine Arts, to play at an official reception at the Louvre. "M. Bizet, *Grand Prix de Rome*, played several very well-chosen selections on the piano," reported the *Revue et Gazette Musicale*, "among them one of his own compositions." ⁿ

On a less grand scale than the Louvre, but "more beautiful than the Tuileries or the Princesse Mathilde's," according to young Paladilhe, was the house of M. and Mme Laurent at 12 rue François Iᵉʳ, where Bizet frequently dined and performed. The hostess was a grand-niece of Schnetz, in whose honor she entertained, early in 1866, a number of former Prix de Rome at a dinner and evening party. Among the guests were Bizet, his friend Paul Dubois the sculptor, and Paladilhe, greatly impressed by the "inconceivable luxury, rows of flunkies and uniformed servants everywhere."

Bizet was also a welcome guest in less formal society. Among the invitations he saved is one from the painter, Eugène Isabey, inviting him "to come most informally—*en botte et en crotte*—any Sunday night," and telling him what "pleasure it will give Mme Isabey and myself to welcome you. I hope my friend Mme Garcia will come tomorrow. . . ." ⁿ Mme Eugenie Garcia, wife of Manuel Garcia, the famous professor of singing and brother of Pauline Viardot, had also become a teacher after retiring from a career as singer at the Opéra-Comique. Her influence enabled her to help young musicians by sending them pupils. Bizet expressed his appreciation by dedicating several songs to her.

Surrounded as he was, then, by the good will of friends and friends of friends, rich in opportunities that less popular young men must have envied, Bizet might well have gained some self-confidence. But social success never served to mitigate his sense of persecution. During the aftermath of his disappointment about *Ivan IV*, he did not even write to Galabert. His letters to Choudens reflect his depression. Early in March he wrote to his publisher: "A slight reproach, *cher ami*. Find my music bad, detestable, whatever you like. That is your privilege and I don't hold it against you. But silence, please! Your role as a friend is to give me your opinions in private and not to express them publicly. I am neither proud nor vindictive. . . . I don't agree with you. I find my music excellent and I am never wrong! Time will tell. In the meantime, see that I'm not *hissed!!!*" ⁿ

If the music in question consisted of *Trois Esquisses musicales,*

Chasse fantastique, or *Chants du Rhin,* which Bizet seems to have been working on at this time, the publisher's opinion was possibly sounder than the composer's. For these compositions for piano were, on the whole, little more than conventional salon pieces. Choudens's public expression of his views may have been provoked by a certain sense of rivalry, for Heugel published these pieces. He paid the composer six hundred francs for *Chants du Rhin: Lieder pour piano* in December 1865. These songs without words were based on six poems by Joseph Méry, the popular poet and librettist of *Erostrate,* with whom Bizet had become friendly during the rehearsals of Reyer's opera in 1862. Heugel apparently accepted without question the trite verses, which were printed as a preface to the score, as well as the banality of the music itself. He protested only one "song," *"La Bohémienne,"* which has also caused disagreement among modern critics. One of them finds it "full of character," showing "great freedom of modulation . . . the most operatic of the set: some nameless José courts the gypsy throughout the last two pages," [n] but another regards it as a feeble reminder of a Chopin mazurka. Bizet had to struggle for its inclusion in the collection.

"I am the least stubborn of composers," he wrote to Heugel, "particularly when good taste and friendship dictate advice. I wish to do everything you want. Nevertheless your disturbing opinion doesn't convince me. I thought I had found an original rhythm; you consider it banal. We might both be right. I shall come to see you tomorrow morning, or the morning after, and we will talk about it and look for the trouble. I have already discussed the subject with several musicians—Gounod, Guiraud, etc. I have played our *Bohémienne* three or four times for several people, and I have been convinced that it will be the success of our publication. (At the moment I am talking about the public.) If you reply that this proves nothing, you are right. So let us look for the trouble and we will find a solution. Perhaps the execution rather than the composition should be modified. . . ." [n]

The collection seemed "charming" to Ambroise Thomas, when Bizet sent him a copy early in March. He found number 3, *"Les Rêves,"* "a pearl that I would like to interpret and play if I were a pianist. Thank you for having thought of me." [n] This "thought" was less a tribute to Thomas than a reminder that Bizet's services were available for the piano arrangements of *Mig-*

non, which was about to go into rehearsal. Bizet was soon commissioned by Heugel to make piano reductions of the score both for solo and for four hands, a task at which he worked on and off for the next nine months.

Besides the hack-work that occupied him at this period, Bizet found time to write a men's chorus commissioned by a choral society in Belgium, where he had served as member of a jury for a competition. Entitled *Saint Jean de Pathmos,* the chorus was set to a poem by Victor Hugo. When Bizet sang it at the piano for Galabert, the latter was "amazed at the high quality and difficulty of the piece." But a modern critic finds the piece "notable for appalling prosody, a second bass part reminiscent of a military band . . . and the only complete fugue that Bizet published—an ingenious but barren monument to his Conservatoire training." [n]

The fee Bizet received for this work did not free him from financial worries. Late in April, when he was going over his accounts before moving to Le Vésinet, he urged his *"caro* Choudens" to do everything possible to save the piano arrangement of Gounod's *Roméo* for him. "It is a matter of major importance to me. If I have that, I can get through this year." When he arrived at Le Vésinet, he found himself with a new neighbor, an extraordinary woman.

Bizet's somewhat primitive attitude towards women was obvious in his Italian diary. In his letters to his mother from Rome he made no effort to disguise his immaturity or his ignorance of matters concerning love and marriage. When the oldest of his Delsarte cousins jilted his fiancée, the daughter of his commanding officer, in order to marry a servant girl whom he had got with child, Bizet commented: ["X. is a boy for whom I have the most profound contempt. I hope to heaven that I shall never be capable of such cowardly behavior. For it is cowardly to renounce his position to wallow in miserable poverty. What unpardonable weakness on the part of his father! That boy should have been driven from the paternal roof forever and ever. If I ever have the *happiness of being a father,* I shall show no such indulgence for my children."] [n] The love affairs of his cousin Gustave Delsarte, Georges regarded more tolerantly. But Gustave, nearer his own age, was the only one of the Delsarte cousins with whom Bizet had a close friendship. This attractive philanderer, endowed with a slight but attractive singing voice and a minor gift for musical composition, had been sent off to Vienna because of the jealousy of his brother, with whose wife he had been flirting. In Vienna he contracted a marriage with the daughter of a doctor. ["I am delighted by what you tell me about Gustave Delsarte, especially as I shan't have to write to him about this matter,"] Bizet wrote. ["After considerable reflection, I decided that I could not bring myself to give advice on such a subject, even to a friend. I deplore, without understanding them, all the transports of the thing known as love. I don't agree with anyone about it, and I am glad of it."] [n]

By 1865, when Bizet first met his new neighbor, popularly known as La Mogador, he had acquired a little more knowledge of "the thing known as love." But the comradeship he shared with this odd woman, who fitted into none of his established categories, served as a prelude to "the transports" he had previously deplored.

Céleste Vénard, who became La Mogador, was a poor man's George Sand. As dynamic if not as prolific as her more illustrious contemporary, Céleste rivaled George Sand's hundred or more volumes of fiction, autobiography, and drama with *Mémoires,* sixteen novels, twenty-six plays, seven operetta librettos, and twenty-nine songs and poems. In contrast to George Sand's romantic relations with her many lovers, self-justified by her belief in a single standard of morals for men and women, Céleste's promiscuity was an economic necessity. The so-called oldest profession offered the only means of livelihood open to her as a young girl.

Born in the slums of Paris in 1824, daughter of a laundress, ignorant even of her father's name, Céleste spent her childhood persecuted by her stepfather. At thirteen, she ran away from home to escape the advances of one of her mother's lovers. Fainting from hunger and cold, she was rescued by the proverbial kindhearted woman of the streets. Subsequently arrested and imprisoned in the Conciergerie, she emerged from prison a *fille inscrite,* a prostitute registered on the police lists. At sixteen, installed in a bordello, she made her first literary acquaintance, Alfred de Musset. His relationship with Céleste exemplified George Sand's prophecy at the time of her final break with the poet: "My God, what kind of life am I abandoning you to? Drunkenness, wine, whores —again and always." [n]

Céleste's account of her episode with Musset, published twenty years later in her *Mémoires,* seemed to her contemporaries shamelessly frank and immoral. Today, a century later, her book exudes the moral tone characteristic of reformed sinners in the novels of Victorian lady writers. "A ghost rather than a man . . . a premature ruin . . . barely thirty years old in spite of the wrinkles that furrowed his face," Musset appeared to Céleste when Fanny, the maid in the brothel, led her into "the little salon" where the poet was quite at home. " 'Where do you come from?' he said, as though waking from a dream. I didn't answer. He started to curse. I blushed and said to him: 'Do I ask you who you are and where you come from? Do I have to have a reference to appear before you? I assure you I have none.' " Disgusted with Musset's bad manners, Céleste ran to complain to the Madam, who insisted that he be "well-treated, as he was her best friend, sometimes spent a week in her house, and besides was . . . one of the greatest writers of the century." Learning of the distinction of her client, Céleste returned after "casting an ironic glance at the Madam and remarking: 'I don't mind taking a look at a great genius. You can always profit by the society of clever people.' " During a series of visits, Musset tried unsuccessfully to force Céleste to drink "rum, brandy, or absinthe" with him, offering her as bait "a fistful of gold pieces" which she accepted while admitting they were unearned. Then he invited her to dine with him. Years later she was able to describe this fantastic outing with total recall:

"He came to fetch me at six o'clock and took me to the Rocher de Cancale. I was very simply clothed in a brand-new dress and hat. I liked the way I looked. I felt a little less sad, perhaps because for the second time I was out of that hateful house. In the beginning I didn't have very much to complain of except for several jokes in bad taste, ungracious to say the least. I restrained myself as best I could. Our waiter brought a bottle of seltzer water. . . . He [Musset] took the siphon as though he were going to pour a drink and, pointing the nozzle at me, drenched me from head to foot. At certain times in my life and in certain states of mind I could have accepted such behavior as a bad practical joke. But then I was so unhappy that this bogus fit of madness exasperated me. I burst into tears of rage. The more I cried, the more he laughed. If I had stayed another minute in that room I would have thrown a carafe at his head in spite of the consequences. Fortunately I reached the door and escaped, vowing that I would kill myself rather than live this life any longer." "

Céleste did eventually escape her bondage to become one of

the famous dancers at the Bal Mabille. Chosen by the proprietor, the notorious Brididi, as his partner in the launching of a new dance, the polka, she had an overwhelming success. Men clamored to dance with her; and Brididi warned her that there was no use in her trying to fight them off. "It would be easier to defend Mogador," the Moroccan city then recently bombarded by a French squadron. Thus Céleste Vénard became "La Mogador" of rapidly spreading fame. The newspapers sang her praises. She was "wasp-waisted, supple as a willow, lively as a linnet . . . just pock-marked enough to suggest a slight resemblance to the Venus de Milo, except that she had two beautiful arms, generously displayed. . . . Proud Mogador voluptuously flaunts curves Minerva might envy." [n]

To the charms of Venus and Minerva she soon added the exploits of Diana. As a brilliant and daring rider at the Hippodrome, La Mogador attracted a variety of admirers, among them a duke who supplied her with her own carriage and horses. Her broadening social life soon led her into the musical world. She became a welcome guest at the *soirées* of Alphonse Royer, for several years director of the Opéra as well as collaborator on or translator of the librettos of *Lucia di Lammermoor, La Favorite,* and *Don Pasquale.* "The circle of witty people delighted me. I listened. . . . For I was so ignorant I would often stop short in the middle of a sentence I didn't dare finish for fear of saying something foolish." At Royer's, Céleste met Hermann Cohen, a favorite protégé of Liszt's, who fell madly in love with her. Cohen, or "Puzzi," as George Sand nicknamed him, was a German Jew, a pianist said to be as gifted as Liszt. An infant prodigy, he had started composing at six, knew Greek, Latin, and French at nine, at twelve made his debut as a concert pianist, and three years later became a professor at the Geneva Conservatoire. When he arrived in Paris a year or two later, Liszt took him under his wing, and he became an intimate of George Sand, Chopin, and Musset. Under the poet's influence, he sank temporarily into a life of gambling, debauchery, and obsessive passion for Céleste, who, while admiring him as a pianist, rejected him as a lover. La Mogador was an admitted anti-Semite. Puzzi, in despair, became a Roman Catholic and four years later entered the priesthood under the name of Père Augustin Marie du Très Saint Sacrement."

A serious accident cut short Céleste's glorious equestrian

career, but she soon became the mistress of a handsome young
nobleman, who, when not hunting at his château in Berry, gam-
bled away his fortune in Paris. Lionel, Comte de Moreton de
Chabrillan, was the son of a former gentleman-in-waiting at the
court of Charles X, grandson of a former ambassador to
Turkey, and a member of the Académie Française. The young
aristocrat's family was less tolerant of their spendthrift son than
was his mistress, who, to supply him with funds, took up acting at
the Variétés. There the younger Dumas encouraged Céleste by
writing a part for her into one of his plays. Thomas Couture, who
had recently painted a portrait of George Sand, fell in love with La
Mogador, made a drawing of her and a cast of her hand which
is in the Carnavalet Museum. To help pay Count Lionel's debts,
she decided to write her memoirs with the aid of a former lover
who was also her lawyer. (She was an indefatigable litigant.) Although she never learned to read with ease or to spell other than
phonetically, she managed to produce an autobiography that had a
considerable *succès de scandale.* "Like Jean-Jacques Rousseau,"
Dumas *père* declared.

In the meantime Céleste's relations with M. de Chabrillan ran
a stormy and frequently interrupted course. After bankrupting his
mistress as well as himself, Lionel departed for Australia. A year
or so later he returned and, after securing the removal of Céleste
Vénard's name from the list of registered prostitutes, married her.
Immediately after the wedding the couple left for Melbourne,
where, through family influence, the count had been appointed
French consul. Departing with two little dogs and a green parakeet,
the Countess returned, after two years, bearing a novel she had
written about life down under. Michel Lévy, the publisher of
George Sand, Flaubert, and Balzac, brought out the book at the
request of Princesse Mathilde's brother, the Prince Napoléon,
better known as "Plon-Plon."

Because of the scandalous gossip her *Mémoires* had aroused,
Mme de Chabrillan feared for the reception of her first novel. But
she had no need to worry. Her friend Dumas *père* praised her book
in his paper, *Le Mousquetaire,* and other important journalists followed suit. Jules Janin, that influential if not wholly reliable critic,
stated: "Only a really gifted, highly intelligent woman could thus
have changed, rehabilitated herself through her intelligence, renounced the life of an adventuress, and won an honorable position

among the distinguished women and good writers of her time." Some fifty years later Marcel Proust rose to the defense of lending libraries because nowhere else could he find such period pieces as the novels of the Comtesse Lionel de Chabrillan.

Her triumph in her own day was marred by the death of her husband in Australia in 1858. A year after his death she started a new career, calling herself merely Mme Lionel in deference to the objections to her use of the title by the Moreton de Chabrillan family. She became director of the Bouffes Parisiens, recently abandoned by Offenbach, and produced over a period of four years a series of operettas for many of which she also supplied the librettos. Driven from this position by the attacks of hostile critics who reminded the public of her unsavory past, Céleste accepted the offer of the manager of a large theatre in Belleville to play the part of a miner in the stage version of her novel *Les Voleurs d'or.*

The night of the opening, May 24, 1864, the theatre was crowded with workingmen on holiday, boisterous, exuberant, and delighted with the play. "Author, author," the audience roared. When the actor chosen to present the author announced, "Madame la Comtesse de Chabrillan," Céleste was horrified. The use of her title in this poor district, where she was born, seemed to her tasteless, and she was afraid that the audience, remembering the exploits of La Mogador, would hiss. But she underestimated the pride of her former neighbors in her success. For four months they crowded the theatre without ever discovering that the real author of the dramatic version of Céleste's novel was Dumas *père.* After the successful run in Belleville, *Les Voleurs d'or* made a triumphant tour of the provinces. Céleste returned to Paris sufficiently affluent to become a landowner.

In September 1865, she bought about an acre and a half of wooded land at Le Vésinet on the Allée Transversale, adjoining Bizet's cottage in the Route des Cultures. The actress and Bizet met on the train between Paris and Le Vésinet while Céleste was supervising the construction of her house, Le Châlet Lionel. The reformed courtesan was forty-one, the composer twenty-seven, unhappy and susceptible to the sympathetic friendship of an experienced older woman. "An aristocratic savage," she called him. "I never saw him laugh outright. Georges Bizet was not very gay at this time. He was still living on hope." In his sadder moods he even confided to her that some of his unhappiness was caused by a love affair. "When you live here, I think Le Vésinet will bore me less," he told her. "We can have music at your house. Do try to get a good piano." She did, and gave him the key so that he could use it in her absence. He came when she was at home, too, and improvised by the hour while she admired the beauty of his hands, of which, she notes, he was well aware. She held her breath lest she interrupt "the master's adorable playing. 'At your house,' " Bizet told her, " 'I can at least hear myself work. My own hole-in-the-wall is so tiny that the sound doesn't rise. . . . It seems as though your presence inspires me. . . . If I see you on the days I go to Paris, I am sure to come back in the evening with good news.' "

Sometimes Céleste was invited to his "modest little cell" to join "a few initmate friends who came to take a cup of tea with him of an evening." She had "the honor," she says, "of being included in this group as a fellow-worker, as I was the only woman he received." The pride and naïveté in Céleste's conception of herself as a "fellow-worker" did not prevent Bizet from expressing his contempt for the *cafés-chantants* where she performed. Indeed, before he went to call on her, he always made sure that none of her colleagues was visiting her, "not even Thérèsa," Céleste remarks with surprise: Thérèsa, the most popular humorous singer of the day, "the Patti of the beer-halls." During her early acquaintance with Bizet, Céleste sang nightly at the Café-Concert du XIXème Siècle.

At 8.45 she sang *"Encore moi,"* at 9.30 *"T'as du chagrin,"* and at 10.15 *"L'Amour c'est des bêtises."* An additional number on the program was *"Ay Chiquita!"* In Bizet's music library there is still a copy of this song by the Spanish composer Sebastián Yradier, from whose *"El Arregilito"* he was to borrow for the *habanera* in *Carmen.* This fortuitous link joining the adventurous courtesan, the popular Spanish ditty, and the enduring *habanera* suggests a more important influence on Bizet's opera than the slight debt to Yradier. Might not Carmen herself have written these words from Céleste's autobiography?

"My character was formed early. I loved passionately or hated furiously. . . . When I hate people, I wish they would die. . . . Moderation is no part of my nature. Joy, sorrow, affection, resentment, laziness, work—I have overdone them all. My life has been one long excess. . . . I feel with a passion that devours me. . . . When I want something, I am willing to gamble ten or twenty years of my life to get it as quickly as possible. . . . When I take up a book, I want to understand it so quickly that the blood rushes to my head. I can't see straight, and I have to stop. Then I go into a ridiculous rage at myself. . . . I beat my brain. When I try to learn to write and my hand disobeys, I pinch my arm black and blue. . . . If my heart rebels against my will, I torture it until it gives in. . . . Two defects in my character have protected me. I have always been capricious and proud. No one, among women whose tendency it is to say *yes*, derives more pleasure than I do from saying *no*. So the men to whom I have given the most are those who asked least of me." ⁿ (*"Si tu ne m'aimes pas, je t'aime,"* *Habanera, Carmen*, Act I.)

Céleste, *"la brave camarade,"* claimed that between her and *"le bon garçon,"* Bizet, only a platonic friendship existed. Yet surely this passionate daughter of the people sowed seeds that flowered, a few years later, in Bizet's masterpiece. "Women are like cats. When you call them, they don't come; when you don't call them, they do," says Don José.

Meanwhile Bizet's neighbor had indeed made life at Le Vésinet less boring. He stayed there steadily until late autumn. Only on Tuesdays and Saturdays did he go to Paris to give lessons, to play an occasional game of baccarat or poker with Meilhac, Halévy, and their friends, to ward off his creditors, and in June 1866 to negotiate with Carvalho the contract for *La Jolie Fille de Perth*.

CHAPTER  XIII

La Jolie Fille de Perth: I

Carvalho's desire for a new work from Bizet at this time corroborated, even more strongly than had his commission of *Ivan IV*
after the failure of *Les Pêcheurs de Perles,* his faith in the young
composer's capacity to create a success. For nothing less than an
overwhelming success could rescue the director of the Théâtre-
Lyrique from his desperate financial straits. On June 15, 1866, he
was said to be one million six hundred thousand francs in debt.
Yet before the end of the month he signed a contract with Bizet
for a four-act opera that would require "superhuman effort," the
latter wrote to Choudens. The libretto, drawn from Sir Walter
Scott's *The Fair Maid of Perth,* bore little resemblance to the novel
except for the names of the chief characters and the title, *La Jolie
Fille de Perth.* But Carvalho had faith in this choice of subject because of the popularity of previous operas based on the Waverley
novels: Boïeldieu's *La Dame blanche,* drawn from *The Monastery*
and *Guy Mannering,* Donizetti's *Lucia di Lammermoor,* and
Flotow's *Rob Roy* among others. The librettists were Jules Adenis,
a dependable workhorse and a friend of Bizet, and Saint-Georges,
whose success for over forty years had been second only to
Scribe's. This indefatigable scribbler was responsible, either singly
or with a collaborator, for the books of nine of Fromental Halévy's
most successful operas, three of Auber's, four of Clapisson's, Balfe's
The Bohemian Girl, Donizetti's *La Fille du Régiment,* Flotow's
Martha, and dozens of others. Saint-Georges prided himself as
much on his accomplishments as a writer (he was elected President
of the Society of Authors six times) as on the achievement of his

position in aristocratic society, a level to which he was better suited.

The *de* in the name of Jules-Henri Vernoy de Saint-Georges did not signify a title. But his lack of birth was compensated for by his splendid appearance—"the perfect gentleman, tall, with a pleasant face and carefully dyed hair, irreproachably dressed, perfumed like a marquis of the *ancien régime,* on whom he patterned himself." ⁿ Accepted as an equal in the aristocratic society of his choice, he was regarded by his peers in the musical world as an amiable, if frequently irritating, figure of fun. "The illustrious poet, the Chevalier de Saint-Georges . . . His Majesty, the Baron, the Marquis, the little Duke, the great Viscount, the young cavalier," as Bizet described him, often retired to the country to visit "*les grands.*" From some remote château he would write to his collaborators in an aristocratically illegible hand, on paper engraved with a gold coronet, explaining his delay in delivering the next act of a libretto. On one occasion, when Scribe had offered to write the second act of an opera, indefinitely delayed because of Saint-Georges's social activities, Halévy had written to him, in a letter dated "The third day of the Empire," "Where are you, oh Saint-Georges? Don't you get tired of being elliptical? Answer me squarely or roundly. When do you return to our Imperial capital? I can understand that the noble graciousness of your good friends delights and detains you, but it is not my fault if I have no castle in which to receive you and offer you princely hospitality. I have nothing but a thatched cottage and a piano . . ." ⁿ doubtless no environment to tempt M. de Saint-Georges.

Indeed, it seems probable that this "last of the Marquis" saw in himself the reincarnation of a *personnage à la mode* of the late eighteenth century known as Le Chevalier de Saint-Georges. Certainly it was the later Saint-Georges's charm and politeness that endeared him to the artists who sang his ridiculous verses, if not to the composers who were forced to set them to music. "Only Saint-Georges can find and handle expertly subjects whose interest springs rather from the sweet surprises of the heart than from the more or less ingenious workings of the mind," said the great tenor, Gustave Roger.

"The sweet surprises of the heart" were hardly Bizet's ideal subject matter, and he cherished no illusions about the stupidity and ineptitude of the libretto that would require his attention for the next six months. But, in no position to turn down the offer of a contract in the hope of finding a better subject, he started work on the score early in July.

"It will be a pretty piece, I hope," he wrote to Galabert, "but what dialogue!"[1] And, a month later," I am fairly well satisfied with my *Fille de Perth*, but it is leading me a dog's life. . . . It resembles the novel very little. It is a trick piece, and the characters are not sufficiently developed. There are lines—well, here at random:

> Catherine
> *Ainsi donc, plus de jalousie!*
> Smith
> *Et vous plus de coquetterie!*
> Cath.
> *C'est convenu.*
> Sm.
> *C'est entendu.*
> *Ah! désormais le bonheur m'est rendu!*

"Or else: *'Quelle est encore cette aventure?*
> *Nous n'en sortirons pas, vraiment!*
> *Je n'y comprends rien! Mais je jure*
> *Que l'ami Smith est innocent!'*

"*L'ami* Smith is delightful.

"Well, I shall have to work on it. I shall not use their words for composing. I couldn't dig up a single note if I did. . . . As for Walter Scott's novel, I must confess myself a heretic. I find it loathsome. But let me explain. It is a loathsome novel, but an excellent book. M. *Ponrail du Tesson* [*sic*],[2] knight of the Legion of Honor, might perhaps write a good novel, yet he will never write anything but contemptible books. You understand I am only trying to excuse Saint-Georges [officer of the Legion of Honor] for not having followed the plot of the English novelist."

Had Saint-Georges merely ignored Scott's plot, he would have sinned, if at all, on the side of wisdom. For Bizet's dictum on the work is sound. The book is good because it is permeated with

---

[1] Bizet, *Lettres à un ami*, 67. Subsequent unidentified quotations in this chapter are from this work. Unpublished portions of the letters are enclosed in square brackets.

[2] Pierre-Alexis, Vicomte de Ponson du Terrail (1829–71), was an extremely successful and prolific novelist who wrote some 73 volumes in two years.

Scott's own virtue, his inborn feeling for his country. But the plot of the novel is tenuously laden with Border feuds and pseudo-Shakespearean royal intrigues, spun out beyond readability. The atmosphere, the local color, is characteristically excellent and the conflicts between the feudal lords and the lower classes could, by a more skillful hand than Saint-Georges's, have been transposed with great success from Scotland to libretto-land. But given such remnants of Scottish, or even British, local color retained or introduced by the librettists as *"du vieux wisky [sic] d'Ecosse"* and *"un* succulent pudding," Bizet can hardly be blamed for having failed to find any musical equivalent for Scottish local color.

The characters, too, in the operatic version, are stripped of the clear-cut, national qualities that Scott gave them, and are transformed into operatic stereotypes. In the novel, the heroine, Catherine, is not unlike Micaëla in *Carmen.* On stage she becomes the familiar comic-opera flirt, a transformation that makes her mad scene in the last act doubly unconvincing. Smith, her suitor, a very upstanding man, well drawn by Scott, is reduced to a foolish, lovelorn simulacrum of a man. The Duke of Rothsay, potentially a Scottish Don Juan or Rigoletto type of duke, merely attempts unsuccessfully the most banal operatic seductions. Louise, the glee-maiden or female wandering minstrel, one of the most original and colorful figures in the novel, is unrecognizably changed into a conventional gypsy, Mab. This substitution of gypsy for Scottish local color had the advantage of enabling Bizet to include the *Danse bohémienne,* one of the best numbers in the opera. It is often used by directors who introduce a ballet into the last act of *Carmen.* Another substitution in the libretto, that of Ralph, the frustrated, unhappy apprentice, for Scott's cowardly disguised Highlander, Conachar, enabled Bizet to use a drinking song as a successful means of characterization. But a reader turning straight from Scott's novel to the book of the opera marvels that the composer could cope with such a flabby, foolish libretto. Cope he did, however. And early in September, after finishing the first act, he sent Galabert a brief résumé of his scenario. The first three scenes are sufficient to give an idea of the caliber of the libretto.

"Characters.

"Smith . . . . gunsmith, tenor

The Duke of Rothsay . . . baritone

Glover . . . . glove-maker
Catherine . . . . . . his daughter
Ralph . . . . Highlander, apprentice
                    to Glover
Mab . . . . Queen of Bohemia, says
                    Saint-Georges, but
                    I say Queen of
                    the Gypsies.

First Act.
Smith's shop. Furnishings ad hoc.
Scene I
Gunsmiths *at work.*
Chorus
Work away, forge away, etc.

Enter Smith.

Sm: Friends, tonight is the carnival. Have fun. Your work is finished, etc.

Exeunt gunsmiths.

Scene II
Smith *alone.*

Here am I left all alone with my love for Catherine. Why wilst thou
not love me? Why dost thou not obey thy father who wouldst have
me for a son-in-law? etc.

Recitative and Romance.

Offstage noise

Sm: What do I hear? . . . Screams! A woman is being insulted, I
fear. I must fly.

He grabs an ax and starts out the door as Mab rushes in.

Scene III

Mab: Save me. I am frightened to death. Some young noblemen
tried to kiss me at your door.

Sm: Fear naught. In my house you are safe.

Mab: Thank you. Then let me render you a service. Show me your
hand and I will read your future destiny.

Sm: My poor child, you are wasting your time. I don't believe in
sorcery.

Mab: *taking Smith's hand,* You are in love with a flirt who wrings
your heart with jealousy, but I assure you that she loves you.
Do not fear Ralph. He loves her, but she loves only you. Wait.
So you will believe my magic powers I tell you that in a mo-

Page showing Bizet's corrections in libretto
of *La Jolie Fille de Perth*, Act III.

Céleste Vénard,
La Mogador.

Céleste Mogador,
Comtesse Lionel de Moreton
de Chabrillan, *c.* 1866.

Marie Reiter, *c.* 1900.

Jean Reiter, 1886.

Esther Halévy.

Jacques Bizet, 1882.

Bizet in National Guard
uniform.

Sketch of Geneviève Halévy
by her mother.

Letter from Bizet
to his wife.

Letter from Bizet to
his mother-in-law.

Mozart

1° Don Giovanni Drame en 2 actes
(S de partition (Paroles franc: ital:) (Richault)

2° Idomeneo res di Creta o sia
Ilia e Idamante, dramma Eroico in 3 atti. (Simrock)
(S de partition)

3° Il flauto magico Dramma jocoso in 2 atti
(S de partition (parole franc: ital:) (Frey)

4° Cosi fan tutte. Dramma jocoso in 2 atti
(S de partition (Breitkopf e Härtel) (paroles all: ital:)

5° Le Nozze di Figaro, Dramma jocoso in 4 atti
(S de partition (Paroles ital: franc:)
(au magasin de musique 76, rue Richelieu)

Page from Bizet's music catalogue.

Alphonse Daudet, *c.* 1870.

Léon Carvalho.

Geneviève Bizet, 1876.
Portrait by Elie Delaunay.

Geneviève Bizet, *c.* 1880.

ment Simon Glover will appear with his daughter and his apprentice to ask you to sup with them.

Sm: Is it possible? Together, etc.

Knocking at the door.

Mab: Here they are.

Sm: But it just occurs to me. Catherine is jealous. Hide yourself, there in that room.

Mab hides. . . .

"I am pleased with the music," Bizet wrote. "I think I have set up my characters well. Ralph is a very grateful character. He will become very important in the second act. I am quite satisfied with the second act, on which I am working, and which I will tell you about in my next letter.

"I no longer go to Paris. I am entirely given over to work."

At the end of September, Bizet was forced temporarily to abandon his opera for a mass of commissioned hack-work. "If, like me," he wrote, "you had just finished orchestrating an ignoble waltz [for Choudens], you would bless your work outdoors. It is maddening to interrupt the work I love for two days to write cornet solos. I have made the orchestration more shabbily vulgar than nature dictated. The cornet utters drunken dancehall yells; the ophicleide and the big drum pleasantly mark the first beat of the bar with bass trombone, 'cellos, and basses, while the second and third beats are pummeled out by the horns, violas, second violins, the two first trombones, and the drum! Yes, the drum! If you could see the saxophone part! . . . Ten pages of it. There are unhappy souls who spend their whole existence producing contraptions like this. Horrible! . . ."

As a relief from this ignominious hack-work, Bizet composed six songs "in a hurry" for Heugel in the autumn of 1866. "I chose the words carefully," he told Galabert, "*Adieux à Suzon* by A. de Musset; *A une Fleur* by the same; *Le Grillon* by Lamartine (a little on the Saint-Georges side); an adorable sonnet of Ronsard's; a charming, fragile little thing by Millevoye, and a wild *Guitare* by Hugo.[3]

"I didn't suppress a line. I put in everything. Musicians shouldn't mutilate poets.

---

[3] During this period, Bizet also composed his best-known song, *"Adieux de l'hôtesse arabe,"* words by Victor Hugo.

"My opera, my symphony, everything is under way. When will I finish? God, it takes a long time, but it is fun. I no longer go to Paris more than once a week. I tend strictly to business and rush back. I behave so well that I hardly recognize myself any more. I like it at home away from bores, idlers, chatterboxes—people, in fact, alas.

"I no longer read the papers. Bismarck irritates me."

The specter of Bismarck and the possible involvement of France in war had, during the summer of 1866, haunted the minds of all intelligent Frenchmen. They were, of course, ignorant of the secret agreement made the year before between Bismarck and Napoleon III. According to its unwritten terms, Napoleon was to abstain from participating in the Prussian-Italian attack on Austria which the Prussian chancellor was then planning, the intention being that the Emperor should serve as mediator in the peace that was expected to follow a long war. For these services, Bismarck had hinted, but never promised, France might be given perhaps the Palatinate, perhaps Luxembourg, perhaps even part of Belgium or Switzerland. But Napoleon's role as peacemaker evaporated when, after only seven weeks, the Austrians were overwhelmingly defeated at the Battle of Sadowa on July 3. Soon after the news of this battle reached Paris, Bizet wrote to Galabert: "In mid-nineteenth century, when a so-called civilized society tolerates, even encourages, stupid, futile, monstrous behavior, odious assasinations going on under our very eyes, and in which our *belle Frrrrance* will doubtless soon participate, decent and intelligent men should get together, come to an understanding, clear things up, love one another, and deplore the 999 thousands of idiots, swindlers, bankers, bores who cover our poor earth! . . . If M. de Bismarck, aided and abetted by the cholera, his worthy colleague in making hash of the world, forces us to give up the exposition, deprives us of our pupils, our publishers, our bread and butter in fact, I shall seek refuge and philosophize with you next year. This year, alas, I can't even think of doing it."

But philosophize by correspondence he did: "I understand perfectly all you say about religion. . . . We agree on a principle that I think can be formulated thus: for the strong, religion is a means of exploiting the weak. Religion is the cloak of ambition, of injustice, of vice. Little by little this progress you mention is destroying all superstitions. The truth emerges, science becomes popular, religion totters; it will fall soon, in a few centuries, that is to say tomorrow. . . . But let's not forget that religion . . . particularly the Catholic religion, has taught us the precepts that enable us to do without it today. Ungrateful children that we are, we beat the breast that fed us, because the nourishment it supplies today is no longer worthy of us. We scorn this false clarity, which has, little by little, accustomed our eyes to seeing the light. . . . Look at that sublime absurdity called the Bible! Isn't it easy to extract from this splendid jumble most of the truths we know today? Then they had to be dressed in the costumes of their epoch. They had to be made to don the livery of error, of falsehood, of imposture. Dogma, religion have had a fortunate, decisive influence on man. If you raise as objection the persecutions, the crimes, the vile deeds that have been committed in their name, I will reply that humanity has burned its fingers at the torch. Millions of men cutting the throats of other men, a drop of water in the ocean, nothing! Man is not yet strong enough, doubtless to cut himself off from faith. . . . Religion is a policeman. Later on, we shall get along without policemen and without judges, too. We have already taken a big step forward since the policeman is almost enough for us. Ask society whether it would rather dispense with bishops or with policemen . . . and you will see how large a majority favors the policeman! Today the helmet is powerful enough to restrain evil passions. The helmet would have had no effect on the Hebrews, who knew nothing about the nature of philosophy. There had to be altars, Sinais with flares, etc. They had to appeal to the eye. Later it was sufficient to appeal to the imagination. Soon we shall need to deal only with reason.

"I believe that the whole future belongs to the perfecting of our social contract (with which politics are always so stupidly confused). Society perfected, no more injustice, therefore no more malcontents, thus no more criminal attempts on the social pact, no more priests, no more policemen, no more crimes, no more adultery, no more prostitution, no more violent emotions, no more passion, but wait—No more music, no more poetry, no more Legion of Honor, no more newspapers (bravo for that), above all no theatre, no fallacies, so no art! To the devil with it! But it's your fault. Unhappy as it may make you, your inevitable, implacable progress kills art! . . . The societies most infected with superstition were the greatest promoters of art. . . . Fantasy, inferno,

paradise, the djinns, phantoms, ghosts, Peri, there is the domain of
art! Prove to me that we shall have the art of reason, of truth, of
precision, and I will come over to your side bag and baggage. But
I search in vain. . . .

"As a musician, I declare that if you suppress adultery, fa-
naticism, crime, fallacy, the supernatural, there is no longer any
means of writing a note. Art has its philosophy, to be sure, but to
define it you have to murder the language.—*The science of wisdom*—. Certainly that's it, except it is just the opposite! Listen, I
am a wretched philosopher (you can see it clearly), but I assure
you that I would compose better music if I believed in everything
that is not true. . . . Art falls to pieces as reason advances. You
don't believe it. *It's true,* nevertheless. Give me a Homer, a Dante
today. With what? Imagination lives off chimeras and visions. You
deny me my chimeras, good-bye imagination. No more art! Science
everywhere! What if you say *where is the harm?* Then I will leave
you in the lurch and not argue any more, *because you are right.*
Just the same it is a pity, a great pity. . . .

"It does me good to write to you. . . . You have wrenched
out of me a devil of a drinking-song that wouldn't come. Now I
have found it. I owe it to you. . . ."

Galabert protested against this painful, but far from inaccurate, prognosis of the future of the arts, and Bizet, in his next letter,
elucidated further. "In spite of my lack of practice in philosophical
jargon, I did not say, nor mean to say, that *science* is the enemy of
art. I said progress, which for me is an entirely different thing. I
spoke of the political, social progress toward which our philosophers are leading us directly. It is a good thing, but American and
not at all artistic."

Revealing as Bizet's letters may be of his intellectual development, they also hint at certain aspects of his personal life hitherto
ignored. His including adultery in the same category as crime and
prostitution is puzzling until one reads an account by Céleste
Mogador of an evening she spent with Bizet during the autumn
of 1866.

"One evening," Céleste wrote, "when he gave an audition of
one of his works for two gentlemen interested in hearing it, Bizet
played the entire score of a comic opera for us. . . . Charmed,
carried away by it, I applauded several times and cried 'Bravo. It is
superb from beginning to end. You will soon be able to build not

just a country house, but a château.' This remark obviously pleased him. Naturally our evening ended late. The gentlemen accompanied me home. It was a superb night. I gave Georges my arm, congratulating him on his inimitable talent. Without realizing it I pressed against him. So, leaning toward me he said, 'I would like to call your attention to the fact that I have always been very guarded with you. Now, tonight you are making advances to me!'

" 'My dear,' I replied laughing, 'my dear, you mustn't misunderstand me. I adore your talent. I am proud of your friendship, of walking arm-in-arm with you by moonlight, but my admiration is absolutely platonic. As for my emotions, I have never dreamed of finding a place in a heart that is like a rooming-house for transient lodgers.'

"He laughed and said, 'I could give notice to my other lodgers.' 'No. One of them has a lease, the wife of your best friend.' [4] 'I think that is finished. I no longer love her.' 'You may love her less, but you are still fond of her. Let it run its course, and we shall see later what to do with our fine, free friendship. But for now let's stay the way we are, good companions. Otherwise it's a hundred to one we'll quarrel later.'

"So the matter was understood and settled—at least for the time being," Céleste concludes." Unlikely as it seems, the relationship may have continued on this innocent level because of family reasons. Bizet's father seemed to Céleste "a saintly man" who respected Georges's independence and was as reverent before him "as the Holy Virgin must have been before her son, conceived by the grace of the Holy Ghost." Bizet's less reverent attitude toward his father appears in his instructions to a friend who was about to lend him some money at this time. After warning him against addressing a letter to M. Bizet, Composer, because in Le Vésinet he "would then be considered mad," Bizet urged him to be sure to include the name Georges on the envelope. "Otherwise," he wrote, "my father will open it, read it, throw it away or forget about it, or use it unopened for baser ends."

Céleste's mother, Mme Vénard, a confirmed slum-dweller, was an ill-tempered woman who resented the need of accepting her daughter's charity and disliked all of her daughter's friends, particularly Bizet, whose casual manners irritated her. Often when

---

[4] This lady has never been identified.

he returned from Paris on the midnight train he would as he passed Céleste's house "rap violently on the shutters with his cane or his umbrella, then continue on his way laughing." The dog would bark and, said Céleste, "we would all wake up with a start, my mother, my adopted daughter, my servant and myself. . . . Everybody would scream from one end of the house to the other, particularly my mother, who was nervous and excessively afraid of being in the country. Once awakened she could not go to sleep again. She had said to me, 'If he plays these practical jokes again he will have me to deal with.'. . . The window of her room was just above mine. One evening when I was writing, Georges saw a ray of light between the cracks of the Venetian blinds . . . and he kept rapping to tell me he had good news. I was more or less undressed, and answered, 'Wait a minute.' At that moment I heard something fall from the window above and Georges crying, 'How stupid! I've been drenched in an unexpected shower.' He yelled, he swore, he stormed out on the avenue while my mother, the little girl, and my maid, all practically undressed, came into my room, where they laughed like idiots escaped from a lunatic asylum. The dog, Blanchette, her hair bristling, her eyes popping out of her head, kept barking in a voice hoarse from yapping.

"And Bizet called from outdoors, 'It is shameful to empty chamber-pots on the heads of poor late passers-by.' My mother replied, 'You should have kept on going, you devil.' " [n]

Bizet's nerves and his relations with Céleste remained unaffected by Mme Vénard's assault. Indeed, during the three months he spent as her neighbor while composing *La Jolie Fille de Perth,* his equanimity remained undisturbed even after an argument with his publisher.

"I have just been talking to your son, and I realize that I made a fool of myself Saturday," he wrote to Choudens after an evening spent in Paris during which there had been discussion of the possible production and publication of the score of *Lohengrin.* "I offer you all my regrets, but let us put things in their proper perspective with no misunderstanding.

"1. To begin with, my opinion is worth no more than any individual's, that is to say, very little. I will explain what I mean. Reyer and Berlioz are great musicians. Yet Berlioz finds Wagner's music abominable, Reyer finds it splendid. It is quite evident that one of them is wholly mistaken. I am not yet either Reyer or Berlioz, and I could be mistaken!!

"2. While not admitting that I am artistically wrong, I do think it's a thousand to one that the public wouldn't agree with me. . . . I admire *Les Troyens*. The public doesn't like it. I adore *La Statue,* and the public is lukewarm. For me *Sapho* is an immortal masterpiece. The public didn't come to see it. In fact, if I had the same taste as the public I wouldn't have done my poor *Shrimp-Fishers,* an opera that one must, alas, confess hardly appealed to the public taste.

"*Requiescat in pace.*

"3. I have never judged an opera I don't know and which may be excellent. Out of eight or nine pieces I do know, three are in my opinion admirable, the rest not good (you see I am not extenuating my original judgment). But what does that show about its chances for success? Absolutely nothing! Four or five fine pieces —you don't need that many for a great success, to be sure. We see it every day.

"In short, *cher ami,* you would be crazy to worry for a moment about *one* opinion based on *one* or *two* auditions of scraps of an opera. So don't think any more about my blundering. When I talk to you, I am aware that I am talking to a friend, an artist (for you have an excellent artistic sense and you are perhaps in a better position than a professional musician like me to judge certain things), and I often forget that I am speaking to a publisher. . . . Don't be upset about it and *go ahead*—that, I think, is the most important thing.

"Once and for all, never attach too much importance to the judgment of musicians, even the best. They identify themselves with the work; they see it from a special point of view. They are prejudiced without knowing they are, and it blinds them. . . ." [n]

When he returned to the turbulent life of Paris in November, Bizet's high spirits rapidly evaporated. His last letter from Le Vésinet in October 1866 speaks of hard work: two acts of *La Jolie Fille* composed, two more to do and nine hundred pages of orchestration. But after only two or three weeks in Paris, he is worn out. "I have been obliged to give up orchestrating my symphony," he complained to Galabert. "As soon as *Fille de Perth* is finished, I shall go back to it, but doubtless too late for a performance this winter. . . . The farther I go, the more I despise our poor human-kind. Except for you, Guiraud . . . and a few rare friends who, unfortunately, are married!!!! I see nobody. And we are all young! . . .

"I am going to bed, *mon cher ami,* I haven't slept for three nights and am becoming too gloomy. Tomorrow I have to write gay music!"

By December matters were worse. "You will forgive me, won't you," he asked his pupil, "for my delay in correcting your *envoi?* If you knew what my existence has been for the last month! I work fifteen and sixteen hours a day, more sometimes, because I have lessons to give, proofs to correct. One must live. Now I am calm. I shall have to spend four or five more nights, but I will have finished. [Carvalho] is being baited by composers who are lending him money. I want to be paid or played. To do this, I have to stick firmly to the terms of the contract. I am well satisfied with my work. It is good, *I am sure.* I am far along with it."

On December 29, just six months after he received the com-mission for *La Jolie Fille de Perth,* Bizet gave the finished score to Carvalho. "Now we shall see," he wrote. "I sense that they want to put me off, but I shall accept no delay. Into rehearsal or into court." But it was beyond Bizet's powers to enforce either alter-native. A long and difficult year would go by before he would finally see his opera performed.

Paul Lacombe: Competition:
Bizet, Music Critic

Early in 1867 an announcement appeared in the *Revue et Gazette Musicale* stating that Christine Nilsson would sing the leading role in *La Jolie Fille de Perth,* to be produced immediately after the *première* of Gounod's *Roméo et Juliette,* which was in rehearsal. A heartening prospect for Bizet, it would seem. But the editors of the *Gazette* omitted mention of the disastrous failure at the Théâtre-Lyrique on January 14 of an opera called *Deborah.* The composer, one Devin-Duvivier, had paid the expenses of producing his work, and Carvalho had mounted it hastily. When, in a masked ball scene, the audience recognized costumes from all the other operas in the repertory, they roared with laughter. Bizet was not amused, In spite of his awareness of Carvalho's financial straits, he was unable to reconcile himself to the director's accepting money from composers. "[*Deborah*] was a ridiculous, shameful failure," he wrote to Galabert. "The same thing will happen to all the works by composers who pay. [Carvalho] asked us *on his knees* to grant him a little more time. He is being hounded by his creditors. Mlle Nilsson is engaged for our work at five thousand francs per month. We will rehearse from March to the end of May. Then Nilsson goes to London for two months and comes back August 15 for *La Jolie Fille de Perth.* All this is subject to a new contract that calls for a 22,000-franc forfeit. The opera will go on or he'll pay. It is sad to have reached this point, but we will fight to the bitter end. This time he keeps his word or we will *kill* him. The ministry, everybody, is for us, and this last concession has made everybody sympathetic to our side. *Sardanapale* will fail; *Cardillac* will fail; Jules Cohen's *Les Bleuets* will fail. Let the usurers, the heartless and talentless, have their day. That's my revenge. The future, our worth, and our conscience will compensate us." [1]

As the winter progressed, there seemed to be little compensation. "My life is insane," Bizet wrote to Galabert in February. "You can judge for yourself. Almost every day I go to Carvalho's, then to Saint-Georges's, from the Châtelet to the rue de Trévise. Every day I dine in town. I have not yet been able to break off certain personal relations. Every day I give lessons. I have to supervise the publication of *Mignon,* reduce the score for piano solo, six hundred pages, two sets of proofs; twelve hundred pages and eight hundred of separate parts, as well as the arrangement for voice and piano, etc., etc. I must slow up. I am ill. [Carvalho] is frightened by the failure of [*Deborah*] and the imminent failure of [*Sardanapale*], and has been hauled over the coals by the ministry, which is indignant that a state-subsidized theatre should be presenting paid works. So, after endless negotiations he has decided to play it safe, and I am about to go into rehearsal. . . . You can't imagine how much intellectual energy and will-power it has taken to achieve this result. To be a musician today you must have either an independent income or a real talent for diplomacy."

This talent, as we have seen, Bizet did not feel called upon to cultivate in his relations with his publisher. "I am completely discouraged," he wrote to Choudens. "I am letting my collaborators change their contract. The public prefers *Deborah, Sardanapale,* and *Les Bleuets* by the usurer, J. Cohen, to my music. So be it. To open in August . . . when nobody will any longer be in Paris, I find deplorable. One would really think that everybody was conspiring to destroy me. Perhaps they will realize, but too late, that admiration based on *convention* and *self-interest* won't bear careful and intelligent scrutiny. . . . If I die of worry, discouragement, and also of hunger one of these fine days, it will occur to someone to do something about *La Jolie Fille* and *Ivan.* If these works ever have any success, the lesson will be useless for the future because

---

[1] Bizet, *Lettres à un ami,* 101–2. Subsequent quotations in this chapter from this work will not be individually noted. Unpublished portions of the letters are enclosed in square brackets.

coterie-praise will continue. The days of the yes-sayers are not numbered, nor of the usurers either." [n]

In spite of his bad temper and anxiety, Bizet continued throughout this long winter to criticize Galabert's work and to set him new exercises. But the time had come when, out of exhaustion or boredom, he was forced to admit to himself that Galabert lacked any creative spark. "You know your craft, and you must no longer write anything that is not felt; I don't believe that you have *felt* this work," he told him. "It is a lesson; it is not music. You have now arrived at the point of being a composer. The fugue will help you to grow, but with the *fugue* you must try to create imaginative works. Forgive my frankness, but as a friend I can't beat around the bush."

Fortunately for Bizet, who could for the time being find little satisfaction in expressing musical ideas to Galabert, a new pupil-correspondent turned up in March whose work he found truly distinguished. Like Galabert, Paul Lacombe was a native of the south of France. Born in Carcassonne the same year as Bizet, he was the son of a wealthy manufacturer and a music-loving, artistic mother. Essentially an *homme de culture* rather than a creative artist, he expressed himself in poetry and prose as well as in music. He traveled through Europe collecting paintings and objects of art to furnish the house in Carcassonne to which he returned from his travels during the eighty-nine years of his life.

Musically he was "ultra-sensitive, nostalgic, eclectic," the embodiment of French "Schumannism." He was influenced, too, by Chopin and by Bizet, who introduced him into the musical world of Paris. Lacombe became a close friend of Massenet and, later, of Chabrier, Vincent d'Indy, and Henri Duparc. He composed more than one hundred and fifty orchestral works, many of which were played in France during his lifetime.

When Lacombe applied to Bizet for lessons in 1867, he had been studying piano, voice, and harmony in Carcassonne with a professor from Paris who had given him a copy of the score of *Les Pêcheurs de Perles*. His admiration for this opera prompted him to seek out Bizet as a teacher. Bizet wrote in reply: "I am twenty-eight years old. My musical baggage is pretty slender. An opera very much discussed, attacked, and defended—a failure in short, honorable, brilliant, if I may use the expression, but still a failure. Some songs—seven or eight piano pieces—some symphonic fragments performed in Paris—and that's all. In some months' time a big work, but that is counting my chickens—don't let's speak of it.—I am known to artists and in Parisian society—a total of about four or five thousand persons whom we call *tout-Paris!*—Did you happen to see the score of my *Pêcheurs de Perles,* and is that the source of the confidence with which you honor me? It would be very flattering—but I doubt it. . . .

"In general, I accept your proposal. But before we start, I must know what you want to do. Judging by the remarkable samples that you sent me, I think you want to go as deeply as possible into the study of your art. Actually, you can.—You have style, you write marvelously.—You know your masters, particularly Mendelssohn, Schumann, and Chopin, whom you seem to cherish with a perhaps slightly preclusive affection.—But I am certainly not courageous enough to reproach you for this preference. Either you have studied counterpoint and fugue or you are specially and extraordinarily endowed. . . . Send me a detailed letter. . . .

"As to terms, sir, I don't know how to answer you. I don't much like dealing with that side of things. If I had any money, I would be happy to devote some of my leisure to you. I should consider myself amply paid by the progress I could help you to make. Unfortunately I have no leisure! Lessons, a vast amount of work for several publishers, too many engagements—all this swallows up my life. I am therefore forced to accept, not the price of my advice, but the price of the time I would devote to you. I charge twenty francs for my lessons. On an average my time is worth fifteen francs an hour to me. Do you want to base our arrangement on this consideration? We shall be able to work out a general average according to the amount of work you send me. . . . The important thing is to avoid discussing it, for I find these details particularly unpleasant." [2]

Lacombe was a tactful man. "Your letter gave me real pleasure," Bizet told him. "If anything can compensate for the indifference of a blasé, uninterested public, it is certainly the approval, the understanding of men of taste and intelligence who, like you, devote the best part of their lives to the highest creed of art. We

---

[2] Hugues Imbert, *Portraits et études,* Paris, 1894, "Lettres à Paul Lacombe," 162–4. Further quotations from this source will not be individually noted in this chapter.

both speak the same language, a language foreign, alas, to most of those who consider themselves artists. Our ideas are the same, in general. But the differences in our backgrounds will sometimes give rise to slight disagreements.—I have lived for three years in Italy and educated myself, not through the shameful musical methods of that country, but through the temperament of some of its composers. Besides, my sensuous nature lays me open to the spell of this music, which is at the same time facile, lazy, amorous, lascivious, and passionate.—By conviction, heart and soul, I am German. But I sometimes go astray in evil artistic haunts.—And I confess to you, in an undertone, that it gives me infinite satisfaction. In a word, I love Italian music as one loves a courtesan; but it must have quality! And when we have cited two thirds of *Norma,* four pieces in *I Puritani,* and three in *La Sonnambula,* two acts of *Rigoletto,* one act of *Il Trovatore,* and about half of *Traviata,* in addition to *Don Pasquale*—we can toss out all the rest. As for Rossini, he has *Guillaume Tell,* his sun, and *Comte Ory,* the *Barber,* one act of *Otello,* his satellites. Because of these, his dreadful *Semiramide* and all his other sins can be forgiven. I felt that I should make this little confession so that the implications in my advice will be wholly clear.—Like you, I place Beethoven above the greatest, the most renowned. The symphony with chorus is for me the culmination of our art. Dante, Michelangelo, Shakespeare, Homer, Beethoven, Moses!—Neither Mozart, with his divine form, nor Weber, with his powerful, colossal originality, nor Meyerbeer, with his overwhelming dramatic genius can, in my opinion, contend for the crown of the *Titan,* the *Prometheus* of music. You see, we still understand each other. . . .

"I shall be perfectly sincere about your *Rêverie.* I really don't like it very much. I hope you won't hold that against me. I owe you the truth, and I shall always tell it to you in spite of everything. . . . In art there should be no indulgence!

"I have no specific criticism to make of this piece. . . . It is soft, dull! The idea is brief. The poetry in it is not exquisite enough for the dreamlike tone that you attempt. There is, doubtless, a certain languor, a certain charm in all this, but not enough. Obviously, it isn't bad, but you should, you could, do much better.—Take my word for it. My criticism will seem severe. But wait a while. Let the thing sleep, and when you see it again after having almost forgotten it, you will agree with me. You will find it rather a *soap bubble!* I have always noticed that the least successful compositions are always those most cherished at the moment of birth. I suspect anything that smells of improvisation.—Look at Beethoven. Take the vaguest, the most ethereal works; they are always deliberate, always sustained. He dreams, yet his idea has body. You can grasp it.—Only one man has been able to do quasi-improvised music, or what seems like it, and that is Chopin. . . . His personality is charming, strange, unique, and one should not try to imitate him. . . .

"Thank you for your photograph. I can't send you one in return, as I haven't any. I have been photographed only once, at the request of Princesse Mathilde, who insists on collecting the heads of her Sunday guests; and my friends have stolen all the prints."

As a postscript to this letter, Bizet, "exhausted" after the opening of Verdi's *Don Carlos,* wrote: "Verdi is no longer Italian; he wants to do some Wagner. He no longer has his weaknesses, but neither has he a single one of his virtues. . . . Artists perhaps will forgive him an unfortunate attempt that gives evidence, after all, of his taste and his artistic integrity. But the dear public came to be amused, and I don't think they will be caught again. The press will be bad."

To Galabert he wrote in much the same vein: "*Don Carlos* is *very bad*. You know that I am eclectic. I adore *Traviata* and *Rigoletto. Don Carlos* is a sort of compromise. No melody, no accent. It aims at a style, but only aims. . . . It was a complete, absolute *failure*. The Exposition may make a semi-success of it; nevertheless it is a disaster for Verdi."

Soon after the opening of *Don Carlos,* Bizet went to Bordeaux to hear the tenor Massy, whom he had engaged for the role of Smith in *La Jolie Fille de Perth.* He was satisfied with this choice, but the uncertainty of the opening date for his opera continued to worry him. His anxiety, as always, intensified his latent sense of persecution. "[The authors of *Roméo*]" he wrote to Galabert, "have done everything possible to postpone and even compromise my work. The human race is ignoble, my poor friend. But I shall have my revenge—and cruelly, I can tell you." As usual the mere utterance of the threat dispelled Bizet's desire for revenge against Gounod. All through the winter months, and even after the opening of *Roméo,* he slaved with the utmost concentration on the piano and voice reductions of the score of Gounod's opera, even writing lyrics to replace the spoken dialogue. After one of the many rehearsals he attended, Bizet wrote to Adenis, a friend who was also one of the librettists of *La Jolie Fille:* "Stormy rehearsal of *Roméo* yesterday! Gounod furious at everybody! Choudens depressed! Carvalho . . . may have enough money to last two or three more weeks, but if there are further delays—who knows? I was not mistaken about *Roméo.* Revenge is starting." "

Bizet continued to feel himself surrounded by enemies. ["I have already quarreled with two-thirds of the musical world,"] he wrote at this time to the Belgian admirer previously mentioned. ["My enemies (I have many) claim that I have a frightfully disagreeable nature. If this rumor reaches you, don't believe a word of it, and continue to feel kindly toward me. The fact is that it is impossible for a high-strung man to regard with composure all the absurdities, all the disloyalties, with which life is graciously studded. They say—and I believe it—that in Belgium the composers and singers are honest, decent people. May I congratulate you on them? Forgive my bad temper, but I don't overcome anger easily."] "

There was nothing in the general atmosphere of Paris in the spring of 1867 to calm Bizet's anger or allay his fears. The much-touted Universal Exposition, which was to usher in a new era of peace and prosperity, was as hopelessly behind schedule as the rehearsals of *Roméo et Juliette.* Visitors to the opening ceremony of the Exposition advised shutting up "the palace and grounds until the works were finished and the place fit for the inspection of the public." Packing-cases lay everywhere. Some countries had not even begun to install a single object when the exhibition was declared open. Nevertheless, the ceremonies to inaugurate the "giant elliptical building shaped like an inverted pie-dish" were not postponed. On April 1, the Imperial party arrived at the Champ de Mars "in three *calèches* with outriders clad in the household liveries of green and gold. They had crossed the Pont d'Iéna under a canopy of cashmere powdered with golden bees. . . . The Emperor, dressed entirely in black, with the Empress leaning on his arm, closely followed by the Princesse Mathilde and a throng of chamberlains, ushers, equerries, and pages, down to footmen and *chasseurs,* moved painfully through the corridors of the elliptical palace, amid echoing applause, loudest from the sections of Egypt and the United States." [n]

The enthusiasm of the British was, naturally enough, restrained, as their exhibits were far from complete. In a despatch written before the Exposition had achieved its eventual success, the reporter of the London *Daily Telegraph* reminded his readers that "each of the Universal Exhibitions within our own generation has been closely followed by a bloody and destructive war. . . . And in 1867, while all the nations are supposed to be basking in the sunshine of peace and amity in the Champ de Mars, there is a prevailing smell of saltpetre in the air and the rumblings of a coming earthquake are distinctly audible." [n]

Bizet was not deaf to these rumblings. But he urged Galabert not to permit the imminence of Bismarck's visit to Paris to discourage him from coming to the Exposition. "It is very well set up," he wrote. "You can eat there very cheaply. *Water-closets* [*sic*], *restaurants* (you know I would start with these), *reading* and *writing rooms, music, lights, cocottes, etc. etc.* They have thought of everything,"—everything, apparently, except the disastrous effect on the theatre of all these rival attractions. *"Don Carlos* is closing at the Opéra after fifteen performances and disgraceful receipts. The Opéra-Comique is closed temporarily; there is nothing on at the Théâtre-Lyrique. So you see, *cher ami,* we can count on nothing. All our hopes are evaporating, vanishing in thin air. . . ."

Although Bizet had no eyes for Norwegian and Swiss châlets, Tartars' tents, Arab mosques, or Rumanian pavilions, he himself was, in a manner of speaking, included in the Exposition. His name appeared—one of the only two young composers mentioned—in the official guidebook. The introduction to this imposing volume was written by no less a person than Victor Hugo. Although the great poet remained in exile, the government, as evidence of its new liberalism, had lifted the ban on his writings. Renan, Sainte-Beuve, Michelet, Gautier, Viollet-le-Duc, the Dumas, father and son, Taine, and Ambroise Thomas also contributed sections to the guidebook. Nestor Roqueplan, who wrote the chapter on the theatre, expressed his loyalty to Carvalho by including a flattering summary of that director's career.

"The sword that hangs over every great enterprise," said

Roqueplan, "fell on M. Carvalho. . . . But now he is back, with his daring, his novelties, his surprises, and his revivals. He has introduced two new composers, Georges Bizet and Barte [*sic*]. . . . I admit my weakness for this indomitable and inventive director, who has done more for the spreading of great music than all the other lyric theatres in Paris put together. He must, at last, hold a trump card and win the *match* [*sic*] in which he is engaged." [n]

The card Carvalho drew was Gounod's *Roméo et Juliette*. Despite a disastrous dress rehearsal, for which no invitations were issued, and despite Gounod's desire to postpone the *première* in order to prevent its conflicting with a great official ball, which he feared would attract most of his audience, the opera finally opened on April 27. Carvalho called its success "pyrotechnical." And *Roméo* was indeed Gounod's first complete triumph in the theatre. Ninety performances drew crowded houses. The critics praised it *en masse*. But in the audience there was at least one dissident voice. "Tunes there are in *Roméo*," wrote Ludovic Halévy, "charming and touching ones, but these melodies are drowned in long recitatives. There is no need to point out that this is Wagner's system, more discreetly used, with concessions to French taste and habits. . . . Roméo and Juliette meet perpetually and talk endlessly about the sun, the moon, and the stars—this becomes monotonous at the end of four hours. Messrs. Barbier and Carré are careful to avoid ordinary expressions. 'Oh, rise, appear, pure, charming star,' means the sun. It could also mean the moon. I find at least twenty or twenty-five apostrophes to the stars of day or night in *Roméo et Juliette*. As for nights of love and nights of madness . . . 'Sweet glances that intoxicate,' 'Flaming kisses,' etc.—they are countless. *Roméo* is not an opera. It is a perpetual love duet. . . . If the duet is interrupted by choruses or entr'actes from time to time, that is to give Mme Carvalho and Michot time to breathe. They catch their breath and repeat, 'Oh, night of madness! . . . One kiss, and I stay. One kiss and I go.' Ah, what kisses! Sung not only in every key, but bestowed by the dozen, right and left and at random. . . . I am sure that Mme Carvalho will receive more kisses from Michot in six months of performances than from Carvalho in ten years of marriage." [n]

At the Opéra-Comique the *première* of *La Grand'tante*, the first theatre work of the twenty-two-year-old Jules Massenet, whose friendship with Bizet began at this time, gave promise of the composer's future success. "Lively, charming, witty, revealing a skillful and talented composer; his personality as a musician is already apparent. . . . An experienced master could not have shown more tact and taste," [n] the critics wrote. But the public remained immune to the charms of this curtain-raiser, which lasted for only seventeen performances. "Massenet, who was supposed to bowl everybody over, had no success, and was played, thanks only to Ambroise Thomas's influence," commented Paladilhe, still waiting hopefully for a performance of his own first opera.

"Massenet was a rival, Bizet a brother," Saint-Saëns remarked more than once. But during the contest that occupied the attention of these young composers throughout the month of May 1867, the prevailing spirit was rivalry rather than brotherhood. A competition sponsored by the Committee for Musical Composition of the Exposition had been announced in February. But only at the last moment did Bizet decide to compete. A month before the deadline he wrote to his friend Ernest L'Epine, acting secretary of the Committee (Gounod and Verdi were the honorary secretaries), to ask for exact details. The subjects for the competition were a hymn "to be sung on international occasions," and a cantata entitled *The Marriage of Prometheus*. The author of the libretto, one Romain Cornut, *fils,* was still a pupil at the Lycée Bonaparte. The prize offered for the hymn was 10,000 francs and a medal worth 1,000 francs. For the cantata, in addition to the thousand-franc medal, the winner was to receive 5,000 francs in cash for each performance of his work. There were also two silver medals offered, two bronze medals, and six honorable mentions. The competition closed on June 5.

During May, when Bizet and Guiraud were slaving over their hymns and cantatas, Galabert paid his annual visit to Paris. Both composers, he says, regarded the cantata as a real opportunity to write good music. He thought that Bizet's cantata, now lost, was excellent. Neither Bizet nor Guiraud took seriously the hymn with fanfare. Dismissing it as a mere chorus for amateurs and schoolchildren, they amused themselves by making their versions as vulgar as possible. Wishing to avoid any risk of his handwriting's being recognized by the jury, Bizet set Galabert to copying his hymn while he and Guiraud orchestrated their cantatas.

"I remember the evening when the three of us worked at the

rue Fontaine. . . ." Galabert wrote. "Guiraud and I sat at either end of the table, with Bizet in the middle, the piano behind him. During the evening he got up, tried some chords several times over, humming them, then turned to us and asked, 'What instruments do you hear in that place? I can't find what I want.' We both told him what we thought, Guiraud rather absentmindedly without interrupting his work, and I curious to know what he would think of my suggestion. He answered, 'Yes, you're probably right—but not quite.' He continued at the piano, and a moment later he said, 'I have it! I have sweetness enough in the horns; but with only two bassoons I won't have enough bite; I'll use four.' He also added the violoncellos, the violas and clarinets in the low register. . . . The proportion of each of these instruments and the combination of them created a new sonority."

Galabert's cooperation extended farther. He permitted the composer, who signed his contributions with the pseudonym Gaston de Betsi, to use his Montauban address as further means of disguising his identity.

"Guiraud and I left our little monstrosities with the *concierge* of the Imperial Commission yesterday afternoon, Wednesday, the 5th, around half past ten," Bizet informed L'Epine. "Because of our appearance, or rather the shape of our packages, this high functionary exclaimed, 'What, again? More music! Everybody in the world is a musician, damn it! There's been enough of this!!!' There were several people in his room. We found ourselves in an intolerable situation, which I resolved by a stroke of genius. 'Not everybody is a musician,' I replied with the air of a lord of the manor, 'and I must ask you to believe that we are not musicians any more than you are. But I am interested in a poor devil who unfortunately is, and I particularly recommend his music to you.' Before my sentence was finished, he had bowed so low that the braid on his cap brushed my knees. All his guests bowed respectfully and said, in an aside, 'He is not a musician.' For everybody knows that not to be a musician these days means that one is either royalty—or a *concierge*.

"Phew, that's over!

"After two unspeakable nights, I am shamelessly writing to call your attention to my little efforts as well as those of Guiraud, whom I forced to compete. In the midst of this free-for-all, they may well have been mislaid or passed over. And it would be

annoying to have sweated that hard without even being considered:

"Guiraud: *Hymne*
    Paix à la Terre et Gloire aux Cieux—Lamartine
    *Cantate—Les siècles à ses pieds comme un torrent
    s'écoulent*—Lamartine
"Bizet: *Hymne*
    Fu il vincer sempre mai laudabit cosa [3]—Ariosto
    *Cantate—J'ai formé l'assemblage des lettres et fixé la
    mémoire, mère de la science et âme de la vie—*
    Aeschylus, *Prometheus*
"So there you are! A thousand thanks in advance.
    "Cordially and affectionately your friend,
        "Georges Bizet" [n]

Bizet's blatant attempt to influence a friend who was also a
member of the jury reflects the standard of ethics prevalent under
the Second Empire. But his maneuvers in his own and Guiraud's
behalf were no less cynical than the little hoax Paladilhe schemed
out for himself. Like Bizet, he wished no one to know he was
competing. But to improve his chances of winning, he submitted
two hymns, signing one of them with the name of his father, to
whom he wrote: "Don't worry. The prize will probably go to one
of the gentlemen of the jury."

Paladilhe's prediction was not far from the truth. For after
only three members of the jury had examined eight hundred and
twenty-three hymns, they declared themselves unable to make a
choice and canceled the competition. While awaiting the decision
of the cantata jury, Bizet went through a series of difficulties
trying enough to warp the judgment and disorganize the nervous
system of a less high-strung person. On the very day the competition closed, the tenor Massy arrived in Paris for rehearsals two
weeks early. Christine Nilsson broke her contract to sing Catherine
in *La Jolie Fille de Perth,* preferring to create the role of Ophelia in
Ambroise Thomas's *Hamlet* at the Opéra. Another prima donna
for *La Jolie Fille* had to be found. Carvalho and Saint-Georges
favored Mme Carvalho for the role, to which she was quite un-

---

[3] "The act of conquest has never been praiseworthy." On the margin of the
original letter, given by L'Epine to Ludovic Halévy many years later, the latter
wrote after this line: "He was conqueror in a thing forever praiseworthy."

suited. Bizet, on the other hand, felt that Jane Devriès was the right singer for the part. While this discussion occupied his days, he spent his nights correcting the final proofs of the piano-and-voice reduction of *Roméo et Juliette.*

"I have passed an atrocious fortnight," he wrote to Galabert, who had returned to Montauban at the end of May. "Saint-Georges has been fluttery. He wanted none of Devriès, who is altogether splendid. But finally everything was arranged this morning. Everybody hugged each other, everybody wept!—We will read Monday, start rehearsing Tuesday, and Thursday we dine together, Saint-Georges, Adenis, Carvalho, and I. Carvalho very nice, truly devoted; Saint-Georges *demanding* and *very malicious;* Adenis still brokenhearted; *me,* irritable and tired; [Choudens] muzzled; Gounod looking up to heaven; Massy no musician, but nevertheless excellent; Devriès superb, very satisfactory execution —that is about how things stand. From two to six months of rehearsals to go, and then—*let come what may!"*

In the meantime, the jury for the cantata had met four times to listen to one hundred and three compositions. Among its members were Auber, who slept most of the time; Ambroise Thomas, who voted for Massenet; Verdi, Félicien David, Théophile Gautier, Saint-Georges; Rossini, who did not appear; and Berlioz who, overjoyed at the victory of his candidate, rushed to the young composer's house to be the first to bring him the news.

"Saint-Saëns has the prize," Bizet rather gratuitously informed L'Epine immediately after the announcement. "I am delighted. Can you, will you tell me, between ourselves, naturally— I promise the most absolute discretion—can you tell me *frankly* the fate of my friend's and my little efforts? Did we rate? Was the rating good or not bad or bad? Burn this note and I will burn yours." [n] The reply, which has not survived, revealed that four of the hundred and three cantatas were "ridiculous," forty-nine passable, thirty-five good, eleven very good, three excellent, one perfect. Bizet was among the last fifteen, Guiraud among the three "excellent." The other two runners-up were Massenet and Weckerlin.

"My copy was supposed to have been recognized," Bizet wrote to Galabert. "M. [Jules Cohen] played me this dirty trick. I howled, and now they don't know what to think. A number of the gentlemen said to me, 'The cantata attributed to you was very good, but not as good as what you ordinarily do.' . . .

"Saint-Saëns wrote his cantata on *English paper,* disguised his copy, and the gentlemen of the jury thought they were awarding the prize to a foreigner!!!!!!" Paladilhe claimed that the paper Saint-Saëns used was German, "which made the jury think that the contribution might be by Wagner. . . . They were disagreeably surprised when they opened the envelope and found the name of Saint-Saëns."

Bizet, on the contrary, found as much satisfaction in Saint-Saëns's victory as his own confused emotions permitted. "A very fine fugue with two choruses gave the prize to Saint-Saëns, and I am delighted," he said. "However, the jury . . . will go blabbering all over that, although Saint-Saëns's work is very remarkable and gives evidence of extraordinary symphonic gifts, it proves at the same time that the composer will never be a theatre man!— Oh, the human race!

"I was annoyed for half an hour. Now it's over. The important thing is that no one should know that I took part in the competition; this has been arranged."

Bizet's congratulations to the victor were despatched before he had wholly recovered from the shock of his defeat: "A thousand compliments, old man. I regret not having competed. I should then have had the honor of being beaten by you. Your friend, Georges Bizet." [n]

Saint-Saëns's official victory profited him little. The announcement of the award was duly made, but no cash prize was forthcoming: by not playing the cantata, the authorities avoided paying the five thousand francs due the winner for each performance. Instead, on the promised date in mid-July at the awarding of the Grand Prizes of the Universal Exposition, an orchestra of three hundred and fifty players and the Opéra chorus of one hundred and fifty voices executed *A Hymn to Napoleon III,* words by Pacini, music by Rossini. The old Italian, after eliminating any conflict of interest by avoiding his duties as juryman in the competition, had gone to the Tuileries to submit his own hymn to the Emperor. "I should prefer to say nothing about the merits of this hymn," one spectator at the ceremony commented. "Some competent critic may inform you whether the jingling tune and puling accompaniment were worthy of a *maestro* who was brother to Meyerbeer and Bellini." [n]

The overwhelming hit of the season was *La Grande Duchesse*

de Gérolstein, libretto by Meilhac and Halévy, music by Offenbach. To the Parisians, "with their long faces, dying of fright without being able to say why," this tuneful satire on war and the stupidity of the military served as distraction and purge. "Because no one has any really clear idea of the danger, everybody is frightened," Prosper Mérimée explained to the mother of the Empress Eugénie in the spring of 1867. "M. de Bismarck has become the universal bogey-man. His words are weighed and reweighed, and people think he wants to swallow us whole. . . . If you could see the way our poor country is split, the lack of patriotism, the love of money and high living, you would not recognize the French of the past and you would dread a war for them, even against an enemy of inferior strength." "

In the imaginary Grand Duchy of Gerolstein there was no threatening exhibit of Herr Krupp's inventiveness, blatantly in evidence at the Exposition. Here the hero was General Boum, a parody of the ineffectual, bombastic commander, eager for war, no matter what the cause, and incapable of planning a campaign or achieving a victory. He delighted the audience as the *reductio ad absurdum* of a figure familiar in real life, and for the time being dispelled their fright. Bismarck, too, enjoyed the spectacle, both for itself and as evidence of the weakness of the French. Indeed, one of the authors gave the Prussian warlord credit for much of the success of *La Grande Duchesse.* "This time it is war we are making fun of," Ludovic Halévy said, "and war is at our gates. . . . People look for and find allusions to absolute power and the military mind. Events are giving our jokes a significance and violence that we had not intended." "

To the fifty-six of the fifty-seven visiting monarchs who repeatedly witnessed Offenbach's piece, its strongest appeal was not political. (The one royal personage who absented himself from the theatre was the Emperor of Austria, in mourning for his brother Maximilian, the news of whose death in Mexico in July cast a fleeting shadow over the festivities.) The magnet attracting the Prince of Wales, the Tsar of all the Russias with his sons, the Sultan, and the many kings was the Grand Duchess herself, played by the brilliant and daring Hortense Schneider. Royal guests flocked to her dressing-room after every performance, and so completely did she identify herself with her role that on her first visit to the Exposition, she ordered her carriage driven to the entrance reserved for royalty. Stopped by the guards, she protested: "But I am the Grand Duchess of Gérolstein," and the gates opened.

On August 3, under the pseudonym Gaston de Betzi (the change of one letter in the name Betsi, which had proved unlucky in the competition, hardly served as a disguise now), Bizet announced, in his first and only published article, that ". . . following the example of Berlioz and Reyer, I have . . . accepted the post of music critic to the *Revue nationale,* which has kindly been entrusted to my inexperience and good will.

"Being a very modest amateur in all that concerns literature, I have never until today taken up the pen except to converse with my friends. . . . So you realize, my dear reader, that you will not find in my column . . . the sparkling wit of Nestor Roqueplan, the enchanting style of Théophile Gautier, the formal elegance and conciseness of B. Jouvin . . . or the caustic vigor of Ernest Reyer, or—but some ill-natured fellow interrupts me and cries, 'Then what *shall* we find, you humbug?' . . . the truth, nothing but the truth, and so far as is possible the whole truth. I belong to no clique, so I have no fellow-members. I have only friends, who will cease to be my friends the day they no longer respect my freedom of judgment and my complete independence. . . . Respect and justice for all, that is my slogan. Neither idolatry nor insults, that is my line of conduct."

Having begun in this hopeful and courageous manner, Bizet launches an attack on "the cult of formula from which springs that barren warfare, those arid discussions which bewilder, sap, and consume the boldest, strongest, and most fertile movements. . . . Quibbling takes the place of progress, wrangling supersedes creation. Composers are growing rare, while factions and sects multiply without limit. . . . We have the music of the future, the music of the present, and the music of the past; then there is philosophical and ideological music, recently discovered by a very talented journalist. . . . We also have melodic music, harmonic music, learned music (the most dangerous of all), and finally, a state-patented brand of cannon music! [4] Tomorrow we shall have nuts-and-bolts music, force-pump music, and double force-pump music—this last above all! How stupid it all is! For me there are only two kinds of music—good and bad."

---

[4] An allusion to Rossini's Hymn for four bass voices and orchestra performed at the Exposition of 1867.

To establish a criterion for discriminating between good and bad music, Bizet quotes the poet Béranger: " 'Art is art, and that's all there is to it.'. . . A poet, painter, or musician devotes the utmost effort of his brain and spirit to the conception and execution of his work; he thinks, doubts, grows enthusiastic, despairs, rejoices, and suffers in turn; and when, more worried than a criminal, he comes to us and says, 'Look, and judge,' we do not let ourselves be moved. We ask him for a passport . . . for his opinions, his contacts and his artistic antecedents. That is not the business of criticism; it is police work. The artist has neither name nor nationality. He is inspired or he is not; he has genius or talent or he has not. If he has, we must adopt him, cherish him, acclaim him; if he has not, we must respect him, condole with him— and forget him. . . . Let us be unaffected and genuine, not demanding from a great artist the qualities he lacks, but learning to appreciate the ones he possesses. When a passionate, violent, even brutal personality like Verdi endows our art with a work that is vigorously alive and compounded of gold, mud, blood, and gall, do not let us confront him and say coldly: 'But, my dear sir, this lacks taste, it is not gentlemanly.' *Gentlemanly!* Are Michelangelo, Dante, Homer, Shakespeare, Beethoven, Cervantes, and Rabelais gentlemanly? Must genius be dressed up with rice-powder and almond icing? Let us rather order our zouaves to storm the battlements in white ties and silk breeches!—Pardon my anger!"

Bizet's anger leads him to speak of that "cruel, terrible, mortal weapon . . . prejudiced criticism." He recalls "all the grief and misery," the "confidences on this subject," he had received as "pupil and friend of Halévy."

Remembering Bizet's inability in the past to make allowances for Halévy's weaknesses and the cool tone of his master's letter at the time of Mme Bizet's death, his change in attitude is worth noting. The antagonistic criticism heaped on him after the first performances of the Scherzo and *Les Pêcheurs de Perles* no doubt played some part in this hitherto unexpressed sympathy. But more probably, Halévy's daughter had kindled the fire of this new warmth: Bizet had just met his future wife for the first time. And what more appealing weapon for a suitor pleading his cause than this public expression of devotion to a lamented father, neglected by that very public? "Neither his high position nor his incontestable reputation could console him for the unjust and odious attacks of

which he was the victim. I do not want to doubt the good faith of
Monsieur X . . . but I could never forgive him the extreme pain
he caused to the famous and revered master whose memory I
cherish."

In concluding his article, Bizet turns to the immediate present.
"The musical program, so slow-moving in ordinary times," he
says, "has been brought to a complete standstill by the fairy-god-
mother known as the Universal Exposition. The cashiers of our
lyric theatres are asking for help: composers without work, please
note! *Don Carlos* and *L'Africaine* at the Opéra; *Mignon* and
L'Etoile du nord at the Opéra-Comique; *Roméo et Juliette* and
Faust at the Théâtre-Lyrique; *L'Oca del Caïro* at the Fantaisies-
Parisiennes; *La Grande Duchesse de Gérolstein* at the Variétés—
such is the musical balance-sheet at present. Meyerbeer, Mozart,
Gounod, Ambroise Thomas, Verdi, Offenbach: two of them dead,
two French, and two foreigners—these are the lucky ones today."

Among the unlucky ones was "Camille Saint-Saëns, who has
two completely finished operas in his drawer: *Samson* and *Le
Timbre d'argent*. Before these works are given the honor of
performance, there will be considerable impatience, disappointment and despair. I tell you in all truth," Bizet concludes, "composers are the pariahs and the martyrs of modern society. Like
the gladiators of old, they cry as they fall, '*Salve, popule! te
morituri salutant!*' [*sic*]. Music! What a splendid art, but what a
sad profession! Still, let us wait in patience, and above all, let us
hope!'" "

CHAPTER  XV

Malbrough s'en va-t-en guerre:
La Jolie Fille de Perth: II

I am completely happy!" Bizet wrote to Galabert after the dress rehearsal of *La Jolie Fille de Perth* on September 10, 1867. "Never did an opera have a better start! The dress rehearsal made a great impression! The piece is really very interesting; the interpretation is more than excellent! The costumes are rich! The settings are new! The director is delighted! The orchestra and singers are enthusiastic! And what matters more than all that, *cher ami,* the score of *La Jolie Fille* is a GOOD PIECE OF WORK! I tell you this *because you know me!!* The orchestra gives it all a color, a relief, that I admit I didn't dare hope for!" [1]

The dress rehearsal of *La Jolie Fille de Perth* elicited the kind of publicity usually reserved for an official *première*. Bizet's likeness, in the form of an amusing caricature, graced the cover of the popular weekly *Diogène* for September 28. The accompanying article admits that it would have been desirable to postpone publication of the cover-portrait until after the opening of the opera. "But," says Félix Jahyer, the editor, "the dress rehearsal was so brilliant we thought we should anticipate the future and tell our readers today of what we regard as an accomplished fact. M. Bizet's new score is the kind that immediately places its composer among the young masters whose future should count.

"The management of the Théâtre-Lyrique, aware of the value

---

[1] Bizet, *Lettres à un ami*, 126. Subsequent unidentified quotations in this chapter are from this source.

of this work . . . has postponed the first performance to mid-November so that 'the really fashionable audience' can be present."

The first two postponements of the opening, each for only a few days, were made in order to permit continued performances of Flotow's *Martha,* in which Christine Nilsson was drawing crowds at the Théâtre-Lyrique. The third postponement, to November 15, was at Bizet's own request because, as he said: "The cosmopolitan public which is honoring us in Paris at the present time runs to famous names and not to new pieces."

The composer, however, underestimated the appeal of his work. For there were visitors in Paris to whom the repeated postponements brought real disappointment. "I have a friend who is mad for Bizet's music," wrote the critic of the *Gazette de Hollande,* "who still rapturously remembers *Les Pêcheurs de Perles,* that undisputed success. This friend hurried to Paris to be present at the *première* of *La Jolie Fille de Perth.* He came from far off, and only with the greatest difficulty arranged to leave his business. Now he is obliged to go back with no game in his bag because of M. Carvalho's postponements. As my friend is stingy, he intends to bring suit for damages against the Théâtre-Lyrique." [n]

Another of Bizet's admirers, forced to leave Paris without seeing his friend's opera, was the young painter, Henri Regnault, whose sketches of Spanish gypsies and bullfighters, and whose singing of folk songs had an authenticity Bizet was to echo in his own portrayal of Spain. Henri Regnault's best-known painting, *Salomé,* which hangs in the Metropolitan Museum in New York, was in its own day as much a target of attack from the critics as *Carmen.* Regnault, who, like Bizet, was destined to die young, loved music and studied singing at the Conservatoire. "He was his own violin," said Saint-Saëns. "Nature endowed him with a tenor voice as enchanting, as irresistibly seductive as his penetrating gaze, his whole personality." This talented young Prix de Rome spent the summer and autumn of 1867 in Paris on leave from the Villa Medici. (Less subject to the spell of Italy than Bizet, he longed to see more exotic countries—Spain, Africa, the Far East. In 1868 he traveled in Spain with Clairin, who later designed Carmen's costumes.) At the Exposition he haunted the East Indian, Egyptian, Turkish, and Persian exhibits, spent days looking at photographs of Indian cities and monuments, nights listening to the music of the Hungarian gypsies.

In September, before the opening date of *La Jolie Fille de Perth* had been finally set, Regnault wrote to Bizet: "I am reminding you, in my name and in the name of Jadin, who lives far from here, that you promised to let us know the date of your *première*. You know how much we count on being present at that celebration, which I hope will be a triumph for you, and consequently for all your friends. Don't forget to tell us ahead of time. You would make us most unhappy if you didn't make use of our paws." [n]

In spite of the disappointment to his friends and admirers (Regnault had to return to Rome early in November) and the inconvenience to himself, Bizet's decision to postpone the *première* was sound. For in October, Paris was as sad as possible, Mérimée wrote. "The society people are away, and the businessmen, who are at present doing the honors, have long, sad faces. Everybody is frightened without knowing why. It's like the sensation Mozart's music makes you feel when the *Commendatore* is about to appear. M. de Bismarck, who is the *Commendatore,* will not, in my opinion, appear, and the rumors of war are not really serious. But there is universal nervous tension. The slightest event is regarded as presaging a catastrophe. In short, one feels stupid and bored." [n]

During this period of nervous tension, Bizet's career as a journalist came to an abrupt conclusion. Crépet, the editor for whom he had written his first article, which had been well received, left the *Revue nationale* in October to be succeeded by one Charpentier, who attempted to censor Bizet's further efforts at criticism. "He tried to keep me from ripping up Azevedo as I wished," Bizet wrote, "and I told him where he could go." When it came to the suppression of part of an article on Saint-Saëns, Bizet resigned. His feelings echoed those expressed by Flaubert to the Princesse Mathilde: "Not to have to write for the newspapers I regard as one of the fortunate things in my life. It lowers my income, but my conscience is clear, which is the principal thing." [n]

Unable to help Saint-Saëns by means of journalism, Bizet made the piano-vocal reduction of his friend's opera, *Le Timbre d'argent.* "It is charming," he said. "True *opéra-comique,* slightly tinged with Verdi. What imagination! What inspired melodies! Of Wagner, of Berlioz nothing, nothing at all. This Saint-Saëns scorns us with his opinions. You will be bowled over.—Two or three of the pieces are a little vulgar in idea, but they are very appropriate, and are saved by the immense talent of the musician. It is a real work and he is a real man, that one." [n] To the man himself Bizet wrote: "I am enchanted by the third act of *Le Timbre.* It has an exquisite tenderness and purity. The end of Hélène's lovely song is indescribably glowing. *It is excellent!* The other big scene is superb, too." [n]

In October, Choudens bought the score of *La Jolie Fille de Perth* on terms rivaling those given to Gounod. Bizet was to receive 3000 francs at the first performance and 1500 at the thirtieth; if the opera was performed 120 times within three years, he would get 16,000 francs in all. Although *La Jolie Fille de Perth* has still to reach its one hundred and twentieth performance, the hopeful prospect led Bizet to plan to marry Geneviève Halévy. "Now forward," he wrote to Galabert, shortly after the dress rehearsal. "I must mount, mount, mount. No more *soirées!* No more sprees! No more mistresses! All that is finished! Absolutely finished! I am saying this seriously. I have met an adorable girl whom I love! In two years she will be my wife! Meanwhile nothing but work and reading; thinking is life. I tell you this seriously; I am convinced! I am sure of myself! The good has killed the evil! The victory is won!" The victory, alas, was of short duration. Less than a fortnight after this euphoric announcement, Bizet scrawled, on the margin of one of Galabert's exercises, "I have just had a terrible blow. My hopes have been crushed. The *family* has withdrawn its consent! I am very unhappy."

The rehearsals of *La Jolie Fille de Perth* were resumed early in November, and simultaneously Bizet became involved in another theatrical venture that caused him additional irritation and anxiety. Largely to make money, he accepted the offer of William Busnach, recently become the director of the Athénée Theatre, to write the score of an operetta entitled *Malbrough s'en va-t-en guerre.* Busnach (cousin to Geneviève Halévy's mother), a good-natured and accommodating man, was regarded by his family as a not unendearing figure of fun, but he lacked, Bizet said, "the authority to help me." The key to Busnach's charm is perhaps most

succinctly expressed in one of the various mottoes he had embossed
in gold on his writing-paper:

> *"J'aime*
> *qu'on m'aime*
> *comme j'aime*
> *quand j'aime."*

An inveterate playwright, he "always had three plays going
simultaneously at three theatres, and ten others in preparation,
each with a different collaborator. Busnach was the type of play-
doctor . . . of carpenter, who rewrites an act in two days, the
petty officer of letters who goes from drama to farce to revue to
café-concert without ever specializing or excelling in any field." ⁿ
Although in later years this artisan was entrusted by Zola
with the dramatization of *L'Assommoir, Nana,* and *Pot-Bouille,*
his position in 1867 was not calculated to aid a young composer
in his resolution to "mount." The previous history of the theatre
Busnach was then directing demonstrates the lack of interest of the
Parisian public in the performance of serious music. Just a year
earlier, Louis-Raphaël Bischoffsheim, a wealthy banker and
naturalized French citizen of German birth, had taken over the
Athénée with the idea of presenting there, at his own expense,
the best music, as well as lecture courses by distinguished scholars.
At the end of one year the disillusioned M. Bischoffsheim abandoned his philanthropic project.

"The Athénée in the rue Scribe has gone over to false gods,"
wrote the critic of *Le Ménestrel.* "In reopening the doors of
this charming theatre, founded by M. Bischoffsheim in honor of
great music . . . the new director, M. Busnach, said to himself
not without reason, that one must keep up with the times. So he has
introduced operetta where the oratorio reigned. . . . The transition is a stiff blow, but it is all to the good, says M. Busnach, and
the public, which remained indifferent to the masterpieces of the
great composers, is entirely capable of proving him right. . . .
The opening piece, *Malbrough s'en va-t-en guerre, opérette-
bouffe* in four acts, has been given to four musicians whose talent
is unquestionable; I shall mention, in spite of the incognito
rigorously maintained by the first of these young masters, Messrs.
Georges Bizet, Emile Jonas, Léo Delibes, and Legouix. M. Léo
Delibes, as a good friend, has taken care of the act that was only

sketched by Georges Bizet, who is wholly given over to *La Jolie Fille de Perth.*" [n]

Bizet's own version of the *Malbrough* affair, which up to now has been accepted as accurate, exists in a letter to Lacombe. "I told them at the Athénée where they could go. But they came to my house, weeping, and I dashed off the first act for them. Legouix has undertaken the second, Jonas the third, and Delibes the fourth. The secret was kept well enough; but it has just been discovered by a woman, and all is lost. I shall disown it shamelessly. I would like to hiss the first act—apart from the fact that the public will do it quite well without me! I have been completely duped. . . . They reproached me for not keeping my word, they wailed, and I *gave* them my first act. It won't bring me a red cent. Decidedly I don't make much progress in business affairs." [n]

The woman in the case appears to have been Mme Trélat, a gifted singer and teacher of singing, hostess of a musical salon, and friend to many young musicians. As part of the "shameless disowning" of his share in *Malbrough s'en va-t-en guerre,* Bizet apparently indulged in exaggerated praise of the work to Mme Trélat, attributing its authorship to Delibes. To the latter composer, Mme Trélat thereupon wrote a letter of congratulations, quoting an unnamed admirer of his work.

"First, *chère Madame,* let me tell you how touched I was by your affectionate letter and the feeling that prompted it," Delibes replied. "But, look, is it really so serious, and isn't the mysterious and kindly 'Someone' our friend Bizet, who wanted to play a joke on me? Then, too, is it really right to label as *opera* or *score* these suites of little pieces, barely sung by the kind of singers who, at the moment, hold sway in all these music-hall ex-theatres?

"Personally I can't complain, for I have gained a certain notoriety through it. But frankly, while bearing in mind what this type of thing requires by way of liveliness and dash, and believing that it permits of the work of a musician, I find that 'M. Someone' grants it an exaggerated artistic importance. . . .

"As for *Malbrough,* here is the truth which I give you *confidentially,* as it seems that the mystery about it must be continued to the end. . . .

"In the beginning I was approached to write the music for this elongated sketch. I was skeptical about the future of the theatre, and only half liked the piece. I hesitated; meanwhile Bizet accepted the job on the express condition that its authorship remain unknown.

"Then Carvalho found out about it and made him see that as his piece at the Théâtre-Lyrique would be done at the same time, his name was bound to be discovered in the end, and that it would do him harm. He agreed, and abandoned the project; nevertheless, he left his first act, but without orchestration (this I have found out since). The rest was offered to two musicians who apparently didn't work quickly enough. For one fine morning Busnach arrived at my house to ask me as a favor to do the fourth act in a few days.

"My name was not to be mentioned, and nobody would know that I had anything to do with the work. I accepted, but once I had finished these few pieces, I wanted to have them executed as well as possible. And as my handwriting had been recognized, I could hardly hide the fact at the theatre that I was the author of one part of this masterpiece. That is how the whole thing was attributed to me.

"But, frankly, I cannot accept the paternity of the first act, which is by Bizet, orchestrated by I don't know whom (I re-did only one piece for Suzanne Lagier); the overture, which is by the orchestra director; the second act, which is by Jonas, the third by one M. Legouix. . . .

"Here, Madame, is the truth about this shady affair." [n]

Malbrough opened on December 13, and had considerable popular success. "Nothing could be more stylish, smarter and, at the same time, more distinguished than the few pieces in the first act by Georges Bizet, who will soon triumph with *La Jolie Fille de Perth*," reported the *Revue et Gazette Musicale*. In addition to its popular success, the operetta achieved a *succès de scandale* caused by a misinterpreted piece of stage business. "One of the actors, Léonce, thought he would produce a comic effect by sneezing into a pocket handkerchief bearing the equestrian figure of Napoleon I. No one dreamed of sedition . . . but one evening a country *sous-préfet*, happening to see the piece, was struck with horror at recognizing the well-known features on the square of cambric applied to the nostrils of Léonce. Fired by patriotic zeal, he returns to his prefecture, and instantly communicates to his chief, the prefect, the horrible incident he himself has witnessed. The prefect . . . addresses a confidential report on the subject to the Minister. . . . The Minister writes to his colleague, another excellency; that excellency summons M. Camille Doucet; notes, legal documents, etc., etc., are exchanged. Léonce, utterly unconscious that his handkerchief has become an affair of State, is informed that if he does not get another one of less seditious import, he will probably be arrested on stage by a company of gendarmes. . . . He now uses a handkerchief on which Croquet, taming his lions, is splendidly printed." [n]

Carvalho was understandably reluctant to jeopardize the future of the one serious opera he counted on to bring him success by having Bizet's name associated with this kind of notoriety. "Carvalho is in a *very low* state (and I don't mean his health)," Bizet wrote only a few days before the opening of *La Jolie Fille.* "I think today he is saved, but we mustn't be too sure. It would have been the last straw to force another postponement."

In October, *Les Bleuets,* by Jules Cohen, whom Bizet despised, had won no praise from critics or audience. The critic of the *Gazette de Hollande* remarked that except for Christine Nilsson, Carvalho had gone to no expense to secure good singers for the opera. "Let us hope he is saving them for M. Bizet's work, about which marvelous things continue to be said, while everyone is impatient at its not having been produced sooner."

Cardillac, by Lucien Daustrême, a politician who subsequently became Minister of Agriculture, of Commerce, and a senator, threatened further delay. But this piece, which opened at the Théâtre-Lyrique on December 11, failed immediately. Bizet's *première* was then set for December 24, only to be postponed once again, this time because of a disturbance chronic in the organization of the lyric theatres.

The male choral singers in the various operahouses also sang in the church choirs of Paris. When a conflict arose between God and Mammon, the performances in the theatres were either cut or hurried. A *première* on Christmas Eve, when the choristers automatically left in time to sing midnight Mass, would have been a disaster, especially as opening performances always ran late. Fortunately for Bizet, the chorus-master of the Lyrique was Henri Maréchal, a young composer who, as a pupil at the Conservatoire, had spent hours in the library studying Bizet's manuscript scores. After rehearsing for months with the composer himself, the chorus-master developed a personal affection for Bizet and a natural desire to see his work succeed. Torn between Carvalho's absolute decision to open on the 24th and the choristers' equal determination to sing at midnight Mass, Maréchal decided to put the matter up to Bizet, who, flanked by his two librettists, confronted the management and declared, "with his habitual brusque frankness," that he was opposed to the 24th as the opening date. After a stormy session, the composer emerged victorious. "On the 24th *Der Freischütz* was played. It even started fifteen minutes early. . . . At quarter past eleven it was over; and half an hour later Weber's huntsmen were singing matins in all the churches of Paris." "

On December 26, after a year of waiting, Bizet at last had the satisfaction of seeing his opera performed. "My work had a genuine and serious success," he wrote to Galabert. "I was not hoping for so enthusiastic, and at the same time so severe a reception. . . . They have taken me seriously, and I have had the great joy of moving, of gripping, an audience that was not wholly predisposed in my favor. I initiated a *coup d'état:* I forbade the leader of the claque to applaud. I know when to leave well enough alone. The press is excellent! Now, will we make money?"

The oldest, but still the most *avant-garde* of the critics, Théophile Gautier, wrote in the official government paper, *Le Moniteur universel:* "M. Bizet belongs to the new school of music and has broken away from made-to-order arias, *strettos, cabalettas,* and all the old formulae. He follows the dramatic action from one end of a situation to the other and doesn't cut it up into little motifs easy to catch on to and hum when leaving the theatre. Richard Wagner must be his favorite master, and we congratulate him on it. His aversion to four-square music, as boring as the alexandrines of ancient tragedy, will perhaps earn him the reproach of a lack of melody. But for this he will easily console himself. Melody does not consist of waltzes and popular folk songs. It blends with harmony as drawing does with color, and doesn't always leap above the orchestra like a ballet-dancer. M. Bizet's orchestration is skillful—we are not using this word in the derogatory sense usually intended—full of ingenious combinations, new sonorities, and unexpected effects. . . .

"In the second act we noted . . . particularly the bacchanale of the gypsies, which recalls with unusual felicity those strangely passionate songs with their mad verve, harsh, savage, yet so sadly tender and melancholy, so nostalgically reminiscent of the

Zigeuner. . . . M. Bizet has wonderfully understood the charming, wild poetry of this music, which, with all the colorful independence of the gypsy, joins voice to note and rejects any regulation of its caprice. Liszt . . . would approve the motifs of such intense local color. . . .

"We must note also all of the St. Valentine piece, with its fresh color, so loving and springlike . . . and the great scene of the challenge, where the composer gives proof of power that would be at home in the vast framework of the Opéra. . . .

"*La Jolie Fille de Perth* was a success, and its career will probably last long enough to permit the production, with all suitable care, of *Lohengrin,* that romantic masterpiece by Richard Wagner, which we are promised in a few months."

One of Bizet's harshest reviewers, a young man his own age, was critical equally of score and libretto. The latter, wrote Eugène Tarbé in the *Figaro,* "completely lacked local color, and had it not been for the costumes and the scenery, it might just as well have been presented under the title of *Mademoiselle de Belle-Isle* as *La Jolie Fille de Perth.* . . . The Scots in the piece are too Frenchified; the rough, harsh side of the half-savage mountaineers is not stressed. They remain the amiable and kindly Scots of *La Dame blanche.*"

Bizet, he continued, was such a skillful musician, such serious hopes were founded on him, that he had the right to severe criticism rather than the circumspection reserved for mediocre composers. After pointing out the improvement over *Les Pêcheurs de Perles* and praising the orchestration, Tarbé maintained that Bizet's vulnerable point was a lack of originality in his conception: "I found nothing new in the score that struck me as bearing the stamp of the composer. . . . M. Bizet has drawn his inspiration from the spring tapped by all the good composers of our epoch. . . . He has absolutely nothing new for us to listen to.

"In a man of his age the lack of creative exuberance is, I fear, an irreparable misfortune, and we dare no longer ask of the author more than what is intrinsic in him: great ability in treatment, a real theatre sense, and great skill."

Ernest Reyer, in the *Journal des Débats,* while praising his friend's many gifts, brings up the question of Bizet's eclecticism and his compromises. "Bizet is at an age," he says, "at which hesitation is permissible; and if his position does not yet justify his being extremely chary of all concessions to the public taste and to the virtuosity of certain singers, these concessions are, in my eyes, nothing more than the shortcomings of youth, which time will correct. . . . He himself, if asked to profess his views on the art of music, would be the first to admit his faults." [n]

The critic on *Le Temps,* Johannès Weber, gave Bizet the opportunity to make this admission. Ignoring the well-known fact that most of the "concessions" in Catherine's role were made for Christine Nilsson's coloratura gifts, Weber admitted that the "disparagement" of Bizet as a Wagnerian was unjustified, that compared with *Les Pêcheurs de Perles,* a "manufactured piece, set to a beginner's music," *La Jolie Fille de Perth* showed "a marked and honorable progress." But, he contended, "there is no reason whatsoever for making Catherine a flirt in order to motivate the jealousy, which is based on apparently sound reasons. Coquetry, however, is a very convenient pretext . . . for launching big pedal-points and for singing bravura melodies. I shan't insist on the theme-and-variations that Catherine spouts in the mad scene. These extravagances, I like to believe, are too outworn for M. Bizet to fall back on. If you must do it, coo in the Italian manner, solely for the pleasure of cooing, but don't pretend to put us off in the style of M. Gounod's ingenues. . . .

"The introduction is well written, but at Catherine's entrance we are subjected to a polonaise full of trills and far-fetched modulations. . . ." In the third act "the entrance of Glover and his daughter produces an ensemble piece in quadrille motif, derived in style from M. Auber, and accompanied by copious cooings from Catherine. Here was something to put M. Wagner to flight.

"After having sunk this low, M. Bizet had some trouble in recovering himself . . . but the last ensemble was excellent. . . .

"In the last act there was a pretty St. Valentine's chorus, but the rest isn't worth mentioning. . . . Of his gift for orchestration there is no question. . . .

"The success of *La Jolie Fille de Perth* will continue for a long time . . . but M. Bizet will never profit by sacrificing to the false gods of the quadrille, the *roucoulade,* and to several others, because they are false gods in which he himself does not believe."

Bizet leaped at the chance to corroborate the critic's claim for him, in a letter unpublished until it appeared seven years later in Weber's obituary notice of the composer: "It is impossible for me, sir, to refrain from telling you how good I think the excellent article that you were kind enough to devote to my new opera, *La Jolie Fille de Perth*. No, sir, no more than you do I believe in false gods, and I will prove it to you. This time, I admit, I have made some concessions that I regret. There are plenty of things I could say in my defense—you can guess them. The School of *flonflons*, of trills, of falsehoods, is dead, dead as a doornail. Let us bury it without tears, without regrets, without emotion and—forward march! Needless to say, sir, I am not, in this letter, trying to curry your favor, which would be as unworthy of my character as of yours. But, I repeat, your criticism pleased me, and I felt the need to tell you so sincerely." [n]

Apart from the stimulus Bizet derived from the published opinions of professional critics, *pro* or *con,* he received personal encouragement from men he respected. Ambroise Thomas praised the opera as a whole and said: "If people talk to you only about your very remarkable *second act* and pass over the rest in silence, you are extremely fortunate in having been able to put into a work a *culminating* point that catches and holds the attention of *all*." [n]

Ernest Beulé, the archeologist who had succeeded Halévy as permanent secretary of the Académie des Beaux-Arts, thanked Bizet for "the great pleasure I experienced last night while listening to your opera, a distinguished original work in which there are many sensitive, happy, fresh things. Your second act delighted me from one end to the other, as it delighted the audience. . . . I was at the *première* of *Les Pêcheurs de Perles; La Jolie Fille* shows that you are growing. I am sure that if it were being played at a theatre less removed from the center of things, your success would increase rapidly. In any case, I hope it will, for you deserve it." [n]

Another of Bizet's elders, one for whom he had very little respect, accorded him polite if reluctant praise. Auber, whose latest work, *Le Premier Jour de Bonheur,* had been recently produced, met Bizet in the street. The old composer, whose tone disclosed that he was merely uttering a well-worn formula, remarked: "Well, I have heard your opera. It's good, it's very good." "I accept your praise," Bizet replied, "but I don't reciprocate it." Then, as Auber scowled, Bizet hastily added: "A simple soldier may receive praise from a marshal of France; he does not return it."

Unfortunately, neither the reactions, personal or in the press, nor the merits of the piece brought success to *La Jolie Fille de Perth*. The Place du Châtelet, to which Carvalho had recently transferred his theatre, was too remote from the boulevards to attract casual theatre-goers. Besides, as Bizet wrote to Galabert in February 1868, "I am unlucky. Barré [who sang the role of the Duke] is ill. I can't cope with these indispositions which continually disrupt my work." Nor did Carvalho have the means to engage substitute singers. He alternated *La Jolie Fille de Perth* with Clapisson's war-horse, *La Fanchonette,* in which Mme Carvalho had won her first triumph. But the audiences for Bizet's opera remained sparse, and after eighteen performances Carvalho withdrew it, leaving the boards to the *chef-d'oeuvre* of Bizet's now-deceased enemy, Clapisson, who thereby achieved posthumous revenge for the premature "burial" celebrated in Bizet's parody.

Bizet's disappointment over the brief run of *Les Pêcheurs de Perles* had been easier for him to bear than the failure of *La Jolie Fille de Perth*. "Without having dreamed of a triumph or riches, he had believed that this time he was sure of a real success," wrote a friend, "and he had the right to believe it. . . . Too full of the sense of his own dignity to complain even to his best friends, he was too conscious of his worth not to feel that he was being denied the rank he deserved, and not to reveal glimpses of his suffering. He braced himself against the injustice, took refuge in work, and prepared himself for the struggle, which he had not foreseen as so rough. But he lost the bloom of his first gaiety, the fine confidence of his early years, and from then on, I noticed on his brow furrows of anxiety he never lost." "

CHAPTER XVI

Mme Trélat: *La Coupe du Roi
de Thulé*: The *Roma* Symphony

Bizet's disappointment over the failure of *La Jolie Fille de Perth*
in Paris was somewhat modified by the success of the opera in
Brussels, where it was first performed on April 14, 1868. Although
the composer was in Belgium at the time, for some reason he
avoided going to the capital. "I hear that *La Jolie Fille* is a success in Brussels," he informed Mme Marie Trélat. "I didn't go
there!—Just a notion!—But I saw the Rubens in Antwerp!—and
the Teniers, some Ostades, some Van Eycks, some Quintin Matzys,
etc., etc." [1] To Lacombe he repeated the report that "the performance of my poor *Jolie Fille* in Brussels was monstrous. In
spite of which it had a really genuine *success*. I have received a
number of encouraging letters. The press was excellent." "

In a year of major projects spun out or abandoned, important compositions unfinished or unsatisfactorily completed,
Bizet needed all possible encouragement. This he received from
Mme Trélat and her husband, Dr. Ulysse Trélat, whom he met
early in 1868. In their household he found a rare kind of friendship. The atmosphere created by this couple was highly stimulating, socially and intellectually, as well as musically rewarding.
Dr. Trélat, a distinguished surgeon, author of a two-volume work,
La Clinique chirurgicale, was the son of a more famous father

---

[1] Bizet to Mme Marie Trélat. Subsequent quotations from letters to Mme
Trélat in this chapter will not be individually noted. These undated, unpublished
letters are in the collection of the author.

who had published a number of books on the subject of insanity; the best known, *La Folie lucide,* is still valued by psychiatrists.

Mme Trélat, born Marie Molinos in 1837, was of Portuguese descent. After her father's death, she started as a young girl to give singing lessons, an occupation she continued throughout most of her life. Her mother, a singer too, had been coached by Rossini, who frequently came to Mme Trélat's house when she was young. Mme Trélat's granddaughter remembers her as a handsome woman, difficult, intense, dominating, with an amazing vitality that she retained to the time of her death in 1914. Passionately interested in politics, patriotic to the degree of chauvinism, she eventually became a strong anti-Dreyfusard. Like the Princesse Mathilde, she preferred the society of men and had little sympathy for the feminine mind.

Dr. Trélat, too, was difficult and forthright. If he found himself displeased by the style of decoration in the house of a wealthy patient, he might well remark: "It's dreadful here. How can you live in the midst of such horrors?" After a lunch party at the "princely palace" of Emile Girardin, George Sand, who had been a fellow-guest, noted that "when the conversation turned to materialism, positivism, nihilism, and spiritualism, Dr. Trélat was very sharp and intolerant." " This attitude hardly served to increase his practice. But Bizet, so often the victim of his own "run-away tongue," found Dr. and Mme Trélat's frankness most congenial. However, it was Mme Trélat's voice that held the greatest attraction for him.

"How you sang the other evening, Madame!" he wrote to her during the winter of 1868. "We were talking about it yesterday . . . and we agreed that nothing is more moving, more poignant than your wonderful talent. *Interpretation* thus conceived becomes *inspiration.*

"I tell you in all honesty that *nobody,* do you hear—nobody *sings, enunciates, feels, expresses,* the way you do. It's *perfect,* it's *true!*

"I am not easily moved. I know several artists who charm me. I know only one whose interpretation is the exact reflection of what I feel, of what I dream! That is you.—I shall tell you this again on Friday. In the meantime accept the great and respectful affection of Georges Bizet."

One of Mme Trélat's pupils, Mme Gaudibert, who studied with her in the eighties still remembers her musical intelligence as prodigious. "Mme Trélat's voice was mezzo, most engaging," she said. "People accused her of working it too hard, but the results were extraordinary. She had a very rare singing legato. She sang Gounod as though she were drawing a bow across a violin. Her best professor, she claimed, was Charles de Bériot." Son of La Malibran and the great Belgian violinist, himself a professor of violin at the Conservatoire, Bériot was greatly admired by Bizet, who dedicated one of the *Chants du Rhin* to him. While listening to the violinist, Mme Trélat would try to imitate the play of the bow on the strings, and she succeeded in achieving a very subtle, if not very strong, sustained tone. "The timbre of her voice was amazing, intensely warm. Her diction was fantastic. She held great store by it and taught her pupils a special system of breathing. Both as professor and as executant she was unique." "

During a large part of 1868 and 1869, Bizet played frequently and with great success at Mme Trélat's musical evenings. Indeed, apart from the many lessons he gave and the various arrangements and transcriptions he made of the score of Ambroise Thomas's *Hamlet,* he seems to have spent much of his time during the winter either at the Trélats' or in the company of Mme Trélat at her friends' parties. The programs for these musicales were most elaborate. One evening in February 1868, *Le Ménestrel* reported: "Two choruses . . . were sung by ladies and gentlemen of the social world, directed by M. Léo Delibes and accompanied by M. Georges Bizet—no less. Among the soloists we must note the voice and talent of Mme Trélat, who, to cap the evening, sang, with that exquisite artistry known to all, the romance from *Mignon* and 'Les Ducats' by Bériot.

"But that was not all: Christine Nilsson, the charmer of the day, delighted all the guests, first with Mme Trélat in a little duet by Blangini, which was encored; then with Delle Sedie in the little duet from *Don Pasquale* which the audience did not dare ask for again, for the rehearsals of *Hamlet* make demands on Ophelia's voice. Our Master, Ambroise Thomas, shone among the listeners. . . . His chorus from *Psyche,* which was so enthusiastically applauded at the Conservatoire concert before last, was sung twice."

At another *soirée* at Mme Trélat's a fortnight later, the *Benedictus* from Mme de Grandval's Mass was sung by the composer, the hostess, and the tenor Pagans. A pianist and a 'cellist played, respectively, a Chopin polonaise, the march from *The Ruins of Athens,* and two 'cello solos. Jane Devriès, the Catherine Glover of *La Jolie Fille de Perth,* sang Schubert's "The Nun." Mme Trélat sang a song from Gounod's *Sapho.* And to top the evening, Delibes directed the Nymphs' chorus from *La Source* and Bizet the St. Valentine's chorus from *La Jolie Fille.* "Both were enthusiastically encored, which was only fair to the young composers and the performers, all of whom were distinguished amateurs!" said *Le Ménestrel.*

Between these two non-professional performances Bizet attended the dress rehearsal of *Hamlet.* "I can't tell you, *mon cher ami,*" wrote Ambroise Thomas in acknowledgment of Bizet's congratulations, "how much I am touched not only by your praise, but by the sympathy, the spontaneous affection, I find in your splendid letter. I thank you and embrace you with all my heart." [n] The opera, which opened on March 9, had a wild success, but because of Christine Nilsson's London engagements was withdrawn after twenty-two performances that brought in 255,000 francs, a record unprecedented in the annals of the Opéra. Bizet, for his three reductions of the score of *Hamlet,* received 900 francs from Heugel.

During the first half of 1868 he composed only short works. He wrote six songs for the publisher Hartmann, among them *"La Chanson du fou"* and *"La Coccinelle,"* to words by Victor Hugo, and *"Berceuse"* to a poem by Marceline Desbordes-Valmore, set to a folk tune used earlier by Couperin, later by Fauré in *"Dolly"* and Debussy in *"Jardins sous la pluie."* "I am afraid I have done only very mediocre things," he wrote to Galabert. "But I need money, always money! To hell with it!" [2] His self-doubting, at least about the *"Berceuse,"* one of the few songs he wrote which bear no taint of salon music, was intensified, no doubt, by Mme Trélat's reaction. She had chosen the lyric, and the song was dedicated to her. "Friday," he told her, "you will have news of your song. I am so ashamed that I prefer not to dwell on the subject, counting on your friendship to excuse me—to forgive me. I am tired half to death. I have finished it for this time, and in spite of your very unsingable assumptions, I am not to blame. . . . I am

---

[2] Bizet, *Lettres à un ami,* 140. Only the unpublished portions of these letters, which are enclosed in square brackets, are individually noted in this chapter.

innocent and unhappy. All I needed was to be crushed by you.

"I do hope that you will be frank and that you will make me start the page over again as many times as necessary. I want to set these little verses to the right, or at least approximately right, music. . . . It is wrong of you not to be willing to sing at the funeral of your thousand times respectful and devoted friend, Georges Bizet."

A few days later, he again complained that he was "going through a dreary time. I am finishing the score of *Hamlet* for four hands. What a job! I am dead of fatigue, of boredom, of discouragement, and of spleen. But in spite of my bad humor Thomas's music has sometimes triumphed! It is really admirable—this *Hamlet*.—I have quite simply cut out four songs. I will come and tell you about it next week."

Early in May 1868 an event occurred which, while shocking Bizet out of his boredom, only added to his depression: Carvalho's long-deferred failure finally materialized. In March, in an effort to ward off bankruptcy, he had rented the Théâtre de la Renaissance, where he proposed to give grand opera and works in translation. He hoped that eventually the Renaissance, which was nearer the center of Paris than the Châtelet, would become his sole investment. In mid-March he opened with *Faust*, half an hour late, in an unheated auditorium. The singers sang badly; the chilled audience applauded Mme Carvalho out of sympathy. On May 6, both the Théâtre-Lyrique and the Renaissance closed, and Carvalho's bankruptcy was announced. Deeply distressed, Bizet wrote to Choudens: "When I left Carvalho yesterday I was convinced that everything was hopeless for him. The announcement in the *Figaro, La Liberté,* etc., is a staggering blow.

"Alas, poor Mme Carvalho!!

"My dear Choudens, God knows what will become of me, but at this moment, I confess, what makes me most miserable is the misfortune of that splendid and unhappy woman. . . . We shall perhaps have to protect ourselves. As for me, I am disposed to move heaven and earth." [n]

Bizet's anxiety about the rights to his works was as natural as it was, alas, unnecessary. For no other director was inclined to take over either of his operas.

Soon after Carvalho's disaster, Bizet escaped to Le Vésinet, where for a short time his spirits revived. "I am working hard," he wrote to Mme Trélat. "I am alone. Nothing bothers me. I hope to have a good summer." Any difficulties Bizet may have feared because of his changed relations with Céleste Mogador were resolved by her having taken a rich lover who spent sufficient time at Le Vésinet to warrant his adding to the Châlet Lionel a stable for his horse and carriage. Bizet did not, however, regain the composure that Céleste's companionship had brought him before he had fallen in love with Geneviève Halévy. His health soon began to show the effects of the strain he had undergone: "Yesterday the heights, today the depths! Thanks to Dr. Trélat's gargle, I am getting over it marvelously—it won't amount to anything, but it is no less true that yesterday's folly is paid for today! What I regret most is not seeing you tomorrow, not being able to express to you again, before you go away, my gratitude for the truly *unique* welcome I have found at your house.

"Both of you gave of your good friendship so openly, so spontaneously, that until now I have been more preoccupied with enjoying it than thanking you for it. But, don't worry. Inside me there is something—I don't know just what—that assures me I am not an ingrate.—A good journey, a good rest, a good Brittany is what I wish you and your dear *babys* [*sic*], Madame.—Come back to us ready to sing often as you sang yesterday. What a marvelous artist you are! . . . A touch of fever is my excuse for this horrible writing."

In July he wrote to Galabert: "I have just been very ill, a very complicated angina [forty tiny abscesses in my gullet, etc., etc.]." I suffered like a dog. Here I am up again, although still very weak. . . ." A month later he had a relapse. But the physical suffering he endured and the heightened awareness resulting from a running fever seem to have stimulated him to compose.

Early in the summer he resumed work on his *Roma* Symphony, which he had laid aside two years before. "I have finished my symphony," he wrote to Galabert. "I eliminated the variations. I think the first movement will be good. The old theme is now . . . preceded by an important quiet introduction, which recurs in the agitation and ends the piece in complete tranquillity. It is no longer at all like any known first movement—it is new and I count on its being effective. . . . It's funny to have looked for this for two years! The middle of the andante is the second motif of the finale, which fits marvelously into this broad movement!—

Curious! Devilish music! One understands nothing about it."

By August it seemed devilish to him, indeed. "I am still down in the dumps. . . ." he wrote to Mme Trélat. "I am very nervous and have been unable to write for the last two days. I must be illegible.

"The finale of my symphony is hateful, and I can't face replacing it. What a profession!"

During his illness, although he complained of having been unable to compose for a fortnight, he finished his *Grandes Variations chromatiques* for piano. This piece, based on a chromatic theme sketched the previous winter, was inspired by his friend Delaborde's playing on one of Erard's pianos. These variations pleased Bizet; he thought them "very boldly treated." While he was ill, he also composed a Nocturne in D major that he regarded as an important piece. But more important than any individual composition created during his illness was the self-revelation it engendered.

"An extraordinary change is taking place in me," he wrote to Galabert in July. "I am changing my skin, both as an artist and as a man. I am purifying myself, I am becoming better; I feel it! Who knows but that I shall find something in myself if I look hard enough? Excuse this slightly mad letter; but I have eaten for the first time today and I am still a little feverish." And two months later, after another bout of illness: "Such a radical change from the musical point of view is going on in me that I cannot risk my new manner without having prepared myself in it several months in advance. I am making use of September and October for this trial."

While these changes in his musical being were taking place, Bizet was searching for some definite general philosophy or faith to sustain him. "For the last two months," he told Galabert, "I have been making a cursory study of philosophy from Thales of Miletus to our own day. I have found nothing enlightening in all this immense jumble of ideas!—Talent, genius, very salient personalities to whom we owe some discoveries, but no philosophic system that will bear scrutiny. With ethics it is different.—*Socrates* (that is to say Plato), *Montaigne* (excellent because he has no system)—but spritualism, idealism, eclecticism, materialism, skepticism—all that is downright useless!—Stoicism, despite its errors, did make men.—In short, true philosophy is: 'to examine known facts, extend scientific knowledge and ignore *absolutely* everything that is not proved, not exact.' That is positivism, the only rational philosophy, and it is odd that the human mind should have taken nearly three thousand years to find this out."

When Galabert, in reply, challenged Bizet's positivism, he further explained his conclusions. "Until now," he wrote, "my studies have been concerned with a very cursory review of everything that is not positivist, and I have rejected it all. I have acquired the conviction (I already had it) that the great practical philosophers, the legislators, the leaders of nations: *Solomon, Confucius, Moses, Zoroaster, Solon,* had no philosophic system whatsoever. They probably didn't know enough about it to be what you call positivist, and they were satisfied with a wholly human moral science, bolstered, sometimes, I realize, by a bogey-man religion as a sop to the masses, almost as foolish then as they are today.—I have also acquired this conviction: that Plato, Aristotle, Zeno, Origen, Augustine, Abelard, Albertus Magnus, Roger Bacon, Ramus, the great Bacon, Hobbes, Descartes, Locke, Helvetius, Spinoza, Malebranche, the admirable Pascal, Bossuet, Leibnitz, Condillac, Hegel, Cousin, Lamennais, etc., etc., will live either by their literary worth, by the errors they have destroyed, or by the progress they have given to science, to human intelligence, but not by their methods and their philosophic systems.— I needn't tell you that I have made this study in a hurry, in great snatches from dictionaries, resumés, etc. I shall retrace my steps on the literary side, but nothing in the world could make me spend my time and strength in a study of what seems to me puerile and senseless. Now I ask nothing better than to be a confirmed positivist."

Bizet's philosophical researches were no aid to him in solving a problem that had troubled him for several months—the choice of a new libretto. In June, Bagier of the Théâtre-Italien had asked him to write an opera in the old Italian style, but the libretto did not suit him, so he rejected it by asking for 6000 francs outright, a demand he knew would be refused. Two other librettos, owned by the Opéra, tempted him. One of them, by Arthur Leroy and Thomas-Marie Sauvage, was still in outline form. But Perrin was very taken with it, sent for Bizet, and urged him to accept it.

" 'Don't hesitate,' he said. 'The piece is superb. Let's go through with it.' 'Is it for me?' I asked. 'Absolutely!' was the answer, and the tone said more than the words," Bizet reported to Galabert.

Before any decision could be reached on this libretto, the outline had to be clothed with words. In the meantime, another libretto became available. This book had been chosen in a competition set by the Opéra a year earlier, at the time when Bizet was recovering from his defeat in the contest for the Exposition cantata. Then he had sworn that if ever again he entered a competition, he would keep the fact secret from everyone but Galabert and Guiraud. Now, attracted to *La Coupe du Roi de Thulé* by Louis Gallet and Edouard Blau, two young writers, Bizet considered setting this prize-winning libretto to music in spite of his aversion to competitions.

"I am very much embarrassed at the moment," he wrote to Galabert. "I don't know what to do. If I compete for the Opéra without getting the prize, I am afraid that the good will in my behalf may be reduced. Winning the prize would postpone my big project for two years, perhaps. If I don't compete, and my big project falls through, I shall fall between two stools." The "big project" was, of course, the untitled opera by Leroy and Sauvage.

Bizet put off his own decision about entering the competition, but sent Galabert a copy of *La Coupe du Roi de Thulé* to use as an exercise. While criticizing Galabert's efforts, he himself gradually became so much interested in the opera that he composed the first act while out walking. This opera is the first major work Bizet attempted after his "change of skin." Although the finished score has vanished, probably destroyed by Bizet after he failed to win the prize, the remaining fragments show that it was a significant work.[3] His detailed criticism of Galabert's version of the opera throws invaluable light on his own approach to the problems of composition.

The heroine of *La Coupe du Roi de Thulé* is Myrrha, a *femme fatale* akin to L'Arlésienne or Carmen. The old King of Thule is dying of love for her, and a young fisherman, Yorick, is also passionately in love with her. She is, however, the mistress of Angus, the king's favorite and presumed successor. The royal

---

[3] For a full account and analysis of *La Coupe du Roi de Thulé*, see article by Winton Dean in *Music & Letters*, XXVIII, No. 4, October 1947.

jester, Paddock, a character somewhat in the tradition of Rigoletto, is the only one at court loyal to his master. Angus and the courtiers are impatient for the king's death. But Myrrha reminds them of the tradition whereby the king, on his deathbed, designates his successor by bestowing on him the golden cup presented to the first King of Thule by Claribel, Queen of the Sea. The King, who has no heir, bestows the cup not on the expectant Angus, but on Paddock, the jester, who throws it into the sea. Myrrha then offers herself and her love to the man who will retrieve the cup. The fisherman Yorick plunges into the sea to find it.

In the depths of the ocean he meets the Queen of the Sea, Claribel, who is possessed of a love for him as vain as his for Myrrha. She offers him immortality, but he asks only for the cup, even though she tries to rouse his jealousy by conjuring up a vision of Myrrha in Angus's arms. Yorick brings the cup back to Myrrha only to have her bestow it, herself, and the throne on Angus. Yorick, in desperation, calls on the siren Claribel for help. She responds by causing the sea to rise and submerge the villains and the corrupt court.

This libretto, with its theme of the simple, honest boy torn between his passion for a bad woman and a good woman's love for him, the basic situation, also, of *L'Arlésienne* and *Carmen*, inevitably attracted Bizet. Before he started work on the libretto, he pointed out to Galabert that "Myrrha, however unsympathetic, is not lacking in a certain color. She is, in my opinion, an old-fashioned courtesan. Her cat side is not sufficiently emphasized by the librettists. It is up to the composer to correct this mistake.— This feline character, terrific in her disappointed ambition, can be very effective: no heart, but a head, and other things, too—which are better than nothing. Think about it. It's important. Myrrha must be well done—or the first act and part of the third are lost."

Later, when Bizet himself was composing music for Myrrha, he scolded Galabert for not doing her justice. "You are a thinker," he wrote, "you are essentially intelligent, you have psychological knowledge rare in a man your age. It is permissible for you to fail in one piece. That, alas, is permitted everybody. But you should not fail in a scene as important as Myrrha's entrance. . . .

"This Myrrha is . . . as sensual as Sappho, as ambitious as Aspasia. She is beautiful, witty, charming. The overwhelming spell she casts over Yorick is proof of it.—Her eyes should have that sea-green look, the sure sign of sensuality and selfishness verging on cruelty.

"Now for her entrance *ritournelle*—Oh, dear!

"Some kind of symphonic idea expressing Myrrha's fascination for Yorick should be the basis of this whole conversation.—This idea should start at 'I tremble at the very sound of her footsteps.'—The snake appears and the bird barely flutters a wing.

"Remember the romance in this symphonic passage; that I am willing to accept. But to my mind Myrrha's entrance should express love in another way.—Alone, Yorick is free; he sings his love passionately, deliriously. He sings *to the clouds,* to the stars. —Myrrha appears—and he is extinguished. . . .

"Another less serious reproach. The entrance is too short. She does not have time enough to enter—*she,* Angus, and the ladies and gentlemen of the court who accompany them. She leans on Angus's arm; she comes in slowly, musing, listless; she lets her eyes wander over the gathering and they come to rest, almost disdainfully, on Yorick. . . .

"Don't be discouraged," Bizet continues, "but let all this convince you that, without your realizing it, you do not put everything you know and everything you are into your music. I'll wager you were thinking about Ténot [4] while writing Myrrha's entrance. I, too, think about it, and I admit that every man of feeling must devote long hours of thought to this compilation of such dry, but instructive facts.—But with Myrrha you must forget it absolutely."

Another character in the opera who appealed to Bizet was Paddock. "The courtiers are all terrified of this jester," he wrote. "He is loyalty and honor; he is *truth;* he is light. You must herald him by a sudden brilliance, by an incisive transition.—Your reentrance of the chorus is too long, ineffectual. . . . You must do a coda for the chorus: there must be a *conclusion.* Paddock is at the back of the stage; he watches, he listens, he scorns! Finish up the chorus well, then a *ritournelle* in the major, sufficiently developed so that Paddock has time to come down the whole stage of the Opéra. In this *ritournelle* you must sketch Paddock's profile. . . ."

The contrast between the characters of the simple lovelorn

---

[4] Pierre-Paul-Eugène Ténot (1839–90) was the author of the recently published *Paris en Décembre, 1851.*

fisherman and the ironical, disillusioned jester is dramatized in a duet that Bizet admits is "horribly difficult to write. The form you have adopted," he continues, "is happy. Only I must reproach you for being satisfied to contrive a piece of music.—All of Yorick's phrases lack flair. Paddock is treated better.

"I rather like 'I loved this old man who has fallen.' The idea in Yorick's reply is weak; besides it is much too high. The beginning of the ensemble works; the end falls into the Rossinian method; your passage in thirds is an old trick. Therefore it lacks enthusiasm. This Yorick is mad with love. He must be radiant. A contrast between Paddock and Yorick was needed. It was difficult, I admit, but I would have preferred too much light on Paddock to not putting enough on Yorick.—Your andante is better, but a little dreary. Yorick is happy over his misfortune.—He is no longer himself. He lives entirely in Myrrha. All his responses should be passionately contemplative. (This is only an apparent, not a real contradiction.) When you have him say: 'The zephyr and the wave and the star,' the picturesque side preoccupies you; that is all right. But above all, love, love! . . ."

"Above all, love," is indeed a new motif for the skeptical, cynical young man who had once admitted his inability to understand "the transports of the thing known as love." Now, having succumbed to the transports only to be deprived of the object of his love, he expresses some of his own emotions in his analysis of a duet in which Paddock, the ironical jester, attempts to dissuade the lovelorn Yorick from his hopeless passion. "The duet should be absolutely fragmentary," he says. "It is melodic declamation. You must find new phrases every minute, and these phrases must always rise, rise.—I would have liked a *pp* coda. Yorick has pulled himself together to reply to Paddock—but little by little— he falls back into his reverie, *into the romance that precedes the duet.* Paddock looks at him, is touched.—Yorick ends by saying: 'Myrrha! Myrrha! I love Myrrha'—and Paddock, who is fond of him, who sees the futility of his efforts, stops taking him to task. He feels sorry for him; he takes his hand.—Yorick, ecstatically, lets him do so. He leans over, puts his head on his friend's shoulder. In Paddock, hatred is for the moment dominated by the sorrow that is inspired in every really sensitive philosopher by the spectacle of human dignity degraded."

In discussing a scene before the palace, Bizet brings life to

the legendary operatic characters by identifying them with contemporary figures. "When the courtiers are at the height of their
enthusiasm and are anticipating proclaiming Angus king, four
officers appear at the top of the stairs. They sound a grave,
lugubrious fanfare. Everybody stops and bows! Harold appears:
'The king is dead!' All the *seigneurs* prostrate themselves: 'Alas!'—
Then, at a sign from Harold, the chamberlains [the Edgar Neys,
the Fleurys], [5] bearing their insignia, leave the palace.—The High
Court, the Court of Appeals, the Senate, the whole kit and caboodle
descend the steps to a solemn *march* and advance to the front
of the stage! Officers carry the crown, the sceptre, all the insignia of royalty.—Paddock follows them, carrying the cup. At the
sight of him there is general astonishment, movement. They are
excited, they rush around to the march, *Glory to the Master of
Thulé*, which this time is loud and pompous."

Bizet's idea of identifying the corrupt courtiers in the opera
with the venal officials of the Second Empire was stimulated perhaps by his enthusiastic reading of a new revolutionary weekly
which appeared early in June. *La Lanterne*, with its bright red
cover showing Diogenes' lantern suspended from a hangman's
rope, was written and published by Henri Rochefort, a brilliant
young republican journalist, driven by a hatred of Napoleon III
as violent as it was articulate. After three numbers, the government
suppressed this radical journal and sentenced Rochefort to three
months in prison. Eluding the authorities, he escaped to Belgium,
where he was welcomed as a son by that greatest of exiles from the
Second Empire, Victor Hugo. Rochefort continued to publish
La Lanterne in Brussels, whence it was smuggled into France
in large numbers. During the whole *affaire Rochefort*, Bizet never
missed a copy of *La Lanterne*, never failed in every letter to
Galabert to express intense enthusiasm for the writer's convictions, admiration for his courage, and outrage at his treatment by
the government.

Bizet's deep sympathy with the republican movement of the
day might well have led him to compose an opera with political
implications if the libretto submitted to him in September of 1868
had been the work of Ludovic Halévy, who was largely responsible

---

[5] These names were deleted from *Lettres à un ami*, 173. Edgar Ney
(1812–82) was general of a division and a senator. Emile-Félix Fleury (1815–84)
was also a general, and in 1867 was appointed Ambassador to Russia.

for the sharp political satire transparently disguised under the classic legends of Offenbach's *Orphée aux enfers* and *La Belle Hélène*. But it was Ludovic's father who now offered Bizet a libretto, *Les Templiers,* on the subject of the Knights Templar. Léon Halévy, brother to Fromental, was essentially a philosopher and classical scholar. As a young man he had been secretary to the philosopher Saint-Simon. A prolific minor poet, author of a French translation of Horace, he was greatly attracted to the theatre. The libretto he offered Bizet, written in collaboration with Saint-Georges, was bound to follow the traditional pattern of *La Juive* or *Le Prophète,* and would inevitably have handicapped Bizet musically. But this offer from Geneviève's uncle could only be welcome to the still hopeful suitor, eager for a gesture of encouragement from a member of the Halévy family.

"Dear Sir," Bizet wrote to Léon Halévy in September, "The bad weather this week and a stubborn cold prevented my risking the considerable distance that separates me from the station at Le Vésinet. This morning, however, I came to Paris. After leaving M. de Saint-Georges, I was about to pay you a visit when an encounter, as unpleasant as it was unexpected, upset my whole day and forced me to leave without seeing you.—I was doubly annoyed by this disagreeable occurrence as I wanted to hear news of Ludovic, and I was most eager and impatient to tell you how enthusiastic I am over your libretto, *Les Templiers.*—It is superb! I spent a week on this scenario. I think I really understand it, and I feel that I am in a position to undertake this big affair.—I shall be sustained, I am sure, by the power, the vividness, the sharpness, the sympathy of the characters.—I need not tell you, Sir, how happy I would be if, in collaboration with M. de Saint-Georges, you should be willing to write a magnificent operatic poem for me. You know all that I owe to the name you bear. I hope to augment my debt! . . . I shall do my best. . . .

"I shall come very soon to discuss with you this subject that interests me so much.—M. de Saint-Georges does not seem to me to feel sufficiently the urgency of this work.—You will help me, won't you, to make him share my impatience?" "

Bizet went immediately to the Opéra to see Perrin, who, he writes to Léon Halévy, received him, "as always, most charmingly. —When M. de Saint-Georges judges the moment opportune, we can start.—As for me, I am doing everything I had to do, but

M. Perrin can give me no answer because he doesn't know the work. . . . It is a long time since I sent the scenario back to M. de Saint-Georges," * into the limbo of whose papers it may well have vanished. For never again does Bizet mention *Les Templiers.*

By October, he was once more in the throes of the conflict that had been disturbing him throughout the summer. "I am still in the depths of the most cruel kind of hesitation," he wrote to Mme Trélat. "Still no finale for my symphony! . . . I am still perplexed about the Opéra! . . . I have my piece, or most of it, but at the same time there is another matter that I don't know how to judge.—With your usual perspicacity you will perhaps help me uncover the truth!—The *truth!* The *truth,* that's what matters—and that's what one spends one's life seeking."

Although the long postponed Leroy-Sauvage libretto was nearly finished in mid-October, "Perrin," Bizet wrote Galabert, "is formally asking me (with the urgent authority the director of the Opéra has over a composer who is under his thumb) to enter the competition for the *Coupe.*—This is what he says: 'You will win the prize. If you don't compete, I shall get a mediocre score, and I shall be brokenhearted not to be able to have the success with the *Coupe* that I dream of.—*You alone* can succeed with this work today.'

"Translated this means: 'I am afraid my competition won't be a success.—If Bizet competes I will have a possible work. If there is something better, I shall be glad enough to drop Bizet.' "

Balanced against the fear of failure in the competition was the fact that he had completed the first two acts of *La Coupe.* "I am extremely happy about them," he continues, ignoring the fact that the patient Galabert had also composed those acts. "They are *much* superior to everything I have done up to this day.—The second act particularly, I think, has come out very well. Yorick and Claribel's whole scene with the vision seems to me not relatively, but *absolutely* a good thing. (With you I am completely frank.)—Guiraud has been successful with this act musically, but in my opinion it is not colorful enough. Altogether I am very much perplexed. . . . Perrin says: 'Don't worry about the jury; whether the work turns out to be German sausage or Italian spaghetti, I'll do what I like with it.'

"To award no prize would be annoying and a bad mark for

the Opéra. If it goes to a gentleman who does less well than myself, it would be trying for me.

"What shall I do?"

He told Guiraud later: "I have reviewed my first act of
La Coupe on two different occasions. The first time I found it
altogether admirable; the second time it seemed to me nauseating."
Nevertheless he finished the score and entered it in the competition, an act that left him with no sense of elation.

"I have been unable to find a note of music for three weeks,"
Bizet wrote to an unidentified woman early in 1869. "I have
several songs to write. Impossible! I don't really know what is
going on in my poor head, but sometimes I ask myself seriously
whether there is a melody left there, or in my heart. I am profoundly discouraged at the moment. The libretto on which I was
counting, and which in scenario form gave high hopes, is a complete failure. I am disgusted with it. . . .

"*Chère Madame,* I would not exchange my troubles for
yours; I would be giving you too sad a gift! I spend my nights
wondering whether life isn't a cruel joke, if intelligence and sensitiveness aren't malformations of the moral system, burdens we
must bear. I have never felt as disgusted as this. I would like to
flee the country, escape from my kind, from this hateful world to
which I am riveted. This so-called artistic *milieu* is no better than
the gutter. I see no one in it I can like or even respect. . . .

"Pasdeloup is rehearsing a symphony of mine. What a
dreary musician!" [n]

As Bizet was not given to introspection it is entirely possible
that he believed that his disappointments in the theatre were the
chief cause of his sterility, his excessive distaste for the world
around him. Or he may merely have been unwilling to admit to
himself or to divulge to another the extent to which "that morbid,
nerve-ridden state termed love" could deplete his whole being, deprive him of the power to compose with the "fantasy, daring, un-
expectedness, enchantment, and above all, tenderness, *morbi-
dezza,*" essential, as he told Galabert, to the musical expression
of love.

Fortunately his disgust for the fellow-members of his profession was not reciprocal, and when the promise to play his symphony, made the previous November, materialized in a perform-

ance on February 28, the composer emerged from the shadows of his private world—if not into the sunlight, at least into the dawn of a new day.

Not that either the performance or the reception of the *Roma* at the Cirque Napoléon was brilliant. The dreariness of Pasdeloup's musicianship was not a mere notion induced by Bizet's passing pessimism. The gifts of the orchestra director were not, unfortunately, on a level with his taste and his courage in introducing new music. In his youth the meagerness of his talent had caused him to abandon his career as a composer. As a conductor, he remained mediocre. "How well Pasdeloup is led by his orchestra," Reyer remarked, and Bizet, after leaving one of the rehearsals of his symphony, wrote to Galabert: "Poor Pasdeloup, will he ever pull it off?"

Pull it off he did, but in his own way. Shortly before the concert, without consulting Bizet, Pasdeloup affixed his own titles to the three movements of the symphony that he chose to play: *"Une Chasse dans la forêt d'Ostie," "Une Procession,"* and *"Carnaval à Rome."* The Scherzo, because of its failure six years earlier, he omitted, much to the composer's distress. "Once the symphony has had the success it deserves," Pasdeloup promised him, "after a third or fourth performance, we will slide in the Scherzo like a letter into a letterbox." No such opportunity arose, for the symphony was not played again until five years after the composer's death. But the reception given the work at its first performance satisfied Bizet, however unsatisfactory it might seem today.

"My symphony went very well," he told Galabert. "First movement: a round of applause, a second round of hisses, third round, a catcall. Andante: a round of applause. Finale: great effect, applause three times repeated, hisses, three or four catcalls. In short, a success."

In the light of the reception accorded the Overture to *Die Meistersinger,* which Pasdeloup played a few months later, Bizet's symphony was indeed favored. The violence of the catcalls and hisses called forth by Wagner's work forced the conductor to stop in the middle to calm the audience by stating that he quite understood that a work of such importance could not be grasped at a first hearing, and that he would therefore repeat it the following Sunday.

"A composer must want to be hissed if he is going to be played by Pasdeloup," Paladilhe admitted while in the process of negotiating with the conductor for the performance of his first symphony. "For most of his audience, which is huge, is composed of subscribers who want only classical music and who raise an uproar over every new name. But the uproar in this instance is an excellent thing because you can show what you are capable of, if only to other musicians." ⁿ

The audience that hissed and applauded Bizet's symphony was at least articulate, in contrast to the press which, with one exception, refrained from comment. The *Revue et Gazette Musicale,* ignoring Bizet's authorship of *La Jolie Fille de Perth,* remarked, "In this new work by the author of *Les Pêcheurs de Perles* there is a very real talent, undeniable skill, and above all a very lively feeling for orchestration. As for the ideas there is nothing absolutely new about them, although none of them is banal. Nor is the style really personal; M. Bizet still remembers the masters too well."

A few weeks after the performance of Bizet's symphony, Pasdeloup, who had succeeded Carvalho as director of the Théâtre-Lyrique, presented Wagner's *Rienzi* there. It caused a sensation. The dress-rehearsal, which Bizet attended, lasted from eight o'clock until two in the morning. "Eighty musicians in the orchestra, thirty on the stage, a hundred and thirty in the chorus, a hundred and fifty extras," Bizet reported to Galabert. "Badly constructed piece. Only one role: Rienzi remarkably played by Monjauze. Nothing can give you an idea of the noise; a mixture of Italian motifs; bizarre, bad style; music of the decadence rather than of the future.—Some detestable pieces, some admirable pieces! On the whole an astonishing work, prodigiously alive: Olympian grandeur, afflatus! Genius without proportion, without order, but genius! Will it be a success? That I don't know.—The theatre was full, no claque! Prodigious effects, disastrous effects! Cries of enthusiasm, then bleak silences for half an hour —Some said: 'it's bad Verdi'; others: 'it's good Wagner!' 'It's sᵤolime!'— 'It's frightful!' 'It's mediocre!'—'It isn't bad!' The public is baffled. It's very amusing.—Few people have the courage to persist in their hatred of Wagner.—The bourgeois and the man about town know that they are dealing with quite somebody, and it leaves them floundering.—We shall see on Tuesday; yesterday's audience of invited guests was forced to be polite. Within the next few days I shall perhaps have come to an agreement with the Opéra-Comique. I'll keep you informed."

A possible commission from the Opéra-Comique had first been broached in February while Bizet's symphony was in rehearsal. "The new director of the Opéra-Comique has asked me in a letter to work for him," he wrote to Galabert. "We are looking for a big piece; three or four acts. It is du Locle, Perrin's nephew (or actually Perrin himself). They want me to do a big thing before the one at the Opéra. I would like to, and I shall be delighted to give up the competition and to try to change the genre of the Opéra-Comique. Down with *La Dame blanche!* . . . Perrin is completely disgusted with Leroy and Sauvage's libretto . . . and has definitely dropped it. The authors are annoyed. . . . Du Locle is in Italy; he returns next week. He is telling everybody that I will be one of the pillars of his structure, etc., etc. The slightest sign of a libretto would suit me better.

"It is true that up to now nobody has one.—Perrin said to me two days ago: 'I have two things in view. As soon as du Locle returns, we will start moving.' He (Perrin) is the one who keeps asking me for things; he reproaches me for my indifference, etc., etc. Choudens is engraving my symphony, *orchestra, arrangements, etc.* In short, I *know* that things are going well for me, but what a long time it takes!"

The cause of Bizet's indifference, his sense of time lagging, arose, no doubt, from the unresolved state of his relations with his future wife. At least, some such conclusion is to be drawn from his remarking to Galabert in April that the Paris weather was "filthy, vile. One might say that it is a faithful reflection of you very well know what." What Galabert knew he never revealed, so the immediate circumstances that led to Bizet's wedding remain as much a mystery as the events surrounding the marriage of his parents.

CHAPTER XVII

Geneviève Halévy

Geneviève Halévy, throughout her long life, attracted men of talent, and even of genius, not so much by her charm and her beauty as by her extraordinary gift for mirroring in her great dark eyes their image of her. To Bizet she seemed ["an admirable creature"] whom he had met by ["a sheer miracle"] and ["whose mind is open to every new kind of progressive reform, who believes neither in the God of the Jews nor the God of the Christians, but in honor, duty; in short, in morality."] [n] The picture of his twenty-year-old wife projected here by Bizet was the ideal embodiment of his own philosophy. The thoughtful intellect with which he endowed her could hardly have been more foreign to her nature. The true portrait of Geneviève was drawn only some thirty years after Bizet's death when Marcel Proust, in creating his worldly, charming, heartless Duchesse de Guermantes, remarked: "I could find my model only in a woman not to the manor born . . . Bizet's widow." But at the time of Geneviève's marriage it was only natural that the question of her religion or lack of it should seem important.[1] The very name Halévy suggested the essence of Judaism. Yet Geneviève's father, Fromental, the composer of *La Juive* and *Le Juif errant,* never practiced any religion, and indeed remained remarkably ignorant of the ritual and dogma of the faith he had inherited from his father.

---

[1] One of Geneviève's witticisms, frequently quoted after her marriage to Emile Straus, was her reply to a woman who wished to convert her to Catholicism: "I have too little religion to change it."

Elie Halévy, originally named Lévy, father of Fromental and Léon, was German by birth. After migrating to France in the late eighteenth century, he married Julie Meyer, a native of the little village of Malzeville, near Nancy. "Our father," wrote Léon Halévy, "was a man much honored among the Israelites because of his character and his learning. . . . He was a profound scholar of Hebrew and very well-versed in Talmudic studies . . . very eager for the complete intellectual emancipation of his co-religionists, who had been made citizens through the Revolution. . . ." [n] Fromental, born in 1799, had for the first sixteen years of his life enjoyed this political and social equality. But with the restoration of the monarchy in 1815, French Jews were again deprived of the rights and privileges that Napoleon had granted them and which were not restored until after the Revolution of 1830. It was natural, therefore, that Geneviève's father, the most conciliatory and adaptable of men, should have preferred to emphasize his French nationality rather than his Jewish origin. Even his best-known work, *La Juive,* is peopled not with characters drawn from authentic Jewish folklore or history, but with operatic lay-figures costumed as Jews or Christians, dwellers in that libretto-land of Scribe's which served as locale for so many operas of the period.

While composing this opera in 1834 and 1835, Fromental Halévy had suffered from a continuous "state of feverish anxiety or rather of actual illness," his brother writes. "His excessive nervous excitement worried not only all of us, but also Halévy himself. . . ." [n] A high-strung, sensitive man, he apparently safeguarded his nervous system by a protective shell of indolence. In the six years following the *première* of *La Juive,* Halévy produced three *opéras-comiques* and four grand operas. Yet Wagner, who was making a piano reduction of Halévy's opera, *La Reine de Chypre,* spoke of "the incorrigible laziness of that peculiarly good-hearted and really unassuming man." This laziness—"*torpeur habituelle*" the director of the Opéra called it—had disturbed Halévy himself long before it irritated his collaborators. As a young man he wrote in his journal: "Often a man seems lazy or indolent, but actually feels himself superior to the position he is supposed to occupy. His activity is merely dormant. If a stroke of luck awakened it, he would shine. It is like a good painting hung in a bad light; the color seems false, the drawing feeble. Hang it where it should be hung in order to judge it properly." "

At the age of forty-three, in 1842, Halévy married a wife who was able to create for him the kind of social background in which he shone. Léonie Halévy, only twenty-two at the time of her marriage, was the daughter of Esther Gradis and Isaac Rodrigues-Henriques, the head of a long-established firm of Bordeaux bankers. The Rodrigues and the Gradis families claimed to have migrated in the year 133 from Palestine to Portugal and thence to Spain, where they remained until they fled from the Inquisition. In 1495 they established themselves in Bordeaux, where the Rodrigues became bankers and the Gradis ship-fitters. According to family tradition, their services to the French navy under Louis XV and Louis XVI were such that the latter offered to ennoble the family, an honor they refused because of their unwillingness to take an oath on a Bible that included the New Testament. In 1826, the widowed Mme Isaac Rodrigues moved to Paris where she, her daughter Léonie, and her son Hippolyte occupied an apartment in the same building with Fromental and Léon Halévy. Other neighbors were Rodrigues cousins and the Péreire brothers. These last, powerful promoters and bankers, notorious for their ruthless business methods in their struggles against the rival Rothschilds, nevertheless assumed a certain responsibility for the material well-being of their less fortunate or less astute co-religionists. Their dealings with the Halévy family would one day add to the complex problems of Bizet's marriage.

Mme Halévy, having grown up in this atmosphere of swelling fortunes, always regarded the spending of money as a form of self-expression. An amateur sculptor, a passionate collector of *objets d'art,* a worldly and successful hostess, she appears to have been excellent company when she was not suffering one of her periodic attacks of insanity.

During the first year of his marriage, Halévy found difficulty in composing the grand opera *Charles VI,* "putting it aside, taking it up again only to abandon it, suffering from one of those attacks of nerves which originate in the mind rather than in the body," his brother said. While he was struggling with this work, which achieved great success, Mme Halévy gave birth to a daughter on June 7, 1843. Esther Halévy was one of those golden children marked for early death whose influence on the lives of others is out of all proportion to their years. Sensitive, intelligent, charming, and selfless, unusually gifted as a musician, Esther Halévy left an indelible memory on all who had known her. In the background of the Bizet household, she hovered, a tragic ghost.

Geneviève Halévy was born on February 26, 1849. A year later she made her first appearance in the family annals when the Halévys crossed the channel to arrange for a production of *La Tempestà,* an Italian version of Shakespeare's *The Tempest* which Halévy had been commissioned to do in London. "We are here in this ancient city," wrote Mme Halévy to her mother, "after an abominable crossing, a tempest indeed. We were all deathly sick, my poor Esther and even my baby . . . and besides, there was the fear of spending a night at sea. But I assure you, I was not a coward. Tonight we are all very well because we are going to the opera. The house we are staying in is charming, but how dull London seems. . . ." [n]

Outside her own Parisian orbit any place was likely to seem dull to Mme Halévy. Even in her own house in the country, she was restless. "I have seen the Halévys twice," wrote their neighbor, Delacroix, from Champigny. "They are leaving already. They are society people who must have their hand-of-cards every evening." In Paris, later, he notes in his journal: "Went to the Halévys'. Always a big crowd, lots of by-play, a true house of Socrates, too small to hold so many friends." (See Appendix I, p. 459.)

If the house was small, the size of the rooms was reduced still further by the clutter of objects crowded into them. "Halévy's house was like an art gallery," said one of his friends. "The walls of his salon were covered with canvases by the masters, or with souvenirs by distinguished amateurs. A watercolor by the Princesse Mathilde was propped against the base of a terra-cotta by Clodien; a seascape by Gudin hung pendant to a sketch by Horace Vernet. And on the console tables and whatnots there were antique masks, statuettes, busts in marble, Florentine bronzes, bowls, vases, *aiguières,* gems of embossed silver, examples of all the arts." [n]

Among these works of art were the paintings by Delacroix of scenes from Halévy's operas *Guido et Ginevra* and *Le Juif errant*. Yet not even the presence of his own work softened Delacroix's judgment of Mme Halévy's taste. "At the Halévy's: suffocating heat," he wrote in his journal. "His poor wife fills the house with old pots and pans and old furniture; this new folly will send her to the poorhouse. He has changed and aged: he has the air of a man seduced in spite of himself. How can he do any serious work in the midst of this hubbub? His new position at the Académie must take a great deal of his time and deprive him more and more of the serenity and tranquillity necessary for work." And again: "How do these Halévys . . . these people, hounded by debts and the demands of family or of vanity, manage a calm and smiling manner through all their troubles? They can be happy only by blinding themselves and ignoring the reefs through which they steer their course, often desperate and sometimes shipwrecked." [n]

Mme Halévy's "folly" did not send the family to the poorhouse (her brother paid many of Halévy's debts), but it did result in her being forced to spend a large part of the year 1853 in a sanatorium. When, the following year, she was well enough to come home, Halévy, planning her welcome, asked his brother-in-law to "be so kind as to come to the house where Bébé will be waiting for her mother." [n] Bébé (the name by which Bizet also called Geneviève) started then, at the age of four, the pattern that long dominated her life—waiting for her mother to be well enough to see her. Not that Mme Halévy failed to recover from her attacks. (See Appendix I, p. 459.) Indeed, her recoveries were always so complete that she retained no memory of her illnesses. But even in periods of good health she was very excitable. "I can hear your wife's cry of terror from here," wrote Scribe to her husband in a letter suggesting their joint departure for Switzerland on a Saturday, "in spite of its being the 13th." [n]

Fortunately, Mme Halévy's health had improved by the summer of 1854, when Halévy became Permanent Secretary of the Académie des Beaux-Arts. This post, eminently suited to his gifts, both scholarly and social, although it brought him welcome recognition, additional income, and living quarters in the buildings of the Institut, also imposed heavier responsibilities. Gradually he became exhausted by his academic obligations, his increasingly neglected duties at the Conservatoire, and the composing of several unsuccessful operas. His last completed work, *La Magicienne,* prompted Gounod to write to Bizet in Rome, in 1858: "You asked me, dear Georges, to tell you about . . . *La Magicienne.* . . . This work, which at times still bears witness to the high intelligence of its author, shows also a lamentable drying-up of the live sources of inspiration: the melody struggles breathlessly between an over-elaborated head and a tail dedicated to the claque. One feels that this man no longer believes in the inherent power of the idea, and that he is looking for effects induced only by whatever potential action they contain. The present weakness of the author of *La Juive* lies in his lack of faith in the Idea, and this lack of faith is, I believe, the result of his failure to consider carefully the intrinsic value of his own ideas. Yes, he could do better, I am sure, if he had more willpower and could exact more from himself. But in the long run, negligence engenders sterility, and I fear that he is not far from it." [n]

Although *La Magicienne,* Halévy's tenth work to be given at the Opéra, had a brief success, it marked the final decline in his career. None of his earlier works except *La Juive* was played during the last years of his life; and in the year and a half before he died, even that opera was given only three times. Increasing anxiety, disappointment, and overwork ruined his health. In a desperate effort to recover, he went, late in December 1861, with his wife and two daughters to Nice. They hoped that the milder climate there would prove beneficial. But the journey was tiring, there were difficulties in finding suitable living quarters, and by the time the family was installed in a villa in the rue de France, Halévy had grown much weaker. And he was bored. "Far from the Parisian world that he loved, far from the diversions that were dear to him," his brother wrote, "he became preoccupied with the symptoms of his illness, which a rigorous diet emphasized. . . . He was careful, in the letters he wrote me, to maintain the most complete silence about his health, and this seemed to me a sad forewarning." [n]

Mme Halévy was less reserved. "Fromental is . . . still weak," she wrote to her brother, Hippolyte Rodrigues, in mid-January, "doesn't very much like prescribed walks, prescribed meat; in fact, he is nervous, and that keeps me from believing the reassurances of the doctor who finds him really better. . . . Two or three people come from time to time to play whist, but we don't want to see anybody else. We want to rest so that as soon as Fromental feels better, he can go back to working on his opera. . . . If he could combine his work with the time he spends out walking, perhaps that would do him more good than anything.

"You see, my dear Hippo, how busy I am kept with my Fromental, with his health, with what he thinks, with what he eats, with what might divert him, so that I no longer have any other ideas in my head. . . ." [n]

Geneviève's little head was full of ideas more suggestive of her future as Proust's Duchesse de Guermantes than as the dutiful wife of an unsuccessful composer. "You may be sure I would have written long ago if I hadn't been afraid of boring you too much," the thirteen-year-old girl wrote her uncle, Hippolyte Rodrigues, during her father's final illness. "We don't do very much here that is worthy of your attention. Yesterday we went to the grottoes of Saint-André. The road was really dreadful, so bad that as soon as we arrived at the entrance to the grotto, we left again quickly so as not to look any longer at such an ugly thing. We had hoped the walk would be great fun, and it was a complete failure. Then, as it was Sunday, we went to listen to the music on the Promenade, which is the Nice version of the terrace at Saint-Germain. They played some of *La Juive,* of *L'Eclair,* and of *Norma.* But you know this happens twice a week, and twice a week there are just as many people. When it is over, you walk up and down until the sun sets at four o'clock. At five minutes past four, no one is left out of doors. That is the chief amusement of the day of the fashionables of Nice. In the evening it is different. First there is the theatre. Six times a week they play Italian opera, and on the seventh usually *Les Doigts de fée.* There are also little dances every Monday at the Prefect's. Next Thursday a grand charity concert given by Mme Vigier and M. Tamburini. Also, the sixth of this month there was a grand ball at the club. We were invited, but you know that we refuse all invitations because we came here to rest. But to return to the ball at the club, there were 1200 people; and it appears to have been delightful. You see that if one wanted to have fun, there are plenty of balls, entertainments, and concerts. But I am afraid I am forgetting myself and boring you horribly." [n]

Disturbing or maddening as the writer of this letter may have become, it is unlikely that she was ever boring. "Esther and

Geneviève bring us their gaiety, which we very much need," her mother wrote during this sad winter. "Esther gives lessons to Geneviève, who adapts herself very well to her strict teacher." Judging by Geneviève's compositions, written under her sister's direction, it was rather the "strict teacher" who adapted herself, at least to the extent of permitting the pupil her own choice of subject. The theme of the first composition Geneviève wrote in her little black, leather-bound notebook embossed with the initials G. H. may have been a reflection of her father's nostalgia for Paris, or perhaps a direct expression of her own feelings.

"Decidedly I say, and I repeat it—there is only one city in the world where one can live, and that is Paris! Put any Parisian whatsoever who is tired of amusements in a charming house on the shore of a lake or a river, and I give even the mortal who most wanted to come a fortnight before he dies of boredom. On the next day he wakes up saying to himself: 'Why don't I go to Paris for a few days?' Then he goes, and if a few months later one of his friends comes up to him laughing in the midst of the round of parties and entertainments to remind him of the beauties of nature, the wholewheat bread, the clotted cream, the wild strawberries that for a moment made him forget Paris, he will make great fun of himself and his poetic aspiration, and he will be right. However, I can't blame the person who does this, because even while saying just the opposite, I feel inside myself that I would do the same thing. I go even farther. I believe . . . it is an affectation of Parisians always to say: 'Mon dieu, how I would like to be shut up in an isolated little blue house, surrounded by stones and decorated with green shutters.' In order to punish them, one should really grant their wish and at the end of a month go and see the faces they make tête-à-tête with their green shutters. I am sure they will look just as sad as a certain farmer's wife who, in a fairy story called the Three Wishes, suddenly found a clothespin at the end of her nose after having dared to make such a rash wish. If I ever become an emperor, or at least an empress, I intend to play this little joke on everyone who complains of crowds and noise. And I shan't let them return to the capital until they are thoroughly convinced that only in Paris can one live; elsewhere one vegetates." [2]

---

[2] Geneviève Halévy, unpublished journal, collection of author. Further quotations from this source in this chapter are not individually noted.

In another of her compositions, Geneviève wrote: "Few people know how to grow old, and when I say few, I am indulgent, because that sounds as though there were some, and I don't think there are any. Let's see. Does the woman who is a coquette know how to age? Certainly not. She tries so hard to make other people believe that she has stayed young that she ends by being convinced of it herself. When she gets to be forty, she will perhaps say to herself some evening when she is going to a ball: 'Maybe I shouldn't dance any longer. But I danced yesterday. I shan't be any more ridiculous today.' As for me, I know some who at the age of sixty still say to themselves: 'I danced yesterday'. . . .

"The unattractive woman knows even less than others how to accept her fate. For she thinks that as she grows older her ugliness is less noticeable . . . and sometimes, if she hasn't dared flirt when she was twenty, she makes up for it at forty.

"But who does know how to grow old? Nobody!—And yet perhaps I am mistaken. There is someone. It is the good mother. She accepts aging easily . . . and when she sees the shining eyes, the thick hair, the rosy cheeks of her daughter, doesn't regret for an instant no longer being pretty. If she has liked society for herself, she likes it even better for her daughter. . . . Decidedly I think I was taking a gloomy view of the world just now when I said that nobody knew how to age. Because fortunately for mankind there are still more good mothers than aged coquettes."

Perhaps this final paragraph was added at the suggestion of her teacher, the sister, of an age to realize that a mother in her forties might well wonder who had served as model for her younger daughter's reflections on the vanity of women.

We find a different, a foreboding note in one of Geneviève's compositions written shortly before her father's death. "He who laughs on Friday will weep on Sunday!" she begins. "Alas, that is the saddest thing that has ever been said, and it is also the truest. As for me, it is a thought that always pursues me so that when I leave a person who is happy and satisfied with his fate, I am always afraid that when I return I shall find him plunged in mourning and in tears. It takes so little to change the loveliest and most hopeful existence into horror, misery, and torment. . . ."

After describing the father of a family who leaves his loving wife and beautiful children to go on a journey of several months, only to find, when he returns, "his house deserted, no echo of voices in the empty halls . . . nothing but inexorable death," she concludes: "I am crazy to talk like this. . . . As we know that eternal happiness does not exist here below, I really can't see how I let myself go so far as to express the dark thoughts that pursue and obsess me at the moment, and which I hope will soon disappear."

Unfortunately, Geneviève's premonition of disaster was sound. Her father's death on March 17, 1862, initiated the series of tragedies that blighted her girlhood. "No gentler, calmer, easier death could be imagined," Ludovic Halévy wrote to his father. "He was so tranquil during his last moments that the doctor had to tell us when it was all over. . . . Esther, who was very strong and courageous, asked to come in for a last time, and after that did not leave Léonie." [n]

Geneviève again was left waiting to see her mother.

Halévy's funeral offered the government officials, theatre directors, and audiences who had neglected the master during his last years an opportunity to pay him posthumous tribute. Fifteen thousand mourners marched in his funeral procession, which reached all the way from the Institut to the Place de la Concorde. Two years after his death, in late March 1864, a monument was dedicated to his memory. At the ceremony, attended by crowds of people, Geneviève and Esther were unaccompanied by their mother.[3] For Mme Halévy had been stricken several months earlier with another attack of insanity, which was to be intensified by the sudden death of her daughter Esther only three weeks after the dedication ceremony.

Esther's death at the age of twenty was a shattering blow to all of her family, particularly to her cousin Ludovic, to whom she was engaged to be married. His life, for several years afterwards, was profoundly affected by this tragedy. On the day that

---

[3] The day after the dedication, Gounod wrote to Esther Halévy: "Yesterday I was conscious of all the empty places around me!—My memories as a pupil and a friend were very close to yours as a daughter, and the father, whom you miss so much, I also missed greatly.

"I would come and take your hand and, in that way, his, too, a little, if I didn't understand that a visit from me at this time would be inopportune. Do feel that I am close to you even if you don't see me; we all bear you in mind. You can't doubt, I am sure, the unfailing and affectionate friendship of your always devoted,

Charles Gounod."

Unpublished letter, collection of author.

Esther died, he wrote some seventy pages in his journal. But later, after his marriage, he tore them all out, noting only: "April 19, 1864, Esther died after a few days' illness."

The actual cause of Esther's death and the circumstances of her illness are lost behind a haze of emotion and secrecy. Mme Halévy, in the red leather-bound, gold-embossed account book that she persisted in keeping both in sickness and in health, noted, after the item for Esther's expenses in 1864: "Illness caused by the inconsistency of my family who put an impressionable girl like my Esther in a nursing home. Unforgivable! They have ruined my life." [n]

After attending Esther's funeral, Emile Paladilhe wrote to his father: "The mother has been mad for several months, and Bébé, who is now a woman, is more and more unbalanced." She had every reason to be. When she left her sister's deathbed to go to comfort her mother, Mme Halévy accused her of being responsible for Esther's death. This obsession of Mme Halévy's precluded Geneviève's continuing to live in the house with her mother; from her fifteenth year to the time of her marriage, she stayed first with one, then with another, of her mother's relatives. The loneliness of these homeless years was interrupted only in the autumn of 1867 by her engagement to Bizet, which was so soon broken off by her family.

Bizet's relationship with Céleste Mogador has been suggested as a cause of the family prejudice against him, and after his marriage he himself said that the relatives of his mother-in-law had always regarded him as a "bohemian" and an outsider. Certainly a weathly family of bankers and brokers could hardly have regarded an unsuccessful composer with no private fortune as the ideal match for a difficult, neurasthenic girl of seventeen who could bring him only a small dowry. Money was of paramount importance to Mme Halévy's family, and her advisers, the Péreire brothers, had every reason to be anxious about her financial situation. At the time of her husband's death the Nice paper, *Le Messager du Midi,* had reported in some detail the cancellation of debts and the contributions made to Mme Halévy by her brother, Hippolyte Rodrigues, by the Baron de Rothschild, and by Emile Péreire. "These tactful gestures," said *Le Messager,* "were made by co-religionists of the illustrious deceased, who left very little money."

In 1867, that war-threatened year, the Péreire brothers' fortune was in jeopardy, and the curtailment of Mme Halévy's resources necessitated the sale of some of her personal property, a procedure she greatly resented. "It is unheard of," she noted in her account book, "that they should dare to sell, in my lifetime, things that belonged to me, that I cared about, when I haven't a single debt and no need of money as my accounts show. Shame on the family council that did such a thing!" Mme Halévy's incapacity to face any reality—least of all her precarious financial situation, the antagonism roused in her by the efforts of the family council to arrange her affairs, their disapproval of Bizet, combined with her irrational attitude toward her daughter, undoubtedly prevented any decision involving Geneviève's marriage and dowry being agreed upon at this time. Geneviève, too, appears to have been rendered indecisive by her own deep unhappiness. Despair and terror were the only continuous emotions she seemed able to feel. In the entry in her notebook at New Year's 1868, only two months after the broken engagement, there is no mention of Bizet's name.

"The years pile up in vain," she wrote, "upon the frightful memory of the cruel moments that have separated me from everybody I loved. . . . Esther, my beloved sister, close to you I could have borne anything. But God has separated us on this earth. Will He give me the strength one day to earn a place beside you? Oh, Lord . . . I have seen my adored father die before I could even grasp all the happiness his affection gave me. And Thou hast taken from me the consolation of the love of my beloved mother and I am not permitted to lighten her suffering and her unhappiness by my care! Thou hast left me alone in the world, oh, Lord, and I knew happiness only before I could appreciate it. . . . Intercede for me, my beloved sister. . . . Send me a little of your heavenly humility, which made the Lord call you to him. . . . And you, my adored father . . . forgive, too, your daughter who suffers, who loves you, and who, if she has not always shown herself worthy of blood like yours, has at least appreciated the incomparable grandeur of your heart."

This craving for fatherly love and reassurance Gounod tried to appease. Although often away from Paris at this time, he continued when possible to give Geneviève piano lessons as he always had. In a letter written to her the day after she had set down her desperate prayer, he tried to offer her the sense of welcome in his household which her own family had failed to give: "My dear little Geneviève, I don't need, I hope, to be very demonstrative to tell you that I am touched by . . . your daughterly little note. . . . You know very well that any paternal feelings that you can *rediscover* in a heart other than a father's, you will find in mine. I need add nothing, I think, to such a declaration except that I expect you Sunday at quarter to five if you feel inclined on that day to resume our dear little meetings. . . ." [n]

Two months later, Geneviève was still torn by unhappiness, but of a less desolate kind. She was experiencing the struggle between the compulsion to continue living in the world of grief and mourning, become familiar and almost safe, and the normal longing of any life-loving person to be happy in spite of all the risks and responsibilities happiness may involve.

"I don't know what to do or what to be. . . ." she wrote in her journal in April 1868. "I can't bear my lonely life; it will break my heart. Nevertheless . . . *life,* so called, is not at the moment showing its thorniest side. . . . What, then, are the consolations that have been granted me? People are kind. . . . I have found some deep and, I believe, lasting affections. . . . But can these affections compare with the tenderness of those I weep for? Have they—I shan't say the blindness—but the indulgence of a mother's, a sister's or a father's love? . . . I am nineteen years old, and I would need to live through only very few more experiences before my death to have run the full gamut of misfortune. So it isn't irrational childishness that makes me suffer. . . . I dread the future, for the past was hardly such as to give me confidence."

Geneviève's intuition was sound in warning her that she would always demand from those who loved her blindness to her faults and indulgence of her wishes. A touching thing about the people who surrounded her was "their care, their skill in sparing her the slightest trouble," wrote Julien Benda, who knew her in her later years. "I would never have been surprised if before I went into the salon one of them had come to warn me: 'Today Mme Straus has decided that 2 and 2 make 5; act as though it were true.'" [n] During her brief engagement to Bizet, Geneviève confided little or nothing to him of the turmoil and tension through which she had passed. He had no hint, therefore, of the problems that were to confront him, no reason for considering the risk he ran from Geneviève's heritage of insanity on her mother's side and of varying degrees of neurasthenia on her father's.

"One sees such strange things," Bizet had written to Mme Trélat less than a year before his marriage. "My friend Ludovic Halévy, whose recent marriage was from every point of view excellent, has left his wife on the pretext that he is not cut out for married life. He is mad, I think, for it would revolt me to believe that he is not an honorable man." Whether Halévy's behavior, which can undoubtedly be attributed to his memories of Esther, bordered on insanity or merely on eccentricity, there is no doubt that Bizet's use of the word "mad" was rhetorical. Not so the remarks of the elder Paladilhe when his son informed him of Bizet's engagement: "As you say, I, too, am glad that it is Bizet, not you, who is marrying Mlle Halévy, although she is the daughter of your master. Even when I knew her as a child, it was not difficult to recognize the seeds of a mental instability that did not bode well for the future. On the other hand, I would have been very happy to see you marry the older sister, who was a charming person apart from the fact that her family would have been an artistic and moral support for you." [n]

The desirability of this family support and prestige has been suggested as one of Bizet's motives in his choice of a wife. And it is probable that if he had fallen in love with a girl of unknown antecedents, he might have investigated her background more thoroughly. But even had he permitted himself to recognize and face the risks he was about to run, it is certain that he was far too much in love with Geneviève to have given her up.

Under what auspices the young couple, after more than a year and a half of separation, again resumed relations has not been disclosed. Only once did Geneviève mention Bizet's name in her journal. In a cramped little scrawl, she wrote: "With all my soul I love my beloved Georges." After his death the picture she retained of her marriage became increasingly idyllic until, finally, in her old age, she invented a remarkable version of how she had become engaged. She told Julien Benda that "one morning her father came into her room and said to her: 'My pupil Bizet would like to marry you. I don't suppose it will suit you. In any case, I have told you about it.'—'It does suit me,' she said quite simply."ⁿ Even had Benda known that Geneviève was barely thirteen years old when her father died, he would no doubt have obeyed the rules of her entourage and accepted this fantasy of a child marriage.

Early in May 1869, Bizet wrote to Galabert: "I am announcing to you secretly the news that will be official next week.

"I am going to be married.

"We love each other.—I am absolutely happy. [We shall be poor for a while, but what does that matter? Her dowry is 150,000 francs plus 500,000 later.]"ⁿ

On May 10, Bizet appeared in the Halévy family box at the Opéra-Comique, not officially as Geneviève's fiancé, but— along with Guiraud, Paladilhe, and Samuel David—as a former pupil of her father's. The revival of Halévy's *Jaguarita l'indienne,* "a true romance à la Fenimore Cooper, but softened and civilized by the muse of the Opéra-Comique," which ran for eighteen performances, was important to Bizet for material as well as for sentimental reasons. On May 31 he signed his marriage contract, to the reading of which he later told his mother-in-law he "listened respectfully without really understanding it." The terms specified that "Mlle Halévy has brought as dowry her rights in the estates of her father and sister, and Mme Halévy, as authorized by the family, has settled as dowry on her daughter . . . 40/84 of the property and the use of the total, without exceptions or reservations, of the royalties of M. Halévy, so that with the rights appertaining to her from her father's and her sister's estates, the said *demoiselle* will receive 70% of the said rights, the 30% being reserved for Mme Halévy, but with the stipulation that the said 70% may be drawn only after the 30% reserved for Mme Halévy has produced an income of at least 3000 francs."ⁿ

One curious circumstance in the plans for the wedding is suggested in a hasty undated note from Gounod to Bizet which appears to have been written at this time. *"Cher petit,"* it runs. "Thank you for your letter, which I have just this instant received. I shan't lose a minute in answering it because of the urgency. Read the enclosed, and have it sent immediately, if you approve of it, to the good *curé* of the Trinité.—So as not to take a moment that might mean losing a whole day, I shan't say anything more. But I embrace you, you and your Geneviève, for everything I have left unsaid. Your old and faithful friend, Ch. Gounod." "

This note implies that Bizet may have wished to be married in a religious as well as a civil ceremony. But only the latter is recorded. It took place on June 3, 1869, in the office of the mayor of the 9th *arrondissement*. No member of Bizet's mother's family attended, nor was Geneviève's mother present. (See Appendix I, p. 460.) Because Mme Halévy was ill in a sanatorium at Ivry, "incapable of giving her permission," the family council had appointed her brother-in-law, Léon Halévy, as official spokesman. The other official witnesses were Bizet's father, Mme Halévy's brother, Hippolyte Rodrigues, "retired stockbroker, aged 57," Emile Péreire, "President of the Compagnie des Chemins de fer du Midi, Commander of the Legion of Honor, aged 68," Adrien Benoit-Champy, "President of the *Tribunal civil* of the Seine, Grand Officer of the Legion of Honor, aged 63," and Adolphe Franck, "member of the Institut, Officer of the Legion of Honor, aged 59." "

In addition to this impressive group of official witnesses, one can only hope that perhaps Gounod or Guiraud or some other friend of Bizet's own age and profession was present to support him.

On the day of the wedding, Ludovic Halévy noted in his journal: "Today Geneviève married Bizet. How happy she is, the poor, dear child! What catastrophes have surrounded her for the last few years. What sorrow and what mourning! If anyone has the right to ask a little peace and happiness of life, it is certainly Geneviève. Bizet has spirit and talent. He *should* succeed." "

C H A P T E R  XVIII

Marriage

I am tremendously happy," Bizet wrote to Hippolyte Rodrigues, at whose house at Saint-Gratien, near Enghien, the young couple spent their honeymoon. "Geneviève is marvelously well.—We love each other and we love you, for it is you who have made our life possible.—Come, come soon. We call you, we long for you. —Here there is happiness for all three of us." "

The gratitude that formed the basis of Bizet's intimate friendship with his wife's uncle sprang from the latter's unique stand in relation to the marriage. As the only member of either the Rodrigues or the Halévy family who favored the match strongly, he overcame the objections raised by the other relatives. The Rodrigues side suspected Bizet of being a fortune-hunter; the Halévys, not given to strong convictions or decisive behavior, remained neutral. In their eyes Rodrigues appeared a somewhat stuffy figure, humorless and slightly ridiculous. Yet Bizet's letters to this new friend during the next few years are as self-revelatory as those to Galabert had been earlier. Although there seems to be little resemblance between the conscientious, provincial, vintner's son and the Parisian financier and scholar, they both possessed the characteristics fundamental to Bizet's conception of friendship: loyalty, reliability, and a "high seriousness" that complemented his own gaiety.

Until 1855, Rodrigues had been a stockbroker on the Bourse. He then retired to write a series of religious books. In 1870 he published *Le Roi des juifs*,[1] which attempts to prove that Jesus of Nazareth was a man crucified for political rather than religious reasons. This radical thesis interested Bizet, and he read the book, a true expression of his gratitude to the author. For the presentation in sparse sentences, connecting long lists of numerical keys to references in the Gospels and in ancient Hebrew documents, savors more of Rodrigues's experience with financial statements and company reports than of any talent for scholarship or the arts. Yet during his long life (he lived until 1898) he wrote some twenty books, including poems and plays. He composed an opera, *David Rizzio,* as well as piano-pieces and songs. As a musician, he was even less talented than Galabert, but letters to him from men as different as Delacroix, Auber, and Ernest Legouvé show that they treated him with cordial respect, combined, perhaps, with appreciation for the help he gave their protégés. Generous and patient, he became in his way indispensable to Bizet.

The atmosphere of Rodrigues's house during the summer of 1869, when he was finishing his *Le Roi de juifs,* offered a congenial setting for the task Bizet undertook immediately after his marriage: the completion of his father-in-law's unfinished opera based on the story of Noah. Halévy himself, just before leaving on his final journey to Nice, had said to another of his pupils, the young Belgian composer, Gevaert: "You will have to do for me what I did for Hérold when he was dying. I finished *Ludovic* for him. You will finish my opera *Noë.*" [n] Yet in 1862, a few months after Halévy's death, it had been Bizet who was summoned to Mme Halévy's house to confer with Ambroise Thomas and the librettist, Saint-Georges, about finishing *Noë*. No decision was reached. In 1868, perhaps in an effort to win Mme Halévy's favor, Bizet again tackled the job. But after a month or two of trying, he wrote to Lacombe: "I have abandoned *Noë* completely, and I think I was right." Now, a year later, when part of the family income depended on the royalties from Halévy's works, he tried again. This time the opera was commissioned by Pasdeloup for the Théâtre-Lyrique. The contract required the completion of the first two acts by mid-September, the third act by October

---

[1] Rodrigues's *Le Roi de juifs* is one of the few books remaining from Bizet's library. Others are Voltaire's *Philosophical Dictionary*, four volumes of Dumas's plays, and a volume of Wagner's librettos, including *Tristan and Isolde, Tannhäuser,* and *Lohengrin.*

25, and the last by November 15. A clause in the contract provided for the postponement of the production until Bizet found suitable singers. "I need a basso and *première chanteuse,*" he told Galabert. "I don't see them anywhere, and if I don't find them, *Noë* will wait." *Noë* waited until ten years after Bizet's death, when it was performed at Karlsruhe in Germany. It was never played in France.

"Apart from the uneven quality of the music, the libretto is among Saint-Georges's more fantastic efforts," writes one critic. "The story, concerned with the sexual digressions of Noah's family and the fallen angel Ituriel (who loses his wings on stage to an orgy of diminished sevenths), reads like a mixture of *Paradise Lost* and *The Country Wife* couched in the most inflated language of Scribe. The behavior of the characters and the landscape is unpredictable in the extreme, and it is not clear who survives the flood which terminates the first scene of Act III." " Halévy had left three acts more or less finished. Bizet composed a fourth act, in which he included parts of *Vasco de Gama* and *Ivan IV,* and orchestrated the whole score.

The last few weeks of work on *Noë* were carried on under considerable stress and strain. The Bizets had taken an apartment in Paris, the furnishing of which required continual journeying between Saint-Gratien and Paris throughout September and October. "I have spent the last six weeks at the upholsterer's, the locksmith's, the carpenter's, etc.," Bizet told Lacombe early in November. And to Mme Trélat he bewailed the horrors of moving: "What a job! It's frightful. We are dead tired at the moment. We spend the day buying casseroles; at night I work on *Noë* . . . for which I have a short-term contract with Pasdeloup which fills me with terror. As soon as there is a pillow under my head, as soon as I have our furniture, I shall come to see you." "

The Bizets moved into an apartment at 22 rue de Douai in Montmartre. The new building had been constructed by a contractor who wished "to demonstrate the highest art of his industry by covering the façade with columns, scrolls, and angels so that it looked like the work of a delirious mason who had passed through Rome." " This gem of architecture stood in a Montmartre very different from the Montmartre of today. In the Place Pigalle, where night clubs now flourish, grass and trees grew in squares and gardens. The Basilique du Sacré-Coeur, that tourist mecca, had not yet risen to dominate the skyline. Indeed Montmartre in the 1870's had something of the atmosphere of a suburb like Passy in the early part of this century. "Artists and a few society people had established themselves there and formed a pleasant, active little republic, a quarter of an hour away from the boulevards." " Ludovic Halévy and his family lived in the apartment below the Bizets. Neighbors in the rue de Douai were Guiraud, Edmond About, Pauline Viardot and her family, Gustave Doré, and the critic Francisque Sarcey. Gounod, Degas, and other friends lived nearby.

Before Bizet became embroiled in the complications of setting up housekeeping, he started searching for new work to do. In August he wrote to Choudens: "You will find me ready, as in the past, to carry out with the usual gusto the artistic and culinary jobs pertaining to our trade." Bizet's "usual gusto," intensified as it was by his personal happiness, stimulated in his imagination as many new projects as he had conceived in his Roman days, the one other time in his life when he was truly happy. During his two and one half years in Italy, ideas for twelve possible compositions had occurred to him; he completed three of them. Now, in the first year of his marriage, at least seven projects, apart from *Noë*, attracted him:

1. *La Mort s'avance:* A paraphrase of two *Etudes* by Chopin, opus 10, No. 1, and opus 25, No. 12, adapted to a sacred text by the Abbé Pellegrin. The choral and orchestral parts were engraved by Hartmann, and the work was offered to a choral society. "Please be assured that no feeling of self-esteem has prompted me in this matter," Bizet wrote to the directors of the society. "To see Chopin's name on your program is the sole desire of your obedient servant." [2] "

2. A grand opera based on the life of Vercingetorix. "I have been tempted by this splendid subject for a long time. What could be greater or more thrilling than that magnificent scene . . . when Vercingetorix, armed, awesome, causing even Caesar to tremble, comes to ask for mercy from his companions! . . . But the obstacles, the

---

[2] "The ingenuity with which Chopin's themes are worked into the texture does not make up for the flatulence of the conception as a whole." (Winton Dean, *Bizet*, 163.)

danger, may be insurmountable—Caesar! These devilish emperors are not generally very musical! Caesar, Charlemagne, Alexander, Napoleon—how can you make them sing?"[3]

3. *"Calendal,* by Mistral, put in operatic form in 4 acts and 6 scenes by Paul Ferrier—a work *commissioned* by the director of one of our important lyric theatres (there are reasons for not divulging its name at the moment.)"[4] The anonymous director, actually Camille du Locle of the Opéra-Comique, was not convinced of the possibilities for success of this opera. Bizet, too, had his doubts. "I have had *Calendal* in mind for a long time," he wrote to Lacombe. "I don't know whether the fublic (*sic*) will agree with me. But there is a score there, and I shall try writing it." Bizet continued to think about *Calendal* for several months, and went so far as to copy out the libretto in various inks, one color for each part. But a false rumor in a gossip column, stating that Gounod had the rights to the libretto recalled to the public mind the failure of his opera *Mireille,* based also on a poem by Mistral, and discouraged still further du Locle's interest in the projected piece. (See Appendix I, p. 460.)

4. *Clarissa Harlowe, opéra-comique* in 3 acts and 5 scenes by Philippe Gille and Jaime the younger.

5. *Rama,* "Opera by M. Eugène Crépet, drawn from the *Ramayana,* the admirable epic poem of India." "

6. *Grisélidis, opéra-comique* in 3 acts, libretto by Sardou. Some twenty-two pages of sketches for this work remain among Bizet's private papers. *"La fleur que tu m'avais jeté"* in *Carmen,* and Fréderi's motif in *L'Arlésienne* were originally, in slightly different versions, part of *Grisélidis.*

7. Songs, "musical interpretations" " of *Pages intimes* by

---

[3] Bizet discussed this project in a letter to Emile Delerot, director of the library at Versailles, translator of the Goethe-Eckermann *Conversations* and author of a libretto drawn from a historical novel on the life of Vercingetorix by Henri Martin, published in October 1869. (Original letter in the Bibliothèque de Versailles.)

[4] Bizet was writing here, early in 1870, to an unidentified editor who wished to list his name "among the young composers who deserve the attention of the directors of our lyric theatres." (Bibliothèque de l'Arsenal.)

Eugène Manuel. This first volume of poems by a thirty-five-year-old professor at the Lycée Napoléon had been awarded a prize by the French Académie. Banal and tepid, these poems have been included for many decades in anthologies for French schoolchildren.

Except for the Chopin paraphrase, never performed, Bizet finished none of these projected works.

The one opera Bizet had finished in the previous three years, *La Coupe du Roi de Thulé,* again occupied his attention this September, when the competition closed and announcement was made of the members of the jury to select the prize-winning score. Knowing Perrin to be "the most volatile, the most capricious, the most changeable of men," [n] Bizet had not taken much stock a year earlier in the director's assurance of his ability to swing the jury; and now that he felt sure only a small minority of the jury would like his work, he reverted to the state of nervous tension which competition always induced in him. "I don't want to hear anything more about this trash. . . ." he wrote to Guiraud. "For two cents, and if I weren't afraid of posing, I would go and take back my little effort.

"It is all settled in advance, you may be sure. They will choose the one that has the most outstanding chance of failure. . . . *Cher vieux,* do go to see Perrin and act as though I had no part in this stupid performance. As for me, I repeat, I will have nothing more to do with all this. I shall not go to the Opéra again for the next two months. I have been very low in my mind ever since the other evening. I am disappointed ahead of time—all the better." [n]

Bizet was, of course, unable to remove his score from the competition. But he did manage somehow before the jury met in October to retrieve the sealed envelope enclosing his name and the address 32 rue Fontaine Saint-Georges, which had been attached to the score when he had entered it in the competition months earlier. Just before the judging, he substituted two envelopes, one inside the other. In the first he wrote: "My name and address are here enclosed; but in case my score, even though it should be judged best in the competition, is not considered worthy of being staged at the Opéra, I wish to remain anonymous and to give up the premium of 3000 francs." [n] In the second envelope he gave his address as 22 rue de Douai.

On the official list of 42 scores submitted in competition Bizet's was listed as "No. 590: *'On confie son secret dans l'amitié, mais il échappe dans l'amour.'* 2 volumes." [n] Bizet's entry was among the final seven, but the winner of the contest was Eugène Diaz, whom Bizet had known in Rome and whose brother he had found most sympathetic. Diaz, a mere amateur, had got into such difficulties while composing his version of *La Coupe du Roi de Thulé* that he asked the advice of Bizet and Guiraud. "Shall I have flute accompaniment here, or the horn?" he wanted to know. Bizet suggested the horn, Guiraud, the flute. At a loss which to use, he consulted his father, a well-known conservative painter, who advised him to avoid any risks by using both. So disgusted with the caliber of the winner were the runners-up, Guiraud and Massenet, that they forbade the Ministry to publish their names. "They do not wish to be ranked with a gentleman whom they do not regard as a colleague," wrote Paladilhe, also a defeated competitor. "Everybody knows that Massé [5] wrote Diaz's score which does not lead me to believe it is very good." [n]

Soon after the announcement of Diaz's triumph, an echo of *La Coupe du Roi de Thulé* occurs in a letter from Bizet to Galabert. "You are reconsidering your plan of taking up farming. *You are right.* I read your second act of *La Coupe.* There are a couple of things in it I will write you about in detail in a day or two. But I will tell you the truth now, or what I believe to be the truth. There is not yet any hope of an *immediate exploiting* of your talent. You understand that I am talking from the business point of view. My friendship for you obliges me to say this: *plan your life* without music, and once your life is arranged, I shan't worry. On the musical side you will achieve excellent results; but not in a way to supply your material needs, to support your family and bring you happiness." [n] When Galabert had become engaged, against his parents' wishes, to his first cousin, who was older than he and who would bring him no dowry, Bizet had expressed some doubts about the wisdom of his friend's choice. "But," he concluded, "I married according to the dictates of my heart, and I am too happy to offer any practical objections. But earning your living is no mean problem." [n]

Understandably enough, the promised detailed criticism of

---

[5] A member of the jury.

La Coupe never materialized. But in June 1870, Bizet sent Galabert ". . . just a note in haste. I am going to Barbizon to spend four months. I am taking with me a charming piece by Sardou (urgent) and also *Calendal* and *Clarissa Harlowe,* etc. What a lot of work!" [n]

After two months in the country, Bizet reported to Rodrigues: "Everything is fine at Barbizon. Geneviève has been rather en-nervated the last few days by the overwhelming heat. Extreme heat is very bad for her, and the news of Prévost-Paradol's death, which we learned from the *Gaulois,* has naturally affected her.[6] I should not, therefore, risk a change at this time. By now I have sufficient experience to know what precautions must be taken for the health of my dear Bébé; and the sun is without doubt our most dangerous enemy.—Her general condition is satisfactory; sleep, appetite, all that is good, which means that, on the whole, news in that quarter is good. When we get back to a temperature of 20 degrees centigrade,[7] we shall share your solitude at Saint-Gratien for a few days.—Besides, by then I shall be far enough along so that an interruption will not seriously interfere with the composing of my *Grisélidis.* I am progressing well enough, and am quite satisfied.—The nature of the libretto requires a clear, easy form, a melodic sound that will, I believe, be accepted with-out difficulty; it is important for me to be ready immediately.—If this horrible war doesn't come and upset everything, I can get through this year, and under circumstances which permit of my hoping for success.—But if the Rhine is against us—good-bye to everything. Theatres closed, art destroyed, life compromised—Let's not even think of it.—But what a sad subject for thought!—To have suffered so much, learned so much, taught so much, experimented so much for so many thousands of years, and to have arrived at this!—Heartbreaking!" [n]

A few hours after this letter was written on July 23, 1870, Napoleon III proclaimed war on Prussia. The Year of Terror had begun.

---

[6] Anatole Prévost-Paradol (1829–70), diplomat and journalist on the staff of the *Journal des Débats,* was a relative and close friend of the Halévy family. While he was Ambassador to the United States, his anxiety over the approaching Franco-Prussian war, combined with the excessive heat of Washington, caused him to commit suicide on July 20, 1870.

[7] 68° Fahrenheit.

CHAPTER  XIX

The Year of Terror I:
The Siege of Paris

At the outbreak of the war, the French had little conception of the seriousness of the situation that confronted them. Unaware of the inadequacy of their army and the inefficiency and corruption of many of their leaders and officers, carried away by a wave of optimistic patriotism, they believed that France would soon, easily and gloriously, conquer Prussia. The *Marseillaise,* which had been banned during the Empire, resounded through the streets and in the theatres.[1] It was first revived at a performance of Auber's opera, *La Muette de Portici,* when the audience, having wildly encored the duet, *"Amour sacré de la patrie"* in the third act, demanded the *Marseillaise* at the end of the performance. Marie Sasse (or Saxe), the prima donna, dressed in white and draped in the folds of the tricolor, responded. After the first stanza, the audience rose in a body and joined in the singing. She repeated the performance nightly until the Opéra closed a few weeks later. And when, coming from the Opéra in her carriage, she was recognized by the crowds in the street, she again sang the forbidden song. At the Opéra-Comique Galli-Marié, the future Carmen, was the first to sing the *Marseillaise;* subsequently a dif-

---

[1] In 1791 the *Marseillaise* was declared the national anthem of France. But after the *coup d'état* of November 1799, it was never legally played or sung under Napoleon or the Bourbons. It was banned under Napoleon III, but again declared the national anthem in February 1879.

ferent singer rendered it every night until that theatre, too, shut
down.

Cries of *"A Berlin!"* in the theatre and on the streets interrupted the performances of *Le Kobold,* a little opera by Guiraud
that opened on July 26. The scene was laid in Alsace, and when
the first false rumors of victory reached Paris de Leuven, one of
the directors of the Comique, had the librettist insert into the
tenor's aria the line: *"Le Rhin à traverser, ce n'est qu'un pas."*
The line was deleted when the first news of German victories
reached Paris. The opera ran for only a few performances.

Bizet, back in Barbizon after a brief visit to Paris for the
opening of his friend's piece, was still able, during the early
days of the war, to remain reasonably cheerful. "Are we in the
National Guard?" he asked Guiraud. "If so, what must I do? . . .
If you have any idea of what is to become of us, it would be nice
of you to let me know. Have Massenet, Paladilhe, and Cormon
been mobilized? We shall be able to sing with variations *'Tutti
son mobile.' "* [n] With the news of three French defeats and the fall
of Alsace, Bizet's debonair attitude soon changed.

"We were so worried and hopeless yesterday," he wrote to
Guiraud a few days later, "that we could no longer tolerate this
awful state of indecision, and we walked to Fontainebleau. There,
in the town hall we read the handful of despatches published in
the *Gaulois.* So, our soldiers fought in three different engagements
one to ten, one to five, one to three! So the Prussian army maneuvers quietly, knowing perfectly where each of our army corps is,
beats them easily, one after the other, and our generals *know
nothing* about it. The Emperor said yesterday: 'I no longer know
where Mac Mahon is.' It's heartbreaking——Lorraine invaded; a
battle imminent between Metz and Nancy, and if we lose them!
——Certainly I am no chauvinist; you know that. But I have been
heartsick and on the verge of tears since yesterday!——Poor country!——Poor army! Governed and led from now on with notorious
inefficiency! This is not the moment for recriminations, but the
uncle [2] at least knew where to find the enemy. . . . I haven't
the slightest idea, not the slightest, what will become of us. But
this is now only a minor question. Why leave the soldiers in the
interior? Why aren't we all busy defending our cities? Is he afraid

---

[2] Napoleon I.

to arm the nation? . . . I need hardly tell you that for three days I haven't written a note! If we lose the big battle, I don't know but what it would be better for me to go back to Paris." "

Bizet's indecision was of short duration. "I am returning to Paris tomorrow morning," he wrote to Galabert a day or two later. "The non-mobile National Guard calls me. . . . Here go tranquillity, order, peace! Today it is a matter of saving the country. But after that, what? [The future is very dark, *cher ami,* and we are getting nowhere. If only your marriage isn't delayed by this call to arms. I hope not. If I weren't married, I would be a mobile, but if I were a bachelor I wouldn't care.]

"And our poor philosophy, our dreams of universal peace, world fraternity, and human fellowship! Instead of all that, we have tears, blood, piles of corpses, crimes without number or end! I can't tell you, *mon cher ami,* into what sadness I am plunged by all these horrors. I remember that I am a Frenchman, but I can't altogether forget that I am a man. This war will cost humanity five hundred thousand lives. As for France, she will lose everything!" "

Although Bizet enlisted in the Sixth battalion of the National Guard as soon as he returned to Paris, his actual training did not start for another fortnight. In the meantime, he proceeded to prepare for the siege. From Galabert, who had been in the habit of paying for his lessons in wine from his father's vineyards, Bizet ordered two casks of wine ["not good enough to be expensive or cheap enough to be poor. . . . No matter what happens, we are all, we artists, commandeered for this winter. . . . *My opera* will not go on; Halévy's works will not be played. There will be no lessons, and I want to organize my year very economically. So how much wine is possible?"] "

Bizet's activities as a soldier began in earnest at the end of August. "Tomorrow morning at 7 I start my military drill," he wrote. "Our guns weigh 14 pounds—that's heavy for a musician. These weapons kick back, spit, do everything possible to be more disagreeable to those who fire them than to the enemy. In short, they are, *par excellence,* Prussian arms." "

At Sedan on September 2, the Prussian army won the decisive victory. The Emperor himself ordered the hoisting of the white flag. The French lost 20,000, the Germans 6,000. Eighty thousand French prisoners were taken, including the Emperor,

who offered his own sword in surrender. The news of the defeat
reached Paris on the 3rd, and a republic was proclaimed the
following day.

At the head of the "Government of National Defense" was
the military governor of Paris, General Louis-Jules Trochu, a
strong critic of the old army. His ministers represented every color
of political thinking: Henri Rochefort, editor of *La Lanterne,*
admired by Bizet and idolized by the working people of Paris;
Jules Favre, Minister of Foreign Affairs, who, on September 6,
issued a circular stating that France would not surrender an "inch
of her territory or a stone of her fortresses"; Léon Gambetta,[3]
Minister of the Interior, in charge of the National Guard, who
believed that it was possible to arm the people against reaction as
well as against the Prussians. The new government seemed to bode
well for the future of France.

"The day of the 4th was splendid," Bizet wrote to Rodrigues,
who had gone to Bordeaux, "no shouting, no noise. The *line*
was the first to cry *'Vive la république!'* I was at the Corps
Législatif with my battalion. I was profoundly moved, I assure
you." [n]

The very depth of Bizet's emotion at the establishment of a
republic, his determination to participate as a citizen-soldier in
defense of Paris and of the new government for which he had
such high hopes, also intensified his family problems. "Your departure has left me with a terrible responsibility," he told Rodrigues. "We think that the disturbance, the misfortunes, the disasters that will come with the siege of Paris might be extremely
dangerous for Mme Halévy. . . ." [n] Dangerous, too, for Geneviève, who refused to be separated from her husband, a decision
in which she was encouraged by Mme de Beaulieu, the cousin
with whom she had lived before her marriage, and whose influence, Bizet complained, ["greatly weakens my authority over
her."] So, although he was able to arrange for Mme Halévy to

---

[3] Léon Gambetta (1838–82), leader of the Left opposition to Napoleon III,
member of the Government of National Defense, had escaped by balloon on
October 7, 1870, from Paris to Tours, the seat of the delegation sent by the
Assembly to represent and act for it during the Siege of Paris. He became
Minister of War and of the Interior. On March 1, 1871, he resigned as Deputy
for the Bas-Rhin and left for San Sebastian, where he remained during the
Commune. He returned to France in June 1871, and was elected Deputy of the
Seine in the July elections.

join her brother in Bordeaux, he was forced to give in to his wife's plea to remain in Paris.

By September 19, the German armies had completely surrounded the city. For four months after September 25 the only means of communication between Paris and the outside was by balloon and carrier pigeon. Nevertheless, Bizet felt "absolutely convinced that citizens between 20 and 35 who have left Paris will regret it bitterly.—The danger for them is greater than for us." [n]

Most of Bizet's friends stayed in Paris. An exception was Gounod, who fled with his family to England. Théophile Gautier, at sixty, with only 900 francs to his name, returned from the safety of his daughter's house in Switzerland, remarking: "When I heard they were beating up my mama I came home." Saint-Saëns joined the National Guard, Massenet and Sardou an infantry regiment. Ludovic Halévy, who had been spending the summer at Etretat with his sister, his wife, and his infant son, Elie, remained there reluctantly and ill at ease. "I so long to be in Paris, if only out of curiosity," he wrote at the beginning of the war to his friend and collaborator, Meilhac. But as the siege of Paris became imminent, Halévy became deeply troubled.

Meilhac attempted to reassure him in a letter written on September 16, three days before the siege started. "I assure you, *mon cher ami,* your reputation has not been attacked, and even if it had, it would be well defended. Anyone who knows you are at Etretat knows why you went there, and from today on I shall announce that you will return as soon as your wife can come with you. As to what you say about your inability to do anything, I offer you a century for the part I am playing. I have been in the National Guard since Saturday, and I still haven't a gun, although I went to ask for one. My Captain asked me to wait and made me a rather pretty little speech about the futility of being rash. . . . France will, I think, succeed, but Prussia does not seem disposed to concede it. She will lose all, and that will be a good thing. . . .

"Last night at nine o'clock we had an alert, and Paris did not cut too bad a figure. I was dining (may the God of battles forgive me—and don't tell this to my godson) with Mlle Beresford, a very pretty English girl, when—*taratata*—we heard the bugle and then loud cries of 'To arms! They are attacking Nogent!' We opened the window, and for a few minutes I saw a rather curious sight. The people in the street, without looking around or changing their direction, started running as fast as they could instead of walking. . . . This didn't last for more than half a minute, but during that half-minute there was at least a semi-panic. I wasn't too displeased with my behavior, although it did not occur to me to take the gun they were making me wait for and go out and fight. But the idea of taking a carriage and going out to look around struck me very forcibly.—Like you, my poor friend, curiosity! After all, it is our nature. . . .

"I think the news of this attack on Nogent was invented by the government to wake Paris up a little and to see how it would behave. . . . It's not courage that is lacking; it is discipline, obedience. The heroes of *La Grande Duchesse de Gérolstein* are not at all cowards, they are just underlings who make fun of their leader. To the extent that we killed respect, we were obviously stupid and didn't see clearly. Respect can be foolish when the objects respected are not respectable, yet it would seem that it is always necessary. When the clergy pass by, one must bow and not laugh at the donkey that carries them. I don't know whether you understand this jumble of words. When I say us, it is clear that I speak of all of us and not of *us two*. But it is evident that *we two* set the tone of this concert. When the people I meet laugh and say that this appalling collapse is our fault, I do not laugh, at least not heartily. Obviously I am not conceited enough to accept the whole responsibility, but I do feel, with all due modesty, that we must accept at least a small part.—And that is too much. Please forgive this page, which sounds like a sermon. It is Miss Beresford's fault. She is a good Protestant, and assures me very seriously that what is destroying France is the lack of religion. The first present she has asked me for is a big Red Cross flag for the dressing-station she is setting up in her salon for the wounded.

At the bottom of this letter, which Halévy copied into his journal, he noted: "Meilhac is wrong to think and talk like this. . . . He finds that we have not sufficiently respected the Empire, the generals, the diplomats, political procedure. I think that we have paid all that too much respect. I saw the Empire at first hand during my intimacy with the Duc de Morny. France never had a worse government; never, never, a weaker one with pretentions to strength." [n]

If Meilhac's letter failed to bolster Halévy's self-esteem, the letter from Geneviève to Ludovic's sister, Valentine, written on the same day as Meilhac's, only added to his anxiety. "Imagine, my dear Bichette, I have spent the last 26 hours all alone. Yes, all alone! Georges was standing guard duty on the fortifications. He left Sunday at 3 o'clock and didn't come back until Monday at 5, after having done sixteen hours of sentry and patrol duty and two of fatigue (that is unloading the heavy weapon teams). He was very tired, but fortunately he takes it all rather well. It doesn't bother him, and after sleeping two full nights, here he is, completely rested. As for me, I found that the time passed slowly, but I think of what it will be like when the Prussians come." [n]

The strain of being left so much alone soon began to tell on Geneviève's health, both mental and physical. She ate less and less, lost weight, and by mid-October was spending much of her time in bed. Bizet evidently tried to disturb her rest as little as possible, for among his papers are several of the little notes he left for her: "My dearest love, I can't see you this morning. I am on sentry-duty at 11 o'clock—and I haven't even time to grab a bite to eat on the run. But I shall come back for dinner. I don't know just what time. In any case, have dinner ready at six o'clock. I love you, my love, with all my soul." [n]

A radical uprising against the provisional government resulted, early in November, in the holding of an election to win a vote of confidence. "Because of the elections, so that the relieving guard can vote, we shall not be relieved until noon or 1 o'clock," Bizet told his wife. "What a nuisance! . . . I will see you tomorrow, darling.—I love you.—It is rather cold out, but I feel fine. Your *bébé* who adores you." [n]

But adoration communicated only at intervals outside her control was insufficient nourishment for Geneviève's well-being. Once more she expresses her insecurity and anxiety in her journal. Again she implores God to relieve her suffering, to find her not unworthy of "the joys I dreamed of." She asks the Lord to "grant me the infinite grace of seeing my mother again and of consecrating my life to her." Mme Halévy, too, wished to re-establish contact with her daughter. Early in November, she wrote to Ludovic Halévy: "If my Geneviève is happy, and her husband loves her, if he likes me a little, if they are well, all my wishes for today and the future will be fulfilled. I live only through them, but they *must live*. Affection is the only thing that helps me. When will it be granted me calmly, without the rumbling of drums, telegraph messages, cries in the street, the gates of Paris closed to me? . . . If only my children, your father, all the rich people in Paris aren't starving! The carefully laid, abundant, succulent tables of Bordeaux reduce me to tears. I would like to make away with the dinner and send it to Paris." [n]

To this cry from the heart, communicated by her cousin, Geneviève replied at the end of November: "We are still perfectly healthy. We are not yet dying of hunger, and I must admit that I have not yet eaten cat or dog or rat or mouse, as is being done in the *best* society; I shall taste some donkey for the first time today. Butter, it is true, is expensive—45 francs per pound. But you do without it, that's all, and don't die of it. We eat even more since this frightful siege, which should really lessen our appetites." [n]

But as all prisoners know, neither the lack of food nor unpalatable meals diminish hunger. "We no longer eat," Bizet wrote in mid-December to Guiraud, who, "threatened by cold, dampness, rice, the Prussians and other vermin . . ." was stationed at a château in the suburbs of Paris. "Suzanne brought me a few horse bones a little while ago which we will share. Geneviève dreams of chicken and lobster every night." [n]

Bizet dreamed that "we were all at Naples, installed in a charming villa; we were living under a purely artistic government. The senate consisted of Beethoven, Michelangelo, Shakespeare, Giorgione, and people like that. The National Guard was replaced by an immense orchestra under the command of Litolff.[4] The vote was denied idiots, spongers, intriguers, and ignoramuses. I need not tell you it was thus the most limited suffrage imaginable.

---

[4] Henry-Charles Litolff (1818–91), a friend of Liszt and of Berlioz, who regarded him as "a composer of the highest order," was *chef d'orchestre* at the Opéra from 1867 to 1870. Bizet had been curious about Litolff since the time the conductor-composer had come to Paris ten years earlier. In 1858, from Rome, Bizet wrote to Gounod asking for information about him. "Litolff:" Gounod replied, "a man who is a remarkable composer: a strong man, with energetic, powerful ideas, often feverish in details, but always deliberate in the *ensemble:* rich orchestration, pungent and gripping: *never boring! . . .* His concerto (4th symphony) is superb, particularly the *Scherzo* and the adagio. His *Overture* of the Guelphs is remarkably fine; the peroration has a colossal effect, stirring, intoxicating." Gounod, *Lettres à Georges Bizet*, 683. (See Appendix I, p. 460.)

Geneviève was a little too friendly with Goethe, but despite this annoyance, waking up was a cruelly bitter business." [n]

As the siege continued and the National Guard increased in numbers, Bizet's military duties occupied less of his time. "I continue to reproach myself for my inactivity," he told Guiraud. "True, my conscience isn't clear, but you know what keeps me here. I blame myself for doing nothing more than the law requires." He did, however, serve as active patron of the dressing-station for the wounded sponsored by the French press. And though he refused to set to music a patriotic poem by Léon Halévy, he did attempt to write a war song. Choudens rejected it.

"Choudens came a little while ago to fetch the songs that I had for him," Bizet wrote to Guiraud. "I was supposed, as usual, to let him see the words in advance. You know Hugo's lines: *'Ceux qui pieusement sont mort pour la patrie—'* I had entitled this piece *'Morts pour la France!'* At this line Choudens interrupts me: 'Very sad, *mon ami,* very sad! But if you don't mind, not that one, *mon ami,* not that one! It would depress me to have it in my shop. When the siege is over, we will eat a leg of lamb, and there will no longer be anything to worry about. I have suffered a great deal in the last three months. I have had the great sorrow of sending my children away from their father. I have eaten poorly. I don't eat at all any more, which is very fattening. I have no coal. My son-in-law has caught cold on the ramparts. If this thing of yours should unfortunately be successful, I would be bored all day long with "Please, monsieur, give me *'Morts pour la France!'* " A bore, *mon ami,* a bore! Sing of the spring, of roses, of love! "Come, oh come into the flowering groves."—Anyway I am a foreigner here; and besides I've paid my debt. I had myself photographed as a sniper. I put on my son-in-law's jacket and a Tyrolean hat that Carvalho loaned me. The photographer will see that I am placed between General Trochu and General Ducrot. *Defense of Paris, 1870* will be inscribed underneath in capital letters! What a monstrosity war is! I have a horror of blood, particularly my own! You know that I am not bellicose. For three months our *fields have been soaked in blood.*—But enough of that! Let's have music, *mon ami,* let's have music! And above all let's sell it, that's what counts. But not that piece, *mon ami,* not that piece I beg of you.' " [n]

Music there was in Paris that winter in spite of the dearth of performers and the lack of heat in the theatres. Almost as an act of mourning for the Empire, all theatres had closed down even before the beginning of the siege. But the authorities soon realized that some form of entertainment was necessary for the morale of both civilian and military population. Pasdeloup, in spite of accusations of frivolity launched against him by the radical Louis-Auguste Blanqui, characteristically made the first attempt to fill the vacuum. On October 23, he resumed his Sunday Concerts Populaires for the benefit of soup-kitchens for the poor. Many soldiers came to the concert, and a lieutenant in the Mobile Guard played a first violin alongside an abbé who addressed a few musico-patriotic words to the audience. The program consisted of the *Marseillaise,* followed by Beethoven's Fifth Symphony. The following Sunday, Pasdeloup played the "Pastoral" Symphony, and a few days later, Georges Hainl, director of the orchestra and chorus of the Société des Concerts du Conservatoire conducted a concert at the Madeleine, with Saint-Saëns at the organ. While the orchestra played the *"Eroica,"* the sum of 2500 francs was collected for the benefit of Bizet's charity, the dressing-station for the wounded run by the French press.

Perrin of the Opéra did not lag far behind. In spite of the limited number of artists, he invited Pasdeloup to conduct a concert early in November. Officers and men, members of the government, and such society people and musicians as remained in Paris crowded the great cold auditorium of the Opéra to listen to excerpts from Gluck's *Alceste,* Rossini's *Guillaume Tell* and Meyerbeer's *Les Huguenots.* At another concert at the Opéra a fortnight later, Hugo's *Les Châtiments* was read to an audience privileged to view a wounded Bavarian prisoner on exhibit in one of the front boxes. Prussian helmets were used to collect the contributions for the wounded.

Music also played its part in the execution of military discipline. On one occasion in this snowy November, eleven men condemned for crimes ranging from murder to theft and desertion were sentenced before 1500 of their fellow-soldiers drawn up in front of the Ecole Militaire. The vans that returned the convicts to prison "were accompanied by a band that played selections from *La Grande Duchesse de Gérolstein,"* [n] a performance which, if they heard of it, may well have assuaged the consciences of Meilhac and Halévy.

The preponderance of works by composers of German origin played while Paris was besieged may well surprise anyone who remembers the violent controversies over the performance of German music during the wars in this century. Indeed, the German love of music inspired one French inventor with a scheme for a "musical *mitrailleuse* that would spray the enemy with machine-gun bullets while playing Wagner, Schubert, and Mendelssohn. According to the inventor: 'The Germans are too fond of music to be able to resist the temptation of listening. They are sure to draw near in thousands when my machine guns are playing. We would have them at our mercy.' " [n]

A French victory at Coulmiers, won by the army of the Loire early in November, heartened the besieged Parisians and increased the prestige and power of Léon Gambetta, who continued to believe in the possibility of an eventual French victory. Gambetta's faith kindled Bizet's ever-latent optimism. "Decidedly three months of the Republic have removed the greater part of the coating of shame and filth with which the Empire whitewashed the country," he wrote to Guiraud. "I have a feeling that Gambetta is really the man we hoped for.—Get rid of the Prussians and keep the Republic! It's hard, but I grow more hopeful each day." [n]

Mme Halévy, too, was exhilarated by Gambetta's presence in Bordeaux, whither the headquarters of the provisional government had now been transferred. "Your poor old aunt sees the Republican court, the city and the suburbs; plebeians and patricians, reacs and democs, everybody goes through my little salon," she wrote to her nephew Ludovic, on New Year's day. "Here is how I have spent the day. Got up at 4 o'clock. At 7 went out to buy a lot of little trifles, presents for the nephews and nieces. . . . At 9 o'clock to the dressing-station. Not a carriage would cross the icy streets of Bordeaux, which are, after all, so pretty. Ice on the ground, sunshine in the air—I find a carriage, and a gentleman inside it. It doesn't matter. I take it, and so does the gentleman. Fortunately he turns out to be one of my relatives. At 11 o'clock I leave my dressing-station. I had taken *twenty-five* presents: cigars, flannel binders, tobacco pouches filled with tobacco, an enormous chicken pâté, cakes, candies, sugar. . . . I was blessed by my 25 soldiers, who promised to defend me if the Prussians come.

"One o'clock I returned exhausted after having gone to wish

a Happy New Year to all my grown-up relatives and lunched with them. Then I dressed in a hurry and went to the prefecture to ask for a private room for my family, the nephews and nieces. . . . I found myself looking down on M. Gambetta's cranium. I listened to his speech, watched his gestures, his enthusiasm. . . . The whole government on the balcony; a crowd of 40,000 people below, open-mouthed, listening to the speeches. As soon as M. Gambetta re-entered the salon, the crowd called for him: 'Gambetta! Gambetta!'—And then they sang the *Marseillaise*. The crowd, excited but peaceful, was superb. Never has Bordeaux had such a celebration.

"In the evening they gave *Charles VI* at the Grand Théâtre. It was a gesture for me by the prefect." [n]

The optimism of Gambetta in Bordeaux was rapidly dispelled in Paris by the bombing of the city, which started on January 5, 1871, and continued almost without interruption until an armistice was signed on January 26. Four days earlier the militant revolutionaries in the National Guard had assembled before the Hôtel de Ville to protest the surrender of Paris. Other members of the Guard, Breton mobiles, put down the demonstration with considerable bloodshed. This sign of internal dissension and the imminence of the Prussian occupation made thousands of Parisians flee the city in panic. Mme Halévy, fearing for Geneviève's safety, asked Bizet to bring her to Bordeaux.

"My dear mother-in-law," he replied, "I can't leave Paris! It's impossible! It would be an act of sheer cowardice! I hope that the government will take the sternest measures against the Parisians who have abandoned us at the critical moment.—I know several strong, healthy men who, like Shakespeare's Falstaff, think that honor is merely a convention. *I wouldn't shake hands with them!*

"You can decide whether I, thinking as I do, have the right to leave Paris! Besides, I repeat, we are *imploring* the government to *brand* or punish the cowards, and it is more dangerous to be chicken-hearted than to do one's duty.—

"As for Geneviève, I offered to let her go.—I begged her to do it—but she has felt, along with many other women . . . that her duty is here.—She has expressed her firm determination to stay, and I have given in. I yielded because I am *convinced* that the situation in Paris is not as dangerous as you picture it.—Inside the city it is absolutely quiet, safe! *Geneviève will be absolutely safe!* Geneviève is my whole life; you know that. Her fate means much more to me than my own.—I know several members of the government who will enable me to shelter my Geneviève from all danger! Have faith in my love for her, set your mind at rest, don't be frightened!—The bad times are over, the future is good. Don't spoil it by exaggerating your anxiety!—The Prussians will not move into our house, and as soon as they have left, the trying part of this ordeal will be over.—The railroads are being used to transport troops and materiel. Passenger traffic will be stopped in a few hours, if it isn't already. It would even be dangerous for Geneviève or you to attempt any sort of journey at this time.—We are happy to know that you are safe near our dear uncle . . . to think that all this is just a bad dream that will end.—The awakening will be all the more joyful!" "

During the year and a half since their marriage, Bizet had taken Geneviève to see her mother only once, a meeting that had been difficult and nerve-wracking. Therefore he was in a state of indecision as to what course to follow, when a plea from Rodrigues, adding his own urgent invitation to Mme Halèvy's, succeeded in breaking down his scruples against leaving Paris. On February 7, he wrote to his uncle: "You are more than right, *mon cher ami,* in supposing that we long to leave Paris. And your letter telling us that you are postponing your return has transformed our longing into decision. You can imagine how overjoyed we are at your kind invitation! . . . All your reasons are too sound not to be enthusiastically accepted. Nevertheless, before we leave it is essential: 1, that my throat should have healed a little, a matter of only a very short delay; 2, that means of travel should be safer and less costly. . . . If I were alone, this consideration wouldn't stop me for a second, but the presence of Geneviève does not permit my starting before I have positive information on the absolute safety of the journey. On the other hand, I know several people (men alone; no woman of our acquaintance has, as yet, dared leave the capital), who were conspicuously exploited. . . . We have decided, Geneviève and I, that no matter what happens, we will draw only on our own regular resources. Not that our self-esteem has ever suffered from the help our loved ones have wished to give us, but as we are in a situation that challenges everyone's status, it is absolutely essential for each of us to act *da se.*—As for the safe-conduct, which is harder to get than you seem to think, at least for those who, because of their opinions, their positions, or their connections are not recognized as belonging to one or another of the monarchist parties,—I have overcome this difficulty. One of my friends in the above-mentioned category, who has great influence with the Prefect of Police, has just brought me two passes. . . . As soon as the officials of the Orléans railroad can give passengers more reliable encouragement than: 'We shall resume operations somehow or other,' we shall leave. . . .

"The *Gaulois* has already brought you news of Bas-Prunay![5] All the occupied houses were, in general, treated respectfully; but the gardeners ·at the Halévy house abandoned their posts, and thanks to the disloyalty and cowardice of these miserable creatures, we can say with the historian: *'Per sex dies ea clade soevitum est!'*". . .

"Geneviève has gone through this ordeal bravely. Her condition is excellent, but her health is always my main preoccupation. Everything else must be subordinated to it; there lies my prime duty. I am sure that we shall agree on this subject, as on all others.

"You count on me, you say, *cher ami.*—I owe you a tremendous debt, the extent of which is proved to me day by day in my increasing happiness. To repay it is impossible! But . . . it is possible to prove to you my true affection, my complete devotion to you. It is possible, in fact, in so far as it lies in my power, to be the friend you hoped I would be, and on whom you pay me the affectionate honor of relying today." [n]

A week or so later the Bizets made the journey to Bordeaux with the intention of spending some time there as guests of Rodrigues. But Geneviève's encounter with her mother proved to be a disaster. A few hours in Mme Halévy's company reduced her daughter to such acute hysteria that very soon after their arrival, Bizet took her back to Paris. On the way, they spent the night at a hotel in Libourne, from which he wrote to Rodrigues: "A better night—a little rest and nourishment. We shall make amends for everything, but she was terribly shaken. This morning she heard someone talking in the corridor of the hotel. If you could have seen how pale she turned, if you could have seen the way she threw herself into my arms screaming: 'She's here! Save me, I'll

---

[5] Bas-Prunay is a village near Paris, on the left bank of the Seine, where the Halévys had a summer house.

die if I see her again,' you would have been frightened of the way she looked. The nature of her distress is shockingly like Ludovic's after his marriage. If my comparison is valid, we can at least hope that we shall not forever have the cruel and savage duty of preventing a mother from seeing her daughter again. In any case, whatever happens will be God's will!" "

Back in Paris, Bizet was confronted with the realization that Geneviève's relatives would demand an explanation of her condition. To Ludovic Halévy, of whose sympathy he was sure, he wrote immediately on his return: "I have just gone through a sad week! I wanted, for Geneviève's sake, for all of you, for myself, to try an experiment, which has, unfortunately, turned out more disastrous than I could have feared. Forty-eight hours spent with her mother have seriously compromised Geneviève's health. It's only in the last few hours that I have assured myself that this sad journey to Bordeaux would leave no after-effects. . . . For the last five months Geneviève has been losing weight. Since the time Mme Halévy re-entered her life, Geneviève has been afraid of the future. Once the blockade of Paris was raised, her dread became morbid. I was in a difficult position. What should I do? Take a stand against Geneviève's visiting her mother? That would have made me seem hateful, which is unimportant. But it would also have left Geneviève in a state of doubt, of remorse even crueller than the crisis we have just gone through. I decided to make the journey. When I have the great pleasure of seeing you, *cher ami,* I shall tell you all the vicissitudes of this personal and sorry drama. Today it is enough for you to know that 22 hours after our arrival, Geneviève, distracted, desperate, said to me: 'Take me away quickly, quickly, or I shall die the way Esther did!' Hippolyte Rodrigues, perhaps more frightened than I was, in a situation he had not foreseen, understood that the only thing to do was to save Geneviève. *That has been done!* Today she is gay again; her appetite, her sleep are excellent. She is still in a state of nervous agitation, the outward manifestations of which are beyond anything you can imagine. . . . As for Mme Halévy, she has graciously accepted her position. I explained Geneviève's attack as a recrudescence of unhappy memories. She does not know the real truth. It is very important, as you will understand, that a mother should never know that her presence might kill her daughter. Besides Mme Halévy does not admit for an instant that her daughter is ill, although she was struck by the change in Geneviève. She attributes this breakdown to a childish indulgence in hysteria and thinks that I am much too gentle with her.—Mme Halévy is cured. She is in high spirits, charming, gay, excessively active. She sculpts, writes ten letters a day, pays ten visits, and receives as many. However, in my opinion, two symptoms of her illness remain:

"1. She is carried away by feelings that are absolutely superficial. She thinks she loves everybody and loves no one. Her daughter is in no way necessary to her. Nobody in the family is spared her stinging criticism, *nobody!* She asks for news of her nephew Alfred . . . with the most affectionate, liveliest interest, and when she is told that the poor creature is in a state of absolute idiocy, she calmly answers: 'Oh, really,' and changes the subject. Her vanity is overwhelming!' 'I am Mme Halévy. Everybody must obey me.' She values people only for their social position. . . .

"2. Money!!!!! Between ourselves, whoever thinks of depriving Mme Halévy of her liberty would be quite simply a monster. But that liberty, I have no doubt, will cause serious difficulties. In a year my financial situation will be reasonably good; Mme Halévy will be debt-ridden. Hippolyte does everything he can to restrain her, and succeeds in doing so only with the greatest difficulty. But he can't spend his life under these conditions; and when Mme Halévy is in her own home—! But all these considerations are secondary. The important thing is her health. It's her life or Geneviève's.—Your heart will tell you what I have suffered in the last twelve days.—Today my mind is at rest. Geneviève feels that she has done her duty; her conscience is clear, and it is a tremendous comfort to her. As for me, I did what I could, what I had to do. Those who approve of me will do me a lot of good, I assure you. Those who blame me will give me a very low opinion of their capacity for feeling and their intelligence, and I have decided to scorn their opinion. Nothing is sadder, *cher ami,* nor worse to behold than a mother *harsh* to her daughter and a daughter *more than cold* to her mother. Their illness (for it is morbid of both of them) excuses everything, but it does not enliven the situation. . . . Geneviève asks for letters and says she will answer in a week. . . ."[n]

Bizet's premonition that certain members of the family would blame him for the whole episode was sound. His inability to ignore their opinions was equally predictable. Soon after his return to Paris, he wrote to Mme Halévy: "I have had to break off relations with M. and Mme Gouin because they questioned my integrity and my scruples. I lunched with them after I came back from Bordeaux. They saw my distress, my anxiety. They knew better than anyone the painful, bizarre situation in which I had been placed by events for which I wished to make allowances. They should have felt sorry for me, instead of which they reproached me violently in terms I shall never forget. Besides, Mme Gouin failed completely to understand my character. She thought me a schemer and was frank enough to tell me so. M. Gouin expressed himself about my behavior with a violence and an ill will that caused me acute distress. . . . If I have taken his attitude seriously, it is because it came from a man I formerly liked, and whom I still respect.—Let's leave the score as it stands.—I am not the composer, and I regret it sincerely.—I love you more than you choose to think and send you the most tender expressions of my filial affection. Geneviève sends you love and kisses." [n]

Fortunately for what little peace of mind Bizet could achieve at this time, his mother-in-law replied kindly to his complaints. "I have just received a long letter from Mme Halévy that touched me profoundly," he wrote to Rodrigues. "I find in it extreme sensitiveness combined with great resignation. . . . Her letter seems to show that her disappointment does not exclude calmness and confidence. You can imagine that this is very gratifying to me. . . . As for Geneviève—at last she has calmed down. I don't leave her for a single instant. I reassure her. I console her. I try to bring her back to herself. She eats a little, she sleeps well enough, but she continues to be profoundly sad, and the external manifestations of her nervous shock are frightening. I can't give you any idea of the extent of the nervous tics.[6] My doctor assures me that in five or six days all will be well; but he does not hide from me the terrible danger that Geneviève ran. Such ordeals are more than she can bear. . . . From now on for some time Geneviève will not read Mme Halévy's letters. I outline them to her briefly. In five or six days I think she will be able to hold a pen (which today is absolutely impossible; her nervous tics preclude any occupation, even if it takes only a few minutes). I shall

---

[6] Geneviève Bizet retained a facial tic throughout her life.

dictate her letters, and thus we can re-establish a correspondence between mother and daughter. . . . Oh, *mon ami,* what a shock this has been! Your heart can tell you what I have suffered and am still suffering.—Still, everything makes me hope that this cruel attack will not have any harmful after-effects. . . . Her nerves will relax and everything will be all right. I shall be rid of this fear, but what fear!" [n]

Rodrigues did his best to reassure his nephew, but with little success. "You tell me, *cher ami,* that my conscience should be clear," Bizet replied. "Alas, no! As long as my poor Bébé's nerves are in this violent state, I shall reproach myself bitterly for having, out of human respect, taken a chance in which the stakes were Geneviève's life. I knew by intuition and from all the doctors I consulted that it was essential for Geneviève never to see her mother again. . . . She has told me a great deal that her extreme sensitiveness kept her from divulging until after she made the supreme effort. Her terror went beyond any bounds we could have imagined. She was perpetually haunted by incessant dreams that were all the more harmful because she didn't dare tell me about them. In short, we have two invalids where we thought we had only one. . . . As for Mme Halévy . . . you describe her condition very well when you say 'a lack of emotional continuity.'

"For my conscience to be clear, I need two things: your approval, which I already have, and Geneviève's complete recovery, which I shall have soon. On that day, and only on that day, shall I again be free of care." [n]

Of his anxiety and distress over his family affairs Bizet revealed nothing to his friends. In a letter to Galabert written in the midst of Geneviève's breakdown he says: "[So you are married, which means that you are happy. My wife has come courageously through these cruel ordeals.] We find ourselves alive, at least more or less so. . . . We shall probably not live long enough to see what the Napoleons have cost us!

"[As for me—I am temporarily ruined. I have just arranged my little business affairs, for better or for worse, to stretch my credit until next winter. If the theatres open in 8 or 10 months, I shall be all right. If not, I shall look for some sort of job to earn my living.] . . . I would like to finish *Clarissa Harlowe* and *Grisélidis* this summer. *Grisélidis* is very far along. Sardou will change the last act. As soon as he is back in Paris, I shall ask him to finish it so that I can do the same. As for *Clarissa,* it is barely started.

"[I don't know what I shall do this summer. Paris and its environs are unhealthy. Perhaps I might come to spend a few months down your way. Could you tell me whether it would be easy to find a nicely situated corner with a little shade, and approximately how much it would cost for rent, living expenses, etc., for my wife, myself, and a maid?]" ⁿ

To Lacombe, Bizet wrote an almost identical letter, only in speaking of summer plans he asked: "Are there forests in the Aude? The woods are prescribed for Geneviève. I would like to settle down in a seaport, but my wife's constitution absolutely prevents it."

The Prussian occupation of Paris was brief and orderly. The armies entered the city on March 1. "We did our duty on this sad occasion," Bizet reported to Rodrigues. "At the first beat of the drum, at 8 o'clock in the morning, we took our guns and went to establish a *cordon sanitaire* around our enemies." To his mother-in-law he wrote more fully: "Paris behaved almost well during the German occupation. I say almost because along with the excellent, there was also disgusting behavior. The *bitter-enders* indulged in warlike demonstrations that could seriously have disturbed anyone unfamiliar with the customary performance of certain portions of the population of Paris. Cannons and machine-guns were paraded. The poor *Marseillaise* was shouted out in strange tonalities, which proved that alcohol was one of the dominant causes of this ill-timed patriotism. . . . The National Guard did its part, the crowd was well-behaved. Their dignity seemed to me to prevail over their curiosity. Some ladies from the 11th *arrondissement* went to present their respects to the enemy. On their return, some polite young men grabbed them and administered that punishment usually reserved for the guileless, punishment that the fair sex should not rate at the very time when they are being only too cooperative. Lots of the spankers tried a little swim.—One of the ladies was slapped and thrown in the water; but it was no more than a bath! However, the spankers and the spanked are of little interest to you, aren't they? And to me, too." ⁿ

While Bizet was performing his military duty, Geneviève again remained at home alone, battling for courage and self-control in a way that corroborates to a certain extent Bizet's prognosis

of the week before: "in five or six days all will be well." Once
more she took out her long unused little notebook and, in a tight,
cramped handwriting, wrote: "March 1, 1871. Entry of the Prussians. Georges left at six o'clock in the morning. Didn't go
out. Wrote to Valentine. Received a letter from Georges. Replied." Following this entry, she devoted a full page to listing the
letters she had written and received. Most of her correspondents
were members of her family, the most frequent being her cheerful cousin, Busnach, the producer of *Malbrough s'en va-t-en
guerre,* and her aunt Mélanie Halévy, whose precarious mental
balance caused her to reside permanently at Dr. Blanche's sanitorium. She and Geneviève exchanged eleven letters. There were
also single exchanges between Geneviève and Delibes, Guiraud,
and Mme Carvalho. As counting and list-making are recognized
forms of therapy, there is something touching about Geneviève's
not too untidy little columns. On March 1, she also listed "Books
read." They included four novels by Victor Hugo, Mérimée's
stories, Dumas's *La Tulipe noire,* and several long-forgotten popular romances.

"Our Geneviève is improving little by little. . . ." Bizet
wrote to her mother. "Unfortunately her nerves are extremely
overwrought. I see to it that she leads a very quiet life without any
emotional strain." This task, even under ordinary conditions,
would seem difficult enough. But the crucial situation in Paris
brought additional strain on Bizet's own nerves. Although the
Germans occupied Paris for only a single day, retiring to the out-
skirts on March 3, revolution was in the air, recognized and
welcomed by the Prussian leaders. They were glad to stand by
and watch the French destroy each other.

Before any plans for the summer could materialize, a revolution far more devastating than the siege, more terrifying than the
occupation by the Prussians, drove the Bizets from Paris.

CHAPTER  XX

The Year of Terror II:
The Commune

The circumstances that brought about the Commune were so complex that Bizet, like most of his contemporaries, failed to understand the events that followed. The Government fell soon after the withdrawal of the Germans from Paris, and the newly elected Assembly was so conservative that Gambetta resigned. Suddenly Adolphe Thiers became the ruler of France.[1] His name was anathema to the workers because of the part he had played in the suppression of the National Workshops in June 1848. Now, after the Minister for Foreign Affairs had secured from Bismarck the right of the National Guard to retain its arms, Thiers, in order to show the authority of the new Assembly, ordered the artillery removed from their control. Indeed, because of their fear of the National Guard, the new deputies refused to move their headquarters to Paris from Versailles, where they were sleeping on camp-beds in the Great Hall of the Palace. The Deputies were sound enough in their presumption that the National Guard, wholly disorganized, would not protect them.

---

[1] Adolphe Thiers (1797–1877), historian and statesman, leader of the Moderate opposition from 1863 to 1870, had been asked by the Empress Eugénie, through Prosper Mérimée, to join the Imperial government in August 1870. He refused, but became a member of the Advisory Council of Defense formed a few days later. On August 24 he took over the planning of the fortification of Paris. On February 17, 1871, Thiers was elected Chief of the Executive Power by acclamation of the National Assembly, and in August 1871 he was given the title of President of the Republic.

"If the National Guard were composed only of honest men
. . . who earn their living," Bizet wrote to Rodrigues in a mood
of obvious tension, a day or two after the withdrawal of the Prussians, "everything would be over. Unfortunately, during the fray,
a good many pickpockets, criminals, or those destined to become
so, have slid in; hence the confusion, which is more apparent than
real. A hundred or more agitators, proclaiming themselves Republicans and holding no recognized variety of opinion, are . . .
the scoundrels in question. . . . They will start an insurrection;
that is clear. But we are no longer under that loathsome Empire
when an honest Republican didn't dare fire at insurrectionists for
fear of killing one of his friends. We have a Republic now; the
Republicans were divided on the subject of war and peace; some
thought war was possible; others, better advised, I think, thought
it wiser to suffer temporary disgrace than to destroy at one blow all
the vital forces of the country. Today the question is settled. The
insurrectionists must be rabble or madmen. *We will kill them.*
. . . There is a great difference between an insurrection, suppressed promptly and completely, with unquestionable effectiveness, and a civil war. . . .

"You know that I have a horror of bloodshed and war! But,
really, I am sick to death of seeing France frightened by a handful of corrupt people. . . . If we are again to suffer the sight of
blood running in the streets of Paris, a sounder order than ever
before will emerge from this ordeal. We all need to work—arti-
sans, manufacturers, businessmen, artists—we all have the same
duty and, I assure you, most of us will not fail in it. . . ." [2]

In his calmer moments Bizet was aware that his grasp of
politics might be inadequate. "We need the perspective of time to
enable us to grasp the whole picture of events as complicated and
vast as those we have just experienced," he explained to his
mother-in-law a day or two later. "Be that as it may . . . what is
needed now, in order to re-establish the equilibrium of the country, is one of those men above ambition and passion, who, by his
character and his gifts, is set so far outside the social scale that he

---

[2] Georges Bizet, "Unpublished Letters," ed. Mina Curtiss, *The Musical
Quarterly*, XXXVI, No. 3, July 1950, 385–6, 394. Subsequent unidentified quotations in this chapter are from this work. Unpublished portions of these letters
are enclosed in square brackets and individually noted.

can neither rise nor fall; a man, in short, who can formulate only one wish: to be useful to the country and to humanity. . . ."

Bizet believed that these qualities of leadership were embodied in Adolphe Thiers, who, unfortunately, was neither unerring nor sensitive enough to cope with the emotions of the Parisians. On the night of March 17, he had the walls of the city placarded with a proclamation appealing to the patriotism and good sense of the people of Paris. It read, in part: "Evilly disposed men, under the pretext of resisting the Prussians, have taken control of part of the city . . . forcing you to mount guard under the orders of a secret committee. . . . Parisians . . . you will approve our recourse to force, for it is necessary at all costs . . . that order, the basis of your well-being, should be reborn."

This threat of force was carried out by the seizure of the guns on the heights of Montmartre. General Lecomte, at the head of a squad of police and a larger body of green troops, succeeded in taking the guns by surprise. But without equipment for hauling them away, the General and his police were soon surrounded by an angry and rebellious crowd of men and women. He ordered his troops to fire on them, but the young soldiers fled and the general was arrested. Later General Clément Thomas was also taken prisoner, and both generals were shot down by unidentified National Guardsmen.

"From a distance it's frightening, isn't it? On the spot it is merely grotesque! Clément Thomas and Lecomte assassinated by snipers and linesmen! It is a horrible, infamous act, but isolated!" Bizet wrote to Rodrigues on March 20, the day after the issuing of a proclamation convoking the inhabitants of Paris to elect a Commune two days later.

"Here's how the scene shapes up: *Thirty thousand* men in Montmartre, Belleville, etc., twenty-five thousand of whom decided to give up at the first gun-fire; a committee embarrassed at this situation and wishing at all costs to rid themselves of the responsibility.

"In Paris, *three hundred thousand* men, a disgrace never to be obliterated, three hundred thousand cowards, three hundred thousand rascals far guiltier, in my opinion, than the lunatics up there. It's unspeakable!—When I say three hundred thousand cowards, I am wrong. I should say two hundred and ninety-five thousand, for about five thousand men (I was among them) went to put themselves at the disposal of the government. In spite of our limited numbers, in spite of our defective arms, in spite of the *lack of munitions* (it sounds insane, but I swear to you it is true), we would have gone into action. They kept us waiting eighteen hours; we didn't see a superior officer, we were not given an order. Our battalion chiefs did not deign to come and find out about us. Mine, M. de Manican, M. Dufaure's son-in-law, appeared briefly around two o'clock, and never came back. At midnight, some sort of staff officer came to advise us to go home.

"All Paris out in the streets, in civilian clothes, smoking cigars, quietly trying to get information. . . . As for the looting, the *Journal officiel* lied a thousand times over! Nobody stole a pin! Up there *they* are disciplined; the first person who stole would be shot. Montmartre is perfectly accessible. The officers of the law go up there to walk around, and are very courteously received. Yesterday, Sunday (it was a beautiful day), the city really had a holiday air! . . . I swear to you on my word of honor that i do not exaggerate! . . .

"Yesterday two of the Montmartre men called to me: 'Hey there, citizen of the Sixth, everything's fine and dandy! Liquidate the reacs, save the social order!' Me: 'My lambs, have you thought of the Prussians?'—'What Prussians?'—'Why, the Prussians from Prussia, *parbleu!* They'll be on our necks!'— 'Word of honor?' —'Word of honor!'—*After a moment's reflection:* 'Bah, this time we'll kick 'em out for you!' . . . 'Yes, but this time' (I replied staring the fellow full in the face), 'this time you mustn't turn tail and run like the first time!' If you could have seen this character's face you would have laughed. His look so clearly said: '*Tiens,* he knows me all right.'

"The shops are open; there is no thought of tomorrow, no-body understands! Paris is foolish, sodden. . . . I confess my mistake. I was correct in my appraisal of the conditions of the insurrection, but I believed that Paris still had a few drops of blood in her veins. . . .

"The *Comité central,* no longer knowing what is to become of it, will try to hold some elections so as to hide behind universal suffrage. We shall see whether Paris is even cowardly enough to take part in this poll. Some kind of scheming reactionaries are hidden in all this disorder. Underneath it all there is something Catholic!

"But don't worry; there is no danger for us. Paris has fallen too low to be bloody. We no longer have revolutions, merely parodies of revolutions! Crime occurs only in the most exceptional cases. The army has left. Good riddance! They were the looters!

"I want to be amusing, but you can read through the lines that I am heartbroken, can't you? We are heading toward a Catholic monarchy, and that is what I dreaded most."

The election that had been scheduled for March 22 was postponed until the 26th because of rioting and disorder. The Commune was proclaimed on March 29, and on April 2 the Army of Versailles attacked and seized Courbevoie, a suburb of Paris through which a large part of the food for the city was brought. All prisoners were shot. The civil war had begun.

"When the gentlemen of the Commune were about to cut off all communications with the rest of the country, I flung myself with Geneviève and Joséphine on the first train I could catch, and here we are at Compiègne," Bizet wrote to his uncle from the Hôtel des Fleurs, near the palace where Napoleon III and the Empress Eugénie had so often held court.

"Ouf! No crime, but raving madness is ruling Paris! . . . We are crushed! What will happen to our books, our belongings, and Mme Halévy's? What will happen to Paris? . . . Where are we going? . . . They are about to dynamite several houses in each street so as to make solid barricades quickly. . . .

"Here, we are deep in Germany. Four thousand Prussians are stationed at Compiègne. They talk a lot about going to Paris. I am forced to admit that the attitude of these enemies makes me blush for our brothers in Paris. Here, women, the family, property are respected. . . .

"I abandoned Paris because I was liable to confinement at home as a suspect, or to be forced to join one of the *right-thinking* battalions. . . . Geneviève was in no condition to bear these new and overwhelming disorders.

"You were right, *cher ami,* a thousand times right. I was blind!—I believed in the integrity of my fellow-citizens. Alas, they are all scoundrels, madmen or cowards!

["I shan't say a word about politics because I am more and

more brokenhearted. I am afraid that the victory of Versailles is not the real end! And besides, the Versailles types are unspeakably foul! All these . . . crooks, these traitors, these panderers of every kind make a strange impression in the palace of the *roi-soleil!* What a mess! . . .

"Our houses are in good condition; they were not pillaged. Yours is in a very safe place, but I am afraid of a huge barricade, a real fortress, only fifty steps away from mine.

"I am glad that your *Saint Peter* is so far along. I shall try to do as you do and work on my *Clarissa Harlowe* while waiting for Sardou to finish our Boccaccio.[3]. . . Geneviève is still nervous, but she is gaining weight and feels better all the time."] "

Within a few days, Bizet, his wife, and her maid were able to take refuge in their cottage at Le Vésinet. "We are camping out here," he wrote to Guiraud, "with no clothes, no books and no way of returning to Paris! There was fighting yesterday. Today the canons are thundering. (Hold tight! Here we go again!) What times! What a country! What people! What morals!" "

Again, a few days later, another letter to Guiraud: "If you have any news of Paris, please be good enough to send it to us.— I read the Versailles papers, which inform the dazed population that France is calm, *excepting Paris.*—Whom do they fool here? I am willing for the Commune to lie; but certainly M. Thiers is not telling the truth.—The day of the 14th . . . we were deafened by cannonading for twelve hours. Some refugees from Courbevoie and Neuilly came here, and all of them agree that the National Guard has the advantage.—Here we are perfectly safe, alas! . . . At Le Vésinet, the Prussians are at home.— Their patrols multiply, but we are not inconvenienced. . . .

"The Seine-et-Oise district is certainly not in favor of the Commune, but they are very much disgusted with Versailles, and actually they have reason to be. M. Thiers's memoranda are, in my opinion, absolute monstrosities, as much from the political as from the humanitarian point of view.

"Neuilly, Courbevoie, Meudon, Clamart have been more destroyed by two weeks of skirmishing than by five months of siege. The Arc de Triomphe has been damaged. My poor friend, I am absolutely discouraged, and I fear that there is no longer any possible future for us!

---

[3] Bizet is referring to the source of *Grisélidis.*

"In a little while I am going to the village to look at a piano. I would like to try to work, to forget. They are making an appeal to all right-thinking members of the National Guard. It's about time! As for me I shan't budge again. The left, the right, the center turn my stomach. . . ." [n]

In the midst of all this sickening disorder, Mme Halévy took to writing impatient letters that upset Geneviève. "The last two letters from Mme Halévy have had a very distressing effect on her," Bizet wrote to Rodrigues. "The letters were, as a matter of fact, rather strange. Mme Halévy seems to have forgotten a number of things, particularly the impossibility of dependable connections with Paris, for she asked us to send her a number of things immediately. Altogether the general tone was, if not disturbing, at least surprising. . . . Geneviève is still obsessed by the idea that her visit to Bordeaux may have harmed her mother. . . . We are living very quietly here in my cottage. We see my father about two hours a day. But he is interested only in how his asparagus grows." [n]

With infinite patience, Bizet explained to his mother-in-law that it took four days for a letter to travel from Le Vésinet to Port-Marly, a distance of less than a mile. "I was arrested yesterday at Saint-Germain," he continues. "They demanded my papers!—Geneviève was sharp with them—and I had to spend several minutes in conversation with a very pleasant police superintendent who laughed a good deal at my mishap. I rarely laugh any more, I confess, and the future seems to me impossible in France. After the insurrection has been put down—and that won't take long in spite of the intellectual weakness of certain generals —everything will again be challenged.

"The clericals will have great vengeance to wreak, and the cruelty of these gentlemen is well known! Between the wrath of the Whites and the wrath of the Reds there will no longer be any place for decent people. Music will have no future here. We shall have to become expatriates. Shall I go to Italy, England, America? [4] These monstrous and brutal questions of existence will con-

---

[4] The idea of going to America may have been suggested to Bizet by the fact that six months earlier Steele Mackaye had tried to persuade François Delsarte to emigrate to the United States to head a conservatory. Cf. *Epoch: The Life of Steele Mackaye,* by Percy Mackaye, New York, 1927; *In the Courts of Memory,* by L. de Hegermann-Lindencrone, New York & London, 1912; *Life of Edwin Forrest, the American Tragedian,* by William Rounseville Alger,

front all of us. The resources left to our poor France will, as usual, be divided between schemers and mediocrities. In short, I am completely discouraged and have no hope for anything more here. Germany, the country of music, is impossible for anyone with a French name and a French heart. This is all very sad! Life had started so well for us! Fortunately, I have some resilience, and when a safe way out comes along, I shall grab it. But will it come? Let us hope so."

Mme Halévy, apparently moved by Bizet's despair, attempted to dispel it by offering to help him achieve a position teaching at the Conservatoire. "Thank you, dear Mme Halévy," he replied, "for the interest you take in my career, in my affairs. To tell you the truth, I have never been spoiled. The reason for this, no doubt, is my rather inflexible character. I have little liking for what is called society, and I admire it even less than I like it. So-called *honors, rank,* titles, etc., would disgust me profoundly if I weren't indifferent to all that. Of all my comrades, I am one of the two or three who have reached some artistic achievement, slight, to be sure, but seriously and honorably acquired. I have seen the Jules Cohens and other jesters to the Imperial court snatch jobs, positions I might have been offered had anyone, for a single moment, been interested in merit or right. (I am not speaking here of honorary positions nor of the Emperor's chapel.) It is true that I twice refused to compose the cantata for the 15th of August. It was important to me that my name, however humble it may be, should not be connected with that of the scoundrel who has led us to ruin and disruption. I am not complaining; had I been less asocial or less honest—it's a matter of values—I should today have the appointments that I don't and probably never shall have.

"The teaching at the Conservatoire is pitiful. Saint-Saëns, Guiraud, Massenet, myself, and a few others could rejuvenate this school, which M. Auber has turned into the kind of establishment I could not describe decently because it isn't decent. There is a professor of singing who indulges in the most unbridled blackmail. A M. Laget forces his pupils to take private lessons at his house at ridiculous prices, and when the pupils can no longer pay, their linen, their clothes, their jewelry are appropriated and sold by Mme Laget to an old-clothes dealer. M. Auber finds this

Philadelphia, 1877; *Delsarte's Own Words,* tr. by Abby L. Alger, New York, 1892.

all right. Professors of this kind don't offend him, so why change? This has been going on for so long.

"As for the theatres, they are theatres; that's all there is to say! Formerly the heads of departments at the Opéra were honorable, decent men, reputable when they entered the theatre and esteemed when they left.

"M. Victor Massé, *chef des choeurs* at the Opéra, does his work in the most shameful, the most immoral way; so do the others.[5] Today it is difficult for even a mildly conscientious man to be anybody. Let us hope that our present honest government will grow strong and raise the moral standards of the arts, which certainly need it.—Today I have some chance of achieving an honorable career. Doors are open to me, and by my own efforts. But as for asking anything of anyone, no matter whom, that is a thing I couldn't do at any price.—Ten years ago I believed in society; I went out in it and, I confess, I was naïvely amused there. Today I am not a misanthrope, I am indifferent; I don't hate, I despise. In short, I don't think I am badly off being what I am. The road I have taken is long, but I know where it leads. Many a person who seems close to achieving the goal never gets there, but if my life runs its normal course, I shall attain mine very soon. And what's more, I am among the twenty or thirty men whom I esteem here below! That is something!

"I have not yet mentioned Geneviève. It is enough to say that she is getting steadily better. I am not yet satisfied with the state of her nerves, but her health is, nevertheless, excellent.

"Read my letter to yourself alone, I beg of you; I never complain, and I should be miserable if anyone thought me dissatisfied with a situation that is as I wish it to be."

Bizet's hyper-sensitiveness about his difficulties is manifest in an account to Rodrigues of a call on Victorien Sardou, the fashionable popular playwright who had written the libretto of *Grisélidis*. When Bizet arrived at Sardou's house in the neighboring village of Port-Marly, he found "an elegant carriage . . . waiting at the

[5] Victor Massé (1822–84), the composer of eighteen operas and many popular songs, had studied composition under Halévy and won the Prix de Rome in 1844. He later became professor of composition at the Conservatoire and *chef des choeurs* at the Opéra. In March 1862, with Gounod, Jules Cohen, and François Bazin, Massé collaborated in composing the *De Profundis* sung at Halévy's grave. In March 1870 he copied a song from his opera *Paul et Virginie* into Geneviève Bizet's autograph album, inscribing it to her in *"hommage affectueux."*

gate, and a flunkey told me that Monsieur was very sorry not to be able to receive me, but he was in conference with a collaborator!! With what collaborator? And how?" ⁿ

Although Bizet did not immediately learn the identity of his rival collaborator, Sardou did write him a letter explaining why he had not returned his visit: "I am waiting daily for horses to replace those which were eaten, but they are slow in arriving. I would have to come on foot, which frightens me not at all as a walker, but very much so as a worker. I am working very hard, at the moment, to make up for lost time, and I shrink from the sacrifice of a lost afternoon. So I shan't come to see you until I have my carriage. If you go to Versailles, stop by and see me. You happened to come on a day when I was in the midst of a collaboration, but a thing like that happens only twice a year, and after half past three I am always free." ⁿ

While waiting to confer with Sardou, Bizet tried to take up work on *Clarissa Harlowe,* but the atmosphere was hardly conducive to concentration. "The cannon keep rumbling with unbelievable violence," he wrote to Mme Halévy on the twelfth of May. "I didn't close my eyes all night. This nocturnal clamor inspired me with some far from cheerful philosophical reflections. I consoled myself with the knowledge that Geneviève was peacefully asleep, and with thoughts of the future that may perhaps compensate us for all our troubles. I have started working again and shall have two operas finished by the end of the summer. . . .

"I came back furious from Versailles two days ago. All the corrupt people in the smart set of Paris were meeting at the Réservoirs. They were talking openly about the return of Napoleon III . . . and in what terms! I couldn't help saying some very tough things to one gentleman who, though he wasn't worth the trouble, is in the habit of pocketing insults without answering back. What will come out of all this muck? . . . *Chi lo sa?*

"Geneviève is getting fat. Her health is *excellentissime.* But her nerves are still extraordinarily on edge. There are no further precautions I can take, for her life is absolutely quiet. . . . I am impatient to see the end of this nervous condition, which might under certain circumstances cause an illness. In the meantime, she is rosy, gay, happy, and not too much affected by the events going on around us.

"I am delighted to see that a taste for the arts still exists in this country and that there is still an audience worthy of appreciating and admiring the masterpiece of our dear Halévy."

In peaceful Bordeaux a revival of *La Reine de Chypre* had been arranged, and Paris, even in the midst of turmoil, managed to have music of one kind or another. The ubiquitous American hostess, Mrs. Moulton, Delsarte's former pupil, gave a party at which "the enjoyment of beautiful music" made the guests forget that they were "in the heart of poor, mutilated Paris, in the hands of a set of ruffians dressed up like soldiers. Bombs, bloodshed, Commune and war were phantoms we did not think of." The magicians who wrought this miracle were Auber, Massenet, François Delsarte, and the hostess herself. The American Minister, Elihu Benjamin Washburne, was also present.

Although the food served at dinner consisted of canned soup, canned lobster, and canned corned beef, the guests were all in evening dress. "Delsarte . . . wore trousers of the workman type, made in the reign of Louis-Philippe, very large about the hips, tapering down to the ankles; a flowing redingote, dating from the same reign . . . a fancy velvet waistcoat, and a huge tie bulging over his shirtfront (if he had a shirtfront, which I doubt). He asked permission to keep on his *calotte* which I fancy had not left his skull since the Revolution of 1848."

Auber and Massenet played piano duets; the hostess sang *"Caro nome"* from *Rigoletto,* accompanied by Massenet. "Delsarte . . . refused to sing *'Il pleut, il pleut, Bergère,'* but condescended to declaim *'La Cigale ayant chanté tout l'été,'* and did it as he alone can. When he came to the end of the fable, *'Et bien, dansez maintenant,'* he gave such a tragic shake to his head that the voluminous folds of his cravat became loosened and hung limply over his bosom." At midnight, when the guests departed, the American Minister "took charge of the now very sleepy Delsarte who declaimed a sepulchral *bonsoir,"* and Massenet escorted Auber." The party had been in the nature of a farewell gathering, for in less than three months both Auber and Delsarte were dead.

The musical entertainment arranged by the Committee of the Commune could hardly be presented under conditions permitting such delightful escapism. A concert at the Opéra on May 16 for the benefit of the widows and orphans of the war resulted in the dismissal of the director, Perrin, accused of insufficient patriotic enthusiasm. An ambitious program was planned for May 22, with the aid of Charles Nuitter, archivist of the Opéra, who had translated *Tannhäuser* and *Rienzi,* and was the author of the scenarios for Delibes's *La Source* and *Coppélia.* The overture to *Der Freischütz* was to open the program. Mme Ugalde would sing the "Jewel Song" from *Faust* and recite Hugo's *Patria.* The young pianist Raoul Pugno was to play *Alliance des peuples,* and after the fourth act of *Il Trovatore,* the fourth act of *La Favorite,* and the trio from *Guillaume Tell,* the concert was to conclude with a chorus by Gossec, *Hymne à la Raison.* This lengthy program was not performed, however. By May 22, the Versailles troops had converted the Opéra into a prison and slaughter-house.

"Two companies, each with a captain, occupied the Opéra, one on the administration side to the right, the other to the left, by the artists' entrance. There was a crowd of prisoners in the courtyard, and more were brought in all the time. The captain on the administration side had the prisoners brought before him locked up in the cellar. The captain on the theatre side had his prisoners shot. Some of them had been caught carrying arms. Others showed no evidence of being combatants. But their shoes were examined. If they were wearing hobnailed boots, they were held. And according to whether luck brought them to the captain on the right or the captain on the left, they were imprisoned in the cellar or shot.

"Why, nobody ever knew.

"The prisoners in the cellar were to be taken to Versailles or to some other station in Paris. Those who were executed were shot right in the courtyard, against the wall, which is now all pierced with bullets. . . . During these sad scenes . . . several young soldiers rested at ease on the outside stairway at the left. Still others, who had discovered in the wings the costumes and properties for *Freischütz* and *Coppélia* (the last two works performed at the Opéra), had taken the skulls, masks, and draperies of Weber's opera-phantoms and brought them out in view of the courtyard. So that there, standing on the steps, watching the shooting of the prisoners, one saw soldiers draped in shrouds, their guns held between their legs, and in their hands, shaking, grimacing death-heads." [n]

The panorama of violence in Paris during the final days of the Commune was less immediately shocking viewed from Le

Vésinet. "We spend our lives climbing up on roofs, terraces, hill-sides, belvederes, and other high places," Bizet wrote to his mother-in-law. "We try, map in hand, to orient ourselves and to guess what is happening to our poor belongings. Up to now, everything is reassuring. . . . The newspapers that exaggerate the extent of our appalling disasters report no fires in our neighbor-hood. The band of incendiaries, of brigands, of cannibals who have swooped down on Paris, and to whom I hope no sane person will attribute any political color, has already seen its chief leaders vanish. . . . Yesterday everything seemed over, and then, at nine o'clock at night we saw a huge fire. . . . Paris will certainly soon be relieved of all the mischief-makers, male and female, who have played any part in this horrible brawl, and we shall at last be able to breathe again. I shall go to Paris as soon as possible. But entry and, particularly, exit are still absolutely forbidden today.

"I learned of Auber's death from you. The poor man couldn't survive the destruction of everything that was his life. If they plan to continue rewarding the musician most in evidence by giving him the directorship of the Conservatoire, Thomas will be named. *Hamlet* is a great work that cancels all the little musical weaknesses of this kind and honorable man. As for the *other*,[6] his private life is really not sufficiently—pure to permit their thinking of trusting him with a school for young girls. This is probably not the opinion of his pushing and tiresome family, but I hope it is what the Minister will think.

"On the other hand, it may be time to realize that the Conservatoire was not created to serve as a reward of merit for some gentleman or other. The talented artist is rewarded by his very talent, and needs nothing else. If our dear Halévy, who was equally good as administrator and musician, were alive, the question would have resolved itself.[7] No other appointment would have been possible. Today (for in spite of our disasters we still bother about these little matters) I know they are thinking of E. Perrin. . . ."

Six years earlier, the appointment of Gounod to the important

---

[6] Charles Gounod.

[7] Auber is reported to have said to M. de Beauchesne, secretary of the Conservatoire during the Second Empire: "Do anything Halévy asks for the students he thinks worth recommending. He is already set to become my successor."

and influential position of director of the Conservatoire would have been Bizet's heart's desire. Now he could not even bring himself to mention his master by name. From 1866 on, when Gounod had become a member of the Institut, his relations with his *"cher enfant"* had waned. In October of that year Bizet had written to Galabert: ["Alas, you would no longer recognize Gounod. The Institut is leading him astray. What a Minotaur that Institut is! Where is the Theseus who will deliver us from it?"] [n] In 1867, when *La Jolie Fille de Perth* and Gounod's *Roméo et Juliette* were both produced at the Théâtre-Lyrique, Bizet, in a state of emotional crisis, was obsessed by the feeling that the older composer had become a hostile or envious rival. In December 1868 he mentioned to Lacombe that Gounod was leaving for Rome supposedly to enter orders. ["Gounod is Catholic to the marrow, a man overboard,"] [n] he wrote Galabert early in 1869.

When, later that year, Bizet's engagement was resumed and he learned of Gounod's kindness to Geneviève during her years of suffering, he made the friendly gesture of producing another arrangement of the master's *Ave Maria,* this time for four hands. But Gounod's conduct during the war served only to alienate Bizet further.

Months before Gounod left for England with his family at the beginning of the war, his state of mind had been desperate and disillusioned. "I am fighting in a void," he wrote to a friend. "I think I have done something tolerable and then, when I re-read it, I find it hateful. My mind doesn't work; I don't know what I'm about. . . . I no longer see clearly. . . . Twenty times a day I am overcome with melancholy; I weep, I am in despair and want to run away. . . ." [n]

In England, Gounod soon began to compose the pieces that the London Philharmonic played at two concerts devoted exclusively to his compositions. One, a *De Profundis,* was, he said, "suggested by all the troubles suffered by our poor country." While composing this patriotic work during the darkest days of the siege of Paris, he had written to the Crown Prince of Prussia asking royal protection for his property at Saint-Cloud. "The letter of the celebrated composer," commented the *Allgemeine Musikalische Zeitung* for January 4, 1871, "is an example of the profound depression into which the misfortunes foolishly instigated by their country plunge men remote from politics. Gounod profoundly deplores the war, of which he disapproved from the start. He says that his own artistic development stems fundamentally from the German spirit, from German art." [n]

The Crown Prince, however, was unable to prevent the inevitable vandalism. The news of serious damage to his property reached Gounod in mid-February, when he was starting to compose *Gallia*, a choral symphony commissioned by the directors of the International Exposition. In this piece, Gounod aimed to portray "France as she then was, not only vanquished, crushed, but also outraged, insulted, violated by the insolence and brutality of her enemy." A more personal inspiration eased the strain of creating this work. For during this same winter Gounod made the acquaintance of Mrs. Georgina Weldon, who was ready and eager to sing the leading role in *Gallia*. Dynamic and ambitious, an amateur singer and professor of singing, this lady, with whose family Gounod made his home for the next three years, soon became the predominant influence in his life. When early in May he moved into her and her husband's house, Mme Gounod returned to Paris, where reports of her husband's new friendship spread rapidly, but did not apparently penetrate into official circles. For on June 10, Gounod received a letter in London, informing him unofficially that he was expected to propose himself as director of the Conservatoire. Also, as a matter of protocol, he was sent an invitation to dinner by Thiers, the acceptance of which would have given him the opportunity to apply for the position directly to the President. After three days' consideration, he replied that he would take no such steps.

Auber's immediate successor, appointed by the administration of the Commune on May 13, had been Salvador Daniel. Formerly head of a choral school in Algiers, and author of a monograph on Arab music published in 1863, he was also music critic on Rochefort's paper, *La Marseillaise*. Although he merely "wanted to reform music and society . . . [and] expressed his very violent theories most gently, insinuatingly, with obsequious, almost oily politeness," [n] he was arrested and shot by the Versailles troops in his apartment in the rue Jacob ten days after he took office.

On May 25 the Versailles government overthrew the Commune with great bloodshed and violence on both sides. Four days later, Bizet wrote to his mother-in-law: "The last cannon-shot was fired Sunday at half past two. . . . The time for recrimination is past. The dissolution of this formidable association of scoundrels of every country is the most urgent issue. The second concern of those who govern us should be not to let themselves be carried away by Catholic reaction. Let us have hope.

"There is no news of the hostages. Has the Archbishop of Paris been shot? [8] . . . What unfortunately seems too certain is the death of my poor and good friend Chaudey, an honest and brave Republican, shot by those bandits! [9] . . . As for us, we have nothing to fear, for we are protected (!) by a German garrison. . . .

"I shan't talk to you about Wagner today. But how unjust you are! . . . Still, it is the fate of great geniuses not to be recognized by their contemporaries. Wagner is no friend of mine, and I am personally quite indifferent to him, but I cannot forget the tremendous enjoyment I owe to his innovating genius. The charm of his music is indescribable, inexpressible. It is *volupté,* it is tenderness, it is love!

"If I played it for you for a week, you would be mad about it! . . . Besides the Germans who, alas, are quite· our equals musically, have understood that Wagner is one of their strongest pillars. The German nineteenth-century spirit is incarnate in that man.

"You know very well, you of all people, what cruelty it is for a great artist to be scorned. Fortunately for Wagner, he is endowed with such overbearing conceit that no criticism can touch his heart —admitting that he has a heart, which I doubt.

"I would not go as far as you do and mention Beethoven's name along with Wagner's. Beethoven is not a man, he is a God! —Like Shakespeare, like Homer, like Michelangelo!—Take the most intelligent public, let them listen to the greatest work in modern art, the Ninth Symphony, and they will understand nothing, absolutely nothing. The experiment has been tried, it is tried

---

[8] Georges Darboy (1813–71), Archbishop of Paris, was arrested April 4 by the Communards, held as hostage, and shot May 24, 1871, by a firing-party composed of National Guardsmen and *Vengeurs de la Commune.*

[9] Gustave Chaudey (1817–71), son-in-law of Jules Barbier the librettist, was a staff-writer on *Le Siècle,* a well-known Republican paper, the only one in Paris during certain periods of the Second Empire. Although violently attacked by the Communard terrorist newspaper, *Père Duchesne,* Chaudey refused to leave Paris, was arrested on April 12, imprisoned at Sainte-Pélagie, and on May 23 was the first hostage to be shot.

every year with the same result. But Beethoven has been dead fifty years, and it is fashionable to find the work beautiful.

"Judge for yourself, forget everything you have heard said, forget the stupid and malicious articles and the even more malicious book published by Wagner, and you will see.[10] It is not the music of the future—an absolutely meaningless phrase—but it is, as you say so well, the music for all time because it is admirable.

"Ouf! . . . you are not convinced, *parbleu,* and you are not the only one. Voltaire didn't understand Shakespeare because he was prejudiced by *conventions* that he believed to be truths. You are prejudiced, too, and there is only one thing you will believe in these last few pages; that is that I love you with all my heart. . . .

"P.S. It is quite clear that if I thought I were imitating Wagner, despite my admiration, I should never write another note in my life. Imitation is a fool's job. It is better to write bad music of your own than to write somebody else's. And besides, the finer the model, the more ridiculous the copy. Michelangelo, Shakespeare, and Beethoven have been imitated! God knows what horrors this passion for imitation has brought us!"

On June 3, the Bizets were able to celebrate their second wedding anniversary in peace. Three days later they returned to Paris, fearing, wondering in what condition they might find their home.

---

[10] *An das deutsche Heer von Paris, January 1871. Eine Kapitulation. Lustspiel in antiker Manier.* Richard Wagner, *Collected Works,* Leipzig, 1888, Vol. 9.

CHAPTER  XXI

Family Problems

I am back from Paris, dear Mother," Geneviève wrote on June 8. "I spent two days there, and you can imagine with what joy I discovered the house still standing and my apartment intact in spite of the fighting that had gone on under my windows. . . . Fortunately our friends and relatives also came out fairly well—a few bullet holes, broken windows, and empty bottles, that's all. . . . Paris looks far less horrible than I had feared. There isn't a single corpse in the streets in spite of what the gentlemen of the press say. And except for two or three hundred houses which, I must admit, were very badly treated, and the Tuileries, the Hôtel de Ville, the Palais-Royal, which are heartbreaking to see, Paris is almost whole. This is a lot, I assure you, after having seen, as we did, the sparks flying for four days over a stretch of nearly a mile and giving us every reason to believe that all was lost. Everything is picking up again little by little. Certain parts of the city are lively, and in spite of the atrocious weather (I am sitting by the fire as I write), the boulevards are almost as crowded as usual. . . . Paris is more disturbing to think about than to see." [n]

Other accounts of Paris immediately after the fall of the Commune indicate that Bizet steered his wife away from the districts where shocking sights were still to be seen. But he was unable to prevent her seeing a letter that announced Mme Halévy's intention of leaving Bordeaux for Versailles, approximately an hour's distance from Le Vésinet. While his wife composed her cheerful letter to her mother, Bizet, without her knowledge, wrote to Rodrigues warning him that the news of Mme Halévy's imminent arrival had given Geneviève "another attack of nervous excitement which has made me tremble. My most pressing duty is to avoid a meeting that would have unpredictable consequences. To prevent this, two courses are open to me:

1. Escape
2. Frankly to tell Mme Halévy the state of things and make her understand that she would be doing her duty, however painful, by not seeing her daughter.

"The first course is very difficult. Under what pretext can I take Geneviève far away? She would know that she was *fleeing,* and *fear* would do her the greatest harm.

"Consequently . . . when Mme Halévy arrives at Versailles, I shall go there at once and make every effort to put an end to this state of terror which is destroying Geneviève's health, and affecting mine, too, which is less important.

"I would prefer a thousand sieges to this anxiety. If you wish to reply in secret, address your letter to Mme Joséphine, the maid, c/o M. Bizet." [n]

Although Rodrigues was apparently able to persuade his sister to stay in Bordeaux, a decision that for a short time allayed Bizet's fears, the respite was brief. For Mme Halévy's relatives, unwilling to reveal to her at long distance the disorganized state of her finances, declared that they would not, in her absence, be responsible for her business affairs. Their refusal naturally placed an additional burden on Bizet.

"The circumstances that give Geneviève her strange terror of me are distressing and painful enough," Bizet wrote to Rodrigues, "without my having to take the *least* responsibility for Mme Halévy's business affairs. If conditions had permitted my being (what I so much wanted to be) Mme Halévy's son-in-law in a normal sort of way, I might have braved the arrogance and scorn of the family. But in the existing situation I am nobody and can be nothing more. . . .

"Outside of family politics, I have the warmest affection for Mme Halévy. . . . I know that she could easily have confidence in me, and that with your moral support we could, perhaps . . . have provided her with an easier, pleasanter existence. All that is impossible, and my *duty* forces me to act in direct opposition to the dictates of my heart. Who knows but that Mme Halévy may one day regard me with horror! . . .

"Also, Geneviève was slightly indisposed and frightened day before yesterday, and said: 'It's strange, but I am depressed and feel the way I did in Bordeaux. I am not yet cured of that feeling.'

"I shall never hesitate to place Geneviève and her health above *every other interest,* but things might come to such a pass that in doing my duty I would be forced to make decisions and sacrifices that would appear impossible in the eyes of outsiders. You and I alone know what this is costing me. As long as no harm comes to Mme Halévy because of it, everything will be all right, and that is the end I have in view. . . ." [n]

For the first time since his marriage, Bizet seems to have become aware of being trapped in a situation from which only a ruthlessness wholly antipathetic to his nature could free him. Even if he had disliked his mother-in-law, his course of action would have been very little simplified. For the depth of his attachment to his own mother had fostered in him the conviction that the very state of motherhood is endowed, if not with virtue, at least with certain rights and privileges. The death of his uncle François Delsarte during the summer (see Appendix I, p. 460) inevitably revived memories of his youth and served, no doubt, to strengthen his attachment to his mother-in-law. Bizet's affection for Mme Halévy, his susceptibility to her charm, seem to have been quite as real and strong as his love for his wife. The patient and fair-minded balance of feeling he maintained toward both women was in itself rare and, perhaps, admirable. But it precluded his observing certain more common emotional reactions in his wife. Apparently it never occurred to him that the very warmth of his affection for Mme Halévy, which gave rise to his fear of becoming an object of "horror" to her, served to intensify Geneviève's own inner conflict. She might well have been shocked if Bizet had hated or been openly antagonistic to her mother. But his equally divided sympathy tended to arouse her latent jealousy and to cause her to identify him with her mother's side of their conflict, thereby inducing the "strange terror" she felt of him at this time.

Had Bizet been able to confide his difficulties to a friend less involved in family matters than Rodrigues, he might have gained some perspective. But his pride forced him to deception, in itself a drain on the moral fibre of so forthright a man. In the midst of this continuing crisis, he wrote to Galabert: "I see that your marriage, like mine, does not interfere with your work. I am finishing my two operas. I read a great deal. I haven't as regulated a plan of reading as yours, but I am beginning to understand quite a lot. The unfortunate thing is that the desire to know comes as one learns; but why unfortunate? I shall live, I shall die with my curiosity unsatisfied. The farther I go, nevertheless, the more childish philosophic systems seem to me." [n]

During the two or three days he spent in Paris, Bizet had seen Pasdeloup and the various theatre directors. Although the latter had not yet been able to surmount the difficulties in the way of re-opening the Opéra and the Comique, Pasdeloup, admitting of no obstacles, resumed his Concerts Populaires on June 19. He played works by Gounod and Massenet, and promised Bizet that he would soon repeat his Symphony. Bizet also learned, while in Paris, of the death of Vauthrot, *chef du chant* at the Opéra for the past fifteen years and professor of singing at the Conservatoire. "As soon as the question of the Opéra is on the carpet," he wrote to Rodrigues, "I shall offer to replace him. The position would free me from any anxiety about my living expenses." [n] It would pay five or six thousand francs a year, and was "a job that neither Hérold nor Halévy scorned." [n]

Mme Halévy was enthusiastic over the news of this project. She wished to muster immediately all possible influence to assure her son-in-law's appointment to both the position at the Opéra and a post at the Conservatoire. Her perspective in the matter was highly personal. A few weeks earlier, on hearing of the destruction of the Thiers's house, she had tried to persuade Bizet to present the President and his wife with a fire-screen she herself had embroidered. Bizet refused. Now she again urged him to take advantage of her friendship with the Thiers and with other important personages.

"I have never misunderstood your intentions," he assured her. "I know many times over that they are as kind, as pure, as the charming heart that inspires them. . . . But your opinion about society and mine are exactly opposite. You regard people in general as kindly, good, generous, sincere, and human. I regard them as almost universally malicious, wicked, greedy, false, and cruel. You have faith in people, I am suspicious of them. . . . I am on the defensive physically and morally, always. I have every reason to be, and it is to my advantage to be cautious. I refused to take your fire-screen to Mme Thiers because a hundred scandalmongers would have slandered me as a result of that simple errand. I do not like to fight. I have applied for a position that only myself, Saint-Saëns, Massenet, and two or three others could suitably fill. It will probably be given to some hanger-on or other. So much the worse for those who perpetrate the injustice. —If I have inside me what I think I have, their action will have been useless. In ten years I shall have the position I desire, and I shall then tell off the obstructionists and self-seekers. . . . Perrin goes to the Français, Halanzier comes to the Opéra. . . ." [n]

No sooner had Bizet started his negotiations with the retiring and the future directors of the Opéra than he discovered that Mme Halévy had written a letter that caused him "the *most intense* and *most serious* annoyance. This business," he told her, "has nothing to do with Mme Perrin, and I had *forbidden* Geneviève to mention it to any of these ladies.—I told Perrin what I wanted.—It was understood between *him* and *me* that I would talk to nobody at all about this arrangement. The steps you have taken have made me break my word. What's more, neither Perrin nor anyone else would believe that you didn't write to Mme Perrin at my request. Everybody in the know in this affair will think that I am playing a role I would never have been willing to accept. I have a horror of being dependent, supported, recommended. I have no *respect* for people who do not conduct their lives entirely independently. Therefore, dear Mme Halévy, I beg of you, I beseech you in the name of our fine and tender affection, never to act in my behalf, never to ask anything for me from anybody at all. Maybe my judgment is not very sound, but I should rather renounce any position than not achieve it *by myself.* . . . I consider deeply everything I do, and an unexpected step in my behalf can really harm me." [n]

Fortunately Perrin, during his long friendship and professional relationship with Halévy, had become inured to Mme Halévy's interfering ways and remained uninfluenced by them, pro or con. Early in July, after Halanzier's installation as provisional administrator of the Opéra, he and Perrin informed Bizet of his appointment as *chef du chant.* "The whole thing is to be kept secret," Bizet told Rodrigues, "until the subsidy has been voted. . . . In the meantime the 2nd *chef du chant* will do the work. . . .

"Halanzier received me with such sympathy, affection, and warmth that I was profoundly touched. This kind and good man knew me as a child, and has never lost interest in me. 'Actions speak louder than words,' he said to me. 'I have a high opinion of you in every way, and soon you will have proof of it.' I was all the more delighted with this evidence of his friendship because Halanzier is not considered exactly a soft-hearted man. His reputation for loyalty and reliability is, on the other hand, solidly built.—Perrin, too, was more than charming, but I have reason to think that Halanzier's friendship did me no harm. . . ." "

Olivier Halanzier-Dufresnoy, "short, stocky, thick-set, heavy-looking, with a very sensitive face, superb eyes and a disposition as affectionate and sympathetic as his body is robust," " was a rarity among the directors of the lyric theatres of Paris. For unlike Véron and Roqueplan, journalists and *boulevardiers,* or Perrin, originally a painter, Halanzier was born to the theatre. The son of a captain in the dragoons and Mme Dufresnoy, the *tragédienne,* he started acting in Lyons in 1824 at the age of four. At fifteen he became the manager of his mother's troupe in Strasbourg, a position he held for thirteen years. Subsequently he managed theatres in Rouen, Bordeaux, Lyons, and Marseilles. Provisional administrator of the Opéra from July 1 to November 1, 1871, when he became provisional director, he was appointed permanent director the following year. His first period at the Opéra was difficult and unpredictable, and before the end of the year Bizet had reason to question Halanzier's judgment and reliability. But now, early in June, he was delighted to be "at last on the verge of a steady and sufficiently well-paid position."

Even more satisfactory was the opportunity to start composing a new opera, scheduled for performance during the autumn season. The directors of the Opéra-Comique, Camille du Locle and Adolphe de Leuven, not yet ready to produce a full-scale opera, commissioned Bizet to write a short work. A triumph for the composer, this commission again showed that the failure of Bizet's operas with the public did not lessen the confidence of the directors in his capacity eventually to achieve success. In order to give Bizet work at this time, du Locle broke a long-standing promise to Delibes, who had been assured that he would be chosen to write the first new work for the Comique. "If it were possible for me to think of a composer new to us for this winter," du Locle told Delibes, "I should feel it my duty to consider someone less fortunate than you. Among others there is a very worthy lad, Bizet, who is living in a hole-in-the-wall with his wife, Halévy's daughter. Do you think it would be decent of you to take precedence over him?" [n]

The libretto offered to Bizet, based on Alfred de Musset's poem *Namouna*, was written by Louis Gallet. It had been for some time in the procrastinating hands of Jules-Laurent Duprato, who had also tarried over *Grisélidis* for a year or two before that libretto had been entrusted to Bizet. Now, when the directors of the Comique discovered that Duprato had managed to write only one aria for *Namouna*, they reclaimed the libretto for Bizet. The title was eventually changed to *Djamileh* at the request of du Locle, who had heard and been enchanted by the name in Cairo, where he was, in a few months, to produce *Aïda*.

"The Opéra-Comique is rushing me to death," Bizet wrote to Rodrigues. "The thing is beginning to take shape, only it goes by fits and starts. In all probability, I should say certainly, *Namouna* will be done in two acts and I will have a cast *de primo castello*. . . . Du Locle is counting heavily on the work, and de Leuven, who hasn't seen it yet (he no longer reads or does anything) overwhelms me with pleasant attentions.—We must begin rehearsals in a month. Du Locle wants to open in November. I may have to start my new job at the Opéra in three or four weeks, so I am working like a slave. As for the Opéra, as the Perrins are telling everybody about my appointment, I can no longer have any doubts. Halanzier is merely a lieutenant of Perrin's. Of that I am at last certain! . . ." [n]

But Bizet was not wholly certain about the suitability for him of the libretto of *Djamileh*. "It's charming," he wrote to du Locle, "but it's horribly difficult. I understand it, I feel it, I see it, but realizing it is troublesome. Therefore I would like your permission to hold on to *Namouna* a few weeks before deciding. In *two* or *three* weeks my score will be sufficiently far along so that I can let you know whether I have succeeded or failed. I am very hopeful but, I repeat, I have never tried anything so difficult.

"You had planned to give the role of Splendiano to M. du Miral. I think that this ex-vice-president of the *corps législatif* would have been inadequate. I see Splendiano as more important than that.—We'll talk it over. . . ." [n]

Djamileh was soon reduced to one act, either because Bizet changed his conception of it or because du Locle needed a curtain-raiser for Donizetti's *La Fille du Régiment*. As his score developed, Bizet saw it as "very distinguished, very noble, very significant artistically. It will enable me to keep from being forgotten by the public, and will at the same time, I hope, be good business." [n]

As soon as Bizet determined to go ahead with the opera, Gallet, the librettist, started to work with him at Le Vésinet. There he found the composer very different from his Paris self. In the city, "he had an habitually serious air and his way of dressing heightened the gravity of his appearance by aging him a little. . . . In order to protect his delicate throat, he wore stand-up collars and high cravats after the fashion of old gentlemen of the previous generation. But he was gay by nature, laughed easily. . . . His eyes shone with mischief; his smile was kind and charming." [n]

In the country, Gallet said: "He walked about in a straw hat and loose jacket with the easy assurance of a country gentleman, smoking his pipe, gossiping gaily with his friends, receiving them at table with good-natured banter, between his charming young wife and his father who . . . spent all day gardening. . . . He had a very gentle, but very acute expression behind his indispensable eyeglasses; his lips were almost continually arched in a rather mocking smile. He spoke quietly, in a slightly hissing voice, with that air of detachment I always noticed in him. He discussed what concerned him with that true and noble honesty which consists not in a man's seeming to doubt his own value, but in letting it be known that while aware of his own worth, he always regrets not having done any given job better." [n]

The joy and relief of having urgent work to do—he mentioned to Galabert du Locle's continual pressure—made him a particularly delightful companion during the summer of 1871. Gallet remembered with special vividness the first day he went to Le Vésinet. Because transportation was still difficult, Bizet took a carriage to meet his guest at a neighboring station. "The day was charming," Gallet wrote, "and *Djamileh* advanced rapidly in a conversation carried on as we strolled along the paths in the garden. For me the chief characteristic of Bizet's temperament was his habit of moving, walking, while dealing with any subject that interested him. I can't remember a single important interview that didn't take place either wandering outdoors or at least standing up or striding back and forth in his study. We talked a long time that afternoon about the destiny of the art of music, already influenced by Wagner's theories, and particularly about the probable reception of the embryonic *Djamileh,* both by the public and even by the management of the Opéra-Comique, split as it then was, into two separate currents—du Locle's, directed toward the future, de Leuven's, in spite of all opposition, turning back to the past." [n]

Bizet's working hours continued to be interrupted by his correspondence with Mme Halévy. The announcement of Ambroise Thomas's appointment as director of the Conservatoire prompted her to write a letter of recommendation for her son-in-law to present to Thomas. Patiently Bizet explained to her: "The rather special quality of my intimacy with Ambroise Thomas imposes a certain reserve. He is fond of me, and every time he talks to me about my music he speaks in terms that would be embarrassing to repeat. If I occupied the musical position assigned to me by Thomas and Reber, I should no longer need to wish for anything. Besides, Thomas is grateful for my attitude at the opening of *Hamlet,* when the musicians were either too stupid or too malicious to do justice to this really admirable work, and I went into such a rage that he heard about it. But he is director of the Conservatoire and, as such, obliged to *conserve.* He is right. The last time I saw him he said to me: 'I have just appointed several professors. I didn't offer you anything because there was nothing worthy of you.' I know how to read between the lines; I understand how I would be most embarrassing to a director. It isn't that my productions frighten Thomas, but he is afraid of my ideas. I understand and approve of this, and I wish to avoid anything that might seem to bring pressure to bear on him in my behalf.—So I shall not present your letter to Thomas because there are things in it which are too flattering to me, and by giving him the letter myself, I could hardly appear to ignore them." [n]

Bizet's remarks about the legitimate conservatism of the Conservatoire, which seem to contradict his recent attack on Auber's administration, stemmed, at least partly, from personal experience. For the past two years he had served on the jury chosen to determine the winner of the Prix de Rome, a function that until a year or two before the war had always been carried out by the Institut. The decisions of the Conservatoire jury had caused heated controversy in the newspapers, and Bizet felt that the responsibility should be restored to the Institut as soon as possible. Also, one of the recurrent commissions to re-organize the curriculum of the Conservatoire, appointed shortly before the war, was about to resume its investigations. Edmond About, a member of the commission, had suggested, "not without malice," the introduction of the study of grammar and handwriting. A class in prosody and literature was also being seriously considered. Bizet may well have wished to reserve his opinions on possible innovations until the commission issued its report.

To Mme Halévy's reproaches at his refusal to make use of her letter to Thomas, Bizet replied: "It is not modesty—I am absolutely devoid of it—but self-respect, that prevents my asking Thomas for the position. I don't think I have had sufficient recognition to warrant my applying for it. Remember that you have to be a Gounod in order to have the right to present pupils to the public. Gounod refuses because as soon as he has an obligation to perform, he is nowhere to be found. Let the Bazins,[1] the Dupratos, the Elwarts,[2] behave as ridiculously as they like (in varying degrees). You are kind, very kind indeed, to have thought of me in this connection; it is an additional proof of your affection, for which I thank you most lovingly. . . ." [n]

Bizet's own letter of congratulation to Thomas has been criticized by certain biographers and commentators as unduly flattering and insincere. "The recognition and common sense of the public so long ago nominated you as director of the Conservatoire," he wrote, "and your admirable *Hamlet* has made any other appointment so absolutely impossible, that congratulations must seem strange to you. Nevertheless, in this odd and surprising country, fairness and justice always bring ineffable satisfaction to people of good will. So my wife and I are very happy to see you receive at last this supreme crowning of so fine, pure, and honorable a career, and we hope that your new duties will not make you forget to give us many more noble works. Please accept, *très cher Maître,* the warm and respectful affection of a household that you know is for many reasons sincerely devoted to you." [n]

---

[1] Bazin succeeded Thomas as professor of composition in 1871; in 1872 he became Carafa's successor as a member of the Académie des Beaux-Arts. See note, p. 21.

[2] Antoine Elwart (1808–77), composer of oratorios, symphonies, church and chamber music, professor of harmony at the Conservatoire from 1840 to 1871, was known primarily as a musicologist and author of textbooks.

This mention of his household is rare in Bizet's official or professional correspondence, and it may well have been a hint of his need for financial security. Yet Thomas had known Geneviève from her childhood and, on his official visit to the young couple soon after their marriage, had inscribed in her album Ophelia's aria from his *Hamlet*. Bizet's often-expressed admiration for this opera was sincere. Perhaps had he lived longer he might have agreed with Chabrier's opinion that "There are three kinds of music: good, bad, and Ambroise Thomas's."

In any case, the response of the new director of the Conservatoire to Bizet's congratulations was cautious and not over-warm. A fortnight after receiving Bizet's note, he wrote: "For the past week I have been overwhelmed with all kinds of work; I am suffocated by examinations at the Conservatoire. I delayed so long in thanking you because I wanted to wait until I could relax. You will understand and forgive my silence, won't you? I was very much touched by your kind and charming letter. My most affectionate remembrances for you and Mme Georges Bizet." [n]

The professorship of harmony left open by Elwart's retirement went to Duprato, who was thus, no doubt, compensated for the loss of his opportunity to write the music for *Djamileh*.

By the end of August, Bizet had finished the major portion of the score of that work, a feat all the more remarkable because he had now to a large extent accepted the responsibility for Mme Halévy's financial affairs. Although he had declared in June that it would be intolerable for him to involve himself in her business arrangements, by July he was taking an architect to Bas-Prunay to estimate the damage to her summer-house and interrupting his work with frequent visits to Paris to negotiate with Maître Delapalme, her *notaire,* a functionary who, in France, combines the duties of accountant, trustee, and notary. This "damned" Delapalme, as Bizet usually spoke of him, became an increasingly prickly thorn. "I am convinced," Bizet wrote to Rodrigues, "that this fantastic *notaire* is an excellent father and a good husband. I find him affable, polite, well educated. I like him and am grateful to him for having spoken so kindly of me. But M. Delapalme's negligence has just made me lose 3000 frs., and his inertia will cost Mme Halévy 2000 frs. per year." [n]

Apart from attempting to straighten out Mme Halévy's finances, Bizet was also saddled with the task of making an inventory and arranging for the packing and transportation to Bordeaux of all her personal possessions. Geneviève did what she could to help him in carrying out this tedious and tiresome duty. Early in August, she wrote to Mme Halévy in Bordeaux: "Dear darling Mother . . . In five or six weeks we shall be starting to think about returning to Paris. . . . You told me you had rented an apartment, and I don't suppose you would mind arranging it a little before our return. Georges has so much work to do, and such difficult things in view, that he would like to get the business of moving settled as soon as possible in order to be completely and quietly settled this winter without having to be preoccupied with additional interruptions to his work."

Geneviève then proceeds to fill some twenty pages with lists of her mother's possessions, concluding with an apology: "Oh, what a serious letter, dear Mama, and how it will bore you to read. I shudder when I think of it. But it was necessary. . . . The hat you gave me continues to be the height of fashion! Brun finds it so pretty he is going to have it copied for his daughter, and the Edouard Rodrigues branch has not criticized it, which is a triumph! Mme de Beaulieu, who is very difficult to please, went so far as to admire it. What a success!!!!!

"Georges is still working hard, making good progress, tires himself terribly, loves you and kisses you affectionately, dear darling Mother. I emulate him and wait for your orders." [n]

To this major effort of his wife's Bizet added a postscript: "I have just read Geneviève's 22 pages.—When you have answered all her questions, I shall immediately make arrangements for this great removal. I can't tell you how very happy I shall be to see you at last again in possession of *yourself*. For all these objects will remind you of great joys and of great sorrows, too. But a heart like yours can find happiness in memories, a satisfaction denied vulgar souls. I was profoundly touched by the presents you gave Geneviève, but I would not want any fear of stripping our house to interfere with your taking back what belongs to you. . . . Our apartment is overcrowded. It is no longer an apartment, but a museum. . . . Need I tell you how happy I am to have Halévy's old piano? Thank you again for all your charming and heartfelt offers. I shall without ceremony take advantage of just one of them. —In your library there are several books in duplicate and triplicate (about a dozen volumes). Could you *lend* me a copy of each of these? . . . There are also *several* dictionaries, books of no value, but which I use a great deal—and finally twenty or so odd volumes, works unfinished in 1862 or still in progress, which I would like to fill in eventually. You see I am asking you quite frankly, and I hope you will reply the same way." [n]

Mme Halévy's reply consisted of further attempts to press gifts upon Bizet. She ignored any reference to a date for the despatch of her belongings, but pelted him with further questions. Indeed, the correspondence exchanged among Bizet and Geneviève and her mother, her uncle, and the notary, Delapalme, bulks about twice as long as the libretto of *Djamileh*. However, the prospect of anchoring his mother-in-law in Bordeaux apparently compensated Bizet considerably for the time and labor lost in writing her almost daily letters. Actually his excursions into these unfamiliar fields so remote from his work seem to have served as a form of relaxation. When Mme Halévy had been too bored, as her daughter suspected she would be, to read her 22-page letter, Bizet assured her: "Decidedly Geneviève does not know how to write business letters. So I shall leave *Namouna* to straighten out for you two or three matters that I see have not been sufficiently explained to you."

First he attempts to make her see the importance to him of an immediate decision on a date for clearing his apartment of her possessions: "You know that your son-in-law is an odd duck, and one of my principles is not to have anything in *my* house that does not belong to *me*. Therefore I shall delay returning to Paris until you are settled. . . . I am something of a maniac on the subject of moving; changing and resettling fills me with horror. . . . Your draperies, your Beauvais tapestries, your rugs, your curtains, your linens, your beds, your Gobelins are none of them any longer in existence. Your pots and pans have suffered the same fate. . . . Your furniture was worm-eaten and falling to pieces. Geneviève tells me that everything was sold at auction five years ago, and she knows that the sale was officially sanctioned by the family council."

Having, of necessity, reminded Mme Halévy of this painful business, passionately deplored by her at the time, but now completely forgotten, Bizet proceeds to re-establish her pride of possession by making a detailed six-page inventory of all the *bibelots* and *objets d'art* Geneviève had omitted from her list. "Ouf!" he exclaimed at the end of his list, and then continued his ungrateful task.

It was now incumbent upon him to shatter Mme Halévy's illusions about the value of a building in the Boulevard Malesherbes which she had inherited from her husband. This boulevard had been cut through in the mid-1850's as part of the Baron Haussmann's great scheme for modernizing Paris. The Péreire brothers, who were among the Baron's financial backers, had persuaded Halévy to invest in this development. But the war and the disorganization resulting from the Commune had wrought havoc with the investment, which in the future, of course, was to become extremely lucrative. In 1871 Bizet felt impelled to ask his mother-in-law: "Do you know to what extent you have been involved in a detestable, deplorable business? Are you aware that the house represents a capital of 5 or 600,000 frs. at the most and that your indebtedness on it is increasing to 6 or 700,000 frs.? That consequently this house can never bring you any income? That the arrangement made by the Messrs. Péreire, by which they accept the rent as interest on the money they have loaned you, is only temporary? That they can change their minds or die, and that then the liquidation would be extremely onerous for you? That it is to your interest to get out of this mess as far as possible? That you would be performing a master stroke if you would take advantage of the friendship they have shown you (the effects of which it is about time for you to understand) by regularizing your position? . . . Do you know all this? Or do you still have illusions about them and ignore what the French have learned at their expense? Keep all this to yourself, dear Mme Halévy. . . . Don't be alarmed. . . . Be clever. Be cautious. Your name is a safeguard. They will not have the impudence to push things too far and show the public that you have been duped by your own good faith and the dishonesty of others. . . . I don't say that M. Emile Péreire's heart is entirely dessicated. His brother is a robber, but his own reputation is a little better. . . . Just remember that it was necessary for the Boulevard Malesherbes to be built rapidly, and that the name of Halévy was not without its uses. Do you understand?

"To sum up, this house is yours without belonging to you. I, simple musician that I am, tell you what I know, what I feel, what I guess. However, public opinion would have enlightened me had I lacked other sources of information. . . ." [n]

To compensate Mme Halévy for the shock of this revelation as well as for the financial loss involved, Bizet offered, although legally prevented from changing his marriage contract, "to modify to your advantage the arrangement that . . . might leave you in slightly straitened circumstances. You understand, don't you, that this is not a favor I am offering you? The letter of the law is not meant for sensitive people. Over and above human rights there is a moral obligation that you and I can feel and understand. In a thing of this kind there need be no spoken agreement. It will take care of itself. We don't even have to discuss it. . . ." "

This generous gesture of Bizet's served to galvanize Mme Halévy into decisive action. By mid-September the load of furniture and bric-a-brac finally left for Bordeaux. No longer was Bizet forced to spend his time traveling between Le Vésinet and Paris and climbing up and down the stairs between his own apartment on the second floor and the maid's room on the sixth, where many of Mme Halévy's things were stored. No longer did he have to supervise the building of crates, the moving down to the street of the various articles, the drawing up of bills of lading. In this nerve-wracking occupation Bizet had taken a certain pride of craftsmanship. Nevertheless, his health was badly affected by the excess of activity. "I have been threatened the last few days with my eleventh attack of angina," he wrote to du Locle in September, "and have more or less conquered it. But I have not wanted to undertake the tiring journey to Paris. However, as soon as you have a clear picture of the cast, don't fail to let me know and I shall come running.

"I have gone as far as I can with the thing but the questions of the range of the voices, and consequently the tonality, have me tied hand and foot. I shall need a day for the links, the transitions, etc., and then I shall finish the work. Think about the *choral* question; it is important. Like you, I should like to eliminate meaningless phrases, but to sing choruses you must have chorus-singers. For the dance I should prefer to do without women and have a sufficient number of men to make the music expressive. Make up your mind about that so that I can write the dance. As for Hassan's friends, don't forget that they have to sing: *Quelle est cette belle,* etc. I venture to hope for a *bis (repetita placent)*, but for that the piece has to be sung!" "

During the summer, in spite of his throat attacks, Bizet had also reworked part of the *Roma* symphony and finished at least one act of *Clarissa Harlowe*. "My wife says it is good," he wrote to Guiraud, "but I absolutely can't tell. I am waiting for your opinion before making up my mind. I am always the same! Yesterday my act seemed to me bad, this morning mediocre, and just now excellent. I am dropping it, and will retain this last impression, which another examination will certainly modify." "

Bizet had no doubts about the other things he composed at this time. He admitted that he liked *Jeux d'enfants* and the *Petite Suite*, based on them.³ These works, composed more or less simultaneously, were sold to Durand on September 28 for 600 francs. The satisfaction he found in composing the suite and in revising the *Roma* caused him to remark that "the symphony, which is to the theatre what the portrait is to *décor*, has got hold of me to the nth degree."

Of all Bizet's projects during 1871, only *Jeux d'enfants* achieved publication. *Grisélidis* was indefinitely postponed because of lack of funds to mount so elaborate a work. *Djamileh* was shelved until the following year. "The directors of the Opéra-Comique . . ." he wrote to Galabert, "are spending all their energies on Jacques Offenbach's *Fantasio,* and my legitimate demands for a cast have slowed things up. . . . But each day I

---

³ To Lacombe, Bizet spoke of "my little suites for orchestra in five pieces. These pieces, which are simple sketches, are accompanied by five others. . . .

"Ten pieces for four hands"

No. 1	*Les Chevaux de bois* (The Rocking-horses)	Scherzo
No. 2	*La Poupée* (The Doll)	Berceuse
No. 3	*La Toupie d'Allemagne* (The Top)	Impromptu
No. 4	*L'Escarpolette* (The Swing)	Rêverie
No. 5	*Le Volant* (The Kite)	
No. 6	*Les Soldats de Plomb* (The Lead Soldiers)	Marche
No. 7	*Colin-Maillard* (Blind-Man's Buff)	Fantaisie
No. 8	*Saute-Mouton* (Leap-Frog)	Caprice
No. 9	*Petit Mari—Petite Femme* (Playing House)	Duo
No. 10	*Le Bal* (The Ball)	Galop

"The orchestral suite is composed of Nos. 1, 2, 3, 9, and 10. The too childish titles I have suppressed." Hugues Imbert, "Lettres à Paul Lacombe," *Portraits et Etudes,* Paris, 1894, 192.

Bizet later added *Les Bulles de Savon* (Soap Bubbles) and *Les Quatres Coins* (Puss in the Corner), which became numbers 7 and 8 in *Jeux d'enfants. Trompette et Tambour,* a march from *Ivan IV,* replaced *Les Soldats de Plomb.* In its final version the *Petite Suite* consisted of *La Toupie, La Poupée, Trompette et Tambour, Petit Mari—Petite Femme,* and *Le Bal.* This finale was substituted for *Les Quatre Coins,* the complete orchestral parts of which exist in manuscript form inscribed in Bizet's handwriting: "Op. 22, *Petite Suite,* No. 5. Final."

am strengthening myself against the minor emotions of life. It is not really a philosophy, but a sovereign scorn that replaces them. . . ." [n]

Much of his scorn he focused on Offenbach. "All the producers of good music must redouble their efforts to fight against the ever-increasing invasion of that infernal Offenbach," he wrote to Lacombe. "The creature, not satisfied with his *Roi-Carotte* at the Gaîté, is going to bestow upon us a *Fantasio* at the Opéra-Comique. Besides, he bought back from Heugel his *Barkouf,* had new words written for all of this trash, and has sold the whole thing back to Heugel for 12,000 frs. The Bouffes-Parisiens will be the first to produce this obscenity." [4] [n]

Bizet's prejudice against Offenbach's minor works was tinged by a natural enough personal resentment. For Sardou was the librettist of *Fantasio,* which like *Djamileh* was based on a poem by Musset; and Offenbach, Bizet no doubt suspected, was the anonymous collaborator whose visit to Sardou during the summer had prevented the playwright's receiving Bizet when he called. So he could hardly be expected to accept cheerfully the indefinite postponement of his and Sardou's *Grisélidis,* while Sardou's and Offenbach's *Fantasio* was given preference over *Djamileh.* Yet, he was not discouraged.

"If I saw my contemporaries outstripping me by several lengths, I should be affected by it, I confess," he wrote to his mother-in-law. "But by proceeding painstakingly and slowly I shall easily have the advantage. Wagner, the great, the tremendous musician whom you would adore if you knew his music, is so far away and above all living composers that one doesn't have to consider him. Besides I don't have to stand in awe of men who are ending their careers. On a lower level than Wagner, Verdi and Gounod are properly enjoying the position their great talents have earned them. . . . Thomas will perhaps write another *Hamlet;*

---

[4] *Barkouf,* produced for the first time on Christmas Eve 1860, was a disastrous failure. The fault lay principally in the libretto by Scribe. The plot centered on a dog, and the music imitated a dog's barking. "The hostile critics described it as a *chiennerie,* and Berlioz in his indignation recalled Offenbach's German origin and put him and Wagner into the same boat. 'Something is definitely disturbed in the brain of some musicians,' he wrote. 'The wind that blows through Germany has made them mad.' In order to rescue his work from oblivion, Offenbach revised it after the War of 1870 and turned the dog into an ox." Sigmund Kracauer, *Orpheus in Paris—Offenbach and the Paris of his Time,* New York, 1938, 210–11.

I hope so for his sake. But he can neither enlarge nor modify his magnificent position. Our turn will come. There are four or five of us, not more, and there is room for all of us.—I do not despise the theatre, I assure you, and to prove it I have three works under way. . . . But now I must quarrel with you . . . not one, but two quarrels!—(I like to battle with you, first because it brings me 'love' letters, and also because you refuse to be convinced! . . .) You said, '*Le Pré aux clercs,*[5] *La Dame blanche, Les Mousquetaires!*'

"*LA DAME BLANCHE!* . . .

"Listen: one day, in front of Halévy, I was expounding some rather subversive theories about *La Dame blanche.* I spoke the simple truth. 'It is a loathsome opera, without talent, with no ideas, no *esprit,* no melodic invention, no anything whatsoever in the world. It is stupid, stupid, stupid!' Halévy, turning toward me with his sly smile, said (I have a witness): 'Well, yes! You are right. Its success is incomprehensible; it is no good. *Only, you mustn't say so.*'

"Doubtless he was right. But let us among ourselves, intelligent people, do justice to this Prud'hommesque nonsense which no longer can amuse anybody but soldiers, children's nurses, and *concierges!* Take your choice: Paul de Kock,[6] Signol,[7] the Empire, anything, anything, anything, but not *La Dame blanche!*

"Now, please consider carefully the great, but too widely ignored truth that I am about to submit to you. *In art* (music, painting, *sculpture particularly*) as in literature, it is the *talent* and not the *idea* that makes success. The public (and I am speaking of intelligent people, the others don't count; that is my own kind of democracy), the public does not understand the *idea* until *later.* To reach this *later* time, the artist's talent must, by means of an

---

[5] *Le Pré aux clercs,* a comic opera by L.-J.-F. Hérold (1791–1833), was performed for the first time December 15, 1832, at the Opéra-Comique, and for the 1,000th October 10, 1871, when Galli-Marié read a poem written for the occasion by Louis Gallet.

[6] Paul de Kock (1794–1871) wrote innumerable popular novels, exaggerated anecdotes, and amusing portrayals of day-to-day bourgeois life, as well as many melodramas, comic operas, pantomimes, etc. Although his style was atrocious, his novels became so famous that at one time, in Spain and Italy, any French novel was attributed to him.

[7] Emile Signol (1804–92), a popular but mediocre painter of religious and historical subjects. His best-known painting, *La Femme adultère,* was hung in the Luxembourg and frequently reproduced.

attractive form, ease the way for him and not discourage him from the very beginning.

"So Auber, who had so much talent with so few ideas, was almost always understood, while Berlioz, who had genius without talent, practically never was. No book, however remarkable its subject matter, is tolerated if it is badly written, while a trivial thing, a bagatelle, is praised to the skies if its style is clear and limpid. Don't talk about method to a musician; what you call 'scholarly music' is merely awkwardly put together. (I am speaking in general.) Mozart and Rossini both had the most prodigious talent imaginable. When they were inspired they created *Don Giovanni, The Magic Flute, The Barber of Seville* (a little dated), *Guillaume Tell.* With talent alone they created all those boring symphonies, *Semiramide,* almost all of *Otello,* etc., etc., etc.—and for a long time the public believed that these scores, which today they will no longer applaud, were the *nec plus ultra* of the idea!

"Now don't go and call me a sectarian. I am eclectic. The beautiful, that is to say the union of matter and form, is always beautiful.

"As for the so-called public, they have no opinions. They are told Michelangelo is a god, and that is true. They believe it, though they are incapable of understanding anything about him.

"Go down into the depths of people's consciousness, and there you will see that Homer, Phidias, Dante, Michelangelo, Cervantes, Shakespeare, Beethoven—the gods, in short, bore the little man in the street, who dares not protest against these recognized truths. Reread Scudéry's letter on *Le Cid.* It's always the same old joke. The artist does not find his true level until a *hundred years* after his death! Is that sad? No. It is merely stupid. So you see, basically we almost agree, and if you knew Wagner well, and Schumann, we should agree altogether. I shall play them for you. You will see!" [n]

This warm mood of Bizet's was soon dispelled by Mme Halévy's acknowledgment of the arrival of her belongings at Bordeaux. Not only were no thanks forthcoming, but she assailed him with a series of complaints about the condition of her furniture and accused him of excessive and careless extravagance and of withholding or losing a number of her possessions. Her ingratitude would have been shocking under any circumstances. But only a short time before, in reply to a protest from her that his refusal to accept additional gifts was hypersensitive and neurasthenic, Bizet had confessed: "I am in no way reluctant to admit the great flaw in my nature. I am, I know, exaggeratedly sensitive; I tend to believe that I am the object of suspicion; I am often conscious of being the victim of persecution that probably exists only in my own mind. It is really an illness, and I can only ask those who love me not to expose a very painful nerve, which some trifling thing quickly sets to vibrating.—It would be useless and would take too long to explain here the reasons for this sensitiveness. . . ." [n]

Now the nerve had been set to vibrating. For the first time he addresses his mother-in-law in a tone that a less patient man would long since have adopted. After filling six pages with figures and details explaining and justifying his procedure and his expenditures in her behalf, he says: "I am only sorry that you did not give me more precise directions. . . . I have succeeded only in satisfying myself, which is not enough, though it is something. If you have communicated your dissatisfaction to your brother, dear Mme Halévy, I should be much obliged if you would also send him this letter. The lack of success of my arrangements affects only my self-esteem, and that is nothing. But the question of the 550 frs. goes farther and has wounded me more deeply than you can believe. . . . I do not offer to help you in your search for the articles you have lost, first because I can think of no way of returning them to you and also because you doubt my ability to do so. Let us hope that this letter is the last I shall write you about your household goods. We will discuss art, a subject which is perhaps less alien to me." [n]

In addition to his disillusionment over his relations with Mme Halévy, Bizet also had to undergo the ordeal of rejecting or being rejected for the position of *chef du chant* at the Opéra. Why he never occupied this post is not clear. No mention of the appointment of which he was so certain has so far been found in the records. But it is possible that he himself refused the position and asked to have his name removed from the books as a protest against the treatment the directors and the singers at the Opéra accorded his friend Ernest Reyer.

Reyer's *Erostrate* was the work chosen to re-open the Opéra. Inevitably Bizet, because of his collaboration with the author nine years earlier, was involved in the Paris *première* of his friend's work. The rehearsals afforded him an opportunity to observe for the first time Halanzier's surprising attitude toward music. Only singing appealed to the director, who dismissed all orchestral music other than accompaniment as *"ritournelle."* In *Erostrate* an orchestral interlude occurs in a scene in which the sculptor, Scopas, first sees Athenaïs, his model for the Venus de Milo, a creation attributed to him by the librettists. After a few bars of the interlude had been played at a rehearsal, Halanzier rapped his cane on the floor, stopped the orchestra, and demanded of Reyer: "What on earth does the woman do while this *ritournelle* goes on?" "She listens to it," the composer replied. The public, no kinder to the opera than the director, reacted against it for different, but no more rational, reasons. Because when *Erostrate* had first been played at Baden-Baden in August 1862, Reyer had dedicated the score to the Queen of Prussia, who then bestowed upon him the Order of the Red Eagle, the Paris audience of October 1871, weary of war and defeat, chose to make a scapegoat of its author.

Those critics who were also composers and had suffered Reyer's unfavorable criticism in the *Journal des Débats* avenged themselves in their reviews of *Erostrate*. But only indirectly was a member of the press responsible for the closing of the work after two performances, an action unprecedented in the annals of the Opéra. Jouvin, of the *Figaro,* compared the heroine to Aphrodite, a word familiar to the singer of the role only in the form of hermaphrodite. Considering herself scandalously insulted, she fomented such rebellion among her already disgruntled fellow-artists that Halanzier removed the piece from the repertory at once, with no warning to the composer. On October 19, Reyer published in his weekly article an open letter to the artists responsible for the disaster: "I am not at all surprised that you are more concerned for your own interests than for the reputation of a composer, but I am none the less distressed to see artists like you treat so disdainfully a work that the public may not have received favorably, I admit, but which the press (that honest, free press which I respect and which I am proud to belong to) has not absolutely condemned. Several of my colleagues regarded *Erostrate* as an honorable attempt; that is enough for me. And however unrewarding the outcome, I shall never deviate from the road I have followed until now, and at the end of which lies, if not success, at least the satisfaction of having remained a conscientious and convinced artist."

Would Bizet's conception of loyalty in friendship and his own standards as an artist have permitted him to become a functionary in an organization capable of such gross injustice and lack of moral standards? One can only guess. On November 1, Hector Salomon, former assistant *chef du chant,* was appointed *chef du chant* at the Opéra at an annual salary of 4000 francs.[8]

---

[8] In May 1868, Hector Salomon presented Bizet with a copy of his *Romances: chansons sans paroles pour piano* inscribed "To my dear friend Georges Bizet, most affectionately."

CHAPTER  XXII

Djamileh

Early in January 1872, the directors of the Opéra-Comique started "harassing" Bizet to put *Djamileh* into rehearsal. "But I am undecided and have no energy," he wrote to Lacombe. "I see so few singers. . . . Offenbach has had three remarkable flops. Is it the end or just temporary exhaustion?" Bizet, of course, did not go to the Gaîté to see *Le Roi-Carotte,* but Flaubert, who attended the opening with Dumas *fils,* wrote to George Sand: "You can't imagine such a stinker. . . . The audience agreed with me completely. Good old Offenbach has also had a failure at the Opéra-Comique with *Fantasio.* Is the public starting to hate trumpery? What a fine step in the right direction that would be!" [n]

Fantasio, which opened on January 18, ran for only ten performances. It was followed by a revival of Auber's *Fra Diavolo,* in which Bizet had the opportunity to see Mme Prelly, the future Djamileh, reveal, for the first time professionally, her extraordinary beauty as well as her striking inability to sing or act. Late in February, Mme Carvalho returned to the stage of the Comique, where her always-ravishing performance of Cherubino only emphasized the poverty of voice and training of the rest of the cast of *Le Nozze di Figaro.* When an important critic, in his review of the Mozart opera, hoped that the directors of the Opéra-Comique would "open their double-doors to new works and call on the young composers," du Locle doubled his pressure on Bizet. The composer, in spite of the dearth of good singers, was caught, and could no longer postpone the casting of his opera.

The rehearsals of *Djamileh* began early in March. Could Bizet have been a mere spectator at these proceedings, they might well have appealed to him as subject-matter for an *opéra-bouffe* in the manner of Mozart's *Der Schauspieldirektor*. For the interplay of directors, theatre personnel, cast, and librettist offered enough farcical material to amuse anyone but the composer himself.

In both appearance and temperament, the two directors exemplified the traditional vaudeville team of opposites. De Leuven, born Count Adolph von Ribbing, had been a close friend and collaborator of Dumas *père*. Dumas *fils* described him as "the strongest and liveliest survivor of a prehistoric age. Tall, dark, lean . . . hardly stooped at all, he looked like the subject of a portrait by Rembrandt who stepped out of his frame to stroll, alone and thoughtful, along the boulevard. His clothes—an ample velvet caftan surmounted by a large mink cap—gave him a strange, bizarre appearance that seemed not at all affected. In the hubbub of Paris his very silence evoked the Norseman he was, son of the brilliant and robust Ribbing who was active in the Swedish plot that resulted in the death of Gustavus III, the hero of Auber's and Scribe's *Bal masqué*.[1] De Leuven's contemporaries were old, but he was archaic." [n]

Archaic, too, his taste in music. The author of dozens of librettos for the successful light operas of Adolphe Adam and Clapisson, he cared only for the familiar, facile, sprightly tunes of his youth. *Djamileh* and "Bizet's ideas, so subtle, so colorful, so seductive, so full of true passion," wrote the librettist Gallet, "fell like dull rain on de Leuven. . . . He didn't understand them or, being of a very shrewd turn of mind, didn't choose to understand them." When the librettist arrived late for rehearsal on one occasion, de Leuven, listening to an aria from the lobby, cornered Gallet and remarked "in his impassive grand manner: 'Splendid, you have arrived just in time for the *De Profundis*.' " [2]

Camille du Locle, short, small, wiry, dynamic, spoke with a nasal twang. The nephew of Perrin, he had from his earliest youth been associated with his uncle in the lyric theatre. His passion, like Carvalho's, for introducing new works arose rather from a taste

---

[1] Also of Verdi's *Un ballo in maschera*.

[2] Louis Gallet, *Notes d'un librettiste*, 20. Unless otherwise noted, the accounts of the rehearsals and performance of *Djamileh* are based on this source.

for novelty and excitement than from any deep-seated interest in contemporary music. But unlike the former director of the Théâtre-Lyrique, who, after his failure as an actor, had restricted his desire for self-expression to the art of directing, du Locle fancied himself as a poet, a librettist, and even as a designer of scenery and costumes. Author (with Méry) of the frequently rewritten libretto of *Don Carlos,* he was responsible, too, for the plotting of the story of *Aïda,* as well as for the French version of that opera. Although more than two years and several visits to Italy were required to persuade Verdi to collaborate with him, du Locle was finally able to arrange for the *première* of *Aïda* in Cairo in December 1871.

For du Locle the chief attraction of *Djamileh* lay in the oriental setting. He had little ear for music and less understanding of the problems of a musician. When Bizet's friend Henri Maréchal was about to play the score of his first opera for the director of the Comique, he discovered that the ivory key of middle C had been removed from the piano for repairs. "It doesn't really matter, does it?" du Locle asked. At the end of an hour, the composer, his thumb bleeding, his fingers sore, waited hopefully to hear du Locle's opinion of his work. After a long silence, the director agreed to produce the opera and suggested the name of a well-known baritone for the part of the lover. "But I have written the part for a tenor," Maréchal pointed out. "That doesn't matter," du Locle replied, "you'll just transpose it, that's all." [n]

In spite of du Locle's insensitiveness to the feelings of composers, he must be granted the distinction of having introduced to the Opéra-Comique *Djamileh* and *Carmen,* as well as early works of Paladilhe, Massenet, and Saint-Saëns. Regarded in the dim light of history, the forces motivating du Locle, sponsor of so many innovations, resemble real courage and a sincere desire to revolutionize the genre of *opéra-comique.* But many of his contemporaries attributed his daring to bravado and the desire, so often cherished by a director, to leave his personal imprint on a work of art he himself was incapable of creating. According to the actor Berton, a friend of Bizet's, du Locle's experiments were the expression of "a sort of dilettantism, a superficial varnish, with no base in solid convictions. Basically he was a skeptic who always lacked the driving force of faith. He was afraid of appearing to believe in anyone or anything, and cared less about the success of one of his projects than about being regarded as an infallible arbiter." "

If, on the opening night, an opera turned out to be a failure, du Locle would stand in the lobby and, beaming, whisper in the ears of his friends: "That was one of de Leuven's pets." At the next failure, de Leuven, rubbing his hands and smiling ironically, would announce that the production was one of du Locle's, who, no more loyal to his singers than to his partner, would ask a member of the audience: "Is the tenor bad enough for you? Well, come back tomorrow night and you'll hear an even worse one."

The fate on stage of any work presented at the Comique lay in the hands of Charles Ponchard, general manager, and Victor, the old stage-manager. Ultra-conservative, old enough to have witnessed the *premières* of *Le Pré aux clercs* and *La Dame blanche*, Victor "regarded Bizet with both indignation and despair. After listening from a corner in the wings to this music, which he found incomprehensible, he would retire to his office, heavy-footed, with a shrug of his shoulders that augured ill."

Charles Ponchard, on the other hand, was a constructive element in this diverse company. Himself a retired tenor with years of success behind him, a sensitive and distinguished artist, Ponchard studied thoroughly each work under production and was able to offer valuable suggestions both to the composer and to the librettist.

Gallet, a sympathetic character, a man of taste, a dabbler in all the arts except music, was amused by, rather than involved in, the conflict around him. "His capacity for work was prodigious," said Saint-Saëns, for whom he supplied librettos for six now long-forgotten operas. "You always found him, pen in hand, scribbling on scraps of paper in his office at the Administration of Assistance to the Poor, compiling reports, writing novels, articles for various reviews, comedies, librettos. . . . There were also speeches in prose and in verse for monument inaugurations, for toasts at literary banquets. . . . To relax, he wrote sonnets." "

Although a conscientious worker, Gallet lacked both a true understanding of music and an instinct for the theatre. In the preface to his libretto of *Thaïs*, he wrote: "A lyrical poem is a work in verse handed over to a musician to convert into prose." A poetic, literary atmosphere, rather than the theatre, was his climate. Charming and well written as is the libretto of *Djamileh*, it lacks action, as Bizet discovered too late. A perfect cast might have disguised this weakness. But Bizet's long search for singers capable of creating the roles proved fruitless. The artists in *Djamileh* could serve only as butts for du Locle's jokes.

The story of the opera has to do with Haroun, a cynical rake who, loving only the idea of love, takes a new mistress every month, at the end of which time he dismisses her with a gift of jewelry. Splendiano, the servant, who resembles Mozart's Osmin, buys his master's favorites in the slave market. Djamileh, at the end of her term, is in love with Haroun and unwilling to leave him. She bargains with Splendiano to disguise her as her successor, and offers herself as his reward if she fails to win Haroun's true love. Splendiano thinks he has a sure thing, but after a struggle Haroun capitulates to Djamileh's love.

Why Bizet should have been charmed by this banal, undramatic little echo of an Arabian Nights' tale is difficult to understand. But he was attracted to Musset's poem *Namouna* before he saw Gallet's libretto. Perhaps the epigraph at the head of the first canto caught his imagination. "A woman is like your shadow: run after it, and it escapes you; run away from it, and it follows." It is a short step from there to Don José's observation in both Mérimée's and Meilhac and Halévy's *Carmen:* "Women are like cats; they don't come when you call them and do come when you don't."

Bizet had wanted Galli-Marié or Priola for the role of Djamileh. But they were both committed to Paladilhe's *Le Passant,* which du Locle also had in rehearsal. This curtain-raiser had its *première* on April 24, a month earlier than *Djamileh.* The libretto of *Le Passant,* a successful play by François Coppée, was chosen by Paladilhe because "it in no way resembles the usual thing at the Opéra-Comique. It is purely poetic, very delicate, with no plot to speak of." Although this precursor of *Djamileh* was not at all a fiasco, the directors closed it after three performances on the pretext of being unable to pay Galli-Marié the sum she demanded, this in spite of an offer from the singer to take a cut in her salary so that *Le Passant* might continue in the repertory. By the time *Djamileh* opened, Galli-Marié was singing in Lyons, a piece of bad luck that can only have increased Bizet's regret at not having held out longer for a better cast.

Even Bizet's first biographer, Pigot, usually hagiological,

blames the composer for his weakness in permitting the management to impose upon him "that sultry Djamileh who had none of the qualities, either vocal or dramatic, necessary to the interpretation of his warm, poetic, passionate music." Mme Aline Prelly, in private life the Baroness de Presles, was a charming society woman who, as Mlle de Pomeyrac, had been a renowned beauty at the court of the Second Empire. Why, with meager voice and almost complete lack of training, she should have taken it into her head to sing at the Opéra-Comique has not been revealed. But it is safe to suspect that strong influences on the political level enabled her to consummate her ambition. "Bizet, unfortunately, did nothing to prevent it," says Pigot. Committed as he was to the directors and burdened with financial and family problems, he had little freedom of choice.

Duchesne, cast as Haroun, was an inexperienced young tenor. Although he later achieved success, his powerful, fine voice, which he had not yet learned to control, was hardly more effective than Mme Prelly's.

Splendiano, the servant, was played by Potel, a mediocre singer, officially classified as *"trial"* or singing actor. Fancying himself as a baritone, he was outraged when he saw his name listed in the proofs of the piano and voice score of *Djamileh* as *"trial."* He tried to persuade first Choudens, then Bizet and du Locle, to change the classification. Unsuccessful in his efforts, he went secretly to the engraver's and himself had the plates changed.

With this cast of characters on stage and off, it is no wonder that Gallet found the rehearsals amusing. "Camille du Locle, as mischievous as a Paris street-urchin, enjoyed fanning Victor's indignation and making fun of de Leuven's solemn scorn. The small, practical details of production enchanted him. Very much the artist, the refined orientalist, he ran around every morning looking for materials, unusual properties, authentic furniture and costumes. I . . . used to tease him from time to time about all this frippery. But he went right on dressing Splendiano-Potel in a fine, heavy blue silk *abail*, gold-striped; Haroun-Duchesne in a jacket that had been superbly embroidered in some fairy-tale Constantinople bazaar; and Djamileh in the ravishing dress of an Egyptian dancing-girl.

"The décor was in Hispano-Moorish style . . . with a backdrop of blue sky. A splendid multi-colored lantern, manipulated on-stage to throw a sunset-light, aroused the admiration of some connoisseurs, but chiefly enchanted the young director, which was the important thing."

On the opening night, May 22, Bizet stationed himself in the prompter's box as the most advantageous spot from which to encourage the singers, give them their cues, and guard against mistakes. Although he was very calm, Gallet decided to stay with him, sitting on a chair in a little narrow passage facing the composer. Bizet's cool assurance amazed him.

Before the curtain rose, the orchestra played several measures of the tenor's opening revery "during which Djamileh silently crossed the stage. Light as a phantom, she bent in adoration of her sleeping lover . . . and vanished with an ecstatic look. . . . This delightful, furtive apparition thrilled the audience. The actress, who hadn't had to sing a note in this scene, won complete approval by her grace and her beauty. Her great dark eyes spoke more eloquently than the sweetest song, and her triumph would have been complete could she have remained silent to the end."

During the first few scenes, everything went well enough; there was even considerable applause. But suddenly Gallet saw Bizet become excited in his little box. "Something had gone wrong, but it was quickly righted. Djamileh had just skipped thirty-two measures in the middle of the Persian song. And the orchestra, spurred on by Deloffre, was racing madly to catch up with the singer. Apart from this accident," says Gallet blandly, "the evening proceeded without further incident, which did not prevent Bizet's leaning over to me towards the end and saying: 'It's a complete flop.' " After the performance, he exclaimed to Gallet: "You see what happens. You wear yourself out, you do your best in vain. If you want to succeed today, you have to be dead—or German."

The day after the opening, composer and librettist presented the singers with souvenirs: a fan to Djamileh, an Arabian knife to Haroun, and an embossed cigar-case to Splendiano. "I have added up our accounts," Bizet wrote to Gallet. "Here they are:

Fan	70 francs
Knife	20 "
Cigar-case	9 "
5 cigars at 0.60 frs.	3 "
	102 francs

"(I smoked the sixth and am considerate enough not to make you pay for it. . . .)

"Another thing. The head of the claque came to annoy me because of his emoluments. De Leuven, whom I consulted, advised me to give fifty francs for the *première* and fifty at the twentieth performance. I will pay the fifty for the *première;* if we go to twenty, it will be your turn to fork out. . . ."

Gallet was safe on this score. After ten performances, *Djamileh* was not performed again until 1938. *"Djamileh* is not a success," Bizet wrote to Galabert. "The libretto is really anti-theatrical, and my singer was even worse than I feared. However, I am very well satisfied with the outcome. The press was very interesting, and never has a one-act *opéra-comique* been more seriously, and I can even say more passionately, discussed. The same old Wagner story continues. Reyer (*Les Débats*), Weber (*Le Temps*), Guillemot (*Journal de Paris*), Joncières (*La Liberté*), (that is to say more than half the daily papers) were very warm.—De Saint Victor, Jouvin, etc., were good in the sense that they admit inspiration, talent, etc., all spoiled by the influence of Wagner. . . . What pleases me more than the opinions of all these gentlemen is the absolute certainty of having found my way. I know what I am doing." "

The "Wagner story" had grown into a case of hiccoughs. Even after Paladilhe's pallid *Le Passant,* one critic had written: "Almost all of our young musicians aspire to the kiss of the modern Germanic muse, who seems to be too little the daughter of Apollo and far too closely related to M. Wagner and his cohorts. The result I would call the school of the *musical labyrinth."* [3] " The derogatory reviews of *Djamileh* were all more or less in this tone. A number of favorable criticisms remarked on the novelty and originality of Bizet's work. But Bizet liked best Reyer's review in the *Journal des Débats.* After reading it, he rushed around to see his friend, who was not at home, but for whom he left a hastily penciled note: "I wanted to shake your hand and thank you, tell you how happy I am over your marvelous review of *Djamileh.* . . . I shan't go to bed until I have seen you." "

Reyer had written: "Here we have true Oriental music, at

---

[3] Massenet's *Don César de Bazan,* which was first played in November 1872, was praised by the critics, one of whom expressed his gratitude to the composer for having "sacrificed nothing whatsoever to the fetishes across the Rhine." Albert Soubies et Charles Malherbe, *Histoire de l'Opéra-Comique: 1860–1887,* Paris, 1893, II, 191.

least as it is understood by visitors to the countries of its origin.
. . . It is true, not through imitation of certain instrumental effects *sui generis,* nor by the use of a scale wholly different from
ours, but by the accompaniment it gives to the landscape our imagination evokes, of the picture it spreads before our eyes. It is a
slightly conventional, slightly dressed up truth, if you like, but a
truth that takes into consideration our ears and the nature of the
musical sensations to which we are accustomed. Besides, don't we
know that all music when it travels changes climate, loses its effectiveness by losing its poetry, and sometimes even changes character? . . . In spite of all the artistry of stage devices or décor,
you cannot make me believe, sitting in a seat at the Opéra-
Comique, that I am in a house in ancient Cairo or on the shores
of the island of Philae. . . .

"Here, in this very civilized environment, it is absolutely necessary, if your Arab music is to charm us, that it, too, become
civilized. It must assume the suavest, most poetic form, whether
under the guise of local color or of originality, I don't know. If
you are realistic, you will wound our ear and bore us to death by
the time you have finished your parody.

"M. Georges Bizet has not made so crass an error. He has
made use of both knowledge and inspiration in writing this curtain-raiser, *Djamileh,* which is incomparably smooth and charming. For that reason I shall compare it with no other work of its
kind.

"Formerly M. Bizet wanted to be more realistic and charmed
us less; then he abandoned the Orient and plunged into the full
tide of Germanism. Should one say Wagnerism? Yes, for I felt
something like a breath of *Die Meistersinger* in certain pages of
Djamileh.

" 'It's a breath of Gounod—'

" 'No,' exclaims a third observer, 'don't you recognize the
style of Robert Schumann?'

"Nowhere can it really be called a reminiscence. It is, if you
like, a preoccupation. And I can hear it said that a man a little
too preoccupied with not being like everybody else always ends by
resembling someone in particular. Wagner, Gounod, and Schumann have their virtues, and I think that the musician who stum-
bles going forward is more worthy of interest than one who shows
us how easily he can go backwards.

"My friend Bizet is not among those who never stumble. But to sustain him both in his daring and in his lapses he has a thorough knowledge of the secrets of his art, a skill, a soundness, possessed to the same degree by only two or three of the younger generation. And he still seems to me to be at the head of the young school. The scores of *Les Pêcheurs de Perles* and *La Jolie Fille de Perth* have given him precedence over less fortunate or less skillful competitors. *Djamileh*, whatever its fate may be, marks a new step in the career of this young master. There is more in this work than the manifestation of a talent; there is the expression of a will. And I believe that if M. Bizet learns of the appreciation of his work by a small number of musicians who judge him without prejudice, he will be much prouder of that than of a popular success."

The praise of Bizet's peers was discerning and, obviously, heartfelt. Massenet, not always given to generosity, said, in a letter at the head of which he had copied a theme from *Djamileh:* "I could have written what I have to say to you, my dear Bizet, five days ago, for I have been reading your score, which Choudens, I suppose, sent me. But I wanted to hear it in the *theatre.* Yesterday I came to spend the day in Paris and went to the Opéra-Comique.

"I knew the music because I had been playing it over and over from the time the score arrived. I like it very much; it is unique and very personal.—Your orchestration is marvelously charming and delicate, and when the action demands it, the accent is penetrating.

"I wanted to see how *Djamileh* looked on the stage, behind the footlights! It was even more effective. For you are a theatre man, and your vision is sound. After that *overture-march,* so picturesque, comes the off-stage chorus, which starts with delicious swirls of sound heard through transparent etched patterns, an *entirely successful* scenic and decorative effect. The *bouffe* chorus of friends that is so melodic and so shrewd, Jouvin claims is *fugué!* It didn't seem so to me! But after all, I forgot what I learned in class long ago!

"Haroun's amorous intoxication is fine, melodic, and envelopingly orchestrated. The end of the comedy is stiff. But what of it? The Turks are lucky to be able to repeat those fine things three times a week. What lovely country!

"You have sometimes told me that you admired me; so read this appreciation and don't make fun of it, for it is sincere." [n]

Saint-Saëns's tribute, more original in form, consisted of a sonnet, a copy of which he himself inscribed in Geneviève's album. He speaks of "the bourgeois, chewing his cud in his narrow box, pot-bellied, ugly, unhappy separated from the herd, opening a glassy eye, eating a sweet, then falling asleep again, lulled by the orchestra. Djamileh, daughter and flower of the sacred Orient . . . is a pearl cast before swine."

Gounod, in England, "read the score with much interest as friend, as artist, and as Frenchman. There is certainly a great deal of talent and value in this work in spite of the slightly uneven style in which it is written. I am sure that, on the one hand, time will affect the author, and that on the other, the public will become more and more qualified to understand better what they find such difficulty in grasping today; that is the story of all new things in this world. . . ." [n]

Curiously enough, the situation that had first established a rivalry between the two composers recurred at this time. Just as in 1867 *La Jolie Fille de Perth* and *Roméo et Juliette* had alternated in the repertory of the Théâtre-Lyrique, so now in June 1872 *Djamileh* and a revival of Gounod's *Le Médecin malgré lui* played on alternate nights at the Opéra-Comique. Unfortunately, each opera achieved only ten performances. Gounod's disappointment at his own failure can hardly have been mitigated by the fact that the score of *Djamileh* was sent to him in England not by Bizet himself, but by Mme Halévy, who, though more or less banished from the family life of her children, still busied herself with Bizet's professional life.

During the winter, Bizet had written to her: "Although you are unaware of it, you are going to be a grandmama which will not age you—quite the contrary. Geneviève is *very well,* and as long as she feels no emotion of any kind, everything goes along splendidly. If you come to Paris in the near future, as you give us reason to hope, let me know of your arrival ahead of time so I can come to see you and we can plan what precautions to take. You remember the unfortunate outcome of our visit to Bordeaux. You know that when Geneviève saw you she also recalled some very unhappy moments! That experience severely compromised her health.—Fortunately, times are better; the after-effects of the anxieties caused by the siege have disappeared, and I have every reason to hope that these strange impressions will not recur.

"However, and I *stress* this essential point, the most scrupulously careful precautions have been recommended to me, and I shall ask you to let me set the stage for this whole thing. As it concerns Geneviève's health, we can only agree.—You can write to me on a separate sheet of paper that I shan't show her.—I will try to use the method you suggest to send you your *bibelots*. . . . The news this letter brings will delight you. As for me, my rejoicing will come later." "

Rejoice he did, during the summer, and with good reason. For du Locle and de Leuven, even before *Djamileh* ended its short run, commissioned Bizet to write a three-act opera. "Meilhac and Halévy will be my collaborators," he told Lacombe. "They will do me something *gay,* which I shall treat as *tightly* as possible. It is a difficult task, but I hope to pull it off."

The libretto for the "gay" work Bizet conceived was not immediately decided upon. The directors as usual had their own ideas on this subject. In June, Bizet wrote to Ludovic Halévy: "M. de Leuven . . . wants to give you three scenarios, one of which is *L'Oiseau bleu.* Will you see him right away? Du Locle advises me to be ready just as soon as possible. . . ." "

The Opéra, too, now wanted a work by Bizet. "The doors are open. It has taken ten years to get there," he told Lacombe. Other doors opened, too. Ernest Beulé, successor to Fromental Halévy as Permanent Secretary of the Académie des Beaux-Arts, invited Bizet to lunch with several members of the Institut—"informally—and you will be free to leave after the cigar." " Beulé's invitation recalls Meifred's prophecy after first hearing the nine-year-old Bizet play the piano when he applied for entrance to the Conservatoire: "That child will one day be a member of the Institut." Although Bizet did not live long enough to be thus honored, he was nominated in July to the jury for a fugue competition at the Conservatoire. "A wrong answer matters very little if the mistakes makes the answer more musical. . . ." he commented to his former teacher, Marmontel. "Long live Bach! Saint-Saëns will probably think as I do but—the others!"

The great event of the summer was the birth on July 10 of a son, Jacques Bizet. At three o'clock in the morning, the great obstetrician of the day, Dr. Devillières, was called in to assist the physician, Dr. Bremond. "Thanks to you," Bizet wrote to Dr. Devillières, "my dear wife had come victoriously through an ordeal we both dreaded. Thanks to you again, a fine *baby* [*sic*] is thriving and growing fat. There is no way of expressing sufficient gratitude for such a service! I shall never forget that night or the part you played in it!" "

After months of anxiety over Geneviève, during which he had given literally hundreds of lessons to earn money for the arrival of his child, Bizet had every reason for optimism. Besides the proposed operas, he planned also to compose oratorios and symphonies. "We must produce," he wrote to Lacombe. "Time is passing and we mustn't *croak* without having given what there is in us."

CHAPTER  XXIII

L'Arlésienne

Even before the birth of his son Bizet had started composing the incidental music for Alphonse Daudet's play *L'Arlésienne*. This work was to be produced in the autumn by Carvalho, who, after his failure at the Théâtre-Lyrique, had become director of the Vaudeville. A fortnight after Jacques's birth Bizet wrote to the director: "At last it's coming! The chorus of the first and the chorus of the second act are finished. The instrumental introduction to the first act is almost set. I have found the motifs for *l'Arlésienne* and *l'Innocent*. I shall take the farandole from the Vidal.[1] In a week, around July 31 or August 1, I shall be able to give you all the necessary information about the orchestra and the choruses. I have been a long time getting at it, partly because of Jacques," " partly, he continues, because of quarrels with Madame Halévy and her family, who have made outrageous demands on his time and rewarded his patience by tearing him to shreds.

But in spite of these difficulties Bizet finished the score by the end of the summer. "It will be better than I had thought," he wrote to Hippolyte Rodrigues late in August. "Mme Halévy still *must* leave. She often goes to the Parc Monceaux [*sic*] to see Jacquot, and absolutely insists on making him eat barley-sugar. Fortunately the wet nurse and the park guard vigorously refused these premature sweets. Geneviève is entirely recovered. She will go out in a day or two, weather permitting. . . . I must leave you quickly be-

---

[1] François Vidal (1832– ?), author of *Lou Tambourin* (1864), a book on the tambourine of Provence and the galoubet pipe.

cause I have a rehearsal tomorrow of all my *mélodrames* with the actors and I still have several hours of work to do. It's midnight." "

The score of *L'Arlésienne* is usually identified with the universally played orchestral suite, drawn from it by the composer himself, and the so-called Second Suite, composed of other excerpts from *L'Arlésienne* and some from *La Jolie Fille de Perth,* which was arranged by Guiraud after Bizet's death. Charming as these almost over-familiar suites may be, they give little notion of the music as Bizet originally wrote it. Only those who have heard the score in relation to the dramatic action can know the delicacy and subtlety of its psychological characterization, the power and beauty of the choruses, the skill and ingenuity with which Bizet orchestrated his score for an ensemble restricted to twenty-six instruments. Unfortunately, like Bizet's original version of *Carmen,* which is played only at the Opéra-Comique, *L'Arlésienne* is rarely given outside the Théâtre de l'Odéon in Paris, where it occupies a permanent place in the repertory. In collaborating with Daudet, Bizet was for the first time associated, not with hack librettists or minor poets devoid of theatre sense, but with a truly talented writer whose play was an expression of his own special gifts as an artist.

Playwright and composer were brought together by Carvalho, who found an outlet for his still adventurous spirit by producing at the Vaudeville such experiments as Flaubert's plays, as well as works by younger writers. Finding *L'Arlésienne* rather serious, even somber, the director decided to carry out an idea he had derived from reading the correspondence of Saint-Evremond. The latter, writing to the Duke of Buckingham in 1687, advised "honest people who delight in the theatre" to resume the custom of introducing dances and music into plays, "which would in no way harm the performance . . . and would satisfy the senses and the spirit." "

The play with background music (or *mélodrame,* as the French call it) had, in 1872, sunk more or less to the level of radio "soap-opera" with "music under." Carvalho therefore, in commissioning as serious a composer as Bizet to inject new life into this form, demonstrated his usual daring. And in spite of the failure of his production of *L'Arlésienne,* he continued to believe that the work itself "typified the happy combination of drama and music." Daudet, too, always retained his enthusiasm for Bizet's contribution to his play.

"I am madly in love with all kinds of music," he admitted, "the sophisticated, the naïve, the music of Beethoven and that of the Spaniards in the rue Taitbout; Gluck and Chopin, Massenet and Saint-Saëns, the *bamboula,* Gounod's *Faust* . . . popular songs, barrel-organs, the tambour-drum, even bells. Music that dances and music that dreams, all of it moves me. Wagnerian recitative takes hold of me, bowls me over, hypnotizes me like the sea; and the zigzag violin-bowings of the Tziganes kept me from seeing the Exposition. Each time those cursed violins caught me as I went by—impossible to go farther. I had to stay there until evening, a glass of Hungarian wine on the table, a lump in my throat, madness in my eyes, my whole body quivering to the nervous beat of the tympani." [n]

Daudet's intense, if eclectic, passion for music was an important element in the rapid ripening of friendship and understanding between him and Bizet. But the rare success of their collaboration grew out of a number of more complex factors. Not the least of these was the capacity both men had of translating into living theatrical expression an intuitive psychological grasp of certain facets of human passion and behavior. This gift neither artist appears to have recognized in himself.

Alphonse Daudet was born in 1840 at Nîmes in Provence. At seventeen, after a miserably unhappy experience as a tutor in a school of unruly boys which remained a nightmare to him all his life, he went to Paris to seek his fortune. "One must know our Provence," Emile Zola said, "to understand the original quality of the poets she sends us. They have grown up down there, in the midst of thyme and lavender, half Gascon, half Italian. The sun is in their blood. . . . They come to conquer Paris with a bold naïveté that is in itself half of their success." [n] Success came very soon to Daudet, in recognition first of his personal charm and later of his talent. At eighteen he published a volume of poems, *Les Amoureuses,* which attracted the attention of the Duc de Morny, who invited him to join his secretariat, which already included Daudet's older brother Ernest, Ludovic Halévy, and Bizet's friend Ernest L'Epine. In the salons, where doors soon opened to him, "he would have had the air of a shepherd in love with the stars or some bold hunter of chamois, had he not worn with such correct ease his yellow gloves and white tie. . . . A young savage who will become a *dandy* [*sic*], that is the impression made by M. Alphonse Daudet, man and writer." " Daudet's "magnificent countenance, small figure, narrow head with a mass of black curly hair, long beard, fine features, resonant voice . . . lively movements" " impressed Sigmund Freud on his first visit to Paris, when he met the writer at the house of Professor Charcot.

Daudet left no record of his impressions of the young Viennese doctor who had not yet started to develop his revolutionary theory, which one day would give to *L'Arlésienne* a significance very different from that conceived by its author. For Daudet had an aversion to the expression of unconscious psychological processes. When a distinguished neurologist mentioned his admiration for the author's intuition in portraying the family relations in *L'Arlésienne,* the playwright "threw up his hands and protested with a sort of horror: 'That's not at all what I intended.' " " Whatever he intended, his deep emotional involvement in the play has been recorded by his wife, who said that *L'Arlésienne* meant more to him than any of his other works.

This story of various levels of disastrous love is laid against the background of Provence, a part of southern France so different in landscape, customs, and speech from the rest of the country that even to Frenchmen it seems strange and exotic. The scenes of the play take place in the courtyard and kitchen of the thriving farm or *mas,* Castelet, and on the edge of a swamp in the Camargue, that strange, wild swampland at the mouth of the Rhône, where wild horses still roam, and bulls are bred for the ring.

The love of Fréderi, the young hero, for the girl from Arles, who never appears on stage, is the main theme. Early in the play, he discovers from her former lover, Mitifio, a *gardien* of horses, a rough and jealous man, that his beloved is faithless and callous. Fréderi's hopeless struggle to conquer his obsessive passion ends in suicide, but not before he has tried to exorcise it by becoming engaged to Vivette, a young girl who has always loved him, the goddaughter of his mother, Rose Mamaï. This woman, who embodies the influence on stage that battles against the magic spell of the invisible girl in Arles, could hardly have failed to strike a chord in the son of Aimée Bizet, whose image had haunted him so threateningly after her death; in the son-in-law of Mme Halévy, whose personality pervaded his household. Rose Mamaï, widowed, young, still beautiful, the dominating force on her farm and in her family, is the mother of two sons. Of Fréderi she says: "He is more than a child to me. . . . When I hear my boy going and coming on the farm, it does something indescribable to me. I no longer feel widowed." Her younger son, Janet, *"l'Innocent,"* she ignores as best she can. For according to superstition the presence of a simpleton protects a house from harm. If he matures, he is no longer a safeguard against disaster. And it is *l'Innocent* alone who senses the danger of Fréderi's desperation. At the end of the play when *l'Innocent* has "awakened," the happiest thing his mother can say to him is: "Do you know you look like Fréderi?"

The element in the play most disturbing to the critics in 1872, the non-appearance of the heroine, expressed an emotional situation that haunted Daudet throughout his life. In one of his first poems, *"Autre Amoureuse,"* he wrote: "While I slept away from you/ In a dream always the same/ I saw you on your knees before me/ Telling me each night: 'I love you!'/ Now that you are mine/ Each night I dream in your arms/ That you are gone, some wretch has taken you/ And when you return I die." [n]

This sad stanza might be dismissed as *vers de siècle* by a romantic young man if in his later writings Daudet had not developed the sentiment into a realistic portrayal of the harm wrought by the magic spell of absent and evil love. Indeed, the very words in which Fréderi, the hero of *L'Arlésienne,* describes in a paroxysm of anguish the hallucinations induced by his frustrated love for the heartless, unseen girl in Arles are taken from an often expurgated passage in Daudet's autobiographical *Le Petit Chose,* published only a year before the author wrote *L'Arlésienne.* And in his last novel, written not many years before he died in 1897, the theme recurred.

Variations on this theme recur in all of the operas Bizet wrote after his "change of skin" in 1868. In *La Coupe du Roi de Thulé* Yorick, the simple fisherman, torn between his longing for the "feline, and terrifying . . . beautiful, quick-witted, alluring" Myrrha and the love of Claribel, the Queen of the Sea, sings ecstatically and freely of his passion for the *femme fatale* when he is away from her. "With Myrrha present, he is extinguished."

The epigraph to *Namouna* or *Djamileh*—"*Une femme est comme votre ombre: courez après, elle vous fuit; fuyez-la, elle court après vous*"—presages perhaps the least-quoted lines about love in Carmen's *habanera:* "*Tu crois le tenir—il t'évite/ Tu crois l'éviter—il te tient!*" The possessive element in jealousy induced by fatal love is expressed in *L'Arlésienne* in a speech of Mitifio's, added in Bizet's handwriting to the working script of the play. The *gardien*, desperate at losing his mistress, shows her letters as proof of her infidelity. "It's cowardly, what I'm doing, isn't it?—" he says. "But this woman is mine and I shall keep her for my own no matter who makes fun of me." [2] In the last act of *Carmen*, Don José says: "Not even if it means shedding blood will you go to his arms and laugh at me."

The psychological subtleties of *L'Arlésienne* afforded Bizet perfect material for musical characterization, and the Provençal background, which had kindled his imagination as a boy on the way to Rome, evoked an authenticity of local color which could hardly have been inspired by the libretto-land versions of Ceylon and Scotland in *Les Pêcheurs de Perles* and *La Jolie Fille de Perth*. Bizet used three traditional Provençal tunes in his score: *Marcho dei Rei*, for the off-stage chorus; *Danse dei Chivau-Frus*, familiar as the farandole in Act III, and the *Er dou Guet* which is played while *l'Innocent* is trying to console Fréderi by telling him the touching fable of *La Chèvre de Monsieur Seguin*. The skill with which Bizet wove these tunes into the score rendered them indistinguishable from the original music he composed for it. Daudet's use in his choruses of words by Mistral, to whose *Calendal* Bizet had given so much thought, undoubtedly gave the composer ease and familiarity with his material, perhaps even the opportunity to use music already conceived. (It will be remembered that Fréderi's theme came from *Grisélidis*.) Composer and playwright worked together on the lyrics, and rapidly achieved a close collaboration. (See Appendix I, p. 461.) Daudet's signature "sincerely yours," in his first letter to the composer, changed in the second to a message to little Jacques: "Please kiss the left eye of the *dauphin* for me."

L'Arlésienne was written in 1869 at Champrosay in Dela-

---

[2] In the published text the final phrase is changed to "by no matter what means."

croix's house, which Daudet had acquired shortly after his marriage in 1867, four years after the painter's death. The playwright
drew the theme of the play from an incident that had recently
occurred: the suicide of a young relative of Mistral's, frustrated
in his passion for a woman of Béziers. "Two women, their hands
shading their eyes in the sunset at the entrance to the Camargue,
calling, one in a high voice, the other low, 'Fréderi,' " " supplied
the name of Daudet's hero and the setting for the second act of the
play.

During the rehearsals, his wife wrote, the author "went
through a variety of phases. . . . 'They are all charming,' he
would say during the first stage. . . . 'They understand, they
project, they bring my characters to life: the grace of Vivette, the
authority of Rose Mamaï.' . . . A week later: 'I am so discouraged! Everything is losing its color. You can no longer tell
whether my play is laid near Arles or Asnières. They either exaggerate the gestures and accent or else everything becomes hopelessly monotonous.' Then, during the final rehearsals, his enthusiasm returned. 'You will see, everything is right. . . . I am
satisfied. Bizet's music is delightful. . . .' " "

L'Arlésienne suffered the disadvantage of opening without
preparatory fanfare. All of the advance publicity dealt with
Madame Frainex, a play by Robert Halt with which Carvalho had
intended to open his season, but which was suddenly banned on
September 21. *L'Arlésienne* opened on October 1.

The usual fashionable opening-night audience had not yet
returned to Paris, and although such admirers and friends of
Bizet as Massenet, Ambroise Thomas, Heugel, and Théodore de
Banville were present, the general atmosphere was frigid and un-
welcoming. Carvalho had spared no expense in staging this
pastoral tragedy in the grand manner. Julia Bartet, who was making
her debut as Vivette, the young farm girl, wore a pink moiré taffeta dress while Rose Mamaï, in black velvet, dragged a long train
after her through the courtyard of the farm and the marshes of the
Camargue. At the appearance of La Renaude—Vivette's grandmother, a character so appealing that many retired actresses of the
Comédie-Française have returned to the stage to play her one
brief scene—Villemessant, the all-powerful editor of the *Figaro*,
slammed the door of his box and exclaimed: "What a bore all

these old women are!" Mme Daudet heard one spectator say: "In spite of this, you know, Daudet isn't a complete fool!" "How could Mme Bizet . . . and I not be reduced to tears at this disaster?" the playwright's wife wrote fifty years later.

Théodore de Banville was shocked by his neighbors, who complained loudly: "Another overture!" each time a piece of music was played without stage action. The members of the audience talked, laughed, went in and out banging doors. "They aren't even listening," Bizet in the wings said despairingly to the conductor, Constantin. By the last act, the house was three quarters empty.[3]

"It was a most dazzling failure," Daudet wrote, "with the most charming music in the world, costumes in silk and velvet, and *opéra-comique* scenery. I left the theatre discouraged, disheartened, with the inane laughter that punctuated the tragic scenes still ringing in my ears, and, without defending myself in the papers—they all attacked this play divested of suspense, this portrait . . . of mores and situations, the absolute truth of which I alone knew—I resolved to write no more theatre pieces, piling up the hostile reviews as a rampart for my will power." "

The review of *L'Arlésienne* by the outstanding dramatic critic Francisque Sarcey coincided with the opinions of his colleagues: "Music is rarely welcome in a drama. Listen to it in *L'Arlésienne;* you will be astonished to see that it is used solely as a stopgap. At the end of the third scene, the actors go offstage to dine; the stage is empty, and the action will not start again until the meal is over. Immediately M. Bizet takes the floor, and there you have a dance of the violins. Very pretty the music may be; useless it certainly is. . . . The fact that all the choruses are sung in the wings goes to prove that the music is not an integral part of the work; it is an ornament appliquéd on as an afterthought. *L'Arlésienne* would

---

[3] Marcel Proust wrote to Daudet's son Lucien, in September 1918: "The story of the last act of *L'Arlésienne* should be called to the attention of all authors so that they may know the futility of writing. I know of nothing so discouraging. And the example strikes me even more forcibly in relation to *L'Arlésienne,* a work in which I have never found solace. The mortal sorrow it engenders is the cause of practically all the follies I have committed in life and of those which are still left for me to commit. Instead of the little boy in my book having been deluded by the example of Swann, *L'Arlésienne* is what I should have said. *L'Arlésienne* and *Sapho,* do you know of any other works that cause such incurable wounds?" Lucien Daudet, *Autour de soixante lettres de Marcel Proust,* Paris, 1928, 212.

not make a good opera; it is unfortunate that it doesn't make a better play." "

At the fourteenth performance (there were twenty-one), a friend of Bizet's sat in the orchestra among only thirty other spectators in that section of the theatre. But the actors played to this nearly empty house "as conscientiously, as earnestly, with as much emotion, as though it were a great opening night. They understood the play and were intoxicated by the music. The few scattered spectators, too, were united by the feeling they shared. There were some among them who had come back for the tenth time." "

Only two music critics reviewed *L'Arlésienne:* Ernest Reyer and Johannès Weber. To the latter, Bizet expressed his thanks: "Leaving aside the sympathy that you show for me, there is still enough praise in your article to give me great satisfaction.—I was happy with this little score of *L'Arlésienne,* as several musicians whose approval I seek have seriously encouraged me." "

Among them was Reyer, who wrote in the *Journal des Débats:* "I take my good where I find it, even at the Vaudeville when they play music there. And with the score of *L'Arlésienne* we are far removed from the folderols of the good old days. . . . The twenty-six musicians played this charming score . . . with rare perfection, an irreproachable ensemble, the most sensitive variations, and exquisite feeling. No one is more skillful nor more ingenious than M. Bizet. What other composer would have made better use of such feeble resources? This handful of virtuosos conducted by M. Constantin's valiant bow should be heard. Obviously if their chief had not told them that they had the work of an eminent musician on their stands, they themselves would have known it. . . . Backstage there is also a harmonium played by a friend of the house; sometimes it is M. Ernest Guiraud, sometimes young Antony de Choudens, and sometimes M. Bizet himself. For twenty-six musicians are included in the budget, and twenty-seven there cannot be. What an odd little economy for M. Carvalho's theatre! . . . The idea of reinforcing such a small orchestra with a piano is excellent. Obviously, arpeggios on the piano do not replace a harp, but the *forte* considerably augments the sonority of the basses and gives more firmness to that of the wind instruments. One need hardly add that M. Bizet did not think of using the piano in any other way, and that in not one piece in the score does the piano serve as an orchestral substitute.

"The music written by M. Bizet for the play *L'Arlésienne* consists of twenty-seven numbers; they are not all of equal importance, but all of them are treated with extreme care, and it is a true feast for a musician to listen to these fine harmonies, these elegantly shaped phrases, and these charming orchestral details. . . . Go and see *L'Arlésienne,* you young musicians who as yet are but a hope to your professors, and perhaps you will feel encouraged and more eager to work when you see the degree of talent reached by one who only a few years ago was sitting like you on the school benches." "

Massenet, after attending the opening, returned to see *L'Arlésienne* a fortnight later. "If your music impressed me and charmed me the first time," he told Bizet, "I have found quite another enjoyment in it since I have come to know the score and have heard again all these lovely, poetic things.—Some of the four-measure *mélodrames* are indescribable pictures, whole landscapes.

"There has been talk of a project for a suite from *L'Arlésienne* using the title of the play. It seems to me *bound* to be *successful,* and I am longing to know the choice of pieces and the sequence. They say that Pasdeloup is enthusiastic over your score. There is not an artist who doesn't place this work in the first rank of new creations.

"To attempt, to *know how to express,* and to *succeed*—that is the goal! . . ." "

Massenet's prognosis of success for the suite Bizet drew from *L'Arlésienne* was wholly accurate. Pasdeloup played it on November 10 to overwhelming applause only three weeks after the closing of the play. Daudet found no such immediate palliative for the failure of his work. "I am sunk in my armchair by my fire with my pipe," he wrote to Bizet, "I am two hundred and fifty-eight years old. And to think of having to start work again! . . . I shan't mention *L'Arlésienne,* for it is dead. *Requiescat!*—but it's hard to bear!" " After the performance of the suite, he wrote: "An echo of your success on Sunday has reached me. We were very happy about it. But ruthless as you are, is it true that they didn't play the lovely entr'acte of the family council? Don't you know that it is wonderfully beautiful, eloquent, heart-rending? When we have dark weather here, I ask my wife to play it; and instantly my heart swells like a sponge.—If ever you come to Champrosay, I will talk to you about an idea for an *opéra-comique* in 3 acts which I have just found in an English novel." [4]

Here again, as after each of Bizet's failures in the theatre, a fresh opportunity was offered him. But by the end of 1872, *Carmen* was already taking shape in his mind.

---

[4] In the copy of the play he presented to Bizet, Daudet wrote: "To my dear companion, Georges Bizet, in friendship and admiration." Bizet, in the presentation copy of the score, wrote: "Let me tell you once again, my dear Daudet, how proud I am to have had my name attached to your admirable play. I shall never forget the days we spent together. Be strong and disdainful. Affectionately yours, Georges Bizet." Bizet's copy of the play in collection of the author. Daudet's copy of the score courtesy of Mrs. Mary A. Benjamin, New York.

CHAPTER  XXIV

Toward *Carmen*

While *L'Arlésienne* was still in rehearsal, Bizet started preparing *Carmen* and thinking of some chamber music he hoped to write during the winter. "I feel that the time for production is here," he wrote to a friend, "and I no longer want to lose a day." [n] But obstacles in the way of composing *Carmen* were many.

There were the more than fifty rehearsals he attended while supervising the revival of Gounod's *Roméo et Juliette* at the Opéra-Comique, a task he had undertaken immediately after the closing of *L'Arlésienne*. Gounod himself, after spending nearly a year at home in an attempted reconciliation with his wife, had fled back to London to the peace and protection of Mrs. Weldon's house in Tavistock Square. Bizet's intimate knowledge of *Roméo* and a desire on Gounod's part again to help his former protégé made him the master's natural choice as deputy.

Bizet, too, had a double motive for accepting the responsibility. He needed money, and, having more or less avoided Gounod during his stay in France, was glad of the opportunity to resume relations with his old friend. But to bridge the gap tactfully and not too evasively was not easy for Bizet. In a letter written in October 1872, he plunged immediately into basic matter that he had apparently never before mentioned to the master: "My dear Gounod, Neither absence nor silence can break the ties that bind us. You were the beginning of my life as an artist. I spring from you. You are the cause, I am the consequence. I can now admit that I was afraid of being absorbed, and you must have noticed the effect of these misgivings. Today I think I am more master of my craft, and I no longer feel anything but the benefits of your salutary and decisive influence. I don't think that I am being ungrateful to our dear Halévy in crediting you with what is so legitimately your due. I know that your fame has nothing to gain thereby. So it is to your heart that I speak, and I am sure of being understood.—I do not know, my dear Gounod, your reasons for staying away from us!—We think of you often. We miss you and love you always. We need you here badly. . . ." "

Gounod purported to feel "profound astonishment" at Bizet's fear of being "absorbed" by him. "A companion, a friend, even a good example," he hoped he had been, but "a cause, a source, a master, to those titles I have no right. . . . Even if I had the slightest claim to the latter, I could not see the legitimacy of your fears. No master, *whoever he may be,* can any more annihilate a personality than he can create one. . . . Personality is the direct expression, the involuntary emanation, the inseparable physiognomy of a being; it is *indelible.* You have too musical a nature not to have *your* own musical nature. Neither your more or less tardy bursting into bloom nor the more or less numerous and complex conditions of assimilation that have *contributed* to your entire development has anything to do with it. . . . Here you are now, *named,* that is to say *distinct,* detached from the mass, emerged from confusion, and your fame will have the right to belong to you as you will have belonged to it." "

If Gounod's professed "astonishment" at learning of Bizet's fear of his musical influence seems obtuse and insincere, Bizet's own profession of ignorance of the motivation of Gounod's personal life certainly laid the disciple open to suspicions of hypocrisy. ["You say: 'I don't know your reasons for staying away from us,'"] Gounod wrote. ["*Cher ami,* I am astonished that you should not know them, having lived as close to me as you did for so long. Are you quite sure of your ignorance?—In that case, it is not up to me to dissipate it. These are things which at the very most one has the right to moan about to those who do know the cause. The key that must open the door to my return is not in my hands. This absence is cruel for me; all the ties that you know I have can leave you no doubts about that. Only the fact that my absence is a necessity and my exile a duty could make me persist in continuing my exile; and this duty, which is incumbent upon me, cannot cease by my will alone."] "

The opening performance of *Roméo et Juliette* at the Opéra-Comique on January 20, 1873, left Bizet theoretically free to devote himself to composing. But his work was continually punctuated by interruptions, not the least among them the presence of a baby in the house. "We had rather a sharp upset this morning," he wrote to his mother-in-law in a hastily scrawled, penciled note. "Jacques seemed to be very ill, and we were worried. Thank heaven, our fears were immediately allayed. Doctors Parrod and Dufour came to reassure us. It's only a bad cold and a slight bronchitis.—I repeat, we are absolutely reassured. . . . but I will not leave my *baby* [*sic*] tomorrow evening. . . . " "

As Jacques grew old enough to crawl, he was allowed to play on the floor of his father's study, where neither the chattering of a pet red-and-gray parrot nor the games Jacques played with Jean, the son of the maid, Marie, lessened Bizet's ability to concentrate. Occasionally, however, a crisis arose. One day when the older boy was amusing the baby by tossing a little balloon to him, the toy hit a candle and exploded. Jacques's tears and cries of disappointment interrupted his father in the delicate task of drying, with a special powder, the parts of a score he had been copying. Bizet leaped up from his desk, took the baby in his arms, and promised him a new balloon immediately. The father's gentleness and good temper on this occasion so impressed the boy Jean that, as an old man, during his final illness he related the incident to his doctor. "

Another adolescent boy retained throughout his long life the memory of a visit to Bizet during the time he was composing *Carmen* and *Patrie*. Jacques-Emile Blanche, son of Dr. Blanche, introduced into Bizet's study by Geneviève's cousin and neighbor, Valentine Halévy, found himself in a room hung with flowered cretonne. The future painter remarked a disorder that seemed to him "artistic" or bohemian. "The beautiful Geneviève, in a dressing-gown, was lying on a sofa," he wrote nearly fifty years later. "I can still see her black eyes, feverish, deep-set. She seemed a sort of gentle Judith, pale as a camelia under her helmet of brown hair; her mouth, with its thick, quivering lips, drooping at the corners. . . . At the piano-desk [1]—an invention of Fromental Halévy's, specially made for him by Erard—Bizet was working.

---

[1] This extraordinary piece of furniture had a piano built into the table on one side and a clavier hidden behind false drawers.

An enormous head, a Diocletian with glasses, hunched up in his pea-jacket, a red scarf around his neck, his feet in Turkish slippers. At the request of Mlle Valentine, he opened the score of his overture, *Patrie,* played for us the instrumental parts of the score, whistling the notes he couldn't play with his hands. I was in an ecstasy, wordless. He asked me whether I liked the music. I dissolved in tears." "

In the apartment above, Henri Ravina, pianist and composer, gave piano lessons continually. But Bizet remained undisturbed. "He was the only composer I have ever known," remarked Charles Lecocq, "who could work while hearing music." " Hardened to such interference from childhood, when he had practiced the piano while his father taught singing in the next room, he was afflicted only by the lessons that he gave to bolster his income. One of his pupils, an American girl, remembered that "M. Bizet did not seem to want pupils. . . . When . . . Mamma asked him if he would take me, he gave an impetuous toss of his head, with an 'Ah!' as if annoyed by such a question. 'Oh, well, I'll try her for a while; you know I don't have much patience with pupils.' . . .

"At first he came to our place. They were half hour lessons and 20 francs. He was supposed to come at three o'clock. You never saw a more irregular man. We would wait, wait, wait; and I was always glad if I thought he was not coming, for I was afraid of him. . . . Not that he ever scolded, but the way he would look at you through those eye-glasses! Our apartment had several rooms strung along one after the other. When M. Bizet arrived he would often have to knock at all the doors and hunt us up. . . . One day he became impatient at finding no one, and we heard him stop in the adjoining room . . . and rap on the floor with his cane, exclaiming: *'Est-ce qu'on m'entend? Qu'est-ce que je viens faire ici? Est-ce qu'on croit que j'ai du temps à gaspiller comme ça?'*

"He would usually go away and leave something in the room —often left on the piano the banknotes that Mamma had paid him; always forgot his overcoat on the rack in the hall, and once in a while the maid would run after him with his hat. He did not appear to relish the idea of receiving pay; apparently disliked to handle money or think of it; treated my lessons as though they were a favor to us. . . . He never seemed to realize that I existed in flesh and blood; scarcely ever looked at me or touched me. . . . I was merely a sort of concept taking a music lesson! He . . . always left me feeling that no one could be doing more wretchedly; that I was utterly stupid, hopeless. Once in a great while, though, he would say: *'Pas mal, pas trop mal,'* and then I felt elated. . . .

"I would practice and work over my lessons, and they were hard ones. Think of Chopin's Second Scherzo all at a clip, fifteen or twenty pages. . . . I would think my lesson was going to be perfect, and then when he would come in, in his handsome, restless way, it was all up with my playing for the day. . . .

"He was as uneasy as a lion in a cage during the lesson; moved about the room, sitting down and getting right up again, looking everywhere but at the piano. I often thought he was paying no attention to my playing and sometimes . . . would make little slips in fingering. Then he would say savagely: *'Je ne dors pas! Je ne dors pas!'* It has been a marvel to me to this day how he could detect the slightest error in fingering, and be looking at a picture on the other side of the room. He never touched my piano, never played a lesson through for me at our house; said that he did not want to make apes of his pupils. . . .

"He had no voice . . . said that if he had one, he would have been a great singer. He hummed, always getting tremendously excited when the music became triumphant. When I would come to the crowning passage in Chopin's Second Scherzo he would become half mad. He would rush up and down the room, crying out to me: 'This is the climax! Throw your whole soul into it! Don't miss a note! Play as if you were saying something.'

"He was very plump and vigorous—a very showy, attractive man without ever thinking that he was or seeming to care what his effect was on the other people. He had light-brown hair and a full beard, almost russet or reddish-brown. His eyes were dark gray or blue. He dressed with extreme care and for his own personal satisfaction. He wore the finest linen I ever saw. His gloves were *gants de Suède*—ladies' gloves—very long, soft, light-brown, with no buttons. And when he would come in and strip off his gloves, throw them on the piano and reveal those beautiful hands! They were hands of shell—the palms all shelvy, with pearl layers of flesh and bluish traceries between. They were chubby, white, soft—not large. He always said that one must have large hands for the piano. . . . He had a lovely complexion—pink and white. But with all his dreaminess, his nonchalant, artistic temperament, he did not impress one as being an ethereal person. He was too healthy, too thoroughly rammed with life, for that.

"And what a gourmand for sweets! He was crazy for bonbons, cakes, *friandises.* . . . He always had *petits fours* at four o'clock. . . . As soon as he saw the bonbon dish at our house he would make for it and eat what there was in it.

"After about a year M. Bizet said one day: 'I am too busy to be giving lessons. If you are to keep on you will have to come *chez moi* hereafter.' . . . At home M. Bizet seemed a different man. When he was *chez nous* he was ill at ease, *gêné,* evidently annoyed at the thought of giving lessons, so he rarely stayed longer than the half hour. *Chez lui* he seemed glad to see us, and wanted to visit, especially when Mamma happened to go with us. He would frequently be half the afternoon giving me my half-hour. He talked, showed pictures, and would bring in his beautiful baby. He was very proud of it. Mme Bizet would almost always come in. . . .

"Here we discovered, too, how he loved to play the piano. . . . He was a pianist of the highest order—superb and brilliant, full of sentiment, *entrain,* fire—spontaneous, colorful, yet having all the technique and precision of the Conservatoire.

"I took my lessons in the salon. His studio was adjoining. . . . Sometimes he would excuse himself during the lesson and go in to the piano in the study, close the door, and work over some strain that would be running in his head. This proved to be *Carmen.* He was full of the airs of *Carmen* at this time, so I heard most of them sooner than almost anyone, but of course I did not know what they were. We only knew he was at work on an opera. He would hum the melodies and develop them on the piano. I recall particularly the Toreador song and *'J'irai danser la séguedille,/ Et boire du Manzanilla!'* " [n]

The early months of work on *Carmen* were interrupted, too, by complications over the playing of his *Petite Suite d'orchestre* from *Jeux d'enfants,* which had been ready for performance since the autumn of 1871, but which was not published until seven years after his death. Pasdeloup had had the work in rehearsal during the season of 1872, but Bizet had withdrawn it. "You were astonished to see me carry off the parts and the score of my

Petite Suite d'orchestre," he wrote to the conductor at that time. "I thought I had let you guess how discouraged I was after the three fruitless rehearsals. I am convinced today that it was all much too small for the Concerts Populaires. You felt it yourself, and only your kindness prevented your letting me know your impressions. . . . I shall not try to hide from you the profound and serious regret I should feel at finding myself banished from the Concerts Populaires. You are, at the moment, the sole resource of musicians who believe! . . ." ⁿ

Fortunately, by 1873 other opportunities were available.² In that year the Concert National (precursor of today's Association Artistique des Concerts Colonne) was founded with the aid of the publisher Georges Hartmann. Edouard Colonne, as director and conductor of these concerts, was very eager to have a new work by Bizet on his first program. Invited by the composer to lunch at his house to discuss the matter, Colonne found some difficulty in concentrating on the subject in hand in the presence of a bored and nervous Geneviève who flipped bread pellets at him during most of the meal. The *Petite Suite d'orchestre* was played at the first Concert National on March 2, 1873. This charming work, which in the twentieth century has supplied the music for at least two ballets, was received with polite applause and not repeated during Bizet's lifetime. It was only the first of many new works by contemporary French composers introduced by Colonne. At a concert of sacred music, on Holy Thursday, 1873, César Franck, at the age of fifty, made his public debut as a composer with the performance of his *Redemption*. After a series of rehearsals that rivaled Pasdeloup's in inefficiency and disorganization, Franck's chorus was performed by an orchestra that disliked the work, a chorus that sang off key, and a soloist who regarded the music as "queer and ineffective." A bored audience dwindled away until, at the end of the concert, only fifty people remained. Not so the following day, Good Friday, when Mas-

---

² Immediately after the war, in February 1871, Saint-Saëns, with the co-operation of Romain Bussine, a professor of singing, Guiraud, César Franck, Fauré, and Lalo, organized the Société Nationale de Musique to encourage the performance of the works of young French composers. Bizet was one of the first members. At the earlier concerts, only chamber music was played, but soon, and for many years thereafter, the society played an important part in winning recognition for French music, giving eight or ten orchestral concerts each year.

senet's *Marie-Magdeleine* had its *première* at Colonne's second concert of sacred music.

This "sacred drama in 3 acts and 4 parts," with a text by Louis Gallet, the author of *Djamileh,* had been ready for performance more than a year earlier. But then, when Massenet played the piece for Pasdeloup, the conductor remained expressionless and silent. At the end of the audition, after Massenet had gathered up his score, the conductor patted him on the shoulder and said: "Well, my boy, you have certainly earned your dinner." But if Pasdeloup regarded the work as "ridiculous and absurd," Pauline Viardot was so much impressed when Massenet played it for her that she offered to come out of retirement to sing the leading role. She was still as powerful as twenty years earlier, when she had helped launch Gounod on his career. Now her influence and personal appearance in Massenet's work also opened the golden gates to him. For *Marie-Magdeleine* was a frantic, hysterical success.

All Paris talked the next day of an oratorio "full of life and love and melody!" Saint-Saëns, who could not be taxed with any prejudice in Massenet's favor, described *Marie-Magdeleine* as "the most audacious experiment made by any musician in Paris since Berlioz's *L'Enfance du Christ.* . . . What is new is the realistic aspect of this work by Messrs. Gallet and Massenet," wrote the author of *Samson et Dalila.* "They have given it an Oriental color . . . have omitted grandeur and *prestige légendaire.* The public, always in quest of dainties, has approved. Massenet's music . . . is Gounod at bottom, but concentrated, refined and crystallized. . . . The pleasing thing about *Marie-Magdeleine* is the felicity with which the composer has expressed sentiments of extreme delicacy. A breath would have tarnished the love of Jesus and Marie Magdeleine. M. Massenet has preserved all its real purity." [n] Ernest Reyer found Massenet's oratorio "powerful and pleasing . . . full of nobility and Christian poetry," and hazarded the guess that *Marie-Magdeleine* would "contribute to the rising fame of M. Jules Massenet what *L'Enfance du Christ* did for the glory of Hector Berlioz." [n]

Bizet's reaction was more personal. "Never has our modern school produced anything comparable," he wrote to Massenet. "You drive me frantic, you rascal! You brazen musician, you!

My wife has just put *Marie-Magdeleine* under lock and key; this is a telling detail. Hanged if you aren't becoming singularly disturbing! . . . No one is more sincere in his admiration and affection for you than your Bizet." [n]

Bizet's admiration for Massenet's oratorio manifested itself in the sincerest form of flattery. Soon after the triumphant success of *Marie-Magdeleine,* he asked Gallet to write him a text based on the life of the patron saint of Paris, to be called *Geneviève de Paris.* (One biographer has suggested that Bizet's choice of saint was a tribute to his wife. The miraculous appearance of St. Geneviève to his aunt, Mme Delsarte, part of the lore he absorbed as a child, may also have given him a certain sense of family feeling for this saint.)

Wholehearted respect for Massenet's talent did not prevent Bizet's recognizing him as a dangerous rival. "That little fellow is about to walk all over us," he remarked to Gallet. Nor, in spite of Bizet's susceptibility to what in his youth he had called "even the externals of friendship," did Massenet's musical gifts or personal charm blind him to his fellow-composer's notorious defects of character. Massenet's devouring ambition and jealousy of his rivals were too strong to be hidden under the excessive flattery he practiced. Indeed, on one occasion his insincerity aroused such rage in Bizet that only his own obvious integrity prevented his alienating his best friend. At a party at Edouard Lalo's, attended by Saint-Saëns, Massenet, Reyer, and many other musicians, Guiraud arrived, as always, very late. His ballet *Gretna Green,* a banal trifle, had just been given at the Opéra. Massenet immediately started overwhelming the shy, retiring Guiraud with egregious flattery. " 'Shut up,' " Bizet shouted at Massenet. " 'Shut up. You make me sick. All of us here love Guiraud as much as you do. As for me, Guiraud is my brother. Nevertheless *Gretna Green* is a failure. We are all miserable because Guiraud hasn't done a better work. But we don't tell him that we admire *Gretna Green* because we *don't.* And you, who don't admire it any more than we do, you call it a masterpiece! You're a false friend. You make me sick.' Massenet, dumbfounded, crushed, tried to defend himself, but in vain. In the meantime Guiraud, the subject of this raging flood of cold water, had the air of a dog under a garden hose." [n]

By the summer of 1873, obstacles over which Bizet had no

control caused him to postpone work on *Carmen*. More, even, than *Djamileh* this new project split the two directors of the Opéra-Comique. When Ludovic Halévy informed du Locle of his and Meilhac's agreement with Bizet to use Mérimée's story as the basis for a libretto, that director approved. "But," he said to Halévy, "de Leuven will be horrified at such a subject. You go to see him. He likes you very much. Perhaps you can convince him." The task was not easy. No sooner had Halévy stated his proposal than de Leuven interrupted him. *"Carmen!"* he protested. "Mérimée's *Carmen?* Isn't she killed by her lover?—And that background of thieves, gypsies, cigar-makers!—At the Opéra-Comique, a family theatre! The theatre where marriages are arranged! Every night five or six boxes are taken for that purpose. You will frighten off our audience.—It's impossible."

Halévy persisted, explained that Carmen would be "softened, toned down," that "a pure *opéra-comique* character had been introduced, a very innocent, very chaste young girl." There were gypsies, he admitted, but "comic" gypsies. As for the inevitable death scene, it would be "sneaked in at the end of a very lively, very brilliant act, played in bright sunlight on a holiday with triumphal processions, ballets, and joyous fanfares." After a long struggle, de Leuven capitulated. But as Halévy left his office, he said: "Please try not to have her die. Death on the stage of the Opéra-Comique! Such a thing has never been seen!—Never! Don't make her die. I beg of you, my dear child, don't." ⁿ

Murder never was committed on the stage of the Opéra-Comique under de Leuven's direction. Six months after this conversation, he resigned, largely because of his antipathy to *Carmen*. Meanwhile he and du Locle were involved in financial difficulties that hampered any immediate plans for the production of a new work and resulted in a lawsuit the following year. Discouraged over this delay, Bizet welcomed a proposal by Jean-Baptiste Faure, the great tenor at the Opéra, who had just sung the role of Paddock in Diaz's prize-winning, but unsuccessful version of *La Coupe du Roi de Thulé.* Faure suggested to Gallet, librettist of *La Coupe,* that he and Bizet collaborate on a grand opera with a heroic leading role. A concentrated search ensued before a subject satisfactory to the tenor could be found. Insufficient charm or nobility of character in the hero caused him to reject a number of Bizet's and Gallet's suggestions. "This Faure wants everything," Bizet remarked. "Not only must he be great, handsome, generous, and strong, but also his praises must be sung even when he is offstage." [3] The composer himself finally resolved the dilemma.

In an old copy of the *Journal pour tous* he found a translation of Guillén de Castro's *La Jeunesse du Cid*. He immediately took the magazine to Gallet and told him, "This is what I want to do. It's not Corneille's *Le Cid*, it's the original *Cid* with its truly Spanish color. There is a scene in it, the scene with the beggar, that is marvelous. Look at it. I am sure Faure will be satisfied. The Cid as a lover, as a son, a Christian, heroic, triumphant—what more could he ask?" Faure's immediate satisfaction with the role of the noble Spaniard enabled Bizet to spend the summer composing the opera, which he called *Don Rodrigue*.

Throughout the summer of 1873, which he spent at Port-Marly, Bizet wrote to the librettist in Paris letters that, in their emphasis on detail, characterization, and the importance of dramatic timing, recall his correspondence with Galabert on the subject of *La Coupe du Roi de Thulé*. (One can only regret that because of Bizet's proximity to Halévy and Meilhac in Paris most of the collaboration on *Carmen* was carried on orally and therefore remains unrecorded.) While *Don Rodrigue* was in progress, Bizet wrote in one of many letters to Gallet: "The fourth act has never worried me (that's the one in which the episode with the beggar takes place), while the love duet has been done so many times and so well—For it is always the same, Roméo and Juliette, Chimène and Rodrigue, Raoul and Valentine, Faust and Marguerite—Always there is the profound sentiment of love—human—which must be expressed in new forms. It is, in short, the real touchstone of the dramatic composer! . . ." On another occasion: "I am really embarrassed at asking so much work of you and upsetting what was so well done, but you can easily rewrite a few lines, while it would be very difficult for me to do over things that I am satisfied with and that came to me with an authority I would call inspiration if the word weren't ridiculously pretentious."

By the end of October, Bizet had *Don Rodrigue* ready to play for Faure and Gallet. His score contained only the vocal

---

[3] Gallet, 63. Unless otherwise noted, the accounts of *Don Rodrigue* are based on this source.

parts; the accompaniment he played from memory. He sang all the parts "in the poorest voice in the world," says Gallet, "but bringing to life each phrase with his own inner passion, hardly stopping between acts, and not leaving the piano until he had played, sung, recited every word of this work, which seemed to us at that time to have definitely come to life." Until long after midnight the three men discussed the work—whether Halanzier would like it, the best way to persuade him to produce it at the Opéra.

The following day, Bizet, after attempting unsuccessfully to see Gallet, wrote to him: "I don't want to go to bed without having a word from you. What is your impression of yesterday's session? What did you talk about on the way home? What do you hope for? What do you fear? And when shall I see you?" A day or two later Faure expressed his satisfaction with the work to Bizet, who "was really touched by his cordial kindness." But more than good will was needed to bring about a production of *Don Rodrigue* at this time. For on October 28, only a few days after Faure had expressed his determination to approach the director, the old Opéra burned to the ground. The present Opéra, which had been in the process of building since before the war, was not yet ready. So, after a few months' hiatus, the company moved to the Salle Ventadour, where traditional works from the repertory were given. When it came to producing a new work, Halanzier gave precedence to *L'Esclave* by Edmond Membrée, a piece distinguished only by its mediocrity and the fact that its fifty-two-year-old composer had been waiting for over twenty years for a production of his opera.

Bizet never finished *Don Rodrigue*, and a modern critic, after examining the manuscript fragments, found them less good than they seemed to Bizet's friends, with "less character than might be expected from a work on a Spanish subject written at the same time as *Carmen*." [4]

While still at work on *Don Rodrigue*, Bizet again undertook to represent Gounod, this time at rehearsals of the incidental music he had written in England for Jules Barbier's play *Jeanne d'Arc*. The producer of the play was Offenbach, who had taken over the Théâtre de la Gaîté, where he hoped to compensate for

---

[4] In 1885, *Le Cid*, music by Massenet, libretto by Gallet, Blau, and Dennery, was given at the Opéra.

his recent failures by giving serious works. Bizet's antipathy to Offenbach was counterbalanced by his satisfaction in doing a service for both Barbier and Gounod, as well as by the opportunity of earning additional money by making a piano reduction of Gounod's choruses. For Barbier the performance of *Jeanne d'Arc* was "the first ray of light that has warmed me for a long time." ⁿ In mourning since the death of his son-in-law, Bizet's friend Gustave Chaudey, the first hostage shot by the *communards,* Barbier was both personally and professionally grateful for Bizet's cooperation.

Jeanne d'Arc, after opening early in November, ran for only thirty performances. Gounod's music received very poor notices, and Offenbach abandoned his grandiose scheme of following *Jeanne d'Arc* with *A Midsummer Night's Dream* to Mendelssohn's music and *The Ruins of Athens* to Beethoven's. Instead he did a revival of *Orphée aux enfers* with a text rewritten by the original librettists, Hector Crémieux and Ludovic Halévy. The latter had, for the time being, finished his part of the work on the libretto of *Carmen.*

Bizet's disappointment over the continued postponement of *Carmen* and the abortive fate of *Don Rodrigue* was somewhat mitigated by a commission for an overture from Pasdeloup, who at the same time asked Massenet and Guiraud for similar pieces to be played in the winter of 1874. For the main theme of this overture, called *Patrie,*⁵ Bizet took a march from the fifth act of *Don Rodrigue. Patrie* dedicated to Massenet, and destined to an even greater popular success than the *L'Arlésienne* suite, is of the genre of Tchaikovsky's *1812.* Echoes of the Russian composer's admiration for Bizet are audible in *1812,* which was written not long after Tchaikovsky spoke of his eagerness to secure a

---

⁵ *Patrie:* "There is some mystery about the title. It has nothing to do with Sardou's play *Patrie,* then being converted into an opera by Paladilhe. Pigot says that this rumor was put about by malignant persons who wished to suggest that Bizet wanted to set Sardou's work, but had been rejected in favor of Paladilhe. . . . Pigot goes on to say that Bizet, though he had the war of 1870 in mind, did not wish to reopen a sore subject in an age of appeasement, and so by poetic fiction substituted for France 'the mighty shade of Poland in her death agony, always conquered but always resurgent, whose ineffaceable memory and sacred name live forever in the hearts of her scattered children.'" Dean, *Bizet,* 83.

In a letter to Lacombe, Bizet wrote in February 1871: "How are they taking down your way the situation of little Poland for whose incidents we are responsible, or rather our stupidity and our immorality?"

score of *Patrie*. But whereas the Russian overture, however hackneyed it may have become, still bears the earmarks of its composer's great gifts, *Patrie* embodies only the weaknesses of Bizet's eclecticism. It is both flamboyant and tired-sounding.

In spite of all his other work, Bizet managed to write enough of *Carmen* so that it seemed timely by the end of the summer to choose the artist to sing the leading role. The first choice for Carmen mentioned in the press was Zulma Bouffar, a popular charmer who had started her career singing risqué French songs in a Cologne café, where she had been discovered by Offenbach. In his and Meilhac and Halévy's *La Vie Parisienne* and *Les Brigands* she had won great success during the previous decade. Bizet's contempt for Offenbach's *Le Roi-Carotte,* in which Bouffar had been playing recently was in itself sufficient reason to suspect the validity of this rumor. It evaporated when a gossip columnist announced that "Meilhac did *not* wish her to play the part because it was out of the question for Zulma to be stabbed." [n]

The first singer seriously considered for Carmen was Marie Roze, who had made her debut at the Comique in 1865 in an opera by Auber in which she sang the part of an English girl. This "charming English vignette," wrote one critic, "is repeating her success at the Conservatoire in the theatre, where her position is progressing as rapidly as the beautifying of the new Paris." [n] More popular with the public than with the management, which found irritating her efforts to surround herself only with admirers, Marie Roze achieved her greatest success in London, where she remained for many years after marrying Henry Mapleson, the well-known impresario. Agreement as to her unsuitability for the part of Carmen followed a single interview. "I am entirely of your opinion," she wrote to Bizet on September 7, 1873. "The tragic end of *Carmen* had made me presuppose dramatic action that would modify the very scabrous side of this character; the explanations you were kind enough to make to me at the outset of our interview having showed me that the character was to be scrupulously respected, I understood immediately that the role would not suit me, or, more accurately, that I would not be suited to it.

"In spite of this conviction, I wanted to have you hear me sing, knowing your fine qualities and valuing your opinion, which I realize was entirely favorable.

"Will you ask Messrs. Halévy and Meilhac to forgive me for having made them climb my five flights of stairs? . . ." "

After Marie Roze's refusal of the part of Carmen, du Locle immediately offered it to Galli-Marié.

Galli-Marié: Delaborde

Galli-Marié, who was on tour when she received du Locle's offer, wrote to her friend Lhérie, the future Don José: "Your little marmoset of a director writes to ask if I wish to create Carmen. What is it?" " This letter to Lhérie she placed by mistake in an envelope addressed to du Locle; Lhérie in turn was surprised to find himself the recipient of a letter from Galli-Marié inscribed to "My dear Director." Fortunately du Locle placed his professional interests above his personal vanity and continued negotiations with Galli-Marié. When she returned to Paris and brought a pet marmoset with her to rehearsals, the director commented: "You're really fond of little marmosets, aren't you?"

Galli-Marié's ignorance of Mérimée's story is surprising, for there appears to have been something about her that suggested the atmosphere of Spain. When her friend George Sand was sent a collection of Spanish folk songs, *Las Muchachas,* she made a point of giving it to Galli-Marié. As early as 1864, a composer visualized her as Carmen. Only two years after her debut at the Comique, Victor Massé had asked Sardou to consider writing a libretto: "I figure that Mérimée's *Carmen* would be an original and remarkable creation for her. . . . Spain would have to be made strikingly true to life. . . . I would flatly accept Mérimée's conclusion. Carmen, as you remember, is killed by her lover." "

Apparently, even as mediocre and unimaginative a composer as Massé saw in Galli-Marié an embodiment of Mérimée's gypsy heroine. "She is small and graceful, moves like a cat, has an impish, pert face, and her whole personality seems unruly and mischievous. She acts as though she had been trained in the sound tradition of Molière; she sings in a full, fresh voice, piquant and mellow," " wrote a critic in 1862 after her overwhelmingly successful debut in Pergolesi's *La Serva Padrona.* In Grisar's *Les Amours du diable* the following year, she was "by turns piquant, tender, sardonic, and impassioned." In *Lara,* by Aimé Maillart, an opera based on Byron's poem, she played her part, dressed as a boy, "with feline grace and fierce energy." *Lara* was "a great success for Mme Galli-Marié, who is decidedly a most remarkable artist," Ludovic Halévy realized as early as 1864. "She sang and played the part with the rarest talent." " In 1866 she created the title role of Thomas's *Mignon,* making it so much her own that when the opera was later revived with another singer one critic protested: *"Mignon is* Galli-Marié; no other artist should sing it." "

Marie-Célestine-Laurence Galli-Marié was born in 1840, the daughter of Claude-Marie-Mécène Marié de l'Isle, who sang at the Opéra under the name of Marié. A very well-rounded musician, he also conducted a small orchestra of amateurs in which Massenet was tympanist while a pupil at the Conservatoire. Trained by her father, Galli-Marié made her debut at Strasbourg in 1859 and next sang in Italian at Lisbon. In 1862 Perrin, then director of the Opéra-Comique, heard her sing Balfe's *The Bohemian Girl* in French at Rouen and immediately engaged her for his theatre. From her first performance at the Comique, she was an outstanding success. Although her mezzo-soprano voice was far less striking than Mme Carvalho's, and she never achieved the status of Nilsson or Patti, she occupied for many years a unique position as singing-actress, not unlike Mary Garden's at a later time.

As a girl of fifteen the future Carmen married a sculptor called Galli, who died in 1861. No rumors about her private life appeared in print until 1951 when the critic Henry Malherbe, Director of the Opéra-Comique from 1946 to 1948, stated in his book, *Carmen,* that Galli-Marié had fallen in love with Bizet, that they often quarreled, that after a particularly violent dispute shortly before Bizet's final illness, they broke off relations. In print, M. Malherbe offers no proof of these statements, but in conversation he gave as authority for this backstage gossip the word of Lhérie, the first Don José, who celebrated his ninetieth birthday in 1934, and of Bouhy, the original Escamillo, who survived until 1929. That the gossip existed, that the company interpreted in the most obvious way the relationship between the composer and the singer who brought his creation to life, is true. The same sort of talk, no doubt, circulated in the wings of the Burgtheater at Vienna some ninety years earlier when Mozart found joy and solace in his relationship with the artist who created the role of Susanna in *Le Nozze di Figaro*. With the words *"Für Mlle Storace und mich,"* he dedicated to her *"Ch'io mi scordi di te,"* a duet for voice and clavier which a recent biographer describes as "a declaration of love in music, the transfiguration of a relation that could not be realized except in this ideal sphere." [n] And at the Opéra-Comique itself, only a little over a quarter of a century after the first production of *Carmen*, it was assumed that the singer who first played Mélisande was inevitably the mistress of Debussy. Mary Garden faced frankly this interpretation of her relationship with the composer. In her autobiography she gives a clear analysis, documented by letters, of the understanding, even the intimacy that is almost bound to arise between a man of genius and the artist who, by bringing perfectly to life a character he has created, becomes a part of himself. Insufficient evidence precludes any specific analogy between Miss Garden's platonic friendship with the composer of *Pelléas et Mélisande* and Bizet's relationship with Galli-Marié.

In September 1873, immediately after playing *Carmen* for Galli-Marié, Bizet decided that she was right for the part. The chief obstacle in the way of a definite arrangement with her was the lack of funds at the Comique and the consequent haggling of the directors over the singer's salary. The composer, helpless in the matter, was obviously afraid that she would refuse the part. *"Cher Monsieur,"* she wrote to Bizet soon after the audition, "How can you possibly doubt my strong and sincere desire to be the interpreter of *your* music, particularly in a work like this one? I shall try to fit it into both my present and future engagements. Forgive me all the trouble I have caused you, and thank you for having thought of me. I assure you it would have been difficult for you to find anyone who admires your work more than your very devoted

Galli-Marié

"Write to me at 18 Cité Malesherbes, Paris. Your letters will reach me sooner."[1]

From Brussels, later in the month, she wrote again: *"Cher Monsieur,* I have received your two letters—the first sent from Paris with my costumes, and your little note yesterday. Tonight I am playing Mignon, and I am in a state of the most profound desolation!! Whom do you think I have for Wilhelm? Little Leroy. Yes, the one from the Opéra-Comique; impossible to get any other! He'd better not come and talk to me today!

"By now you should at last have arrived at a solution. I must say that I am waiting most impatiently, for I absolutely must reply to two or three directors who need to know for the sake of their repertoire whether or not I am coming. I have asked them for another week's delay. When that week is over, I can accept, can't I? If you happen to speak to that awful de Leuven, tell him that . . . *I do not know la demoiselle Paola Marié*[2] (a family affair too long to explain here). How odd of him to have had *that idea! Au revoir, cher Monsieur.* Quick, quick, quick, a reply, and you will oblige more than she can say your sympathetically devoted

Galli-Marié

"I am at the Hotel de Suède, but as I don't intend to stay here, address my letters to the theatre. I will tell the *concierge* to watch for them."

On her return to Paris from Brussels, Gali-Marié saw the composer, who had apparently, for the time being, been reassured by du Locle. Early in October, she wrote to Bizet from Mentone: *"Cher Monsieur,* When I saw you in Paris you told me that the question of salary was decided, that only the date was undecided, and that you asked only one thing of me—not to sign anything for after December 15. I have kept my word, and here I am, thunderstruck at your woebegone letter!! Everything you have been told is true, as it repeats what I told you in Paris—and besides your letter is so ambiguous that to tell the truth I didn't really understand it. Can you reply *immediately, poste restante* here, and express yourself more clearly? If you want my word of

---

[1] Galli-Marié to Bizet, n. d. Unpublished letter in collection of the author. All letters from Galli-Marié to Bizet in this chapter are unpublished and in collection of the author.
[2] Her sister.

honor not to tell anyone what you write me, I give it to you in advance. To make things surer for you, do you want me to make a final concession *for your work?*: a two- instead of a three-year contract and one month of leave per year, *in winter,* instead of four months' leave. If the month in winter is too difficult to get, replace it by two in summer.—So it's understood: an engagement for two years at 3000 frs. per month, one month of leave in winter every year or two months in summer. And lest you think this is a small concession, let me tell you that each of my months of leave can bring and has brought me 6 or 8000 frs.

"I assure you that I am profoundly sorry; nevertheless I have major reasons for being inflexible in the matter of salary!— If you were in Venice, as you say, we would have your *Carmen* translated, and I promise you that we would give it a great launching! For I am negotiating with Marini, the impresario of the Fenice.

"I assure you that I am less mercenary than I appear to be. I am very sorry that you are so unhappy, and I shall continue to hope that some way will be found to arrange all this.
Sympathetically and devotedly yours,
Galli-Marié

"Another idea: do you think it would be possible for me to sign a contract to play only your piece? And for how long might that be?"

From Mentone, Galli-Marié proceeded to Venice, where the picture of her in the city that he loved so much obviously aroused Bizet's emotions. *"Cher Monsieur,"* she wrote from the Hotel Royal Danieli on October 21, 1873. "Almost at the same time as your letter I had one from M. du Locle. . . . He talks about *Carmen,* and most pleasantly insists that I hasten my return, but in the long run he comes to no conclusion, and the fundamental question still remains in doubt. I know very well that M. du Locle is only ½ director, as he writes me, which is all the worse for me. For I am very sure that if it were otherwise, he would not hesitate so much over a matter of seeding for future harvest.—You ask me if I value you at all. You know very well that I understand and like your school and I should be very happy to interpret a work from it, particularly one signed by you, whose last two scores I know almost entirely by heart, both voice and accompaniment. The best proof I can give you is my *waiting* as I am

doing until the thing is decided in your favor before I reply to
the *bona fide* offers that have been made me. This having been
said, I shall not mention it again; these matters of advantage are
extremely distasteful to me, and it is agonizing for me to have to
consider and maintain my stand so firmly.—

"Your Venice is still worthy of the memory you have kept
of it. Its aspect is still as strange, its calm of a flooded city still
the same, and its gondolas, still as softly upholstered, continue to
be graciously guided by the calls of their gondoliers. I sprinkle
all this with lovely sunlight or a beautiful moon, and exclaim as
you do: how fortunate I am to be in Venice!

"However, *horresco referens!* Some little motorboats are
venturing into the *Gran Canale,* and the tower at the base of the
St. Mark campanile is being demolished to make way for . . .
who knows what! Oh, civilization!!!! As for the Church of San
Giovanni de Paolo, its Carpaccios are safe and sound; only the
Rosario chapel attached to it was burned down with its mag-
nificent Titian among other things and the inimitable bas-reliefs
that you must remember. The loss is estimated at 26 millions.
. . . In the church there are still some Tintorettos and two
Carpaccios of the greatest beauty.

"As I do not intend to return directly to Paris when I leave
Venice and cannot tell you ahead in what city in Italy I shall
be on a given day, be kind enough, if you have to write to me, to
address me at 18 Cité Malesherbes, from where your letter will
surely be forwarded."

Galli-Marié's uncertainty about her future plans grew out of
exigencies both personal and professional. She was not traveling
alone. Her companion was in all probability Emile Paladilhe, in
whose first opera, *Le Passant,* she had appeared a month before
the opening of *Djamileh.* It may be remembered that in spite of
Galli-Marié's offer to continue to sing in it at a greatly reduced
salary, the work ran only three nights. After this fiasco, Galli-
Marié continually tried to persuade directors to include *Le Passant*
in the repertoire of the provincial opera houses where she sang.
Most probably one of "the major reasons" she mentions for being
"so inflexible" in the matter of salary was her desire to maintain her
financial independence in order to help her lover's career. Not
long after her last letter to Bizet from Venice, she was again
touring the provinces. From somewhere in France in November

1873, she wrote to the painter Elie Delaunay, a close friend of Paladilhe and Bizet, as well as a great admirer of Geneviève, expressing the delight she and *"le doux Emilio"* felt at hearing that the artist had finished painting her portrait. "Show it, show it, by all means," she writes. "Make me very beautiful! But how can it resemble me? If I remember correctly, I gave you only two or three sittings. Would you like my big picture as Mignon, a life-size photograph? . . . That fire at the old Opéra must have been an enormous challenge to you. Lazy master that you are, that must have roused you a little! Now, at last we shall see your masterpieces! [3] As for me, I work, I work. . . . We have just been playing *Le Passant* with great success for our two friends: Emilio and Zanetto." [n] (Zanetto was the part Galli-Marié sang and that Sarah Bernhardt had acted in the play by François Coppée on which Paladilhe's opera was based.)

When Galli-Marié and Paladilhe became lovers no one can tell. As early as 1867 she had sung his song *"Mandolinata"* at a benefit, with such success that it achieved the popularity of a folk song. Shortly before the Siege of Paris in September 1870, she took refuge at Montpellier, where Paladilhe had rejoined his family. In the summer of 1872, she was forced to rest, having temporarily lost her voice, "worn out," as one critic said, "by the tearful airs of the eternal Mignon." From Switzerland, giving her address as "Mme Paladilhe, Hôtel Beau Rivage à Montreux," she wrote to Delaunay: *"Amico nostro,* Is it true for a moment that you have had the idea, the happy idea of coming to see us for a few days? Come right along. Our house is admirably situated, and don't be afraid of embarrassing us. We are a young couple, but also an old married pair. Do come. You would make us very happy.—The hotel is not too expensive and such a beautiful view, the lake, there at the bottom of the garden; opposite, and on both sides, the great mountains, most of them snow-covered—and the huge black pine trees! And close by, the old castle of Chillon! And above all the tranquillity, the great, the rare tranquillity! I am sure that if you came, you would leave here full of good ideas. . . . We are taking a room for you. . . . The maestro joins me in an affectionate handshake and we say: *au revoir.* Your trusty [*sic*] Galli-Marié." [n]

---

[3] Delaunay was one of the many artists engaged in painting murals for the new Opéra.

In December 1873, Galli-Marié was on tour, but her negotiations with du Locle on the subject of *Carmen* continued.
Early in the month, addressing him as "Hypersensitive Director!" she wrote: "What will happen to you if I accept, and you
see me next displaying the savage charms of pretty Carmen! A
fire at the Opéra-Comique, and we shall all be lost!!!

"Grant me time to send a telegram, to receive a reply and I
shall write to you again at once. Yours ever [*sic*], Galli-Marié." "

On December 18, she came to terms with du Locle: "Yes,
cher Monsieur, I accept—2500 per month—four months—
October 1874, November, December and January—12 times a
month—to create the *Carmen* of Messrs. Bizet, Meilhac, and
Halévy—

"Is that it, are you satisfied? That will make very nice performances at 208 frs. 33 cent. a piece!! *Misère* as they say in
the *faubourg* Antoine [*sic*]!

"However if the piece is successful, and if you prolong my
engagement, I want a little more, and you won't find me unfair,
will you . . . if I ask for 300 per night; for if it doesn't succeed,
all is over between us! Come now, grant me this right away for
once, without dragging me through the dust! (Particularly as in
this weather it is more likely to be mud!)

"How you have made my self-esteem suffer! How you despise the good Lord's poor actors!! Nevertheless I am inclined
to agree with you! But, look, what honorable trade is there that
brings in 12,000 francs in twenty-eight days? What a chatterbox,
what a chatterbox I am! The hope of seeing you again in 10
months makes me garrulous!

"I cannot accept your nice proposal to come back to Paris
for the month of January, because if I am not in Brussels I shall
be in Antwerp (still for 1000 an evening). . . . My best wishes
to M. Bizet. (I am sure that he will dine well tonight.)" "

A few days later, when Galli-Marié spent a day in Paris
to pick up her costumes at the Opéra, she saw neither Bizet nor
du Locle. But she wrote to the latter on January 2, 1874, from
Ghent: "I have signed with the Monnaie for a new series of 15
performances. It is no longer a matter of the anodyne, peaceful
role of Marguerite (in which, by the way, I have just had a
triumph here . . .) but of *Le Prophète, La Favorite, Il
Trovatore,* etc., etc. And I am not afraid of them!

"And by the way, it seems that you are very much entertained at the idea of my playing *Faust* and are promising yourself even more entertainment when you hear me sing it! If you will lend me Lhérie and Bouhy, somewhere near Paris so as not to tire you with a long journey, we will make you laugh indeed!!

"As for coming to Paris to talk to the kind authors of *Carmen,* I can't give you a definite date. Day before yesterday I gave up a fee to come and spend a few hours in my beloved city! Tell M. Bizet to use the *tessitura* of Marguerite for that part of my role not already done. His Mignon *tessitura* is too commonplace and rather bothers me. . . ." [n]

Not until the following spring or summer is there any evidence that Bizet again saw Mme Galli-Marié.

In the meantime, on February 15, 1874, he had one of the few triumphs of his lifetime. The audience that listened to Pasdeloup play the *Patrie* overture greeted that very minor work with even more enthusiasm than they had lavished on the suite from *L'Arlésienne.* Both Pasdeloup and Colonne performed *Patrie* a number of times that year, and it remained in the concert repertory for many seasons. Bizet had dedicated the work to Massenet, who wrote to him the day after the concert, which he had been unable to attend: "I have heard from *everybody* of your *great* success and the *salvos of applause.* In spite of your habitual attitude, you must be really happy about that day, and I want to express to you my sincere joy, *cher ami.* The work is so beautiful!—I saw my name beside yours, and again I tell you how flattered I am. . . . My wife is clamoring for your overture. Do sign a copy, which I shall go and pick up at Choudens's. Don't forget to give me this additional pleasure." [n]

Massenet is not alone in referring to Bizet's "habitual" melancholy during the year preceding the *première* of *Carmen.* Another composer, Henri Maréchal, on his return in 1874 from the Villa Medici, went immediately to call on Bizet, who questioned him with the utmost nostalgia about all the beloved landmarks in Rome. He asked to see the works that the younger man had composed "there, under the umbrella pines, of his cherished villa. To arrange this," Maréchal wrote, "we decided to lunch together every Sunday. . . . Lunch was always gay. . . . After lunch, Bizet would sit down at the piano and decipher the manuscripts I had brought with me. . . . Without hesitation, he would play an orchestral score on the piano with prodigious skill. . . . Then we would go into his study; pipes were lighted and our talk about art, about what audiences wanted, would last far into the afternoon. . . . During these conversations, I often sensed tears in his voice, but an immediate effort at self-control quickly suppressed them. . . . Many people had started to have doubts about this musician; he was aware of it . . . a secret sorrow that could not escape his friends. He smiled as he talked about all this . . . but underneath his laughter, the wound remained apparent." [n]

Maréchal, in omitting any reference to Geneviève at this time, was concurring in an unexpressed agreement among Bizet's close friends to reveal nothing of the increasingly strained relations between him and his wife. All but a handful of family letters written between the time of Jacques's birth and Bizet's death have been destroyed. The faithful Galabert, who until his death in 1913 treasured every word and note his master had written, kept no letters from Bizet written after 1873 because, as he told his son, he felt that they revealed facts about the marriage which Bizet would have wished to remain secret. But Bizet's letter to Carvalho in the summer of 1872 gave warning of a situation that was bound to worsen.

Early in 1874, Bizet and Geneviève spent two or three months apart. She went to Saint-Germain while he stayed in Paris.[4] One letter that he wrote to her during this period remains: "Dear Baby [sic], Your mother . . . tells me that she wants to have the child either constantly with her or not at all. We came to the latter arrangement.—Do give me the satisfaction of keeping Jacquot or sending him elsewhere. Your mother has informed Mme Brun [5] of the decision. So the question is settled, and I have had enough of this subject, which is beginning to besmirch me singularly.

"And how is your little head—in good order? I love you, I love you, I love you. Don't worry. Good-bye for the present. *Ton* baby [sic]." [n]

---

[4] On February 6, 1874, Bizet paid 28 francs to a lending library for a two-year subscription in the name of his wife. The address 22 rue de Douai has been crossed out on the receipt, and instead Mme Bizet's address is given as 6 Route de Versailles, St. Germain, the home of Ludovic Halévy. The fact that the subscription is for two years suggests that at that time the duration of the separation was undecided.

[5] The daughter of Hippolyte Rodrigues.

The news, in the spring of 1874, that *Carmen* was again postponed (rehearsals, which were to have started in August, were put off to October) hardly lessened the impact on Bizet of a very severe attack of throat angina. "I am not dawdling over my convalescence," he wrote in reply to an affectionate note from Mme Halévy. "Cutlets and roasts will take care of that! I shall come to see you Saturday perhaps. I am getting up to-morrow!—These abscesses have made me suffer acutely. But that is in the past—so it no longer exists." In a postscript he added: "I shall go to look at Bougival Sunday. . . ." [n]

The yellow brick villa-style house at Bougival where Bizet and his wife spent the summer of 1874 stands on a high bluff above the Seine. The garden reaches down to the river, where the composer greatly enjoyed swimming with his friend and neighbor, the pianist Delaborde. Among the many other artists who spent their summers at Bougival, a small town near Versailles, were Pauline Viardot, Turgenev, and Guiraud. In two months during the summer, Bizet orchestrated the full score of *Carmen*—1200 pages. This process seems somewhat to have restored his self-confidence, for he said to a friend at this time: "People make me out to be obscure, complicated tedious, more hampered by technical skill than lit by inspiration. Well, this time I have written a work that is all clarity and vivacity, full of color and melody. It will be entertaining. . . ." [n]

Bizet's work was interrupted several times in June by visits to Paris to confer with Saint-Georges and the influential critic, Blaze de Bury, on the possibilities of reviving one of Fromental Halévy's operas. (This inopportune notion had occurred to Mme Halévy during Bizet's recent illness.)

Galli-Marié, too, was in Paris during the early summer, and it seems probable that at this time Bizet's already warm feeling toward her as an artist crystallized into an attachment to the woman herself. In any case, it is clear from the change of tone in her letters to him that she did not reciprocate whatever emotion he may have felt. In addressing him she no longer uses the more friendly *"Cher Monsieur,"* but begins her letters with a formal *"Monsieur."* On June 25 she wrote: "I shall be at your house at 22 rue de Douai on Monday at 1 o'clock. I have no place of my own at the moment; I have moved, and nothing is yet in-stalled in my new apartment; that is why I am taking the liberty of making the appointment at your house. If, however, this doesn't suit you, please send me word at 18 Cité Malesherbes. I remain, *Monsieur,* sincerely yours, Galli-Marié."

On July 9: *"Monsieur,* I am waiting impatiently for the pieces we read at sight recently. If you will have them sent to 18 Cité Malesherbes, they will be given to me when I come there. I shall have the time to study them and tell you if anything troubles me. Many thanks in advance and all good wishes, Galli-Marié."

Bizet did not send the pieces before the singer left Paris for the summer. It was rumored that she was ill. From the safe distance of the country near Bordeaux she permitted herself, on July 22, to write a more personal letter: *"Monsieur,* Rest assured that I was never in better health. During the winter I agreed *verbally* to several engagements for this summer, and in order to resume the freedom that was required of me in another quarter, I had to say I was ill so as not to have to sign and carry out those contracts. That is the origin of the news that worried all those who are interested in my health. I am leading a charmed existence. I have let myself be carried off to a lovely château, in the midst of beautiful country with water and great trees. A dream of Eden, in fact—and I no longer think of the theatre at all, not at all. What a blessing! I even left my name with my costumes in the rue Favart shop. Here I relish the pleasures of incognito. I call myself Mme Cipriani.[6] So if you want to give me something to study, that is the name by which to address me at Château de Puygaland, Mérignac near Bordeaux. I intend to stay here until October.

"With best wishes, I am sincerely yours,
Galli-Marié
"Please keep all these details between ourselves."

This letter seems to have stimulated Bizet to suggest his bringing in person to Galli-Marié her entire part as Carmen, a favor that she makes it quite clear is unwelcome. *"Monsieur,"* she writes on August 15, "I wish absolutely to work only on the difficult passages in my role and not on the role as a whole, which I shall read at sight on October 1, the day my contract starts. So if you would be kind enough to send me *by mail* (to the same

---

[6] Galli-Marié borrowed her pseudonym from the Castello di Cipriani in *Mignon.*

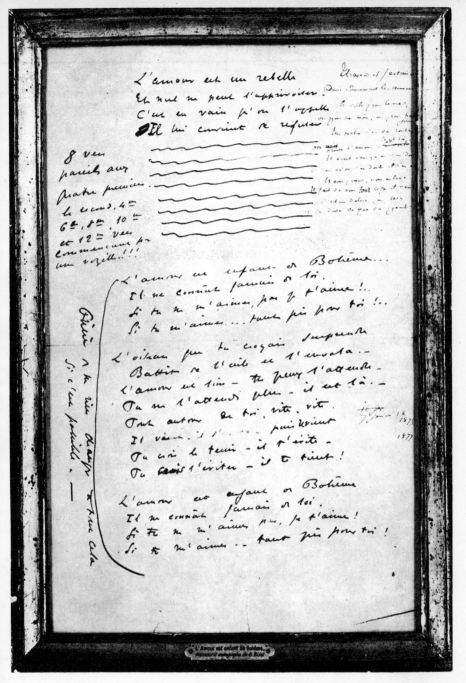

Manuscript of the "*Habanera*" from
Carmen in Bizet's handwriting.

Henri Meilhac and Ludovic Halévy, 1866.

Camille du Locle.

Galli-Marié
in unidentified role.

Galli-Marié
as Carmen.

Lhérie as Don José.

Page from manuscript of *Grisélidis* showing original version
of "*La fleur que tu m'avais jetée*" from *Carmen*.

Proofsheet of piano score of *Carmen*.

Georges Bizet, 1875.

Telegram from Ludovic Halévy to Hippolyte
Rodrigues announcing Bizet's death.

Geneviève Bizet-Straus, 1886.
Portrait by Auguste Toulmouche.

address) the pieces I went over with you, and any others that are difficult either in intention or execution, I should be most grateful.—I shall get a metronome at Bordeaux.—I am no less grateful for your offer and remain, *Monsieur,* sincerely yours, Galli-Marié (Cipriani)."

This letter was followed a week later by one less sharp in tone: *"Monsieur,* I think perhaps you have lost my address and that is why you have sent me nothing; so, as I shall be traveling a large part of September, I should be grateful if you would send me the principal pieces of my part which are not at all like an andante by Mozart, so that I can study them a little. As the opera is apparently to go on very soon, I shall hardly have time to do serious work on it if I have to rehearse on stage every day and play on alternate nights.—I don't think my request can annoy you, but if it should, please forgive me and consider it withdrawn. Sincerely yours, Galli-Marié (Cipriani)."

While Bizet was occupied in orchestrating his opera, and was, no doubt, preoccupied with thoughts of the singer, who, in her own way, appears to have been quite as free and independent as his gypsy heroine, his neighbor Delaborde became an intimate member of the Bizet household. The "assiduities" toward Geneviève of this virtuoso pianist are believed by the same biographer who claims that Galli-Marié "fell in love" with Bizet, to have been in part responsible for the unhappiness that hastened Bizet's death. This assumption could hardly be farther from the truth. For Bizet himself had long been aware of, and not unamused by, his wife's tendencies to flirtation. Soon after their marriage, indeed, had not "the inconvenience of Geneviève's being a little too friendly with Goethe" wakened him from his wartime dream of Utopia? Now, when he had lost any illusion that his marriage could ever be a happy one, the convenience of having a trusted and admired friend to relieve him of the burden of his wife's perpetual need for attention could only be welcome.

Elie-Miriam Delaborde was no Goethe, but on his own level he was indeed a "multiple man." A year younger than Bizet, he was said to be the illegitimate son of the pianist Valentin Alkan, who began to give him piano lessons when he was only five years old. Later he studied with Moscheles. Success as a concert pianist in the tradition of the *"haute école"* came early to Delaborde. He was particularly popular in French provincial cities and in the British Isles. The war years he spent in London accompanied by his hundred and twenty-one parrots and cockatoos. In Paris he lived in a large studio, where he painted the pictures that he showed each year at the Salon under the name of Miriam. A close friend of Manet's and influenced by him, Delaborde was said to have "a real vocation for painting." He had been appointed piano professor at the Conservatoire in 1873.

"Activity was always essential to him; relaxation he found exhausting. He gave himself wholly to any task he undertook." An experienced fencer, an intrepid oarsman, he also shared Bizet's passion for swimming. He was extraordinarily well read and a brilliant conversationalist. His favorite topic, according to Marmontel, was "the parallel between the art of symphonic and the art of dramatic music," a subject of the greatest interest to Bizet at this time.

Like Bizet, Delaborde was frank and given to "instinctive antipathies and impulsive antagonisms." If at times superficially brusque, at others he was "exquisitely urbane, considerately polite and given to delicate attentions. . . ." A short man, with a very striking head—"the face of an artist slightly tinged with a nuance of Rabelaisianism"—Delaborde found life "fair and smiling." [n] His presence relieved the tension in the Bizet household during the summer of 1874.

C H A P T E R  X X V I

Carmen I: Rehearsals

Carmen is in rehearsal at the Opéra-Comique," is the first sentence of a page Ludovic Halévy wrote in his journal on September 1, 1874. The rest of the page was crossed out many years later. For although he was a passionate archivist, Halévy, when his mind and memory had weakened with age, mutilated large parts of the journal he had kept so assiduously. After writing the *Famille Cardinal,* charming little sketches based on conversations with ballet dancers and their parents backstage at the Opéra, and *L'Abbé Constantin,* a proper little tale that paved his way into the French Académie, he seems to have wished to destroy the image of himself as a theatre man. Had he not become obsessed by this unfortunate notion, he might have left the fullest and liveliest possible account of the French dramatic and lyric theatre between 1862 and 1888. Instead, there remain many small volumes, tantalizingly slashed, with lines or paragraphs inked out or whole pages lacking, cut out with a scissors. For many subjects, including non-controversial theatrical events, this source remains invaluable. On the turbulent rehearsals of *Carmen* it throws no positive light. As a contemporary record of that stormy period, we have, apart from gossip, only the calendar of rehearsals listed in the logbook of the Opéra-Comique. There we find that on October 2, Galli-Marié arrived thirty-five minutes late for the sight-reading of her part with Bizet. The following day, the composer met with the four principals. Between October 5, when Galli-Marié sang in the 344th performance of *Mignon,* and October 20, there were no rehearsals. On the 25th Ludovic Halévy noted in his journal: "Reading of *Carmen* at the Opéra-Comique today. Only the music was in rehearsal. . . ." At that point, four and a half lines are blotted out, but he later admitted that the music had then seemed to him "complicated and distorted."

Starting on November 12, there were rehearsals practically every weekday throughout the rest of the year. Bizet was present at all but two or three. The usual absences of various members of the cast because of illness are listed in the logbook. Only one entry suggests an "incident." On December 9, "Mme Galli did not appear. She sent a message. M. Bizet said that without Mme Galli and without the singers in *Le Domino noir,* the rehearsal was useless." That evening Mme Galli sang in *Les Dragons de Villars.* There is mention, too, that Meilhac and Halévy were absent from the reading "to collate the roles" of the libretto.

These prolific playwrights were far too busy elsewhere during these autumn months to spare time for the early rehearsals of *Carmen.* On September 23, their one-act comedy *L'Ingénue* opened at the Variétés. One critic compared it to the exquisitely mounted semi-precious stone worn by a duchess who, noted for her pearls and diamonds, found it *chic* occasionally to leave her valuable jewels at home in the strongbox. Early in November, these indefatigable collaborators presented a three-act comedy. *La Veuve,* "embroidered on an imperceptible plot, comes to life, so to speak, only through the timing and the wit its two charming authors have been able to put into it. The action is so feeble it is practically non-existent. . . . M. Meilhac persists in his desire to have the piece played at the Théâtre-Français. M. Halévy is hesitant and more or less refuses." [n] At the Palais-Royal theatre, frivolous neighbor of the Comédie-Française, *La Boule,* also a three-act comedy, had its *première* late in the month. The first week in December, *Les Brigands,* libretto by Meilhac and Halévy, music by Offenbach, was revived at the Variétés. With four works in performance, the librettists managed to attend three rehearsals of *Carmen* during the final month of 1874.

Paradoxically enough, although Meilhac and Halévy were the only thoroughly competent librettists Bizet ever had, their established reputation for success in the boulevard theatres diminished initially the chances of an equal success for *Carmen,* their first work to be played at the Opéra-Comique. According to one critic, the public pictured them as privileged creatures who used the laps of duchesses for desks, writing only with pens taken from the brilliant plumage of rare Asiatic birds. They were actually so professionally skillful that they could turn out articles, plays, and librettos with the facility and speed of ordinary hackwriters. (Between 1855 and 1875 they collaborated on most of their works, forty or more of a total of seventy-five.) Apart from the fact that production at the Opéra-Comique was a step up from the Bouffes-Parisiens, to them *Carmen* was simply another show. "There are some very, very lovely and charming things in the score," Halévy wrote, shortly before the opening, "and I dare hope for a happy evening for Bizet. His interests alone matter in this instance. The thing has little importance for Meilhac and me. If *Carmen* does open on Wednesday we shall have a *première* and a hundredth performance on the same night, *Carmen* and *La Boule*." [n] Both librettists lived long enough to appreciate the irony of this scale of values. The posthumous success in 1881 of *Les Contes d'Hoffmann*, Offenbach's most serious work, written after they had refused to supply him with further librettos, and the successful revival of *Carmen* two years later, may well have made Halévy and Meilhac suspect that their fame would depend largely on the juxtaposition of their names with those of their musical collaborators.

Halévy's concept of success or happiness changed gradually. At twenty-nine, in 1863, he had found the mere fact of being back in Paris an "enchantment" after a holiday "monotonous and empty," dutifully spent at Etretat with his family: "My home, my books, my *faïences*, my little balcony, my boulevards, my Opéra, my Paris, in short—all this I have seen again with the joy of a child. . . . I arrived . . . in the midst of the heat and the celebration for the 15th of August. . . . The heat did not exasperate me and I didn't mind the celebration. I went with . . . Meilhac . . . to see the fireworks . . . the *Bal* Morel, the illumination of the Champs-Elysées . . . the whole celebration in the midst of dust and crowds of people from the provinces. Then home at midnight, exhausted, worn out, but perfectly happy I read fifty pages of Heine and two acts of *Le Bourgeois-Gentilhomme*. I lay on my big bed, my window open, the murmur of the crowds outside. That is true happiness: to love your parents, your friends, your books, and your home." [1]

Three years later, the death of the President of the *corps législatif,* the powerful Duc de Morny, whose secretary Halévy had been, left him, at 32, confronted with the need of deciding his future career. He sought counsel in Joubert's *Pensées,* which he reread for the twentieth time: "How happy that man must have been and how enviable his destiny! He had only *pure passions:* his family, his friends, his writing. . . . He asked for no outside success. . . . He liked to think, to read, to write, but for himself alone. . . . He looked at the world from on high with sincere detachment. 'A passion for the welfare of the public,' he wrote in 1797, 'would be foolish at this time. . . . I far prefer the man who without pretension amuses himself in his spare time by skimming stones in his pool. At least he knows that he is expendable.'

"To realize that you are expendable! . . . There is true philosophy and true wisdom. . . . Never to give in to the foolish ambitions and puerile excitements of life. . . . To regard this spectacle with curiosity, but never to permit one's self to be frightened or moved by it.

"As for me, I became inevitably involved in risks and adventures. The luck that made me an intimate of M. de Morny opened wide to me the gates of ambition and wealth. That I was hesitant and apprehensive before these gates I can do myself the justice of admitting. . . . The evaporating of these opportunities left me wholly indifferent. I immediately made a new program for my life. . . . Of my own free will I renounced the future opportunities offered by my position at the *corps législatif.* With no difficulty at all I devoted myself eagerly to my work in the theatre and quickly I achieved security and independence in my life. If I died today I should leave some fifty thousand francs. . . . To give my family a happier and broader life is my great ambition. For myself I wish for nothing."

Consistent with this attitude was Halévy's refusal three months later of Perrin's offer of the assistant-directorship of the Opéra. When his uncle Fromental had continued to hold this post long after the success of *La Juive* had relieved him of the necessity, he

---

[1] The source of the account of Halévy's career in this chapter is Ludovic Halévy, *Carnets,* I and II.

had given as the reason: "A man can't write operas all day long." Ludovic, on the other hand, in rejecting Perrin's offer said: "My freedom, my complete freedom is what I want," freedom, actually, to write as much as and whatever he liked. That this freedom of choice would inevitably be limited by unpredictable circumstances Halévy soon realized. For after the presence of Bismarck and Moltke at a performance of *La Grande Duchesse de Gérolstein* during the Exposition of 1867 gave that operetta a significance not intended by the authors, Meilhac and Halévy sensed that the era of frivolity, of parody, of *opéra-bouffe,* was drawing to a close. That same summer, Halévy, who had several years earlier been awarded the Cross of the Legion of Honor, deplored the long delay preceding Meilhac's decoration: "Certain people have made up their minds to treat our plays as though they were show-pieces or vaudeville acts. I know very well that it is our success that avenges us, but this business of the Cross has saddened and discouraged Meilhac."

To overcome the prejudice of the powerful minority against their operettas and farces, Meilhac and Halévy wrote their first serious non-musical work, *Froufrou,* a more or less realistic comedy-melodrama in five acts. Performance of the play was delayed for over a year. In the meantime Halévy underwent a dramatic psychological experience that caused him to ruminate for some time on the subject of relative values and reality. One evening in June 1869, during the revolutionary riots that accompanied the campaign in which Rochefort and Gambetta were elected to the Chamber of Deputies, Halévy was attending a performance of *Faust* at the Opéra. Back in the wings singers and dancers were chatting gaily, more interested in the activity in the streets than in the performance which absorbed the audience. Halévy, who went out on a balcony from which he could see the military subduing the rioters, was struck by the juxtaposition of the Soldiers' Chorus on stage and the maneuvers of the mounted troops forcing back the mobs singing the forbidden *Marseillaise* in the streets below. "This mixture of rioting and opera," he wrote in his journal the following day, "of Rochefort and Gounod, of *Faust* and *La Lanterne,* seemed to me a strange and violent contrast. . . ."

Froufrou, a play with its own "strange and violent contrast," had its *première* at the Gymnase four months later. Today this

play by Meilhac and Halévy seems in its wit a pale shadow of
Marivaux or Musset, in its structure less skillful than Sardou, as
melodrama an echo of Dumas *fils*. The first three acts tell the
story of an irresponsible, frivolous, willful young woman, the
swish of whose taffeta petticoats, as enchanting and provocative
as her charm, explains her nickname, Froufrou. In the two final
acts she experiences an awakening of conscience. The guilt she
feels over the havoc she brings into the lives of her family and her
lover drives her into devoting herself to acts of charity. As a result
of her visits to the poor, she contracts a fever and dies on stage in
a simple little black frock with no taffeta petticoats. Froufrou's
change of personality, unconvincing though it may be, is perhaps
the unconscious expression of her creators' desire—or at least of
Halévy's—to metamorphose themselves, if not into reformers, at
least into purveyors of a respected form of entertainment.

"Yesterday *Froufrou, Froufrou, Froufrou, Froufrou, Froufrou!*" Halévy wrote the day after the *première*. "How happy I
am! A great, great, great success!" And a week later: *"Froufrou, Froufrou, Froufrou!* Ah, what a pleasant sound, what a
lovely noise success makes. To stroll in the boulevards . . . and
see everybody come up to you naturally, frankly, openly. These
compliments are not merely polite and automatic. . . . The newspapers are unanimous in calling it . . . *'Masterpiece'! Froufrou,
Froufrou!* Oh, but it's nice, it's sweet—the noise that success
makes. *Froufrou, Froufrou!*

"However one mustn't become intoxicated. Have we really
done a masterpiece? That's what Meilhac and I have quite frankly
and simply been asking ourselves every evening. When it comes to
answering this question we are embarrassed. . . . No, *Froufrou*
is not a masterpiece . . . but it is, I really believe, a very accurate
and faithful picture of society today. At least the first three acts
are. We have a great success on our hands, a success both in
honor and in money. Let's try to do two or three more *Froufrous*.
That's what's important."

The crowning glory for *Froufrou* was two visits from the
Emperor, on the second of which he was accompanied by the
Empress, who "wept, wept, wept, wept more than any woman has
wept at *Froufrou* and that's saying a lot . . ." Halévy exulted.
"The Empress started weeping . . . at the beginning of the third
act . . . and didn't stop until the death of Froufrou. By the fifth

act there were floods of tears. The Empress sat motionless, utterly crushed. . . . When the Emperor tried to speak to her, she didn't reply or even turn her head. . . ." After the performance, when their Majesties received the players, they found the Empress's face streaked with tears, her eyes bloodshot, her make-up zigzagging her face in red, white, and black stripes. The Emperor, who teased her about her excessive emotion, remarked to one of the actors: "The fact is it's a very charming, very witty, and very touching play."

Bizet was apparently insufficiently attracted to *Froufrou* to wish to set it to music. For had he wanted it, du Locle would probably not have offered it to Verdi early in December 1869. "I read the play at one sitting," Verdi told the director. "If . . . the whole thing were as distinguished and original as the first three acts, it would be extremely fine; but the last two acts descend to the commonplace, though they are effective, extraordinarily so. Good as *Froufrou* is, I would, if I had to work for Paris, prefer to Meilhac and Halévy's *cuisine* (as you call it) . . . a more refined, more piquant one: that of Sardou, with du Locle to write the verse!" ⁿ

Froufrou, whatever its limitations, marked the turning point in the theatrical careers of its authors. They had shown their capacity to write a successful serious work; more, they had challenged contemporary dramatic tradition by bringing down their final curtain on the death, not of a *Dame aux camélias* or a Violetta, but of a lady, the wife of a respected member of the diplomatic corps. In permitting a prodigal wife to expiate the sin of infidelity by dying on stage at a popular boulevard theatre, Meilhac and Halévy showed their determination to break with the past. But a war, a defeat, and a revolution occurred before they dared present as a finale at that stronghold of domesticity, the Opéra-Comique, a renegade soldier murdering his gypsy mistress. And indeed, from time to time, their courage wavered.

Meilhac could not bear the idea of a pretty woman being stabbed. And he cared neither for scenery nor for music. "When he goes to the *première* of a musical show," said a friend, "he generally stays in the back of the box, *listening to the dialogue.* The audience may well have swooned over the more or less successful parts of the score, or have encored the songs, applauded the sets and the costumes if the dialogue did not amuse them. But

Meilhac says, 'There's a success that can't last.'. . . Meilhac . . .
adores the Folies-Bergères. Clowns afford him unmixed delight.
. . ." ⁿ Unlike Halévy, he was neither an intellectual nor a family
man. A confirmed Parisian, a bachelor, a *bon vivant,* expert at
billiards but less accomplished at whist and *écarté,* games at which
Bizet usually beat him, happiest in the society of young ladies of
the chorus (*"ingénues"*), he was a high-strung and restless man.
At rehearsals he could never stay still; coming and going, sometimes sitting in the orchestra, at others wandering backstage, he
would suggest a word or a line from time to time, then vanish and
reappear.

Meilhac, who was some seven years older than Bizet, had
started his career as a bookseller. Subsequently he drew caricatures
and wrote articles for various humorous journals. His contribution
to the dramatic works in which he collaborated was largely the
planning of the plot and the writing of the prose dialogue. Because *Carmen* is played as a grand opera, with recitatives replacing the spoken passages in every country but France,² where even
at the Opéra-Comique many speeches are omitted, little of Meilhac's work remains discernible. His greatest gift was for humorous
characterization; Halévy had been quite sincere when he assured
de Leuven that humorous roles would be introduced into *Carmen*
to lighten the atmosphere of the piece. In the original version,
Meilhac's touch was easily recognizable in the characters of Le
Dancaïre and Le Remendado, the two chief smugglers, whose
amusing horseplay is typical of traditional vaudeville farce. It is
probable, too, that Meilhac wrote the verses for the quintet in
Act II in which the two smugglers, Mercédès, and Frasquita mock
Carmen for refusing to go away with them because she is in love.
During the two months before the *première,* Meilhac attended most
of the rehearsals.

Although Meilhac derived no pleasure from music, he was
loyally devoted to Bizet, and was consequently shocked at du

---

² Covent Garden has recently begun using a version of *Carmen* that includes some dialogue. In December 1957, the Carl Rosa Opera Company presented at Wolverhampton, England, a version of *Carmen* "restored" by the
Dutch orchestra conductor, Maurits Sillem. Mr. Sillem's version was based on a
comparison of the published orchestral scores of the opera with Bizet's manuscript. He restored the score and libretto to the condition in which they had
been before Bizet himself, the conductor Deloffre, Guiraud, and a fourth, unidentified person made considerable alterations. See article by Paul Chr. Van
Westering in the *Haagse Post* (The Hague), December 21, 1957.

Locle's attitude during the rehearsals of *Carmen*. Sole director now of the Opéra-Comique, having bought out de Leuven's interest for 300,000 francs early in 1874, du Locle could no longer blame failures, artistic or financial, on his partner. Alone responsible for the gradually diminishing receipts at the box office—over 182,000 francs less in 1875 than in 1872—he was hard put to it to find novelties to attract his dwindling audiences. The "entertainments" that sold out the house in 1874 turned out to be seven concert performances each of Massenet's *Marie-Magdeleine* and of Verdi's Requiem with the composer conducting. In the spring of 1875, when *Carmen* was playing to half empty houses, Verdi returned to Paris and conducted seven more performances with as great success as in the previous year. "It's odd that it took a mass for the dead to revive the Opéra-Comique," said one critic as he left the theatre. This sort of remark du Locle preferred to make himself.

Not only had he lacked faith from the beginning in the potential success of *Carmen,* but also his part of the direction of it did not afford him the compensating self-expression he had found in *Djamileh.* No longer could he pick up here and there the costumes that amused him or plan the stage-effects in which he delighted. Galli-Marié's costumes were designed by Clairin, Henri Regnault's companion on the journey to Spain from which that gifted young painter had brought back the vivid sketches that Bizet had probably seen. Detaille, a young pupil of Meissonier's, who in his early twenties had won fame for his war paintings, designed the uniforms for the dragoons. The only remaining outlet for du Locle was the upholding of his reputation as a prophet. Preferring omniscience to loyalty, he did not hesitate to indulge in derogatory remarks in the hearing of the authors and singers. He told all and sundry that Bizet's music was "Cochin-Chinese and utterly incomprehensible." The effect of the director's attitude permeated the whole company, thereby rendering unbearably difficult the composer's efforts to control the rebellious musicians and singers. "For the only time in his life, during the rehearsals of *Carmen,* Ludovic Halévy, that wisest, most balanced, most philosophical of men, lost his composure," a friend has written. "But he felt what we all did, and Bizet more than any of us, that for the composer this was the decisive test, the turning point in his career. His emotion was as profound as his hopes were high. The slightest shock set him to vibrating like a taut wire. The theatre gossip that seeped through the half-open door of the director's office and whistled through the wings and the dressing-rooms like a threatening wind before a storm, shook his confidence for the first time." "

On all but one day during the first week in January 1875 there were daily rehearsals of *Carmen* with authors and composer present. On that day, Tuesday, January 5, a long-awaited event occurred, the inauguration of that eighth wonder of the world, the *palais* of the architect Charles Garnier, the new Opéra, the cornerstone of which had been laid thirteen years earlier. Outside, in the new Place de l'Opéra, great crowds watched the arrival of the guests for the gala performance: the Lord Mayor of London in full regalia descending from a coach and four manned with lackeys "bedecked in gold braid and wearing pink silk stockings;" the Lady Mayoress glittering in a diamond diadem and an emerald bracelet recently presented to her by Queen Victoria; the King and Queen of Spain, the latter in puffed pink satin; the King of Hanover; and some two thousand other fortunate guests. A specially prepared illustrated volume enabled the press to inform the public of the splendors in store for them: the most miraculous stage machinery ever invented; the thousand-step marble staircase; the sculpture and the murals that covered walls and ceilings and had long occupied most of the former Prix de Rome. (See Appendix I, p. 462.) But while the eyes of the audience were regaled with novel splendors, their ears were assailed only by familiar sounds. For the Académie Nationale de Musique had commissioned no new opera to celebrate French musical genius at this historic inauguration.

The program planned for the gala occasion consisted of the overtures to Auber's *La Muette de Portici* and Rossini's *Guillaume Tell,* the first two acts of *La Juive,* the third and fourth acts of Thomas's *Hamlet,* the church scene from Gounod's *Faust* and the second act of Delibes's ballet, *La Source.* But a fit of temperament on the part of the star imported for the occasion resulted in Delibes's being the only living composer to uphold the glory of French music.

At the dress rehearsal the night before the *première,* while the auditorium was filling with some two thousand invited guests, there was chaos backstage. The ladies of the chorus were threatening to strike because they had been forced to rehearse on a Sunday. But far more serious was the dereliction of Christine Nilsson, who was to have sung Ophelia and Marguerite. This *prima donna* disliked the tenor with whom she was to sing, but gave as excuse for her refusal to appear her objection to rehearsing before an audience. The scenes from *Faust* and *Hamlet* had to be striken from the program and were replaced for the *première* by a scene from *Les Huguenots.* The orchestra conductor, Deldevez, after surmounting the obstacles of this eventful evening, was rewarded for his efforts by two Sèvres figurines, presented by the Minister of Public Instruction, and the congratulations of Messrs. Ludovic Halévy and Georges Bizet for "the fine performance of *La Juive.*"

To console Thomas for the disaster that had befallen him (he had not been reticent in expressing the opinion that the new Opéra should open not with a potpourri, but with all five acts of his *Hamlet*), du Locle quickly whipped up a revival of *Le Caïd,* an *opéra-comique* first played in 1849. A few days after its revival on January 18, Bizet wrote to Thomas: *"Carmen* doesn't leave me a moment's peace. I am doing the accompanying myself. I am doing the reduction myself. . . . Your *Caïd* the other evening delighted me. It is still young and witty and so skillful! . . ." [n]

On January 15, Bizet, signing for the librettists as well as for himself, sold the score of *Carmen* to Choudens for 25,000 francs.[3] (The royalties from performances abroad were to be divided equally among Choudens, Bizet, Meilhac, and Halévy.) The publisher was said also to have offered a large bonus to the authors if their opera ran for fifty performances. But the increasing tension of the rehearsals at this point afforded little hope of success. On January 27, Halévy filled several pages of his journal with notes about the rehearsal, all of which he later excised with a scissors. Thirty years later, at the time of the 1000th performance of *Carmen,* he stated that the training of the chorus was the greatest obstacle facing the authors. "Most of the singers were bewildered and threatened to strike. After two months of rehearsal, they insisted that the two first-act choruses were unperformable: the entrance of the cigarette girls and the scuffle around the officer after the arrest of Carmen. These two choruses, very difficult to play . . . necessitated not only singing, but at the same time motion, action, coming and going—life, in short. This was with-

---

[3] In the library of the Opéra there is a copy of the voice and piano score of *Carmen* inscribed by Bizet "To the godfather of my four children as a token of my great affection." It seems probable that the godfather was Choudens.

out precedent at the Opéra-Comique. The members of the chorus were in the habit of singing the ensembles, standing motionless in line, their arms slack, their eyes fixed on the conductor's baton, their thoughts elsewhere." [n] They resented Bizet's desire to have them enter by ones and twos rather than in the traditional mass formation, and in this protest du Locle upheld them. It must therefore have been with trepidation that Bizet wrote to the director in mid-February: "As you are making great sacrifices for *Carmen,* please allow me to do one small thing to assure the proper execution of my women's choruses in the first act. Meilhac and Halévy want faces, and I would like some voices! Authorize me to take six additional first-upper-voices and four second-upper-voices. I can still hear the performance of the first chorus of *Mireille,* and I feel that a similar performance would be effective for my two choruses of cigarette-girls. If the execution is brilliant at the first three performances, it need be only adequate later on. What I am asking should not delay you for five minutes. The women are there. I will rehearse them myself tomorrow, *Sunday,* and the *day after, Monday!* They can take their places on stage *Tuesday.* I shall do *everything necessary* so that the choruses will be ready in three days. Please forgive my frenzy, but don't think that I am selfish; if I were alone before the enemy, I should be less disturbed. But you are with me; you are risking more than I am. I sense a possible victory, I assure you, and I know that you will be repaid by it. It's a matter of honor, and also, *cher ami,* of feeling." [n]

Du Locle's reply was cool. After asking Ludovic Halévy whether it was really necessary to add singers for "these *diabolic* choruses," he wrote to Bizet: "What you ask does not seem to me very reasonable. In spite of what you say, you are condemning us to at least a week's delay by adding singers to the choruses of *Carmen.* I am writing to Ludovic to ask him to see you tomorrow and talk to you about it. What you decide will be done Monday if it takes place. Yours, Camille du Locle." [n] The phantom of the havoc wrought by Sunday rehearsals at the Opéra surely lurked in the mind of the director of the Opéra-Comique.

But "Bizet insisted," Halévy writes, again thirty years later. "It was necessary—and Camille du Locle provided the additional voices. There were also difficulties with the orchestra; certain details in the orchestration they declared *unplayable,* but after more than the usual number of rehearsals, these musicians, excellent on the whole, succeeded in playing what had seemed unplayable." ⁿ

If Bizet had been confronted only with technical musical problems, his task in projecting *Carmen* as he conceived it would have been far less difficult. The librettists, however, with their long history of pleasing the public, were now afraid of shocking the members of the Opéra-Comique audience, who were more interested in using their boxes for match-making than for listening to music. Having accepted the basic violence of their subject, Meilhac and Halévy wished to dilute its effect as much as possible. They stopped Escamillo at his first entrance from patting the cheeks of some of the gypsy chorus-girls. They carried on a running battle with Galli-Marié in an attempt to persuade her to tone down her acting, which they regarded as vulgar and unrestrained. But they met with no success. She and Lhérie continued to believe in the eventual success of *Carmen,* and stood by Bizet throughout his struggles.

A short time before the opening, du Locle decided that the ending must be changed. Bizet held out "ferociously" (there is no record of the librettists' attitude, but at best they probably remained neutral), and Perrin, then director of the Comédie-Française, was called in to arbitrate. He loathed the piece, insisted that it would be a failure and a scandal, ruinous to the reputations of both Bizet and the Opéra-Comique. At this point, Galli-Marié and Lhérie declared that they would resign their parts rather than accept any changes whatsoever. The directors had no choice but to give in. When they asked Bizet to shorten what they considered the "too naturalistic" duet in Act II and to break it up to allow for applause, he flatly refused. Yet he made many more than the usual number of changes during rehearsals.

In the first act, a number that appears in the first edition of the piano reduction as well as in the libretto was omitted from the orchestral score: a typical little *opéra-bouffe* pantomime in which a young woman on the arm of her elderly husband flirts with her lover as they cross *la place* while the brigadier, Moralès, describes the episode in song. Bizet is said by Guiraud to have rewritten the *habanera* thirteen times before it satisfied him and Galli-Marié. He also willingly changed parts of duets at the request of Lhérie. Of the many changes and additions to text and stage directions which Bizet made in the original manuscript, the two most striking are in the lyrics of the *habanera* and in Carmen's part of the card trio in the third act. The final version of both songs was entirely Bizet's.

In the margin of the manuscript page of the *habanera*, he bracketed the last three stanzas with the words: "Please do not change any of this." Also written in the margin is a request to Halévy for "8 lines like the first four, the second, 4th, 6th, 8th, 10th, and 12th lines starting with a vowel!!" On the reverse side Halévy scribbled: "Here are the twelve lines you asked for. Is the feeling right? I did some tenderer ones, but I don't think that in the beginning Carmen should be given too melancholy a tinge. A little banter won't hurt. . . ." " Here are the two versions:

Halévy:

Illusion (?) et fantaisie,
Ainsi commencent les amours,
Et voilà pour la vie,
Ou pour six mois ou pour huit
*   jours*
Un matin sur sa route
On trouve l'amour—Il est là.
Il vient sans qu'on s'en doute
Et sans qu'on s'en doute il s'en
*   va*
Il vous prend, vous enlève,
Il fait de vous tout ce qu'il veut.
C'est un délire, un rêve
Et ça dure ce que ça peut.

Bizet:

L'amour est un oiseau rebelle
Que nul ne peut apprivoiser
Et c'est bien en vain qu'on l'ap-
*   pelle*
S'il lui convient de refuser.
Rien n'y fait, menace ou prière;
L'un parle bien, l'autre se tait;
Et c'est l'autre que je préfère,
Il n'a rien dit, mais il me plaît.[4]

It is hardly necessary to point out the superiority of Bizet's version: Halévy's difficult repetition of *"sans . . . s'en doute"* as against Bizet's immediate and profound characterization of Carmen in the line: *"Rien n'y fait, menace ou prière."* Here, while incorporating Halévy's idea of a bantering tone, he immediately introduces Carmen's sense of fatalism, of the futility of "threat or prayer." This is intensified in the card song, in which Bizet retained

---

[4] In the original manuscript version the word *"oiseau"* was omitted in line 1. Line 2 read *"Et nul ne peut l'apprivoiser."* In line 3 *"et"* and *"bien"* were omitted. In line 4 *"S' "* was omitted. In the refrain, *"L'amour est enfant de Bohême,"* line 4, *"Si je t'aime, prends garde à toi,"* read: *"Si tu m'aimes, tant pis pour toi!"*

the most telling lines in Halévy's version, but by the insertion of a number of concrete details changed Carmen's fatalism from passive resignation to rebellious acceptance:

Halévy:

Mais qu'importe après tout si par cette menace
Mon coeur n'est pas troublé
Cette mort qui m'attend je la re-garde en face
Carmen n'a pas tremblé
Pourquoi se révolter? Aucune force humaine
Ne peut rien à cela
Je suis prête. J'attends—que le destin me mène
Ou bon lui semblera.
Il faut savoir mourir si le mot redoutable
Est écrit par le sort—
(Consultant encore ses cartes)
J'ai beau recommencer, La carte impitoyable
Répète encore: La mort. "

Bizet:

En vain pour éviter les réponses amères
En vain tu mêleras,
Cela ne sert à rien, les cartes sont sincères
Et ne mentiront pas.
Dans le livre d'en haut, si ta page est heureuse
Mêle et coupe sans peur,
La carte sous tes doigts se tour-nera joyeuse
T'annonçant le bonheur.
Mais si tu dois mourir, si le mot redoutable
Est écrit par le sort,
Recommence vingt fois—la carte impitoyable
Dira toujours: la mort!

Three extant versions of the introduction to the *seguidilla* show variations in text typical of the many changes Bizet himself made in the manuscript score. The details in the original version of this scene in Act II are taken from Mérimée's story, and are included in the spoken dialogue of the opera. Carmen welcomes Don José back from prison, not as she does in the grand opera version by immediately flinging herself into the dance, but by ordering Lillas Pastia to bring in a splendid supper of oranges, candied fruits, sweets, and Manzanilla wine. "Let's eat it all, all of it," Carmen cries and sets to eating greedily as Don José watches her. "You crunch that candy like a child of six," he says. "That's because I like it." During the brief repast, she flirts, she teases, she shows a kind of pure animal earthiness much simpler than the wild, voluptuous charm she displays in the rest of the opera. After taunting Don José by telling him that she has danced

for his officers, she jumps up to dance for him, can't find her
castanets, takes a plate off the table, and breaks it in half. Here
are the three versions of her introduction to the dance.

Original Manuscript Score.

"Carmen: (avec une solennité comique)
           Je vais danser en votre honneur
           Et vous verrez, Seigneur,
           Comment je sais [claquer ces morceaux de faïence.]
           Mettez-vous là, brigadier, je commence."

The phrase *"claquer ces morceaux de faïence"* Bizet crossed
out, and in a footnote he wrote: "This part should be added to the
role of Carmen. But if the singer does not know how to play this
instrument, she should mime the gestures, and the castanets will
be played by a musician in the percussion section of the orchestra."

Piano and Voice score. (First Edition)

"Carmen: *Je vais danser en votre honneur*
           Et vous verrez, Seigneur,
           Comment je sais moi-même accompagner ma danse.
           Mettez-vous là, Don José, (avec une solennité comique)
           je commence."

In the piano score the footnote reads: "The part of the
castanets engraved in small type is to be performed either in the
orchestra by one of the percussion players or on stage by the
artist who plays Carmen. In that case the rhythm could be
modified to suit the singer."

Original libretto, still in print and on sale
at the Opéra-Comique.

"Carmen: *Je vais en ton honneur danser la Romalis*
           Et tu verras, mon fils,
           Comment je sais moi-même accompagner ma danse
           Mettez vous là, Don José, je commence." (Stage direc-
           tion omitted.)

During rehearsals, early in February, Bizet was notified that
he had been awarded the Cross of the Legion of Honor. "A big

piece of my ribbon belongs to your husband," he wrote to Mme Carvalho, "for it is to HIM that I owe it. I am not *forgetting* it and I shall NEVER FORGET IT." " Toward the end of the month, Bizet wrote in the postscript of a letter to Rodrigues: "The Marshal has signed my decoration, so it is completely sure. Only it will not be officially announced for several days because Baudry's promotion to the rank of Commander necessitates some formalities that delay the insertion of the awards granted by the Minister des Beaux-Arts. —Therefore let's not talk about it yet."

The body of this note, which was sent in an envelope marked "Urgent," informed Rodrigues that "Geneviève has an abscess in her right eye. It doesn't amount to anything, but the eye is absolutely closed. So our Bébé does not intend to go out for several days.—I try to dine with her, as at the moment I am out from 8 in the morning to 6 at night, but I shall ask you for lunch one of these days. Come to see Geneviève. . . ." "

Thus afflicted, Geneviève was probably unable to attend the *première* of *Carmen*. No comment of hers on the occasion has been recorded. Bizet's nomination to the Legion of Honor was announced the morning of March 3. That night, one member of the audience was heard to say: "They announced it this morning because they knew that by tonight it would no longer be possible to give him a decoration!"

CHAPTER  XXVII

Carmen II: Première

During the winter of 1875, while the rehearsals of *Carmen* were in progress, Bizet attended César Franck's organ class at the Conservatoire. As a student of sacred music in the peaceful confines of the academic, Bizet appears at first glance to have sought a somewhat quixotic escape from the tension of the Opéra-Comique and the daily disputes over the profane or "scabrous" nature of *Carmen*. But in the back of Bizet's mind, his oratorio *Geneviève de Paris* was already taking shape. Early in the year he had told Gallet, the librettist, that since the orchestral score of *Carmen* had to be ready by May 1, he would plan to work on the oratorio during May, June, and July. The libretto had been approved by Charles Lamoureux, director of the Société de l'Harmonie Sacrée, who at this time was rehearsing Massenet's *Eve*. Bizet's determination to compete with Massenet in a field for which he knew he was ill equipped explains his "scrupulous and deferential attention" in listening to César Franck's course in religious music.

A member of Franck's class, Vincent d'Indy, remembered more than half a century later that none of the pupils had known the identity of the silent, bearded visitor until the day before the *première* of *Carmen*, when Bizet introduced himself to the class. He wished, he said, to express his gratitude for what he had learned from their studies by giving them tickets to the opening of his opera: "But there are eight of you and I have only two tickets. Unfortunately that is too few; but you know even the most beautiful girl in the world can give no more than she has." ⁿ The two tickets, drawn by lot, went to Camille Benoît and Vincent d'Indy, who were probably the youngest musicians present at the Opéra-Comique on the night of March 3, 1875.

The presence of Gounod, Ambroise Thomas, Delibes, Offenbach, Massenet, and Charles Lecocq, Bizet's earliest rival, whose *La Fille de Madame Angot* had been the hit of Paris for nearly two years, was mentioned in the newspaper accounts. But composers were in a minority. The public before whom *Carmen* was first performed was neither primarily musical nor intellectual; nor was it typically Opéra-Comique. Du Locle, afraid of a scandal, had frightened off the usual family parties. When asked for a box for the *première* by a member of the ministry, the director had advised him to come to the dress rehearsal to decide for himself the suitability of *Carmen* as a background for the arrangements of his daughter's marriage. A large part of the audience consisted of Meilhac and Halévy's devoted followers: Offenbach's stars, Hortense Schneider, Zulma Bouffar, and his latest discovery, Mme Judic, who postponed her departure for St. Petersburg for the occasion. Jean-Baptiste Faure and a number of other singers from the Opéra were able to be present, for an epidemic of head-colds among the tenors had caused a week's unprecedented closing of that theatre. Music publishers were there *en masse:* Heugel, Choudens, Hartmann; Pasdeloup, to whom the score of *Carmen* was dedicated;[1] Prince Troubetzkoi; Alphonse and Ernest Daudet; Dumas *fils*, who rarely attended openings, and whom Bizet greatly admired. Besides the whole band of music critics, the higher echelons of the press were represented by Hébrard of the *Temps,* who entertained a party in his box, and Villemessant of the *Figaro,* accompanied by four members of his staff. The audience, in short, was mixed, fashionable, replete with *boulevardiers* who, having been warned by the journalists in attendance to expect a scandalous work, were only too eager to be shocked and to condemn. The word "immoral" was bandied about in the lobbies during the intermissions not merely by the ultra-bourgeois, but by members of the artistic and social worlds as well.

The first act, which ran for fifty-eight minutes, was well re-

---

[1] On March 1, 1875, Pasdeloup wrote to Bizet: "I am happy to accept for my wife and myself. Let me tell you how happy and grateful I am for the proof of your affection that you give me by dedicating *Carmen* to me. . . ." Unpublished letter, collection of author.

ceived. The *habanera* and the duet for Micaëla and José were applauded. At the end of the act, the applause was warm and the
singers were recalled.[2] During the half-hour intermission, the
stage was crowded with people congratulating Bizet. The entr'acte
was encored, and the second act began brilliantly. The Toreador
song evoked tremendous enthusiasm; when composing this piece
Bizet had remarked: "So they want trash (*de l'ordure*)? All right;
I'll give them trash." The lively quintet of the smugglers, Mercédès, Frasquita, and Carmen also pleased the audience. But José's
Flower song and his duet with Carmen were greeted with increasing coolness. "As Bizet deviated more and more from the traditional form of *opéra-comique,* the public was surprised, put out,
baffled." [n] The absence of a ballet obviously disturbed a reporter
accustomed to the Bouffes-Parisiens or the Variétés. "In the second act," he wrote, "the Opéra-Comique produced its whole *corps
de ballet,* which is composed of two pretty dancers. In his box
Offenbach . . . smiled compassionately. M. du Locle's ballerinas
have, however, solved the rather difficult problem of dancing in a
space no larger than a pocket handkerchief." [n]

In the second half-hour interval fewer people went backstage. Among them was the fourteen-year-old Jacques-Emile
Blanche, who, having wandered away from his family, had been
taken under Gounod's wing. In honor of the occasion, the master
coined a new phrase. Instead of disguising his opinion of a rival's
opera by his habitual "It's monumental," he forestalled the ques-
tioning critics by exclaiming: "What a work this is!" He flung his
arms around his *"cher* Georges," professing the greatest admiration for the opera. "However," Blanche remembered, "if a friend

---

[2] Cast of *Carmen* as listed in
original piano and voice score

Characters	*Singers*
Don José	Messrs. Lhérie
Escamillo	Bouhy
Le Dancaïre	Potel
Le Remendado	Barnolt
Zuniga	Dufriche
Moralès	Duvernoy
Lillas Pastia	Nathan
Un guide	Teste
Carmen	Mme Galli-Marié
Micaëla	Melle Chapuy
Frasquita	—Ducasse
Mercédès	—Chevalier

Mise en scène by M. Charles Ponchard

told Gounod that a number of the themes, indeed the best pieces in the score, had been 'stolen' from his works or from Wagner or were simply Spanish, Gounod protested, but weakly." [n] During the third act, Blanche sat in Gounod's box: "Micaëla sang her now well-known air, which the public encored. Gounod leaned forward in his box and applauded enthusiastically so that all could see. Then he took his seat again and sighed: 'That melody is mine! Georges has robbed me; take the Spanish airs and mine out of the score, and there remains nothing to Bizet's credit but the sauce that masks the fish.' It would have been better had I been in bed that night," Blanche concludes, "for the embraces which I . . . had witnessed on the stage were my first lesson in duplicity. . . ." [n]

The third act, with its wild mountain setting, immediately evoked invidious comparison with *Les Brigands,* the Meilhac-Halévy-Offenbach comic opera that had recently been revived with great success at the Variétés. "When the curtain went up . . ." wrote one commentator, "we asked our neighbor to pinch us, thinking that we were the victim of a dream. It is the décor of the first act of *Les Brigands,* slightly modified." [n] Only Micaëla's aria, Gounodesque indeed, was applauded.

In the final interval, which fortunately lasted only twenty-four minutes, very few people went backstage. Outside in the rue Favart, d'Indy and Benoît found Bizet pacing the street with the publisher Hartmann. "Both of them seemed melancholy and dejected," d'Indy wrote. " 'My poor children,' Bizet replied to our timidly proffered praise, 'you are really very kind, but . . . I sense defeat. I foresee a definitive and hopeless flop. This time I am really sunk.' " [3]

The reaction of the audience to the fourth act was "glacial" from the first scene to the last. "They did not seem to want to enjoy themselves," said Barnolt, the singer who played Le Remendado. After the final curtain nobody remained "except three or four faithful friends. They all had reassuring things to say, but the look in their eyes was sad. *Carmen* had not been a success," Halévy wrote to a friend the day after the *première.* [n]

---

[3] D'Indy, writing more than half a century after the event, places this episode after the first act and quotes Bizet as saying: "Your congratulations are probably the only ones I shall receive this evening." But Halévy, in a letter written the day after the *première,* speaks of Bizet's receiving congratulations on stage during the first interval.

Bizet, taking refuge in du Locle's office, tried unsuccessfully to hide his feelings. Among the few well-wishers who sought him out was Benjamin Godard, who often in later years spoke of the pain he had experienced at seeing so great a composer in such despair." To one well-intentioned person who congratulated him on the "success" of *Carmen,* Bizet is said to have replied: "Success! Don't you see that these bourgeois have not understood a word of the work I have written for them?" " Arm-in-arm with the faithful Guiraud, who had seen him through so many other crises, he left the theatre to wander through the streets of Paris until dawn.[4] A day or two later, he had sufficiently regained his equilibrium to take steps to improve the performance of *Carmen.*

Except for the brilliance of Galli-Marié and the sound singing and acting of Bouhy as Escamillo and Mlle Chapuy as Micaëla, the interpretation had been mediocre. The orchestra, at first rebellious against "the complexity" of Bizet's score, gradually, with great effort, overcame their prejudice and managed, at the *première,* to play moderately well. There was only one mishap. At a point when Galli-Marié was singing *pianissimo,* the bass-drum player, miscounting his bars, beat two loud bangs. This accident was less disastrous to the performance than the detachment of the ladies of the chorus, who continued to be resentful of the demands made upon them. As they were unaccustomed to acting as individuals, shocked at the very idea of violent behavior, and rendered dizzy by the cigarettes they were made to smoke, their quarreling among themselves and with Carmen was, to say the least, listless. Yet after the performance, Bizet wrote to the *chef des choeurs* of the Opéra-Comique: "Will you once more give your courageous artists all my thanks for the hard work my *Carmen* imposed on them? Without their understanding, without their adaptability, we would never have got the good performance that we achieved. Tell them all of the sincere gratitude of your friend, Georges Bizet." "

To overcome Lhérie's most blatant weakness in the part of Don José, Bizet employed more drastic measures. Shortly after the opening night, he reappeared at César Franck's organ class, announcing that he had come to ask a favor; he needed someone

---

[4] Ludovic Halévy, thirty years later, said that Bizet went home to 22 rue de Douai with him and Meilhac. But his memory often played him false at this time. Guiraud, who in the eighties supplied firsthand information to Bizet's first biographer, Pigot, often mentioned this painful experience.

to play the harmonium backstage at every performance of *Carmen.*
Lhérie could act adequately and sing correctly when he was on
stage, Bizet explained. "But he is incapable of singing accurately
in the wings in the second act, '*Halte-là! qui va là?/ Dragon
d'Alcala!*' He starts in G and finishes in E major—or else in E
minor . . . and even, unbelievably, in E flat minor!!! A few peep-
peeps on the harmonium will keep him on pitch and will give him
the indispensable assurance, the hope that one day he will be
capable of grasping solfeggio!" Vincent d'Indy was delighted to
undertake this task. Having already acted as pianist, organist,
horn-player, and drummer at the Théâtre-Italien, as well as tympanist at the Colonne concerts, he now played the harmonium in
the wings of the Opéra-Comique for thirty performances of *Carmen.* "I saw the house gradually empty," he said. "I was present
at the last performance in February 1876." [n]

At the second performance, two nights after the *première,*
one gentleman, after groaning and moaning through the first act,
walked out in a huff in the second act when Galli-Marié broke the
plate she was about to use for castanets. The rest of the audience,
however, was entranced throughout the evening. A friend of
Bizet's, Pierre Berton, unable to attend the *première,* had been
shocked and grieved at the reports of the icy coldness of the first
night audience. On the second night, "I arrived," he said, "very
sad, very depressed . . . trying to figure out the reason for this
cruel disappointment. The first measures of the prelude and the
raising of the curtain dispelled the gloom. . . . Throughout the
first act, I remained in that state of delicious intoxication which
hearing a new and delightful work induces. . . . What had my
friends been talking about? What had happened to the resistance
of the audience, the glacial chill they had told me so much about?
Here, tonight, I was not alone under a spell. The whole audience
had vibrated in unison. Everything had been understood, appreciated, emphasized! The choruses at the beginning had been applauded, the famous couplets encored, the seduction scene and
Carmen's amusing escape greeted with bravos. This crowd with
which I rubbed elbows in the corridors and lobbies, whose naïve
appreciation I overheard, seemed quite as enchanted as I was.
How could it have been otherwise night before last? Perhaps, after
all, the effect of the other acts would not live up to the success of
the beginning.

"But this was not so. The second act went over like the first, without raising any of the prudish revulsion that du Locle had so inopportunely predicted. In the third act, the card scene made the greatest impression. In the fourth, the audience was carried away by the final duet and the death of Carmen; and when the curtain fell the applause was aimed quite as much at the composer as at the interpreters. . . . The people there seemed a little surprised at enjoying themselves. But enjoy themselves they did, nevertheless; and if they had not been informed of the coldness of the *première,* they would have been even more enthusiastic. I left delighted, but less and less able to explain what could have happened at that first performance. My friends, whose acumen and whose sympathy for Bizet were beyond question, had told me of a failure, and I had just been present at a success." [n]

Berton, a distinguished, experienced actor, and at this time a member of the Comédie-Française, knew very well how successes were launched. He believed that the director of the Comique was responsible for the failure of *Carmen:* "The great, the real, culprit was du Locle. In Perrin's hands the success would have been unquestionable. He knows how to control an audience and how to handle the press. Among the most severe critics of *Carmen,* I could name those who are notoriously venal. I could say exactly how much it would have taken to transform their attacks into dithyrambic eulogies and even by what intermediaries these delicate negotiations could have been carried out." [n]

Distasteful as this procedure would have been to Bizet had he been aware of it, and shocking as it is to realize that certain journalists of the Third Republic were no less corrupt than those so vividly portrayed by Balzac under the reign of Louis-Philippe, it is nevertheless true that if the daily papers that appeared between the first two performances of *Carmen* had not treated it primarily as a shocking and immoral spectacle, favorable word-of-mouth reports would gradually have counteracted the attacks of the popular press. By the third performance, which took place on Sunday, March 8, many of the better-class weeklies had come out with their reviews. Most of the adverse critics merely rehashed what they had said about Bizet's previous work. A few discriminating and respected writers, among them Victorien Joncières, praised the opera wholeheartedly. By the end of the week, however, it was too late for the harm wrought by the early press reports to be undone. The fact that *Carmen* was performed forty-eight times in six months has been used as an argument to prove that it was not really a failure in the beginning. But the records show that the auditorium was never filled and that the box-office receipts did not pay the cost of production.

Halévy, who with Meilhac was already busy working on *Le Passage de Vénus,* a one-act comedy to be given at the Variétés early in May, wrote in his journal, after the sixth performance of *Carmen,* his own explanation of the failure: "During rehearsals I went through a series of very different impressions of this piece. At first the music seemed distorted, complicated. Little by little . . . the performers began to be able to see the delicate and original things with which this very curious, very special score was filled. . . . The final rehearsals were *excellent.* The audience consisted of members of the staff who had lived with this music for three or four months, and who consequently had had time enough to be pervaded by its beauty. We were full of confidence the opening night. But, alas, the same thing that had happened to us in the beginning also obviously happened to the public. It took a little time for us to get to like and admire this score. At the outset we were more astonished than enchanted by it. Such was the evident impression on the audience the first evening. The effect of the performance was uncertain, indecisive. Not bad, but not good either." [n]

Of Bizet's peers only two felt impelled to inform him in writing of their impressions of *Carmen.* No word from Gounod or Ambroise Thomas. Delibes, on the day of the dress rehearsal, after the announcement of Bizet's election to the Legion of Honor, sent a message on a calling-card: "Sincerely happy about the good news, my friend. Good luck for tomorrow evening, Affectionately yours, L.D." [n] On the same day, Ernest Reyer, with what would seem like almost brutal obtuseness, sent Bizet a request to arrange an audition with du Locle for two "charming and talented" singers, because, he said: "Your relations with the director of the Opéra-Comique are of the all-powerful kind that insure success." In a postscript he added: "Try to get *Carmen* to me tonight or tomorrow morning. Thanks for the box. . . ." [n]

In the matter of seating, Massenet had been less fortunate. Nevertheless, at two o'clock in the morning after the *première* he sent Bizet a characteristic note: "How happy you must be at this time!—*It's a great success.* When I have the good fortune to see you, I shall tell you how happy you made me—and this happiness cancels somewhat the pain I felt at having been completely forgotten by you or by M. Camille du Locle in the matter of tickets. But you must have had your hands full with requests from friends!—Besides, I am being a nuisance. Again bravo with all my heart. Your devoted friend, J. Massenet." [n]

Saint-Saëns, who had been unable to go to a performance until a week after the *première,* wrote to Bizet: "At last I have seen *Carmen.* I found it marvelous and I am telling you the truth." [n] "Those three lines," Bizet replied, "signed by a master, by a man of honor like you, console me immeasurably for the insults of the Comettants, the Lauzières and other arses. You have made me proud and happy and I embrace you with all my heart." [n]

Bizet's use of the word "insult" to describe the adverse criticism of ·hostile journalists sprang rather from a sense of personal injury than from any hypersensitiveness about his music. For one can only be insulted by a peer and Bizet knew well that the musical endowment, intelligence, and taste of Comettant and Lauzières were negligible, their influence limited. Yet, though their attacks on his music were no more stupid, banal, or prejudiced than criticism of his earlier works, Bizet had lost the capacity to accept it philosophically. *Les Pêcheurs de Perles* he could regard as an "honorable" failure. After *La Jolie Fille de Perth,* he could count on the moral support of Mme Trélat. *Djamileh* failed while his marriage was still happy, and the disastrous reception of *L'Arlésienne* was mitigated by his joy at the birth of his son. Now Bizet's self-confidence, both as a man and as a musician, was undermined. His desperate need of reassurance naturally enough has given rise to the legend that, like Keats, "that fiery particle, snuffed out by an article," Bizet, too, was the victim of his critics. Actually their onslaughts on his integrity and taste as an artist, his talent and ability as a musician, were merely a minor element in the tension and strain that resulted in his illness and death. Yet the tone pervading all but three or four of the reviews of *Carmen* explains Bizet's unprecedented vulnerability. The flow of angry words in the newspapers stemmed not from any honest attempt to appraise a work of art, but from resentment at the idea of change or innovation that required new eyes and ears in the theatre.

"Decidedly the forerunners of the revolution had no conception of the violence of the passions they would have to curb . . ." Bizet, while still a student in Rome, had commented on a letter in which Beaumarchais described his escape from rioters. And later, when first commissioned by du Locle, he had written to Galabert: "I shall be delighted to try to change the genre of the Opéra-Comique." But he learned quickly, with breathtaking impact, that the process of launching a revolution more or less singlehanded was not enjoyable. Nor did he live long enough to realize that an innovation he had envisioned as purely artistic would seem an affront to the moral and social standards of the public. The invasion of the stage of the Opéra-Comique, that bulwark of bourgeois security, by lifelike, working-class characters ruled only by their passions introduced a kind of realism for which both audience and critics were as little prepared as for the originality of Bizet's music.

Even Ernest Reyer, who might have been expected to rally to his friend's support, allotted to the music only the two final paragraphs of a 2500-word review. "Must one now," he asked "give a detailed analysis of the score of *Carmen?* The reader, I know, has no excessive interest in the kind of analyses that require the use of technical terms. I prefer to mention the pieces that the audience particularly liked and which, therefore, should be the most successful." ʺ

A comparison of Reyer's article on *Carmen* with his review of Gounod's *Faust* accentuates his inability to appreciate Bizet's score. For his entire review of *Faust* was devoted to an analysis of Gounod's music. The libretto, that sugary version of Goethe's great poem, Reyer accepted without comment. But this tolerance was perhaps characteristic of a certain chauvinism that also blinded French critics to the feeble operatic versions of *Hamlet* and *Romeo and Juliet*. Goethe and Shakespeare were, after all, foreigners. Mérimée, although a minor writer, was a Frenchman. And had Reyer been writing of an adaptation to the operatic stage of a play by Corneille or Racine, he could have treated it with no more hallowed respect than he accorded Mérimée's short story. Yet without the addition of Bizet's music, would the original *Carmen* have found many readers outside of France? Reyer stood almost alone in believing that the defects in the libretto lay in Meilhac's and Halévy's "whitewashing" of the heroine, their sentimentalizing of Don José, and the introduction of Micaëla. This fair-haired maiden, whose existence Mérimée mentioned in a single sentence, seemed to the other critics the only character suited to the stage of the Opéra-Comique.

In the original story, Don José had committed two murders before he killed Carmen. At her behest and out of jealousy he knifed her husband (in the libretto, Carmen is, of course, unmarried). He ran his sword through an officer and nearly killed an English *milord* whose mistress Carmen had been and whom Don José helped her to rob. The Carmen of Mérimée was an adulteress, a wanton, a thief, a witch, and a devil who valued riches as much as she valued her freedom. In the time-span of months used by Mérimée for his story, Carmen's evil ways were counterbalanced in the reader's mind by her powers of enchantment. Transferred into the more restricted time limits of the theatre, she would have appeared as an unmitigated and unconvincing monster, had her character not been simplified and deepened.

The libretto of *Carmen* has long been recognized as one of the five or six perfect examples of its kind, yet only one contemporary critic, Théodore de Banville, himself a poet and a playwright, showed any grasp of the requirements for adapting a piece of literature, whether a play, a poem, or a story, to the operatic stage. A lucid summary of this problem at an earlier period exists in Lorenzo da Ponte's introductory remarks to the original libretto of Mozart's opera based on Beaumarchais's play *Le Mariage de Figaro:* "The duration prescribed for a stage performance by general usage," he wrote, "and the given number of roles to which one is confined by the same, as well as several other considerations of prudence, of costume, of place and public, constituted the reasons why I have not made a translation of that excellent comedy, but rather an imitation, or let us say an extract.

"For this reason I was compelled to reduce the sixteen original characters to eleven . . . and to omit in addition to one whole act, many highly effective scenes and many witty lines. . . . For these I have had to substitute *canzonette,* arias, choruses, and other thoughts and words susceptible of being set to music— things that can be handled only with the help of poetry and never with prose. . . ." Da Ponte then expresses his and Mozart's hope that the changes they had made would be excused by "the variety of development of this drama," their desire "to paint faithfully and in full color the divers passions that are aroused, and to realize our special purpose, which was to offer a new type of spectacle to a public of such refined taste and such assured understanding." " No controversy arose over da Ponte's omission of the essentially political aspect of Beaumarchais's play.

Deviations from the original were not, however, the problem that troubled most of the critics of *Carmen*. Many of them felt that no treatment could have made the work suitable for presentation to the audience at the Opéra-Comique. The two critics whose "insults" Bizet so strongly resented were the most savage advocates of this point of view. Achille de Lauzières, Marquis de Thémines, critic for *La Patrie*, apart from his ancient title, could boast of several unpublished operas, one of which had been performed at the Théâtre-Italien. Also, between 1844 and 1875, he had translated into Italian some dozen operas, including *Martha, Faust, Dinorah, Don Carlos,* and *Hamlet*. As a barely recognized composer who never achieved a performance at the Opéra-Comique, as an artistocrat who believed that a change in the existing hierarchies in the theatre would result in the dissolution of the established social order, Lauzières, naturally enough, resented Bizet and his innovations.

M. de Thémines, as he signed himself in *La Patrie,* claimed at the outset of his review of *Carmen* that courtesans had more and more usurped the stage. "This is the class from which writers enjoy recruiting the heroines of our dramas, our comedies and even our *opéras-comiques,*" he wrote. "And when once an author has become fouled in the social sewer, he is forced to descend . . . to the lowest level for a choice of models. . . . He feels in duty bound to outbid his predecessors. Marion Delorme, Manon Lescaut, Marguerite Gauthier . . . milestones on this unhappy route, are outdistanced. One of them claimed that love restored her virginity, another gave youthful inexperience as an excuse, still another expiated her folly by a great sacrifice. . . . As all of them pleaded their passion in extenuation, . . . one is forced to conclude . . . that they were merely pseudo-courtesans, that they didn't trail enough mud after them, that better ones must be found. . . .

"This 'better' one . . . is a *'fille'* in the most revolting sense of the word; a woman, mad over her body, giving herself to the first soldier who comes along, out of caprice, bravado, by chance, blindly. Then, after having lost him his honor, treated him with scorn, she deserts him to run after a handsomer fellow whom, in turn, she will leave when she likes. In the meantime she makes it her business to sleep with customs officials in order to facilitate the exploits of smugglers. . . . A savage; half gypsy, half Andalusian; sensual, mocking, shameless; believing neither in God nor in the Devil . . . she is the veritable prostitute of the gutter and the crossroads."

To avoid attributing any responsibility to Mérimée for this evil creation, Lauzières places that author's "subtly written" story in the category of a "phenomenon in the pathological library of a scholar . . ." comparable to "the limbs or viscera . . . revealed by an anatomist as he traces the ravages of gangrene."

Had the "very talented and witty" librettists chosen to treat "the love affair of a bad soldier, a bad son who ends as a murderer, with a working-girl in a tobacco factory . . . who begins by slashing with a knife . . . and ends stabbed by a dagger," as a melodrama for a boulevard theatre, the noble Marquis admits that his objections would have been less vehement. But the presentation of these vulgar, low-class characters at the Opéra-Comique signified the current degradation of society and of the arts. What was one to expect, he asked, in a period when only money mattered, when even the Opéra and the Comédie-Française opened their doors to works that had found success among the common people of the boulevards?

In an inverted form, Lauzières's snob values also conditioned his criticism of the score of *Carmen*. Bizet's widely circulated remark that he wrote only for the four or five people who could understand his music riled M. de Thémines. Would the composer "return to his earlier manner when he was still writing for the public," the critic wondered, "or would he persist in . . . writing only for his little group, 'the twenty-four persons who alone are able to understand him.'" Having added some twenty members to the comprehending audience the composer had allotted himself in a moment of anger and despair, the critic proceeds by indirection to imply that Bizet's music is easily understandable because he had plagiarized parts of it, notably the Toreador song, from popular sources. Then, more or less contradicting himself, Lauzières goes on to say, in discussing the "local color" in *Carmen:* "It would have been easy for him to take one of the thousand Spanish melodies everybody is singing and playing on guitars, to have assimilated it more or less and interpolated it into his score. He did it only once. He was right. But he could have given to the entire work the warm tone of the sun of Spain . . . (as he did in the *habanera* sung by Mme Galli-Marié) and for which one looks in vain in the score as a whole." [*]

Curiously enough, Lauzières was the only contemporary reviewer who brought up the subject of Spanish sources in Bizet's music, a topic that has preoccupied a number of modern scholars. No research was necessary to discover the derivation of the *habanera* from Yradier's *El Arreglito.* It was acknowledged in 1875 in a note in the first edition of the piano-and-voice reduction of the score of *Carmen.* But modern musicologists have worked long and laboriously to discover: (1) that the Prelude to Act III contains the opening bar of a *"Canción de cuna,"* a folk song included in Volume I of Pedrell's *Cancionero Musical Popular Español,* [*] a collection probably unknown to Bizet; and (2) that the entr'acte before Act IV was based on a *polo* taken from a *tonadilla* or short dramatic dialogue by the Spaniard, Manuel García, father of La Malibran and Pauline Viardot. The question of whether the *polo* Bizet used came from *El Criado Fingido,* as claimed by Julien Tiersot, or from a very similar *tonadilla, El Poëta Calculista,* reopens a musicological problem. For the latter work was included in a collection of Spanish folk music owned by Bizet. In the exhaustive catalogue he made of his music library, which remains among his papers, he has listed *Echos d'Espagne: Chansons et danses populaires, recueillies et transcrites par Lacome et Puig Absubido. (Texte espagnol, traduction française de Lacome et le Comte de Lusignan.)* He listed separately, in ink differing from that used in the earlier entries: *"El Poëta Calculista, Opéra,"* the only signed work in the volume of anonymous folk music. In spite of the closer technical resemblance between *El Criado Fingido* and the entr'acte before Act IV of *Carmen,* it seems probable, therefore, that Bizet made use of the *polo* included in the collection he owned.

So much, then, for the traceable sources of actual Spanish influence in the score of *Carmen*.[5] The opera-goer, amateur musician or music-lover, more fortunate than the musicologist, may fall unreservedly under the spell of Bizet's imagined Spain. The nature of the exoticism in Bizet's music is perhaps best explained by Reyer in a review previously quoted. The score of *Djamileh,* he said, is truly Oriental in the sense that it is native music "as it is understood by visitors to the countries of its origin . . . not through imitation of certain instrumental effects *sui generis* . . . but by the accompaniment it gives to the landscape our imagination evokes, of the picture it spreads before our eyes. It is a . . . slightly dressed-up truth, if you like, but a truth that takes into consideration . . . the nature of the musical sensations to which we are accustomed."

To earlier authors and composers who had laid their scenes in Spain, authenticity in local color had not been a problem. The Seville of Beaumarchais and Mozart or Beaumarchais and Rossini was a stage-setting in the classic tradition. But to the romantics and their followers, Spain was no longer a symbol or a convention. It was a strange and magical land, yet a country with a true existence. The projection on the stage of Spanish customs and folklore required a previously unknown degree of realism. In the unrestricted medium of prose fiction, Mérimée, who knew and wrote in Spain, a country Bizet never visited, could invent a device that permitted him, as a French narrator, to emphasize the essential Spanishness of his subject. Bizet, within the limits imposed by the operatic form, could only develop a synthesis of his own conception of Spanish music and feeling. Yet the local color in his opera gives the illusion of authenticity in every country but Spain. There *Carmen* is regarded as essentially French opera, which, of course, it is. The realism and truth of *Carmen* lie not in any literal depiction of Spain or Spanish life, but in the depth and universality of the passions of its characters.

The striking vividness of these characters elicited from the critic, Comettant, "insults" that wounded Bizet more deeply than Lauzières's. For Jean-Pierre-Oscar Comettant was a far abler and

---

[5] For further information on this subject, see Julien Tiersot, "Bizet and Spanish Music," in *The Musical Quarterly,* XIII, October 1927; Domenico de Paoli, "Bizet and His Spanish Sources," *The Chesterian,* XXII, No. 153; Gilbert Chase, *The Music of Spain,* New York, 1941; Carl Van Vechten, *The Music of Spain,* New York, 1918.

more intelligent journalist than his colleague. Educated at the Conservatoire under Elwart and Carafa, he achieved some reputation as a pianist and a composer before going to the United States, where he had spent three years traveling in the 1850's. His entertaining, if somewhat superficial, account of that journey launched him on a career of journalism, and for many years he was music critic on *Le Siècle,* one of the few papers that remained liberal under the Second Empire.

In his review of the libretto of *Carmen,* Comettant wasted no space on a discussion of Meilhac and Halévy's deviations from Mérimée. Indeed his attack on their version of the story could be interpreted as an unconscious tribute to its success. "Friends of unrestrained Spanish gaiety must have been delighted," he wrote. "There were Andalusians with sun-burned breasts, the kind of women, I like to think, who are found only in the low cabarets of Seville and lovely Granada. A plague on these females vomited from Hell! . . . this Castilian licentiousness! It is a delirium of castanets, of leers *à la Congreve,* of provocative hip-swinging, of knife-stabs gallantly distributed among both sexes; of cigarettes roasted by the ladies; of St. Vitus dances, smutty rather than sensuous. . . . To preserve the morale and the behavior of the impressionable dragoons and toreadors who surround this *demoiselle,* she should be gagged, a stop put to the unbridled twisting of her hips; she should be fastened into a straitjacket after being cooled off by a jug of water poured over her head.

"The pathological condition of this unfortunate woman, consecrated unceasingly and pitilessly to the fires of the flesh . . . is fortunately a rare case, more likely to inspire the solicitude of physicians than to interest the decent spectators who come to the Opéra-Comique accompanied by their wives and daughters. . . ."

In Comettant's long, detailed summary of the libretto, Carmen becomes in Act I *"la terrible espagnole* who leaps like a tiger-cat, writhes like a snake." In Act II he fears that "Mmes Galli-Marié, Ducasse (Frasquita), and Chevalier (Mercédès), who are not used to shaking themselves to the sound of castanets, will break their backs." Micaëla "is the only decent and sympathetic character in the midst of this inferno of ridiculous and uninteresting corruption."

"A libretto like this could hardly inspire a composer. . . ." Comettant declares. "Its essence is sensuality. . . . If Rossini

. . . had been forced when he was twenty-five to compose a score for the libretto of *Carmen,* he would have pulled off this difficult task by being lavish with spontaneous melodies . . . with a new twist. . . . Ingenious orchestral details, risky dissonances, instrumental subtlety, cannot express musically the uterine frenzies of Mlle Carmen and the aspirations of her ribald followers. Melody, independent melody . . . is the only thing suited to Messrs. Meilhac and Halévy's brutally realistic characters.

"This does not mean that there are no so-called themes in M. Bizet's score; unfortunately they lack novelty and . . . distinction. There is neither plan nor unity in the style of this opera, the greatest defect of which is that it is neither scenic nor dramatic. M. Bizet, who has nothing more to learn that can be taught, unhappily needs to find out things that cannot be studied. His essence, rather staled by the school of dissonance and research, needs to regain its musical virginity."

Comettant also recommended a purifying of Galli-Marié's interpretation of Carmen. "This distinguished artist," he felt, "could have corrected what was shocking and antipathetic in the character of this heartless, faithless, lawless gypsy. She has, on the contrary, exaggerated Carmen's vices by a realism that would at best be bearable in an operetta in a small theatre. At the Opéra-Comique, a subsidized theatre, a decent theatre if ever there was one, Mlle Carmen should temper her passions." Yet, shocked and disturbed as he was by the impurity of the music, the libretto, and the performance of Bizet's opera, Comettant concluded his review with the promise that "we shall go back to see *Carmen,* if it is played again, and we shall return to that score." "

Because of the rarity of Puritanism among the French, for whom *le plaisir* requires no justification, one can only suspect that the emphasis on sexuality in both Lauzières's and Comettant's criticism of *Carmen* was in large part a barricade erected against the threat of further revolutionary violence at the Opéra-Comique. Bizet's failure to grasp this aspect of the critics' animus gives rise to the question of whether the distress caused him by their attacks was not personal and psychological in origin, rather than professional. Subjected to the discord in his family life, accused of attacking bourgeois morality by presenting a prostitute as heroine, he was bound, consciously or unconsciously, to question the validity of his own moral standards and judgment.

Comettant and Lauzières both stated that as an operetta played in a "small theatre" of the sort that, say, Céleste Mogador had directed, *Carmen* might have been acceptable. This theory was, of course, based on the time-worn formula that only two categories of women exist—good or bad—"and never the twain shall meet." Bizet's own acceptance of the basic truth of this formula had restricted his experience with women, until his mid-twenties, to association with prostitutes. If his affair with a friend's wife opened the way to doubts of the validity of his simple code, his partner must nevertheless in his opinion have forfeited her original status as a good woman when she became an adulteress. His relationship with Céleste Mogador, the former *fille inscrite* who by dint of hard work had managed to achieve the more or less independent status of author and actress, probably caused him further self-questioning. One need only reread Céleste's self-portrait to know what Bizet himself may not have realized—that good or bad or both, she figured in his conception of the character of Carmen.

The only undeniably "good" woman Bizet ever loved was his wife. Yet his past experience had hardly prepared him for the responsibilities of marriage to so young, inexperienced, and complex a creature. Inevitably, situations arose which brought into question certain moral standards. At the high point of happiness in his marriage, Bizet's mother-in-law had questioned him about the suitability of Geneviève's calling on the wife of Dumas *fils*. "Calm yourself, dear Mme Halévy," Bizet wrote in the winter of 1872. "I am so rigid that I revolt my friends. I agree with Alex. Dumas that a gentleman who is unfaithful to his wife is no more an upright man than a wife unfaithful to her husband is a decent woman. Mme Dumas has been *exemplary* since she's been with Dumas. I consider her a decent person. . . . I would not permit Geneviève to see Mme (illegible). She could no doubt, for she is and will be a woman like you, above all evil. But I am unwilling to have a woman whom I know to be of doubtful reputation set foot in my house. As for women of the theatre, under no circumstances will one of them cross my threshold. You see that I am *inflexible*—so much so that Geneviève calls me M. Prud'homme," [n] —the satirical character invented by Henry Monnier to epitomize the qualities of the dull, respectable bourgeois husband.

After attending a performance of one of the plays in which

Dumas advocated a single standard of morals for men and women, Bizet wrote to Dumas: "I can't resist the desire, or rather the pressing need, to thank you for the profound emotion I experienced yesterday through your prodigious wit and your immense talent. . . . You believe that before tending to your own business, you must tend to the business of the social system. You have understood that in order to regenerate, you must stigmatize, and at the risk of your popularity you have dared to tell the truth. . . . I still remember, and always shall, the impression your prefaces made on me. You were the first to trace a clear line of demarcation between the absolutely and the relatively upright man. I have profited by the lesson. . . . We both admire you, my little Geneviève and I; but we esteem and love you even more. To be the wittiest gentleman of his day is indeed splendid; but also to be the most honest man is even better. Be lenient to my musician's prose, and be assured that those who say all this better than I do believe it no more firmly." "

Bizet's conception of the nature and function of women which began to change at the time of his engagement to Geneviève in 1867 had probably crystallized into a new pattern by the time *Carmen* was produced. He had learned that a "good woman" does not necessarily make a good wife, that women like his wife and his mother-in-law, though "above all evil," could be more harmful than the "bad" women he had known. His prejudice against "women of the theatre," none of whom was ever to be permitted to "cross his threshold," was obviously dislodged by his attachment to Galli-Marié. Throughout the embattled rehearsals of *Carmen,* it was not the composer's wife who sustained him either as a man or as an artist. It was Galli-Marié, the woman of the theatre, who became the embodiment of his creation by her own gifts, her faith in his talent, her fierce loyalty to his conception of the interpretation of her role, and her willingness to make sacrifices for it rather than compromise—it was she who gave him wholehearted support. How then must he have felt when he read the virulent personal attacks by Comettant and Lauzières on the character she portrayed with such faithful adherence to his conception that she herself became Carmen? And if the singer's interpretation represented the tangible, visual aspects of Bizet's heroine, it is probable that spiritually and musically Carmen was the realization of Bizet's own unconscious longing.

"I like my freedom . . . my individual liberty," he had

written to his mother before leaving Rome when he had hoped for living quarters apart from his family. And from the time of his mother's death until his marriage, he led the free Bohemian life of an artist. When he had enthusiastically resolved to transform himself into a good husband, he could hardly have envisaged the extent to which this duty would impinge upon his time, cut off his freedom of movement. Even before he started to compose *Carmen,* he had already begun to admit to himself that his family life was becoming unbearable. By the time the opera was finished, he sensed that the loss of his liberty of spirit threatened his future creative life. Even in the days when he was free from emotional anxiety and responsibility, a lack of self-confidence had periodically dogged him. Now that he was caught in the conflict between his love for his wife and his distress at the thought of leaving her, he could express his deepest feelings only in his music.

In one of the less-remarked but most moving arias in his opera, *"Là-bas, là-bas, dans la montagne,"* Carmen tries to seduce Don José from his duty by evoking the free, wandering life of the gypsy: *"Le ciel ouvert, la vie errante/ Pour pays l'univers, pour loi ta volonté,/ Et surtout la chose enivrante,/ La liberté.–. La liberté!"* This motivating passion for liberty is the element Bizet contributed to the characterization of Carmen. In Mérimée's story no emphasis is placed on her need for freedom beyond the remark that "to people of her blood, liberty is everything, and they would set a town on fire to save themselves one day in prison." From this tribal feeling, Bizet, by the dramatic intensity of the music to which he has set the simple and telling words, raises an almost animal instinct against being trapped to the poetic human need for identification with the unconquerable freedom of nature itself. Carmen, in Lillas Pastia's dark tavern, at the height of her love or infatuation for Don José, her desire unquenched, visualizes the consummation of her passion "in the mountains . . . under the open sky." Love under any laws except her own will is inconceivable to her. She is herself a force of nature, uninhibited, uncompromising. Mérimée's Carmen, out of an inborn fatalism, resigned herself to being killed. Bizet's Carmen chose death in preference to a loss of freedom. Thus the "devil . . . sorceress . . . witch" of Mérimée is transformed by Bizet's music into a true *femme fatale,* as destructive to herself as to her lover. Is it illogical then to suppose that the liberty-loving Bizet, whose happiest days had been spent wandering in the mountains of Italy, and who was now caught in a situation from which he could free himself only by a ruthlessness equal to Carmen's, should create in his music the embodiment of his own needs and desires? *"Madame Bovary, c'est moi,"* said Flaubert. *"Carmen, c'est moi,"* would explain the power over the composer of the small-minded men who, by attacking his heroine and her interpreter, unwittingly hit him at the deepest level of his own nature. How else explain the fact that the review by the one truly distinguished writer who treated *Carmen* as a work of art compensated the composer so little for the "insults" of his inferiors that he dismissed it as a charming gesture on the part of a critic who was also a friend?

To the poet Théodore de Banville, in acknowledgment of his piece in *Le National* on March 8, 1875, Bizet wrote: "There is no way of thanking you for the charming article you devoted to *Carmen*. I am very proud to have inspired this delightful fantasy. . . ." [6]

Banville, in his article, describing the impact of *Carmen* on the opening night, wrote: "This thing is so new that the audience . . . cried, 'Oh, oh, what is this? Here I am, resentful, excited, alive, in tears, engrossed in these people: I have been tricked.'" One senses that Bizet dismissed as a "delightful fantasy" the only review that envisaged the artistic significance of *Carmen* as a whole because, in a perverse way, he felt cheated by this single drop of nectar in so much poison; that like the audience at his opera, he too was unwilling to enjoy himself; that only by fighting an enemy could he convince himself of the value of his own work. For there was nothing fantastic or whimsical about Banville's very long, discerning, and lively review.

"The Opéra-Comique," he wrote, "the traditional theatre of kind-hearted brigands, languorous maidens, rose-water loves, has been forced, violated, stormed by a band of unbridled ro-

---

[6] Bizet to Théodore de Banville, n. d. Unpublished letter in New York Public Library. Although this letter is addressed merely to *"Monsieur et cher maître,"* it could not refer to any but Banville's review of *Carmen*. On March 23 [1875], Banville wrote to Bizet: "Our friend Cressonnois tells me of the great effort you have generously made for him. As I am his accomplice, having supplied him with the canvas, it seems that I have the right to add my thanks to his. I am a great admirer of your talent. That in itself tells you how happy I am to be indebted to you for something and that I am very sincerely, warmly, and gratefully yours, Théodore de Banville." (Unpublished letter in collection of the author.) Jules-Alfred Cressonnois (1823-83) was writing the incidental music for Banville's comedy *Déidemia,* which was produced in 1876.

mantics headed by M. du Locle; then Georges Bizet, Wagnerian, who is set against expressing passion in songs set to dance tunes; Meilhac and Halévy, who build windmills as high as the tower of Babel solely to toss their caps over them, and finally Mme Galli-Marié, who has devoted herself to the mission of performing poetry, Goethe and Musset, Mignon and Fantasio, in the one place in the world most antagonistic to poetry. . . . Either Seville . . . the *posada* drenched in aloes, the oleanders and the cigarette-smoke . . . Carmen murdered, bathed in her own blood, must disappear, put to flight by the muse that inspired M. de Saint-Georges . . . or *Fra Diavolo* must return to the vague regions of faded fabrications and empty shadows! All the more so because the bold attempt of the insurgents has left no door open for conciliation. . . . If we aren't careful they will end by so thoroughly corrupting our second lyric theatre, formerly such a sweet, well-behaved child, that we shall even hear beautiful lines there, which would affect the late Scribe as a good bath in holy water affects the devil. . . .

"M. Georges Bizet," Banville continues, "is one of those ambitious men for whom . . . music must be, even in the theatre, not an entertainment, a way of spending an evening, but a divine language expressing the anguish, the folly, the celestial aspirations of the being who . . . is a wanderer and an exile here below. . . .

"Instead of those pretty sky-blue and pale-pink puppets who were the joy of our fathers, he has tried to show real men and real women, dazzled, tortured by passion . . . whose torment, jealousy . . . mad infatuation are interpreted to us by the orchestra turned creator and poet. . . . To bring about such a *coup d'état* M. Bizet . . . found the only associates who could have the idea, the courage, and the audacity to give him enough range by throwing out the window all the old rubbish and the old ghosts of the Opéra-Comique. . . . Take care, M. du Locle, M. Bizet, M. Meilhac, M. Halévy, for Lady Macbeth was right. In spite of all the perfumes of Araby the odor of blood will always be there. How in the future can . . . *La Dame blanche* . . . ever be brought back?" "

CHAPTER  XXVIII

Death of Georges Bizet

In spite of the preponderantly adverse criticism of *Carmen,* du Locle, soon after the *première,* commissioned another opera from Bizet and his librettists. The director also scheduled fourteen performances for April, three more than had been given in March. At the end of two months, therefore, *Carmen* had been performed more often than any of Bizet's previous works. This achievement might well have encouraged him, had financial success not been so essential to his peace of mind at this time. For the profound melancholy that struck his friends so sharply arose largely from his anxiety over the insecurity of his marriage, which deprived him of self-confidence, destroyed his natural resilience, and engendered an unprecedented bitterness. If his friends were aware of his domestic situation, they did not feel free to record it.

A few days after the second performance, Berton, still in the throes of the emotion *Carmen* had aroused in him, met the composer in the street. Sensing Bizet's depression, he immediately launched into a description of the enthusiastic second-night audience, its intelligent appreciation of the score, the impact on it of the whole opera. "He listened to me," Berton said, "without interruption, his eyes fixed on mine, his manner serious and attentive. But not one of my encouraging words drew a smile from him, and when I had finished he alluded indirectly, but not without bitterness, to the attitude of the musical press."

Berton thereupon enlarged upon the various reviews that had horrified him, pointed out how false they had been proved by the performance of *Carmen* he himself had seen. "This second part of my discourse—" he continues, "I can use this term because the whole time I was talking Bizet remained silent—was even more vehement than the first. I gave full vent to my indignation, which was intensified by the painful inertia that congealed my poor friend. I would like to have seen him carried away, joining in my indignation as he formerly had done so brilliantly on similar occasions when he was not the person involved. I would have given anything in the world to force out of him one violent word, a single gesture of revolt, a cry of rage. But no; he remained silent, his features . . . immobile . . . retaining the same sad, serious expression. He replied to my excited words only by pressing my hand from time to time . . . and I felt all the more the internal tempests hidden behind this stoical façade; the wavering of his spirit, torn between the raging desire to curse his judges and his terror of believing them. Finally he shrugged his shoulders in a gesture of profound weariness and said . . . 'Perhaps they are right.' " "

Soon after this incident, toward the end of March, Bizet was stricken with an attack of the throat angina to which he had long been subject and which, as we have seen, frequently followed an emotional crisis. In the past, in spite of the acute pain caused by the abscesses, he had recovered rapidly. But this time, when he was worn out on every level of his being, his recovery was only apparent. "You wouldn't believe how old I feel," he remarked to a horrified friend. For his stocky build, his rosy face, his spontaneous gaiety, his love of life had always given an impression of health in spite of his never strong constitution.

Early in April, Maréchal again lunched at the Bizets' one Sunday. As host the composer managed a superficial liveliness during the meal. But the conversation in his study afterwards was evasive, touching on anything but the subject both men had in mind. "Then suddenly Bizet put down his pipe on the mantelpiece, slapped his sides, and, speaking sharply, said: 'I've had enough of writing music to impress three or four friends who thumb their noses at me behind my back! I now see what the public wants. Very well then, I'll give them what they want.' " "

There was no question that spring of what the public wanted. At the Opéra-Comique the first two performances of Verdi's Requiem, again conducted by the composer, met with the same success as the year before, and du Locle arranged for five additional performances. Massenet's oratorio *Eve*, played for the first time at the Cirque des Champs-Elysées a fortnight after the *première* of *Carmen,* was welcomed by a large audience with only slightly less enthusiasm than had been accorded *Marie-Magdeleine.* In writing of "the great joy and profound emotion" he had experienced in listening to *Eve,* Gounod told Massenet that "the triumph of one of the elect should be an occasion for rejoicing in the Church. You are one of the elect, *mon cher ami*: Heaven has marked you with the sign of her children. I feel it in everything your beautiful work has stirred in my heart. Prepare yourself for the role of martyr . . . but don't complain and don't be sad. . . . Spread your wings boldly and put your trust in the upper regions where base lead shot from the earth cannot reach the bird in the sky." "

Both the baser lead and more precious metals were of great importance to Gounod at this time. After quarreling with the directors of the Albert Hall, having been sued for libel by his English publishers, and having become involved in a variety of legal complications over matters of copyright and taxation, the wandering master had returned suddenly to France in June 1874 in a state of acute nervous breakdown. Dr. Blanche's ministrations and Gounod's distaste for the scandal caused by his three years with Mrs. Weldon in England resulted in his once more taking up residence with his wife several months after his return to France. In January 1875, writing to *"Mon* Bizet" and signing himself *"Ton* Gounod *qui t'aime,"* he thanked his disciple for arranging a meeting with Colonne, who wished to play a manuscript piece of Gounod's: "The fraudulence of the music business (which has subjected me to the most perfidious chicanery) is such a consummate art today that I shall never again permit public performance of any work until after it has been engraved and is ready to face the dangerous obligations of copyright and registration." "

Gounod's rancor soon strained his relations with Choudens to such a degree that Bizet was called upon to act as intermediary, a role that inevitably resulted in Gounod's identifying him with the enemy. "Have you any information to give me of the intentions, inclinations or decisions of Messrs. Choudens (father and son) on the subject of the *pure and simple* suppression I have asked for, of three pieces that they have unwarrantedly published *under my name* in a collection of *Quinze duos* by Ch. Gounod?" he demanded of Bizet.

"I shall have to be informed so that I can instruct my solicitor and my attorney if Messrs. Choudens persist in the *absolutely illegal* continuance of this defamatory publication. The Messrs. Choudens have no right whatsoever to submit, as a condition of the suppression of the above-mentioned pieces, my providing them with *new* ones to replace them. It is as though one said to somebody: 'I will give you back ten thousand francs that belong to you if you give me thirty thousand that don't belong to me.' A word in reply, please. Yours, Ch. Gounod." [1] This final letter from the master to his disciple, written on May 5, is indeed proof of the pitiful level to which their friendship had dwindled. Bizet had become the scapegoat. Yet Gounod could hardly have written such a letter had he known that Bizet was suffering a new attack of illness at the time.

"Colossal angina," he wrote to Guiraud. "Imagine a double pedal from A flat to E flat going through your head from ear to ear. Don't come Sunday. No more now. I'll write to you." " In addition to the abscesses in his throat, an abscess at the root of his tongue added greatly to his suffering. Yet the inflammation resulting from this acute septic condition soon disappeared, and for about a fortnight no new symptoms appeared. Bizet's attitude, however, remained far from normal, and for the only time in his life he engaged in a personal dispute with an adverse critic.[2]

One day, early in May, when Comettant was standing in the lobby of the Conservatoire with several musicians, he saw Bizet "furious, with bloodshot eyes, descending upon him and looking as though he intended to strangle" him. "He restricted himself," wrote Comettant, "to reproaching me in far from restrained language and in a tone of voice that revealed unknown echoes under the vault of that temple of harmony. I tried to make him understand that it is a critic's function to say what he thinks about au-

---

[1] Gounod to Bizet. Unpublished letter in collection of the author. On April 26, 1875, Gounod had written the following note to Bizet: *"Cher ami,* The letter from Messrs. Choudens, father and son, is a *masterpiece!* Can you give me a moment's interview so I can tell you in detail of their extreme scrupulousness and no less touching magnanimity! I embrace you and your Geneviève. Ch. Gounod." Unpublished letter in collection of the author.

[2] After *Djamileh,* he wrote to an unidentified critic: "I read with lively interest your evaluation of *Djamileh.* Your criticism, although severe, is evidently marked with good will and I wish to thank you warmly." Bizet to unidentified correspondent, n. d. Unpublished letter in collection of the Metropolitan Opera of New York. Kindness of Mrs. O'Donnell Hoover.

thors . . . that I had in no way exceeded my right to judge and that I owed him no redress. I added, however, that if he was set on cutting my throat, I would consent to it, but only to please him and thus to prove to him how much I esteemed his great talent and his honorable character. . . . M. de Saint-Georges was kind enough to assume the role of arbitrator." ⁿ He wrote to Bizet on May 26: "I think the discussion you had with a M. Comettant was the result of your mistake in supposing that his article had the same malicious imputation as M. de Lauzière's. Considering our artistic standing and dignity, your reproaches to M. Comettant about his criticisms were out of place. It is not proper for us authors to defend our own works. I can't see that there is any objection to your *admitting your mistake* by writing M. Comettant a short, polite explanation of the misunderstanding between you. Send me this letter and I will make use of it in a suitable way that will reflect neither on your character nor your dignity." ⁿ The suggested letter was never written.

Bizet's already irritable state of mind was intensified by the restriction of *Carmen* to seven performances during May. Because Galli-Marié played the leading role in the *première* of *L'Amour africain* on May 8, she was unable to sing as often in *Carmen*. This new opera in two acts by Emile Paladilhe, with a libretto by Ernest Legouvé, whose granddaughter the composer later married, had no success, and was played only six times. This failure, in addition to that of *Don Mucarade* by Ernest Boulanger, which opened on May 10 and ran for only eight performances, and the questionable *succès d'estime* of *Carmen,* had a dire effect on the finances of the Opéra-Comique as well as on its director's never robust health. Du Locle therefore decided to shut down his theatre from June 16 to August 15 and to remove *Carmen* from the repertory during June. As a result of this decision, Galli-Marié wrote to the composer: "My dear M. Bizet, M. du Locle has just informed me that I shall be free the first of June. Didn't you wish to have *Carmen* continue until the closing of the theatre? It seems that I am very odd because I prefer my own enjoyment to money. This explains why, up to the present time, I have refused to go to London in the hope that I would be playing Carmen until June 15. —Do you think it is the question of salary that bothers M. du Locle? If so, couldn't you arrange with Choudens, for instance, to act as my cashier for those two weeks? Make up your mind quickly because I need hardly tell you that without your Carmen I shall hasten to accept London, as everyone tells me I am wrong to refuse. . . . Believe me your wholly devoted Galli-Marié." " *Carmen* continued in the repertory until the closing, perhaps with the aid of Choudens, who was determined that the opera should have fifty performances before he published the orchestral score.

Toward the end of May, Bizet's spirits improved, although the muscular rheumatism to which he had long been subject increased in intensity. (It seems probable that this chronic disease was the result of a childhood attack of rheumatic fever.) Because the abscesses in his throat and mouth had healed, he felt that he was on the way to recovery. Around May 20, Gallet went to see him to discuss work on *Geneviève de Paris*. "I found him slightly tired, his smile still somewhat melancholy, but full of enthusiasm at the thought of working again. Seated in his invalid's chair, he talked to me at length both of his past suffering and of his dreams for the future. He made light of his illness, saying that he had conquered it. . . . All his reviving strength as a composer, all his renewed ardor, centered on *Geneviève*. . . . It was the only time, I think, that Bizet did not talk to me standing up. . . ." " Gallet laid no stress on this inactivity at the time; after Bizet's death he realized how ill he had been at that final meeting. Because Gallet had only the manuscript copy of the libretto of *Geneviève,* Bizet asked him to have it copied quickly and sent to Bougival.

St. Geneviève, whose faith saved Paris from the Huns, appears as a sort of precursor of St. Joan in the script, which is somewhat reminiscent of *Clovis et Clotilde,* the cantata with which Bizet won the Prix de Rome. Gallet's libretto, although more sophisticated in its simplicity, could hardly have inspired Bizet to another *L'Enfance du Christ.* The copy of *Geneviève de Paris* was sent to Bougival promptly, but by the time it arrived, Bizet was too ill to look at it.

During the few days late in May before he left for the country, Bizet's condition did not improve. He complained of fits of suffocation. The severity of his rheumatism caused him to fall one morning when getting out of bed. He asked Marie Reiter, who nursed him as she had his mother in her final illness, to promise that she would not mention this accident to anyone: "If you do, they won't let me leave Paris, and this air is poisoning me." He spoke of turning over to her the funds she had always entrusted to his care. "And I must arrange a little remembrance for you," he added, "in case something should happen to me." *

A premonition of death recurs in an incident remembered by the critic, Blaze de Bury, who had written one of the more favorable reviews of *Carmen*. "The last time we saw Bizet," he says, "he was running through the score of *Carmen* with a young girl whose voice and rare musical gifts had charmed him. . . . All of a sudden he stopped playing, rose and said: 'Now, Mademoiselle, sing me some Schumann.' While she sang *'Iche grolle nicht'* and *'Aus der Heimat,'* Bizet sat at the other end of the room listening, his head in his hands. 'What a masterpiece,' he exclaimed, 'but what desolation. It's enough to make you long for death!' Then he went back to the piano and played the Funeral March by the same master, then Chopin's, which a few days later was played at his own funeral." *

Bizet continued to insist upon leaving Paris in spite of the objections of his friends and family. Dr. Dufour, his own physician, was out of town, so Geneviève consulted a doctor who neither knew Bizet's medical history nor paid him a personal call. He advised the move to Bougival on the general principle that for a convalescent the country is better than the city. The night before the departure, Guiraud called at Bizet's request to play parts of *Piccolino,* the opera on which he was working at the time: "I sat down at the piano and had hardly started to play the first piece when he put his hand on my shoulder and said: 'Wait. I can't hear anything in that ear; I'll sit on the other side.' The shrill, shaky tone of his voice made me wince. I turned quickly. The man I saw was no longer Bizet, the friend full of youth and vigor I had always known. The peaked, sickly look he had at that moment made a profound impression on me. I was struck by a horrible vision, quick and fleeting, like lightning. Bizet had . . . seated himself on my left, near the piano; he was all attention. I had regained my composure, and without showing any of the terror that had gripped me, I started playing. . . . He listened attentively, told me what he thought about each piece with that freedom of expression, that charming frankness, that admirable sincerity which endeared him to all of us. Then, when he had exhausted that subject, we talked about other things, both trivial and serious. Hours went by. At midnight I got up to leave and we shook hands. He lighted a candle to show me the way, for the gaslight on the stairs had been extinguished. I went down, but at the bottom I suddenly remembered something I had promised myself to talk to him about and which, in the excitement of our conversation, I had forgotten. . . . Our talk continued at a distance; he stood at the top of the stairs, leaning toward me, wrapped in his dressing-gown in spite of the warm weather, his candle in his hand and I, downstairs looking up at him. We chatted like that for about twenty minutes. Then, after a final good-night I left, thinking no more of the strange terror that had shaken me." "

Bizet still felt ill the night before he left for Bougival when he wrote to du Locle: "I would have liked to shake your hand, but nothing in the world would make me risk exposing you to the illness with which I am still afflicted. . . . I shan't thank you again; but how well you have stood up for me! And how touched I am by all the proofs of your affection. I should have liked to do more!—I hoped for something better, I admit. It has made me very unhappy, not for myself—as far as I am concerned I am more than satisfied —but for you. Kiss your two lovely daughters for us and tell Mme du Locle how sorry I am to leave so impolitely. Your friend, Georges Bizet." [3]

On Friday, May 28, the Bizets moved to Bougival. Besides the composer, his wife, and their little son Jacques, who was now nearly three years old, the household consisted of Marie, her son Jean, Geneviève's maid Eliza, and Eliza's daughter. From Le Pecq, where the railroad line then terminated, they made the journey in an open carriage. The family dined at the Hôtel de Madrid which stood in a cool, breezy bend in the Seine. The country air immediately revived Bizet's spirits. He could breathe freely. The rheumatic pains seemed to vanish. On Saturday he went for a walk along the river bank with his wife and Delaborde. Later the two men went for a swim in the river. (From the time when he had started bathing on the Italian coast he had developed a passion for swimming in cold water. He had even installed a sort of shower behind curtains in his study, which he enjoyed when the weather prevented outdoor bathing.) On Sunday, May 30, Bizet developed an acute rheumatic attack, with high fever, extreme pain, and almost total immobility of his arms and legs. His con-

[3] Bizet to Camille du Locle, unpublished letter, n.d. Inscribed on the envelope by Mme du Locle, "Sent on the eve of his departure for Bougival, May 27, 1875." Courtesy of Mme Vouillon.

dition changed little during Monday, but the muscular inflammation diminished and he could move a little more easily. During
the night between Monday and Tuesday, however, he had an
extremely painful heart attack that caused him to suffer great
agony and fear of imminent death. A Dr. Clément Launay, probably called by Delaborde from Rueil, a nearby town, arrived at one
o'clock in the morning. By that time the attack had diminished
and Bizet was resting quietly. The doctor stayed for some time,
and left only after having put a blister on the region of the heart.
He returned at eight the next morning, Wednesday, June 2, and
said: "The crisis is over; there is no more danger." Shortly after
his departure, Ludovic Halévy, who since Bizet's illness had been
coming on horseback each day from Saint-Germain-en-Laye to
Bougival, arrived and found "Geneviève in tears, Bizet feverish,
troubled." During the day, although his fever remained high,
Bizet gradually calmed down, and in the early evening he seemed
to feel better, less depressed. About half past eight, little Jacques
and Jean Reiter, who was now thirteen years old, went into his
bedroom for their daily visit. "Off to bed with you, my fine fellows,"
he said as he kissed them good-night. At about ten o'clock he
seemed very quiet and said: "Perhaps I can sleep a little." An
hour later he had another heart attack, as violent and agonizing as
the previous one. "Delaborde," he cried. "Go and fetch Delaborde
at once."

His calling for Delaborde was undoubtedly motivated by a
final desire to protect Geneviève. For according to those who were
closest to Bizet, any jealousy he may have felt of Delaborde earlier
had changed to resignation and, indeed, to relief. Knowing that
in any crisis Geneviève was likely to suffer another nervous collapse, he felt that he could count on Delaborde to give her the
necessary care and attention.

The shock his father would suffer also occupied Bizet's
thoughts. While waiting for the arrival of Delaborde and the doctor,
Marie stayed at Bizet's bedside. "My poor Marie," he said to her,
"I am in a cold sweat. It is the sweat of death. How are you going
to tell my poor father?" Then he lost consciousness.

Delaborde arrived an hour or more before the doctor, who
seemed to take an interminable time. When Dr. Launay finally
entered the sickroom, Delaborde said to him: "He has fainted.

What can we do?" "Nothing," replied the doctor, after a moment. "He is dead."

At three o'clock in the morning, Ludovic Halévy, who had been only half asleep in a guestroom, heard a voice calling, " 'Monsieur Ludovic, Monsieur Ludovic!' It was Geneviève's maid. Geneviève had to be removed from that house," he wrote in his journal." The three lines explaining this statement are inked out. Halévy immediately took Geneviève to his house at Saint-Germain-en-Laye; and from there at 8.30 in the morning on June 3, he telegraphed the tragic news to Hippolyte Rodrigues, Ernest Guiraud, and Camille du Locle. "The most horrible disaster," he wired Rodrigues. "Bizet died last night." "

The exact hour and the precise cause of Bizet's death are not known. Halévy believed that he died at three o'clock, the hour at which the maid called him. The death certificate gives the hour as two o'clock. But as Bizet had been in a coma from midnight on, two hours before the doctor arrived, he may have died immediately after midnight. In 1911 Bizet's widow, when asked by Pigot the nature of her first husband's fatal illness, attributed his death to a heart attack. A year or two before her own death in 1926, she told another biographer that Bizet had died of a tumor in his ear which surgeons regarded as inoperable, but which they hoped would be absorbed.

The most reliable diagnosis was given by the late Dr. Eugène Gelma, formerly Professor of Psychiatry at the University of Strasbourg. Dr. Gelma spent many years of his life collecting information from everyone who might throw light on the subject. His most valuable informant was Jean Reiter, who was in the house at Bougival the night of Bizet's death. When he himself died in 1939, he was under the care of Dr. Gelma. Although he never stated openly to the doctor, as he had to Henry Malherbe, that Georges Bizet was his father, Dr. Gelma assumed this to be true on the basis of recollections his patient confided to him.

"Bizet succumbed to a cardiac complication of acute articular rheumatism. Without the febrile polyarthritis following on a chill, he would not have died during a convalescence from a recurrent throat angina," Dr. Gelma believed." He did not include among the fatal symptoms the tumor or abscess in Bizet's left ear which had caused his deafness, and which had apparently burst while he was in coma. Traces of the excretions of pus and blood, still visible on his neck the following morning when Antony de Choudens viewed the body, led him to think that Bizet had cut his throat. Because no member of the family was present to contradict this erroneous conclusion, it became the basis of the rumor that Georges Bizet had committed suicide.

The only suicidal aspect of Bizet's death was his swimming in the Seine after so many days of illness. This kind of recklessness was more responsible for the tragedy of Bizet's unhappy life and early death than any pathological factors. He lacked the instinct for self-preservation. Only shortly before his death, if then, did he learn that to live long and freely enough to carry out the concepts in his imagination, an artist has only two alternatives: either he cultivates his sense of self-protection to a degree that may well make him seem a monster of selfishness to non-creative human beings; or, if he is incapable of the ruthlessness necessary to protect the integrity of his inner core from the onslaughts of daily existence, he compensates for this lack by finding the right person to protect him. In France it is an accepted idea that a man of genius needs a *"protectrice."* Bizet, on the other hand, became, by his marriage, the protector and guardian of a mother and daughter incapable of conducting their own lives, unaware of or indifferent to the burden they imposed on others. Although Mme Halévy and Geneviève nibbled away Bizet's time and his vitality by the importunate demands of their neurasthenic natures, they cannot be blamed for his early death, which could have been warded off only by a self-protective ruthlessness, an egotism stronger than theirs. And this life-preserver he lacked.

At approximately the moment when Bizet lost consciousness, the curtain fell on the last act of the thirty-third performance of *Carmen.* Galli-Marié had arrived at the theatre "in a state of indescribable hyper-excitement and enervation; before going on stage . . . she had great difficulty in restraining her tears. Camille du Locle, who attributed her mood to some momentary annoyance . . . perhaps a lovers' quarrel, tried to calm her. 'Listen, my child,' he said in a kindly, but somewhat ironic tone. 'It will blow over. Calm yourself. By tomorrow everything will be all right again.' 'No,' she replied, 'it's not what you think; there's nothing the matter with *me,* nothing at all.' " "

She apparently managed to collect herself sufficiently to go through the first two acts without difficulty. But in the third act, when Carmen foresees her own death in the card trio Galli-Marié's heart beat, she said, "as though it would break, and she seemed to feel a threatening chill in the air. She mustered enough self-control to finish the scene, and then fainted in the wings. After she had been revived, when other members of the cast tried to calm and reassure her . . . she insisted that it was not for herself she feared." "

A sixth sense has been attributed to Galli-Marié by a number of Bizet's biographers. The literal-minded, however, may be inclined to accept du Locle's more realistic explanation—that the singer was troubled by problems in her personal life. Certainly it was complex. Whatever the status of her liaison with Paladilhe may have been at this time, the failure of his opera could only cause her unhappiness. The knowledge that she was scheduled to sing *Carmen* only five more times would also inevitably distress her for both Bizet's sake and her own. And Galli-Marié, when in distress, was prone to fainting. When George Sand's *La Petite Fadette,* set to music by one Théophile Semet, had achieved a *première* in 1869 after more than the usual number of delays and complications, "Mme Galli-Marié showed herself a remarkable protagonist in spite of the uneasiness or emotion which . . . caused her to faint during an entr'acte." " After the performance, when George Sand came to congratulate the singer, she found her "in the wings, talking of death. She said it was the only good thing in life!" "

On learning of Bizet's death, Galli-Marié developed a high fever that prevented her from singing the night of June 3. Instead of the scheduled performance of *Carmen, La Dame blanche* was played. *"Mort à La Dame blanche!* . . .*[4]* I shall be delighted to try to change the genre of the Opéra-Comique," Bizet had said five years earlier. His success in achieving this aim was recognized only gradually. But the *Dame blanche* who appeared on the night after Bizet's death was a portent and a ghost. She had suffered her death blow three months earlier by the murder on stage at the Opéra-Comique of the phoenix Carmen.

---

[4] The year after Bizet's death, when Galabert was preparing Bizet's letters for publication, Guiraud asked him to suppress the words *"Mort à La Dame blanche"* lest the son of the composer Boïeldieu defend his father's reputation by attacking Bizet's. Guiraud withdrew his objection before publication of the brochure in 1877.

Bizet's funeral took place on Saturday, June 5, at the Church of La Trinité in Paris. Four thousand people attended the services: the whole company of the Opéra-Comique, a number of the actors who had played in *L'Arlésienne*, the music critics en masse, Dumas *fils*, and the rest of *"le Tout-Paris."* Galli-Marié and Mlle Chapuy (Micaëla) were noted sitting together "utterly crushed." Among the flowers that covered the coffin was a wreath from the Prix de Rome contestants who were *en loge* and could not attend the ceremony. Pasdeloup, who had been conducting a music festival in Caen at the time of Bizet's death, hurried back to Paris and "in a few hours" arranged the musical program. The entire orchestra of the Concerts Populaires took part.

As prelude, the organist improvised on themes from *Les Pêcheurs de Perles*. The orchestra then played *Patrie*, which was followed by a *Pie Jesu* adapted by Guiraud from the duet in *Les Pêcheurs*, sung with tears in their voices by Duchesne (Haroun in *Djamileh*) and Bouhy (Escamillo). "In the nave of the church," wrote Reyer, "Bizet's songs had a quality of grandeur, an elevation of thought, a nobleness of form that they had never had in the theatre or the concert hall." As the service drew slowly to a close, performers and congregation wept. The chant of the priests alternated with the sound of the orchestra and the voices of the singers. Lhérie (Don José) sang the *Agnus Dei,* the orchestra played the *andante* from the Prelude to *L'Arlésienne* and the *adagietto*. A grand fantasy on themes from *Carmen* was improvised by the organist during the absolution. The cortège left the church to the strains of Chopin's Funeral March.

At the head of the procession were the pallbearers: Gounod, Ambroise Thomas, Camille Doucet, and du Locle. The chief mourner, Bizet's father, followed on the arm of Ludovic Halévy. Then came Ludovic's father, Léon Halévy, and Bizet's close friends: Guiraud, Delaborde, Massenet, literally in tears, and Paladilhe with eyes red from weeping. The catafalque, covered with white flowers and bouquets of *immortelles*, was temporarily placed in Montmartre Cemetery. Jules Barbier, representing the Commission of Dramatic Authors and Composers, du Locle, and Gounod were the eulogists. Du Locle, the second speaker, concluded, "And so the road that he followed from childhood with such energy and force, that road has led to this grave! . . . He marched at the head of that young pleiad from which our com-

posers of tomorrow will emerge; he fell on the eve of victory. After
having long since conquered the discerning and the literate, he was
moving toward the conquest of the crowd, not by descending to it,
but by forcing it to raise itself up to him." "

Gounod delivered the final eulogy. "He was only able to speak
a few words before his voice broke with emotion," reported the
Figaro. "Gentlemen," he said, "I shall not hold you for long
around this too-early opened tomb, which engulfs so many hopes,
so much future, and so much happiness. Georges Bizet is dead at
the age of 37 [*sic*] at the moment when, after twenty years of
patient and courageous effort, he was at last enjoying that regard
which means even more than success itself, which is attached only
to true artists, and which ends by conferring upon those chosen
the name of master. At the outset of this arduously glorious route,
death has struck him down. It has struck him, too, at the time of
his heart's great joy. Married for six years to Geneviève Halévy,
daughter of his illustrious master, who was also mine, he leaves in
the heart of his widow regrets that are a greater tribute than any
of the wreaths placed on his grave in his memory. May I be permitted, gentlemen, to repeat here the testimonial, both sorrowful
and consoling, which came to me from the lips of that young woman
whose despair is so heartbreaking because it is so simple and so
true. 'Of the six years I spent with him,' she told me, 'there is not a
single minute, not one, which I am not still grateful for and happy
to remember.' " At this moment Gounod broke down and was unable to pronounce the final sentence of the prepared draft of this
singular speech: "Gentlemen, there you have the measure of everything that mattered in the present and in the future to the man
and the artist we mourn." "

At the burial of Berlioz six years earlier, Bizet had been in-
furiated by Antoine Elwart's eulogy because that trivial composer dared speak of the great dead musician as "our colleague."
At Bizet's own funeral, had he been able to listen to Gounod, he
would no doubt have made allowances, as always, for the successful master who grudgingly admitted his disciple to the bottom
rung of the ladder; for the unfaithful husband who gauged the
significance of a composer's present and future by the statement of
an unsuccessful wife in words that after only two days of widow-
hood seem too opportune to carry conviction. Geneviève, utterly
prostrated in bed at Saint-Germain, unable to attend her husband's

funeral, could hardly have been in any condition to receive Gounod.

"What we did was very natural," Pasdeloup wrote to Ludovic Halévy after the funeral. "For a long time we have belonged to Bizet as he belonged to us. We grew up together and today only God knows how far he could have gone! . . . If I do not go to call on Mme Bizet, it is out of discretion, for she needs as much calm as your affectionate care can give her. Pay her my respects and ask her to kiss her son for me." "

The night of the funeral, *Carmen* was performed at the Opéra-Comique. "All the singers wept on stage. The evening was too devastating to discuss. Only a great painter could reproduce so moving a sight." " Performances of *Carmen* scheduled for June 8 and 11 were canceled because Galli-Marié was unable to sing. She made her final appearance of the season on June 13.

The nature of the obituary notices devoted to Bizet was predictable. An almost enviable wave of hypocrisy or change of heart swept over his adverse critics. Those who had labeled him a "savage Wagnerian," a man without original talent, now crowned him "master" in a frenzied flow of oratory. Here we shall quote only the words of two friends, critics who were also composers. Ernest Reyer, slightly guilty perhaps over his lukewarm review of *Carmen*, said: "I did not wait until Georges Bizet was dead to praise him." He concluded by pointing out that ". . . the Opéra . . . never deigned to cast an eye on this great, solid musician. . . . History will deal more severely than is now believed with the indifference of an omnipotent organization, proud of its profits, which sees withering all around it talents that a little care would have developed promptly . . . and to which it leaves no consolation other than . . . a love of this art which interests so few people." "

Victorien Joncières wrote: "Bizet was the first who had the courage to embrace the new doctrines, and at a time when even more than today he ran the risk of remaining alone and misunderstood. His boldness will clear the way for the musicians of his generation, who, stirred by his example, will follow him on the road along which he advanced so resolutely. All of us, we young composers, might never have abandoned the monotonous paths so often traveled by our precursors had Bizet not preceded us in the unexplored territory of the new art." "

On October 31, 1875, the eve of All-Souls' Day, Colonne

dedicated his opening concert "To the Memory of Georges Bizet."
Beethoven's Seventh Symphony, the interlude from Gluck's *Orphée,* and Saint-Saëns's Fourth Piano Concerto formed the first
part of the program. After the intermission, following a *Lamento*
specially written for the occasion by Massenet, Galli-Marié read a
poem by Louis Gallet in memory of Bizet. (See Appendix I,
p. 463.) As accompaniment to her recitation the orchestra played,
"as if in a mysterious distance," the *adagietto* from *L'Arlésienne.*

On All-Souls' Day 1954, "the director of the Opéra-Comique,
who had gone to kneel at the grave of Georges Bizet, was struck
by the state of complete abandon of this funerary monument. He
intends to inform the Association of Dramatic Authors and the
Commission des Beaux-Arts of the Municipal Council of its condition. Without delay this tomb must be restored in a manner
worthy of perpetuating the memory of the author of *Carmen* and
Les Pêcheurs de Perles, works that are the backbone of the Salle-Favart." ⁿ

Bizet might well have smiled at the picture of the successor
to Carvalho and du Locle giving thanks at his grave for the support his works continued to bring to the Opéra-Comique, which
brought him so little remuneration in his lifetime. An unassuming
man, always interested in the logic of history, he would hardly have
been surprised at the neglect of the "outward and visible symbol"
of his existence as a man. This monument, erected in Père-Lachaise Cemetery by his friends and relatives, many of whom believed that his final work had killed him, bears little relation to
the immortality he shares with *Carmen.*

CHAPTER  XXIX

Carmen III: Success

Less than a month after Bizet's death, eight years before Paris would acclaim his work, an incident in London gave the first hint of the future recognition of *Carmen*. When Mlle Chapuy, the original Micaëla, appeared as Rosina in *Le Barbier de Séville* at the Drury Lane Theatre in July 1875, London admirers presented her with a bouquet tied with tri-colored streamers. Attached to the ribbon was a small silvered laurel wreath enclosing the words: "Micaëla. *Carmen*. Georges Bizet. Regrets!"

Early in August, the Vienna Opera House started rehearsals of *Carmen*. The first performance took place on October 23, 1875, two days before the thirty-seventh anniversary of Bizet's birth. Jauner, the director, had originally planned to produce *Carmen* as grand opera with recitatives by Guiraud. But shortly before the *première* he decided to retain the spoken dialogue for all the personal or humorous scenes. This last-minute change may have been necessitated by Guiraud's well-known procrastination. For not until after September 25 did he send off the recitatives for *Carmen* and the orchestration of the two *airs de ballet* taken from *L'Arlésienne*, intended for a ballet inserted into the second act, for which the *Danse bohémienne* was actually used. (See Appendix I, p. 462.) The Viennese public loved *Carmen*, but the city's foremost critic, Eduard Hanslick, was restrained in his appreciation. Brahms, on the other hand, went twenty times to hear the opera and remarked, it is said, that he would have gone to the ends of the earth to embrace Bizet. Wagner, a visitor in Vienna at this time, exclaimed after a performance of *Carmen:* "Here, thank God, at last for a change is someone with ideas in his head!" Liszt was merely tolerant of the work. Although he said that he was not bored by the music and even found it skillfully written, he thought it was the kind of opera that would be most successful in Paris.

Paris, however, had no interest in reviving *Carmen*. Without Galli-Marié's urgent persuasion, du Locle would probably not have scheduled the opera for the winter season of 1875–6. From Puygaland, the château near Bordeaux where her doctor had ordered her to go to rest and prepare for "a brilliant campaign for next winter," the singer wrote to the director: "I very much want to oblige *both of us* by staying at the Opéra-Comique. On the other hand, I am being strongly urged to go to Brussels to create Carmen there. They are offering me 800 fr. a performance, with ten performances a month assured. I am asking you for only 400 fr., so will you please be as kind as always and reply at once so that I can decide and put my mind at rest. A very important step in regaining my health! My voice is stronger and fuller than ever." " When the director had not yet replied nearly three weeks later, she threatened to leave the Opéra-Comique: "Joking aside, I am extremely eager to be helpful to you by staying in Paris under your direction and this time I think we have the piece that the Opéra-Comique needs and which can be paired with *Mignon*. . . ." "

As a final gesture, before being forced out of the directorship of the Comique for financial reasons and because of ill-health, du Locle revived *Carmen* on November 15. The original company remained intact. But the feeling that prevailed in the theatre resembled a wake rather than a resurrection. "All of the friends of Georges Bizet met there," said the *Ménestrel*. "The house was crowded, but the atmosphere was heavy with mourning." " A member of the audience at one of the twelve performances that followed, Piotr Ilyitch Tchaikovsky, "could scarcely restrain his excitement, first over the opera as such, and then over Galli-Marié's interpretation." [1] *Carmen* was played for the last time for eight years on February 15, 1876.

---

[1] Herbert Weinstock, *Tchaikovsky*, New York & London, 1946, 115. In a letter to Mme von Meck, Tchaikovsky wrote: "Carmen is a masterpiece in every sense of the word; that is to say one of those rare creations which expresses the efforts of a whole musical epoch. . . . Bizet is not only a composer essentially of our time, but he is also an artist who feels deeply, a master. . . . I am convinced that in ten years *Carmen* will be the most popular opera in the whole world." Henry Gauthier-Villars, *Georges Bizet*, Paris, 1928, 103–4.

A week before it was dropped from the repertory of the Opéra-Comique, *Carmen* had its *première* in Brussels at the Théâtre de la Monnaie. "There was nothing enthusiastic about the success," said the critic of *Le Guide musical.* "Bizet's music is too personal, too original, too much *off the beaten track* not to disturb somewhat a public accustomed to the hackneyed formulas of modern opera. But the audience was frank, spontaneous, unanimous, and no one failed to recognize the superior merit of the work." " The following year Galli-Marié and then Minnie Hauk sang Carmen at the Monnaie. Thereafter the opera remained permanently in the Brussels repertory.

In 1878 *Carmen* became a popular success throughout the Western world. In London two separate productions were announced. At Covent Garden, Adelina Patti and Nicolini were to have sung the leading roles, and at Her Majesty's Theatre, Minnie Hauk and Campanini. The young American singer won all the laurels, however, for Patti's rejection of the role of Carmen on the grounds that it was unsuited to her voice resulted in the cancellation of the Covent Garden production. At Her Majesty's the opera, sung in Italian, achieved immediate success. From London the troupe went to Dublin, where enthusiastic crowds waited outside the theatre to escort the triumphant Miss Hauk to her hotel.

"What a pity I never met Bizet!" she said to her manager. "But you did meet him," he replied, and reminded her of a party at Théophile Gautier's in Paris in 1869. Miss Hauk then recalled that "a program had been arranged and I sang several arias—among them *'Caro Nome'* from *Rigoletto.* A young man played my accompaniments, but I paid no special attention to him. . . ." " The young man was Georges Bizet.

During her career as a singer, Minnie Hauk sang Carmen some five hundred times in French, German, Italian, and English. In New York, at the Academy of Music on October 23, 1878, she introduced *Carmen* in the Italian version to the American public, duplicating her triumph in London and Dublin earlier that year. The next year Miss Hauk threatened to bring suit against *The New York Herald* for preferring Marie Roze's performance to hers. Mlle Roze, no longer finding the "scabrous" role distasteful, played it with great success in San Francisco.

At St. Petersburg, the Russians, whose passion for *Carmen* and interest in Bizet has never diminished,[2] also heard the opera for the first time in 1878, in an Italian version translated by Lauzières who, apparently, had no scruples against spreading corruption among the barbarous Slavs.

In this same year Marseilles, Lyons, and Angers, by welcoming *Carmen,* corroborated the truism that Paris is not France. Although notoriously oblivious to outside opinion, the Parisians could hardly ignore the success in their own country of a work the capital had found scandalous. The triumph of *Carmen* in the provinces caused Ludovic Halévy to make another attempt to bring *Carmen* back to Paris. Since Carvalho had succeeded du Locle as director of the Opéra-Comique in 1876, Halévy had tried and failed to persuade him to revive *Carmen.* In a rehash of the accepted clichés, Carvalho had flatly refused. Although he loved Bizet, he disliked *Carmen,* found the work immoral and unsuitable for a respectable family theatre. When Halévy approached him in 1878, he expressed a certain willingness to give the opera if only he could find a singer for the role of Carmen. Galli-Marié, he claimed, had been "too realistic." He would have to find a "calmer" interpreter. During the five-year interval before Carvalho was prodded into producing a substitute, Galli-Marié sang Carmen in Bordeaux and Brussels, Naples and Genoa, where an inexperienced Don José stabbed her in the cheek. Performances of *Carmen* were given in Florence and Milan; in New York, Boston, Philadelphia, Chicago, New Orleans, and other American cities; in Hanover, Mainz, and Berlin. In the German capital in 1881 *Carmen* was played twenty-three times as against thirteen performances of *Lohengrin,* nine of *Tannhäuser,* and six of *Der Freischütz.*

Bizet, both as man and as artist, has always commanded more interest and admiration in Germany than elsewhere. The relation to music of the *Schadenfreude* of the Germans has been analyzed too frequently to necessitate any summary here. Suffice it to say that Hans von Bülow found the score of *Carmen* "heavenly . . . bewitching," and termed it his *"Lieblings-oper";* that Bismarck,

---

[2] Three biographies of Bizet by Russian writers have been published in Russia since 1935. In the summer of 1957 at the first exhibition of modern "bourgeois" paintings at the Gorki Park in Moscow a young man, defending the new works, was heard to shout at an adversary: "Tell me this. Do you like and listen to Bizet? Well do you know that every leading critic said he was no good when Bizet's music was first performed?" *The New York Times,* August 9, 1957.

whom Brahms regarded as "the best amateur judge of music" he had ever met, went to see *Carmen* twenty-seven times; that Nietzsche, by 1888, had attended twenty performances. "Through it one almost becomes a 'masterpiece' one's self . . ." he wrote in *The Case of Wagner.* "Bizet's music seems to me perfect. It comes forward lightly, gracefully, stylishly. It is lovable, it does not sweat. 'All that is good is easy, everything divine runs on light feet': this is the first principle of my aesthetic. This music is wicked, refined, fatalistic. . . . Have more painful, more tragic accents ever been heard on the stage? And how are they obtained? . . . Without counterfeiting of any kind! Free from the *lie* of the grand style!— In short, this music assumes that the listener is intelligent even as a musician. . . .

"I become a better man when Bizet speaks to me. Also a better musician, a better *listener.* . . . With Bizet's work, one bids farewell to the *damp* north and to all the fog of the Wagnerian ideal. . . . Above all else it has that dryness of atmosphere, that *limpidezza* of the air which belongs to sub-tropical zones. . . . The music is gay, but not in a French or a German way. Its gaiety is African; fate hangs over it, its happiness is short, sudden, without reprieve. I envy Bizet for having had the courage of this sensitiveness, the southern, tawny, sunburned sensitiveness that hitherto in the cultured music of Europe has found no means of expression. . . . And finally love, love translated back into *Nature!* The love whose means is war, whose every essence is the *mortal hatred* between the sexes!—I know no case in which the tragic irony that constitutes the kernel of love is expressed with such severity, or in so terrible a formula as in the last cry of Don José with which the work ends:

> *'Oui, c'est bien moi qui l'ai tuée,*
> *O ma Carmen, ma Carmen adorée!' "* [n]

"Long live the sun and love!" Bizet had written to Galabert in 1865.

From Barcelona in August 1881, Galli-Marié wrote to Bizet's widow: "I am very happy to be able to tell you that we have had another great success, this time in Carmen's own country. . . . I shall be playing Carmen at Dieppe the eighteenth of this month. —Dieppe is very near Paris! If you would care to come there it would please me to give a performance especially for you! . . . If you see Messrs. Meilhac and Halévy, please tell them the good news." "

The demand for *Carmen* among music-lovers, particularly of the younger generation, had gradually become articulate in Paris. In 1882, when both the Opéra and the Opéra-Comique celebrated Auber's centenary by gala performances of his works, Maurice Lefevre, making his debut as critic on *Le Clairon*, concluded his review by deploring the fact that "M. Carvalho leaves a masterpiece like *Carmen* in his desk drawer while wasting his time by reviving the *'pantalonades'* of M. Auber." Other newspapers followed suit, and, encouraged by the general hue and cry, Lefevre went to see Carvalho and Meilhac and Halévy in an attempt to discover the reasons for their lack of initiative in restoring *Carmen* to the repertory of the Opéra-Comique.

Carvalho had reverted to the stand he had expressed to Halévy six years earlier. He told Lefevre that a revival of *Carmen* was out of the question, that Lillas Pastia's tavern was nothing more than a brothel, and that never as long as he was director would a brothel be put on the stage of the Opéra-Comique. Meilhac and Halévy claimed that they would be delighted to have *Carmen* revived, but, reiterating the objection made by Carvalho in 1878, they asked: " 'What woman is there to sing the role?' 'Mme Galli-Marié, of course,' " Lefevre replied timidly. " 'Don't mention that woman to us,' said the librettists. 'It was her fault that the piece failed. Her interpretation of the part was too realistic. . . . Mme Galli-Marié may perhaps have played Mérimée's Carmen, but she did not play ours.' " "

The singer herself was making every effort to be reinstated in the role at the Opéra-Comique. Early in June 1882, she wrote to Geneviève Bizet: "I hear on all sides that *Carmen* is being seriously considered, but no gesture has been made in my direction. Until now I have refused without regret all other engagements (some of them very advantageous) in order to be at your disposal. I played Carmen with great success this winter in Italian at Genoa, then later at Lyon and at Liège in Belgium.—Last summer, without mentioning you, whom I have always felt to be on my side, I saw Carvalho. He couldn't have been kinder, nor could Choudens. Meilhac and Halévy, however, I found a little cold. Will the danger be from that side? You, who are bound to see them frequently, must know. If they think my acting is beyond the pale, let them re-direct me among ourselves at the theatre in Chateaudun, for instance, where the director is a friend of mine. I shall have an excellent tenor as partner (a friend of Guiraud, and now in negotiation with Carvalho). In that way they can see the new manner I have adopted, which seems to me less harsh than the first (which, however, they let me use in the beginning with no objections). I am going to Belgium for a fortnight. . . . Please ask M. Halévy not to permit anyone to be engaged. Certainly if poor Bizet were still among us, I would be the only one to revive the piece he wrote specifically for me and to which I am so attached. —I am wracking my brain to figure out the cause of the hostility I feel but can't uncover! My dear Madame, will you continue your kind support and defend me? With your help I shall be strong and shall not have to bear the heartbreak of seeing my dear Carmen go to another!

"I wish very much that you would have M. Halévy read this letter so that he will say why he is angry at me. If he is right, I promise not to bother you any more and to keep my troubles to myself.—*Au revoir,* Madame. I can't help being sad after all the success I have had everywhere else to think that I am obliged to be such a beggar here! . . ." "

Less than a year after Mme Galli-Marié made this offer, *Carmen* was revived at the Opéra-Comique in an ill-timed, poorly rehearsed, shabby, badly cut production. The pressure brought to bear on Carvalho by the subscribers, the press, various members of the government, and the directors of the Beaux-Arts had driven him, in self-justification, to whip up a hasty production of Bizet's work which he presented at a most inopportune moment. This second *première* took place on April 21, 1883. The contrast between the freshness and taste in the décor of Delibes's *Lakmé,* presented for the first time a week earlier, and the shabby sets and faded costumes provided for *Carmen* proved only an initial shock to the audience. For Carvalho had tampered with both the score and the libretto of Bizet's work.

The tempos were slowed down, the rhythms over-stressed. In the second act, Lillas Pastia's *posada* became a respectable inn. Instead of the wild gypsy dancers, modestly clothed ballerinas frolicked. The duel scene between Don José and the lieutenant was in large part cut. Mlle Adèle Isaac, whose excellent soprano voice was said to bring out elements in the music not revealed by

Galli-Marié's mezzo, had been chosen for the bland restraint of her interpretation. She was surrounded by third-rate singers. Carvalho, in his haste to rid himself of the obligation to present *Carmen*—and it seemed as though Carvalho's own distaste for the work made him want to kill it once and for all—left the opera comparatively unrehearsed. The first and second acts were ready on the opening night, the third was more or less so. But the fourth was incoherent. The singers muffed their lines; Don José twice let his dagger fall and twice interrupted his duet with Carmen to lean down and pick it up. This disastrous playing of the last act brought the audience to its feet in a rage against Carvalho. Yet in spite of all the defects in the production Bizet's music had conquered the house, and for the rest of the season *Carmen* was a great box-office success.

The critics, on the whole, manifested more tolerance of the production than it deserved. Forced to admit that eight years earlier their judgment of Bizet's score had been mistaken, they now chose to blame the failure of *Carmen* on Galli-Marié's interpretation. They handled Mlle Isaac with a gentleness suitable to her purification of the role. Some of them avoided the issue by substituting personal recollections of Bizet for criticism. Comettant divided his article into an account of Bizet's quarrel with him, a defense of his first review, and a reiteration of his earlier attack on Galli-Marié. He concluded, however, by saying that "although the new cast of *Carmen* leaves something to be desired . . . we believe and heartily wish that Bizet's masterpiece will never again leave the repertory of the Opéra-Comique. It is a living work, and it will live." [*]

Johannès Weber, who had previously been one of the severest critics of *Carmen*, permitted himself in a very brief review to deride the past charges of Wagner's influence on the composer. "I shall never forget," he wrote, "the restraint Bizet exercised by merely shrugging his shoulders and making a slight face when I talked to him about the accusations of Wagnerism." [*]

Ernest Reyer, like all of Bizet's friends, made a strong personal attack on Carvalho. Yet, after admitting that *Carmen* "is the work of one of the most distinguished, skilled, ingenious, and knowledgeable musicians who would be in the top rank today," he decided that perhaps the time had come to confess that he had never been "a warm partisan of *Carmen*. While doing justice to the undeniable merit of the work, I regretted not finding in it a high enough affirmation of the doctrines the young composer professed. . . . He set himself to playing castanets and watching his rhythms. He wrote songs and *seguidillas* for Carmen, and for Escamillo *'Toréador en garde!'* In short he, the composer of *Djamileh* and *L'Arlésienne,* became the author of a Spanish *opéra-comique.* I cannot say that . . . in *Carmen* one finds the culmination of Bizet's genius. Of his talent, at most.

"*Carmen* is obviously the work of the most skillful of masters. And I can't understand why the public . . . did not in the first place make it a great success. . . . The work was written for them. How did they fail to see it?" "

Both the public and Carvalho recognized their mistakes, and after seventeen successful performances of *Carmen* during the spring season the director finally, on October 22, 1883, gave it the production it deserved. The score was played as Bizet wrote it. The original costumes and sets were revived. Galli-Marié triumphed.[3] The receipts at the box office were 201,803 francs 50 centimes for twenty-six performances between November 3 and December 31.[4] At the hundredth performance, on December 23, a replica of Paul Dubois's bust of Bizet in the Père Lachaise Cemetery was placed in the lobby of the Opéra-Comique.

In reviewing the second revival of *Carmen,* the critics acted as though Bizet's opera had no previous history. In the *Moniteur universel,* Edouard Thierry wrote: "*Carmen* is a masterpiece. Might one not say that the musician who composed it, because of a foreboding of the few days of life left to him, hastened to put into his score all that he could preserve of his youthful genius?" " The *Figaro* reported that "Mme Galli-Marié's success was complete. . . . In the last act when Carmen flees from José . . . Mme Galli-Marié translated the terror that drives the poor creature mad into an attitude and a facial expression so intense and so lifelike that the whole audience burst into applause." " And Comettant

---

[3] On November 25, 1892, when Emma Calvé first sang Carmen at the Opéra-Comique, Galli-Marié went backstage to congratulate her successor. " 'Bravo,' she said. 'The way you have played the part is highly interesting, very original, never trivial, although very bold. And what a lovely voice you have!' Then, with a sigh: 'This is the first time I have consented to be present at this opera which reminds me so poignantly of all my youth.' " Emma Calvé, *"Souvenirs d'une grande Cantatrice," Le Figaro,* June 9, 1939.

[4] Approximately $40,300.

finally turned tables completely. "Mme Galli-Marié is the personification of Carmen as Mérimée conceived her. This incarnation at first seemed shocking to the decent audience of the Opéra-Comique, which today accepts it without reservation. . . . Mme Galli-Marié was recalled as much as three times in rapid succession. Carmen, the most hair-raising strumpet of Moorish blood . . . but also the most live and 'thrilling' of creatures, has finally gained her naturalization papers at the bourgeois, prudish Salle-Favart. Bizet's work has liberated it from all obstacles and it has definitely entered the repertory of the Opéra-Comique." [5] "

During the next five years, performances of *Carmen* were given in English in Australia, in Czech in Prague, in Spanish in Mexico, in French and Italian in Rio de Janeiro, Buenos Aires and Santiago, Chile, in Lettish at Riga, and in Esthonian at Reval. By 1888, the semi-centenary of Bizet's birth, *Carmen* had been performed three hundred and thirty times at the Opéra-Comique. Wishing to celebrate Bizet's anniversary, the editor of a magazine asked one of his staff to write a brochure about the composer and his work. When he had completed his piece, the writer asked the editor what the title should be. "But you've called it 'Georges Bizet.' Why won't that do?" the editor asked. "I don't know why," the writer replied, "but I think it needs something like 'The Author of *Carmen*' or 'Bizet and *Carmen*,' or 'The Father of *Carmen*.' Bizet without *Carmen* says nothing." The skeptical editor then led the writer into an outer office where several stenographers were at work. "Do you know *Carmen*?" the editor asked the first girl. "Certainly I do," she said. "It's so beautiful." "By whom is it?" he asked. "By whom? But—but, I don't know, sir." A second typist made the same reply. A third girl boasted, "I know. It was written by Gounod." "

Between the fiftieth and hundredth anniversaries of Bizet's birth, *Carmen* was sung on all five continents in English,[6] Italian,

---

[5] As this book goes to press, March 1958, the French government is threatening to close the Opéra-Comique. The repertory of the Comique, it is said, will be transferred to the Opéra. Thus, eighty-three years after Bizet's death, his wish to be played at the Opéra would be automatically granted. But it remains to be seen whether *Carmen* will be given with Guiraud's recitatives substituted for the spoken dialogue. If this grand-opera version should be used, the only production of *Carmen* as Bizet wrote it would go out of existence with the theatre for which it was written.

[6] John Galsworthy, who found *Carmen* "such a jolly good story with such perfect tunes," made an English translation of the libretto, published in 1932. Mrs. Galsworthy, who collaborated with her husband on the translation, wrote

Russian, Swedish, Croatian, Slovenian, Bulgarian, Rumanian, Ser-
bian, Lithuanian, Ukrainian, Hebrew, Chinese, and Japanese. A
performance of *Carmen* in Norwegian celebrated the opening of the
State Opera House at Oslo in 1912. In 1938, the centenary of
Bizet's birth was celebrated throughout the world. *Carmen* in a
new production was played for the two thousand two hundred and
seventy-first time at the Opéra-Comique.[7] *Les Pêcheurs de Perles*
was also provided with new sets and costumes, and *Djamileh* was
revived for eleven performances. The Bibliothèque de l'Opéra held
an exhibition of Bizetiana consisting of 231 items. Journalists, musicologists, and composers filled newspapers and magazines with accounts of Bizet's life, résumés of the original reviews of *Carmen*,
discussions of the relative merits of the *artistes* who had interpreted
the immortal gypsy.

"Bizet has conquered the universe," Reynaldo Hahn wrote in
Le Figaro. "He has conquered not only by his talent, but also by
the sympathy, the warmth, the profoundly human quality of that
talent. His soul showed through his music—that sensitive, loyal,
generous soul; that spontaneous, kind, uncomplicated character
that all those who knew Bizet enjoyed praising. And just because
it is reflected so faithfully in his music, the resistance of which he
was the victim is difficult to understand." " This very personal
quality may indeed be the clue to the critical antagonism to Bizet,
which continued to exist even some sixty years after his death.

"Bizet who achieved early success through docile and uninspired exploitation of the conventionally proper, remains insignificant as a personality," wrote Georges Jean-Aubry. "Two indisputable
masterpieces, *L'Arlésienne* and *Carmen*, will probably keep the
name of Bizet alive; but henceforth his name, which does not recall a lofty mind, a life of experience, nor a great soul, will for us
possess no reality!" " Since the Second World War, another school
of criticism has arisen in France. In the summer of 1957, the critic
on *Le Figaro* objected to the portrayal of Carmen and of Don
José by an American soprano and an Italian tenor because, he said:

to a friend: "*Carmen* is drawing to a close; it is a tough job, especially to keep
Jack duly aware that there is a rhythm in music as well as in poetry. I don't
know that I think it was worthwhile, but it has been great fun." H. V. Mariott,
The Life and Letters of John Galsworthy, London, 1935, 633.

[7] As of January 1, 1958, *Carmen* had been played 2,897 times at the
Opéra-Comique.

"*Carmen* is the 14th of July of music; let us keep that day to our-selves." ⁿ

That *Carmen* should become synonymous with a national holi-day, the annual celebration of the storming of the Bastille, is not wholly paradoxical. For like all revolutions in recent French his-tory, Bizet's revolutionizing of the genre of *opéra-comique* resulted in the eventual triumph of the *bourgeoisie*. The Opéra-Comique re-mains a stronghold of domestic respectability. But instead of *La Dame blanche, Carmen* initiates young people into the realm of music. At any one of the bi-weekly performances of *Carmen* one is likely to see schoolboys and young girls *en famille*. Oblivious to the worn scenery and shabby costumes, the mediocre singing, unrehearsed chorus, and tired orchestra, they sit absorbed, en-chanted by the magic of Bizet's music.

In a dark corner of the basement lobby of the Opéra-Comique stands a large marble statue of Bizet.[8] The bust of the composer, raised on a large block of marble, is flanked on one side by a semi-nude virginal muse bearing a stringed instrument. At the base of the statue sits an elegantly dressed Spanish gypsy, the ultimately rehabilitated Carmen. This tribute is dust-covered and half-hidden behind three box offices. The few members of the audience who dislike crowds spend the intermission in this sparsely peopled lobby and its tiny adjoining bar. A careful observer at some twenty performances of *Carmen* has yet to see a single person cast a glance at the image of Georges Bizet.

---

[8] This statue by Jean-Alexandre-Joseph Falguière (1831–1900) was pre-sented in 1889 to the Opéra-Comique by Bizet's family and friends to replace the bust by Paul Dubois, presented in 1876 and destroyed in the fire of 1887.

In 1925 a memorial plaque was dedicated to François Delsarte at Solesmes. The inscription read: "In this house was born in 1811 François-Chéri Delsarte, celebrated professor of Lyric Declamation whose sister, Aimée Del-sarte, was the mother of Georges Bizet, the immortal author of *Carmen* and of *L'Arlésienne*."

Some years after the success of *Carmen* a street in Paris, running between the Avenue Marceau and the Avenue d'Iéna was named rue Georges Bizet.

CHAPTER  XXX

Postscript

All the members of Bizet's immediate family lived to see the success of *Carmen*. After Georges Bizet's death, his father spent the winters at 22 rue de Douai, the summers at Le Vésinet. In 1879, Mme Halévy acquired the property at Le Vésinet from Adolphe Bizet in exchange for an annuity of 2000 francs; she died in 1884. Jacques Bizet inherited the little cottage where, during his boyhood, he spent several summers with his grandfather. He attended the Lycée Condorcet and studied medicine briefly at the University of Paris. He became interested in the automobile industry and founded Unic, the first garage in France to let cars for hire. Attractive, charming, and witty, he was unfortunately weak in character. Twice married, once divorced, he committed suicide in 1922 because of an unhappy love affair. In 1908 he asked Romain Rolland to write a biography of his father. (See Appendix I, p. 463.)

Jean Reiter, after four years as a journeyman printer, became at the age of twenty-nine director of the press of *Le Temps,* where he worked for over fifty years. He was an Officer of the Legion of Honor and died at the age of 77 in 1939. Much of their lives he and his family lived at Le Vésinet, where his mother, Marie, died in 1913.

In 1886, Geneviève Bizet married Emile Straus, a connection of the Rothschild family, a very rich lawyer, counsel for the Société des Auteurs. After the success of *Carmen,* which was to make her independently wealthy, she led a very gay and active social life, courted by many suitors, one of whom was Guy de Maupassant. As the wife of Straus, she became one of the foremost hostesses of

Paris, "devoured by society," according to Degas, an old family friend.[1]

Mme Straus's salon and Sunday lunch parties soon became celebrated both through her charm and wit and the distinction and talent of her guests. Among her personal friends and admirers were such aristocrats and men of wealth as Prince Auguste d'Arenberg, the Comte d'Haussonville, Baron Edmond de Rothschild, Comte Pierre de Polignac (later Prince de Monaco), General Galliffet, Adrien Hébrard, editor of *Le Temps*, the Princesse Mathilde, and the poetess Anna de Noailles. The devotees of her salon were the most successful and popular novelists and playwrights of the day—Paul Bourget, Paul Hervieu, Abel Hermant, Tristan Bernard, Alfred Capus, Georges de Porto-Riche, Robert de Flers, and Henri Bernstein. Mme Straus owned a number of paintings by Monet, but he rarely went to her house. The art of painting was represented in her salon by Jean-Louis Forain, the art of music by Reynaldo Hahn. She welcomed, too, many of her son's friends, including Marcel Proust and the Marquis de Lauris, who in his memoirs has described Mme Straus's salon at its height:

"Mme Straus, at her house in the rue de Miromesnil, played the leading role. . . . At the time of the Dreyfus Affair, her salon was of the greatest importance. This was inevitably surprising because the mistress of the house was admittedly frivolous and pleasure-loving. But she forfeited many amusing relationships that she seemed to value.[2] . . . She would tell you frankly, in justifying the presence of a serious scholar, that he wasn't a bore. And, indeed, this was always true. . . . Her own witticisms, when repeated, are often disappointing. But they always evoked a smile, broke off a conversation before it became too serious or remained too long on the same note. . . .[3] Marcel Proust, her friend, said

---

[1] She met him in the street one day and was able to persuade him to accompany her to a fitting at one of the great dressmaking houses because, as he said: "It was the only time she had free and I had abandoned her so completely that I had to give in." Thereafter he frequently went to fittings with her. When she asked him what continued to attract him about these occasions, he replied: "The chapped, red hands of the little girl who holds the pins." *Lettres de Degas,* ed. Marcel Guérin, Paris, 1931, 147.

[2] Forain and Bourget were among the anti-Dreyfusards.

[3] Typical of the graciousness of Mme Straus's wit is a remark she made shortly before her death to Mme Sibilat, the fair-haired, blue-eyed Danish bride of Emile Straus's nephew and heir, René Sibilat. Mme Straus's house

to me one day: 'Why is it that we prefer the conversation of Mme
Straus, who is basically so little interested in what we care about,
to that of Mme X, who is so well-versed in matters of literature
and art?'. . .[4]

"I can still see, at her Sunday lunch parties," M. de Lauris continues, "Jacques Bizet, who looked so like the pictures of his
father . . . Joseph Reinach, whose bulky physique did not prevent his casting flirtatious glances emphasized by rather too broad
a smile. He enjoyed provoking Straus's jealousy. The latter was
proud of his wife, of her salon, of her collections; proud, too, of
the roses on his property at Trouville. But all his proprietary instincts were not without their painful side. . . . He would have
liked to exercise a certain tyranny. But that was impossible with
Mme Straus, who took such successful refuge in her nervous ills.
After her friends departed, she was wholly given over to anxiety
about her health." [n]

Mme Straus died at the age of seventy-seven in 1926. Neither
she nor her son had ever catalogued Bizet's manuscripts. A number of them she gave away as souvenirs. Others, with his private
papers, were left to her second husband. The original score of
Carmen, however, went to the Conservatoire; the royalties from
the performances were left to the Fondation Ophtalmologique
Rothschild. In her will, Mme Straus also established a foundation
for a Georges Bizet prize of 10,000 francs "to be awarded annually to a composer (male) who had produced a remarkable
work within the previous five years and who was not over forty
years of age." (In 1926 10,000 francs equalled $2,000. In 1958
it is worth approximately $30.)

There is as much difficulty today in ascertaining detailed information about the conditions attached to the Prix Georges Bizet
as there was a century ago when Bizet himself described the regu-

----

was filled with hideous dark-brown or gloomy gray Copenhagen figurines of
animals which she disliked but felt obliged to display because they were the
gifts of the Baroness de Rothschild, a frequent caller. When Mme Sibilat entered the salon, Mme Straus turned to her husband and said: "At last we
have a true and charming piece of Copenhagen."

[4] In 1920 Proust wrote to Mme Straus: "My friends . . . will also rediscover in the *Côté de Guermantes* witticisms of yours over which they have laughed
when I repeated them and which I am having the Duchesse de Guermantes
say . . . without mentioning you, as you asked me not to put your name in the
novels but to keep it for the *pastiches* present and future. [See Proust's *Pastiches
et Mélanges,* Paris, 1919, 79.] But everyone knows the witticisms and will mention
your name." Marcel Proust, *Correspondance générale,* VI, 232–3.

lations for the Rodrigues prize as "extremely complicated. But," he added, "it doesn't matter, for the prize exists. . . ." The Prix Georges Bizet was first awarded in 1931 to Francis Bousquet. Among the well-known musicians who have won the prize since are Tony Aubin, Jean-Michel Damase, Henri Dutilleux, and Jean Martinon.

Bibliographical Notes

CHAPTER I
The Bizets and the Delsartes

p. 6 l. 22 M. Roland to François Delsarte, n. d. Unpublished letter, collection of Mme Bouts Réal Del Sarte.

p. 9 l. 18 Abbé Delaumosne, *Delsarte System of Oratory*, New York, 1892.

p. 9 l. 22 Angélique Arnaud, *François Delsarte*, Paris, 1882, 28.

p. 10 l. 21 Charles Boissière, "François Delsarte," *La Ruche Parisienne*, n. d., 5–6.

p. 10 l. 27 *L'Indépendance Belge*, March 14, 1880.

p. 10 l. 37 Ibid.

p. 12 l. 5 Camille Saint-Saëns, *Ecole buissonnière*, Paris, 1913, 243–9.

p. 12 l. 17 Eugène Delacroix, *Journal*, Paris, 1950, I, 338.

p. 14 l. 19 L. de Hegermann-Lindencrone, *In the Courts of Memory*, New York and London, 1912, 78–9.

CHAPTER II
The Conservatoire

p. 16 l. 10 Charles Pigot, *Georges Bizet et son oeuvre*, Paris, n. d. (1911), 3–4.

p. 16 l. 22 Pierre-Joseph-Emile Meifred to François Delsarte, June 1, 1848. Unpublished letter, collection of Mme Bouts Réal Del Sarte.

p. 17 l. 25 Madeleine Réal Del Sarte, unpublished journal, collection of Mlle Géraldy.

p. 17 l. 30 Hugues Imbert, "Lettres à Paul Lacombe," *Portraits et Etudes*, Paris, 1894, 175.

p. 18 l. 18 Jules Massenet, *Mes Souvenirs*, Paris, 1912, 15–16.

p. 18 l. 28 See René Dumesnil, *Le Monde*, November 24, 1950.

p. 19 l. 26 Quoted in unpublished journal of Ludovic Halévy, collection of M. Daniel Halévy.

p. 20 l. 3 Hegermann-Lindencrone, 316.

p. 20 l. 25 Georges Bizet, *Lettres, Impressions de Rome (1857–1860)*, *La Commune (1871)*, Paris, 1907. Unpublished portion, letter XXXI, 117, collection of author.

p. 20 l. 35 Antoine-François Marmontel, *Les Pianistes célèbres*, Paris, 1888, 202–4, 210.

p. 21 l. 2 Bizet, *Lettres*. Unpublished portion, letter XXXI, 117.

p. 21 l. 30 Antoine-François Marmontel, *Symphonistes et Virtuoses*, Paris, 1881, 257.

p. 22 l. 25 Ignaz Moscheles, *Life of*, by his wife, London, 1873, I, 269.

p. 22 l. 39 Saint-Saëns, *Ecole buissonnière*, 41.

p. 23 l. 13 Ibid., 12–13.

p. 23 l. 37 Edouard Monnais, *Souvenirs d'un ami*, Paris, 1863, 29.

p. 24 l. 8 Bizet, *Lettres*. Unpublished portion, letter XXII, 88 and 90.

p. 24 l. 33 Charles Sainte-Beuve, *Nouveaux Lundis*, II, Paris, 1883, 227 f., 240–3.

p. 25 l. 28 Bizet, *Lettres*, 117.

CHAPTER III
Bizet and Charles Gounod

p. 26 l. 16 Marmontel, *Les Pianistes célèbres*, 207.

p. 28 l. 4 Sebastian Hensel, *Die Familie Mendelssohn*, Berlin, 1880, II, 139.

p. 30 l. 35 Edmond Got, *Journal*, Paris, 1910, 272 f.

p. 31 l. 10 Henri Meilhac to Geneviève Bizet-Straus, n. d. Unpublished letter, Bibliothèque nationale.

p. 31 l. 27 Camille Saint-Saëns, *Portraits et Souvenirs*, Paris, n. d. (3rd edition), 43.

p. 31 l. 36 Hector Berlioz, *Les Musiciens et la musique*, Paris, 1903, 116.

p. 31 l. 40 Moscheles, II, 89 f.

p. 32 l. 9 Saint-Saëns, *Ecole buissonnière*, 217.

p. 32 l. 13 Henry James, *Letters*, ed. Percy Lubbock, London, 1920, I, 45.

p. 33 l. 10 Ludovic Halévy, *Carnets*, Paris, 1935, II, 114 f.

p. 33 l. 22 Henri Blaze de Bury, *Meyerbeer et son temps*, Paris, 1865, 525.

p. 35 l. 15 Edmond et Jules de Goncourt, *Journal, 1ère Série, 1862–1865*, Paris, 1887, II, 322.

p. 35 l. 23 Saint-Saëns, *Portraits et Souvenirs*, 85.

p. 35 l. 31 Ibid., 55, 118.

p. 36 l. 6 Hector Berlioz, *Mémoires de*, Paris, 1887, II, 313.

p. 37 l. 4 Mina Curtiss, "Gounod before *Faust*," *The Musical Quarterly*, XXXVIII, No. 1, January 1952, 65.

CHAPTER IV

Symphony in C: *Le Docteur Miracle:* Prix de Rome

p. 40 l. 22 Charles Gounod, "Lettres à Georges Bizet," *Revue de Paris*, Vol. 6, December 1899, 682 f.

p. 41 l. 7 Jacques Offenbach, *Le Figaro*, July 17, 1856.

p. 41 l. 22 Louis Schneider, *Hervé et Lecocq*, Paris, 1924, 135.

p. 43 l. 4 "Lettres inédites de Lecocq à Saint-Saëns," *Revue Musicale*, Vol. 5, February 1, 1924, 124.

p. 44 l. 1 Henri Maréchal, *Souvenirs d'un Musicien*, Paris, 1907, 32.

p. 46 l. 9 Francis Toye, *Rossini: A Study in Tragi-Comedy*, New York, 1934, 214.

p. 46 l. 32 Berlioz, *Mémoires*, I, 122.

p. 47 l. 2 Gounod, "Lettres à Georges Bizet," 679.

p. 47 l. 20 Amédée Burion, *Clovis et Clotilde, Cantate à trois voix*, Bibliothèque du Conservatoire.

p. 47 l. 39 Gounod, "Lettres à Georges Bizet," 679.

p. 48 l. 5 Berlioz, *Mémoires*, I, 126.

p. 48 l. 37 Gioacchino Rossini to Francesco Florimo, December 15, 1857. Unpublished letter, collection of author.

p. 48 l. 39 Giaocchino Rossini, *Lettere di*, ed. G. Mazzatinti, Florence, 1902, 230–1.

p. 50 l. 12 Bizet, *Lettres*, 222–3.

p. 50 l. 23 Auguste Laget, *Le Chant et les Chanteurs*, Paris, n. d., 349–50.

p. 50 l. 27 Julien Tiersot, *Hector Berlioz et la Société de son Temps*, Paris, 1904, 217.

CHAPTER V

Villa Medici: Victor Schnetz: Edmond About

p. 52 l. 32 Edmond About, *Rome Contemporaine*, Paris, 1861, 344.

p. 53 l. 35 Ibid., 58 f.

p. 54 l. 34 E. Beulé, *Notice sur Victor Schnetz*, Institut de France, Académie des Beaux-Arts, Paris, 1871, 18 ff.

p. 54 l. 38 Charles Gounod, *Mémoires d'un artiste*, Paris, 1896, 135–6.

p. 55 l. 3 Beulé, op. cit.

p. 55 l. 9 Eugène Delacroix, *Correspondance Générale 1850–1857*, Paris, 1937, III, 391–2.

p. 55 l. 17 Henri Maréchal, *Lettres et Souvenirs*, Paris, 1920, 109.

p. 55 l. 34 Henry d'Ideville, *Journal d'un diplomate en Italie: Rome 1862–1866*, Paris, 1873, 55–6.

p. 56 l. 15 Gounod to Georges Bousquet, February 6, 1841. Unpublished letter, Bibliothèque du Conservatoire.

p. 56 l. 23 Henry Lapauze, *Histoire de l'Académie de France à Rome*, Paris, 1924, II, 263.

p. 56 l. 39 Bizet to Emile Paladilhe, October 8, 1860. Unpublished letter, Paladilhe collection.

p. 59 l. 8 Bizet, *Lettres*. Unpublished portion, letter IX, 42.

p. 60 l. 13 Ibid. Unpublished portion, letter XIV, 59.

p. 62 l. 15 Ibid. Unpublished portion, letter XII, 55.

p. 63 l. 25 D'Ideville, 55.

p. 65 l. 32 Emile Paladilhe to his father, n. d. Unpublished letter, Paladilhe collection.

p. 66 l. 14 Pierre Berton, *Souvenirs de la Vie de Théâtre*, Paris, 1913, 217.

p. 66 l. 36 Bizet to Clapisson, n. d. Unpublished letter, collection of author.

p. 67 l. 18 Winton Dean, *Bizet,* London, 1948, 41.

p. 67 l. 29 Charles Baille, "Le Peintre, Félix Giacomotti," *Mémoires de l'Académie des Sciences, des Belles Lettres, et des Arts de Besançon,* 1910.

CHAPTER VI

Rome: *Don Procopio:* Italy

p. 71 l. 4 Gounod, "Lettres à Georges Bizet," 685–6 n.

p. 71 l. 29 Baille, op. cit.

p. 77 l. 16 Marc Delmas, *Georges Bizet,* Paris, 1930, 15–17.

p. 78 l. 4 Gounod, "Lettres à Georges Bizet," 682–3.

p. 80 l. 36 Bizet, *Lettres.* Unpublished portion, letter XXXV, 132.

p. 81 l. 29 Gounod, "Lettres à Georges Bizet," 685–8.

p. 83 l. 31 Curtiss, "Gounod before *Faust,*" 50–1.

p. 86 l. 15 Bizet, "Notes de voyage," unpublished diary, collection of author.

p. 88 l. 34 Bizet to his father, n. d. Unpublished letter, collection of author.

p. 89 l. 4 Bizet to Hector Gruyer, n. d. Ibid.

p. 89 l. 23 Curtiss, "Gounod before *Faust,*" 51.

CHAPTER VII

Vasco de Gama: Return from Rome

p. 94 l. 10 *Report of Proceedings* of the Académie des Beaux-Arts, September 17, 1859.

p. 102 l. 38 Bizet to his father, n. d. Unpublished letter, collection of author.

p. 104 l. 21 Gounod, "Lettres à Georges Bizet," 690. Unpublished portion in square brackets. Original letter, collection of author.

CHAPTER VIII

Death of Aimée Bizet

p. 106 l. 27 Bizet to Ernest L'Epine, n. d. Unpublished letter, collection of M. Daniel Halévy.

p. 107 l. 6 Bizet to Ludovic Halévy, n. d. Ibid.

p. 108 l. 16 H. Sutherland Edwards, *Famous First Representations,* London, 1886, 231–2.

p. 109 l. 9 Pigot, 113–14.

p. 109 l. 30 Berton, 217–18.

p. 110 l. 38 Georges Bizet, *Lettres à un ami,* intro. by Edmond Galabert, Paris, 1909, 31 f.

p. 111 l. 13 Gounod, "Lettres à Georges Bizet," 691–2.

p. 111 l. 27 Fromental Halévy to Georges Bizet, n. d. Unpublished letter, collection of author.

p. 111 l. 40 Gounod, "Lettres à Georges Bizet," 693.

p. 112 l. 11 Edmond Galabert, "La Maladie et la mort de Bizet," *Le Passant,* February 1888.

CHAPTER IX

Gounod's *La Reine de Saba:* *Erostrate* by Ernest Reyer

p. 113 l. 5 Gustave Flaubert, *Oeuvres complètes, Correspondance, 1862–1868,* Paris, 1929, V, 16–17.

p. 113 l. 12 Charles Baudelaire, *Correspondance générale,* Paris, 1948, II, 99.

p. 114 l. 23 Gounod, "Lettres à Georges Bizet," 693.

p. 114 l. 31 Jacques Barzun, *Berlioz and the Romantic Century,* Boston, 1950, II, 210–11.

p. 118 l. 25 Gounod, "Lettres à Georges Bizet," 694.

p. 118 l. 32 J. G. Prod'homme et A. Dandelot, *Gounod,* Paris, 1911, II, 45 *n.* 1.

p. 119 l. 19 Ibid., II, 45.

p. 120 l. 5 "Baden Vanity Fair," *Dublin University Magazine,* January 1864, 703 f.

p. 120 l. 21 Ernest Reyer, *Notes de Musique,* Paris, 1875, 374 f.

p. 120 l. 27 Ernest Reyer, *Quarante Ans de Musique,* Paris, 1909, 304.

p. 121 l. 32 Pigot, 43.

p. 123 l. 15 Bizet to Antoine de Choudens, n. d. Unpublished letter. Copies of original correspondence in Bibliothèque de l'Opéra.

p. 123 l. 27 *Report of Proceedings* of the Académie des Beaux-Arts, October 4, 1862.

CHAPTER X

Scherzo: *Les Pêcheurs de Perles:* Choudens

p. 127 l. 12 Berlioz, *Les Musiciens et la musique,* 309–11.

p. 128 l. 23 *La Revue et Gazette Musicale,* Vol. 30, January 25, 1863.

p. 129 l. 21 Saint-Saëns, *Portraits et Souvenirs,* 173 f.

p. 129 l. 28 Pierre Lalo, *De Rameau à Ravel,* Paris, 1947, 94.

p. 130 l. 33 *La Revue et Gazette Musicale,* Vol. 30, February 15, 1863.

p. 132 l. 40 Gounod, "Lettres à Georges Bizet," 695–7.

p. 133 l. 7 E. de Lacroix to Bizet, dated Perpignan, October 11, 1863. Unpublished letter, collection of author.

p. 133 l. 16 Gounod, "Lettres à Georges Bizet," 695–7.

p. 134 l. 34 Bizet to Choudens, n. d. Unpublished letter, Bibliothèque de l'Opéra.

p. 135 l. 7 Choudens to Bizet, August 26, 1863. Ibid.

p. 136 l. 2 Lalo, 91.

p. 138 l. 22 Berton, 211–12.

p. 139 l. 39 Bizet, *Lettres à un ami,* 15.

p. 141 l. 6 Berlioz, *Les Musiciens et la musique,* 343–5.

p. 141 l. 21 Ludovic Halévy, *Carnets,* I, 4–5.

p. 141 l. 38 Emile Paladilhe to his father, October 12, 1863. Unpublished letter, Paladilhe collection.

p. 142 l. 36 Berlioz, *Mémoires,* II, 377.

p. 143 l. 8 Barzun, II, 240.

p. 143 l. 23 Berlioz, *Mémoires,* II, 379.

p. 143 l. 34 Ludovic Halévy, unpublished journal.

p. 144 l. 22 Victor Chéri to Bizet, n. d. Unpublished letter, collection of author.

p. 144 l. 30 Gounod to Ludovic Halévy, n. d. Unpublished letter, collection of M. Daniel Halévy.

p. 145 l. 32 Emile Paladilhe to his father, December 8, 1863. Unpublished letter, Paladilhe collection.

p. 145 l. 38 Imbert, 162.

CHAPTER XI

Meyerbeer: Galabert: *Ivan IV*

p. 147 l. 36 Adolphe Jullien, *Hector Berlioz, Sa Vie et ses oeuvres,* Paris, 1888, 291.

p. 147 l. 38 Berlioz, *Les Musiciens et la musique,* ed. André Halley, xxxii.

p. 148 l. 8 Saint-Saëns, *Ecole buissonnière,* 284.

p. 148 l. 17 Martin Cooper, "Giacomo Meyerbeer" in *Fanfare for Ernest Newman,* ed. Herbert van Thal, London, 1955, 46.

p. 149 l. 34 Ludovic Halévy, unpublished journal.

p. 149 l. 39 Ernest Newman, *The Life of Richard Wagner,* New York, 1941, III, 221 *n.* 20.

p. 153 l. 7 Léon Carvalho, *Le Matin,* March 9, 1895.

p. 153 l. 9 Bizet to Jacques-Léopold Heugel, n. d. Unpublished letter, Heugel collection.

p. 154 l. 19 Goncourt, II, 261–2.

p. 154 l. 30 André Coeuroy, "Théodore de Banville contre l'Opéra," *Revue Musicale,* May 1, 1923.

p. 155 l. 16 Camille Doucet to Minister des Beaux-Arts, December 11, 1863. Unpublished letter, collection of author.

p. 155 l. 27 Bizet to Emile Perrin, n. d. Unpublished letter, Bibliothèque de l'Opéra.

p. 157 l. 3 Bizet to Choudens, n. d. Ibid.

CHAPTER XII

The Princesse Mathilde: Céleste Mogador

p. 158 l. 18 Bizet to Choudens, March 31, 1866. Unpublished letter, Bibliothèque de l'Opéra.

p. 159 l. 30 Alfred Godard to Bizet, February 6, 1866. Unpublished letter, collection of author.

p. 159 l. 35 Gounod to Bizet, February 17, 1866. Unpublished letter, collection of author.

p. 160 l. 6 Gounod to Meilhac, March 16, 1866. Unpublished letter, collection of M. Daniel Halévy.

p. 160 l. 20 Bizet to unidentified Belgian composer, n. d. Published in part in Henry Malherbe, *Carmen*, Paris, 1951. Unpublished portion of letter in square brackets. Collection of M. Albert Willemetz.

p. 161 l. 34 Hegermann-Lindencrone, 68 ff.

p. 162 l. 4 *Revue et Gazette Musicale*, Vol. 33, March 18, 1866.

p. 162 l. 20 Eugène-Louis-Gabriel Isabey to Bizet, n. d. Unpublished letter, collection of author.

p. 162 l. 39 Bizet to Choudens, n. d. Unpublished letter, Bibliothèque de l'Opéra.

p. 163 l. 18 Dean, *Bizet*, 116.

p. 163 l. 34 Bizet to Heugel, n. d. Unpublished letter cited in Tausky Catalogue, 1955.

p. 163 l. 38 Ambroise Thomas to Bizet, March 7, 1866. Unpublished letter, collection of author.

p. 164 l. 14 Dean, *Bizet*, 126.

p. 164 l. 35 Bizet, *Lettres*. Unpublished portion, letter XII, 54.

p. 165 l. 9 Ibid., letter LXVIII, 252.

p. 165 l. 37 George Sand et Alfred de Musset, *Correspondance de,* ed. Félix Décori, Brussels, 1904, 225.

p. 166 l. 39 Céleste Mogador, *Mémoires*, Paris, 1854, II, 139 ff.

p. 167 l. 13 A. Delvau, *Les Cythères Parisiennes: Histoire Anecdotique des Bals Parisiens,* Paris, 1864, 71 f.

p. 167 l. 39 Thérèse Marix-Spire, *Les Romantiques et la musique: Le Cas de George Sand,* Paris, 1954, 451–2 *n.* 128.

p. 171 l. 11 Mogador, I, 93, 115, 245, 275; II, 58.

Chapter XIII
La Jolie Fille de Perth: I

p. 173 l. 7 Léon Carvalho, *Le Matin,* February 9, 1895.

p. 173 l. 25 Fromental Halévy to Saint-Georges, December 4, 1851. Unpublished letter, collection of author.

p. 181 l. 22 Jeanne Marix, "Séjour de Bizet au Vésinet, d'après les 'Mémoires inédits' de Céleste Mogador, Comtesse de Chabrillan," *Revue de Musicologie*, No. 68, November 1938, 149 ff.

p. 182 l. 24 Ibid.

p. 183 l. 31 Bizet to Choudens, n. d. Unpublished letter, Bibliothèque de l'Opéra.

Chapter XIV
Paul Lacombe: Competition: Bizet, Music Critic

p. 187 l. 2 Bizet to Choudens, n. d. Unpublished letter, Bibliothèque de l'Opéra.

p. 191 l. 9 Bizet to Jules Adenis, n. d. Ibid.

p. 191 l. 21 Bizet to unidentified Belgian composer, op. cit.

p. 192 l. 3 James Pope-Hennessy, *Monckton-Milnes: The Flight of Youth,* London, 1951, 202 ff.

p. 192 l. 13 George Augustus Sala, *Notes and Sketches of the Paris Exhibition,* London, 1868, 192–3.

p. 193 l. 8 *Paris Guide: Première Partie—La Science—L'Art,* Paris, 1867, 828–9.

p. 193 l. 38 Ludovic Halévy, *Carnets,* I, 156–7.

p. 194 l. 5 Albert Soubies et Charles Malherbe, *Histoire de l'Opéra-Comique: 1860–1887,* Paris, 1893, II, 127.

p. 196 l. 14 Bizet to Ernest L'Epine, n. d. Unpublished letter, collection of M. Daniel Halévy.

p. 197 l. 31 Bizet to L'Epine, n. d. Ibid.

p. 198 l. 23 Bizet to Saint-Saëns, n. d. Musée Saint-Saëns, Dieppe. Published in *Musica,* June 1907.

p. 198 l. 39 Sala, 297.

p. 199 l. 13 Prosper Mérimée, *Lettres à Madame de Montijo,* Paris, 1936, 316–17.

p. 199 l. 28 Ludovic Halévy, *Carnets,* I, 156.

p. 202 l. 26 *La Revue Nationale et Etrangère,* August 3, 1867.

CHAPTER XV

Malbrough s'en va-t-en guerre:
La Jolie Fille de Perth II

p. 204 l. 21 *La Gazette de Hollande,*
October 5, 1867, 71.
p. 205 l. 11 Henri Regnault to Bizet,
n. d. Unpublished letter, collection of author.
p. 205 l. 24 Prosper Mérimée, *Lettres*
à une autre Inconnue, Paris,
n. d., 126.
p. 205 l. 37 Flaubert, V, 199–200.
p. 206 l. 7 V. Wilder, "Georges
Bizet," *Le Ménestrel,* July 18,
1875, 258.
p. 206 l. 11 Bizet to Saint-Saëns, n. d.
Unpublished letter, Musée Saint-
Saëns, Dieppe.
p. 207 l. 12 Schneider, 139.
p. 208 l. 2 *Le Ménestrel,* XX, December 15, 1867, 20.
p. 208 l. 14 Imbert, 180.
p. 209 l. 24 Léo Delibes to Mme
Trélat, n. d. Unpublished letter,
collection of Mlle Letellier.
p. 210 l. 8 A. B. N. Peat, *Gossip from*
Paris, London, 1903, 275–6.
p. 211 l. 10 Maréchal, *Souvenirs d'un*
Musicien, 228–30.
p. 213 l. 5 Reyer, *Quarante Ans de*
Musique, 282.
p. 214 l. 12 Pigot, 103.
p. 214 l. 19 Ambroise Thomas to
Bizet, January 7, 1868. Unpublished letter, collection of author.
p. 214 l. 30 Ernest Beulé to Bizet,
n. d. Ibid.
p. 215 l. 28 Berton, 227 ff.

CHAPTER XVI

Madame Trélat: *La Coupe du*
Roi de Thulé: The *Roma* Symphony

p. 216 l. 12 Imbert, 185.
p. 217 l. 23 George Sand, *Agendas*
de, May 29, 1868. Ms. Bibliothèque nationale.
p. 218 l. 16 Conversation with Mme
Gaudibert.
p. 219 l. 17 Ambroise Thomas to
Bizet, March 4, 1868. Unpublished letter, collection of author.
p. 220 l. 35 Bizet to Choudens, n. d.
Unpublished letter, Bibliothèque
de l'Opéra.

p. 221 l. 26 Bizet, *Lettres à un ami.*
Unpublished portion, 145.
p. 229 l. 36 Bizet to Léon Halévy,
n. d. Unpublished letter, collection of M. Daniel Halévy.
p. 230 l. 3 Ibid.
p. 231 l. 26 Bizet to unidentified correspondent, n. d. Unpublished
letter, Cornuau Catalogue for
sale held February 15, 1935.
Contributed by M. Marc Pincherle.
p. 233 l. 8 Emile Paladilhe to his father, February 12, 1869. Unpublished letter, Paladilhe collection.

CHAPTER XVII

Geneviève Halévy

p. 235 l. 8 Bizet, *Lettres à un ami,*
189. Unpublished portion in
square brackets.
p. 236 l. 10 Léon Halévy, *F. Ha-*
lévy, sa vie et ses oeuvres, Paris,
1863, 7.
p. 236 l. 27 Ibid., 26–7.
p. 237 l. 2 Mina Curtiss, "Fromental Halévy," *The Musical Quarterly,* XXXIX, No. 2, April 1953,
204.
p. 238 l. 18 Léonie Halévy to her
mother, n. d. Unpublished letter,
collection of author.
p. 238 l. 38 Léon Escudier, *Mes Souvenirs,* Paris, 1863, 186–7.
p. 239 l. 15 Delacroix, *Journal,* II,
313, 231.
p. 239 l. 22 Fromental Halévy to
Hippolyte Rodrigues, n. d. Unpublished letter, collection of author.
p. 239 l. 31 Georges Bizet, "Unpublished Letters," ed. Mina Curtiss,
The Musical Quarterly, XXXVI,
No. 3, July 1950, 381.
p. 240 l. 15 Curtiss, "Fromental
Halévy," 211.
p. 240 l. 33 Léon Halévy, 69.
p. 241 l. 8 Léonie Halévy to Rodrigues, n. d. Unpublished letter,
collection of author.
p. 241 l. 38 Geneviève Halévy to
Rodrigues, n. d. Unpublished letter, collection of author.
p. 244 l. 15 Léon Halévy, 73–4.
p. 245 l. 11 Léonie Halévy, account
book, collection of author.

p. 247 l. 9 Charles Gounod to Geneviève Halévy, January 2, 1868. Unpublished letter, collection of author.

p. 247 l. 38 Julien Benda, "Un Régulier dans le siècle," *La Nouvelle Revue Française,* January 1, 1938, 84.

p. 248 l. 22 Alcide Paladilhe to Emile Paladilhe, May 22, 1869. Unpublished letter, Paladilhe collection.

p. 249 l. 2 Benda, 84.

p. 249 l. 11 Bizet, *Lettres à un ami,* 186. Unpublished portion of letter in square brackets.

p. 249 l. 31 Léonie Halévy, account book.

p. 250 l. 3 Gounod to Bizet, n. d. Unpublished letter, collection of author.

p. 250 l. 19 Marriage Certificate of Alexandre-César-Léopold Bizet and Marie-Geneviève-Raphaëlle Halévy. *Préfecture de la Seine, 9ème Arrondissement.* Document B. No. 0938073.

p. 250 l. 29 Ludovic Halévy, *Carnets,* I, 104.

CHAPTER XVIII

Marriage

p. 251 l. 6 Bizet to Rodrigues, "Unpublished Letters," 378.

p. 252 l. 24 B. Jouvin, *Le Figaro,* March 24, 1862.

p. 253 l. 17 Dean, *Bizet,* 163.

p. 253 l. 31 Bizet to Mme Trélat, postmarked Enghien-les-Bains, October 8, 1869. Unpublished letter, Saffroy Catalogue, No. 34, 1955.

p. 253 l. 37 Daniel Halévy, *Pays Parisiens,* Paris, 1932, 28–9.

p. 254 l. 6 Ibid.

p. 254 l. 31 Bizet to unidentified correspondent, September 12, 1869. Unpublished letter, collection of Maître Roger Hauert, Paris.

p. 255 l. 26 Bizet to unidentified editor. Unpublished letter, Bibliothèque de l'Arsenal. (See note 4, p. 255.)

p. 255 l. 33 Bizet to Eugène Manuel, n. d. Unpublished letter, New York Public Library.

p. 256 l. 13 Sardou to du Locle, n. d. Unpublished letter about *Grisélidis,* Archives nationales.

p. 256 l. 28 Imbert, 209.

p. 256 l. 39 Unpublished document, Archives nationales.

p. 257 l. 3 Report on competition, Archives nationales.

p. 257 l. 18 Emile Paladilhe to his father, November 29, 1869. Unpublished letter, Paladilhe collection.

p. 257 l. 31 Bizet to Galabert, n. d. Unpublished letter, courtesy of the late M. F. Galabert.

p. 257 l. 37 Bizet to Galabert, December 31, 1869. Ibid.

p. 258 l. 5 Bizet, *Lettres à un ami,* 191.

p. 258 l. 31 Bizet to Rodrigues, "Unpublished Letters," 379.

CHAPTER XIX

The Year of Terror I: The Siege of Paris

p. 260 l. 18 Imbert, 205–6.

p. 261 l. 3 Louis Gallet, *Notes d'un librettiste,* Paris, 1891, 51.

p. 261 l. 19 Bizet, *Lettres à un ami,* 191–2. Unpublished portion in square brackets.

p. 261 l. 30 Ibid., 192.

p. 261 l. 36 Bizet to Rodrigues. "Unpublished Letters," 380.

p. 262 l. 20 Ibid., 381.

p. 262 l. 28 Ibid., 380.

p. 263 l. 9 Ibid., 381.

p. 264 l. 40 Meilhac to Ludovic Halévy. Copied in Ludovic Halévy's unpublished journal.

p. 265 l. 12 Geneviève Bizet to Valentine Halévy. Ibid.

p. 265 l. 22 Bizet to his wife. "Unpublished Letters," 381.

p. 265 l. 29 Bizet to his wife, n. d. Unpublished letter, collection of author.

p. 266 l. 7 Léonie Halévy to Ludovic Halévy, n. d. Copied in Ludovic Halévy's unpublished journal.

p. 266 l. 16 Geneviève Bizet to her mother. Ibid.

p. 266 l. 23 Gallet, 55.

p. 267 l. 2 Dean, *Bizet,* 67.

p. 267 l. 39 Gallet, 54–6.

p. 268 l. 38 Hon. Captain Bingham, *Journal of the Siege of Paris,* London, 1871, 132.

p. 269 l. 11 Melvin Kranzberg, *The Siege of Paris: 1870–1871,* Ithaca, New York, 1950, 91.

p. 269 l. 21 Gallet, 53.

p. 270 l. 13 Léonie Halévy to Ludovic Halévy. Copied in Ludovic Halévy's unpublished journal.

p. 271 l. 14 Bizet to Mme Halévy. "Unpublished Letters," 382.

p. 272 l. 26 Bizet to Rodrigues. Ibid., 382–3.

p. 273 l. 6 Bizet to Rodrigues, n. d. Unpublished letter, collection of author.

p. 274 l. 38 Bizet to Ludovic Halévy, February 24, 1871. Unpublished letter, collection of M. Daniel Halévy.

p. 275 l. 18 Bizet to Mme Halévy, n. d. Unpublished letter, collection of author.

p. 276 l. 7 Bizet to Rodrigues, n. d. Unpublished letter, collection of author.

p. 276 l. 26 Bizet to Rodrigues. "Unpublished Letters," 384.

p. 277 l. 8 Bizet, *Lettres à un ami,* 193–4. Unpublished portions enclosed in square brackets.

p. 277 l. 37 Bizet to Mme Halévy. "Unpublished Letters," 388.

CHAPTER XX

The Year of Terror II: The Commune

p. 284 l. 12 Bizet to Rodrigues. "Unpublished Letters," 391. Unpublished portion in square brackets.

p. 284 l. 18 Gallet, 57.

p. 285 l. 5 Ibid., 58.

p. 285 l. 18 Bizet to Rodrigues, n. d. Unpublished letter, collection of author.

p. 288 l. 3 Bizet, *Lettres.* Unpublished portion of letter, 296.

p. 288 l. 15 Sardou to Bizet, n. d. Unpublished letter, collection of author.

p. 289 l. 33 Hegermann-Lindencrone, 308–9.

p. 290 l. 38 Charles Nuitter, quoted in Louis Gallet, *Guerre et Commune,* Paris, 1898, 315.

p. 292 l. 8 Bizet, *Lettres à un ami.* Unpublished portion of letter, 88.

p. 292 l. 15 Ibid., 182.

p. 292 l. 29 Prod'homme et Dandelot, II, 116.

p. 293 l. 3 Ibid., 123.

p. 293 l. 35 Henri d'Almeras, *La Vie Parisienne pendant le Siège et la Commune,* Paris, n. d., 441.

CHAPTER XXI

Family Problems

p. 296 l. 18 Geneviève Bizet to her mother, June 8, 1871. Unpublished letter, collection of author.

p. 297 l. 18 Bizet to Rodrigues, June 8, 1871. Unpublished letter, collection of author.

p. 298 l. 10 Bizet to Rodrigues, "Unpublished Letters," 399–400.

p. 299 l. 6 Bizet, *Lettres à un ami,* 195–6.

p. 299 l. 18 Bizet, *Lettres,* 315–16.

p. 299 l. 20 Bizet, *Lettres à un ami,* 196–7.

p. 300 l. 9 Bizet to Mme Halévy, "Unpublished Letters," 398–9.

p. 300 l. 30 Bizet to Mme Halévy. Ibid., 406.

p. 301 l. 8 Bizet to Rodrigues. Ibid., 407.

p. 301 l. 11 G. Weldon, *Gounod en Angleterre,* London, 1875, 10.

p. 302 l. 3 Camille du Locle to Léo Delibes, July 11, 1871. Unpublished letter, Archives nationales.

p. 302 l. 26 Bizet to Rodrigues, n. d. Unpublished letter, collection of author.

p. 302 l. 38 Bizet to du Locle, n. d. Unpublished letter, Bibliothèque de l'Opéra.

p. 303 l. 5 Bizet to Mme Halévy, "Unpublished Letters," 401.

p. 303 l. 14 Berton, 214–16.

p. 303 l. 27 Gallet, 14.

p. 304 l. 7 Ibid., 14–15.

p. 304 l. 32 Bizet to Mme Halévy, "Unpublished Letters," 402.

p. 305 l. 21 Ibid., 401–2.

p. 305 l. 35 Marc Pincherle, ed., *Musiciens peints par eux-mêmes,* Paris, 1939, 166–7.

p. 306 l. 18 Ambroise Thomas to Bizet, July 31, 1871. Unpublished letter, collection of author.

p. 306 l. 38 Bizet to Rodrigues, June 26, 1871. Unpublished letter, collection of author.

p. 307 l. 24 Geneviève Bizet to her mother, August 9, 1871. Unpublished letter, collection of author.

p. 308 l. 5 Bizet to Mme Halévy, n. d. Unpublished letter, collection of author.

p. 309 l. 40 Bizet to Mme Halévy, n. d. Unpublished letter, collection of author.

p. 310 l. 10 Bizet to Mme Halévy, n. d. Unpublished letter, collection of author.

p. 310 l. 39 Bizet to du Locle, n. d. Unpublished letter, Bibliothèque de l'Opéra.

p. 311 l. 7 Pigot, 285-6.

p. 312 l. 3 Bizet, *Lettres à un ami*, 196-7.

p. 312 l. 12 Imbert, 191.

p. 314 l. 32 Bizet to Mme Halévy, "Unpublished Letters," 405.

p. 315 l. 9 Ibid., 407.

p. 315 l. 27 Bizet to Mme Halévy, September 28, 1871. Unpublished letter, collection of author.

Chapter XXII

Djamileh

p. 318 l. 11 *Correspondance entre George Sand et Gustave Flaubert*, Paris, n. d., 296.

p. 319 l. 22 Alexandre Dumas, *Henri Blaze de Bury*, Paris, 1885, 278-9.

p. 320 l. 25 Maréchal, *Souvenirs d'un musicien*, 218 ff.

p. 321 l. 2 Berton, 239.

p. 321 l. 34 Saint-Saëns, *Portraits et Souvenirs*, 180 ff.

p. 325 l. 22 Bizet, *Lettres à un ami*, 199.

p. 325 l. 28 Soubies et Malherbe, II, 185.

p. 325 l. 36 Bizet to Ernest Reyer, n. d. Unpublished letter, New York Public Library.

p. 328 l. 2 Jules Massenet to Bizet, May 28, 1672. Unpublished letter, collection of author.

p. 328 l. 17 Gounod to Mme Halévy, June 7, 1872. Unpublished letter, collection of M. Daniel Halévy.

p. 329 l. 10 Bizet to Mme Halévy, n. d. Unpublished letter, collection of author.

p. 329 l. 22 Bizet to Ludovic Halévy, n. d. Unpublished letter, collection of M. Daniel Halévy.

p. 329 l. 28 Ernest Beulé to Bizet, n. d. Unpublished letter collection of author.

p. 330 l. 6 Bizet to Dr. Devillières, n. d. Unpublished letter, collection of author.

Chapter XXIII

L'Arlésienne

p. 331 l. 12 Bizet to Léon Carvalho, n. d. Unpublished letter, courtesy of Mme de Juge.

p. 332 l. 2 Bizet to Rodrigues, n. d. Unpublished letter, collection of author.

p. 332 l. 32 Léon Carvalho, "Chant et Dialogue," *Le Matin*, June 22, 1895.

p. 333 l. 15 Léon Pillant, *Instruments et Musiciens avec une préface par* A. Daudet, Paris, 1880, iii-iv.

p. 333 l. 32 Emile Zola, *Les Romanciers naturalistes*, in Elsa Fricker, *Alphonse Daudet et la Société du Second Empire*, Paris, 1937, 5.

p. 334 l. 4 Théodore de Banville in *Le National*, February 4, 1878, quoted ibid.

p. 334 l. 6 Ernest Jones, *Life and Works of Sigmund Freud*, New York, 1953, I, 187.

p. 334 l. 17 Jacques-Henry Bornecque, "Alphonse Daudet et l'Amour fatal," *Le Monde*, February 6, 1951.

p. 335 l. 21 Alphonse Daudet, *Les Amoureuses: Poèmes et Fantaisies, 1857-1861*, Paris, 1895, 55-6.

p. 337 l. 7 Léon Daudet, *Quand vivait mon Père*, Paris, 1940, 21-2.

p. 337 l. 20 Mme Alphonse Daudet, "La Cinquantenaire de *l'Arlésienne*," *Les Annales*, October 1922.

p. 338 l. 20 Alphonse Daudet, *Quarante Ans de Paris: 1857-1897*, Geneva, n. d., 211.

p. 339 1. 2 Frans Gerver, *Georges Bizet,* Brussels, 1945, 74.

p. 339 1. 10 Berton, 234.

p. 339 1. 16 Bizet to Johannès Weber, facsimile in Julius Rabe, *Georges Bizet, En Minnestechning,* Stockholm, 1925.

p. 340 1. 10 Reyer, *Quarante Ans de Musique,* 285 ff.

p. 340 1. 24 Massenet to Bizet, October 16, 1872. Unpublished letter, collection of author.

p. 340 1. 33 A. Daudet to Bizet, n. d. Unpublished letter, collection of author.

Chapter XXIV
Toward *Carmen*

p. 342 1. 4 Bizet to unknown correspondent, n. d. Unpublished letter, Bibliothèque nationale.

p. 343 1. 8 Bizet to Gounod, n. d. Unpublished letter.

p. 343 1. 24 Gounod, "Lettres à Georges Bizet," 700–1.

p. 343 1. 40 Ibid. Unpublished portion of letter, collection of author.

p. 344 1. 11 Bizet to Mme Halévy, n. d. Unpublished letter, collection of M. Daniel Halévy.

p. 344 1. 25 Dr. Eugène Gelma, "Un Centenaire: Quelques Souvenirs sur Georges Bizet," *Extrait de La Vie en Alsace,* December 1938.

p. 345 1. 7 Jacques-Emile Blanche, *La Pêche aux Souvenirs,* Paris, 1949, 110–11.

p. 345 1. 11 "Lettres inédites de Lecocq à Saint-Saëns," 223.

p. 347 1. 33 Stuart Henry, *Paris Days and Evenings,* London, 1896, 192–202.

p. 348 1. 9 Bizet to Pasdeloup, n. d. Unpublished letter copied from catalogue. Source lost.

p. 349 1. 32 Henry T. Finck, *Massenet and His Operas,* London and New York, 1910, 46–8.

p. 349 1. 36 Reyer, *Quarante Ans de Musique,* 337.

p. 350 1. 4 Arthur Pougin, *Massenet,* Paris, 1914, 49.

p. 350 1. 39 Lalo, 112–13.

p. 351 1. 25 Ludovic Halévy, "La Millième Représentation de *Carmen,*" *Le Théâtre,* January 1905, 5–6.

p. 353 1. 33 Dean, *Bizet,* 82.

p. 354 1. 6 Maréchal, *Souvenirs d'un Musicien,* 181.

p. 355 1. 17 Albert de Maugny (pseud. "Zed"), *Le Demi-Monde sous le Second Empire,* Paris, n. d., 196.

p. 355 1. 23 Soubies et Malherbe, II, 96–7.

p. 356 1. 2 Marie Roze to Bizet, n. d. Unpublished letter, collection of author.

Chapter XXV
Galli-Marié: Delaborde

p. 357 1. 4 Berton, 237 ff.

p. 357 1. 22 Victor Massé to Sardou in Victor Degrange Catalogue No. 47, May 15, 1938.

p. 358 1. 5 Soubies et Malherbe, *passim.*

p. 358 1. 13 Ludovic Halévy, unpublished journal.

p. 358 1. 16 Georges Duval, *L'Année Théâtrale,* Paris, 1875, 89–90.

p. 359 1. 14 Alfred Einstein, *Mozart,* London, 1948, 74.

p. 363 1. 13 Galli-Marié to Elie Delaunay. Unpublished letter, collection of author.

p. 363 1. 38 Ibid.

p. 364 1. 8 Galli-Marié to du Locle. Unpublished letter, Bibliothèque de l'Opéra.

p. 364 1. 32 Delmas, 51–2.

p. 365 1. 11 Galli-Marié to du Locle, January 2, 1874. Unpublished letter, Bibliothèque de l'Opéra.

p. 365 1. 29 Massenet to Bizet, February 24, 1874. Unpublished letter, collection of author.

p. 366 1. 10 Maréchal, *Souvenirs d'un Musicien,* 232–4.

p. 366 1. 35 Bizet to his wife, n. d. Unpublished letter, collection of author.

p. 367 1. 10 Bizet to Mme Halévy, n. d. Unpublished letter, collection of M. Daniel Halévy.

p. 367 1. 24 Dean, *Bizet,* 84.

p. 370 l. 23 Antoine-François Marmontel, *Virtuoses Contemporains*, Paris, 1882, 159 ff.

CHAPTER XXVI

Carmen I: Rehearsals

p. 372 l. 29 Duval, 296.
p. 373 l. 17 Daniel Halévy, "Souvenirs de Famille," *Revue de Musicologie*, No. 68, November 1938, 130–1.
p. 377 l. 20 *Verdi: The Man in His Letters*, ed. Franz Werfel and Paul Stefan, New York, 1942, 267.
p. 378 l. 3 (Arnold Mortier), *Les Soirées Parisiennes de 1874: par Un Monsieur de l'Orchestre*, Paris, 1875, 379–80.
p. 380 l. 3 Berton, 239 ff.
p. 381 l. 19 Bizet to Ambroise Thomas. Unpublished letter, Cornuau catalogue of sale November 16, 1935. Supplied by M. Marc Pincherle.
p. 382 l. 4 Ludovic Halévy, "La Millième Représentation de *Carmen*," 8.
p. 382 l. 26 Bizet to du Locle, n. d. Unpublished letter, Bibliothèque de l'Opéra.
p. 382 l. 34 Du Locle to Bizet, February 13, 1875. Unpublished letter, collection of author.
p. 383 l. 2 Ludovic Halévy, "La Millième Représentation de *Carmen*," 8.
p. 384 l. 12 Ludovic Halévy to Bizet. Unpublished note, collection of author.
p. 385 l. 23 Original manuscript, collection of author.
p. 387 l. 3 Bizet to Mme Carvalho, n. d. Unpublished letter, courtesy of Mme de Juge.
p. 387 l. 16 Bizet to Rodrigues, n. d. Unpublished letter, collection of author.

CHAPTER XXVII

Carmen II: Première

p. 388 l. 26 Delmas, 43 ff.
p. 390 l. 13 Ludovic Halévy, "La Millième Représentation de *Carmen*," 8.
p. 390 l. 19 Unidentified clipping, Bizet scrapbook, collection of author.
p. 391 l. 3 Blanche, *La Pêche aux Souvenirs*, 111–12.
p. 391 l. 12 Jacques-Emile Blanche, *More Portraits of a Lifetime: 1918–1938*, London, 1939, 156–7.
p. 391 l. 20 Bizet scrapbook.
p. 391 l. 36 Ludovic Halévy, "La Millième Représentation de *Carmen*," 8.
p. 392 l. 5 Mary Garden and Louis Biancolli, *Mary Garden's Story*, New York, 1951, 111–12.
p. 392 l. 8 D. C. Parker, *Bizet*, London, 1951, 40–1.
p. 392 l. 33 Facsimile, Rabe, *Georges Bizet*.
p. 393 l. 15 Delmas, 45–6.
p. 394 l. 14 Berton, 243–4.
p. 394 l. 25 Ibid., 259 ff.
p. 395 l. 24 Daniel Halévy, "Souvenirs de Famille," 130–1.
p. 395 l. 31 Delibes to Bizet, n. d. Unpublished letter, collection of author.
p. 395 l. 37 Reyer to Bizet, n. d. Ibid.
p. 396 l. 7 Massenet to Bizet, March 4 [1875], 2 a.m. Ibid.
p. 396 l. 11 Saint-Saëns to Bizet, n. d. Collection of author. This letter, incorrectly translated, has frequently been published.
p. 396 l. 14 Bizet to Saint-Saëns, n. d. Unpublished letter, Musée Saint-Saëns, Dieppe.
p. 397 l. 24 Reyer, *Quarante Ans de Musique*, 300.
p. 399 l. 5 Alfred Einstein, *Mozart: His Character, His Work*, New York and London, 1945, 430–1.
p. 401 l. 10 Achille de Lauzières de Thémines, *La Patrie*, March 8, 1875.
p. 401 l. 21 See Domenico de Paoli, "Bizet and His Spanish Sources," *The Chesterian*, XXII, No. 153.
p. 404 l. 28 Oscar Comettant, *Le Siècle*, March 8, 1875.
p. 405 l. 37 Bizet to Mme Halévy, n. d. Unpublished letter, collection of author.
p. 406 l. 16 Bizet to Dumas *fils*, n. d. Unpublished letter, Marc Loliée Catalogue No. 90, Supplement.
p. 409 l. 36 Théodore de Banville, *Le National*, March 8, 1875.

CHAPTER XXVIII

Death of Georges Bizet

p. 411 l. 16 Berton, 259 ff.
p. 411 l. 35 Maréchal, *Souvenirs d'un Musicien*, 235–6.
p. 412 l. 13 Pougin, 55–6.
p. 412 l. 31 Gounod to Bizet, January 24, 1875. Unpublished letter, collection of author.
p. 413 l. 17 Gallet, 92.
p. 414 l. 6 Oscar Comettant, *Le Siècle*, April 23, 1883.
p. 414 l. 16 Saint-Georges to Bizet, May 24, 1875. Unpublished letter, collection of author.
p. 415 l. 3 Galli-Marié to Bizet, n. d. Unpublished letter, collection of author.
p. 415 l. 20 Gallet, 93–5.
p. 416 l. 2 Pigot, 248.
p. 416 l. 15 Henri Blaze de Bury, *Musiciens du Passé, du Présent et de l'Avenir*, Paris, 1880, 326–7.
p. 417 l. 9 Pigot, 244–5.
p. 419 l. 7 Daniel Halévy, "Souvenirs de Famille," 130.
p. 419 l. 12 Ludovic Halévy to Hippolyte Rodrigues. Collection of author.
p. 419 l. 37 Dr. Eugène Gelma, "La Mort du Musicien Georges Bizet," *Cahiers de Psychiatrie*, No. 2, Strasbourg, 1949.
p. 420 l. 39 Pigot, 247 *n*. 1.
p. 421 l. 8 Reyer, *Quarante Ans de Musique*, 308–9.
p. 421 l. 23 Soubies et Malherbe, 149.
p. 421 l. 25 Sand, *Agendas*, op. cit., September 26, 1869.
p. 422 l. 20 Reyer, *Quarante Ans de Musique*, 305–6.
p. 423 l. 4 Pigot, 251.
p. 423 l. 29 Charles Gounod. Draft of address given at funeral of Georges Bizet, collection of M. Daniel Halévy.
p. 424 l. 8 Pasdeloup to Ludovic Halévy, n. d. Unpublished letter, collection of M. Daniel Halévy.
p. 424 l. 12 *Le Ménestrel*, June 13, 1875. Quoted Pigot, 251.
p. 424 l. 30 Reyer, *Quarante Ans de Musique*, 308.
p. 424 l. 39 Pigot, 219 *n*. 1.
p. 425 l. 17 *L'Aurore*, November 2, 1954.

CHAPTER XXIX

Carmen III: Success

p. 427 l. 17 Galli-Marié to du Locle, July 10 [1875]. Unpublished letter, Bibliothèque de l'Opéra.
p. 427 l. 22 Galli-Marié to du Locle, July 28, 1875. Ibid.
p. 427 l. 29 Pigot, 257.
p. 428 l. 8 Ibid., 258.
p. 428 l. 28 Minnie Hauk, *Memories of a Singer*, London, 1925, 51.
p. 430 l. 31 Frederick Nietzsche, *Complete Works of*, ed. Dr. Oscar Lay, London, 1911, Vol. 8, *The Case of Wagner*, 1–4.
p. 431 l. 2 Galli-Marié to Geneviève Bizet, August 7, 1881. Unpublished letter, collection of author.
p. 431 l. 27 Maurice Lefevre, *Musica*, June 1912, No. 117, 102.
p. 432 l. 21 Galli-Marié to Geneviève Bizet, June 6 [1882]. Unpublished letter, collection of author.
p. 433 l. 28 Oscar Comettant, *Le Siècle*, April 23, 1883.
p. 433 l. 34 Johannès Weber, *Le Temps*, April 24, 1883.
p. 434 l. 12 Ernest Reyer, *Le Journal des Débats*, April 29, 1883.
p. 434 l. 28 Edouard Thierry, *Le Moniteur universel*, October 29, 1883.
p. 434 l. 33 Auguste Vitu, *Le Figaro*, October 28, 1883.
p. 435 l. 10 Oscar Comettant, *Le Siècle*, October 28, 1883.
p. 435 l. 30 René Péter, *Le Théâtre et la vie sous la Troisième République: Première Epoque*, Paris, 1945, 53–4.
p. 436 l. 22 Reynaldo Hahn, "Propos sur Bizet," *Le Figaro*, October 27, 1938.
p. 436 l. 31 G. Jean-Aubry, "Bizet or Luckless Good Fortune," *The Chesterian*, November–December 1938, 40.
p. 437 l. 2 Bernard Gavoty (Clarendon), "Aix-en-Provence nous offre *Carmen* aux étoiles," *Le Figaro*, July 15, 1957.

Chapter XXX
Postscript

---

p. 440 1. 16 Georges de Lauris, *Souvenirs d'une belle époque*, Paris, 1948, 152 ff.

Appendix I

UNPUBLISHED LETTERS

CAMILLE DELSARTE TO HIS BROTHER, FRANÇOIS / Addressed to: M. Delsarte, professor of singing / rue de Larochefaucauld [sic] 22 or 26 Paris

Mézières
March 8, 1841

My dear brother,

I am taking advantage of the departure for Paris of Mme Paquet to whom you gave lessons, to write you a few words. I hope that this time you will really answer me, because for 18 months I have had no word of you. I do not think however that anything has happened to make you cross with me. I would have been pleased to have a few words from you, for since I have seen you I have been the most unfortunate of men; also my health has improved. I have been several times in the hospital where I had to fight both illness and boredom. Having barely left Lille where I was ill for 4 months, I arrived at Mézières where further suffering was in store for me. Conscripted, I had to go twice a day for exercises no matter what kind of weather, subject to the rudeness and threats of stupid corporals who made my life as a soldier so hateful that I don't know to this very day how I stood it. It is true I had an uncle who consoled me and kept up my courage, but you know he has been taken from us, regretted by the numerous friends drawn to him by his kindness. During his illness, which lasted two months, I didn't leave him for an instant. My experience in that hospital was very sad and has left me with painful memories. Here I am now without relatives. Fortunately my uncle's friends are mine, for everything connected with the Rolland [sic] family is very precious to them; but here I am far away from such thoughts. All my officers are interested in me; General André himself has commiserated with me over my fate. He has granted me several favors which are not to be dismissed lightly when one is a miserable pioupiou [foot soldier]. My sister must have told you that I am giving lessons. I am the fashion in our two little cities of Mézières and Charleville. At the moment I have twelve pupils; besides I know other people who will soon be taking from me. Not having anyone to count on, I am saving money this way which will later help me to retire from the service. . . . I hope in a little while to have a fine nest egg, if only I don't get orders to leave, and can establish myself in this part of the country. I urge you again to answer promptly and to give me news of all of you, so that Mme Paquet's kindness may not be futile.

If by any chance you see my sister, give her my greetings and kiss her for me.

Your brother
Delsarte

P.S. My address is M. C. Delsarte, care of M. Becherel, Commanding Officer, Retired, Mézières.

CAMILLE DELSARTE TO FRANÇOIS DELSARTE / Addressed to M. Delsarte, professor of singing / 16 rue de la Pépinière, near the railroad, right bank

My good brother,

I don't know whether you received the letter that I sent to you by one of my friends, who was perhaps careless about delivering it. I told you of my débuts which were magnificent, particularly in lucie [sic]. The person who gives you this letter will tell you all the details of what is going on. He is a friend of our director who is going to Paris to engage a number of singers to replace those who have fallen by the wayside. If among your pupils there are any who need work, and whom you regard as able to play the roles, send them to us. Above all don't forget my request that you should call on Mme Vacher, 48 rue Lafitte. She is the aunt of the person I am supposed to marry. She knows nothing of my success and expects your visit. Also please make my excuses to Halévy. You see him now; you can do much for my future.

Kiss my nephews and Mme Delsarte for me. Thank you for the leads you have given me. I shall thank you when I return from Saint-Hubert.

Your brother Camille Delsarte, 1st tenor at Rheims. Write to me; tell me about your visit.

Collection of
Mme Bouts Réal Del Sarte

AIMÉE BIZET TO HER HUSBAND

[Probably 1846 or 1847]

I arrived last night, my dear friend, but too late. Our poor grandmother was no longer alive 2 hours after the letter my godfather wrote me. It is he who told me this bad news. He, too, regrets it deeply. My arrival brought back all the pain he had suffered and was terrible for me. Poor woman! She was so happy at Samer.[1] All the time she kept repeating to my godfather: "Never since I was born have I had such happiness." They could neither of them have been happier. For three weeks she was very well. They had brought her an *armoire*; her things were all in order. She was sick only four or five days and the illness was only a slight fever of the kind she so often had. Doctors were called right away, to her great regret, for she said to my cousin Genan that it was nothing and that she had no need of all these people around her. Nevertheless the four doctors all agreed that this was a woman who was dying and that for a long time only her energy had kept her alive. They all said that the jour-

ney had not affected her illness, but that the joy she felt and the serenity of mind which was not habitual with her had caused her death a few days sooner. Her end was as peaceful as possible. Two hours before she drew her last breath she was still talking, not for a moment aware of her condition. All this I was told yesterday. My cousin had told me that she immediately had everything sealed. My godfather has just this instant told me in tears that in her last moments Grandma called him and gave him all the money she possessed as well as the papers which are the deeds she had made out to him and the acknowledgment of the 6 thousand francs that cousin Genan has, in addition to 2 thousand francs that came from my aunt and which are also deposited at Samer in a way that Mme Genan says is safe. As for the house, I have found out its value—it is not valued at more than 2000 francs. It is rented for 150 to someone who will probably never leave it. It seems to me that these things had better be left as they are. After the taxes are paid and the repairs made, there will always be at least 100 f. net from this house. From the 100 f. from this house, the 100 f. income from the 2000 f. which I spoke of above, the 200 f. of the 6000 f. that my godfather draws every year and, added to that, nearly 300 f. from his pension—all this added up gives him, if I am not mistaken, 700 f. As for the income from the 5000 f., he tells me that he does not need it, that we can do what we like with it. He wants to stay at Mme Genan's where he is happy and overwhelmed with attention. He wishes, he told me, to end his days there quietly and never to move away. It seems to me that with his staying at Samer it would be best to leave matters as they are, while at the same time placing the deeds in safe hands, because I don't understand why my godfather took them. As for all the money, it is in the hands of M. Genan. It was not placed under seal. I asked him what he had. He replied that he didn't know exactly but that things were not as good as we thought.

---

[1] Mme Roland had very recently moved from Raillencourt.

The inventory includes everything except what belongs to my godfather, and his bed and bedding which he must, of course, be allowed to keep. What to do with the rest which consists of bedding and a lot of useless old things? I think it would be best to sell it. As for the linens, I think we would make very little from selling them and since they are always very useful it would be better to divide them up. In any case, see my brothers at once. You know I can do nothing without the powers of attorney of you 3. Send them to me promptly for I can accomplish nothing here until I have them. Or perhaps my brother would prefer to come. But it would be an expensive journey, besides all the time he would lose which would be tremendous. In any case, have him do what he wants about this. Have him write me everything he wishes if he doesn't come. I don't mention Camille because I imagine they are consulting each other about everything. Tell them to hurry. I am longing to be back with my poor little Georges and with you, my friend.

Au revoir; I embrace you with all my heart.

Your friend
Aimée

Take good care of Georges. I have not seen a single soul here except my cousin Genan and her husband who are splendid people and fill one with confidence in them.

*Collection of
Mme Bouts Réal Del Sarte*

ADOLPHE BIZET TO AUBER

Oct. 3, 1849

My good friend,
I did not see the première of *La Fée*.[2] M. Perrin asked me yesterday what I thought of this piece. I answered that having been unable to find a seat I saw nothing. He said: "Ask me for one tomorrow and I will give it to you." I am carrying out his wishes by asking you for two orchestra seats this evening. If you could give them to Marie you would oblige your devoted Bizet.

Archives nationales

EUGÈNE DELACROIX TO MME HALÉVY
October 14

Madame,
I am taking the liberty of asking you for the recipe of the famous tomato *hors-d'oeuvre*. You would be more than kind if you would give it to me in writing. I would have come to ask for it today, but I have to leave for Paris, but not quite for good. Perhaps I shall be obliged to stay two or three days, so will you be kind enough to ask Halévy, in case he was thinking of doing an errand at Champigny, to wait until my return.
Sincerely yours,
E. Delacroix

Collection of author

MME HALÉVY TO EMILE AUGIER
[Probably 1854]

My dear M. Augier, Master of Masters, I have just spent a long month at home in my room. I was very unwell, and without you I think I should have died. I have read and reread you, and Philiberte Giboyer has been my only medicine.[3] That's why I am cured, and admire you and feel the need of telling you so. I am proud to know you. You are really the only one who speaks to the heart. Everything I admired about you previously fills me with even more enthusiasm today. Your works are like the pictures by our great painters; they continue to grow on you. There are some that I reread every week and that I would like to read every day. Forgive me my admiration. I am still a little weak and couldn't restrain it.
Friendly greetings
L. Halévy

Collection of author

[2] Halévy's *La Fée aux Roses* was given October 1, 1849.

[3] Augier's drawing-room comedy, *Philiberte,* had been produced in 1853.

BIZET TO UNIDENTIFIED EDITOR.

[Early 1870]

Sir,

You announce in your theatre gossip column that M. Gounod is putting aside his *Polyeucte* to caress a *Calendal* grand opera in five acts.

M. Mistral, the author, and consequently the only owner of the rights to *Calendal*, has given them to M. Paul Ferrier to write a libretto for an opera based on that admirable poem. These gentlemen, with the directors of one of our lyric theatres, have commissioned me to write the score.

M. Gounod has been informed of my negotiations, and his well-known loyalty makes it unthinkable that he would for a single instant have considered a libretto which he knew to be reserved for one of his best friends.

Would you be kind enough to insert this little correction in your paper?

Sincerely yours,
Georges Bizet
22 rue de Douai

Library of Congress

BIZET TO CHOUDENS

[Early 1869]

Cher Ami. . . . I would like to have something of mine played at the Opéra concerts. Unfortunately I can ask nothing of M. Litolff, who denies me even the elementary politeness of a *greeting!* Will you talk to him?—He will certainly refuse, but if by some impossible chance, he should regard the request favorably, suggest to him the *Prelude* and the *Ballet* music from *La Jolie Fille.* The *Prelude* is absolutely symphonic and would regain in a concert hall everything it loses in the theatre.

Under no circumstances would I conduct the orchestra, for two reasons: 1. M. Litolff is an *admirable* conductor; I am a cardboard conductor; 2. I have a horror of making an exhibition of myself. . . . Do try to have *La Jolie Fille* given in Brussels. . . .

Your friend, Georges Bizet

Bibliothèque de l'Opéra

BIZET TO FRANÇOIS DELSARTE

My dear Uncle,

The newspapers played me the trick of mentioning my marriage before I was in a position to announce it myself.

I am marrying Mlle Geneviève Halévy. I passionately desire this union which will make me a perfectly happy man. I don't doubt that you and my aunt will be pleased to learn of this happy event.

Always your most devoted nephew
G. Bizet

*Collection of
Mme Bouts Réal Del Sarte*

BIZET TO MME DELSARTE

July 23, 1871

My dear Aunt,

My father's maid, who was sent to Paris this morning, brings us back two sad letters this evening! One of them informs me of the illness, the other of the death of my poor uncle. You must know how much we share your cruel sorrow. We are heartbroken not to have been able to be with you at this sad time. . . . We didn't know of his illness, so the news of his death made us realize with a shock all that you must have suffered during the last three months. As for me, I shall regret eternally the position in which circumstances outside my control have put me today. My place was beside you, and I regret terribly not having been able to be there. I shall come to Paris tomorrow to see you and to express more adequately in person my very real and very sincere sorrow. Until tomorrow then, until tomorrow. My regards to all and to you, my dear aunt, my most respectful affection.

Georges Bizet

*Collection of
Mme Bouts Réal Del Sarte*

ALPHONSE DAUDET TO BIZET

My dear M. Bizet,

We are lunching together Thursday at Carvalho's and I shall return to you your Vermillon couplets in two versions. You will choose. In the meantime here are the couplets in blank verse which are sung in the wings in the first act.

Grand soleil de la Provence
Gai compère du Mistral,
Toi qui siffles la Durance
Comme un coup de vin de Crau.
Allume! Allume!
O grand soleil
Allume ton flambeau vermeil.

O Soleil, ton feu nous brûle,
Et pas moins quand vient l'été
Avignon, Arles et Marseille
Te reçoivent comme un Dieu
Allume! Allume!
O grand soleil
Allume ton flambeau vermeil.

This is a popular song from down there by Frédéric Mistral.

Here are the 4 lines for the end of Act 4.

Bon Saint-Eloi qu'on fête en Messidor
Soyez béni, père du labourage
Pour avoir mis à l'abri de l'orage
Nos blés serrés et pleins et couleur
d'or! . . .

The *Noëls* by Saboly are on their way to Paris. It is more difficult to get the *Tambourin* by Vidal which is out of print!

However I shall have it for you.

Yours,

Alphonse Daudet

Collection of author

ALPHONSE DAUDET TO BIZET

Here, my dear Bizet, are some rhymes strung together for better or for worse.—Carvalho has asked me to make it very short, very airy, with lists of names! There is no way of putting real poetry into it.

Choeur des Fillettes
Pour cueillir le vermillon
Nous nous levons à la fraîche.

On s'habille, on se dépêche,
Ruban neuf, fin cotillon,
Et l'on marche en bataillon
Hé! Robert, Annie, Mion!—(Mi-on)
vite au vermillon—
Dans les chaudes plaines
au bord des chemins,
sous les chênes-nains,
sous les petits chênes,
à hauteur des mains
le vermillon bouge
Dans l'ombrage clair
comme un corail rouge
au fond de la mer
                    Reprise:
Pour cueillir le vermillon etc.

Carvalho sees this like a *flight* of birds—Frrrrt—I rather agree with him, which is why instead of the more developed chorus with an andante which I had done, I am sending you these verses. If you need another couplet, say so.

Please kiss the left eye of the *dauphin* for me.

Alphonse Daudet

Collection of author

ALPHONSE DAUDET TO BIZET

Here, *mon cher ami:*

Pour cueillir le vermillon
Nous nous levons à la fraîche
On s'habille, on se dépêche
Ruban clair, fin cotillon.
Nos chants de toute la route
La perdrix dans le sillon
Les répète, et le grillon
au bord des blés les écoute . . .
Pour cueillir le vermillon etc. . . .
Par les chaudes plaines
au bord des chemins
sous les petits chênes
à hauteur des mains
le vermillon bouge
sous l'ombrage clair
comme un corail rouge.
au fond de la mer.
vite les corbeilles!
allons! détachez
les graines vermeilles
des rameaux penchés.
                or
vite les corbeilles!

Et plus de chanson
Des graines vermeilles
faisons la moisson.

If this doesn't work, let me know. I will rewrite them as often as you like.

Cordially yours,
A. Daudet

[On the back of this letter Bizet has written: *3 contre Basses—1 Saxophone alto—1 piano—1 hautbois—2 flûtes—2 clarinettes—2 cors—1 alto —5 violoncelles—1 basson—7 violons—26*

In another handwriting: *2 flûtes —1 cor anglais—2 clarinettes—2 basson—1 timbalier—7 violons*]

Collection of author

BIZET TO ELIE DELAUNAY

Cher ami,

If you are not too disdainful of the praise of a musician let me tell you that I am very taken with your paintings. You have a great success on your hands and you owe it to your work alone, for never has an artist despised sensationalism, pulling strings and publicity more than you. It is absolutely pure and of an exquisite charm. When I went to see the third act of *La Juive* the other night I looked at your work—and I had the pleasure of seeing my impression shared by everybody. Bravo, *cher ami*, it is fine and solid.

Your Bizet

Collection of author

CAMILLE SAINT-SAËNS TO EMILE STRAUS

October 22, 1919

Dear Sir,

Since by a fortunate chance we met and I was able to chat with you I am taking the opportunity now to discuss a subject that has obsessed me for some time.

For several years now the management of the theatre has had the strange idea of adding a ballet to the last act of *Carmen*. A procedure of this kind would be understandable if it had to do with a work that needed

support. But *Carmen!* Is there a more brilliant success? This addition of a ballet is in no way justified. How does it happen that Mme Straus has not opposed it?

The worst of it is that Choudens, who should have held out against this unpardonable nonsense, lent himself to it. And to do this he took pieces from Bizet's works that are not at all Spanish in character and are therefore a hideous blemish in that masterpiece.

It would be bad enough if they had taken fragments from the first three acts. The unity of the work would not then have been destroyed. This is a task I would gladly undertake without, naturally, any advantage to myself. I shouldn't even want my name divulged.

But it would seem better to suppress this useless, scandalous ballet.

Please remember me most cordially to Mme Straus.

Yours sincerely,
C. Saint-Saëns

Rue de Courcelles 83 bis. (17ème)

P.S. Did you see the article in the *Annales* in which I defended Halévy against that abominable Lalo?

Collection of author

CAMILLE SAINT-SAËNS TO MME STRAUS

October 26, 1919

Chère Madame,

It is not only in Paris but in the whole world that this unfortunate ballet disfigures the last act of *Carmen*. The guilty one is the publisher who probably finds it to his advantage. The only recourse is through the Société des Auteurs. Our agent, M. Bloch, is an extremely intelligent and wholly honest man, incapable of considering anything but the interests of the authors. I can't urge you enough to deal with him directly and to ask his advice before going straight to the committee of the Société. This group, unfortunately composed of a large majority of *authors* and a feeble minority of *musicians,* does not always defend the latter as it should.

Thank you so much for the photograph; such a good likeness of my friend and comrade. For me he was a brother-in-arms and a comfort rather than like so many others, a rival, and often even an enemy under the guise of a friend!

Your letter, dated from a sanatorium, shows me how much your health still leaves to be desired. With all my heart I wish you a prompt and complete recovery.

Affectionately and respectfully yours,
C. Saint-Saëns

Addressed to the Sanatorium de la Malmaison, Rueil, S & O

Collection of author

ADOLPHE BIZET TO GENEVIÈVE BIZET
[Probably 1882]

A thousand thanks, my dear daughter, for the supplement you have added. You seem to give me lots of money and I hope that it doesn't embarrass you too much.

I am very much pleased with Jacques. He works well. He does one or two lessons every day. We also go for piano lessons to Mme Boton's with whom we are going to lunch in the forest of Saint-Germain.

I embrace you affectionately.
Your very devoted father,
A. Bizet

A mother's handwriting is never illegible.

Collection of author

ROMAIN ROLLAND TO JACQUES BIZET
Monday, Nov. 16, 1908

My dear Bizet,

I am very sorry not to be able to accept your invitation nor the task that you are friendly enough to ask of me. At the moment, as the year's courses are again beginning, I find myself taken up by so many tasks that my days aren't long enough to accomplish them; and it is impossible for me to do any more.—It is my intention, later at my leisure, to do a study of all the works and of the life of your father. But for the time being I could only write something hasty and mediocre; and that is just what I do not want to do—above all on such a subject. If I do not come to see you it is because I haven't an instant to myself. I stop one piece of work only to take up another, and never go out, so to speak, except to my courses. . . .

Very cordially yours,
Romain Rolland

Collection of author
By permission of
Mme Rolland

Poem by Louis Gallet, recited by Galli-Marié at Memorial Concert, October 31, 1875

Georges Bizet!—Ce nom tout à coup prononcé
Met, avec un frisson un doute dans notre âme;
Nous nous demandons si tant de force et de flamme
Dorment réellement dans l'ombre du passé,
Si nous n'allons point voir, rayonnante de vie,
Se lever parmi nous cette figure amie,
S'il est vrai que ce coeur soit à jamais glacé!

Oui, les rêves parés d'irrésistibles charmes
Ont brusquement fini dans le deuil et les larmes,
Cet esprit que suivait le nôtre s'est éteint.
Oui, tout est vrai: la mort, le coup rapide et rude
Pesant de tout le poids aveugle du destin
Sur un calme bonheur, pur dans sa plénitude,
Sur une jeune gloire à son premier matin.

Sa muse était charmante; elle aimait la lumière,
L'azur, le pourpre, l'or, les fleurs et les parfums!
Le front plein de lueurs, en sa grâce première,
On la voyait marcher hors des sentiers communs.
Elle chantait l'amour, la joie et l'espérance
Et des brumes d'Ecosse aux soleils d'Orient,

Des beaux jardins d'Asie aux déserts
de Provence,
Elle allait, tour à tour rêvant et
souriant.

Sa tendresse parfois et même sa folie
Mettaient en leur accent quelque
mélancolie:
On eût dit qu'elle avait comme un
pressentiment
Et qu'elle entrevoyait, sur la route
trop brève,
Cet abîme où devait s'ensevelir son
rève,
Cette ombre, où l'attendait le fatal
dénoûment.

Et sa voix s'élevait plus vibrante et
plus fière;
La foule le suivait déjà sur les
sommets.
Carmen jetait au vent sa chanson
familière;
Le maître avait conquis sa place
désormais.

Plus haut, plus loin encore l'entraînait
sa pensée,
A de nobles accents son coeur avait
battu:
Il voulait nous parler d'héroïque vertu,

Nous montrer la patrie affaiblie et
blessée
Et le rude Attila par le Ciel abattu.

Mais la mort vint, avant la tâche
commencée.
Le silence se fit . . . On annonça
tout bas
Ce malheur, si cruel que l'on n'y
croyait pas!

O toi que nous pleurons, jeunesse
épanouie,
Ame ardente, gardien des purs trésors
de l'art,
Dors en paix maintenant; ne crains
point qu'on oublie
Ou qu'on fasse à ton nom une trop
faible part.

Non! Les chants envolés de ton âme,
ô Poète,
Revêtent la splendeur auguste du
tombeau
Et le temps sacrera ton oeuvre, où se
reflète
La lumière du vrai, comme l'amour
du beau!

Louis Gallet,
Notes d'un librettiste

Appendix II

WORKS OF GEORGES BIZET CHRONOLOGICALLY LISTED WITH DATES OF COMPOSITION AND PUBLICATION

DRAMATIC

Published

Don Procopio, Opéra-bouffe; Text, Carlo Cambaggio, 1858–9. Choudens, 1905 (vocal score only).

Les Pêcheurs de Perles, Opera; Text, Michel Carré and E. Cormon, 1862–3. Choudens, 1863 (vocal score only; full score posthumously published).

Ivan IV, Opera; Text, Arthur Leroy and Henri Trianon, 1865. Choudens, 1951.

La Jolie Fille de Perth, Opera; Text, J. H. Vernoy de Saint-Georges and Jules Adenis, 1866. Choudens, 1868 (vocal score only; full score posthumously published).

Noé, Opera; Text, J. H. Vernoy de Saint-Georges. Completion of F. Halévy's opera, 1868–9. Choudens, 1885 (vocal score).

Djamileh, Opéra-comique; Text, Louis Gallet, 1871. Choudens, 1872 (vocal score), 1892 (full score).

L'Arlésienne, incidental music; Text, Alphonse Daudet, 1872. Choudens, 1872 (vocal score; full score later).

Carmen, Opéra-comique; Text, Henri Meilhac and Ludovic Halévy, 1873–4. Choudens, 1875 (vocal score which contains passages omitted in all later scores). Orchestral score, 1880 (?).

Unpublished

La Maison du docteur, Opéra-comique; Text, Henry Boitteaux. Very early. Ms. at Conservatoire.

Le Docteur Miracle, Operetta; Text, Léon Battu and Ludovic Halévy, 1856 or 1857. Ms. at Conservatoire.

La Guzla de l'Emir, Opéra-comique; Text, Jules Barbier and Michel Carré, 1861–2. Probably destroyed.

Malbrough s'en va-t-en guerre, Operetta; Text, Paul Siraudin and William Busnach, 1867. Act I only by Bizet. Probably destroyed.

La Coupe du Roi de Thulé, Opera; Text, Louis Gallet and Edouard Blau, 1868. Fragments of Ms. at Conservatoire and in collection of author.

Clarissa Harlowe, Opéra-Comique; Text, Philippe Gille, 1870–1. Ms. sketches at Conservatoire.

Grisélidis, Opéra-Comique; Text, Victorien Sardou, 1870–1. Ms. sketches in collection of author.

Sol-si-ré-pif-pan, Operetta; Text, William Busnach, 1872. Probably destroyed.

Don Rodrigue, Opera; Text, Louis Gallet and Edouard Blau, 1873. Unfinished Ms. at Conservatoire.

ORCHESTRAL

Published

Symphony in C major, 1855. Universal, 1935.

Scherzo and *Marche funèbre* (F minor), 1860–1. Scherzo used in *Roma* Symphony. Ms. of *Marche* at Conservatoire.

Symphony in C major (*Roma*), 1860–8, revised 1871. Choudens, 1880.

Marche funèbre (B minor), 1868. Choudens, 1881.

Petite Suite, 1871. Durand, 1882. Arrangement of 5 piano pieces from *Jeux d'enfants.* Nos. 2, *La Toupie;* 3, *La Poupée;* 6, *Trompette et Tambour;* 11, *Petit Mari, Petite Femme;* 12, *Le Bal.* On an unpublished Ms. orchestration of No. 8, *Les quatre coins,* in collection of author, Bizet has written: "op. 22, *petite suite d'orchestre,* No. 5, *final.*"

Suite, *"L'Arlésienne,"* 1872. Arr. of 4 pieces from *L'Arlésienne.* 2nd suite arr. by Guiraud. Choudens, 1876 (?).

Overture, *"Patrie,"* 1873. Choudens, 1874.

Unpublished

Overture, *"La Chasse d'Ossian,"* 1861. Lost.

Overture in A minor-major. *c.* 1855. Ms. at Conservatoire.

KEYBOARD

Published

Chasse fantastique, 1865 (?). Heugel, 1865.

Chants du Rhin, 6 Lieder for piano, based on poems by J. Méry, 1865. Heugel, 1865.

Trois Esquisses musicales pour orgue expressif, 1866 (?). Heugel, 1866.

Marine, 1868 (?). Hartmann, 1868.

Variations chromatiques de concert, 1868. Hartmann, 1868. Orchestrated by Weingartner, 1939.

Nocturne in D major, 1868. Hartmann, 1868.

Jeux d'enfants (12 pieces for piano duet) 1871. Durand, 1872.

Unpublished

Four Preludes (C major, A minor, G major, E minor), very early. Ms. at Conservatoire.

Valse in C major, very early. Ms. at Conservatoire.

Thème brillant in C major, very early. Ms. at Conservatoire.

Caprice original, No. 1, in C sharp minor, very early. Ms. at Conservatoire.

Romance sans paroles in C major, very early. Ms. at Conservatoire.

Caprice original, No. 2, in C major, very early. Ms. at Conservatoire.

Grande Valse de concert in E flat major, 1854. Ms. at Conservatoire.

Nocturne in F major, 1854.

Fugue in 4 parts. Inscribed *"Concours de Fugue, le dimanche 9 Juillet 1854 à onze heures ½ du soir."* Collection of author.

Fugue in 4 parts, 1854. 2nd prize. Ms. at Conservatoire.

Fugue in 4 parts on theme of Auber, 1855. 2nd prize. Collection of author.

Various fugues and exercises. Mss. at Conservatoire.

SONGS

Published

1 *Petite Marguerite,* Words by Olivier Rolland, 1854 (?). Cendrier, 1854.

2 *La Rose et l'abeille,* Words by Olivier Rolland, 1854 (?). Cendrier, 1854. Reissued by Choudens 1888 as *"Rive d'amour"* and *"En Avril."*

3 *Vieille Chanson,* Words by Millevoye, 1865 (?). Choudens, 1865.

4 *Adieux de l'hôtesse arabe,* Words by Victor Hugo, 1866. Choudens, 1867.

5 *Après l'hiver,* Words by Victor Hugo, 1866. Choudens, 1867.

6 *Douce Mer,* Words by Lamartine, 1866. Choudens, 1867.

7 *Chanson d'avril,* Words by Louis

Bouilhet, 1866 (?). Choudens, 1867.

8 *A une fleur,* Words by Alfred de Musset, 1866. Heugel, 1866.

9 *Adieux à Suzon,* Words by Alfred de Musset, 1866. Heugel, 1866.

10 *Sonnet,* Words by Ronsard, 1866. Heugel, 1866.

11 *Guitare,* Words by Victor Hugo, 1866. Heugel, 1866.

12 *Rose d'amour,* Words by Millevoye, 1866. Heugel, 1866.

13 *Le Grillon,* Words by Lamartine, 1866. Heugel, 1866.
Numbers 8 through 13 published together as *Feuilles d'album.*

14 *Pastorale,* Words by Regnard, 1868. Hartmann, 1868.

15 *Rêve de la bien-aimée,* Words by Louis de Courmont, 1868. Hartmann, 1868.

16 *Ma vie a son secret,* Words by Félix Arvers, 1868. Hartmann, 1868.

17 *Berceuse,* Words by Marceline Desbordes-Valmore, 1868. Hartmann, 1868.

18 *La Chanson du fou,* Words by Victor Hugo, 1868. Hartmann, 1868.

19 *La Coccinelle,* Words by Victor Hugo, 1868. Hartmann, 1868.

20 *La Sirène,* Words by Catulle Mendès, 1868. Dramatic fragment from *La Coupe du Roi de Thulé.* Choudens, 1886.

21 *Le Doute,* Words by Paul Ferrier, by 1868. Choudens, 1886.

22 *L'Esprit Saint,* Words by ?, ?. Choudens, 1869.

23 *Absence,* Words by Théophile Gautier, ?. Choudens, 1872.

24 *Chant d'amour,* Words by Lamartine, ?. Choudens, 1872.

25 *Tarantelle,* Words by Edouard Pailleron, ?. Choudens, 1872.

26 *Vous ne priez pas,* Words by Casimir Delavigne, ?. Choudens, 1873.
Numbers 3, 4, 5, 6, 7 and 14 through 26, as well as three songs from operas, were in-

cluded in *Vingt Mélodies,* Choudens, 1873.

27 *Voyage,* Words by Philippe Gille, ?. Choudens, 1886.

28 *Aubade,* Words by Paul Ferrier, ?. Choudens, 1886.

29 *La Nuit,* Words by Paul Ferrier, 1868. Choudens, 1886.

30 *Conte,* Words by Paul Ferrier, ?. Choudens, 1886.

31 *Aimons, rêvons!* Words by Paul Ferrier, 1868 (?). Choudens, 1886.

32 *La Chanson de la rose,* Words by Jules Barbier, ?. Choudens, 1886.

33 *Le Gascon,* Words by Catulle Mendès, 1868 (?). Choudens, 1886.

34 *N'oublions pas!* Words by Jules Barbier, 1868. Choudens, 1886.

35 *Si vous aimez!* Words by Philippe Gille, ?. Choudens, 1886.

36 *Pastel,* Words by Philippe Gille, ?. Choudens, 1886.

37 *L'Abandonnée,* Words by Catulle Mendès (original words by Philippe Gille), 1868 (?). Choudens, 1886.
Numbers 20, 21 and 27 through 37 are included in *Seize Mélodies,* a posthumous collection, many of which are excerpts from unfinished dramatic works.

38 *Sur la Grève,* Words by ?, ?. 'L'Age d'Or' Collection, Piano and voice. Choudens, n.d.

Unpublished

L'âme humaine est pareille au doux ciel, Words by Lamartine, very early. Ms. at Conservatoire.

Le Colibri, Words by Alexandre Glass, *c.* 1868–73. Ms. at Conservatoire.

Oh, quand je dors, Serenade; Words by Victor Hugo, ?. Ms. at Conservatoire.

Voeu, Words by Victor Hugo, ?. Ms. at Conservatoire.

MISC. VOCAL WORKS

Published

Vasco de Gama, Ode Symphony; Text by Louis Delâtre, altered by Bizet, 1859–60. Choudens, 1880.

Le Golfe de Bahia, soprano or tenor, chorus and piano, by 1865; Words by Lamartine. Choudens, 1880. (Used in *Ivan IV.*)

Saint-Jean de Pathmos, part-song for male voices; Words by Victor Hugo, 1866 (?). Choudens, n.d.

Chants des Pyrénées, French version of traditional; Words by M. J. Ruelle. Flaxland, 1867. Accompaniment to 6 *Mélodies Populaires.*

Ave Maria, Words by Charles Grandmougin, ?. Choudens, n.d.

La Fuite, Words by Théophile Gautier, ?. Choudens, 1872.

La Chanson du rouet, solo voice, chorus and piano; Words by Edouard Blau, probably 1857. Choudens, 1880. (*Le Chanson du rouet,* by Leconte de Lisle, was set as text for chorus in the Prix de Rome competition of 1857.)

Unpublished

Choeur d'étudiants, male chorus and orchestra; Words by Scribe, early. Ms. at Conservatoire.

L'Ange et Tobie, Cantata; Words by Léon Halévy, *c.* 1855–7. Unfinished. Ms. at Conservatoire.

Le Retour de Virginie, Cantata; Words by Rollet, *c.* 1855–7. Ms. at Conservatoire.

Clovis et Clotilde, Cantata; Words by Amédée Burion, 1857. 1st Prix de Rome. Ms. at Conservatoire.

Te Deum, soli, chorus and orchestra, 1858. Ms. at Conservatoire.

La Mort s'avance, Words by Abbé Pellegrin, ?. Ms. at Conservatoire.

Geneviève de Paris, Oratorio; Words by Louis Gallet, 1874–5. Projected. Probably not begun. Ms. of libretto in collection of author.

CHIEF TRANSCRIPTIONS OF WORKS BY OTHER COMPOSERS

Charles Gounod

Ulysse, 6 Transcriptions for piano solo. Choudens, 1852.

Symphony No. 1 in D major, Transcription for 4 hands. Choudens, 1855.

La Nonne sanglante, Piano and voice transcription. Choudens, 1855.

Philémon et Baucis, Piano and voice transcription. Choudens, 1859.

La Reine de Saba, Piano and voice transcription. Choudens, 1862.

Ave Maria, Piano solo transcription. Heugel, 1865.

Six Choeurs Célèbres, Piano solo transcription. Choudens, 1866.

Roméo et Juliette, Voice and piano transcription for 4 hands. Choudens, 1867.

Méditation sur le 1er Prélude de J. S. Bach, Piano transcription for 4 hands. Heugel, 1869.

Jeanne d'Arc, Piano solo transcription. E. Gérard, 1873. Piano and voice transcription. Choudens, 1877.

Gallia: Lamentation, Transcription for 4 hands. Choudens, n.d.

George Friedrich Handel

L'Harmonieux forgeron, Piano transcriptions for 4 hands. Choudens, n.d.

Benedetto Marcello

Salmo, Signore non tardi dunque, Piano solo transcription. Edouardo Songogno, Milan, n.d.

Victor Massé

Le Fils du brigadier, Piano solo transcription. Choudens, 1867.

Jules Massenet

Scènes hongroises, Suite for Orchestra, No. 2. (Work dedicated to Bizet.) Heugel, n.d.
Scènes de Bal, Op. 17, Piano solo transcription. Heugel, n.d.

Wolfgang Amadeus Mozart

Don Juan, Piano solo transcription of complete score. Heugel, 1866. Transcription of Overture and excerpts for 2 and 4 hands. Heugel, n.d. (Probably 1867.)
L'Oie du Caïre, Piano solo transcription. Heugel, 1867.

Otto Nicolai

Les Joyeuses commères (The Merry Wives of Windsor), Piano and voice transcription. Choudens, 1866 (?).

Ernest Reyer

Erostrate, Piano solo transcription. Choudens, 1862.
La Statue, Piano and voice transcription. Choudens, 1889.

Camille Saint-Saëns

Le Timbre d'argent, Piano and voice transcription. Choudens, 1879.
Concerto No. 2 for piano and orchestra, Piano solo transcription. Durand, n.d.
Introduction and Rondo capricioso for violin and orchestra, Piano solo transcription. Durand, n.d.

Robert Schumann

Six Etudes en forme de canon pour Piano à pédales, Op. 56, Transcription for 4 hands. Durand, n.d.

Ambroise Thomas

Mignon, Piano solo transcription. Heugel, 1867.
Hamlet, Piano and voice transcription. Heugel, 1869.

Collections

Don Juan de Mozart: Richard Coeur-de-Lion de Grétry: Le Barbier de Séville de Rossini, Three duets for *orgue expressif* and piano. Régnier et Canaux, 1858.
Le Pianiste chanteur, 6 volumes. Famous works of Italian, German, and French Masters. Piano solo transcription. Heugel, 1865.
Thalberg, (Sigismond) *L'Art du Chant appliqué au Piano,* Simplified edition for 2 and for 4 hands. Heugel, 1872.
Cent Fragments tirés de divers auteurs (Weber, Chopin, Beethoven, etc.) Girod, n.d.

Unpublished

Trio pour Violon, Piano, et Orgue sur Guillaume Tell de Rossini. Mss. at Conservatoire.

Appendix III

POSTHUMOUS PRESENTATIONS OF BIZET'S WORKS

DRAMATIC

Don Procopio. First performed at Monte Carlo, March 13, 1906, in a version revised by Charles Malherbe which differs considerably from the original. On February 6, 1958, *Don Procopio* in the original version was performed at the Théâtre Municipal in Strasbourg.

Les Pêcheurs de Perles. Revived in Paris at the Gaîté April 20, 1889, at the Opéra-Comique April 24, 1893, March 17, 1932, and October 27, 1938. Since then, it has remained in the repertory of the Opéra-Comique. Since 1886 it has been played in every country in Europe, in the Argentine, in Mexico and the United States. The Sadler's Wells Opera revived *The Pearl Fishers* in 1956. On January 1, 1958, *Les Pêcheurs de Perles* had been performed 359 times at the Opéra-Comique.

Ivan IV. The posthumous history of *Ivan IV* is too complicated to recount in detail here. For sixty years the score was thought to be lost. But at the death of Émile Straus in 1929 it passed to the Paris Conservatoire, where it was discovered in 1933 and discussed in an article by Jean Chantavoine in *Le Ménestrel*. In 1938, it was displayed at the Bizet centenary exhibition at the Bibliothèque de l'Opéra. The score lacked title page and list of characters, and the orchestration for the last act was incomplete. During the German occupation of Paris, Ernst Hartmann, a German music teacher and musicologist, completed the orchestration. The Germans had the score microfilmed. Schott of Mainz commissioned a German translation and had a vocal score engraved. But after the German defeat, Choudens, who had hitherto ignored the existence of the work, brought suit against Schott and obtained exclusive publication rights.

Ivan IV was first performed privately in 1946 at Mühringen Castle near Tübingen. It had a new libretto and was called *Ivan le terrible,* a title that Bizet never used. The first performance in France took place at the Grand Théâtre in Bordeaux on October 12, 1951, in the Choudens version "revised" and completed by Henri Busser. The first public performance in Germany occurred on April 6, 1952. To at least one member of that audience *Ivan IV* seemed theatrically more effective than *Les Pêcheurs de Perles* although musically the influence of Meyerbeer, Gounod, and Verdi is more easily discernible. Bizet used some of the music from *Ivan IV* in *La Jolie Fille de Perth.* He also incorporated part of *Vasco de Gama* into the score of *Ivan.* The *Trompette et Tambour* march, which was put into *Jeux d'enfants,* is brilliantly used in a scene laid on the walls of the Kremlin. *Ivan IV* was also given in Berne, Switzerland, in December 1952. For full details of the history of this work and an analysis of the score see Winton Dean, "Bizet's *Ivan IV"* in *Fanfare for Ernest Newman,* 58–85.

La Jolie Fille de Perth. Revived at the Opéra-Comique on November 3, 1890, and played the same year in Barcelona. It was given at Weimar and Vienna in 1883, at Kiev in 1887, and in English at Manchester and London in 1917. The Oxford University Opera Club revived what one reviewer called *"The Girl Friend from Perth"* in 1955. The following year the opera was broadcast by the BBC.

Noë. This opera by Fromental Halévy, completed by Bizet, was first performed in Karlsruhe in 1885, and later in several other German cities. It was played in Polish in Warsaw in 1887, but has never been performed in France.

Djamileh. First revived in Stockholm in a Swedish version in 1889. From then on it was played in many cities in Europe, including Rome, St. Petersburg, and Barcelona. It was played in Dublin in 1892, in Manchester the same year, in London in 1893 and 1919, and at the Hintlesham Festival in July 1957.

L'Arlésienne. First revived in Paris in 1885 at the Théâtre de l'Odéon, where it remains in the repertory. A version of Daudet's play in Italian by L. Marenco was set to music by Francesco Cilea. At the *première* in Milan in 1898, Enrico Caruso had his first success in the part of Fréderi.

ORCHESTRAL

Symphony in C. Eighty years after its composition, this symphony was discovered in the library of the Conservatoire by D. C. Parker, the first English biographer of Bizet. It had been part of a collection of Bizet's manuscripts including the original score of *La Jolie Fille de Perth* which his widow had given to Reynaldo Hahn. Hahn, without apparently having examined the unpublished works, presented the collection to the Conservatoire in 1933. Mr. Parker, soon after discovering the symphony, called it to the attention of Felix Weingartner, who played it for the first time at Basle on February 26, 1935. Since then, it has taken its place in the repertory of orchestras throughout the world. The score has been used by Georges Balanchine for the ballet, *Symphony in C,* which was first performed at the Paris Opéra in 1947.

Roma. This work was played in full for the first time in Paris by Pasdeloup on October 31, 1880. Colonne played it twice in January 1885, and since then it has been included from time to time in Paris programs. It is played infrequently elsewhere, and there is considerable difference of opinion about its value. Mahler liked it. Hanslick said that it contained "much attractive, witty, and even dazzling music, delightfully orchestrated." Hans von Bülow regarded the whole symphony as *"Schweinerei."* Nietzsche found it "extraordinarily charming . . . naïve and at the same time subtle as, indeed, is everything composed by this last master of French music." Georges Balanchine admires the work and used it for the ballet *Roma,* first played at the New York City Center in 1955.

Appendix IV

BIZET'S MUSIC LIBRARY

Bizet's music library and the *catalogue raisonné* that he wrote out meticulously in longhand over a period of years still exist. The former is now part of the library of the Comtesse de Chambure; the catalogue is in the collection of the author. It consists of 267 loose leaf pages, 9″ x 7″, enclosed in a cardboard folder covered with red marbled paper, backed with green velvet and tied with linen tapes. The library consists of volumes uniformly bound in green marbled boards with green calf backing. It includes compositions by two hundred and thirty-six composers, a few of Bizet's own works, and all of his piano reductions, as well as such publishers' collections as *Echos de France*, *Echos d'Espagne*, *Echos d'Italie*, *Echos d'Allemagne*, each item in which is separately listed under the composer's name.

Opera and other vocal music naturally enough predominates. Auber, for example, is represented by fifteen operas in full score, including *La Muette de Portici* and *Fra Diavolo*.

Of Bach's works, Bizet had only the Czerny edition of *Das wohltemperirte Clavier* and seven transcriptions, six of them by Saint-Saëns. Beethoven occupies twelve pages in the catalogue: *Fidelio* in piano score, full scores of all the symphonies and concertos, complete or nearly complete collections of the string quartets and trios, the duos and piano trios, the piano sonatas and other piano pieces, four-hand transcriptions of the overtures, and numerous other works.

Of Berlioz, Bizet owned a full score of *L'Enfance du Christ*, piano scores of *Les Troyens*, *Benvenuto Cellini*, and *Béatrice et Bénédict*. Of Brahms, two sets of *Ungarische Tanze* for four hands; of Cherubini, full scores of

Démophon and *Lodoïska* and three Masses. The Chopin section includes the *Préludes* and *Etudes* complete, but only the B flat minor Sonata and only the F minor Concerto.

Seventeen of Delibes's songs appear, including *"Les Filles de Cadix."* Several Donizetti operas are represented by arias and concerted numbers, but the only complete score is that of *La Favorite*. There are six songs by Fauré, among them *"Dans les ruines d'une abbaye"* and *"Lydia."* César Franck's *Ruth* and *Rédemption* are here, as are six organ pieces. Bizet had full scores of Gluck's *La Rencontre imprévue*, *Armide*, *Orphée et Eurydice*, *Cythère assiégée*, *Iphigénie en Tauride*, and *Alceste; Iphigénie en Aulide* is represented by a single aria. Two catalogue pages are taken up with songs and piano pieces of Benjamin Godard, most of which were presentation copies from the composer.

Interesting to Americans especially is the listing of three piano pieces by Louis Moreau Gottschalk: *"Le Bananier," "La Moissonneuse,"* and *"Le Mancenillier."* Gounod's works outnumber all but Beethoven's and Schumann's. Besides the compositions Bizet reduced for piano, there are full scores of both symphonies, and a large number of piano pieces, choruses, songs, and *"cantiques,"* many of which were presentation copies. Grétry is represented by ten operas in full score (including *Zémire et Azor*, *Richard Coeur-de-lion*, and *Les Deux avares*) and there is a full score of Handel's *Messiah*.

There are eight Haydn violin sonatas and thirty-one piano trios, but no symphonies, string quartets, or choral works. There are dozens of compositions by Stephen Heller, a composer whom Bizet knew and warmly admired, and by such other piano-playing virtuoso-teachers as Czerny, Herz, Hummel, Kalkbrenner, Moscheles, and Thalberg. Lalo, a personal friend, is represented by the piano score of his Schiller opera, *Fiesque* (and Massenet's piano transcription of its orchestral *Divertissement*) and six songs, presentation copies. The page devoted to Liszt contains the full scores of a Mass, the "Dante" and "Faust" symphonies, *Die Ideale*, and *Prometheus;* three *"Mélodies hongroises"* for piano, and the transcriptions of the *Lohengrin* Bridal Chorus and *Faust* Waltz.

Lully's *Armide, Phaëton,* and *Cadmus* are present in full score, as are *Euphrosine, ou le Tyran corrigé, La Journée aux aventures,* and *Melidore et Phrosine* by Méhul. Bizet owned Mendelssohn's *St. Paul* (piano score with French text), seven collections of *Lieder ohne Worte,* a full score of the incidental music for *A Midsummer Night's Dream* the "Scottish," "Italian," and "Reformation" symphonies, and seven string quartets. Of Meyerbeer's works he had full scores of *Les Huguenots, Robert le Diable,* and *Le Prophète,* and piano scores of *L'Africaine, L'Etoile du nord,* and *Il Crociato in Egitto.*

Mozart as opera-composer is naturally well represented: full scores of *Don Giovanni, Idomeneo, Die Zauberflöte* (text in French and Italian), *Così fan tutte, "Peines d'amour"* (an adaptation of the *Così fan tutte* music to a Barbier-Carré libretto based on Shakespeare's *Love's Labour's Lost*), and *L'Oie du Caïre,* as well as many separate arias. The Mozart items also include twelve symphonies in full score, five string quartets, nine piano trios, eighteen violin sonatas, and a collection of overtures transcribed for piano, four-hands.

The piano scores of Offenbach's *La Belle Hélène, La Grande-Duchesse de Gérolstein, Le Soixante-six, La Vie parisienne, Le Roi Carotte,* and *Fantasio* precede in the catalogue five pi-

ano scores of Palestrina Masses. There is a full score of Pergolesi's *La Serva Padrona,* but of Rameau, besides a full score of *Hippolyte et Aricie,* only two airs and three pieces for piano, violin, and violoncello. Rossini is represented by full scores of *Le Comte Ory, Guillaume Tell, Moïse,* and *Le Siège de Corinthe,* as well as a piano score of *Tell* and a piano transcription of the *Semiramide* overture, but oddly enough no score of *Le Barbier de Séville.*

There are full scores of Jean-Jacques Rousseau's *Le Devin du village* and Sacchini's *Dardanus.* The piano score of *La Princesse jaune,* the only Saint-Saëns opera produced during Bizet's lifetime, is included in the catalogue, as are a full score of the A minor violin concerto and piano scores and four-hand arrangements of a number of other works by Saint-Saëns.

No work by Alessandro Scarlatti is listed, and Domenico Scarlatti is represented by a single Sonata in A. Forty songs by Schubert (French texts) and four-hand piano transcriptions of the overtures to *Alfonso und Estrella, Rosamond,* and *Fierrabras* are listed, but no symphonies or chamber music.

Schumann, like Beethoven, occupies twelve pages in the catalogue; there are full scores of *Das Paradies und die Peri* and the four symphonies; piano scores of *Des Sängers Fluch,* the *Introduction und Allegro Appassionato,* the Piano Concerto, *Das Paradies und die Peri, Scenes from Goethe's "Faust,"* and *Music to Byron's "Manfred";* more than one hundred songs; *Papillons,* the *Davidsbündlertänze,* the Toccata, *Carnaval, Kreisleriana,* the *Fantaisie;* the three piano sonatas, the violin sonatas, the piano trios, the Piano Quintet, the Piano Quartet; and four-hand piano transcriptions of the *Overture, Scherzo, and Finale* (op. 52), the *Overture to Schiller's "Braut von Messina,"* and the *Kinderscenen.* Bizet also owned full scores of three operas by Spontini: *Julie ou le pot de fleurs, La Vestale,* and *Fernand Cortez*, but of Verdi's works only a transcription by Jules Cohen of the *Miserere* from *Il Trovatore* is listed.[1]

Weber is represented by a full score and piano score of *Der Freischütz*, three piano sonatas, the *Aufforderung zum Tanze*, miscellaneous operatic transcriptions, and a collection of ten overtures arranged for piano, four

hands. Although Bizet owned no full score of any of Wagner's operas, he had an orchestral score of the overture to *Die Meistersinger*, piano scores of *Tannhäuser, Lohengrin, Rienzi*, and *Der fliegende Holländer*, three songs, and four-hand piano transcriptions of the *Lohengrin* Bridal Chorus (Liszt) and the overture to *Tannhäuser* (Bülow).

Yradier, whose *El Arreglito*, was the source of the *habanera* in *Carmen*, is represented by five songs, four of which are included in *Echos d'Italie: La Colasa, El Jaque, El curro marinue, La Calesera. Aÿ Chiquita* (French text), published by Heugel as a supplement to *Le Ménestrel*, is unbound and remains among Bizet's papers.

---

[1] "In 1872, Bizet wrote the following note to the critic Victor Wilder: 'If you are not busy, come as soon as possible this evening. I have the score of *Aïda*. You will see things in it that will astonish and enchant you.'" *Le Ménestrel*, July 18, 1875, Vol. XLI.

Appendix V

SELECTED LIST OF READING
ON THE LIFE AND WORKS
OF GEORGES BIZET

BAILLE, CHARLES: "Le Peintre, Félix Giacomotti," Mémoires de l'Académie des Sciences, des Belles Lettres, et des Arts de Besançon. 1910.

BELLAIGUE, CAMILLE: Georges Bizet, sa vie et son oeuvre. Paris, 1891.

BERTON, PIERRE: Souvenirs de la vie de théâtre. Paris, 1913.

BIZET, GEORGES: (Gaston de Betzi): "Causerie Musicale," La Revue Nationale et Etrangère, August 3, 1867.

———: Lettres, Impressions de Rome, 1857–60, La Commune, 1871. Ed., Louis Ganderax, Paris, 1907.

———: Lettres à un ami, 1865–72. Ed., Edmond Galabert, Paris, 1909.

———: "Unpublished Letters by Georges Bizet." Ed., Mina Curtiss. The Musical Quarterly, Vol. XXXVI, No. 3, July 1950.

Exposition Georges Bizet au Théâtre National de l'Opéra, illustrated catalogue, Paris, 1938.

Briefe aus Rom, 1857–1860. Ubertragen und mit einem Vorwort von Walter Klefisch. Hamburg, 1949.

BLAZE DE BURY, HENRI: Musiciens du Passé, du Présent et de l'Avenir. Paris, 1880.

BLOCK, L.: "Die Instrumentation der Carmen," Blätter der Stadtsoper, Vol. X, No. 28.

BRUK, MIRA: Bizet. Moscow, 1938.

CHANGEUR, JEAN-PAUL: Six articles on Ivan IV, La Vie Bordelaise, October 12 to November 16, 1951.

CHANTAVOINE, JEAN: "Quelques Inédits de Georges Bizet," Le Ménestrel, Vol. 95, August 4 to September 22, 1933.

CHARLOT, ANDRÉ and JEAN: "A propos de la Millième de Carmen," L'Art du Théâtre, January 1905.

CHARPENTIER, GUSTAVE: "La Millième de Carmen," Le Figaro, December 23, 1904.

CHASE, GILBERT: The Music of Spain. New York, 1941.

COOPER, MARTIN: Georges Bizet. London, 1938.

CURTISS, MINA: "Bizet," Die Musik in Geschichte und Gegenwart: Allgemeine Enzyklopädie der Musik. Kassel und Basel: Barenreiter-Verlag, 1951–

———: "Bizet, Offenbach, and Rossini," The Musical Quarterly, Vol. XL, No. 3, July 1954.

———: "Fromental Halévy," The Musical Quarterly, Vol. XXXIX, No. 2, April, 1953.

———: "Gounod before Faust," The Musical Quarterly, Vol. XXXVII, No. 1, January 1952.

DAFFNER, HUGO: "Nietzsche und Carmen," Blätter der Stadtsoper, Vol. IX, No. 7.

DEAN, WINTON: Bizet. London, 1948.

———: "Bizet," Grove's Dictionary of Music and Musicians, I, 5th ed., New York, 1955.

———: "Bizet and La Coupe du Roi de Thulé," Music and Letters, Vol. XXVIII, October 1947.

———: "Bizet's Ivan IV," Fanfare for Ernest Newman. Ed., Herbert Van Thal. London, 1955.

———: Carmen by Prosper Mérimée with a study of the Opera of the same name, with Goya drawings. London, 1949.

———: Introduction to the Music of Bizet. London, n.d. [1950].

DELMAS, MARC: Georges Bizet. Paris, 1930.

FAURÉ, GABRIEL: "La Millième Représentation de Carmen," Le Figaro, December 23, 1904.

———: Opinions Musicales. Paris, 1930.

GALABERT, EDMOND: *Georges Bizet, Souvenirs et Correspondance.* Paris, 1877.

———: "La Maladie et la Mort de Bizet," *Le Passant,* February, 1888.

GALLET, LOUIS: *Notes d'un librettiste.* Paris, 1891.

GATTI, GUIDO M.: *Giorgio Bizet.* Turin, 1914.

GAUDIER, CHARLES: *Carmen de Bizet.* Paris, 1922.

GAUTHIER-VILLARS, HENRY: *Bizet.* Paris, 1911.

GELMA, EUGÈNE: "Un Centenaire: Quelques Souvenirs sur Georges Bizet," *La Vie en Alsace,* December 1938.

———: "La Mort du Musicien Georges Bizet," *Cahiers de Psychiatrie,* No. 2, Strasbourg, 1949.

GOUNOD, CHARLES: "Lettres à Georges Bizet," *Revue de Paris,* Vol. 6, December 15, 1899.

HALÉVY, LUDOVIC: "La Millième Représentation de *Carmen,*" *Le Théâtre,* January 1905.

HARTMANN, LUDWIG: *"Die Perlenfischer," "Djamileh," Historisch-Äesthetistche Einführung,* Leipzig, 1900.

HENRY, STUART: *Paris Days and Evenings.* London, 1896.

HÜHNE, FRITZ: *Die Oper Carmen als ein Typus musikalischer Poetik.* Greifswald, 1915.

IMBERT, HUGUES: *Médaillons contemporains.* Paris, 1903.

———: *Portraits et études, Lettres inédites de Georges Bizet.* Paris, 1894.

IMSAN, DORA: *Carmen, Charakter—Entwicklung für die Bühne.* Darmstadt, 1917.

ISTEL, EDGAR: *Bizet und Carmen.* Stuttgart, 1927.

———: "*Carmen,* novel and libretto —a dramaturgic analysis," *The Musical Quarterly,* Vol. VII, No. 4, October 1921.

———: "Die Uraufführung der *Carmen,*" *Blätter der Stadtsoper,* Vol. IX, No. 7.

KAPP, J.: "Einführung in *Djamileh,*" *Blätter der Stadtsoper,* Vol. VIII, No 2.

KLEIN, JOHN W.: "Bizet's Admirers and Detractors," *Music and Letters,* Vol. XIX, October 1938.

———: Bizet's Early Operas," *Music and Letters,* Vol. XVIII, April 1937.

———: "Bizet—Opportunist or Innovator," *Music and Letters,* Vol. V, July 1924.

———: "Bizet and Wagner," *Music and Letters,* Vol. XXVIII, January 1947.

———: "Nietzsche and Bizet," *The Musical Quarterly,* Vol. XI, No. 4, October 1925.

KREMLEV, J. U.: *Georges Bizet.* Leningrad, 1935.

LALO, PIERRE: *De Rameau à Ravel: Portraits et Souvenirs.* Paris, 1947.

LANDORMY, PAUL: *Bizet.* Paris, 1924.

LAPARRA, RAOUL: *Bizet et l'Espagne.* Paris, 1935.

MALHERBE, HENRY: *Carmen.* Paris, 1951.

MARÉCHAL, HENRI: *Paris: Souvenirs d'un musicien.* Paris, 1907.

MARMONTEL, ANTOINE: *Symphonistes et Virtuoses.* Paris, 1881.

MASTRIGLI, LEOPOLDO: *Giorgio Bizet: la sua vita e le sue opere.* Rome, 1888.

MORTIER, ARNOLD: *Les Soirées Parisiennes de 1875: par un Monsieur de l'Orchestre.* Paris, 1876.

MOSER, FRANÇOISE: *Vie et aventures de Céleste Mogador.* Paris, 1935.

Musica, special Bizet number, June 1912.

NIETZSCHE, FRIEDRICH: *Randglossen zu Bizet's Carmen.* Ed. by Hugo Daffner. Ratisbon, 1912.

PARKER, D. C.: *Georges Bizet, his Life and Works.* London, 1951.

PIGOT, CHARLES: *Georges Bizet et son oeuvre.* Paris, 1886; 2nd ed. with additions, Paris, 1911.

POUGIN, ARTHUR: "Le Légende de la chute de *Carmen* et la mort de Bizet," *Le Ménestrel,* Vol. 69, February 15, 1903.

RABE, JULIUS: *Georges Bizet.* Stockholm, 1925.

Revue de Musicologie, No. 68. *Numéro consacré à Georges Bizet.* November 1938.

REYER, ERNEST: *Quarante Ans de Musique.* Paris, 1910.

ROLLAND, ROMAIN: *Musiciens d'aujourd'hui.* London, 1918.

SAINT-SAËNS, CAMILLE: *Portraits et Souvenirs.* Paris, 1900.

SHAW, G. B.: *London Music in 1888–89 as heard by Corno di Bassetto.* London, 1937.

SOUBIES, ALBERT: *Histoire du Théâtre-Lyrique, 1851–70.* Paris, 1899.

—— and MALHERBE, CHARLES: *Histoire de l'Opéra-Comique: 1860–1887.* Vol. II. Paris, 1892.

STEFAN-GRUENFELDT, PAUL: *Georges Bizet.* Zürich, 1952.

TIERSOT, JULIEN: "Bizet and Spanish Music," *The Musical Quarterly,* Vol. II, No. 4, October 1925.

——: *Un Demi-siècle de musique française, 1870–1917.* Paris, 1918.

VAN VECHTEN, CARL: *The Music of Spain.* New York, 1918.

VOSS, PAUL: *Georges Bizet.* Leipzig, 1899.

WEISSMANN, ADOLF: *Bizet.* Berlin, 1907.

WILDER, VICTOR: "Georges Bizet," *Le Ménestrel,* Vol. XLI, July 1875.

Index

Abbé Constantin, L', *see* Halévy, Ludovic
Abdul-Aziz, Sultan of Turkey, 199
About, Edmond: *quoted* 53; friendship
   with B., 62–4, 68, 74; mentioned, 43,
   75, 254, 305
   Gaëtana, 114
   Grèce contemporaine, La, 62
   King of the Mountains, The, 62
   Tolla, 62
Absubido, Puig, 401
Académie des Beaux-Arts: Fromental
   Halévy secretary of, 32, 239; reports
   on B.'s works, 89–90, 93–4, 107, 112,
   123, 130; mentioned, 39, 47, 67, 68, 95,
   214, 329
Académie Française, 168, 371
Académie Imperiale Française in Rome,
   3, 48, 53–64 *passim*, 97; *see also* Villa
   Medici
Académie Nationale de Musique et de
   Danse, 124, 380; *see also* Opéra
Academy of Music, New York, 428
Adam, Adolphe, 39, 107, 126, 319
Adenis, Jules, 172, 191, 197, 465
Aeneid, see Virgil
Aeschylus, 74, 196
Africaine, L', see Meyerbeer
Aïda, see Verdi
Albano, Gaston d' (pseud. of Mlle de
   Montréal): *David*, 40
Albano, Italy, 69
Alceste, see Gluck
Alexander I, Tsar of Russia, 160
Alexander II, Tsar of Russia, 199
Alizard, Louis, 15
Alkan, Charles-Henri-Valentin, 22, 369
Allgemeine Musikalische Zeitung, 292
Amour africaine, L', see Paladilhe, Emile
Amour-peintre, L', see Molière
Amoureuses, Les, see Daudet, Alphonse
Amours du diable, Les, see Grisar
Ampère, Jean-Jacques, 60n
Andrien, Atala-Thérèse-Annette, 12n
Andrien, Martin-Joseph, 12
Andrien, Mme Martin-Joseph, 13
Anzio, Port of, 85, 86
Archives du Chant, see Delsarte, François
Arenberg, Auguste-Marie-Raymond, Prince
   d', 439
Argentina Theatre, Rome, 73
Ariosto, 196
Arles, 52, 334, 335, 337
Arnaud, Angélique, 9
"*Arregilito, El*," *see* Yradier
Arvers, Félix, 467
Assisi, 100
Assommoir, L', see Zola
Athenée, Théâtre de l', 206–8 *passim*
Auber, Daniel-François-Esprit: Director
   of Conservatoire, 19–20, 22; B. men-
   tions, 90, 95, 286; praises B., 214;
   during Commune, 289; death, 291;
   on Halévy, 291n; letter from Ad-
   olphe Bizet, 459; mentioned, 18, 41, 43,
   78, 108, 126, 136, 141, 144, 149, 197,
   213, 252, 293, 355, 431, 466, 472
   Bal masqué, Le, 319
   Domino noir, Le, 372
   Fra Diavolo, 19, 318, 409, 472
   Muette de Portici, La, 259, 380, 472
   Premier Jour de Bonheur, Le, 214

Aubin, Tony, 441
Augier, Emile, 31, 34, 459
   Philiberte, 459n
Autre Amoureuse, see Daudet, Alphonse
"*Ave Maria*," *see* Gounod
Avignon, 52
"*Ay Chiquita!*" *see* Yradier
Azevedo, Alexis, 205

Bach, Johann Sebastian, 29, 56, 109, 329,
   472
   Well-Tempered Clavier, The, 110, 472
Baden-Baden, 103, 115–20 *passim*, 130,
   131, 139, 316
Badenblatt, 117
Bagier, M., 223
Bal masqué, Le, see Auber
Balanchine, Georges, 471
Balfe, Michael William: *The Bohemian
   Girl*, 172, 358
Ballo in Maschera, Un, see Verdi
Balzac, Honoré de, 35, 133, 168, 394
Bambini, Signor, 8
Banville, Théodore de: at *L'Arlésienne*,
   337, 338; on *Carmen*, 398, 408–9; let-
   ter from B., 408; letter to B., 408n
   Déidemia, 408n
Barbier, Jules: librettist of *La Guzla de
   l'Emir*, 107, 465; eulogist at B.'s fu-
   neral, 422; mentioned, 193, 295n, 467,
   473
   Jeanne d'Arc, 353–4
Barbier de Séville, Le, see Beaumarchais,
   also Rossini
Barbizon, 258, 260
Barbot, M., 83, 84
Barkouf, see Offenbach
Barnolt, M., 390n, *quoted* 391
Barré, M., 215
Bartet, Julia, 337
Barthe, Adrien, 71, 193
Bas Prunay, 272, 272n, 306
Battera, Princess, 119
Battu, Léon, 41, 465
Baudelaire, Pierre-Charles, 113, 113n
   Fleurs du Mal, Les, 113
Baudry, Paul-Jacques-Aimé, 387
Bazin, François-Emmanuel-Joseph, 21n,
   287n, 305, 305n
   Maître Pathelin, 21n
   Voyage en Chine, 21n
Béatrice et Bénédict, see Berlioz
Beauchesne, Mme de, 291n
Beauharnais, Stephanie, Grand Duchess of
   Baden, 119
Beaulieu, Mme de, 262, 307
Beaumarchais, Pierre-Augustin-Caron de,
   74–5, 397–9 *passim*, 402
   Barbier de Séville, Le, 74–5
   Mariage de Figaro, Le, 74, 398
Beethoven, Ludwig von: B. on, 72, 79,
   189–90, 201, 266, 294–5, 314; men-
   tioned, 56, 109, 128, 132, 148, 149,
   333, 469, 472
   Egmont Overture, 127
   Eroica, 79, 268
   Fifth Symphony, 67, 268
   Ninth Symphony, 294
   Ruins of Athens, The, 219, 354
   Seventh Symphony, 425

Beethoven (continued)
    Sixth Symphony ("Pastoral"), 268
    Thirty-two Variations, 110
Belle Hélène, La, see Offenbach
Belleville, 169, 281
Bellini, Vincenzo, 48, 198
    Norma, 135, 189, 241
    Puritani di Scozia, I, 189
    Sonnambula, La, 189
Belval, M., 111
Bénazet, Edouard, 115–20 passim
Benda, Julien, quoted, 247, 248–9
Benoist, François, 22
Benoît, Camille, 389, 391
Benoit-Champy, Adrien, 250
Béranger, Pierre Jean de, 201
Beresford, Mlle, 263, 264
Bériot, Charles de, 218
    "Les Ducats," 218
Berlioz, Hector: controversy with Del-
    sarte 11; B. mentions, 20, 95, 101,
    182–3, 200, 206, 314; on Pauline Vi-
    ardot, 31; and La Nonne sanglante
    libretto, 35–7; on Prix de Rome 45,
    48; on Carafa, 50; on La Reine de
    Saba, 114; on condition of concert
    stage, 126–7; letter to Marmontel,
    131n; on Les Pêcheurs de Perles,
    140–1; on Les Troyens, 142–3; on
    Meyerbeer, 147; on Barkouf, 312n;
    funeral, 423; mentioned, xii, 33, 65,
    84, 93, 108, 115, 129, 132, 136, 139,
    197, 266n, 472
    Béatrice et Bénédict, 116–21 passim,
    472
    Enfance du Christ, L', 36, 146, 349,
    415, 472
    "Marche au Supplice," 148
    Prise de Troie, La, 110
    "Queen Mab Scherzo," 120
    Troyens, Les, 137, 139, 142–5, 183, 472
Bernard, Paul, quoted 128
Bernard, Tristan, 439
Bernhardt, Sarah, 363
Bernstein, Henri, 439
Bertin, Armand and Edouard, 11, 12
Berton, Pierre, quoted 320, 393–4, 410–11
Berton, Gustave, 139
Beulé, Ernest, 149, 329, qouted 214
Bischoffsheim, Louis-Raphael, 207
Bismarck, Otto Edward Leopold, Prince
    von, 178, 192, 199, 205, 279, 375, 429
Bizet, Adolphe Amand (father): birth
    and ancestry, 5, 5n; marriage, 5–6;
    B.'s relationship with, 6, 12, 121–3,
    181, 418; takes B. to Conservatoire,
    15–16, 15n; his pupil Gruyer, 78; life
    at Le Vésinet, 150, 153, 285, 303;
    "saintly," 181; at B.'s funeral, 422;
    life after B.'s death, 438; letter to
    Auber, 459; to Geneviève Bizet, 463;
    see also Bizet, Georges: Letters
    Imogine, 7n
Bizet,   Aimée-Marie-Louise-Léopoldine-
    Josephine Delsarte (mother): birth and
    ancestry, 3–5; marriage, 5–6; teaches B.,
    7, 13; her nature, 51; ill health, 73, 92,
    101–2, 106–7; death, 111, its effect on
    B., 112; letter to husband, 458–9; men-
    tioned, 27, 63, 121, 201, 437n; see also
    Bizet, Georges: Letters
Bizet, Geneviève Halévy (wife): life be-
    fore marriage, 235, 238–49; birth, 238;
    death of father and sister, 244–5; mar-
    riage, 249–50, 460; neurasthenia, 245,
    248, 265, 272–8, 283, 287, 297–8, 328–9,
    440; relationship with mother, 239,

Bizet (continued)
    271–6, 285, 297–8; in Paris during Siege,
    262–3, 270–1; B.'s dream, 267; returns
    to Paris, 296; birth of son, 329–30; at
    L'Arlésienne première, 338; appearance,
    344; strained relations with B., 366,
    366n, 369, 407, 410; B.'s conception of
    good woman, 405–6; during B.'s illness
    and death, 416–19, 423; quoted by Gou-
    nod in eulogy, 423; letter from Galli-
    Marié, 431–2; marriage to Emile Straus,
    438–40; her salon, 439; friendship with
    Marcel Proust, 439–40; death, 440; her
    will, Prix Georges Bizet, 440–1; letters
    from Saint-Saëns, 462–3; from Adolphe
    Bizet, 463; to Hippolyte Rodrigues,
    241; to Valentine Halévy, 265; to
    mother, 266, 296, 307–8; Journal,
    quoted 242–4, 246–7, 265, 278; men-
    tioned, xii–xiii, 206, 221, 229, 300–8
    passim, 311, 328, 347, 369, 413n, 420

BIZET, GEORGES (Alexandre-César-
    Léopold)
LIFE
    Birth and baptism, 3; ancestry, 3–6; rela-
    tionship with father, 6–7, 12, 121–3, 181,
    418; relationship with mother, see Let-
    ters and Bizet, Aimée; first lessons, 7,
    13; and Delsartes, 7, 12–13, 16, 111, 460
    Financial problems: determination to earn
    money, 7, 74; aversion to discussing,
    122, 150, 152, 188, 345; insecurity,
    122–3, 159, 164, 171, 245, 276, 299, 301,
    306, 342, 345, 410; income, 153, 159,
    206, 219, 381; dowry, 249; posthumous
    fortune, 438; see also Halévy, Léonie
    Anti-clericalism, 7, 52–3, 61, 71, 178–9,
    235, 283, 294
    Enters Conservatoire, 14–18, 21–3; impact
    of Revolution of 1848, 16–17; appear-
    ance, 17, 58–9, 138, 170, 303, 345,
    346–7, 411; on his teachers: Zimmer-
    man, 20, Marmontel, 21, Halévy, 24,
    80; wins prizes at Conservatoire, 20, 22,
    40; interest in literature, 24, 151
    On Gounod, 25, 63, 78–9, 82, 83–4, 89, 91,
    95, 291–2, 305, 312; influence of Gou-
    nod, 25, 38–9, 77, 79, 82, 89, 139, 213,
    342, 470; friendship with Gounod, 26,
    39–40, 48, 77–84 passim, 88–9, 91, 103–4,
    291–2, 342–3; arrangements of Gounod's
    works, 34, 37–8, 38, 106, 112, 114, 292,
    468
    Hackwork, 34, 122–3, 146, 153, 159, 164,
    177, 206, 218
    Receives Offenbach prize, 40–3; social life,
    43–4, 57–60, 90, 160, 218; and Rossini,
    44, 46, 48–9; wins Prix de Rome, 46–8;
    journey to Rome, 51–3; personality, 51,
    58, 129, 138, 156, 303, 346–7; relation-
    ship with Schnetz, 54, 56, 59; on life
    at Villa Medici, 57; starts Te Deum 57,
    63, and finishes 68; on politics, 57, 228,
    269, 280–5 passim, 288, 294
    Illness, 60–1, 71, 85–9 passim, 94, 221–2,
    271, 310, 367, 411–15 passim
    Friendship with About, 62–4; fellow Prix
    de Rome: Colin, 64–5, 73, David, 80–1,
    90–1, Guiraud, 96–7, 100; parody on
    Clapisson, 65–7, 215; character, 66, 129,
    303, 420; enters Rodrigues competition,
    68, and loses, 71; on Rome, 69, 96, 97;
    travels in Italy, 69–70, 84–8
    On his own works: 70, 79–80, 84, 162–3;
    Te Deum, 68; Don Procopio, 90; Vasco
    de Gama, 93, 95; Les Pêcheurs de

BIZET, GEORGES (*continued*)
Perles, 145; "*La Bohémienne*," 163; *La Jolie Fille de Perth*, 177, 203, 211; *Roma* Symphony, 222, 232; *La Coupe du Roi de Thulé*, 230–1; *Djamileh*, 303; *Clarissa Harlowe*, 311; *Jeux d'enfants*, 311; *L'Arlésienne*, 339; *Carmen*, 367; on composing, 70, 76–7, 83–4, 153, 183, 189–90, 200–1, 295, 314–15

Starts *Don Procopio*, 70, and receives report, 89–90; on religious music, 71, 94; reaction to competitions, 71, 197–8, 224, 256; on art and artists, 72, 79, 99–101, 179–80, 201, 314; on Verdi, 72, 81–2, 95–6, 190; temperament, 73, 101–2, 121, 134; quarrelsomeness, 73, 102, 120–1, 134, 350, 413–14; authors read, 74–6, 222–3; enjoyment of swimming, 85, 86, 100, 370, 417; on Austro-Sardinian War, 85, 87; considers new projects, 86–7, 93–5

On women, 90, 97–8, 106, 164–5, 404–6; on friendship, 91, 97; love affair with "Zeph," 92, 98; petitions to stay in Italy, 92; starts *Vasco de Gama*, 92–3, and receives report, 107; returns to Paris, 97–103, 105–6; conceives symphony (*Roma*), 101; writes *La Guzla de l'Emir*, 107, 110, 123; on Wagner, 107, 233, 294–5, 312; meets Liszt, 108–9; as pianist, 109–10, 146, 160, 162, 347, 365–6; death of mother, 111–12; *Scherzo* performed, 112, 127

Friendship and correspondence with Reyer, 115–19; as rehearsal director of *Erostrate*, 114, 115, of *Roméo et Juliette*, 342, of *Jeanne d'Arc*, 353–4; birth of Jean Reiter, 121–2; conference about *Noë*, 123; as conductor, 128, 460; friendship with Saint-Saëns, 128–30; writes *Les Pêcheurs de Perles*, 131–8 *passim*; works on *Ivan IV*, 130–1, 142, and takes it to Perrin, 154–5; supposed influence of Wagner, 139, 211, 213, 325, 391, 409, 433; and *Les Troyens*, 143–4; influence of Meyerbeer, 148

Moves to Le Vésinet, 150; Galabert visits, 150–1, 153; as teacher of Galabert, 151–3, 187, of children, 152, of Lacombe, 187–90, of American pupil, 345–7; lack of self-confidence, 151, 162, 396, 407; meets Roqueplan, 154; sense of persecution, 158, 162, 190–1, 299, 315; plays at Princesse Mathilde's, 160–1; friendship with Céleste Mogador, 165, 169–71, 180–2, 405; on love, 165, 227, 231; love affair, 169–70, 181, 181*n*

Negotiates with Carvalho on *La Jolie Fille de Perth*, 171–2, starts, 174, on plot and characters, 174–7, finishes, 184, difficulties, 196–7, rehearsals, 210, *première*, 211; philosophy, 178–80, 222–3, 299; leaves Le Vésinet, 183; on Carvalho, 185–6, 387; on Exposition, 192; mentioned in guidebook, 192; enters Exposition contest, 194–6, and is defeated, 197–8; as critic, 200–2, 205

Plans marriage, 201, 206; on Saint-Saëns, 206, 300; *Malbrough s'en va-t-en guerre* episode, 206–9; visits Belgium, 216; friendship with Trélats, 216–18; resumes work on *Roma*, 221, performed, 231–3; finishes *Grande Variations Chromatiques*, 222; his "change of skin," 222, recalled, 335; offer from Théâtre-

BIZET, GEORGES (*continued*)
Italien, 223; offer of Leroy-Sauvage libretto, 223–4, 230

Enters *La Coupe du Roi de Thulé* competition, 224–31, is defeated, 256–7; offered *Les Templiers*, 229–30; approached by du Locle, 234; "delighted to try to change the genre of the Opéra-Comique," 234, 397, 421; on Ludovic Halévy's marriage, 248, 273

Wedding, 249–50; honeymoon, 251; friendship with Rodrigues, 251; commissioned to finish *Noë*, 252–3; moves to 22 rue de Douai, 253; projects for possible works, 254–6; spends summer at Barbizon, 258; on Franco-Prussian War, 260–1; in National Guard, 261, 265–7

And Mme Halévy, 262, 271–6, 285; rejects her help in getting positions, 286–7, 299–302; affection for her, 295, 297–8; handles her finances and household affairs, 297, 306–10, 314–15; *see also* Halévy, Léonie

His Utopian dream, 266–7; "*Morts pour la France*," 267; refuses to leave Paris, 270; anxiety about wife's health, 272–8 *passim*, 284–8 *passim*, 297, 328–30, 387; goes to Bordeaux, 272; on Paris during occupation, 277; on National Guard, 280–2; at Compiègne, 283; on future of music, 285–6; on Conservatoire, 286, 291; on theatres, 287; and Sardou, 287–8; works on *Clarissa Harlowe*, 288, and finishes one act, 311; on Paris during Commune, 291; returns to Paris, 295; applies for Opéra position, 315–17; and is rejected, 315–17; *Djamileh* commissioned, 301–3, casting and rehearsals, 319, 322–3, *première*, 324–5; on Prix de Rome jury, 304–5

Reworks *Roma* and writes *Jeux d'enfants*, 311; on Offenbach, 311–12; on *La Dame blanche*, 313; and Galli-Marié, 322, 358–62, 367–9, 406; *Carmen* commissioned, 329; nominated to Conservatoire jury, 329; birth of son, 329–30; composes *L'Arlésienne*, 331, *première*, 337–8; friendship with Daudet, 333, 336; reaction to criticism, 339, 396, 404, 406, 408, 413, 413*n*; starts *Carmen*, 342; *Petite Suite* withdrawn from Pasdeloup, 347, played by Colonne, 348; on Massenet, 349–50; asks Gallet for libretto (*Geneviève de Paris*), 350; works on *Don Rodrigue*, 351–3; *Patrie* overture commissioned, composed, 354, and played, 365; melancholy, 365, 410–11

Strained relations with wife, 366, 366*n*, 369, 407, 410; goes to Bougival, 367; friendship with Delaborde, 369–70; at rehearsals of *Carmen*, 371–2, 379, 382–3; *Carmen* contract, 381; changes libretto, 383–6; receives Legion of Honor, 386–7; plans *Geneviève de Paris*, 388; attends César Franck's organ class, 388; at *Carmen* première, 390–2; tries to improve production of *Carmen*, 392–3; new opera commissioned by du Locle, 410; final correspondence with Gounod, 412–13; argument with Comettant, 413–14

Final illness, 415–18; premonition of death, 415–16; expresses appreciation to du Locle, 417; moves to Bougival, 417; death, 418–19; cause of death, 419–20; suicide rumor, 420; funeral, 422–4;

BIZET, GEORGES (*continued*)

Gounod's eulogy, 423; obituary notices, 424; memorial concert, 424–5; posthumous fame, 435–7; posthumous presentations of works, 470–1; music library, 472–4

LETTERS

To Marmontel, 21; to mother, 20–1, 49–50, 52–65 *passim*, 68–74 *passim*, 78, 80–97 *passim*, 100–2, 105–7, 164–5; to Gounod, 39, 70–1, 342–3; to Emile Paladilhe, 56; to father, 60, 84, 88, 102; to Clapisson (draft), 66; to Diaz, 76–7; to Gruyer, 78–80, 88–9; to L'Epine, 106, 195–6, 197; to Ludovic Halévy, 107, 273, 329; to Choudens, 122–3, 134, 156–7, 158, 162, 182–3, 186–7, 220, 254, 460

To Galabert, 150–2, 154, 156, 174, 175–80, 183–7, 190, 192–3, 197–8, 203, 211, 215, 219, 221–8 *passim*, 230–5 *passim*, 249, 253, 257–8, 261, 276–7, 292, 298–9, 311–12, 325, 397; to Heugel, 163; to Adenis, 191; to Perrin, 155; to Belgian admirer, 160, 191; to Lacombe, 187–90, 208, 252, 253, 255, 277, 311*n*, 312, 318, 329, 330, 354

To Saint-Saëns, 198, 206; to Weber, 213–14, 339; to Mme Trélat, 216–22 *passim*, 230, 248, 253; to Léon Halévy, 229; to unidentified woman, 231; to Rodrigues, 251, 258, 262, 271–3, 275–6, 277, 280–5 *passim*, 296–300 *passim*, 302, 306, 331–2, 387; to directors of choral society, 254; to Délérot, 254–5, 255*n*; to unidentified editor, 255, 255*n*, 460; to Manuel, 255; to Guiraud, 256, 260–1, 266–7, 269, 284–5, 311, 413; to Opéra jury, 256

To wife, 265, 366; to Mme Halévy, 270–1, 275–81 *passim*, 285–8, 291, 293, 299–300, 303–15 *passim*; 328–9, 344, 367, 405; to du Locle, 302, 310, 383, 417; to Thomas, 305, 381; to Gallet, 324–5, 353; to Dr. Devillières, 330; to Carvalho, 331; to Massenet, 349–50; to Mme Carvalho, 387; to *chef des choeurs* of *Carmen*, 392; to Dumas *fils*, 406; to Banville, 408; to unidentified critic, 413*n*; to François Delsarte, 460; to Mme Delsarte, 460; to Delaunay, 462

Lettres, Impressions de Rome (*1857–1860*), *La Commune* (*1871*), 51, 52*n*, 68*n*, 92*n*, 105*n*, 106*n*

Lettres à un ami, intro. by Edmond Galabert, 153*n*, 174*n*, 186*n*, 203*n*, 219*n*, 228*n*, 421*n*

WORKS

(For works not mentioned in the text and chief transcriptions of works of other composers, see Appendix II, 465–8)

DRAMATIC

Arlésienne, L': commissioned, 331; use of background music, 332; plot, 334–5; presages *Carmen*, 336; musical sources, 336; Daudet on rehearsals, 337; *première*, 337–8; reviews, 338–40; mentioned, 35, 38, 224, 225, 255, 342, 396, 422, 426, 434, 436, 437*n*, 465, 471

Carmen: recitatives, 96, 378, 378*n*, 426; dedicated to Pasdeloup, 127, 389, 389*n*; commissioned, 329; work on, 341–7 *passim*, 351, 367–9; libretto, 351, 383, 398; collaboration, 352, 372–3, 377, 383; casting, 355–62, 364–5, 390*n*, 392;

BIZET, GEORGES (*continued*)

rehearsals, 371–2, 379–83 *passim*, 395; costumes, 379; contract with Choudens, 381; B.'s versions of libretto, 384–5; *première*, 387–92; failure, 391, 395, 414; second performance, 393–4, 410; reviews, 394–404, 408–9; B.'s reaction to critics, 396, 404, 406–8, 410–11, 413–14; Spanish sources, 401–2, 474; performance night of B.'s death, 420–1, night of funeral, 424; themes played at funeral, 422; posthumous success, 426–38; ballet, 426, 462; Hanslick on, 426; Brahms on, 426; Wagner on, 426; Liszt on, 427; Tchaikovsky on, 427*n*; von Bülow on, 429; Bismarck on, 429–30; Nietzsche on, 430; number of performances, 436*n*; mentioned, 31, 35, 39, 107, 108, 129, 148, 170, 171, 175, 204, 224, 225, 255, 320, 322, 332, 353, 412, 416, 425, 440, 465

Clarissa Harlowe, 255, 258, 276–7, 284, 288, 311, 465

Coupe du Roi de Thulé, La, 224–8, 230–1, 256–8, 335, 352, 465, 467

Djamileh (*Namouna*): commissioned, 301–2; casting, 302, 322–3; Gallet librettist, 303–4; postponed, 311–12; rehearsals, 318–20, 323; libretto, 321–2; *première*, 324–5; reviews, 325–8, recalled, 336; revival, 436, 471; mentioned, 306, 308, 329, 349, 351, 362, 379, 396, 402, 413*n*, 434, 465

Docteur Miracle, Le, 41–3, 62*n*, 465

Don Procopio, 70, 82, 84, 89–90, 94, 465, 470

Don Rodrigue, 352–3, 354, 465

Grisélidis, 255, 258, 276, 284*n*, 287, 302, 311, 312, 465

Guzla de l'Emir, La, 107, 110, 123, 465

Ivan IV, 130–1, 145, 146, 148, 153–6 *passim*, 162, 172, 186, 253, 311*n*, 465, 468, 470–1

Jolie Fille de Perth, La: commissioned, 171–2; libretto, 173–7; work on, 182, 183; finished, 184; casting, 185, 190, 196–7; rehearsals, 203, 206; postponed, 204–5; *première*, 211; reviews, 211–14; "concessions to public taste," 213; "false gods," 213–14; failure, 214–15; mentioned, 186, 208, 209, 219, 233, 292, 327, 328, 332, 336, 396, 460, 465, 470, 471

Leïla, see *Pêcheurs de Perles, Les*

Malbrough s'en va-t-en guerre, 206, 207–10, 278, 465

Noël, 123, 252–3, 254, 465, 471

Pearl-Fishers, The, see *Pêcheurs de Perles, Les*

Pêcheurs de Perles, Les: commissioned, 131; Gounod's letter on, 131–2; B.'s irritation with Choudens over delay, 133–5; rehearsals, 135; libretto, 135; *première*, 137–8; reviews, 138–41; financial failure, 142, 145; mentioned, 121, 131*n*, 146, 148, 153, 172, 183, 187, 201, 204, 212, 213, 215, 233, 327, 336, 396, 422, 425, 436, 465, 470

KEYBOARD

Chants du Rhin, 163, 218, 466; "La Bohémienne" from; 163; "Les Rêves" from, 163

Chasse d'Ossian, La, 112, 466

Chasse Fantastique, 163, 466

Grandes Variations chromatiques, 222, 466

BIZET, GEORGES (*continued*)
Jeux d'enfants, 152, 311, 311*n*, 347, 466, 470
Nocturne in D major, 222, 466
Pianiste Chanteur, Le, 153, 159, 469
Trois Esquisses musicales, 162, 466

MISCELLANEOUS VOCAL
Clovis et Clotilde, 46–7, 415, 468
Geneviève de Paris (planned), 350, 388, 415, 468
Saint Jean de Pathmos, 164, 468
Te Deum, 57, 63, 68, 69, 71, 468
Vasco de Gama, 93, 95, 107, 130, 253, 468, 470

ORCHESTRAL
Arlésienne Suite, *L'*, 332, 340, 365, 466
"*Danse bohémienne*" (from *La Jolie Fille de Perth*), 175, 426
Marche funèbre, 112, 465
Mort s'avance, La, 254, 254*n*, 468
Patrie, 344, 354–5, 365, 422, 466
Petite Suite, 311, 311*n*, 347–8, 466
Scherzo (from *Roma*), 112, 127–8, 130, 201, 232, 465
Symphony in C major, 38–9, 465, 471
Symphony in C major (*Roma*), 38, 101, 221, 232–3, 299, 311, 465, 471

SONGS
A une Fleur, 177, 467
Adieux à Suzon, 266, 467
Adieux de l'hôtesse arabe, 177*n*, 466
Berceuse, 219, 467
Chanson du fou, La, 219, 467
Coccinelle, La, 219, 467
Grillon, Le, 177, 467
Guitare, 177, 467

Bizet, Georges, Prize, 441
Bizet, Guillaume-Michel-Jérôme, 5
Bizet, Jacques (son): birth, 329–30; illness, 344; B.'s relationship with, 344; at B.'s death, 418; later life, 438, 440, 463; letter from Romain Rolland, 463; mentioned, 331, 336, 366, 417
Bizet, Louis-Guillaume, 5
Blanche, Dr. Antoine-Emile, 48, 141, 159, 278, 344, 412
Blanche, Jacques-Emile, *quoted* 344, 390–1
Blangini, Felice, 218
Blanqui, Louis-Auguste, 268
Blau, Edouard, 224, 353*n*, 465, 468
Blaze de Bury, Ange-Henri, 367, *quoted* 416
Bleuets, Les, see Cohen, Jules
Bloch, M., 462
Boccaccio, Giovanni, 284
Boccherini, Luigi, 11
Bohemian Girl, The, see Balfe
Boieldieu, François-Adrien, 126
Dame blanche, La, 172, 212, 234, 313, 321, 409, 421, 421*n*, 437
Boitteaux, Henry, 465
Bologna, 101
Bologna, Giovanni da, 101
Bonaparte, Hortense, Queen of Holland, 14
Bonaparte, Jérôme, King of Westphalia, 160
Bonaparte, Prince Jérôme (Plon-Plon), 168
Bonaparte, Princesse Mathilde, 62, 160–2, 168, 190, 191, 205, 217, 238, 439
Bonaparte, Napoleon I, 54, 124, 160, 318, 255, 259*n*, 260*n*

Bonaparte, Napoleon III, 10, 14, 34, 56, 87, 108, 124, 160, 178, 228, 258, 259*n*, 260, 261, 262*n*, 283, 288, 376–7
Bonnet, Paul, 64
Bordeaux: Mme Halévy joins brother in, 263; government in, 269; B. and wife visit her mother, 272–3
Boton, Mme, 463
Bouffar, Zulma, 355, 389
Bouffes-Parisiens, 40, 169, 312, 373, 390
Bougival, 48, 367, 415, 416, 417, 419
Bouguereau, Adolphe William, 63
Bouhy, Joseph, 359, 365, 390*n*, 392, 422
Bouilhet, Louis, 466–7
Boulanger, Ernest: *Don Mucarade*, 414
Boule, La, see Halévy, Ludovic
Bourey, Comte de, 159
Bourgeois Gentilhomme, Le, see Molière
Bourget, Paul, 439, 439*n*
Bousquet, Francis, 441
Bousquet, Georges, *quoted* 27–8
Brahms, Johannes, 426, 430, 472
Brandies, Louis, 149
Bremond, Dr., 330
Brididi, M., 167
Brigands, Les, see Offenbach
Brun, M., 307
Brun, Louise, 366
Brussels, 118, 216, 427, 428
Buckingham, Duke of, 332
Bülow, Hans von, 108, 429, 471, 474
Burion, Amédée, 46, 468
Busnach, William, 206–7, 209, 278, 465
Busser, Henri, 470
Bussine, Romain, 348*n*
Byron, George Gordon, Lord, 358

Cabaret, Le, 122
Caïd, Le, see Thomas
Calendal, see Mistral
Calvé, Emma, 434*n*
Cambaggio, Carlo, 465
Cambrai, 3
Camões, Luiz Vaz de: *The Lusiade*, 93
Campanini, Italo, 428
Cancionero Musical Popular Español, see Pedrell
Cape Circe, 86
Capus, Alfred, 439
Carafa di Colobrano, Michele Enrico Francesco Vincente Paola, 49–50, 95, 403
Thérèse, 50
Cardillac, see Daustrême
Carmen (book), *see* Malherbe, Henry
Carmen, see Bizet, Georges: *Carmen*
Carmen Saeculare, see Horace
Carpaccio, Vittore, 362
Carré, Michel, 107, 132, 135, 193, 465, 473
Caruso, Enrico, 471
Carvalho, Caroline Miolan- (Mme Léon), 136, 137, 146, 193, 196, 215, 220, 278, 318, 358, 387
Carvalho, Léon: commissions *Les Pêcheurs de Perles*, 131; identified and described, 135–7; commissions *Ivan IV*, 142, 154; produces *La Jolie Fille de Perth*, 171–2, 184–6, 196–7, 204, 211, 215; financial problems, 185–6, 191, 210, 220; Roqueplan on, 192–3; produces *L'Arlésienne*, 331, 332, 337, 339; letter from B., 331; refuses to revive *Carmen*, 429, 431; revives *Carmen*, 432–4; mentioned, 82, 142–4 *passim*, 193, 209, 267, 319, 425, 461
Case of Wagner, The, see Nietzsche

Castro y Bellvís, Guillén de: *La Jeunesse du Cid,* 352
Catherine, *see* Bizet, Georges: *La Jolie Fille de Perth*
Catherine II, Empress of Russia, 76
Cazaux, M., 117
Cercle de l'Union Artistique (Cercle des Mirotons), 112
Cervantes Saavedra, Miguel de, 201, 314
    Don Quixote, 89
Cerveteri, 98
Chabrier, Alexis Emmanuel, 187, *quoted* 306
Chabrillan, Comtesse Lionel de, *see* Mogador, Céleste
Chabrillan, Lionel, Comte de Moreton de, 168
Chambure, Comtesse de, 472
Champrosay, 336, 340
Chantavoine, Jean, 470
Chapuy, Mlle, 390*n,* 392, 422, 426
Charcot, Jean-Martin, 334
Charles VI, see Halévy, Fromental
Charles X, 168
Charpentier, Gervais, 205
Charton, Mlle, 119
Chateaubriand, François-René, Vicomte de: *Itinéraire de Paris à Jerusalem,* 75
Châtelet, Théâtre du, 215, 220
Châtiments, Les, see Hugo
Chaudey, Gustave, 294, 294*n,* 354
Chéri, Rose, 144
Chéri, Victor, 143–4
    "Turlurette," 144
Cherubini, Maria Luigi Carlo Zenobus Salvatore, 12, 18, 19, 50, 71, 125, 472
Chevalier, Mlle, 390*n,* 403
Chimay, Princess de Caraman-, 9
Chiusi, 99
Chopin, Frédéric-François, 14, 32, 56, 163, 167, 187, 188, 190, 219, 254, 254*n,* 256, 333, 469, 472
    Funeral March, 110, 416, 422
    Second Scherzo, 346
Choudens, Antoine de: publishes B.'s works, 37, 106, 159, *La Jolie Fille de Perth,* 206, *Roma,* 234, *Carmen,* 381, 381*n,* 414–15; B. negotiates with, 122–3; relations with Gounod, 133–4, 412–13, 413*n;* B. argues with, 134–5, 156–7, 158; B. reproaches, 162–3; B. apologizes to, 182–3; refuses B.'s patriotic song, 267; mentioned, 117, 118, 172, 177, 191, 197, 323, 327, 365, 389, 431, 462, 465–70 *passim; see also* Bizet, Georges: Letters
Choudens, Antony de, 134, 339, 420
Choudens, Paul de, 134
Christophe Colomb, see David, Félicien
Cid, Le, see Corneille, *also* Massenet
Cilea, Francesco, 471
Cinq-Mars, see Gounod
Cipriani, Comtesse de, *see* Galli-Marié
Cirque d'hiver (Cirque Napoléon), 127, 232
Citta della Pieve, 99
Civita Vecchia, 98
Clairin, Georges-Jules-Victor, 204, 379
Clairon, Le, 431
Clapisson, Antoine-Louis, 65–7, 90, 95, 136, 141, 172, 215, 319
    Fanchonette, La, 65–7, 136, 215
    Gibby la cornemuse, 65, 66
    Promise, La, 66
Clinique chirurgicale, La, see Trélat, Ulysse
Cohen, Hermann ("Puzzi"), 167

Cohen, Jules, 197, 286, 287*n,* 474
    Bleuets, Les, 186, 210
Colin, Charles, 48, 52, 64–5, 73, 80, 85, 96
Colombe, La, see Gounod
Colonne, Association Artistiques des Concerts, 348, 393
Colonne, Edouard, 348, 365, 412, 424, 471
Comédie-Française, 34, 55, 74, 300, 383, 394, 400
Comettant, Jean-Pierre-Oscar, 396, 406, 413–14; *quoted* 402–5, 433, 434–5
Compiègne, 283
Comte Ory, Le, see Rossini
Concert National, 348
Concerts Populaires, 127, 268, 299, 348, 422
Congreve, William, 403
Conservatoire: B. at, 15–18, 43, 388; criticism of, 18; curriculum, 18–19; under Auber, 19–20; Fromental Halévy at, 23–5; B. on, 286, 291, 304; B. nominated to jury, 329
Constantin, M., 338, 339
Contes d'Hoffmann, Les, see Offenbach
Cooper, James Fenimore, 249
Coppée, François, 322, 363
Coppélia, see Delibes
Coquelin, Benôit Constant, 9
Cormon, Eugène (pseud. of Pierre-Etienne Piestre), 135, 260, 465
Corneille, Pierre, 397
    Cid, Le, 314, 352
Cornu, Catherine Geneviève, 5
Cornut, Romain, *fils: The Marriage of Prometheus,* 194
Corot, Jean-Baptiste, 62, 145
Così fan tutte, see Mozart
Côté de Guermantes, see Proust
Country Wife, The (William Wycherley), 253
Couperin, François, 219
Courbevoie, 283, 284
Courmont, Louis de, 467
Cousin, Victor, 223
Couture, Thomas, 168
Covent Garden, 378*n,* 428
Creation, The, see Haydn
Crémieux, Hector, 354
Crépet, Eugène, 205
    Rama, 255
Cressonnois, Jules-Alfred, 408*n*
Criado fingido, El, see García, Manuel
Croharé, Professor, 21
Croquet, M., 210
Czerny, Karl, 472, 473

Daily Telegraph, 192
Dalicot, M. and Mme, 31
Damase, Jean-Michel, 441
Dame blanche, La, see Boieldieu
Dancaïre, Le, *see* Bizet, Georges: *Carmen*
Daniel, Salvador, 293
Dante, Alighieri, 100, 101, 180, 189, 201, 314
Da Ponte, Lorenzo, *quoted* 398–9
Darboy, Georges, Archbishop of Paris, 294, 294*n*
Daudet, Alphonse: love of music, 331; identified, 332; described by Zola, 333, by Banville, 334, by Freud, 334; mentioned, 106*n,* 389
    Amoureuses, Les, 333
    Arlésienne, L', 331–40, 461–2, 465, 471
    "Autre Amoureuse," 335
    Petit Chose, Le, 335
    Sapho, 338
Daudet, Mme Alphonse, *quoted* 337–8

Daudet, Ernest, 333, 389
Daudet, Lucien, 338n
Daustrême, Lucien: *Cardillac*, 186, 210
David, see Albano, Gaston d'
David, Félicien, 139, 197
   Christophe Colomb, 130
   Desert, Le, 93
   Symphony in E Flat, 130
David, Jacques Louis, 55
David, Samuel, 80–2, 85, 90–1, 96, 141, 249
   Genies de la terre, Les, 80, 91
David d'Angers, Pierre Jean, 48
David Rizzio, see Rodrigues, Hippolyte
Dean, Winton, xiii, 224n, 471
De Profundis, see Gounod
Deborah, see Devin-Duvivier
Debussy, Achille-Claude, 96, 359
   "Jardins sous la pluie," 219
   Pelléas et Mélisande, 359
Degas, Hilaire-Germain-Edgard, 254, 439, 439n
Déidemia, see Banville
Delaborde, Elie-Miriam: identified and described, 369–70; mentioned, 222, 367, 418, 422
Delacroix, Eugène, 12, 34, 55, 63, 238–9, 336–7, 459
   Journal, 3, 12, 239
Delapalme, Maître, 306, 308
Delâtre, Louis, 92–3, 468
Delaunay, Elie, 363, 363n, 462
Delavigne, Casimir, 467
Deldevez, Edouard, 381
Délérot, Emile, 255n
Delibes, Léo, 43–4, 208–9, 218, 219, 278, 301, 380, 389, 395, 472
   Coppélia, 44, 290
   Lakmé, 432
   Source, La, 219, 290, 380
Delle Sedie, Enrico, 218
Deloffre, M., 324, 378n
Delsarte, Adrien, 13
Delsarte, Aimée-Albertine Roland, 4–5
Delsarte, Camille, 4, 4n, 457–8
Delsarte, François-Alexandre-Nicolas-Chéri: childhood, 8–9; as teacher and performer, 9–12, 289; treatment of pianos, 13–14; assists B., 14, 16; military service, 17; death, 298, 460; memorial plaque, 437n; letters from Camille Delsarte, 457–8; from B. 460; mentioned, 3, 4n, 5, 7, 29, 83; *see also* Bizet, Georges: and Delsartes
Delsarte, Gustave, 13, 164–5
Delsarte, Henri, 13
Delsarte, Jean Nicolas Toussaint, 4, 4n, 5
Delsarte, Dr. Nicolas, 4
Delsarte, Rosine-Charlotte Andrien, 12–13, 350, 458, 460
Del Sarto, Andrea, 4
Demidov, Count Anatole, 160
Dennery, Adolphe-Philippe, 353n
Desbordes-Valmore, Marcelline, 219, 467
Désert, Le, see David, Félicien
Detaille, Jean-Baptiste-Edouard, 379
Devillières, Dr., 329–30
Devin-Duvivier, M.: *Deborah*, 185–6
Devriès, Jane, 197, 219
Diaz, Emile, 76
Diaz, Eugène, 257
   Coupe du Roi de Thulé, La, 351
Didier, Jules, 85, 87
Dinorah, see Meyerbeer
Diogène, 203
Djamileh, see Bizet, Georges: *Djamileh*
Dogs, 87, 153, 182

Doigts de fée, Les, 241
Dolly, see Fauré
Domino noir, Le, see Auber
Don Carlos, see Verdi
Don César de Bazin, see Massenet
Don Giovanni, see Mozart
Don Juan, see Mozart: *Don Giovanni*
Don Mucarade, see Boulanger
Don Pasquale, see Donizetti
Don Quixote, see Cervantes Saavedra
Donizetti, Gaetano, 48, 472
   Don Pasquale, 70, 167, 189, 218
   Favorite, La, 167, 290, 364, 472
   Fille du Régiment, La, 172, 303
   Lucia di Lammermoor, 167, 172, 457
   Parisina, 70, 86
Doré, Gustave, 254
Douai, 22 rue de, 253–4, 256, 367, 392n, 438
Doublemard, Amedée-Donatien, 73
Doucet, Camille, 145, 145n, 155, 210, 422
Dragons de Vilars, Les, see Maillart
Dreyfus Affair, 439
Dubois, Paul 87, 162, 434, 437n
Ducasse, Mlle, 390n, 403
"Ducats, Les," *see* Bériot
Duchesne, M., 323, 422
Ducrot, General Auguste Alexandre, 267
Dufaure, Armand Jules Stanislas, 282
Dufour, Dr., 344, 416
Dufresnoy, Mme, 301
Dufriche, M., 390n
Dukas, Paul, 96
Du Locle, Camille: produces *Djamileh*, 301–3, 310, 318; produces *Aïda*, 302, 320; described, 319–23 *passim*; commissions *Carmen*, 329, 351; financial difficulties, 351, 379, 414; negotiates with Galli-Marié, 356, 357, 360–1, 364; produces *Carmen*, 379, 382–3, 389–97 *passim*, 409, 417; eulogist at B.'s funeral, 422–3; revives *Carmen*, 427; mentioned, 136, 234, 255, 304, 377, 381, 411, 419, 420, 421, 425, 429
Dumarsais, Abbé, 28
Dumas, Alexandre, 161, 168, 169, 192, 319
   Tulipe noire, La, 278
Dumas, Alexandre, *fils*, 137, 161, 168, 192, 252n, 318, 319, 376, 389, 405–6, 422
Dumas, *fils*, Mme Alexandre, 405
Du Miral, M., 302
Duparc, Henri, 187
Duprato, Jules-Laurent, 302, 305, 306
Dutilleux, Henri, 441
Durand, Marie-Auguste, 311, 466, 469
Duvernoy, M., 390n

E Flat Symphony, *see* Mozart
Echos d'Espagne, 401, 472
Eclair, L', see Halévy, Fromental
Education sentimentale, L', see Flaubert
Edward, Prince of Wales, 199
Egmont Overture, *see* Beethoven
Eichthal, Eugène d', 109
1812, see Tchaikovsky
Elwart, Antoine-Aimable-Elie, 305, 305n, 306, 403, 423
Enfance du Christ, L', see Berlioz
Epreuve Villageoise, L', see Grétry
Erard, Pierre, 22, 222, 344
Eroica, see Beethoven
Erostrate, see Reyer
Escamillo, see Bizet, Georges: *Carmen*
Esclave, L', see Membrée
Esmeralda, see Hugo
Etoile du Nord, L', see Meyerbeer

Etretat, 263, 373
Etude de Chasse, see Heller
Eugénie, Empress of France, 160, 199, 279n, 283, 376-7
Eve, see Massenet
Exposition of 1867, 191-2, 199, 202, 204; competition, 194-8, 224

Fair Maid of Perth, The, see Scott
Falguière, Jean-Alexandre-Joseph, 437n
Famille Cardinal, La, see Halévy, Ludovic
Fanchonette, La, see Clapisson
Fantaisies Parisiennes, 202
Fantasio, see Offenbach
Fauré, Gabriel-Urbain, 348n, 472
  Dolly, 219
Faure, Jean-Baptiste, 9, 351-3 *passim,* 389
Faust, see Gounod
Faust Symphony, *see* Liszt
Favorite, La, see Donizetti
Favre, Jules, 262
Fée aux Roses, La, see Halévy, Fromental
Fernando Cortez, see Spontini
Ferrara, 101
Ferrier, Paul, 255, 460, 467
Ferrière, M., 17
Fifth Symphony, *see* Beethoven
Figaro, Le, 220; quoted 40, 121, 139, 212, 316, 337, 389, 423, 434, 436
Fille de Madame Angot, La, see Lecocq
Fille du Régiment, La, see Donizetti
First Symphony in D, *see* Gounod
Flandrin, Hippolyte, 52
Flaubert, Gustave, 115, 136, 161, 168, 332, 408; quoted 62, 113, 205, 318
  Education sentimentale, L', 161
  Madame Bovary, 113, 408
  Salammbô, 115
Flers, Robert-Pellevé de la Motte-Ango, Marquis de, 439
Fleurs du Mal, Les, see Baudelaire
Fleury, Emile-Félix, 228, 228n
Florence, Italy, 53, 118
Florimo, Francesco, 48
Flotow, Friedrich, Baron von:
  Martha, 172, 204, 399
  Rob Roy, 172
Flying Dutchman, The, see Wagner
Folie lucide, La, see Trélat, Achille
Fontaine Saint-Georges, 32 rue, 141
Forain, Jean-Louis, 439, 439n
Fourth Piano Concerto, *see* Saint-Saëns
Fra Diavolo, see Auber
France: war with Prussia, 258-64; defeat at Sedan, 261; proclamation of republic, 262; radical uprising, 265; government at Bordeaux, 269-70; Versailles government, 279, 279n, 280-4, 293; civil war, 283-5, 293-4
France musicale, La, quoted 36
Franck, Adolphe, 250
Franck, César, 16n, 129, 348n, 388, 392, 472
  Redemption, 348, 472
Franz Joseph, Emperor of Austria, 199
Frascati, 69
Frasquita, see Bizet, Georges: *Carmen*
Freischütz, Der, see Weber, Karl Maria von
Freud, Sigmund, *quoted* 334
Froufrou, see Halévy, Ludovic
Fughette, see Paladilhe, Emile
Funeral March, see Chopin; *also* Schumann

Gaëtana, see About
Gaîté, Théâtre de la, 312, 318, 353, 470

Galabert, Edmond: on B., 109-10, 164, 194-5; identified and described, 150-2; visits Le Vésinet, 153; on B.'s marriage, 366; mentioned, 112, 162, 187, 224, 228, 251, 252, 303, 352, 421n; *see also* Bizet, Georges: Letters
Imogine, 151
Gallet, Louis: librettist of *La Coupe du Roi de Thulé,* 224, 465, of *Djamileh,* 302, 322, 325, 465, of *Geneviève de Paris,* 350, 388, 415, 468, of *Don Rodrigue,* 351-3, 465; on B., 303-4, 319, 353, 415; described by Saint-Saëns, 321; on rehearsals and *première* of *Djamileh,* 323-4; author of poem for Memorial Concert, 425, 463-4; mentioned, 313n, 349, 353n
Galli, M., 358
Galli-Marié, Marie-Célestine-Laurence: negotiations on *Carmen,* 356, 357, 359-62, 364-5; description and biographical sketch, 357-8; relations with B., 358-9, 367-9, 406; and Paladilhe, 362-3; at *Carmen* rehearsals, 371-2, 383; as Carmen, 390n, 392, 393, 401, 403, 404, 409, 414, 428, 429; reaction to B.'s death, 420-1, 424; at Memorial Concert, 425, 463; attempts to continue and revive *Carmen,* 427, 430-2; Mlle Isaac compared to, 432-3; in revival of *Carmen,* 434-5; with Calvé, 434n; letters to B., 359-62, 367-9, to Delaunay, 363, to du Locle, 364-5, 427, to Geneviève Bizet, 430-2; mentioned, 313n, 322, 379
Gallia, see Gounod
Galliffet, Gaston-Alexandre-Auguste, Marquis de, 439
Galsworthy, John, 435n
Galsworthy, Mrs. John, *quoted* 435n
Galuppi, Baldassare, 12
Gambetta, Léon, 262, 262n, 269-70, 279, 375
Garcia, Eugénie, 162
García, Manuel:
  Criado fingido, El, 401
  Poëta Calculista, El, 401
Garcia, Manuel, the younger, 162
Garden, Mary, 358, 359
Garibaldi, Giuseppe, 87, 100
Garnier, Charles, 380
Gaston de Betsi *or* Betzi, *see* Bizet, Georges: as critic
Gaudibert, Mme, 218
Gaulois, Le, 258, 260, 272
Gaumont, Charles, 5
Gautier, Théophile, 161, 192, 197, 200, 263, 428, 467, 468; *quoted* 34, 35, 148, 211-12
Gay, Abbé, 28
Gazette de Hollande, quoted, 204, 210
Gelma, Eugène, 419
Genan, M. and Mme, 458, 459
Génies de la terre, Les, see David, Samuel
Genoa, 53
Gensano, 69
George III, King of England, 160
George Sand (pseud. of Aurore Dupin, Baroness Dudevant), 165, 167, 168, 318, 357, 421, *quoted* 217
  Petite Fadette, La, 421
Georges Bizet, rue, 437n
Géricault, Jean-Louis-André-Théodore, 55
German music during Siege, 269
Germany, 92; Gounod on, 103-4
Gevaert, François-Augustus, 63, 252
Giacomotti, Félix-Henri, 58

Gibby la cornemuse, see Clapisson
Gille, Philippe, 255, 465, 467
Giorgione, Il, Giorgio Barbarelli, called, 266
Giotto di Bondone, 100, 101
Girard, Mlle, 130
Girardin, Emil, 217
Glass, Alexandre, 467
Globe, The, 60*n*
Glover, *see* Bizet, Georges: *La Jolie Fille de Perth*
Gluck, Christoph Willibald, 8–9, 10, 125, 148, 333, 472
  Alceste, 268, 472
  Iphigénie, 11, 472
  Orphée, 11, 425, 472
Godard, Alfred, 159
Godard, Benjamin, 392, 472
Goethe, Johann Wolfgang von, 60*n*, 151, 267, 369, 409
Goldoni, Carlo, 98
Goncourt, Jules and Edmond, 35, 63
Gossec, François-Joseph: *Hymne à la Raison,* 290
Got, Edmond, *quoted* 30
Gottschalk, Louis Moreau, 472
Gouin, M. and Mme, 275
Gounod, Anna Zimmerman (Mme Charles), 26, 83, 141, 293
Gounod, Charles: B. on, 25, 38–9, 63, 78–9, 82, 83–4, 89, 91, 95, 291, 291*n*, 292, 305, 312; influence on B., 25, 38–9, 77, 79, 82, 89, 139, 213, 342–3, 470; friendship with B., 26, 39–40, 48, 77–84 *passim,* 88–9, 91, 103–4, 291–2, 342–3; early life, 26–31, 39; on art and artists, 30; appearance, 30; personality, 31; failure of *Sapho* and *Ulysse,* 33–5; Berlioz and *La Nonne sanglante,* 35–7; nervous attacks, 48, 141, 159, 412: gives B. work, 106, 110–12, 114; sympathy at death of B.'s mother, 111; at Baden, 118; on Berlioz, 119; relations with Choudens, 133–4, 412–13; failure of *Mireille,* 146–7; at time of B.'s wedding, 249–50; flees to England, 263, 292–3, again, 342; on *Djamileh,* 328; asks B. to supervise *Roméo et Juliette* revival, 342–3; represented by B. at *Jeanne d'Arc* rehearsals, 353–4; at *Carmen première,* 389, 390–1; final correspondence with B., 412–13; at B.'s funeral, 422; eulogy, 423–4; mentioned, xii, 20, 41, 43, 56, 107, 108, 129, 131, 135, 144, 155, 159–61 *passim,* 163, 194, 197, 202, 206, 218, 254, 255, 287*n*, 299, 349, 375, 412, 435, 460, 468, 472
  Letters to B., 40, 46–7, 77–8, 81, 103, 111, 114, 118, 131–2, 133, 159, 240, 249–50, 266*n*, 343, 412–13, 413*n*; to Meilhac, 159–60; to Esther Halévy, 244*n*; to Geneviève Halévy, 246–7; to Massenet, 412; *see also* Bizet, Georges: Letters
  "Ave Maria," 153, 292, 468
  Cinq-Mars, 160
  Colombe, La, 103, 160
  De Profundis, 292
  Faust; B.'s interest in, 57, 70, 77, 80; B.'s opinion of, 78, 84; production of, 78, 81–4, 88; mentioned, 34, 122, 131, 133–4, 143, 148, 161, 202, 220, 290, 333, 365, 375, 380, 381, 397, 399
  First Symphony in D, 38, 468
  Gallia, 293, 468
  Hymne à la France, 39

Gounod *(continued)*
  Jeanne d'Arc, 353–4, 468
  Médecin malgré lui, Le, 77, 328
  Mémoires d'un artiste, 27, 27*n*
  Mireille, 131, 133, 146–7, 255, 382
  Nonne sanglante, La, 35–7, 38, 154, 468; *"La Symphonie des Ruines"* from, 37; *"La Marche des Morts"* from, 37
  Philémon et Baucis, 106, 122, 468
  Pierre l'Hermite, 36
  Polyeucte, 160, 460
  Reine de Saba, La, 111–21 *passim,* 131, 468
  Roméo et Juliette: B. arranges, 164, 191, 197, 468; success, 193; B. supervises revival, 342; mentioned, 34, 148, 159, 161, 185, 202, 292, 328, 344, 397
  Sanctus, 48
  Sapho, 26, 30–6, 38, 219; B. on, 34, 183
  Sérénade, 48
  Six Famous Choruses, 159, 468
  Tribut de Zamora, Le, 133–4, 160
  Ulysse, 34–5, 468
  Vive l'Empereur, 39
Gounod, François, 27
Gounod, Mme François, 26–8 *passim*
Grand Théâtre, Bordeaux, 470
Grande Duchesse de Gérolstein, La, see Halévy, Ludovic
Grandmougin, Charles, 468
Grand'tante, La, see Massenet
Grandval, Vicomtesse de, 146
  Messe, La, 146*n*, 218
Grazia, Maria, 55
Grèce contemporaine, La, see About
Gregorovius, Ferdinand, *quoted* 60*n*
Gretna Green, see Guiraud
Grétry, André-Ernest-Modeste, 77, 469, 472
  Epreuve Villageoise, L', 137
Grimm, Baron von, *Correspondence of,* 76
Grisar, Albert, 36
  Amours du diable, Les, 358
Gruyer, Hector, 78–83 *passim,* 88, 104
Guardi, *see* Gruyer
Guermantes, Duchesse de (*Côté de Guermantes*), 235, 241, 440*n*
Guide musical, Le, quoted 428
Guido da Siena, 99
Guido et Ginevra, see Halévy, Fromental
Guillemot, M., 25
Guiraud, Ernest: identified and described, 96; friendship with B., 96–7, 100–2 *passim,* 144, 224, 350; works on cantata, 194–6; *La Coupe du Roi de Thulé,* 230; arranges Second Suite by B., 332, 466; after *Carmen première,* 392, 392*n*; during B.'s illness, 416–17; at funeral, 419, 422; writes recitatives for *Carmen,* 426; mentioned, 105, 141, 146, 150, 151, 163, 184, 249, 250, 254, 257, 278, 286, 339, 348*n*, 354, 367, 378*n*, 383, 432
  Gretna Green, 350
  Kobold, Le, 260
  Piccolino, 416
  Sylvie, 147
Guiraud, Jean-Baptiste, 96
Guizot, François-Pierre-Guillaume, 60*n*
Gustavus III, 319
Gymnase Théâtre, 375

Hahn, Reynaldo, 439, 471; *quoted* 436
Hainl, Georges, 268

Halanzier-Dufresnoy, Olivier, 300–2 *passim*, 316, 353
Halévy, Daniel, xi
Halévy, Elie (son of Ludovic), 263
Halévy, Elie (father of Fromental and Léon), 236
Halévy, Esther: birth, 237, description, 237–8; engagement to Ludovic Halévy, 244; letter from Gounod, 244*n;* death, 244–5; mentioned, 242, 246
Halévy, Fromental: as teacher, 23–5, 42–3; B. on, 24, 95, 201, 289, 291; secretary of Académie des Beaux-Arts, 24, 239, 329; life and character, 25, 235–9; *chef du chant* and vice regent of Opéra, 25; on Offenbach competition jury, 41–2; reports on *Vasco de Gama,* 107; introduces B. to Liszt, 108; death and funeral, 114, 243–4; marries Léonie Rodrigues, 237; finances, 239, 309; letters to B., 80, 111, to Saint-Georges, 173; mentioned, xii, 12–13, 18, 36, 57, 96, 126, 149, 172, 214, 229, 261, 287*n,* 291*n,* 299, 313, 343, 344, 367, 374, 458, 459, 462
  Charles VI, 43, 237, 270
  Eclair, L', 241
  Fée aux Roses, La, 459, 459*n*
  Guido et Ginevra, 238
  Jaguarita l'indienne, 249
  Juif errant, Le, 235, 238
  Juive, La, xii, 23, 25, 96, 140, 229, 235, 236, 240, 241, 374, 380, 381, 462
  Magicienne, La, 239, 240
  Mousquetaires de la Reine, Les, 313
  Noë, 123, 252–3, 254, 465, 471
  Reine de Chypre, La, 7*n,* 25, 236, 289
Halévy, Geneviève, *see* Bizet, Geneviève Halévy
Halévy, Julie Meyer, 236
Halévy, Léon, 229, 237, 250, 267, 422, 468; *quoted,* 236, 240
  Templiers, Les, 229–30
Halévy, Léonie Rodrigues (Mme Fromental): biographical sketch, 237–9; mental illness, 239, 245, 250, 274, 276; *quoted* 241–2, 245; financial problems, 245–6, 249, 297, 306, 309–10; moves to Bordeaux, 262; relationship with Geneviève Bizet, 271, 272–6 *passim,* 285, 297–8; B. on, 273–4, 275–6; tries to help B., 286, 299–300, 304–5; B.'s affection for, 275, 297–8; household affairs, 307–8, 310, 314–15; difficulties with B., 314–15; 331; later life and death, 438; letters to Rodrigues, 240–1, to Ludovic Halévy, 265–6, 269–70, to Augier, 459, from Delacroix, 459; mentioned, 123, 252, 328, 335, 367, 420; *see also* Bizet, Georges: Letters
Halévy, Ludovic: on Roqueplan, 32–3; on Baudelaire, 113*n;* on Mme Carvalho, 137; on *Les Pêcheurs de Perles,* 141; on *Les Troyens,* 143; on *Mireille,* 147; on Meyerbeer, 148–9; on *Roméo et Juliette,* 193; on war, 199; on Fromental Halévy's death, 244; engagement to Esther Halévy, 244–5; marriage, 248, 273; on B.'s marriage, 250; on Second Empire, 264; collaborates on *Carmen,* 329, 351, 364, 379, 465; on Galli-Marié, 358; life, description, and works, 371–7; at rehearsals of *Carmen,* 371, 372, 381–3 *passim;* his versions of libretto, 384–5; on *première,* 391, 391*n;* on failure, 395; mentioned in criticisms, 397, 403, 404, 409; at B.'s death, 418–19, and funeral,

422; letter from Pasdeloup, 424; attempts to revive *Carmen,* 429, 431–2; mentioned, 41, 43, 106–7, 160, 171, 196*n,* 228, 229, 254, 263, 265, 268, 269, 333, 366*n,* 378, 381, 465
  Abbé Constantin, L', 371
  Belle Hélène, La, see Offenbach
  Boule, La, (with Meilhac) 372–3
  Famille Cardinal, La, 371
  Froufrou, (with Meilhac) 119, 375–7
  Grande Duchesse de Gérolstein, La, (with Meilhac) 198–200, 202, 264, 268, 375, 473
  Ingénue, L', (with Meilhac) 372
  Passage de Venus, Le, (with Meilhac) 395
  Veuve, La, (with Meilhac) 372
Halévy, Mélanie, 278
Halévy, Valentine, 265, 278, 344
Halt, Robert: *Madame Frainex,* 337
Hamlet, see Thomas
Handel, George Friedrich, 468, 472
Hanslick, Edouard, 426, 471; *quoted* 45–6
Haroun, *see* Bizet, Georges: *Djamileh*
Hartmann, Ernst, 470
Hartmann, Georges, 219, 254, 348, 389, 391, 466, 467
Hauk, Minnie, 428
Haussmann, Georges-Eugène, Baron, 309
Haussonville, Comte d', 439
Haussonville, Comtesse d', 9
Haydn, Joseph, 11, 56, 119, 128, 472
  Creation, The, 119
  Quartet No. 6, 127
Hébrard, Adrien, 389, 439
Heim, François-Joseph, 52
Heim, Joseph, 51, 69, 105
Heine, Heinrich, 373, *quoted* 24
Heller, Stephen, 473
  Etude de Chasse, 110
  Nuits Blanches, 110
Hensel, Fanny Mendelssohn, *quoted* 27
Her Majesty's Theatre, 428
Hermant, Abel, 439
Hérold, Louis-Joseph-Ferdinand, 126, 136, 149, 299
  Ludovic, 252
  Pré aux clercs, Le, 7, 313, 313*n,* 321
Hervieu, Paul, 439
Herz, Henri, 473
Heugel, Henri, 134, 153, 159, 163, 177, 219, 312, 337, 389, 466–9 *passim,* 474
Hintlesham Festival, 471
Hoffman, Dr., 31
Hoffmann, Ernst Theodor Amadeus: *Le Tonnelier de Nuremberg,* 86
Homer, 86, 180, 189, 201, 294, 314
Horace, 74, 229
  Carmen Saeculare, 94–5
Hugo, Victor, 35, 164, 266, 192, 219, 228, 267, 278, 466–8 *passim*
  Châtiments, Les, 268
  Esmeralda, 79, 86
  Patria, 290
Huguenots, Les, see Meyerbeer
Hummel, Johann Nepomuk, 473
Hymne à la France, see Gounod
Hymne à la Raison, see Gossec
Hymne à Napoléon III, see Rossini

Imogine, see Bizet, Adolphe, *also* Galabert
Indy, Vincent d', 187, 388, 389, 391, 391*n,* 393
Ingénue, L', see Halévy, Ludovic
Ingres, Jean-Auguste-Dominique, 9–12 *passim,* 34, 56, 104

Institut de France, 16, 46, 50, 65, 72, 96, 149, 239, 292, 304–5, 329
Iphigénie, see Gluck
Isaac, Adèle, 432–3
Isabey, Eugène, 162
Ismaël, Jean-Vital-Ismaël Jammes, called, 139
Italy, 51, 55, 56, 71, 87, 97, 100, 101, 103, 189, 204
Itinéraire de Paris à Jerusalem, see Chateaubriand

Jadin, Emmanuel, 205
Jaguarita l'indienne, see Halévy, Fromental
Jahyer, Felix, *quoted* 203–4
Jaime, Adolph, the younger, 255
James, Henry, *quoted* 32, 62
Jane Eyre, 8
Janin, Jules, *quoted* 168–9
"*Jardins sous la pluie," see* Debussy
Jauner, M., 426
Jean-Aubry, Georges, *quoted* 436
Jeanne d'Arc, 98
Jeanne d'Arc, see Gounod
Jesus, 252, 349
Jeunesse du Cid, La, see Castro y Bellvis
Jockey Club, 108
Jonas, Emile, 208, 209
Joncières, Victorien, 325, 394, *quoted* 424
Sardanaple, 186
José, Don, *see* Bizet, Georges: *Carmen*
Joseph, see Méhul
Joubert, Joseph: *Pensées,* 374
Journal de Paris, 75, 325
Journal des Débats, 11, 115, 145, 258n, 316; *quoted* 140, 211, 325–7, 339–40
Journal pour tous, 352
Jouvin, Benjamin, 118, 316, 325, 327; *quoted* 121, 139
Judic, Mme, 389
Juif errant, Le, see Halévy, Fromental
Juive, La, see Halévy, Fromental
Julien, Louis-Antoine, 23

Kalkbrenner, Christian, 473
Karlsruhe, Germany, 253, 471
Keats, John, 396
King of the Mountains, The, see About
Kisseleff, Comte de, 59, 59n, 60, 96
Kobold, Le, see Guiraud
Kock, Paul de; 313, 313n
Krupp, Alfred, 199

La Bruyère, Jean de, 24
Lacombe, Paul, 187–90, 208, 216, 252, 253, 277, 311n, 312, 318, 329, 354n
Rêverie, 189
Lacome, Paul, 401
Laget, Auguste, 286
Lagier, Suzanne, 209
Lakmé, see Delibes
Lalo, Edouard-Victor-Antoine, 348n, 350, 473
Lalo, Pierre, 462
Lamaquais, Comte de, 76
Lamartine, Alphonse-Marie-Louis de Prat de, 35, 177, 196, 466–8 *passim*
Voyage en Orient, 75
Lamartine, Mme Alphonse de, 9
Lamennais, Félicité-Robert de, 223
Lamoureux, Charles, 388
Lanterne, La, 228, 262, 375
Lara, see Maillart
Launay, Clément, 418
Laurent, M. and Mme, 162

Lauris, Georges, Marquis de, *quoted* 439–40
Lauzieres, Achille de, Marquis de Thémines, 396, 399–401, 404, 406, 414, 429
Lecocq, Charles, 41–3, 41n, 389, *quoted* 345
Fille de Madame Angot, La, 41, 389
Petit Duc, Le, 41
Lecomte, General Claude-Martin, 281
Leconte-de-Lisle, Charles, 468
Lecuyer, M., 150
Lédentu, M., 74
Lefevre, Maurice, 431
Legouix, M., 207–9 *passim*
Legouvé, Ernest, 252, 414
Leibnitz, Gottfried Wilhelm, Baron von, 223
Leïla, *see* Bizet, Georges: *Les Pêcheurs de Perles*
Lemorne, M., 115, 117
Léonce, M., 209–10
L'Epine, Ernest, 106, 106n, 194, 195–6, 196n, 197, 333
Leroy, Arthur, 131, 223, 224, 230, 234, 465
Leuven, Adolph de (Count von Ribbing): described, 321; mentioned, 145, 260, 301, 302, 304, 319, 323, 325, 329, 351, 360, 378
Lévy, Michel, 113n, 168
Lhérie, Paul, 357, 359, 365, 383, 390n, 392–3, 422
Liberté, La, 220, 325
Lillas Pastia, *see* Bizet, Georges: *Carmen*
Lind, Jenny, 9
Liszt, Franz von, 45, 108–9, 149, 167, 212, 266n, 427, 473, 474
Faust Symphony, 148, 473
Litolff, Henry Charles, 266, 266n, 460
Lohengrin, see Wagner
Lombardy, 87
Louis XIV, 120, 124
Louis XV, 237
Louis XVI, 237
Louis Philippe, 10, 55, 125, 289, 394
Love's Labour's Lost, see Shakespeare
Lovy, J., *quoted* 127
Lucia di Lammermoor, see Donizetti
Lucretia, 98
Lucretius, 94
Ludovic, see Hérold
Lully, Jean-Baptiste, 124, 473
Lusiade, The, see Camões
Lusignan, Comte de, 401
Lyons, 52

Mab, *see* Bizet, Georges: *La Jolie Fille de Perth*
Mac Mahon, Marie-Edme-Patrice-Maurice, Comte de, 87, 260
Madame Bovary, see Flaubert
Madame Frainex, see Halt
Maësen, Léontine de, 137
Magenta, Battle of, 85, 87
Magic Flute, The, see Mozart: *Die Zauberflöte*
Magicienne, La, see Halévy, Fromental
Mahler, Gustav, 471
Maillart, Aimé:
Dragons de Villars, Les, 372
Lara, 358
Maître Pathelin, see Bazin
Malesherbes, Boulevard, 309
Malibran, La (Maria Garcia), 9, 31, 218, 401
Malherbe, Charles, 470
Malherbe, Henry, 358, 419
Carmen, 358

"Mandolinata," see Paladilhe, Emile
Manet, Edouard, 62, 370
Mangin, the beggar, 142
Manican, M. de, 282
Manon, see Massenet
Manuel, Eugène, 256
  Pages intimes, 255
Mapleson, Henry, 355
Marcello, Benedetto, 468
"Marche au supplice," see Berlioz
"Marche des Morts, La," see Gounod
Maréchal, Henri, 210–11, 320, 365–6, 411
Marenco, L., 471
Mariage de Figaro, Le, see Beaumarchais, also Mozart
Marié, Paola, 360
Marié de l'Isle, Claude-Marie-Mécène, 358
Marie-Magdeleine, see Massenet
Marini, Signor, 316
Marivaux, Pierre Carlet de Chamblain de, 376
Marmontel, Antoine-François, 16–22 *passim,* 26, 96, 131n, 329, 370
Marmontel, Jean-François:
  Contes moraux, 21
  Mémoires d'un père pour servir à l'instruction de ses enfants, 21
Marriage of Prometheus, The, see Cornut
Marseillaise (anthem), 259, 259n, 268, 270, 277, 375
Marseillaise, La (newspaper), 293
Martha, see Flotow
Martin, Henri, 255n
Martinon, Jean, 441
Mascagni, Pietro, 43
Massé, Victor, 257, 287, 287n, 357, 469
  Paul et Virginie, 287n
Massenet, Jules: friendship with B., 193–4; in competitions, 193, 197, 257; in National Guard, 260, 263; B. on, 286, 300, 349–50; on *Djamileh,* 327; on *L'Arlésienne,* 337, 340; B.'s annoyance with, 350; B. dedicates *Patrie* to, 365; to B. on *Carmen,* 395–6; at B.'s funeral, 422; mentioned, xii, 129, 187, 299, 320, 333, 354, 358, 389, 425, 469, 473
  Cid, Le, 353n
  Don César de Bazin, 325n
  Eve, 388, 411–12
  Grand'tante, La, 193–4
  Manon, 136
  Marie-Magdeleine, 349–50, 379, 412
  Thaïs, 321
Massy, M., 190, 196, 197
Mathilde, Princesse, *see* Bonaparte, Mathilde
Maupassant, Guy de, 438
Maximilian, Archduke of Austria and Emperor of Mexico, 199
Mayrargues, Nephtali, 144
Meck, Natasha von, 427n
Médecin malgré lui, Le, see Gounod
Méhul, Etienne Nicolas, 473
  Joseph, 137
Meifred, Pierre-Joseph-Emile, 15–16, 329
Meilhac, Henri: to Halévy on war, 263–4; librettist of *Carmen,* 322, 329, 351, 352, 364, 373, 381, 397, 403, 404, 409, 465; at *Carmen* rehearsals, 372, 382, 383; description and biographical sketch, 277–8; contribution to *Carmen,* 378; attempts to revive *Carmen,* 431; mentioned, 31, 160, 171, 268, 356, 373, 375, 389, 392n; *see also* Halévy, Ludovic, for works

Meissonier, Jean-Louis-Ernest, 379
Meistersinger, Die, see Wagner
Membrée, Edmond: *L'Esclave,* 353
Mémoires d'un artiste, see Gounod
Mendelssohn, Felix, 44, 128, 188, 269, 473
  Midsummer Night's Dream, A, 110, 354, 473
  Songs without Words, 110
Mendès, Catulle, 467
Ménestrel, Le, 127, 134–5, 138, 139, 142, 207–8, 218, 219, 427, 470, 474
Mercadante, Giuseppe, 49
Mercédès, *see* Bizet, Georges: *Carmen*
Mérimée, Prosper: on *Tannhäuser,* 108; on war and Bismarck, 199, 205; author of *Carmen,* 322, 351, 357, 385, 397–8, 402; plot of *Carmen,* 398, criticisms, 400, changes by B., 407; mentioned, 278, 279n, 431, 435; *see also* Bizet, Georges: *Carmen*
Merry Wives of Windsor, The, see Nicolai
Méry, Joseph, 115, 117, 120, 163, 466
Messager du Midi, Le, 245
Messe, see Grandval
Metternich, Princess Pauline, 107–8
Meyerbeer, Giacomo: B. on, 72, 79, 89, 189; death, 147, 148–50; influence, 147–8, 470; mentioned, xii, 33, 109, 125, 144, 154, 198, 202, 473
  Africaine, L', 148, 148n, 149, 155, 156, 202, 473
  Etoile du Nord, L', 202, 473
  Huguenots, Les, 79, 147, 148, 268, 381, 473
  Pardon de Ploërmel, Le (Dinorah), 147, 399
  Phophète, Le, 33, 74, 150, 229, 364, 473
  Robert le Diable, 148, 150, 473
Micaëla, *see* Bizet, Georges: *Carmen*
Michelangelo Buonarroti, 72, 79, 147, 189, 201, 266, 294, 295, 314
Michelet, Jules, 192
Michot, M., 193
Midsummer Night's Dream, A, see Mendelssohn
Mignon, see Thomas
Millevoye, Charles-Hubert, 177, 466, 467
Mireille, see Gounod
Mistral, Frédéric, 255, 337, 460, 461
  Calendal, 255, 460
Modena, 87
Mogador, Céleste, 165–71, 180–2, 221, 245, 405
  Voleurs d'or, Les, 169
Molière (pseud. of Jean-Baptiste Poquelin), 358
  Amour peintre, L', 93, 94
  Bourgeois Gentilhomme, Le, 39, 373
Moltke, Helmuth, Count von, 375
Monastery, The, see Scott
Monelli, M., 108n
Monet, Claude, 439
Moniteur universel, Le, 63, 211, 434
Monjauze, M., 233
Monnier, Henry, 405
Montauban, 150–2 *passim,* 195, 197
Montespan, Françoise-Athénaïs Rochechouart, Marquise de, 124
Montmartre, 253–4, 281, 282
Montréal, Mlle de, *see* Albano, Gaston d'
Montretout, 47
Morales, *see* Bizet, Georges: *Carmen*
Moreau, Gustave, 60n
Morini, M., 140
Morny, Charles-Auguste-Louis-Joseph, Duc de, 106n, 264, 333, 374
Moscheles, Ignaz, 473; *quoted* 22, 31

Moses, 189, 223
Moulton, Mrs. (L. de Hegermann-Linden-
   crone), 289
Mousquetaire, Le (newspaper), 168
Mousquetaires de la Reine, Les, see
   Halévy, Fromental
Mozart, Wolfgang Amadeus: Rossini's
   opinion of, 45, 49; B. on, 71, 72, 79,
   84, 96, 100, 189, 314; relationship
   with Anna Storace, 359; mentioned,
   12, 18, 56, 109, 125, 128, 148, 149,
   205, 322, 369, 402, 469, 473
   Così fan tutte, 44, 96, 136, 153, 473
   Don Giovanni (Don Juan), 96, 153,
      159, 314, 469, 473
   E Flat Symphony, 127
   Nozze di Figaro, Le, 79, 96, 137, 142,
      153, 318, 359; da Ponte's introduction
      to, 398-9
   Oca del Caïro, L' (L'Oie du Caïre),
      202, 469, 473
   Requiem, 71
   Schauspieldirektor, Der, 319
   Zauberflöte, Die (The Magic Flute),
      153, 314, 473
Muchachas, Las, 357
Muette de Portici, La, see Auber
Musset, Alfred de, 31, 75, 165-6, 167, 177,
   312, 376, 409, 467; quoted 120
   Namouna, 302, 308, 332, 336; see also
      Bizet, Georges: Djamileh

Nadir, see Bizet, Georges: Les Pêcheurs
   de Perles
Namouna, see Musset; also Bizet, Georges:
   Djamileh
Nana, see Zola
Naples, 87-8, 103, 266
Nathan, M., 390n
National, Le, 408
National Guard, 16, 260-3 passim, 266,
   270, 277, 279-80, 284-5
Neuilly, 284
New York City Center, 471
New York Herald, The, 428
Ney, Edgar, 228, 228n
Nice, 52, 105, 240, 241, 252
Nicolai, Otto: Joyeuses Commères, Les
   (The Merry Wives of Windsor), 122,
   469
Nicolini (Ernest Nicolas), 428
Nietzsche, Friedrich Wilhelm, quoted 471
   Case of Wagner, The, quoted 430
Niewekerke, Alfred-Emilien, Comte de,
   161
Nilsson, Christine, 159, 161, 185, 196, 204,
   210, 213, 218, 219, 358, 380
Ninth Symphony, see Beethoven
Noailles, Anna, Comtesse de, 439
Nocturne, Third, see Paladilhe, Emile
Noë, see Halévy, Fromental; also Bizet,
   Georges
Noëls, see Sabol
Nonne sanglante, La, see Gounod
Norma, see Bellini
Norma, Italy, 69
Nôtes sur le théâtre grec et sur le théâtre
   latin, 74
Nourrit, Adolphe, 9
Nozze di Figaro, Le, see Mozart
Nuits Blanches, see Heller
Nuitter, Charles, 290
"Nun, The," see Schubert
Nydahl, Kapten Rudolph, 42n

Oca del Caïro, L', see Mozart
Odéon, Théâtre de l', 332, 471

Offenbach, Jacques: holds competition,
   40-3, 62n; his parties, 43; B. scorns,
   311-12, 354; Flaubert on, 318; pro-
   duces Jeanne d'Arc, 353-4; at Car-
   men, 389, 390; mentioned, 25, 62,
   126, 169, 202, 473
   Barkouf, 312, 312n
   Belle Hélène, La, 34, 229, 473
   Brigands, Les, 355, 372, 391
   Contes d'Hoffmann, Les, 96, 373
   Fantasio, 311, 312, 318, 409, 473
   Grande Duchesse de Gérolstein, La, see
      Halévy, Ludovic
   Orpheé aux enfers, 34, 229, 354
   Roi Carotte, Le, 312, 318, 355, 473
   Vie Parisienne, La, 355, 473
Offenbach, Mme Jacques, 62
Ollivier, Emile, 149
Opéra: history, 124-5, 155-6, 353; B.'s
   contacts with, 155-6, 223-4, 229-31, 234,
   329, 353, 460; competition, 224, 256-7;
   B. on, 287; during Siege and Commune,
   289-90; possible position for B., 299-
   302, 315-17; opening of new Opéra,
   380-1
Opéra-Comique: commissions La Guzla
   de l'Emir, 107; history, 125-6, 192, 359,
   429; and "freedom of the theatres," 145;
   possible commission for B., 234; commissions Calendal, 255; commissions
   Namouna (Djamileh), 301-2, 318; directors described, 304, 319-21, 351, 379;
   puts pressure on B., 318; a family
   theatre, 351, 377, 383, 397-9, 403, 404,
   408-9, 437; logbook, 371-2; Carmen at,
   382-3, 388-90, 392, 400, 414, 424; revival of Carmen, 427, 431-6 passim;
   Auber centenary, 431; statue of B., 434,
   437, 437n; revival of Les Pêcheurs de
   Perles, 470
Orlando, 99
Orléans, Ferdinand-Philippe-Louis-Charles-
   Henry, Duc d', son of Louis Philippe,
   10, 55
Orphée, see Gluck
Orphée aux enfers, see Offenbach
Orvieto, 99
Otello, see Rossini
Ourliac, Edouard: Susanne, 113n
Oxford University Opera Club, 471

Pacini, Antonio Francesco, 133
Pacini, Emilien, 120-1, 198
Padua, 101, 102
Pagans, M., 219
Pages intimes, see Manuel
Pailleron, Edouard, 467
Paladilhe, Alcide, 43, 44
Paladilhe, Emile: identified, 43; at Ros-
   sini's, 44-5, 49; B.'s advice to, 56; B.
   mentions, 101, 260; on Les Pêcheurs
   de Perles, 141; in competition, 196,
   198; on Geneviève, 245; relations with
   Galli-Marié, 362-3, 421; at B.'s fu-
   neral, 422; quoted, 145, 162, 194, 233,
   257; mentioned, 150, 249, 320, 354n,
   414
   Amour africaine, L', 414
   Fughette, 44
   "Mandolinata," 363
   Nocturne, Third, 43, 44
   Passant, Le, 322, 325, 362-3
Palestrina, Giovanni, 29, 49, 473
Palo, 98
Paradise Lost, 253
Pardon de Ploërmel, Le (Dinorah), see
   Meyerbeer

Paris: B. born, 3; Orphéon de la Ville de, 39; Gounod on, 104; Flaubert on, 113; Baudelaire on, 113; Geneviève Halévy on, 242; Siege of, 262–70 *passim;* music during Siege and Commune, 267–9, 289–90, 299; Prussian occupation, 277–8; under Commune, 279–85, 289–91, 293–4; Haussmann's plan, 309; Ludovic Halévy on, 373

Parisina, see Donizetti

Parker, D. C., 471

Parma, 87

Parrod, Dr., 344

Pasdeloup, Jules: directs Jeunes Artistes, 126–7; conducts B.'s works, 127, 323, 340, 347, 365, 471; *Carmen* dedicated to, 127, 389, 389*n;* as musician, 231–3; commissions completion of *Noë,* 252–3; directs Concerts Populaires, 268, 299; commissions *Patrie,* 354; arranges music for B.'s funeral, 422; letter to Ludovic Halévy, 424; mentioned, 144, 349

Passage de Venus, Le, see Halévy, Ludovic

Passant, Le, see Paladilhe, Emile

Pastiches et Mélanges, see Proust

"Pastoral" Symphony (Sixth), *see* Beethoven

Patria, see Hugo

Patrie, see Sardou; *also* Bizet, Georges

Patrie, La (newspaper), 399

Patti, Adelina, 159, 170, 358, 428

Paul et Virginie, see Massé

Pedrell, editor: *Cancionero Musical Popular Español,* 401

Pelléas et Mélisande, see Debussy

Pellegrin, Abbé, 254, 468

Pensées, see Joubert

Père Duchêne, Le (newspaper), 295*n*

Péreire, Emile, 245, 250, 309

Péreire brothers, 237, 247, 309

Pergolesi, Giovanni Battista: *La Serva Padrona,* 358, 473

Perrin, Emile: and *L'Africaine,* 149, 155–6; negotiates with B., 155–6, 223, 229–30, 234; controls competition for *La Coupe du Roi de Thulé,* 230, 256; B. applies for Opéra position, 300–1, 302; loathes *Carmen,* 383; mentioned, 136, 154, 268, 289, 291, 301, 319, 358, 375, 459

Perrin, Mme Emile, 300

Perugia, 99–100

Perugino, Il, P. Vanucci called, 52, 99

Petit Chose, Le, see Daudet, Alphonse

Petit Duc, Le, see Lecocq

Petite Fadette, La, see George Sand

Phaon, 34

Philémon et Baucis, see Gounod

Philiberte, see Augier

Philosophical Dictionary, see Voltaire

Piccinni, Niccola, 125

Piccolino, see Guiraud

Piedmont, 52, 86, 87

Pierre l'Hermite, see Gounod

Pigot, Charles, 15–16, 322, 354*n,* 392*n,* 419

Piombo, Sebastiano del, 98

Pius IX, Pope, 54, 59*n,* 61, 100

Poëta Calculista, El, see García, Manuel

Poland, 354*n*

Polignac, Edmond, Prince de, 112

Polignac, Pierre, Comte de, 439

Polyeucte, see Gounod

Pompeii, 88

Ponchard, Charles, 321, 390*n*

Poniatowski, Jözef Michal, Prince, 112

Port-Marly, 285, 287, 352

Porto-Riche, Georges de, 439

Pot-Bouille, see Zola

Potel, M., 323, 390*n*

Pré aux clercs, Le, see Hérold

Prelly, Aline (Baroness de Presles), 318, 323

Premier Jour de Bonheur, Le, see Auber

Prévost-Paradol, Anatole, 258, 258*n*

Priola, Mlle, 322

Prise de Troie, La, see Berlioz

Prix de Rome competition: B. wins second prize, 39–40; B. enters, 46, and wins first, 47–8; described by Berlioz, 46, 48; program, 48; recipients and Théâtre-Lyrique, 145; B. on Jury, 304; mentioned, 18, 25

Promise, La, see Clapisson

Prophète, Le, see Meyerbeer

Proust, Marcel, xi, xii, 169, 235, 241, 338*n,* 439–40

Côté de Guermantes, 440*n*

Pastiches et Mélanges, 440*n*

Provence, 52, 333, 334

Prud'homme, M. Joseph, *see* Monnier

Prussia, 258–63 *passim,* 282

Prussia, Augusta, Queen of, 316

Psyche, see Thomas

Pugno, Raoul, 290

Puritani di Scozia, I, see Bellini

Quartet No. 6, *see* Haydn

"Quatrelles" (pseud.), *see* L'Epine

"Queen Mab Scherzo," *see* Berlioz

Rabelais, François, 201

Rachel (Elisa Félix), 9

Racine, Jean-Baptiste, 397

Ralph, *see* Bizet, Georges: *La Jolie Fille de Perth*

Rama, see Crépet

Ramayana, 255

Rameau, Jean Philippe, 124, 473

Ramo da Siena, 99

Raphaël (Raphaël Sanzio), 72, 79, 99

Ravenna, 101

Ravina, Henri, 345

Réal Delsarte, Madeleine, 8n

Reber, Napoléon-Henri, 11, 95, 304

Redemption, see Franck, César

Regnard, Jean François, 467

Regnault, Henri, 204–5, 379

Reinach, Joseph, 440

Reine de Chypre, La, see Halévy, Fromental

Reine de Saba, La, see Gounod

Reiter, Jean, 121, 344, 417–19 *passim*

Reiter, Marie, 121–2, 344, 415–18 *passim,* 459

Rembrandt van Ryn, 319

Remendado, Le, *see* Bizet, Georges: *Carmen*

Renan, Joseph-Ernest, 161, 192

Requiem, see Mozart; *also* Verdi

Rêverie, see Lacombe

Revolution of 1848, 16, 133, 289

Revue de musicologie, 131*n*

Revue et Gazette musicale, 185; quoted 127, 128, 130, 162, 209, 233

Revue nationale et étrangère, La, 200, 205

Reyer, Ernest: identified and described, 115; friendship with B., 115–18; on *Béatrice et Bénédict,* 118–19; on B.'s temper, 120–1; on Carvalho, 135–6; B. on, 182, 200; on *La Jolie Fille de Perth,* 212–13; on Pasdeloup, 232; B. resents Opéra's treatment of, 315–16; on *Djamileh,* 325–7, 402; on *L'Arlé-*

Reyer (continued)
  sienne, 339–40; note to B., 395; on
    Carmen, 397, 433–4; on music at B.'s
    funeral, 422; obituary of B., 424;
    mentioned, 129, 137, 143, 349, 350,
    469
  Erostrate, 115–18, 120, 122, 163, 315–16,
    469
  Statue, La, 115, 121, 135, 137, 183, 469
Ribbing, Comte de, 319
Rienzi, see Wagner
Rietri, 87
Rigoletto, see Verdi
Rimini, 100
Rob Roy, see Flotow
Robert, Léopold, 55
Robert le Diable, see Meyerbeer
Rochefort, Henri, 228, 262, 293, 375
Rodrigues, Edouard, 307
Rodrigues, Jacob-Hippolyte: helps Halévys
    financially, 245; identified and de-
    scribed, 251–2; difficulty with Mme
    Halévy, 273–4, 297; letters from Mme
    Halévy, 240–1, from Geneviève Ha-
    lévy, 241, mentioned, 237, 250, 272,
    298, 366n; see also Bizet, Georges:
    Letters
  David Rizzio, 252
  Roi des Juifs, Le, 252, 252n
  Saint Pierre (Saint Peter), 284
Rodrigues Prize, 68, 71, 441
Rodrigues-Henriques, Esther Gradis (Mme
    Isaac), 237
Rodrigues-Henriques, Isaac, 237
Roger, Gustave, quoted 173
Roi-Carotte, Le, see Offenbach
Roi des Juifs, Le, see Rodrigues, Hippolyte
Roland, Mme, 5, 6n, 458, 458n
Rolland, Olivier, 466
Rolland, Romain, 438, 463
Romances: chansons sans paroles pour
    piano, see Salomon
Romani, Felice, 48
Rome: B. goes to, 48, 51; Carnival, 57–8;
    Holy Week, 61; B.'s feeling for, 69, 70,
    92, 96, 97; B.'s first year in, 74, 76;
    Gounod on, 103–4, 118
Roméo et Juliette, see Gounod
Ronsard, Pierre de, 177, 467
Roqueplan, Nestor, 32–3, 35, 36, 54, 64,
    125, 136, 137, 154, 192–3, 200, 301
Rossini, Gioacchino: his parties, 44–6;
    advice, 48–9; and Carafa, 49–50; B.
    on, 72, 79, 84, 89, 96, 189, 314; men-
    tioned, xii, 125, 129, 133, 197, 217,
    402, 403, 473
  Barber of Seville, The, 189, 314, 426,
    469, 473
  Comte Ory, Le, 189, 473
  Guillaume Tell, 79, 189, 268, 290, 314,
    380, 469, 473
  Hymne à Napoléon III, 198, 200n
  Otello, 189, 314
  Semiramide, 189, 314, 473
Rossini, Olympe (Mme Gioacchino), 45, 46
Rothsay, Duke of, see Bizet, Georges: La
    Jolie Fille de Perth
Rothschild, Baron de, 245
Rothschild, Baroness de, 439n
Rothschild, Edmond, Baron de, 439
Rothschild, Fondation Ophtalmologique,
    440
Rothschild family, 237, 438
Rouen, 5
Rousseau, Jean Jacques, 76, 168, 473
Royer, Alphonse, 108n, 167
Roze, Marie, 355–6, 428

Rubinstein, Anton, 45
Ruelle, M. J., 468
Ruins of Athens, The, see Beethoven

Saboly, Nicholas: Noëls, 461
Sacchini, Antonio Maria Gasparo, 473
Sadler's Wells Opera, 470
Sadowa, Battle of, 178
Saint-Cloud, 47, 133, 292
Saint-Evremond, Charles, Seigneur de, 332
Saint Francis, 100
Saint-Georges, Jules-Henri Vernoy de:
    librettist of Noë, 123, 252–3, 465; de-
    scribed, 172–3; librettist of La Jolie Fille
    de Perth, 172–6 passim, 186, 196, 197,
    465, of Les Templiers, 229–30; arbitra-
    tor in dispute between B. and Comettant
    414; mentioned, 149, 177, 367, 409
Saint-Germain-en-Laye, 285, 366, 366n,
    418, 423, 463
Saint-Gratien, 251, 253, 258
Saint John, 94
Saint Mark's Square, 102, 103
Saint Paul, 94
Saint Peter, see Rodrigues, Hippolyte
Saint Peter's Square, Rome, 61
Saint-Saëns, Camille: quoted 11–12, 22,
    31–2, 35, 204, 321, 349; as conductor,
    128; on B., 128–9, 194; described,
    129–30; visits Le Vésinet, 153; wins
    cantata competition, 198–9; B. on,
    202, 300, 329; suppression of B's
    article on, 205; tribute to Djamileh,
    328; to B. on Carmen, 396; letters re-
    garding Carmen ballet, 462–3; men-
    tioned, xii, 42, 136, 146, 263, 268,
    320, 333, 348n, 350, 469, 472, 473
  Fourth Piano Concerto, 425
  Samson et Dalila, 202, 349
  Tarantella, 45
  Timbre d'argent, Le, 136, 202, 205–6,
    469
Saint-Simon, Claude-Henri de Rouvroy,
    Comte de, 229
Saint Victor, Paul de, 325
Sainte-Beuve, Charles, 161, 192, quoted 24
Sainte Geneviève, 13, 350, 415
Salammbô, see Flaubert
Salomon, Hector, 317
  Romances: chansons sans paroles pour
    piano, 317n
Sampayo, Antoine-François-Oscar, 59,
    59n, 90
Samson et Dalila, see Saint-Saëns
Sanctus, see Gounod
Sand, George, see George Sand
Sapho, see Gounod; also Daudet, Alphonse
Sappho, 34, 225
Sarcey, Francisque, 254; on L'Arlésienne,
    338
Sardanapale, see Joncières
Sardou, Victorien, 255, 258, 263, 276, 284,
    287–8, 312, 357, 376, 377
  Patrie, 354n
Sasse, Marie, see Saxe, Marie
Satie, Erik, 96
Sauvage, Thomas-Marie, 223, 224, 230,
    234
Savona, 52
Saxe, Marie, 117, 148, 259
Scarlatti, Alessandro, 473
Scarlatti, Domenico, 473
Schauspieldirektor, Der, see Mozart
Schiller, Johann Christoph Friedrich von,
    151, 473
Schneider, Hortense, 199, 389

Schnetz, Victor, 54–6, 58–60 *passim*, 63–5
passim, 67
Schott & Söhne, 470
Schubert, Franz, 269, 473
"The Nun," 219
Schumann, Robert, 127, 132, 188, 314,
326, 416, 469, 472, 473
"*Aus der Heimat*," 416
Funeral March, 416
"*Ich grolle nicht*," 416
Scott, Sir Walter, 174–5
Fair Maid of Perth, The, 172
Guy Mannering, 172
Monastery, The, 172
Scribe, Eugène, 19, 36, 41, 120, 172, 236,
239, 253, 312*n*, 319, 409, 468
Scudéry, Georges de, 314
Second Scherzo, *see* Chopin
Sedan, 261
Ségur, Monseigneur de, 82
Sellier, Charles, 51, 58
Semet, Théophile, 421
Semiramide, see Rossini
Sérénade, see Gounod
Serva Padrona, La, see Pergolesi
Seventh Symphony, *see* Beethoven
Seville, 402, 403, 409
Shakespeare, William, 189, 201, 266, 270,
294, 295, 314, 397
Love's Labour's Lost, 136, 473
Tempest, The, 238
Shanet, Howard, 39*n*
Sibilat, Magda (Mme René), xii-xiii, 439*n*
Sibilat, René, xii, 439*n*
Siècle, Le, 294*n*, 403
Signol, Emile, 313, 313*n*
Signorelli, Luca, 99
Silem, Maurits, 78*n*
Simart, Mme Benjamin, 44
Siraudin, Paul, 465
Six Famous Choruses, see Gounod
Sixth Symphony ("Pastoral"), *see* Beetho-
ven
Smith, *see* Bizet, Georges: *La Jolie Fille
de Perth*
Société des Auteurs, 172, 438, 462
Société de l'Harmonie Sacrée, 388
Société des Concerts du Conservatoire,
18, 126, 268
Société des Jeunes Artistes, 126–7
Société Nationale de Musique, 348*n*
Société Nationale des Beaux-Arts, 128,
130
Socrates, 222, 238
Solesmes, 3, 4, 437*n*
Songs without Words, see Mendelssohn
Sonino, 86
Sonnambula, La, see Bellini
Soumy, Joseph, 54
Source, La, see Delibes
Splendiano, *see* Bizet, Georges: *Djamileh*
Spontini, Gaspare, 125, 473
Fernando Cortez, 130, 474
Vestale, La, 135, 473
Statue, La, see Reyer
Stern, Georges, *see* Lecocq
Storace, Anna, 359
Straus, Emile, xii, 235*n*, 438, 440, 462, 470
Straus, Mme Emile, *see* Bizet, Geneviève
Halévy
Susanne, see Ourliac
Sylvie, see Guiraud
"*Symphonie des Ruines, La*," *see* Gounod
Symphony in E Flat, *see* David, Félicien

Taine, Hippolyte-Adolphe, 161, 192
Tamburini, Mme, 241

Tannhäuser première, 107–8; *see also*
Wagner
Tarantella, see Saint-Saëns
Tarbé, Eugène, 212
Tchaikovsky, Peter Ilitch, 354, 427, 427*n*
1812, 354
Tempest, The, see Shakespeare
Templiers, Les, see Halévy, Léon
Temps, Le, 325, 389, 439; quoted 138, 213
Ténot, Pierre-Paul-Eugène, 226, 226*n*
Terracina, 85
Terrail, Pierre-Alexis, Vicomte de Ponson
du, 174, 174*n*
Teste, M., 390*n*
Thaïs, see Massenet
Thalberg, Sigismund, 469, 473
Variations, 153
Théâtre de la Gaîté, 312, 318, 353, 470
Théâtre de la Monnaie, Brussels, 364, 428
Théâtre de la Renaissance, 220
Théâtre de l'Athénée, 206–8 *passim*
Théâtre de l'Odéon, 332, 471
Théâtre des Variétés, 144, 168, 202, 372,
390, 391, 395
Théâtre du Châtelet, 215, 220
Théâtre du Vaudeville, 332, 339
Théâtre-Français, 372; *see also* Comédie-
Française
Théâtre-Italien, 126, 148, 159, 223, 393,
399
Théâtre-Lyrique: description and history,
126, 136–7, 145, 220, 233; financial
straits, 154–5, 172, 185; *see also* Car-
valho, Léon, *and* Bizet, Georges: *Les
Pêcheurs de Perles, La Jolie Fille de
Perth*
Théâtre Municipal, Strasbourg, 470
Thérèsa, Emma Valadon, called, 170
Thérèse, see Carafa
Thierry, Edouard, quoted 434–5
Thiers, Adolphe, 60*n*, 279, 279*n*, 281, 284,
293, 299
Thiers, Mme Adolphe, 299
Thomas, Ambroise: member of juries, 22,
41, 95, 197; report on B.'s *envoi*,
93–4; on B.'s songs, 163; on *Les
Pêcheurs de Perles*, 214; letter to B.,
219; B. on, 291, 304, 312; appointed
Director of Conservatoire, 304–5;
mentioned, 43, 67, 123, 141, 192, 194,
202, 337, 389, 395, 422, 469
Hamlet, 196, 218–30 *passim*, 291, 304,
305, 306, 312, 380–1, 397, 399, 469
Mignon, 163–4, 202, 218, 358, 368*n*,
371, 409, 469
Psyche, 218
Thomas, General Clément, 281
Tiersot, Julien, 401
Timbre d'argent, Le, see Saint-Saëns
Tintoretto, Il, Jacopo Robusti, called, 362
Titian (Tiziano Vecellio), 362
Tivoli, 69
Tolla, see About
Tonnelier de Nuremberg, Le, see Hoff-
mann
Torlonia, Donna Francesca, 59*n*, 90
Toulon, 52
Tour d'Auvergne, 26 rue de la, 3
Traviata, La, see Verdi
Trélat, Achille: *La Folie lucide*, 217
Trélat, Marie Molinos (Mme Ulysse),
208, 216–19, 221–2, 230, 253, 396
Trélat, Ulysse, 216–17, 221
Clinique chirurgicale, La, 216
Trianon, Henry, 131, 465
Tribut de Zamora, Le, see Gounod
Tristan and Isolde, see Wagner

Trochu, General Louis-Jules, 262, 267
Troubetskoi, Prince, 389
Trovatore, Il, see Verdi
Troyens, Les, see Berlioz
Tulipe noire, La, see Dumas, Alexandre
Turgenev, Ivan, 31, 367
"Turlurette," see Chéri, Victor
Tuscany, 84, 87

Ugalde, Mme, 290
Ulysse, see Gounod
Umbria, 84

Variations, Thirty-two, see Beethoven
Variétés, Théâtre des, 144, 168, 202, 372, 390, 391, 395
Vatican, 64, 82
Vaudeville, Théâtre du, 332, 339
Vauthrot, Professor, 299
Vénard, Céleste, see Mogador, Céleste
Vénard, Mme, 181-2
Venice, 101-3 passim, 361-2
Vercingetorix, 254, 255n
Verdi, Giuseppe: B. on, 72, 81-2, 95-6, 107, 121, 190, 201, 312; his influence on Les Pêcheurs de Perles, 140; on Froufrou, 377; mentioned, xii, 36, 45, 56, 90, 148, 155, 194, 197, 202, 206, 233, 320, 470, 474
   Aïda, 302, 320, 474n
   Ballo in Maschera, Un, 82, 319n
   Don Carlos, 190, 192, 202, 320, 364, 399
   Requiem, 379, 411
   Rigoletto, 45, 95, 189, 192, 289, 428
   Traviata, La, 95, 189, 192
   Trovatore, Il, 95, 189, 290, 364, 474; About's parody, 43
Vernet, Horace, 53
Véron, Dr. Pierre, 54, 125, 136, 301
Versailles, 279, 284, 288, 290, 296
Vésinet, Le: purchase of property at, 150; Galabert describes, 153; Céleste Mogador's house, 169; Gallet visits, 303; mentioned, 151, 164, 170, 171, 181, 183, 220, 229, 284, 285, 291, 296, 310, 438
Vestale, La, see Spontini
Veuve, La, see Halévy, Ludovic
Viardot-Garcia, Pauline, 31-3 passim, 162, 254, 349, 367, 401
Victor, M., 321, 323
Victor Emmanuel II, 87
Victoria, Queen of England, 380
Vidal, François: Lou Tambarin, 331, 331n, 461
Vie Parisienne, La, see Offenbach
Vienna Opera House, 426
Vigier, Mme, 241
Villa Medici, 53-60 passim, 64, 65, 67, 73, 74, 80, 204, 365; see also Académie Imperiale Française in Rome

Villemessant, Jean-Hippolyte-Auguste Cartier de, 337, 389
Viollet-le-Duc, Eugène-Emmanuel, 192
Virgil (Publius Virgilius Maro), 75, 94
   Aeneid, 74, 88, 142
Viterbo, 98
Vive l'Empereur, see Gounod
Voleurs d'or, Les, see Mogador
Voltaire, François-Marie Arouet, called, 86, 295
   Philosophical Dictionary, 252n
Voyage en Chine, see Bazin
Voyage en Orient, see Lamartine

Wagner, Richard: B. on, 74, 107, 121, 182, 294-5, 312, 314; letter to Royer, 108n; supposed influence on B., 112, 139, 148, 211, 213, 325, 326, 391, 409, 433; on Meyerbeer, 147-8; on Fromental Halévy, 236; on Carmen, 426; mentioned, 25, 109, 132, 136, 149, 190, 193, 198, 206, 213, 269, 304, 312n, 474
   Flying Dutchman, The, 107
   Lohengrin, 107, 147, 182, 212, 252n, 429, 474
   Meistersinger, Die, 232, 326, 474
   Rienzi, 233, 290, 474
   Tannhäuser, 107-8, 108n, 121, 147, 252n, 290, 429, 474
   Tristan and Isolde, 252n
Wartel, Pierre-François, 12n
Washburne, Elihu Benjamin, 289
Weber, Johannès, 325, 339, 433; quoted 138-9, 213
Weber, Karl Maria Friedrich Ernst, Baron von, 125, 153, 189, 469, 474
   Freischütz, Der, 211, 290, 429, 474
Weckerlin, Jean-Baptiste-Théodore, 197
Weingartner, Felix, 466, 471
Weldon, Mrs. Georgina, 293, 342, 412
Well-Tempered Clavier, The, see Bach
Wilder, Victor, 474n
Württemberg, Catherine, Princess of (wife of Jérôme Bonaparte), 160

Yradier, Sebastien, 170, 474
   "Ay Chiquita!" 170, 474
   "El Arregilito," 170, 401, 474

"Zeph," 92, 98
Zimmerman, Pierre-Joseph-Guillaume, 20-1, 26, 77n
Zimmerman, Mme Pierre, 20
Zola, Emile, quoted 333
   Assommoir, L', 207
   Nana, 207
   Pot-Bouille, 207
Zuniga, see Bizet, Georges: Carmen
Zurga, see Bizet, Georges: Les Pêcheurs de Perles

A NOTE ON THE AUTHOR

Mina Kirstein Curtiss was born in Boston. She attended Smith College (B.A.), Radcliffe College, and Columbia University (M.A.). From 1920 to 1934 and again from 1940 to 1943 she was an associate professor of English at Smith. In 1942–3 she served as a radio-script writer in the overseas branch of the Office of War Information. Mrs. Curtiss edited the anthology *Olive, Cypress and Palm* (1930) and *Letters Home,* a collection of enlisted men's letters (1944); edited and translated *Letters of Marcel Proust* (1949); and wrote a novel, *The Midst of Life* (1933). She divides her time between homes in New York and in Ashfield, Massachusetts.